WINDOWS PROFESSIONAL COMPLETE

SAN FRANCISCO ▸ LONDON

Associate Publisher: Joel Fugazzotto

Acquisitions and Developmental Editor: Ellen L. Dendy

Compilation Editor: Pat Coleman

Editor: Cheryl Hauser

Production Editor: Dennis Fitzgerald

Technical Editor: Emmett Dulaney

Book Designer: Maureen Forys, Happenstance Type-o-Rama

Electronic Publishing Specialists: Nila Nichols, Judy Fung

Proofreaders: Emily Hsuan, Dave Nash, Yariv Rabinovitch, Nancy Riddiough

Indexer: Ted Laux

Cover Designer: Design Site

Cover Illustrator/Photographer: Will Crocker, The Image Bank

Library of Congress Card Number: 2001098064

ISBN: 0-7821-2985-4

Manufactured in the United States of America

10 9 8 7 6 5 4 3 2

Acknowledgments

This book is the work of many, both inside and outside Sybex including the publishing team members Joel Fugazzotto and Ellen Dendy, and the editorial/production team of Cheryl Hauser, Dennis Fitzgerald, and Nila Nichols.

Pat Coleman deserves particular thanks for making sure all of the material in this book was up-to-date, organized, and flowed together in a cohesive manner. She was ably assisted by revisers Faithe Wempen and Guy Hart-Davis. Emmett Dulaney provided a technical review of some of the chapters.

Finally, our thanks to those contributors who agreed to have their work excerpted into *Windows XP Professional Complete*: Mark Minasi, Guy Hart-Davis, Peter Dyson, Pat Coleman, Faithe Wempen, and Peter Hipson.

CONTENTS AT A GLANCE

CONTENTS

Part iii ▸ Multimedia in Windows XP Professional 507

INTRODUCTION

Windows XP Professional Complete is a one-of-a-kind computer book—valuable both for the breadth of its content and for its low price. This book, a compilation of information from some of Sybex's very best books, provides comprehensive coverage of Windows XP Professional. Unique in the computer book world, *Windows XP Professional Complete* was created with certain goals in mind:

- To offer a thorough guide covering all the important user-level features of Windows XP Professional at an affordable price
- To acquaint you with some of our best authors, their writing styles and teaching skills, and the level of expertise they bring to their books—so that you can easily find a match for your interests and needs as you delve deeper into Windows XP Professional

Windows XP Professional Complete is designed to provide you with all the essential information you'll need to get the most from Windows XP Professional and your computer. At the same time, *Windows XP Professional Complete* will invite you to explore the even greater depths and wider coverage of material in the original books.

If you have read other computer "how to" books, you have seen that there are many possible approaches to effectively using the technology. The books from which this one was compiled represent a range of teaching approaches used by Sybex and Sybex authors. From the quick, concise Simply Visual to the wide-ranging, thoroughly detailed Mastering style, you will be able to choose which approach and which level of expertise works best for you. You will also see what these books have in common: a commitment to clarity, accuracy, and practicality.

In these pages, you will find ample evidence of the high quality of Sybex's authors. Unlike publishers who produce "books by committee," Sybex authors are encouraged to write in their individual voices, voices which reflect their own experience with the software at hand and with the evolution of today's personal computers, so you know you are getting the benefit of their direct experience. Nearly every book represented here is the work of a single writer or a pair of close collaborators. Similarly, all of the chapters here are based on the individual experience of the authors, their first-hand testing of pre-release software, and their subsequent expertise with the final product.

In adapting the various source materials for inclusion in *Windows XP Professional Complete*, the compilation editor preserved these individual voices and perspectives. Chapters were edited to minimize duplication, omit coverage of non-essential information, update technological issues, and cross-reference material so you can easily follow a topic across chapters. Some sections may have been edited for length in order to include as much updated, relevant, and important information as possible.

Who Can Benefit From This Book?

Windows XP Professional Complete is designed to meet the needs of a wide range of computer users working with the newest version of Microsoft's operating system. *Windows XP Professional Complete* provides an extraordinarily rich environment, with some elements that everyone uses, as well as features that may be essential to some users but of no interest to others. Therefore, while you could read this book from beginning to end—from upgrade decisions, to installation, through the features, and on to expert tinkering—you may not need to read every chapter. The contents and the index will guide you to the subjects you're looking for.

Beginners Even if you have only a little familiarity with computers and their basic terminology, this book will start you working with Windows XP Professional. You'll find step-by-step instructions for all the operations involved in running application programs and managing your computer system, along with clear explanations of essential concepts. You'll want to start at the very beginning of this book, Part I, which covers the basics.

Intermediate Users Chances, are you already know how to do routine tasks in Windows 9*x*/Me and have a head start when in comes to XP. You know your way around a few productivity applications, use e-mail extensively, browse the Web a little, and maybe have a favorite game or two. You also know that there is always more to learn about working more effectively, and you want to get up to speed on the new Windows XP features. Throughout this book, you'll find instructions for just about anything you want to do. Nearly every chapter has nuggets of knowledge from which you can benefit.

Power Users Maybe you're a hardcore multimedia fiend looking to take advantage of Windows XP's expanded capabilities, or the unofficial guru of your office, or an Internaut ready to try Web publishing. There's plenty for you here, too, particularly in the chapters from the Mastering book.

This book is for people using Windows XP Professional in any environment. You may be a SOHO (small-office/home-office) user, working with a stand-alone computer or a simple peer-to-peer network with no administrators or technical staff to rely on. In that case, you'll find plenty of information about maintaining and troubleshooting your computer. Or you may be working with a larger network and simply want to get a leg up, quickly and inexpensively, as your office migrates to the new operating system.

How This Book Is Organized

Here's a look at what *Windows XP Professional Complete* covers in each part:

Part I: Windows XP Professional Essentials The 11 chapters in this part of the book are designed to take you step by step through installing Windows XP Professional and to introduce you to the basic features of Windows XP Professional. You'll learn how to manage files, folders, and disks; how to customize Windows XP Professional; how to print and manage printers; and how to set object properties and share data.

Part II: Communications and the Internet Windows XP Professional includes an extensive set of communications tools that you can use to browse the Web, send and receive e-mail, access newsgroups, send and receive faxes, and so on. This part begins with a discussion of how to connect to the Internet by means of a broadband device or a dial-up modem. Later chapters show you how to use some new features introduced in Windows XP Professional: Windows Messenger (an instant messaging application) and Remote Desktop Connection.

Part III: Multimedia in Windows XP Professional With features built in to Windows XP Professional, you can now create and edit videos, burn data and audio CDs, edit photos and other images, play audio and video, and make you own audio recordings. The chapters in this part of the book are extensively illustrated, which helps even a novice user acquire multimedia skills easily and quickly.

Part IV: Networking Windows XP Professional One of the most powerful features of Windows XP Professional is its capability to attach to and become part of a networking environment. This part of the book begins with a couple of chapters that explain how networks work. The remaining chapters show you how to set up a local peer-to-peer network, how to connect to a domain, how to secure your network with rights and permissions, and how to telecommute securely.

Part V: Working with the Registry The Registry is a hierarchical database of all the settings required by your installation of Windows and the programs installed on your system. This part of the book explains exactly what the Registry is, how and when you should use it, how to use it safely, and how to use it to get the most out of Windows XP Professional.

Part VI: Maintaining and Troubleshooting Windows XP Professional Windows XP Professional is arguably the most stable operating system to date in the family of Windows operating systems. Nevertheless, occasionally things do go wrong. The chapters in this part of the book deal with this eventuality and show you how to use features of Windows XP Professional to restore your system, to manage disks and drives, to manage hardware, drivers, and power, and to troubleshoot and optimize Windows XP Professional.

A Few Typographic Conventions

When a Windows operation requires a series of choices from menus or dialog boxes, the ➢ symbol is used to guide you through the instructions, like this: "Choose Start ➢ All Programs ➢ Accessories ➢ System Tools ➢ System Information." The items the ➢ symbol separates may be menu names, toolbar icons, check boxes, or other elements of the Windows interface—anyplace you can make a selection.

`This typeface` is used to identify Internet URLs and HTML code, and **`boldface type`** is used whenever you need to type something into a text box.

You'll find these types of special notes throughout the book:

TIP

You'll see a lot of these Tips—quicker and smarter ways to accomplish a task, which the authors have based on many hours spent testing and using Windows XP Professional.

NOTE

You'll see Notes, too. They usually represent alternate ways of accomplishing a task or some additional information that needs to be highlighted.

WARNING

In a few places, you'll see a Warning like this one. There are not too many because it's hard to do irrevocable things in Windows XP Professional unless you work at it. But when you see a Warning, do pay attention to it.

YOU'LL ALSO SEE SIDEBAR BOXES LIKE THIS

These sections provide added explanations of special topics that are referred to in the surrounding discussions, but that you may want to explore separately in greater detail. The Mastering series also includes Expert Knowledge sidebar boxes, which as the title implies, provides information for expert-level users, or those who are just curious about learning more on the topic.

For More Information

See the Sybex Web site, `www.sybex.com`, to learn more about all the books contributed to *Windows XP Professional Complete.* On the site's Catalog page, you'll find links to any book you're interested in. Also, be sure to check out the Sybex site for late-breaking developments about Windows XP Professional itself.

We hope you enjoy this book and find it useful. Happy computing!

PART I

WINDOWS XP ESSENTIALS

Chapter 1

Introducing Windows XP Professional

This chapter discusses what Windows XP Professional is, what it does, and who it's for. It covers in some detail the features and improvements in Windows XP Professional, so that you'll know what the operating system offers.

The chapter then discusses whether you should upgrade from your current version of Windows. As you might imagine, the answer depends on which version of Windows you're currently running, what you're trying to do with it, and what degrees of success and satisfaction you're experiencing. But for most people who have adequate hardware, Windows XP offers significant improvements over all previous versions of Windows.

At the end of the chapter, you'll find a discussion of the main ways in which Windows XP Professional differs from Windows XP Home. If you're already up to speed on all of Windows XP's features, skip straight to the next chapter and get started on installing XP.

Revised and adapted from *Mastering Windows XP Home Edition* by Guy Hart-Davis

ISBN 0-7821-2980-3 1024 pages $39.99

What Is Windows XP Professional?

In a nutshell, Windows XP Professional is the latest version of the Windows NT family of operating systems (which includes Windows 2000). Windows XP Professional comprises a feature set designed for business users, while its less powerful (and less expensive) sibling Windows XP Home edition offers features designed for consumers, or home users.

If you've used Windows before, or if you're currently using Windows, you may wonder what the big deal is. The good news is that Windows XP *is* a big deal, especially if you've had less than satisfactory experiences with Windows in the past. Windows XP isn't the be-all and end-all of operating systems, but it's a great improvement on its predecessors.

As you probably know, through the second half of the 1990s and up until 2001, Microsoft offered two main categories of Windows versions for personal computers: the Windows 95 family and the Windows NT family. In the Windows 95 family were Windows 95 itself, naturally enough; Windows 98; Windows 98 Second Edition, which (despite its unassuming name) was a major upgrade to Windows 98; and Windows Millennium Edition, also known as Windows Me. In the Windows NT family were Windows NT versions 3.1, 3.5, 3.51, and 4, each of which came in a Workstation version and a Server version, and then Windows 2000, which came in a Professional version and several Server versions.

The Windows 95 family, widely referred to as Windows 9*x* in a brave attempt to simplify Microsoft's inconsistent naming, offered impressive compatibility with older hardware (*legacy hardware*, as it's sometimes politely termed) and software (*legacy software*), including full (or full-ish) DOS capabilities for running games and character-based programs. These versions of Windows kept their hardware demands to a reasonable minimum. They were aimed at the consumer market. When things went wrong (which happened regrettably often), they became unstable. And they crashed. Frequently.

Many of those people—both professionals and home users—who couldn't stand or afford to lose their work because of Windows 9*x*'s frequent crashes migrated to Windows NT instead. (Others tried OS/2 while it lasted, then returned disconsolately to Windows. Others went to Linux, and mostly stayed with it.) NT, which stands for New Technology, had a completely different underpinning of code than Windows 9*x*. NT was designed for stability, and as a result, it crashed much less frequently than Windows 9*x*. Unfortunately, though, NT wasn't nearly as compatible as Windows 9*x* with legacy hardware and software. Most games and much audio and video software wouldn't run on NT, and it was picky about the hardware on which it would run. (Actually, this wasn't unfortunate at all—it was deliberate on Microsoft's part, and probably wise. But the result was far from great for many users.)

So for the last half-dozen years, users have essentially had to decide between stability and compatibility. This led to a lot of unhappy users, some of whom couldn't run the software they wanted, and others who kept losing work or at least having to reboot their computers more than they should have had to.

The Windows 9*x* line culminated in Windows Me, which tacked some stability and restoration features onto the Windows 9*x* code base. NT culminated in Windows 2000 Professional, which featured increased compatibility with programs over NT (which wasn't saying all that much), a smooth user interface, and usability enhancements.

Windows 2000 Professional was arguably the most stable operating system that Microsoft had produced until Windows XP came along. (Some old-timers reckoned Windows NT 3.51 was more stable.) But Windows 2000 Professional's stability came at a price: It had no interest in running any games or other demanding software that wouldn't conform to its stringent requirements. And while it was compatible with quite an impressive range of legacy hardware, many items still wouldn't work. Even up-to-date hardware could be problematic, especially if it connected via USB.

Since the late 1990s, Microsoft had been promising to deliver a consumer version of Windows that melded the stability of NT and the compatibility of Windows 9*x*. In Windows XP Home Edition, that version of Windows is finally here. According to Microsoft, Windows XP Professional is a strict superset of Home Edition, as well as of all the desktop clients that preceded Professional.

What's New in Windows XP Professional?

This section outlines the most striking and appealing new features in Windows XP, starting with installation and upgrading, moving through the user interface and visible features, and ending with the features hidden under the hood.

Some of these new features fall into convenient categories, and this section presents them in categories. Others don't; this section presents these features individually.

Easier Installation and Updating

Windows XP includes several features designed to make it easier to install and keep up to date. These include Dynamic Update and Windows Update; the Files and Settings Transfer Wizard; more Wizards for a variety of tasks; a wider selection of device drivers; simplified installation for multifunction devices; and effective uninstall back to Windows 98 and Windows Me.

Dynamic Update and Windows Update

If you're installing Windows XP, one of the first new features that you'll notice is Dynamic Update, which runs during setup and offers to download the latest patches, packages, and fixes so that they can be installed during the setup process.

Dynamic Update may prove to be a great feature. It goes hand in hand with its terrible twin, Windows Update, which runs periodically after setup and offers to download the latest patches, packages, and fixes and install them so that your copy of Windows is as up to date, secure, and compatible as possible. (You can also run Windows Update manually whenever you want to.)

Files and Settings Transfer Wizard

Making its debut in Windows XP is the Files and Settings Transfer Wizard, a feature that Windows users have been demanding for a good 10 years. The Files and Settings Transfer Wizard provides a way of transferring designated files and settings from one computer to another or from one installation of Windows to another on the same computer. You'll still need to reinstall all your programs on the new computer or new installation of Windows, but you can transfer your data and a good amount of information about your work environment easily.

If you're migrating from an old computer to a new computer, or if you're installing Windows XP as a dual-boot with an existing version of Windows, you can use the Files and Settings Transfer Wizard to clone your existing Desktop and files and transfer them to the new computer or new version of Windows.

More Wizards to Make Tasks Easier

Windows XP includes a slew of Wizards designed to walk you through complicated processes (and some that aren't so complicated). Perhaps most welcome are the improvements to the Network Setup Wizard, which provides effective configuration of simple networks and Internet connection sharing, and the two Hardware Wizards, the Add Hardware Wizard and the Found New Hardware Wizard.

On the less useful front, Windows XP also includes Wizards such as the Desktop Cleanup Wizard, which pops out periodically like the neighborhood dog and tries to persuade you to let it herd the stray icons on your Desktop into a folder where they'll be available but less obtrusive. If you refuse, it wags its tail and goes away for a while.

More Device Drivers

Windows XP comes complete with drivers for a large number of devices, including scanners, digital still cameras, digital video cameras, printers, and so on. So there's a better chance than with another version of Windows (say Windows Me or Windows 2000) that when you plug in a new device, Windows XP will be able to load a driver for it and get it working without any fuss.

You'll probably want to take this improvement with a grain of salt. It's great when Windows XP installs a new device without any effort on your part. But to enjoy the latest features and the best performance from a new device, you may well need to install the driver that comes with the device or (better) download the latest version from the manufacturer's Web site rather than wait for updated drivers to filter through Windows Update.

Simplified Installation for Multifunction Devices

Apart from having more drivers (as described in the previous section), Windows XP makes it easier to install multifunction devices–for example, a multifunction printer/scanner/fax device (the kind that people sometimes call *hydra* machines), a PC Card that combines a network interface card with a modem, or a sound board with extra features.

Previous versions of Windows tended to recognize the component pieces of multifunction devices separately in sequence. If you installed a hydra, Windows would recognize the printer and demand the installation software for it. Once that was done, Windows would recognize the fax and demand the software for *that*. After that, it would recognize the scanner and suggest you might want to install yet more software. Windows XP improves on this social ineptitude by recognizing multifunction devices as such the first time you introduce it to them, and so it demands the installation software only once.

Effective Uninstall Back to Windows 98 and Windows Me

Windows XP Home provides an effective uninstall feature for rolling back the Windows XP installation to your previous installation of Windows 98, Windows 98 Second Edition, or Windows Me. However, you can't revert to a previous installation of Windows NT or Windows 2000 Professional.

Effective Multiuser Capabilities

Windows XP provides far better multiuser capabilities than Windows 9*x*. You'll notice this at once when you start Windows XP, because by default the Welcome screen that's displayed when Windows starts lists each user who has an account on the computer.

While Windows 9*x* let anybody log on to the computer by creating a new account, Windows XP requires an existing account in order to log on. By default, no account has a password in Windows XP, though, so in effect anybody can log on using one of the existing accounts until you require passwords–and you ought to require passwords immediately to protect your data.

Windows 9*x* let you create a profile for each separate user, so that each user could have their own Desktop, Start menu, and set of programs; but it didn't offer any features for preventing one user from seeing another user's files. By contrast, Windows XP takes the approach of NT and Windows 2000, which keep each user's files separate, letting you set Windows up so that no user can see another user's files unless they have been shared deliberately.

Windows XP goes further than NT and Windows 2000, though, in that it lets multiple users be logged on at the same time, each with programs running. Only one user can be actually *using* the computer, or *active* in Windows XP parlance, at any one time, but the other user sessions continue running in the background (*disconnected*, in Windows XP parlance). When you've finished with the computer for the time being, you can log off Windows, just as you did in previous versions of Windows. Logging off closes all the programs you were using and frees up the memory they took up. But if you stop using the computer only temporarily, you may prefer to *switch user*, which leaves your programs running but lets someone else use the computer in the interim. Further encouraging you to switch user, Windows' default screen saver setting is to display the Welcome screen after 10 minutes of inactivity, performing the equivalent of a Switch User command as it disconnects the user but leaves their session running hidden in the background.

Enhanced User Interface

Windows XP has a completely revamped user interface with a large number of visual enhancements and improved functionality. Some of the visual enhancements improve usability, while others are mere eye candy. But the overall effect is mostly easy to use and mostly looks good–and if you don't like the look, you can restore the "classic" Windows look with minimal effort.

The following sections discuss the main changes to the user interface.

Redesigned Start Menu

Windows XP sports a redesigned Start menu that's supposedly easier and quicker to use. Whether you find it so depends on your experience with the Start menu found in Windows 9*x* and Windows 2000. But don't worry if you like the "classic" Start menu–you can restore it easily enough with a few clicks of the mouse.

The Start menu appears as a panel containing two columns (shown in Figure 1.1). The right-hand column remains the same unless you customize it. The left-hand column starts off with items Microsoft thinks you ought to know about immediately after installation. It then automatically reconfigures itself to show your most used programs. You can pin an item to the Start menu to prevent it from moving and keep it available.

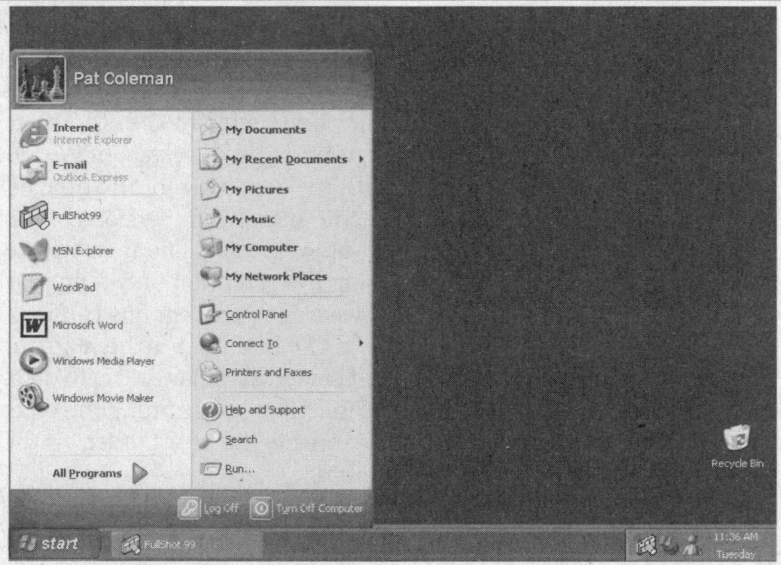

FIGURE 1.1: The redesigned Start menu contains a static column of choices on the right and a variable column of choices on the left.

As you can see in the figure, the current user's name appears in a bar across the top of the Start menu, and the Log Off button and Turn Off Computer button appear at the bottom of the menu.

Redesigned Explorer

Explorer windows use a pair of technologies called WebView and ListView to present context-sensitive lists of tasks you may want to perform or other locations you may want to access. If that sounds a bit vague, that's because WebView and ListView mean that what you see in an Explorer window changes depending on the item that's displayed.

For example, when you select a file (as in Figure 1.2), you see a list of File and Folder Tasks (including links for Rename This File, Move This File, and Delete This File), a list of Other Places (other folders you may want to access from this folder), and a list of Details (which contains information about the file selected and is off the screen in the figure). When you select a folder, Explorer displays a list of File and Folder Tasks (including links for Rename This Folder, Copy This Folder, and Publish This Folder to the Web). When you select your My Network Places folder, you get a Network Tasks list (including links for View Network Connections and Set Up a Home or Small Office Network). When you select the Recycle Bin.... Okay, you get the idea.

Shortcut menus (right-click menus) in Explorer are also improved, with more context-sensitive commands added where appropriate. But most of the action takes place in the Tasks list for the selected item. That's because some 80 percent of users apparently weren't using the shortcut menus successfully—an impressive and frightening statistic thrown up by Microsoft's research on Windows users.

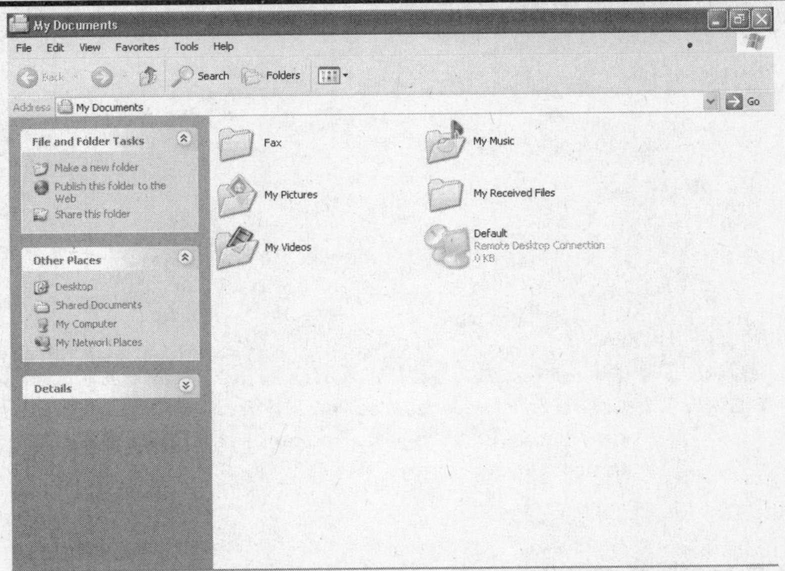

FIGURE 1.2: Explorer windows use the new WebView and ListView technologies to present lists of tasks associated with the selected item.

Redesigned Control Panel

Windows XP also has a redesigned Control Panel (shown in Figure 1.3) that uses WebView and ListView technology to present Control Panel as categories of items and actions you can take with them. (If you regard Control Panel as an oddly behaved Explorer window, it should come as no surprise after reading the previous section that Control Panel uses WebView and ListView.)

New users will likely find the Category view of Control Panel easy to use. Users comfortable with the regular manifestation of Control Panel in Windows 9*x*, Windows NT 4, and Windows 2000 will probably prefer to use the Classic view.

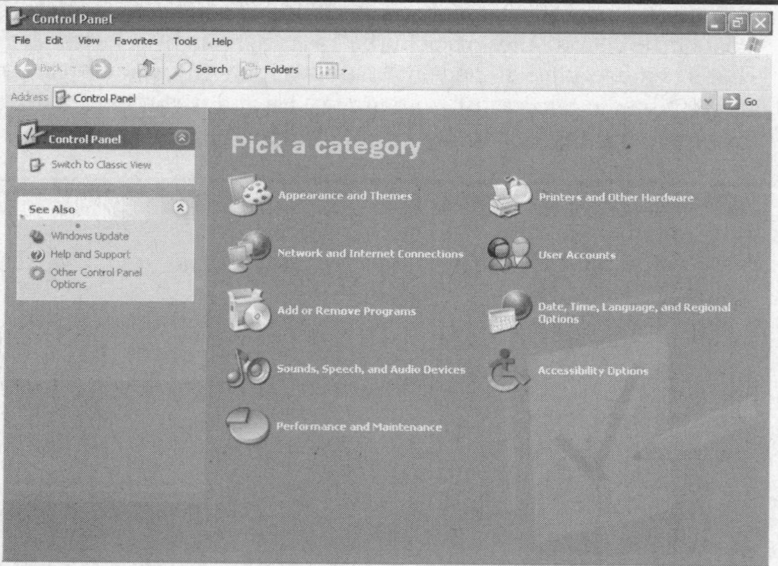

FIGURE 1.3: Control Panel also uses WebView and ListView by default, dividing its bevy of icons into categories. You can use the Classic view to see all the icons at once.

Eye Candy

To complement its highly graphical interface, Windows XP includes a dangerous amount of eye candy. Most people will like at least some of it. Some people will love it all. And no doubt some people will claim to detest every pixel of it.

The prime example of eye candy is the My Pictures Slideshow screen saver, which lets you set up an automated (or mouse-controlled) slideshow of designated pictures instead of a regular screen saver. This feature seems destined to be widely popular.

Less assured of a rapturous welcome are the staggering amounts of adornment in the interface, such as shadows under the mouse pointer and under menus; the color gradient in the title bar of windows; and the effect of sliding icons, controls, and Taskbar buttons. This overbearing emphasis on graphics places heavy demands on your graphics card and processor, and if your computer's hardware tends to the lukewarm rather than the hot, you may find that the eye candy exacts an unacceptable performance penalty. Microsoft has had the sense to let you set performance options to balance the demands of appearance against your need for performance, so you can turn off the least necessary effects and speed up your computer.

Taskbar Changes and Enhancements

Windows XP includes a number of tweaks to the Taskbar. These seem designed for beginners, so if you're an experienced Windows user, you may find some good and others bad. Fortunately, you can change the Taskbar's behavior back to how it was in previous versions of Windows.

Taskbar Locking

By default, the Taskbar is locked so that you cannot resize it or move it. Presumably this is intended to help prevent users from dragging their Taskbar to an inaccessible line at the edge of the screen, but it will annoy experienced users who want to be able to resize and move their Taskbar freely. (You can unlock it easily enough.)

Taskbar Scrolling

If you read the previous paragraph, you probably started raising objections: If the Taskbar is a fixed size, the buttons for the running programs must become tiny and useless as soon as you've got 10 or more programs running.

Two other changes come into play here, of which the first is Taskbar scrolling. When the Taskbar is locked, Windows keeps the buttons bigger than a minimum size. To accommodate the buttons, Windows increases the depth of the Taskbar, but displays only its top row. On the displayed portion of the Taskbar, Windows puts scroll buttons so that you can scroll the Taskbar up and down one row of buttons at a time.

Taskbar Button Grouping

The second change that makes Taskbar locking reasonable is Taskbar button grouping.

By default, Windows XP groups related Taskbar buttons once you've opened enough windows to more or less fill the Taskbar. Whereas other versions of Windows displayed one Taskbar button for each program window, Windows XP groups them onto a pop-up menu from a single Taskbar button. For example, if you open nine Internet Explorer windows in Windows 98, Windows displays nine Internet Explorer buttons on the Taskbar. Having all these buttons can make it easy to find the window you want, but the buttons take up a lot of space (or each button on the Taskbar gets shrunk to a tiny size to fit them all in).

In Windows XP, if the program has multiple open windows, the Taskbar button displays the number of windows, the title of the current active window or last active window, and a drop-down arrow. To access one of the other open windows, click the Taskbar button. Windows displays a list of the windows by title. Select the window you want, and Windows displays it.

Notification Area

By default, Windows XP collapses the notification area (previously known as the System Tray or the status area) so that only the icons you've used most recently are displayed. To display the other icons in the notification area, click the < button at the left end of the notification area.

Better Audio and Video Features

Windows XP includes a slew of new features and improvements for audio and video. These include a new version of Windows Media Player; better features for grabbing and handling images from digital input devices such as scanners and cameras; and Windows Movie Maker, a modest video-editing program.

Windows Media Player Version 8

Front and center among the improved audio and video features of Windows XP is Windows Media Player version 8, which combines a video and DVD player, a CD player, an Internet radio tuner, and a jukebox for playing and organizing digital-audio files such as Windows Media Audio (WMA) files and MP3 files. Windows Media Player 8 comes with a number of visually interesting *skins* (graphical looks) that you can apply at will. You can even create your own skins if you have the time and talent to invest.

All in all, Windows Media Player 8 is a huge improvement over the 98-pound weakling version of Windows Media Player shipped with all previous versions of Windows except Windows Me. (Me included Windows Media Player 7, which offered many of the features of version 8.) Windows Media Player can even burn audio CDs at the full speed of your CD-R or CD-RW drive.

Windows Media Player is a strong program, but two missing features will disappoint many users:

- Windows Media Player has no codec (coder/decoder) for playing back DVDs. If you want to watch DVDs, you'll have to add a codec of your own—and almost certainly pay for the privilege.
- Windows Media Player can encode audio to the universally popular MP3 format—but only if you add a third-party encoder. You'll probably have to pay for this too.

My Music Folder and My Pictures Folder

Like several of its predecessors, Windows XP uses custom folders for music (the My Music folder) and pictures (the My Pictures folder). Again like its predecessors, it tries none too subtly to persuade you to save your music in these folders. But Windows XP goes further, in that it makes these folders much more useful than they were in earlier versions of Windows.

As you'd expect, the My Music folder and the My Pictures folder use WebView and ListView to present customized lists of actions you can take with music files and picture files. Some of these actions tend to the commercial—for example, the Order Prints Online link in the Picture Tasks list, and the Shop for Music Online link in the Music Tasks list. But others are solidly useful—for example, the Play All link in the Music Tasks list, which lets you play all the music in a folder without spelunking into it, or the View As a Slide Show link in the Picture Tasks list, which lets you set a whole folder of pictures running as a slideshow with a single click.

Not surprisingly, the My Music folder works hand in hand (or is it glove?) with Windows Media Player. Windows Media Player is definitely happy for you to keep your music in the My Music folder, though it will let you keep your music elsewhere as well. Better yet, Windows Media Player's features for cataloging music tracks are flexible enough to keep track of music files even when you move them from one folder to another.

The My Pictures folder works closely with Windows Image Acquisition, Windows Picture and Fax Viewer, and Paint (all three of which are discussed in the next section). The folder includes a slideshow applet and a filmstrip view, and it can publish your pictures to the Web.

Better Image Acquisition and Handling

Windows XP provides strong features for capturing images from scanners, still cameras, and video cameras. It also provides better throughput for video streams, though unless you have a duplicate computer running an older version of Windows to use as a benchmark, you could be forgiven for failing to go into raptures over the improvement. Less cynically, the improvement in throughput is unquestionably a good thing, and on decent hardware, Windows XP delivers adequate to impressive video performance; but the chances of your confusing your PC with your Dreamcast remain poor.

One of the central tools for image acquisition and handling is the Scanner and Camera Wizard. This Wizard has a variety of duties, including transferring image files from still cameras and digital media (for example, CompactFlash cards and SmartMedia cards) to the computer. Most of its capabilities stay on the useful side of the esoteric. For example, you can scan multiple pages into a single image file, an ability that can come in handy in both home and business settings.

Windows XP provides some basic tools for handling still images. As mentioned in the previous section, the My Pictures folder acts as a default repository for images and provides some basic image-handling abilities, such as rotating an image. Windows Picture and Fax Viewer feature lets you examine an image (and annotate a fax). And Paint, the basic image-manipulation and drawing package that's been included with Windows since Windows 3.*x*, has been beefed up as well. Paint can now open—and save—JPEG, GIF, TIFF, and PNG images as well as Windows bitmap (BMP) files, making it about five times as useful as before.

Windows Movie Maker

Windows XP includes Windows Movie Maker, a basic package for capturing video, editing video and audio, and creating video files in the Windows Media format. You won't find yourself making the next *Timecode* or *Traffic* with Windows Movie Maker, but it's good enough for basic video editing. You can also create video slideshows with still images.

CD Burning

Windows XP comes with built-in CD-burning capabilities. You can burn CDs from an Explorer window with minimal effort. You can also burn CDs directly from Windows Media Player, which lets you easily create audio CDs that you can play in regular CD players.

Compressed Folders

Windows XP has built-in support for compressed folders in both the ubiquitous ZIP format and the Microsoft Cabinet (CAB) format. You can create ZIP folders containing one or more files or folders. Better still, you can view the contents of a ZIP or CAB folder seamlessly in Explorer as if it were a regular folder.

Improved Features for Sending Attachments

Windows XP includes improved features for sending files and folders as attachments to e-mail messages. Instead of blindly attaching the files and folders identified by the user, Windows offers to optimize the file size and display size of the pictures so that they transfer faster and fit onto the recipient's screen when they arrive. If the recipient is using Windows XP, they get to choose whether to open the file or files at the original size or at the optimized size.

Because this feature can actually change the files sent, it seems suspect. But if it reduces the number of multimegabyte digital pictures landing on your ISP's mail server, you may well find it a positive feature—even if you choose never to use it yourself.

Chapter 14 discusses how to use Outlook Express for e-mail, including attachments.

Search Companion

Windows XP includes Search Companion, an enhanced search feature for finding information both on your PC and in the wider world. You can use Search Companion to search for files, for computers or people online, or for information in Help and Support Center. Search Companion brokers the search requests that you enter and farms them out to the appropriate search mechanisms.

You can choose between having Search Companion appear in a straightforward and unexceptionable window and having it manifest itself using one of various animated characters reminiscent of the Microsoft Office Assistant.

Easy Publishing to the Web

Windows XP makes it easier to publish files or folders to a Web site by using a Web-hosting service. Windows XP includes a feature called Web Digital Authoring and Versioning (WebDAV for short) that lets you save information to the Web from any program rather than having to use the regular Web-publishing protocols. Windows XP Professional also includes Personal Web Server and Internet Information Services, which let you run a modest-scale Web server on XP.

A Sane Implementation of Autoplay

If you've used Windows 9*x*, NT 4, or 2000, you'll know all about the Autoplay feature and how it used to drive people crazy. You remember Autoplay—the moment you insert a CD, it starts playing the music from it or installing any software it contains. By default, Autoplay was enabled, so you had to switch it off (or override it by holding down the Shift key while closing the CD tray) to prevent this from occurring.

Windows XP includes a new version of Autoplay that's improved in several ways. First, you can customize it. Second, you can configure it to take different actions depending on what the CD (or other medium) contains. For example, you might want Windows to play your audio CDs automatically when you insert them (okay, you don't—but you *might*), or you might want Windows to display a slideshow automatically when you insert a CD containing nothing but pictures.

What's that about *other medium*? That's the third thing: In Windows XP, Autoplay works for CDs, DVDs, assorted flash cards (including CompactFlash, Memory Stick, and SmartMedia), PC Cards, Zip and other removable disk drives, and FireWire hot-plug external drives.

More Games

Windows XP includes more games than previous versions of Windows. Some of these are single-player games (for example, Spider Solitaire). Others are multiplayer games that you can play across the Internet via MSN's Zone.com Web site.

Remote Desktop Connection

Windows XP includes Remote Desktop Connection, a technology that lets you use your computer to access a remote computer (for example, your computer at the office) that's running Windows XP Professional. Once you've connected to the remote computer, you can control it as if you were sitting at it.

A More Useful Winkey

A what? *Winkey*, pronounced "win-key" rather than as the diminutive of *wink*, is the Windows key on the keyboard–the key with the Windows logo. Most keyboards have one or two Winkeys, usually located next to the Alt key or keys.

Windows XP includes more functionality for the Winkey. You can still press the Winkey to open or close the Start menu, but you can also use it in a number of key combinations. For example, pressing Winkey+M issues a Minimize All command (showing the Desktop), and pressing Winkey+Shift+M issues an Undo Minimize All command.

Improvements for Portable Computers

Windows XP includes several improvements for portable computers.

Windows XP supports processor power control, which lets the computer make use of features in chips such as Intel's SpeedStep, in which the processor runs at full speed when the computer is plugged into the main power supply (or told that it's plugged in) but at a lower speed to save power when it's running on battery power (or told that it is).

Throttling back the processor like this reduces the computer's power usage a bit, improving battery life, but in most portables, the screen consumes far more power than the processor. Windows XP also targets the screen, providing a couple of features designed to reduce power use when the computer is running on battery power. First, Windows XP turns off the display when the user closes the computer's lid, on the basis that the user probably isn't looking at the display. Second, it runs the screen at a dimmer brightness when the computer is running off the battery. The cynical among you will point out that the better-designed portables implement both these functions already in hardware. Still, it shouldn't do any harm to have Windows help out for the manufacturers who design their machines a little less carefully.

Windows XP also includes some other less obvious visual enhancements, such as support for ClearType, a Microsoft text-display technology that improves the look of fonts on LCD screens that have digital interfaces. While these screens aren't strictly confined to portables, that's where the bulk of the market is.

Faxing

Windows XP contains a built-in fax client that's more than adequate for most home needs and many home-office needs. You can send faxes from any program that supports printing, and you can specify whether to print out incoming faxes automatically or store them in a folder. You can even configure different fax/modems to take different roles. For example, if you use faxes extensively, you might want to keep separate incoming and outgoing fax lines. You'll need a modem for each of the phone lines involved, but that's about as difficult as it gets.

Windows XP Professional also lets you share a fax/modem with other computers: Your computer can provide fax services to other computers to which it is networked, or your computer can send a fax via a fax/modem on another computer. These features can save a great deal of time and effort, not to mention phone lines.

More Help

Windows XP delivers more help–and more different types of help–than any other version of Windows.

If you've searched fruitlessly for information in the past, you'll be aware that Windows' Help files have never exactly delivered the ultimate in user satisfaction. Digging information out of Help often felt so difficult that if you knew Windows well enough to find help on the right topic, you could probably solve the problem without Help's assistance.

Windows XP takes a new approach to help. There are Help files on your hard drive still, but they're integrated into a program called Help and Support Center. Help and Support Center not only works with the Help files but also with the Microsoft Knowledge Base (a database of support queries) and other online sources of information. For example, if you run a query within Help and Support Center to find information on hardware, it might return some information from local files, some information from the Microsoft Web site, and some information from hardware manufacturers' Web sites, all packaged into one window so that you can access the information conveniently.

Help and Support Center also provides a gateway to other areas of support, including Microsoft Assisted Support and Microsoft Communities, and to programs that you can use to get help from other users (such as Remote Assistance) and troubleshoot your computer (such as System Configuration Utility and System Restore).

Figure 1.4 shows the home page of Help and Support Center.

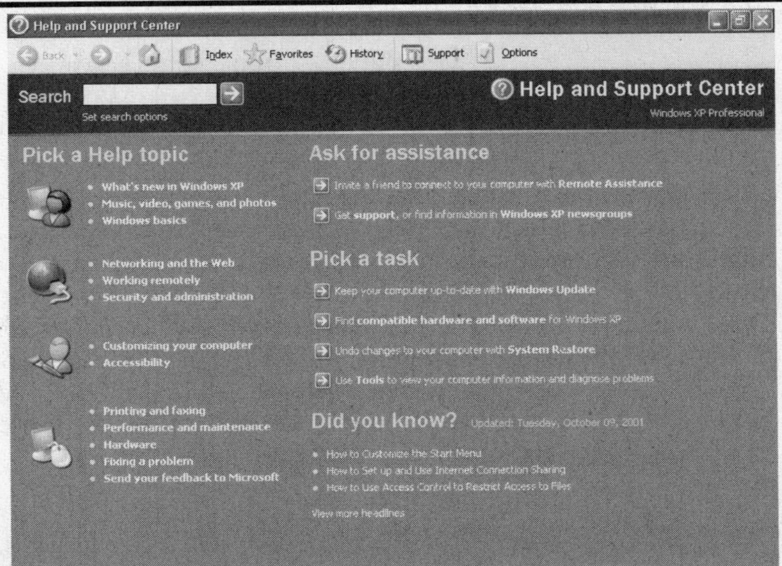

FIGURE 1.4: The home page of Help and Support Center

Microsoft Assisted Support

Windows XP's Microsoft Assisted Support feature lets you automatically collect information on a problem you're having and submit it to Microsoft electronically. A Microsoft technician then sends a solution, which appears as a pop-up in your notification area. You can read the response in the Help and Support Center window and apply the wisdom it contains to fix the problem.

Microsoft Assisted Support is designed to bypass the problems inherent with tech support via phone call, namely that it's difficult for the user to tell the help technician what's wrong with their computer; it's even harder for the technician to get a good idea of what's going wrong without knowing a fair bit of technical information about the computer; and waiting on hold for tech support is nobody's idea of fun, especially if you're paying for a long-distance call as well as for the support.

Windows Newsgroups

Instead of contacting a Microsoft technician via Microsoft Assisted Support, you can try to get support from the Windows Newsgroups, which are Microsoft-hosted newsgroups dedicated to Windows. Your mileage *will* vary in the Windows Newsgroups depending on whether helpful users answer your query soon and whether the stars have decided to shine on your horoscope for the day.

Remote Assistance

Remote Assistance is an ingenious feature by which you can get assistance from a friend or other knowledgeable person remotely by computer.

Here's the brief version of how Remote Assistance works. You send out an invitation file via e-mail, via Windows Messenger instant messaging, or via a file saved to the network (for example, in a business environment) or floppy disk. Your helper receives the invitation and responds to it. Remote Assistance sets up a secure connection between their computer and yours, using a password to verify their identity. Your helper can then view your screen remotely and chat with you (via text chat and voice). If you trust your helper, you can even let them control your computer so that they can take actions directly.

Help Queries: Errors, Events, and Compatibility

You can use Help queries to search for information on error messages, event messages, and compatibility. Help and Support Center's integrated approach lets you search seamlessly across multiple Web sites (for example, the Microsoft Knowledge Base and the hardware manufacturer's Web site) to find the information you need.

Tools Center

Help and Support Center includes a Tools Center that gives you quick access to information about your computer (My Computer Information and Advanced System Information) and its configuration (System Configuration Utility); network diagnostic tools (Network Diagnostics); the System Restore feature; and more. In addition to the tools that Microsoft makes available in the Tools Center, OEMs (original equipment manufacturers) can add tools of their own, so you may also find custom tools provided by your computer manufacturer.

Many of the tools accessible through the Tools Center are also accessible in other ways through the Windows interface. For example, Windows XP includes an improved version of Disk Defragmenter, which you can use to keep your hard disk from becoming fragmented (fragmentation decreases performance). You can run Disk Defragmenter from Tools Center, but you can also run it from the System Tools submenu of the Start menu (choose Start ➢ All Programs ➢ Accessories ➢ System Tools ➢ Disk Defragmenter). Similarly, you can run Windows Update from inside Help and Support Center. This can be convenient, but it offers no great advantage over running Windows Update from the Start menu.

Fixing a Problem Tool

Help and Support Center includes an area called Fixing a Problem that contains a number of troubleshooters for walking you through the steps of diagnosing and curing various common problems. Fixing a Problem isn't a panacea, but it's a good place to start, and it can save you a call to a guru or even a trip to your local computer shop.

Device Driver Referral Site

Help and Support Center contains a system for referring searches for drivers that don't come with Windows or with the hardware device. When you plug in a new hardware device, and Windows finds that it doesn't have a driver for it and you can't supply a driver, Windows invites you to send information about the hardware to Microsoft. Once you've sent the information, you can take a variety of actions depending on what information is available. For example, you might be able to view a list of compatible devices (if any), search for information on compatible devices or Knowledge Base articles about the hardware, or find a link to the vendor's Web site.

Other Help Improvements

Help and Support Center includes assorted other help improvements that can save you time. For example, you can print out a whole chapter of help information at once instead of having to slog through it screen by screen. And you can open multiple Help and Support Center windows at the same time. This makes it easier to pursue different avenues of exploration for the information you need. When you find useful information, you can create a favorite for it so that you can access it quickly again when you need it.

Network Connectivity

Windows XP provides various improvements in network connectivity, from creating a home or home-office network to joining a computer to two separate networks. There are also great improvements in Internet connectivity, discussed in the next section.

Network Setup Wizard

The Network Setup Wizard simplifies the process of creating a network; sharing printers, Internet connections, and other resources; and configuring protocols and security.

All-User Remote Access Service

The All-User Remote Access Service lets you create a credential for all users of the computer so that they can share a connection. For example, you can make your high-speed Internet connection available to all the users of the computer without divulging the account password to them. The name is a bit intimidating and the acronym is nonsensical, but the process is easy.

Alternative TCP/IP Configuration

Windows XP provides an alternative TCP/IP configuration that allows you to connect to a network that has a DHCP server and to a network that doesn't without changing your TCP/IP settings. For example, you might use a laptop at work (where the network has a DHCP server) and at home (where your network doesn't).

This feature is (jargon alert) transparent to the user—in other words, you won't usually notice it.

Network Bridging

Windows XP's network-bridging capability lets you use a computer with two or more network adapters to join two separate networks. You're perhaps unlikely to have two (or more) networks at home or in a small office—unless you have a wired network to which you've added a wireless component to provide roaming capabilities for some of the computers.

Internet Connectivity and Web Browsing

Windows XP provides a number of enhanced features for Internet connectivity and Web browsing, from Internet connection sharing and firewalling to a new version of Internet Explorer.

Internet Connection Sharing and Internet Connection Firewall

Like Windows 98 Second Edition, Windows Me, and Windows 2000, Windows XP includes an Internet Connection Sharing (ICS) feature that lets you share an Internet connection on one computer with one or more networked computers. Windows XP's version of Internet Connection Sharing has some tweaks, such as that you can disconnect the shared Internet connection from another PC if necessary—for example, if you need to use the phone line that the connection is using. Windows XP includes a Quality of Service Packet Scheduler that works to optimize the utilization of a shared Internet connection.

Internet Connection Sharing is a great convenience, particularly if you have a high-speed connection such as a DSL or a cable modem—but it lays your network open to assault from the Internet. Windows XP goes one better than its predecessors by including a firewall (called Internet

Connection Firewall) to protect the Internet connection (whether shared or not).

New Version of Internet Explorer

Windows XP includes Internet Explorer 6, the latest version of Internet Explorer. Even if you feel you've already had it up to here with new versions of Internet Explorer, stifle your impatience, because Internet Explorer 6 offers a number of welcome innovations, including the following:

- You can save images, music, and videos more easily to your computer.
- The new Media bar lets you listen to streaming audio directly in Internet Explorer and (perhaps a less welcome feature) access WindowsMedia.com easily.
- Internet Explorer provides better handling of cookies and digital certificates for securing information transfer and authenticating content.
- Internet Explorer can automatically resize an image you've displayed directly. If you've ever used Internet Explorer to open a digital photo, and found it displayed bigger than your screen so that you could see only part of it, you may appreciate this feature. (But you'd be better off opening the photo in Paint in the first place.)
- Internet Explorer 6 has more integrated functionality for handling different file types. This won't strike you over the head; you'll simply find that more file types open without your being prodded to download and install extra components. For example, Internet Explorer 6 has built-in support for Macromedia Flash and Shockwave animations, and support for Cascading Style Sheet (CSS) Level 1. The net result is that more animations will play without your needing to add software, and documents formatted with CSS1 style sheets will be displayed as their authors intended. (They may still look horrible, but at least you'll know that they're meant to look that way.)

Chapter 13 discusses how to configure and use Internet Explorer.

MSN Explorer

Windows XP includes MSN Explorer, an Internet client dedicated to MSN. If you don't have an ISP, you may want to use MSN Explorer to connect to the Internet.

.NET Passport Integration

In order to implement many of its Internet services, Windows XP relies heavily on Microsoft's .NET Passport feature. For example, you need to get a .NET Passport in order to use Windows Messenger for instant messaging, to use Hotmail (Microsoft's Web-based e-mail service), to create Web pages on MSN, or to visit a Web site that requires a Passport sign-in (for instance, to download certain files from the Microsoft Web site).

.NET Passport (or, more simply, just *Passport*) is an electronic identifier that's associated with your user account on your PC. (If you use the same Passport with multiple PCs, it can be associated with multiple user accounts.) You can sign up for a Passport by using an existing e-mail account. If you don't have an e-mail account, Microsoft encourages you to base your Passport on a Hotmail account or an MSN account.

Passport enables many cool features—but it also locks you into using Microsoft technologies when you may not want to use them. Worse, it can (or *could*) give Microsoft a way to track some of your actions online. Microsoft protests that it is committed to your online privacy, and does give you the choice of opting out of some of the tracking features, but you don't need to be paranoid to find Passport's possibilities frightening.

You can use Passport Wallet features to (in Microsoft's words) "simplify your online shopping experience"—in other words, spend money faster online and with less effort. You get to decide whether this is a good idea. (Hint: Evaluate Passport Wallet carefully. Don't rush into anything.)

What's Hiding under the Hood

The features mentioned so far catch the eye—some even on a cursory scan of the Windows XP Desktop and interface.

Less glamorous, but more important in the long run, are the enhancements hiding under Windows XP's hood. This section discusses the major enhancements that you probably *won't* see.

Protected Memory Management

Windows XP improves on Windows 9*x* (Windows 95, 98, and Me) by offering fully protected memory management. Windows 9*x* didn't protect the areas of memory used by the operating system. This meant that if a program tried to store information in memory already used by another program or by the operating system, the program could crash not only itself but also the operating system. If you've used any version of Windows 9*x* for any length of time, you're probably familiar with these crashes. Typically, you see a succession of instances of the Blue Screen of Death with assorted error messages, and eventually have to perform a warm reboot (Ctrl+Alt+Delete) or a hard reboot (by powering the computer down and back up again). In the meantime, you lose any unsaved work in the programs you're using.

With protected memory management, Windows XP can handle memory errors with more aplomb. When a program tries to access memory that doesn't belong to it, Windows XP can close the program without affecting any other running program. You still lose any unsaved work in the guilty program, but all your other programs continue running.

While Windows XP is dealing with the misbehaving program, you can move the program's window so that it doesn't obstruct your view of any other programs you have open.

System File Protection

Windows XP offers a feature called System File Protection that protects your system files from ill-advised actions on your part.

Windows XP tries to persuade you not to view the contents of folders that you probably shouldn't be messing with, by refusing to show them to you until you demand it show them. You can then delete system files if you want (except for any file that's actively in use, which is locked automatically). But the next time that Windows boots, or if it catches the damage you've done before you reboot it, it replaces the files you deleted without notifying you.

System Restore

Windows XP offers a System Restore feature similar to but more effective than the System Restore feature in Windows Me. System Restore automatically creates restore points both periodically and each time you make a change to the system—for example, by installing a program or a driver.

You can also create system restore points manually. When one of your changes leads to an unwelcome result, such as your computer failing to work as well as it did before, you can use System Restore to roll back the change to an earlier point at which the system was working properly.

Device Driver Rollback

Device drivers have long been the bane of Windows–okay, *one* of the banes of Windows. By installing the wrong driver, or a buggy driver, you could render your computer useless until you reinstalled Windows (or turned in frustration to another operating system).

Windows XP tracks the drivers you install and lets you roll back the installation of the driver–in other words, you can revert to the driver you were using before.

Better yet, Windows XP stores details of the previous driver in what's called the Last Known Good Configuration–the configuration used the last time the computer seemed to be running okay. This means that if installing a new driver prevents your computer from booting as normal, you can use the Last Known Good Configuration to restore the previous driver.

NTFS

Whereas Windows 9*x* versions used the FAT (File Allocation Table) and VFAT (Virtual File Allocation Table) file systems, Windows XP prefers NTFS, the NT file system. NTFS provides security features (including file-level security) and stability that FAT and VFAT do not.

Chapter 2 discusses how to install (or upgrade to) NTFS.

Compatibility with Windows 9x Programs

Windows XP aims to be able to run all programs that would run on Windows 9*x*, Windows NT, and Windows 2000. As you'll know if you've struggled to run a Windows 9*x* program on NT or Windows 2000, this is quite a challenge. NT-based operating systems (including Windows XP) handle memory and hardware access in a different way than Windows 9*x* operating systems. These differences mean that programs designed for Windows 9*x* often won't run satisfactorily on NT and Windows 2000.

Being able to run these legacy programs is a big feature of Windows XP–but because Microsoft has implemented this feature very successfully, it remains hidden most of the time. Usually, you can simply install a legacy program and run it without complications. Behind the scenes, Windows XP may be running the program in its Compatibility mode or applying one of its new AppFixes to the program (to prevent it from detecting the wrong operating system and from causing problems such as referencing memory once it's been freed up), but you often won't know about it. You may need to specifically run some programs in Compatibility mode, and you may see Windows Update automatically downloading new information for AppFixes to keep your copy of Windows up to date, but most of the time, your old programs will simply work—which of course is the way it should be.

Should You Upgrade to Windows XP Professional?

Whether you should upgrade to Windows XP Professional depends on your needs, how well your current version of Windows is fulfilling them, and whether your hardware is up to the test. The decision is wholly yours (of course), but the following sections offer some suggestions, depending on where you're coming from.

Intended Usage

As its name suggests (and is designed to suggest), Windows XP Professional is geared toward use in a professional setting—for example, in an office or in a corporate setting. That doesn't mean you can't use it at home if you want, just that it has features designed for use in office and corporate settings. For example, it's designed to connect to Windows 2000 servers running Active Directory domains, and it has features for being managed remotely by administrators. Professional also has features for using a portable computer as a complement to a desktop computer (rather than instead of a desktop computer) and lets you easily synchronize files between two computers.

Cost

As you'd expect, Windows XP Professional is more expensive than Windows XP Home, though if you need the extra features it offers, it's affordable enough. But you'll certainly want to avoid first buying Windows XP Home and then upgrading to Windows XP Professional.

Hardware Requirements

Windows XP Professional runs adequately on the same hardware as Windows XP Home. While Professional doesn't actually *need* better hardware than Home, it probably *appreciates* better hardware more than Home does, because its extra features can use some extra memory and processing power.

Upgrade Paths to Windows XP

You can upgrade to Windows XP Professional from Windows 98, Windows 98 Second Edition, Windows Me, Windows NT 4 Workstation, and Windows 2000 Professional.

WHAT'S NEXT?

The next chapter discusses how to install Windows XP Professional, both as an upgrade and as a clean installation from scratch. It also describes system requirements and how to prepare for installing a new operating system.

Chapter 2

Installing Windows XP

This chapter discusses how to install Windows XP Professional in each of the three ways in which you may want to install it: as an upgrade to Windows 98 or Windows Me; as a new installation on a computer that already has installed an operating system that you want to keep; and as a clean installation on a computer that doesn't have an operating system installed (or a computer whose operating system you want to wipe). Each of these installation paths starts in a distinct way, and the chapter covers these separately. Toward the end of the installation, all three installation paths join each other for the last few steps, so the chapter covers these steps only once.

At the end of the chapter, you'll find a discussion of how to perform an unattended installation, which can be useful if you need to install the same operating system multiple times.

Revised and adapted from *Mastering Windows XP Home Edition* by Guy Hart-Davis

ISBN 0-7821-2980-3 1024 pages $39.99

The Order of Business

Here's the order of business for installing Windows XP successfully:

- First, make sure that your computer will be able to run Windows XP Professional. Start by comparing your system specifications with the minimum requirements, and see if you need to upgrade any components.
- Then—assuming your computer has an operating system loaded already—load the Windows XP CD in your computer and run the Windows Upgrade Advisor.
- If you want to perform a new installation or a clean installation of Windows XP rather than an upgrade, but you want your new installation or clean installation to pick up your current settings and some of your files, run the Files and Settings Transfer Wizard to save the settings from your current version of Windows.
- Then perform the upgrade, new installation, or clean installation.
- If you ran the Files and Settings Transfer Wizard, run it again to apply your settings to Windows XP and to make your files available.

Will Your Computer Be Able to Run Windows XP Professional?

First, make sure that your computer will be able to run Windows XP Professional. The following sections discuss the main requirements.

Processor

Windows XP requires a minimum of a Pentium II processor running at 233MHz. But realistically, you'll want a 600MHz or faster processor for the kind of performance you'll need in a business setting.

If you don't know what processor your computer has, watch the information that comes up as it boots. This will give you at least the processor speed, though it may give an incorrect classification of the chip. For example, some systems classify Celeron chips as Pentium III chips.

(Midrange Celeron chips *are* in fact cut-down Pentium III chips, but your system should really know the difference.)

RAM

Windows XP requires a minimum of 64MB of RAM to install and run. This too is an absolute minimum and delivers poor performance unless your processor is extremely fast (in which case the lack of RAM cannibalizes processor performance). You'll get good performance for one concurrent user session if you have 128MB of RAM. For multiple concurrent user sessions, get 256MB or more RAM. (At this writing, 256MB RAM modules are selling for prices as low as $45, so upgrading your RAM is relatively painless.)

NOTE

Windows XP Professional can access a maximum of 4GB of RAM.

If you don't know how much RAM your computer has, watch the count of RAM when you boot. If the number is in kilobytes, divide by 1024 to get the number in megabytes. Alternatively, click Start, right-click My Computer, and choose Properties from the shortcut menu. Windows displays the System Properties dialog box with the General tab foremost. At the bottom of the page is a readout of the amount of RAM in the computer.

EXPERT KNOWLEDGE: GET PLENTY OF RAM

Huh, you may be thinking: *that's* "expert knowledge"? Everyone knows that you need plenty of RAM to run Windows. That's true—up to a point. But most people still have too little RAM in their computers.

Windows XP will run—well, more like stagger along—on 64MB RAM. If the computer has a fast processor, and if you don't use any large programs or large files, performance may be tolerable. But the hard disk will be kept busy as Windows continually uses virtual memory to store the information that won't fit in the RAM.

CONTINUED →

If you're buying a new computer, you'll be much better off saving a little money on the processor and putting it into RAM. Unless you're running the latest 3D games or performing terrain mapping or other advanced imaging, you'll notice little benefit from having a few hundred extra megahertz on your processor. But another 128MB (better, another 256MB) of RAM will make a huge difference over 64MB on a system with just about any processor.

Windows XP runs adequately on an antiquated processor such as a Pentium II 266 provided the computer has enough RAM—128MB for a single user session running a "normal" number of programs, 192MB for a single user session running a heavy number of programs, and 256MB or more for multiple user sessions running concurrently.

Given this, it's sad to see that many companies that should really know better—including IBM, Dell, and Compaq—are plugging computers with gigahertz-plus processors and 64MB RAM. They'll happily sell you as much extra memory as you specify, of course—but the implication is that a computer with 64MB RAM is adequately configured to run Windows, which it isn't.

Free Disk Space

Windows XP requires approximately 650MB of free disk space to install on a 2GB hard drive. If you're installing over a network, you'll need more free space. In addition, there has to be space for your paging file (by default, 1.5× the amount of RAM in your computer) and for your hibernation file (the same size as the amount of RAM) if your computer supports hibernation. On top of that, you'll need space for any programs you want to install and any files you want to create.

In practice, it's a good idea to have at least 1GB of free space on the drive on which you install Windows XP, plus space for your programs and files. To see how much space is free on a drive, right-click the drive in an Explorer window and choose Properties from the shortcut menu. The General tab of the resulting Properties dialog box for the drive shows how much free space it has.

SVGA-Capable Video Adapter and Monitor

Your video adapter and monitor need to be capable of SVGA (Super Video Graphics Array) resolution (800×600 pixels) with 256 or more colors for you to enjoy Windows XP in all its glory. Beyond that, just about any PCI (Peripheral Component Interconnect) or AGP (Accelerated Graphics Port) video adapter should work (drivers permitting, of course), as should any CRT (cathode ray tube) or LCD (liquid crystal display) monitor.

CD Drive or DVD Drive

You need a CD drive or DVD drive, or access to one or the other, to install Windows XP. If the drive is on another computer, you can install across a network or copy the files to your local drive and run them from there.

Checking System Compatibility

To check whether Windows XP thinks your computer will be able to run it, run the Windows Upgrade Advisor program by following these steps:

1. Insert the Windows XP CD. If your computer doesn't automatically start running the CD, open an Explorer window, navigate to the CD, and double-click the `SETUP.EXE` program.
2. On the opening screen, click the Check System Compatibility link. Setup offers the choices Check My System Automatically and Visit the Compatibility Web Site.
3. Click the Check My System Automatically link.
4. If an Internet connection is available, Setup runs Dynamic Update to download any new files that may help with the installation. It then runs the Windows Upgrade Advisor program and displays the Upgrade Report page of the Microsoft Windows Upgrade Advisor. Figure 2.1 shows an example of an upgrade report.

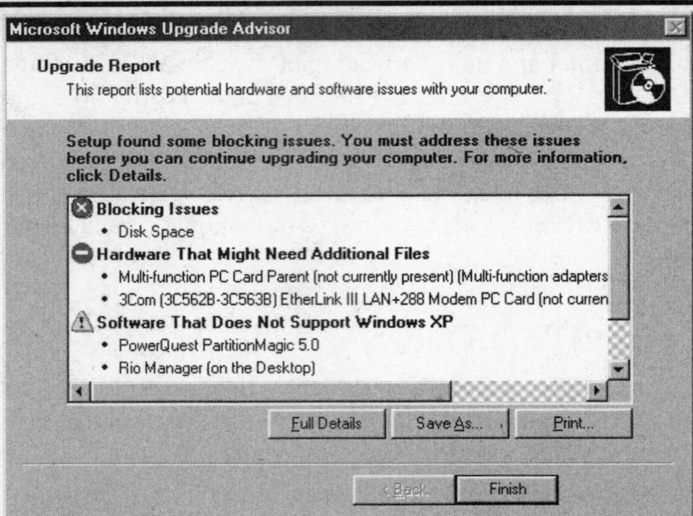

FIGURE 2.1: Use the Microsoft Windows Upgrade Advisor to check whether your computer will be able to run Windows XP.

5. If your computer seems to be fit for Windows XP, the report tells you that the check found no incompatibilities or problems. Any problems are listed in the list box in summary form. Click the Full Details button to view the details (broken up into categories such as Blocking Issues, Warnings, and Helpful Information) and advice on what to do about the problems. (Click the resulting Summary button to return to the summary view.) Click the Save As button to save the information to file, or click the Print button to print a copy of it.

6. Click the Finish button. Windows closes the Microsoft Windows Upgrade Advisor.

Follow the Upgrade Advisor's advice to get your computer ready for upgrading to Windows XP. In particular, you need to take care of any blocking issues that the Advisor has identified. An example of a blocking issue is not having enough disk space to install Windows XP. You might need to remove some existing files, or reconfigure your partitions (for example, by using a tool such as PartitionMagic), in order to resolve such an issue.

Choosing a Method of Installing Windows XP

Once you've decided to install Windows XP, your next decision is how to install Windows XP on your computer. You can install Windows XP in three ways:

Upgrade If you have Windows 9*x*, Windows NT 4 Workstation (including service packs), or Windows 2000 Professional (including service packs), you can perform an upgrade, essentially overwriting the previous version of Windows with Windows XP. (It's not entirely overwritten, because you can restore it if you so choose.) Upgrading like this transfers all your files, settings, and programs to Windows XP, so (in theory) you can pick up your work or play straight away in Windows XP where you left off.

New installation You can install Windows XP alongside your current version of Windows. Windows XP creates a dual-boot setup (or modifies an existing dual-boot setup to create a multi-boot setup) so that you can run either operating system. Installing like this lets you compare Windows XP with your previous version of Windows. You can use the Files and Settings Transfer Wizard to copy your files and settings from your previous version of Windows to Windows XP.

Clean installation You can install Windows XP from scratch on your computer, setting it up as the only operating system but not upgrading from your current operating system. Again, you can use the Files and Settings Transfer Wizard to copy your files and settings from your previous version of Windows to Windows XP. You'll need to install all the programs you want to use after you install Windows XP.

Which type of installation to perform can be a tricky decision. The longer you've been running Windows on this computer since installing it, the stronger the arguments are for both an upgrade and a clean installation:

- By now, you've probably installed all the programs you need and got them working together. By upgrading, you can transition your whole work environment to Windows XP, so that your Desktop, Start menu, and folder structure retain their current settings and your programs all work as before.

- Then again, you probably have programs that you no longer use, or programs that no longer work. By performing a clean install, you can strip your system down to only the software you need. It'll take longer, but the result may be better. Similarly, your data folders could probably do with some cleaning out and archiving.

If you need to install a new hard drive as your main hard drive, you'll need to perform a clean install. (The exception is if you use a hard drive cloning or migration package such as DriveImage or Ghost. These packages are often used for upgrading the hard drives in laptops, where the lack of expansion room forces you to replace the current hard drive rather than add a drive, but some of them work for desktops as well.)

Preparing for Installation

Once you've established that your computer should be able to run Windows XP, prepare for installation by taking those of the following steps as are applicable to the type of installation you're planning (upgrade, new installation, or clean installation).

Back Up All Your Data Files

For safety, back up all your data files shortly before installation using your usual backup medium.

Write Down Internet Connection Information

If you're planning a new installation or clean installation rather than an upgrade, and you use a dial-up Internet connection, write down the information you need to create the connection: your ISP account username, your password, your ISP's phone number, and your ISP's primary DNS server and secondary DNS server. If you connect to the Internet through a broadband connection that requires some configuration and/or that you log on, make a note of all these settings.

Plug In and Switch On All Hardware

Make sure that all the hardware you intend to use with the computer is attached to it and powered on. For example, if you'll use a printer and scanner with the computer, make sure these devices are attached to the computer and powered on, so that Setup can detect them if it's smart enough.

Use the Files and Settings Transfer Wizard to Transfer Settings

Windows XP includes a Wizard for transferring files and settings from one computer or operating system to another. You don't need to use this Wizard, which is called the Files and Settings Transfer Wizard, if you're upgrading Windows 98 or Windows Me to Windows XP, because Windows automatically transfers all your settings when you perform an upgrade. But the Wizard can save you a great deal of time when you want to transfer files and settings either to a new computer that's running Windows XP or to a new installation of Windows XP on the same computer on which you've kept your previous installation of Windows as a dual-boot. For example, if you choose to test Windows XP on a new partition before committing yourself to it, you can use the Files and Settings Transfer Wizard to transfer your work environment to the new partition so that you can use your regular settings and files.

Before you use the Files and Settings Transfer Wizard, make sure you've connected any network drive you want to use, or that you have a removable disk or recordable CD ready. To transfer files and settings, you'll need plenty of storage. You can save settings files to a floppy drive, but most data files will be too big.

To use the Files and Settings Transfer Wizard, follow these steps:

1. Insert the Windows XP CD. If your computer doesn't automatically start running the CD, open an Explorer window, navigate to the CD, and double-click the SETUP.EXE program. Windows displays the Welcome to Microsoft Windows XP screen.

2. Click the Perform Additional Tasks link.

3. On the next screen, click the Transfer Files and Settings link. Setup starts the Files and Settings Transfer Wizard.

4. Click the Next button. If this computer is running Windows XP, the Wizard displays the Which Computer Is This? screen. If it does, select the Old Computer option button and click

the Next button. (If this computer isn't running Windows XP, the Wizard knows it's the old computer.) The Wizard then displays the Select a Transfer Method page (shown in Figure 2.2).

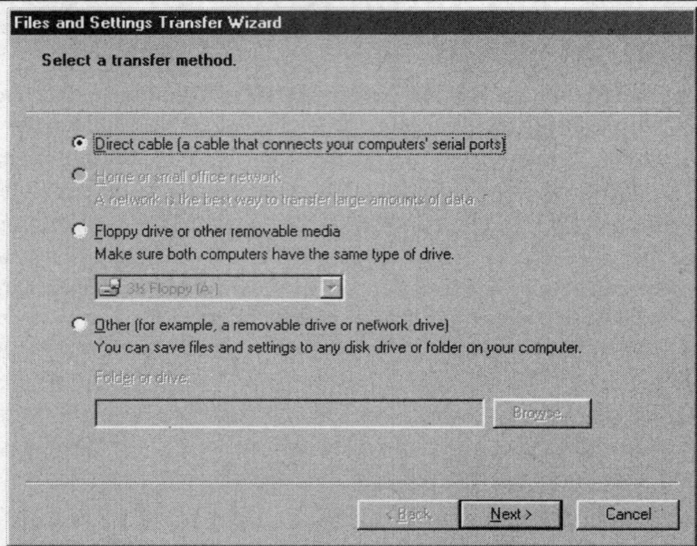

FIGURE 2.2: On the Select a Transfer Method page of the Files and Settings Transfer Wizard, specify how you want to transfer files and settings from the old computer to the new computer.

5. Select the Direct Cable option button, the Home or Small Office Network option button (if it's available), the Floppy Drive or Other Removable Media option button (select the drive in the drop-down list), or the Other option button as appropriate. The Other option button lets you use the Browse button and the resulting Browse for Folder dialog box or the Folder or Drive text box to specify a removable drive or a network drive.

6. Click the Next button. The Wizard displays the What Do You Want to Transfer? page (shown in Figure 2.3).

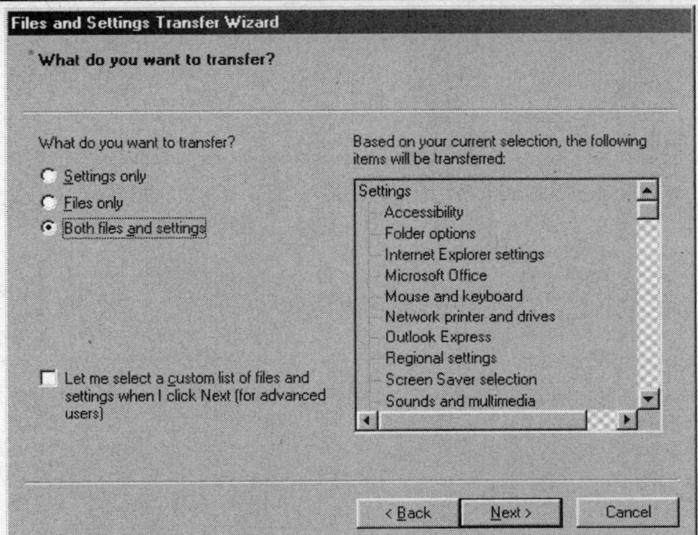

FIGURE 2.3: On the What Do You Want to Transfer? page of the Files and Settings Transfer Wizard, specify which settings and files you want to transfer to the new computer (or to Windows XP).

7. In the What Do You Want to Transfer? list, select the Settings Only option button, the Files Only option button, or the Both Files and Settings option button as appropriate. The list box on the right side of the dialog box lists the types of settings and files that will be affected.

8. If you want to customize the list of settings, files, or both, select the Let Me Select a Custom List of Files and Settings when I Click Next check box. Customizing the list of files lets you specify particular folders for transfer. By default, the Wizard transfers the `\Desktop\` folder, the `\Fonts\` folder, the `\My Documents\` folder, and the `\Shared Desktop\` folder.

9. Click the Next button. If you selected the Customize check box, the Wizard displays the Select Custom Files and Settings page (shown in Figure 2.4).

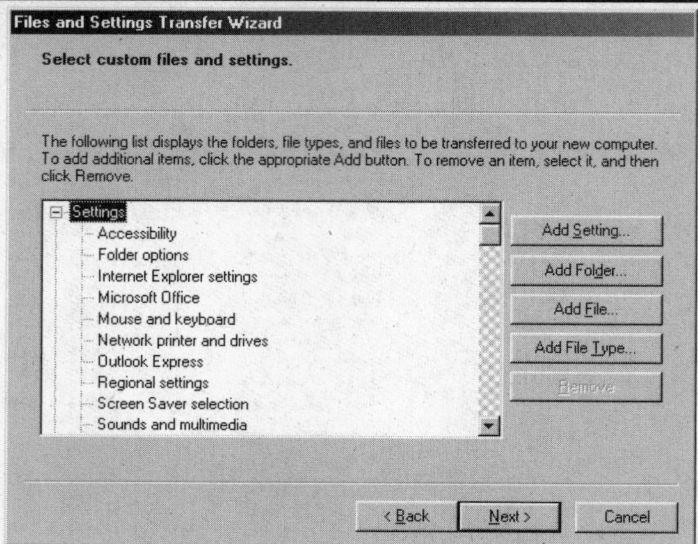

FIGURE 2.4: On the Select Custom Files and Settings page of the Files and Settings Transfer Wizard, choose the files and settings to transfer.

10. Select the files and settings to transfer:
    - To add a setting, click the Add Setting button. The Wizard displays the Add a Setting dialog box. Select the setting or settings in the list box and click the OK button. The Wizard closes the Add a Setting dialog box and adds the setting or settings to the list.
    - To add a folder, click the Add Folder button. The Wizard displays the Browse for Folder dialog box. Select the folder and click the OK button. The Wizard closes the Browse for Folder dialog box and adds the folder to the list.
    - To add a file, click the Add File button. The Wizard displays the Add a File dialog box (a common Open dialog box in disguise). Select the file and click the Open button. The Wizard closes the Add a File dialog box and adds the file to the list.
    - To add a file type, click the Add File Type button. The Wizard displays the Add a File Type dialog box (shown in Figure 2.5). Select the file type in the Registered File

Types list box; if it's not listed there, enter its extension in the Other text box. Then click the OK button. The Wizard closes the Add a File Type dialog box and adds the file type to the list.

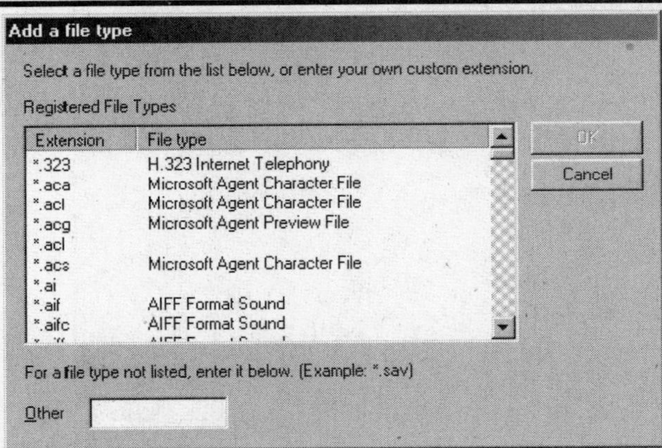

FIGURE 2.5: Use the Add a File Type dialog box to add a file type to the list of file types to transfer.

- To remove a setting, folder, file, or file type, select it in the list box and click the Remove button.

11. Click the Next button. The Wizard may display the Install Programs on Your New Computer page, suggesting some programs that you may want to install on your new computer (or new installation of Windows) before transferring settings. If so, note these suggestions.
12. The Wizard then displays the Collection in Progress page (shown in Figure 2.6) while it collects your files and settings. It then displays the Completing the Collection Phase page.

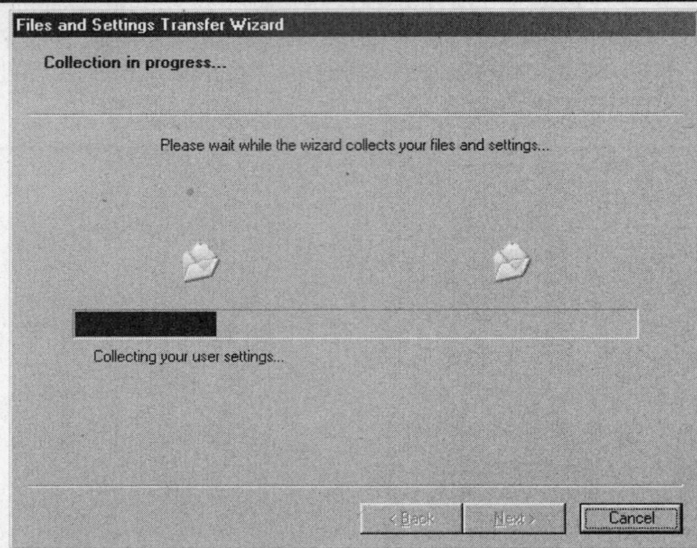

FIGURE 2.6: The Wizard collects the files.

13. Click the Finish button. The Wizard closes itself.

For details of how to apply your saved files and settings to your new installation of Windows, see "Applying Your Files and Settings" later in this chapter.

Stop Any Antivirus Software or Disk Utilities

Stop any antivirus software or disk utilities before running the Windows installation, because the installation process needs direct access to your hardware.

Upgrading Windows to Windows XP

When you upgrade, the installation procedure copies the settings from your current version of Windows and applies them to the installation of Windows XP. If the installation doesn't work correctly, or if you find

Windows XP doesn't suit you, you can uninstall it and revert to your previous installation unless you are upgrading from Windows NT or Windows 2000 Professional.

To perform an upgrade, take the following steps:

1. Insert the CD in a CD drive or DVD drive. If Autoplay is enabled on your computer, Windows displays the introductory screen (shown in Figure 2.7). If not, open an Explorer window and double-click the CD. This should trigger the Autoplay action. If it doesn't, double-click the SETUP.EXE file on the CD to run it.

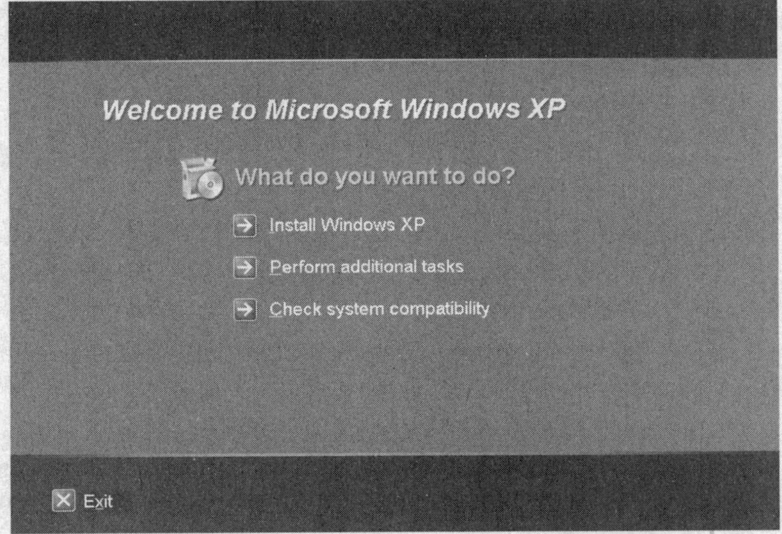

FIGURE 2.7: To start the upgrade, select the Install Windows XP link.

2. Click the Install Windows XP link. Setup displays the Welcome to Windows Setup page (shown in Figure 2.8).

FIGURE 2.8: On the Welcome to Windows Setup page, choose the Upgrade item in the Installation Type drop-down list.

3. In the Installation Type drop-down list, choose the Upgrade item.
4. Click the Next button. Setup displays the License Agreement page. Read it.
5. If you agree to the license, select the I Accept This Agreement option button and click the Next button. (If you don't agree to the license, Setup exits.) Setup displays the Your Product Key page.
6. Enter your product key and click the Next button. Setup displays the Upgrade Report page (shown in Figure 2.9).

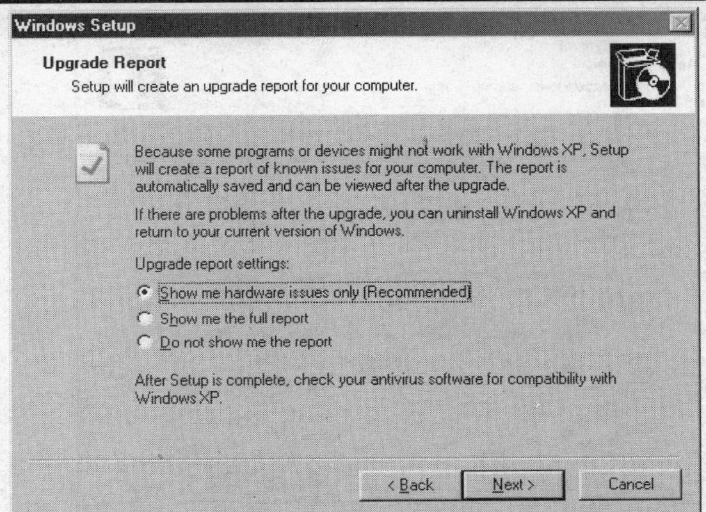

FIGURE 2.9: On the Upgrade Report page of Setup, choose the type of upgrade report you want for this computer.

7. Choose the type of upgrade report you want by selecting the Show Me Hardware Issues and a Limited Set of Software Issues option button, the Show Me the Full Report option button, or the Do Not Show Me the Report option button.
8. Click the Next button. Setup displays the Get Updated Setup Files page (shown in Figure 2.10), which lets you choose whether to use Dynamic Update to download any new Setup files that Microsoft may have released since your copy of Windows XP was pressed.

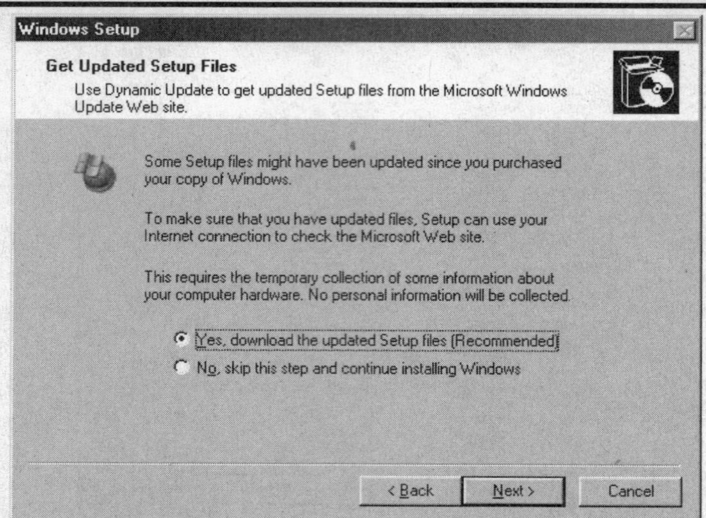

FIGURE 2.10: On the Get Updated Setup Files page of Setup, choose whether to let Dynamic Update download the latest Setup files.

9. To download any available files, leave the Yes, Download the Updated Setup Files option button selected, as it is by default. To skip Dynamic Update, select the No, Skip This Step and Continue Installing Windows option button.

NOTE

You can download any updated files by using Windows Update after you finish installing Windows XP. The only advantage to Dynamic Update comes if the new files are needed for any of the hardware on your computer during installation.

10. Click the Next button. If you chose to use Dynamic Update, Setup contacts the Microsoft Web site and downloads any relevant files. Setup then starts analyzing your computer for possible problems in upgrading to Windows XP.

    - If you don't have enough space to install Windows XP, you'll see a Windows XP Setup dialog box such as that shown in Figure 2.11 warning you of the problem. Click the Quit Setup button, retire disconsolately from the fray, and return when you've made more space available.

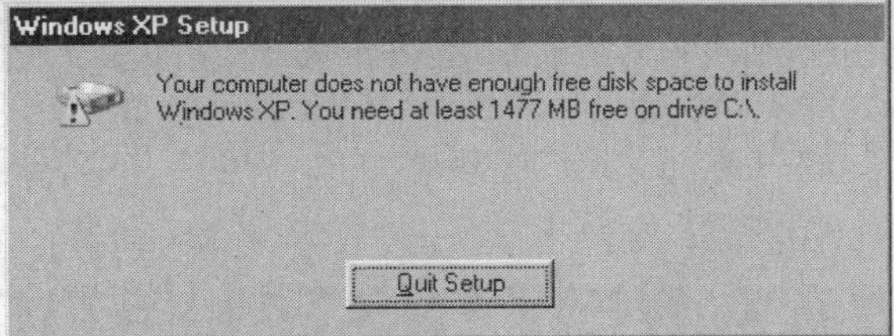

FIGURE 2.11: Setup warns you if you don't have enough space available to install Windows XP.

11. If you have any incompatible hardware or software, Setup displays the Upgrade Report page (of which Figure 2.12 shows a sample). You can click the Full Report button to view the details of the hardware and software, click the Save As button to save the information to file, or click the Print button to print a copy of it. If you don't take up one of these options, Setup displays the Windows XP Setup dialog box, which warns you that some devices on your computer may not work with Windows XP and offers you a View Report button, a Continue button, and a Quit Setup button. Click the Continue button if you want to continue.

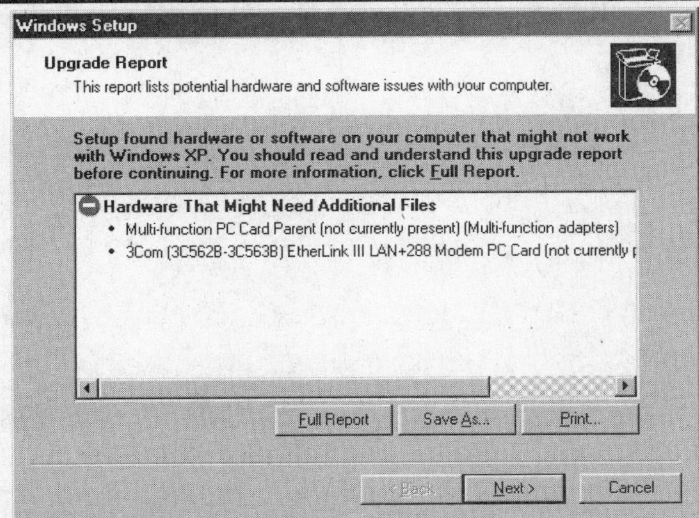

FIGURE 2.12: The Upgrade Report page of Setup summarizes any potential hardware and software upgrade problems you may face.

12. Click the Next button. Setup continues running the setup routine, reboots your computer, and takes the installation all the way to the Welcome to Microsoft Windows screen. Skip ahead to "The Installation Paths Converge" later in the chapter.

Performing a New Installation of Windows XP

To perform a new installation of Windows XP (without upgrading your current version of Windows), follow these steps:

1. Insert the CD in a CD drive or DVD drive. If Autoplay is enabled on your computer, Windows displays the introductory screen (shown in Figure 2.13). If not, open an Explorer window and double-click the CD. This should trigger the Autoplay action. If it doesn't, double-click the SETUP.EXE file on the CD to run it.

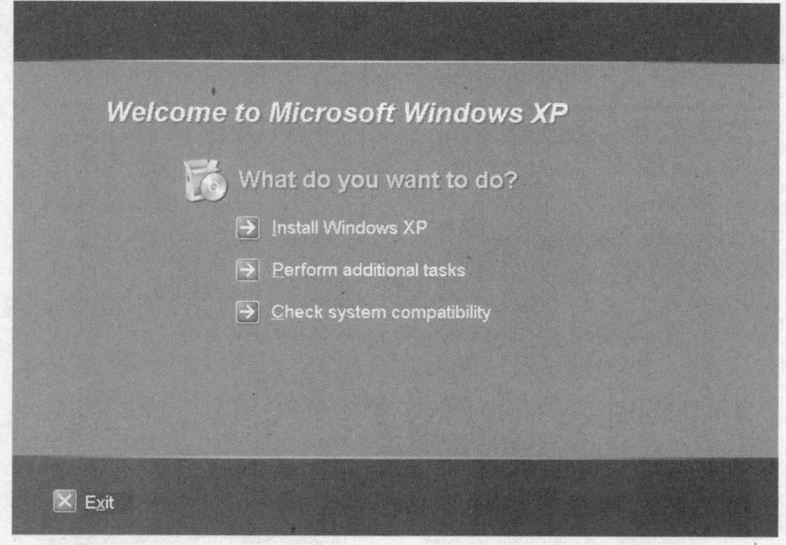

FIGURE 2.13: To start the upgrade, select the Install Windows XP link.

2. Click the Install Windows XP link. Setup displays the Welcome to Windows Setup page (shown in Figure 2.14).

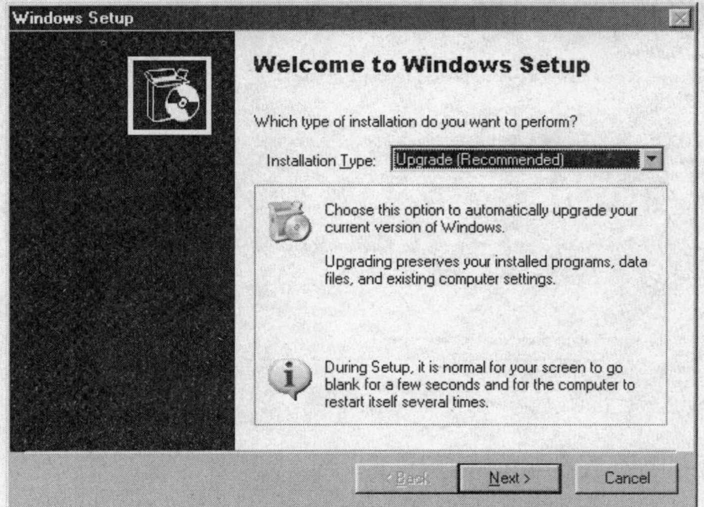

FIGURE 2.14: On the Welcome to Windows Setup page, choose the New Installation item in the Installation Type drop-down list.

3. In the Installation Type drop-down list, choose the New Installation item.
4. Click the Next button. Setup displays the License Agreement page. Read it.
5. If you agree to the license, select the I Accept This Agreement option button and click the Next button. (If you don't agree to the license, Setup exits.) Setup displays the Your Product Key page.
6. Enter your product key and click the Next button. Setup displays the Setup Options page (shown in Figure 2.15). From this page, you can choose language options, installation options, and accessibility options.

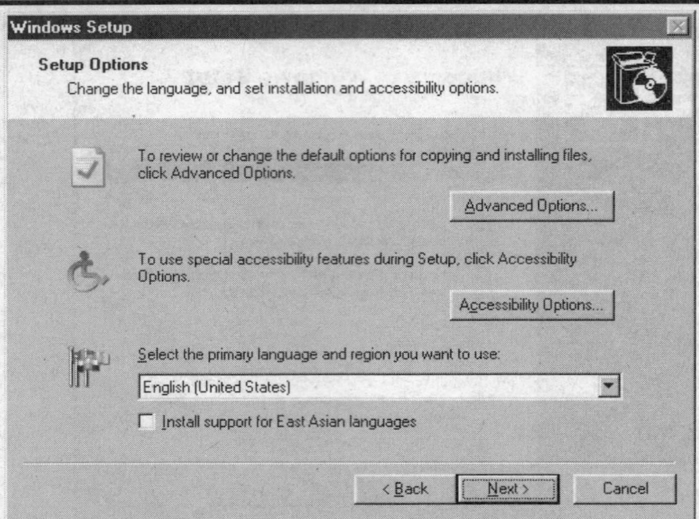

FIGURE 2.15: When you perform a new installation, Setup displays the Setup Options page, on which you can choose advanced options and accessibility options.

7. To change the language used, select the language in the Select the Primary Language and Region You Want to Use drop-down list. If you want to install support for East Asian languages, select the Install Support for East Asian Languages check box.

8. To set the advanced options, which let you control the installation folder and specify that you want to select the installation partition, click the Advanced Options button on the Setup Options page. Setup displays the Advanced Options dialog box (shown in Figure 2.16), which offers the following options:

   - The Copy Installation Files from This Folder text box lists the path from which you ran the Setup program (or it ran itself). Usually, you won't need to change this path, but you can if necessary.

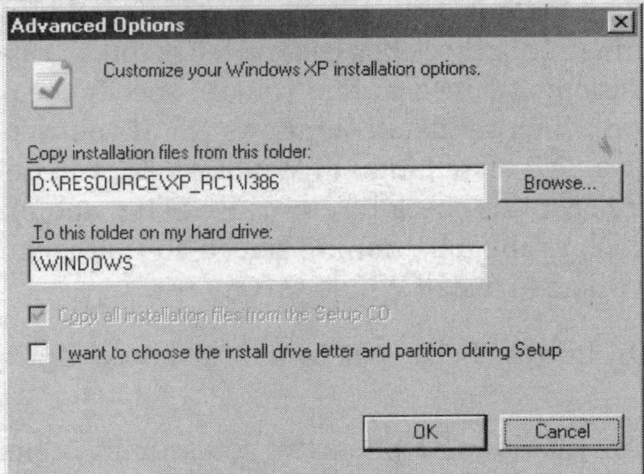

FIGURE 2.16: In the Advanced Options dialog box, you can specify the installation folder and tell Setup that you want to choose the installation partition.

- The To This Folder on My Hard Drive text box shows the location to which Setup is planning to install Windows XP: your current Windows folder. If you don't want Windows XP to overwrite your current version of Windows, choose a different folder. For example, you may want to create a dual-boot setup so that you can compare Windows XP to your current version of Windows without yet removing the latter from your computer.
- The Copy All Installation Files from the Setup CD check box enables you to force Setup to copy all its files to the hard drive rather than leaving them on the CD. Use this option when installing Windows XP from a CD that will not be available after Setup reboots the computer. For example, when installing Windows XP on a laptop computer using an external CD drive (such as a parallel-port drive, a USB drive, or a PC Card–connected drive), you'll probably need to copy all setup files to the hard drive because the CD drive will not be available from the reboot until Setup is complete. You may also need to use this option if your CD drive will not read the Windows XP CD reliably during the setup routine after the reboot. (This shouldn't happen, but it does. After the reboot, Setup uses a different CD driver that apparently disagrees with some CD drives.) By default, this check box is cleared unless you're installing from a network drive, in which case it's not available (as in Figure 2.16).

- The I Want to Choose the Install Drive Letter and Partition during Setup check box lets you tell Setup to display the partitioning screen so that you can specify the partition on which to install Windows XP. If you're performing a new installation of Windows XP, you don't need to select this check box, because Setup automatically displays the partitioning screen so that you can specify where to install Windows XP.

9. Click the OK button. Setup closes the Advanced Options dialog box.

10. During Setup, Windows XP offers two accessibility options, Magnifier and Narrator. Magnifier is designed for people with limited but viable vision and displays an enlarged version of the selected portion of the screen. Narrator is designed for the blind and those with more limited vision. It reads the contents of the screen aloud. To use these options, click the Accessibility Options button on the Setup Options page. Setup displays the Accessibility Options dialog box (shown in Figure 2.17). Select the Use Microsoft Magnifier during Setup check box or the Use Microsoft Narrator during Setup check box as appropriate. Then click the OK button. Setup closes the Accessibility Options dialog box and applies your choices.

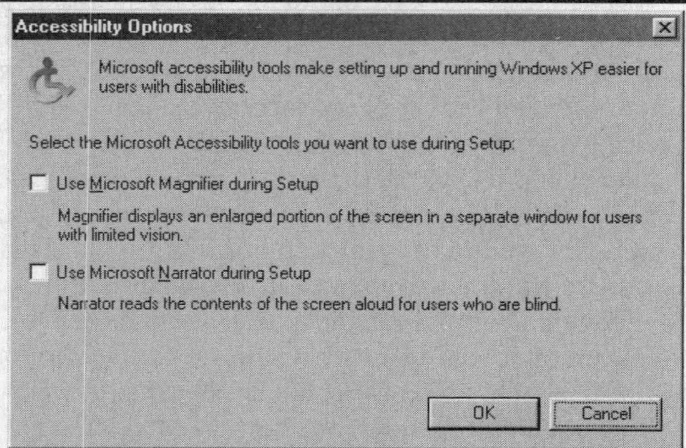

FIGURE 2.17: Setup offers Magnifier and Narrator accessibility options for those with limited vision and the blind.

11. Once you've finished choosing special options, click the Next button on the Setup Options page. Setup displays the Get Updated Setup Files page (shown in Figure 2.18), which lets you choose whether to use Dynamic Update to download any new Setup files that Microsoft may have released since your copy of Windows XP was pressed.

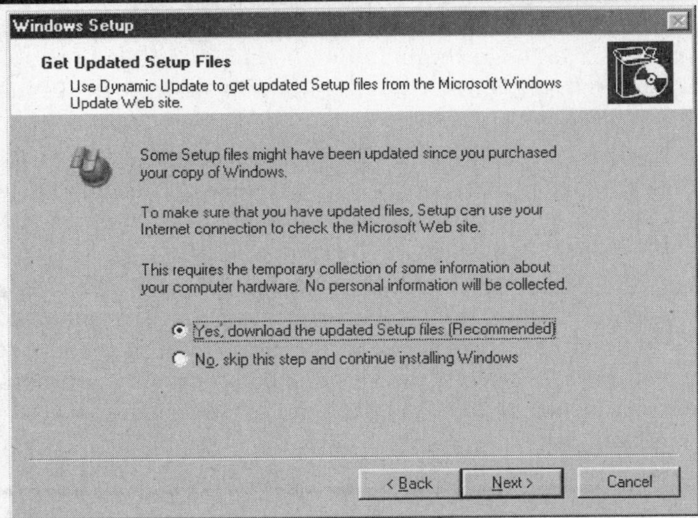

FIGURE 2.18: On the Get Updated Setup Files page of Setup, choose whether to let Dynamic Update download the latest Setup files.

12. To download any available files, leave the Yes, Download the Updated Setup Files option button selected, as it is by default. To skip Dynamic Update, select the No, Skip This Step and Continue Installing Windows option button.

13. Click the Next button. If you chose to use Dynamic Update, Setup contacts the Microsoft Web site and downloads any relevant files. Setup then continues running the setup routine, reboots your computer, and displays the partitioning screen. Go to the "Choosing a Hard Disk Partition" section in the "Performing a Clean Installation of Windows XP" section, a little later in this chapter.

EXPERT KNOWLEDGE: WHY IS THE FOLDER CALLED I386?

If you're looking at the Advanced Options dialog box, the Copy Installation Files from This Folder text box is probably listing a path that ends in `\i386\`. What's this all about?

i386 stands for Intel 386. The 386, as you'll remember if you've been computing for a while, was Intel's hottest processor at the end of the 1980s. But it's also the descriptor for the entire family of chips that has continued through the 486 chips and Pentium chips (renamed from 586, which wasn't trademarkable) to the Pentium IV chips of today.

But why is i386 there? Why's the folder not called something intuitive like *Files*? It's because NT was originally written to be processor independent so that it could run on various types of processor without major rebuilding.

The early version of NT ran on Intel chips, Alpha chips, MIPS chips, and PowerPC chips. The installation CD came with a separate folder for each of these. Over the years (or, more correctly, over the versions of NT), Microsoft gradually dropped support for processors other than the Intel 386 family. But the `\i386\` folder survives as a hangover of the old days.

Performing a Clean Installation of Windows XP

To perform a clean installation of Windows XP, put the Windows XP CD in your CD-ROM drive or DVD drive and boot from it. (You may have to change the boot settings in your computer's BIOS to boot from the CD.) Setup automatically launches itself.

First, Setup displays the Welcome to Setup screen. From here, press the Enter key to start the installation. (Press the F3 key if you've reached this stage by mistake and need to quit.) Setup displays the partitioning screen.

Choosing a Hard Disk Partition

The partitioning screen lets you create and delete partitions as well as specify the installation partition. The screen lists the current partitions on the disk, their label, their type (for example, *NTFS* for an NTFS partition, *FAT32* for a FAT partition, and *Raw* for a new, unformatted partition), their size, and the amount of space free on each. Any unpartitioned space is listed as such. Any space you've deliberately left unpartitioned will of course be free, but there will often be a few megabytes of unpartitioned space left over after you've tried to allocate all the space on the disk.

To choose an existing partition for the installation, use ↑ and ↓ to move the highlight to it. Then press the Enter key.

To create a new partition, select some unpartitioned space and press the C key. Setup displays a details screen. Specify the size of the partition in megabytes and press the Enter key.

If you want to install Windows XP and use up the full amount of unpartitioned space, you don't need to explicitly create a partition first. Just select the Unpartitioned Space item and press the Enter key to start the installation.

To delete an existing partition, select it in the list and press the D key. Setup displays a screen confirming the action. Press the L key. If the partition is a system partition, Setup displays a more extensive warning. And if the partition is the partition on which Setup has installed its temporary files for carrying out the installation of Windows, Setup refuses to delete the partition.

Once you've chosen a partition, Setup proceeds. If the partition is a new partition, Setup offers you the choice of formatting it with NTFS or with FAT. For each, there's the option of a quick format. A full format includes a scan of the disk for bad sectors; a quick format skips this scan. Unless you're in a tearing hurry and have checked the disk recently for bad sectors, go with the full format.

NOTE

If you choose to install Windows XP on a partition that already contains another operating system, Setup displays a page warning you that this may cause problems. Press the C key if you're prepared to continue. Press the Esc key to return to the partitioning screen and select another partition.

Converting the Partition to NTFS

If you're installing Windows XP on an existing partition that uses FAT, Setup offers you the option of converting the installation partition to NTFS. Think seriously about doing so, because NTFS is one of the major improvements in Windows XP Professional over Windows Me and other Windows 9*x* versions.

NTFS offers two compelling advantages over FAT. First, NTFS has security features (including auditing) that FAT does not. And second, NTFS keeps a log of activities so that it can restore the disk to order after a hardware or power failure; FAT simply loses your data instead.

WARNING

If you're creating a dual-boot configuration with a version of Windows 9*x*, remember that Windows 9*x* cannot read NTFS partitions. If this doesn't matter to you, go right ahead and convert the partition to NTFS.

Next, you see the license agreement. Read it and press the F8 key if you agree and want to proceed. Press the Esc key to cancel installation.

Choosing Regional and Language Options

After this, Setup entertains itself for a few minutes as it performs part of the installation. Next, you see the Regional and Language Options page. From here, you can change the computer's standards and formats setting so that it displays numbers, currencies, and dates in the appropriate formats for the country or user. You can also change the default keyboard layout.

To change the standards and formats setting, click the Customize button. Setup displays the Regional and Language Options dialog box with the Region Options tab foremost, as shown in Figure 2.19. In the Standards and Formats section, select the language and locale you want to use. The text boxes in the Samples area show samples of a number, a currency, a time, a short date, and a long date for that language and locale. (You can change these by clicking the Customize button and working in the Customize Regional Options dialog box.) In the Location drop-down list, select your geographical location so that Windows knows which part of the world you're in when its services try to present you with local information. Click the OK button. Setup closes the Regional and Language Options dialog box.

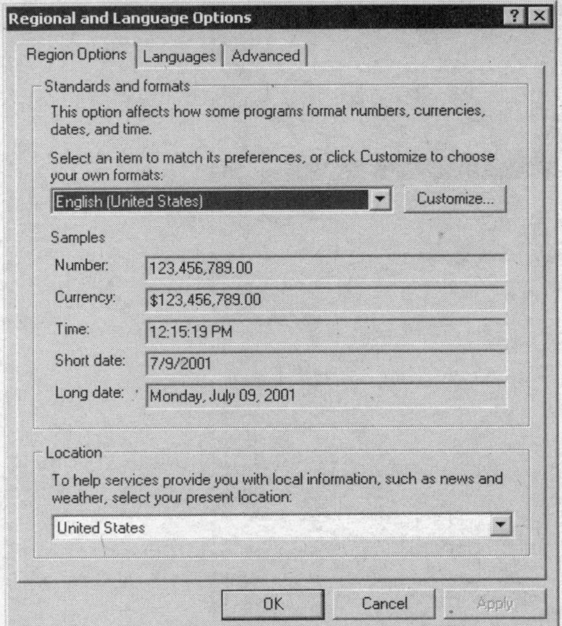

FIGURE 2.19: On the Region Options tab of the Regional and Language Options dialog box, specify the standards and formats setting to use and tell Windows your location.

To change the keyboard layout, click the Details button. Setup displays the Text Services and Input Languages dialog box (shown in Figure 2.20). Select the language in the Default Input Language drop-down list. To add an input language, click the Add button and use the resulting Add Input Language dialog box to specify the input language and keyboard layout. For example, if you use the Dvorak layout for your keyboard, set it as the default keyboard layout. Then click the OK button. Setup closes the Text Services and Input Languages dialog box.

Click the Next button to continue the setup process.

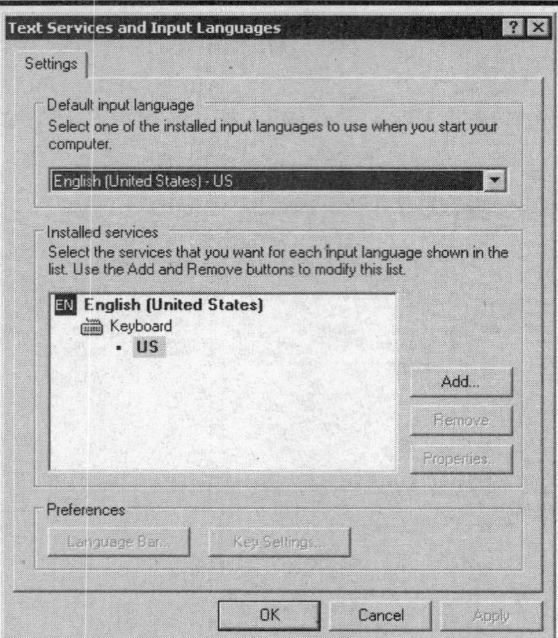

FIGURE 2.20: Use the Text Services and Input Languages dialog box to change your default input language.

Entering Your Name and Organization

Next, Setup displays the Personalize Your Software page, which demands your name and your organization's name. Enter these with due care and consideration, as they get deeply buried within the Windows Registry. (Part V discusses the Registry.) You must enter some text in the Name text box, but you can leave the Organization text box empty if you want.

Click the Next button to proceed.

Entering Your Product Key

Next, for a clean installation (but not for a new installation), Setup displays the Your Product Key page. Enter the 25-character product key (it should be on a yellow sticker on the back of the folder or CD box your Windows CD came in) and click the Next button to proceed.

TIP

If there's any risk of your misplacing your product key, write it on the Windows CD using a permanent pen.

Entering the Computer Name

Next, Setup displays the What's Your Computer's Name? page. By default, Setup suggests a complex and unmemorizable name that starts with the first part of the organization name you entered on the Personalize Your Software page. Change this name to something descriptive that you'll be able to remember and associate easily with this computer. The name can be up to 63 characters long, but you'd do well to keep it shorter than this to make it manageable. Names of more than 15 characters will be visible to other computers only via TCP/IP; via other network protocols, they won't be visible.

Click the Next button once again.

Entering the Modem Dialing Information

Next, if the computer has a modem that Setup was able to detect, Setup displays the Modem Dialing Information page. Specify your country or region (for example, United States of America), your area code (which is compulsory), any number you dial to get an outside line, and whether the phone system uses tone dialing or pulse dialing. Then click the Next button to proceed.

Checking the Date and Time

Next, Setup displays the Date and Time Settings page. Check the date, time, and time zone, and select or clear the Automatically Adjust Clock for Daylight Saving Changes check box as appropriate. Then click the Next button.

Specifying Networking Settings

Next, Setup installs some networking components and attempts to detect any network cards installed in your computer. Setup then displays the Networking Settings page, which offers you the choice of Typical Settings or Custom Settings.

The Typical Settings option installs the Client for Microsoft Networks, the QoS Packet Scheduler, File and Print Sharing for Microsoft Networks, and TCP/IP with automatic addressing. You can install other services after Setup completes (or remove these services), of course, but usually you'll be better off choosing the Custom Settings option and specifying suitable settings as described in the rest of this section.

If you select the Custom Settings option button and click the Next button, Setup displays the Networking Components page.

You can adjust the default settings by adding other services, uninstalling the default services, or choosing not to apply the selected services to this network adapter. When you remove a service, you make it unavailable to any of the network or dial-up adapters on your computer. So if you need to install a service but not use it for your primary network connection, let Setup install it, but clear its check box on the Networking Components page.

Uninstalling a Service

To uninstall one of the services, select it and click the Uninstall button. Setup displays a confirmation message box warning you that uninstalling the component removes it from all network connections. Click the Yes button if you want to remove the service.

Adding a Service

To add other services to the default services, follow these steps:

1. Click the Install button. Setup displays the Select Network Component Type dialog box.
2. Select the type of component you want to add–Client, Service, or Protocol–and click the Add button. Setup displays the Select Network Client dialog box, the Select Network Service dialog box, or the Select Network Protocol dialog box, as appropriate.
3. Select the client, service, or protocol in the list box. To add an unlisted client, service, or protocol that you have on disk, click the Have Disk button and use the resulting Install from Disk dialog box to identify the file.

4. Click the OK button. Setup installs the client, service, or protocol and closes the Select Network Component Type dialog box.

Configuring TCP/IP

Some of the network components have parameters you can configure. Of these, the key component is TCP/IP, the Internet protocol suite. If you don't run Internet Connection Sharing (ICS) on this computer, connect to the Internet through a computer running ICS, or connect to a DHCP server, you'll probably want to configure TCP/IP manually.

To configure your TCP/IP settings for the primary network card, follow these steps:

1. Select the Internet Protocol (TCP/IP) item in the list box on the Networking Components page.
2. Click the Properties button. Setup displays the Internet Protocol (TCP/IP) Properties dialog box.
3. On the General tab, select the Use the Following IP Address option button.
4. Enter the IP address in the IP Address text box (for example, `192.168.0.11`).
5. Enter the subnet mask in the Subnet Mask text box (for example, `255.255.255.0`). Setup automatically enters a suggested subnet mask appropriate to the IP address you enter, but you may need to change it.
6. Enter the IP address of the default gateway in the Default Gateway text box.
7. Select the Use the Following DNS Server Addresses option button.
8. Enter the IP address of your primary DNS server in the Preferred DNS Server text box.
9. Enter the IP address of your secondary DNS server (if you have one) in the Alternate DNS Server text box.
10. Click the OK button. Setup closes the Internet Protocol (TCP/IP) Properties dialog box and applies your settings.

NOTE

If necessary, you can also set advanced TCP/IP settings by clicking the Advanced button on the General tab of the Internet Protocol (TCP/IP) Properties dialog box and working in the resulting Advanced TCP/IP Settings dialog box.

Click the Next button to proceed with the installation. You've now chosen all the custom options.

Changing Display Settings

If Setup detects that your screen has a recommended resolution (for example, if it is an LCD panel), or if it detects that you were using the 640× 480 screen resolution, Setup displays the Display Settings dialog box, which announces that Windows will automatically adjust your screen resolution to improve the appearance of visual elements. Click the OK button. Windows adjusts the resolution and displays a Monitor Settings dialog box asking if you want to keep the change. Click the OK button if you do. If not, click the Cancel button or (if the screen isn't legible after the change) wait 30 seconds, after which Windows restores the previous screen resolution.

The Installation Paths Converge

The installation paths converge at the Welcome to Microsoft Windows screen, at which Setup starts playing active elevator music while an animated help logo struts its stuff. Click the Next button to move along.

Setting Up Your Internet Connection

Setup then tries to get you connected to the Internet. It tests any detected network adapter to see if it can find an Internet connection. If it detects an Internet connection, Setup displays the Will This Computer Connect to the Internet Directly, or through a Network? screen. Select the Yes, This Computer Will Connect through a Local Area Network or Home Network option button or the No, This Computer Will Connect Directly to the Internet option button as appropriate. (To skip the step of connecting to the Internet, click the Skip button.) Click the Next button. Setup displays the Ready to Activate Windows? screen.

If Setup doesn't detect an Internet connection, it displays the How Will This Computer Connect to the Internet? screen, which offers three options: the Telephone Modem option button, the Digital Subscriber Line (DSL) or Cable Modem option button, or the Local Area Network (LAN) option button.

Select the appropriate option button. If you don't want to configure an Internet connection at the moment—for example, you don't have your ISP or network information—click the Skip button.

The following sections describe what happens when you select each of these options.

Telephone Modem

If your computer connects with a telephone modem, select the Telephone Modem option button, then click the Next button. Setup displays the Ready to Activate Windows? screen.

After the step of activating Windows (or your turning down the invitation to do so), Setup displays the Do You Want to Set Up Internet Access Now? screen, which asks if you want to set up your computer to connect to the Internet. Select the Yes, Help Me Connect to the Internet option button or the No, Not at This Time option button as appropriate.

If you choose the Yes option button, Setup displays the Let's Get on the Internet screen. This offers three choices: The Get Online with MSN option button, the Use My Existing Internet Account with Another Service Provider (ISP) option button, and the Create a New Internet Account after I Finish Setting Up Windows option button. Select the appropriate option button and click the Next button to proceed.

If you choose the Get Online with MSN option button, Setup walks you through the process of signing you up for a new account on MSN (the Microsoft Network) or letting Windows know the details of your current MSN account.

If you choose to use your existing Internet account, Windows displays the Do You Want Help Finding an Internet Service Provider? screen. If you want assistance setting up your account, select the Yes, I Need Help Finding Information about My Account option button. When you click the Next button, Setup dials a toll-free number to the Microsoft Referral Service to walk you through the steps of identifying your ISP. If you know the details of your account, select the No, I Have My User Name, Password, and My ISP's Name and Phone Number Handy option button.

When you click the Next button, Windows displays the Set Up Your Internet Account screen.

Enter your username, password, and ISP phone number. By default, Windows selects the Obtain IP Automatically (DHCP) check box and the Obtain DNS Automatically (DHCP) check box. If you need to specify a static IP address rather than have the IP address be assigned automatically, clear the Obtain IP Automatically (DHCP) check box and enter the IP address in the Static Internet Protocol (IP) Address text box. Similarly, if your ISP does not supply DNS information automatically, clear the Obtain DNS Automatically check box and enter the IP addresses of the primary and secondary DNS servers in the Preferred DNS text box and the Alternate DNS text box.

When you click the Next button, Setup displays a Congratulations screen telling you that you can connect to the Internet using your phone line. Bear in mind that this isn't necessarily true–you've entered the information, but Windows hasn't checked that it works.

If you choose to create a new account, Setup walks you through the process of selecting an ISP from Microsoft's list and entering the connection information for it.

Digital Subscriber Line (DSL) or Cable Modem

If your computer connects with a DSL or cable modem, select the Digital Subscriber Line (DSL) or Cable Modem option button, then click the Next button. Setup displays the Do You Use a Username and Password to Connect to the Internet? screen. Select the Yes, I Use a Username and Password to Connect option button or the No, This Computer Is Always Connected to the Internet option button as appropriate. Click the Next button. Setup displays the Ready to Activate Windows? screen.

Local Area Network (LAN)

If your computer connects through a local area network (LAN), select the Local Area Network (LAN) option button, then click the Next button. Setup displays the Setting Up a High Speed Connection screen.

If your network is set up to automatically supply an IP address and Domain Name System (DNS) information, this screen is easy: Select the Obtain IP Automatically check box and the Obtain DNS Automatically check box, and you're all set. If your network isn't set up to deliver the goods, leave these check boxes cleared and enter your static IP address, your subnet mask, and your default gateway in the left stack of text boxes; your primary DNS server's IP address in the Preferred DNS text box; and your secondary DNS server's IP address (if you have one) in the Alternate DNS text box.

Click the Next button to proceed. Setup displays the Ready to Activate Windows? screen.

Activating Windows

Next, Setup displays the Ready to Activate Windows? screen, prompting you to activate Windows. Select the Yes, Activate Windows over the Internet Now option button or the No, Remind Me Every Few Days option button as appropriate.

Activation is a one-time procedure that you need to perform within 30 days of installing Windows. If you don't activate Windows, it stops working. The activation procedure is intended to reduce software piracy. A side effect is to increase the annoyance to legitimate software users.

In theory, setup is a convenient time for activating Windows, because you get the activation out of the way once and for all. But it's best to wait until you're sure that all your hardware works before activating Windows. This needn't take long, and it's much better than needing to get your activation revoked because you need to install Windows on another computer instead. If you don't activate Windows at setup, it reminds you every few days until you activate it or your grace period ends.

Activation is a little creepy, even though it doesn't involve supplying any personal information. Windows creates what it calls "a unique hardware configuration that represents the configuration of the PC at the time of activation." At this writing, it's hard to tell how many problems upgrading your PC will cause if you need to reinstall Windows.

The Windows Product Activation Privacy Statement reassures you that "Windows can detect and tolerate minor changes to your PC configuration" and that only a complete overhaul will need reactivation. But you have to wonder: If you upgrade, say, the BIOS, the processor, and the network card, how will Microsoft be able to tell that it's the same computer? Doubtless there will be plenty of horror stories about activation going wrong—and pirates will offer hacks and cracks for circumventing activation.

NOTE

Product activation does not apply if you have a corporate license for Windows XP Professional.

Registering Windows

During activation, you're heavily encouraged to register your copy of Windows XP with Microsoft.

If you've already registered on Microsoft's Web site, your Windows registration information gets merged into your current information. If you haven't registered, Microsoft creates a new profile for you with a personal information number (PIN) and adds the PIN to your hard drive in a cookie file. When you then visit the Microsoft Web site, it prompts you to create a Registration ID (not usually acronymed to RID). You can keep a profile with personal information—and you can opt out of the communications that Microsoft and the other companies it "occasionally" allows to offer its customers information will bombard you with.

Creating User Accounts

When you've finished with activation and registration, or when you've skipped both, Setup displays the Who Will Use This Computer? screen, which provides an easy way of setting up accounts for one to five users. This screen contains five text boxes. The first is named Your Name; the rest are numbered 2nd User through 5th User.

NOTE

When you're upgrading from Windows *9x*, Setup creates an account for the username under which you upgraded if you yourself forget to do so.

Enter the names of the users in the text boxes. Each name can be up to 20 characters long, and each must be unique. Names cannot use the characters " * + , / : ; < = > ? [ ] \ or |, and no name can consist of all spaces, all periods, or a combination of the two.

Click the Next button. Setup displays the Thank You! screen telling you you're ready to start using Windows.

Click the Finish button. Setup completes a few odds and ends, and then displays the Welcome screen for you to log in. Turn ahead to the next chapter for coverage of this and other basic Windows procedures.

APPLYING YOUR FILES AND SETTINGS

To apply the files and settings you saved by using the Files and Settings Transfer Wizard to your new installation of Windows, take the following steps:

1. Choose Start ➢ All Programs ➢ Accessories ➢ System Tools ➢ Files and Settings Transfer Wizard. Windows starts the Files and Settings Transfer Wizard, which displays the Welcome to the Files and Settings Transfer Wizard page.
2. Click the Next button. The Wizard displays the Which Computer Is This? page.
3. Select the New Computer option button.
4. Click the Next button. The Wizard displays the Do You Have a Windows XP CD? page, which offers to create a Wizard disk that you can use to collect the information from your old computer.
5. Select the I Don't Need the Wizard Disk. I Have Already Collected My Files and Settings from My Old Computer option button.
6. Click the Next button. The Wizard displays the Where Are the Files and Settings? page (shown in Figure 2.21).

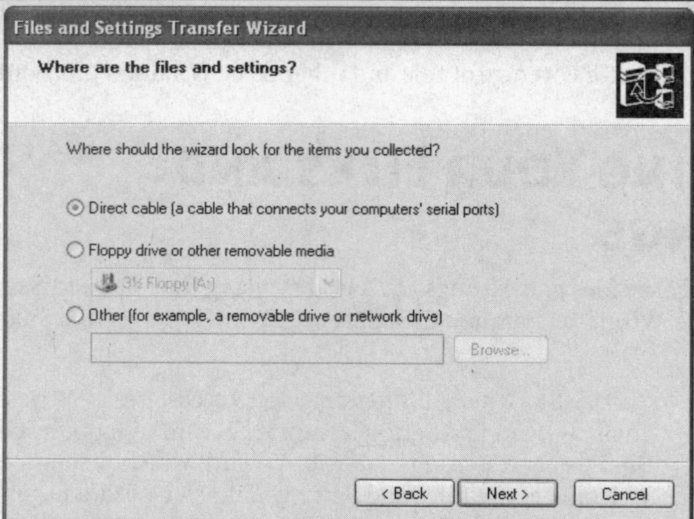

FIGURE 2.21: On the Where Are the Files and Settings? page of the Files and Settings Transfer Wizard, tell the Wizard where you saved the files and settings.

7. Select the Direct Cable option button, the Floppy Drive or Other Removable Media option button, or the Other option button as appropriate.
   - If you select the Floppy Drive or Other Removable Media option button, select the drive in the drop-down list.
   - If you select the Other option button, use the text box and (if necessary) the Browse button and the resulting Browse for Folder dialog box to specify the location of the files and settings.
8. Click the Next button. The Wizard displays the Transfer in Progress page (shown in Figure 2.22) as it transfers the files and settings.

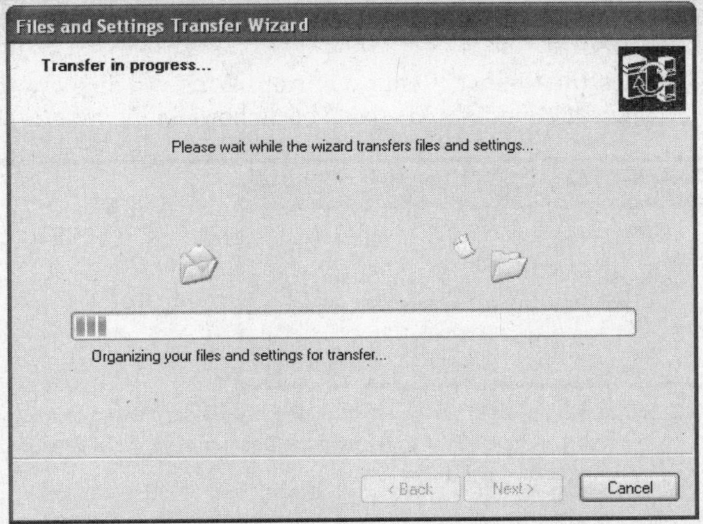

FIGURE 2.22: The Files and Settings Transfer Wizard transfers the files and settings.

9. If the Wizard displays a dialog box telling you that you need to log off for the settings to take effect and inviting you to log off now, choose the Yes button. The Wizard logs you off and finishes applying the settings.
10. Log back in, and your files and settings are available.

Uninstalling Windows XP and Reverting to Windows Me or 98

If you upgraded from Windows Me or Windows 98 to Windows XP, you can uninstall Windows XP and revert to your previous version of Windows if necessary. To do so, take the following steps:

1. Choose Start ➢ Control Panel. Windows displays Control Panel.
2. Click the Add or Remove Programs link. Windows displays the Add or Remove Programs window with the Add or Remove Programs page foremost.

3. Select the Windows XP Uninstall item. Windows displays its details, including a Change/Remove button.
4. Click the Change/Remove button. Windows displays the Uninstall Windows XP dialog box (shown in Figure 2.23).

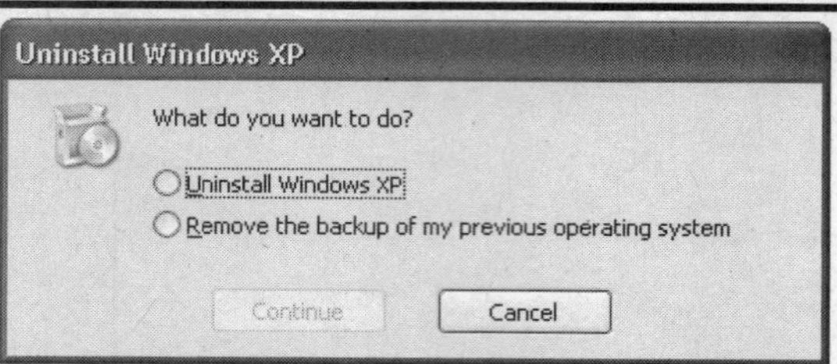

FIGURE 2.23: In the Uninstall Windows XP dialog box, choose whether to uninstall Windows XP or to remove the backup of your old version of Windows.

5. Select the Uninstall Windows XP option button.
6. Click the Continue button. Windows displays a confirmation dialog box checking that you're absolutely sure.
7. Click the Yes button. Windows closes, runs the uninstall procedure, and automatically restarts your computer with your previous version of Windows.

Removing Your Old Version of Windows

If you decide to stick with Windows XP after upgrading to it, you can reclaim the space taken up by the backup of your old version of Windows. To do so, follow the first four steps in the previous section but select the Remove the Backup of My Previous Operating System option button in the Uninstall Windows XP dialog box. Click the Continue button and confirm your choice, and Windows deletes the backup of your previous operating system.

Keeping Windows Updated

Windows XP includes a feature called Windows Update that's designed to keep Windows up-to-date by automatically downloading Windows updates, such as patches and fixes for security holes, and offering to install them. If you need to run old programs that have compatibility problems, Windows Update may be of particular interest, because it also includes new fixes for programs to run on Windows XP.

There are several things you should know about Windows Update before you find it springing into action: how it works, how to configure it, and what to do when an update presents itself.

When Windows Update Runs

By default, Windows Update runs automatically, but only when an Administrator user is logged in. (Microsoft assumes that you don't want Limited users–let alone guests–to install or refuse updates.) If multiple Administrator users are logged on to the computer at the same time, Windows Update runs for only one of them.

You can also run Windows Update manually by choosing Start ➢ All Programs ➢ Windows Update. (If you prefer to run Windows Update manually, you may also want to turn off automatic updating. Read on.)

Windows Update's default setting is to automatically download updates when they're available (and an Administrator user is logged on) and then invite the Administrator to install them. You can change this default behavior, as described in the next section.

Here's what happens:

- Windows Update decides it's time to run (or an Administrator runs it manually).
- Windows Update goes online and checks which updates are available, then compares the list to those that have already been applied to the computer and those that have been offered to the computer but refused by an Administrator.
- If update files are available, Windows Update downloads them in the background, using bandwidth-throttling technology to make sure it doesn't prevent you from using your Internet connection by grabbing all bandwidth when you need it. (*Bandwidth-throttling* means that Windows Update throttles back the amount of

bandwidth the download is taking up, not that it throttles your bandwidth.) If you're not using your Internet connection, Windows Update downloads the update files as fast as possible.

- Once the update files are downloaded, Windows Update notifies you (assuming you're an Administrator) that they're available and invites you to install them.

Configuring Windows Update

To configure Windows Update, follow these steps:

1. Press Winkey+Break. Windows displays the System Properties dialog box. (Alternatively, click the Start button to display the Start menu, then right-click the My Computer item and choose Properties from the shortcut menu.)
2. Click the Automatic Updates tab, as shown in Figure 2.24.

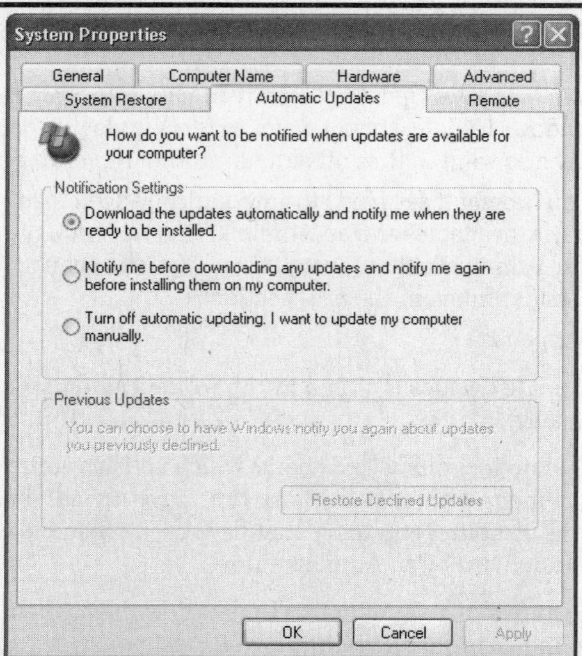

FIGURE 2.24: You can configure Windows Update on the Automatic Updates page of the System Properties dialog box.

3. In the Notification Settings section, choose one of the three option buttons:

   Download the Updates Automatically and Notify Me When They Are Ready to Be Installed The default, this setting is convenient if you want to use automatic updating and you have a fast Internet connection.

   Notify Me before Downloading Any Updates and Notify Me Again before Installing Them on My Computer Use this setting if you want to use automatic updating but want to be aware of when Windows Update is downloading updates. You might want to know this because your Internet connection isn't fast enough to support your surfing (or downloading MP3s) at the same time as Windows is trying to squeeze a large update through it, or because you don't like unexplained activity across your Internet connection.

   Turn Off Automatic Updating. I Want to Update My Computer Manually Select this option button if you prefer to control not only when Windows Update downloads and installs updates but when it checks for them—or if you don't want to use Windows Update at all.

4. If you have previously declined updates that Windows has offered you, you can click the Restore Declined Updates button in the Previous Updates section to make them available again. (Until you've declined an update, the Restore Hidden Items button is unavailable.)

5. Click the OK button. Windows closes the System Properties dialog box.

Running Windows Update Manually

If you don't want to wait for Windows Update to run automatically on schedule, or if you don't like to have your computer calling Microsoft secretly in the wee hours of dark and stormy nights, you can run Windows Update manually. You can do so either from the Start menu (choose Start ➢ All Programs ➢ Windows Update) or from the Help and Support Center window.

EXPERT KNOWLEDGE: AUTOMATING THE INSTALLATION OF WINDOWS XP

The installation procedure described in this chapter is effective and relatively straightforward once you know what the options mean. But it still takes between 45 and 90 minutes to complete, depending on the speed of your computer, and requires you to be there at odd moments to answer prompts, so it's a bit of a waste of time.

Still, you need to run the installation procedure only once on any computer. Or do you? Some people find that they need to install Windows multiple times on the same computer. Every installation of Windows gradually accumulates unneeded programs, files, and settings. These can cause Windows to slow down or even become unstable. Windows 98 was so notorious for this that the joke went that its name specified the number of days that you could reasonably run it before expecting enough trouble to set in that would require a reinstall to fix.

Windows XP improves your chances of not needing to reinstall by providing tools such as System Restore, device driver rollback , and Disk Cleanup and Disk Defragmenter to keep your system in working order. But even these can't fix every problem. If you need a fresh start, or if you maintain a test computer, you may want to blow away all the old files and settings and virtual dust-bunnies by performing a new installation.

To help you do so, Windows XP includes a tool for performing an unattended installation. (You can, of course, use these tools to set up Windows XP the first and only time, but most people don't find it worth their while to do so.)

If you had to guess at how the procedure works, you'd probably figure that it'd consist of creating a file ahead of time that gives Windows the information for which it normally prompts you during setup, and then feeding that file to the Setup procedure. That's just how it works. The file is called an *answer file* for obvious enough reasons. There's a Wizard to help you create the answer file, but then you may want to edit it a bit by hand.

CONTINUED →

To perform an unattended installation, take the following steps:

1. Extract the tools from the `\Support\Tools\Deploy.cab` folder on the CD to a convenient location. If you already have Windows XP installed on one of your computers, you can extract these files by using Explorer. If you have an earlier version of Windows, use a Zip program (for example, WinZip) from Windows or the EXTRACT command from a command prompt instead.
2. Open an Explorer window to the folder to which you extracted the files.
3. Double-click the SETUPMGR.EXE program. Windows starts the Windows XP Setup Manager Wizard, which displays its first page.
4. Click the Next button. The Wizard displays the New or Existing Answer File page.
5. Leave the Create a New Answer File option button selected (as it is by default) unless you already have an answer file that you want to tweak. In that case, select the Modify an Existing Answer File option button and enter the path and filename in the text box, either by typing or by clicking the Browse button and using the resulting Open dialog box.
6. Click the Next button. The Wizard displays the Product to Install page (shown below).

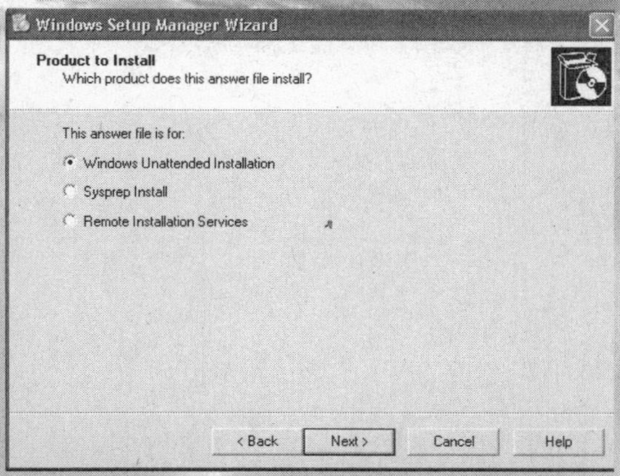

CONTINUED ➞

7. Make sure the Windows Unattended Installation option button is selected.
8. Click the Next button. The Wizard displays the Platform page (shown next).

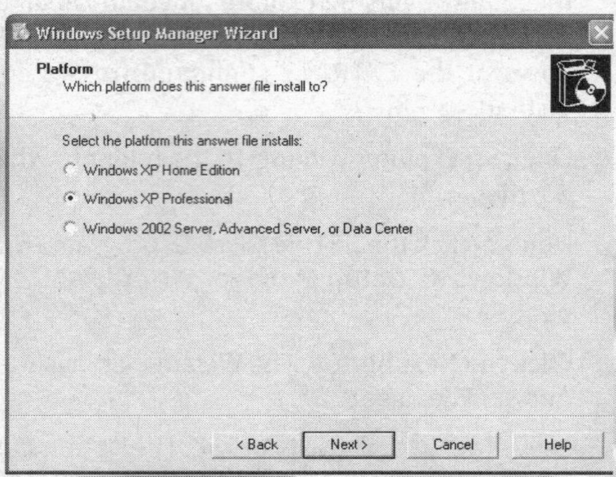

9. Select the Windows XP Professional option button.
10. Click the Next button. The Wizard displays the User Interaction Level page (shown below).

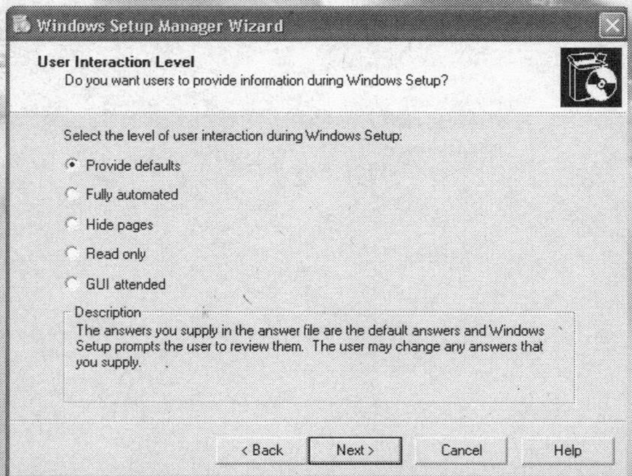

11. Select the Fully Automated option button.

CONTINUED →

12. Click the Next button. The Wizard displays the Distribution Folder page, which lets you specify that the Wizard create a distribution folder on your computer or on a networked drive containing the Windows source files.

    ▸ Creating a distribution folder lets you not only install without the CD but also add extra files (such as device drivers) to the custom installation. If you like unattended installation so much that you'd like to buy the company that made it—that is, if you want to run unattended installations frequently and you have a convenient drive or folder—you'll probably want to try this option. For the moment, we'll stick with installing from the CD.

13. Select the No, This Answer File Will Be Used to Install from a CD option button.

14. Click the Next button. The Wizard displays the License Agreement page.

15. Select the I Accept the Terms of the License Agreement check box and click the Next button. The Wizard displays the Windows Setup Manager window (shown below).

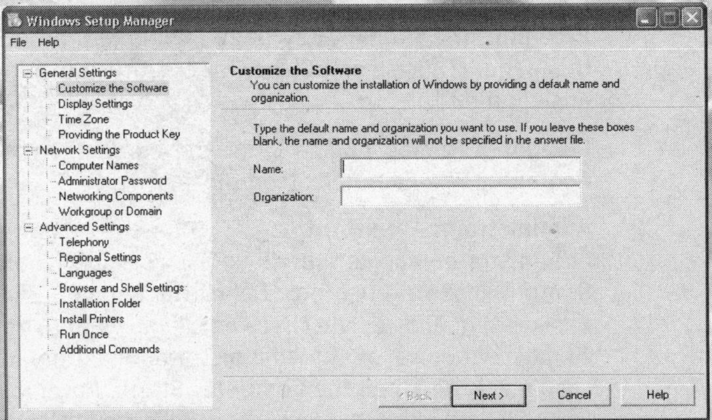

CONTINUED ➞

16. Select each page in turn and specify those settings applicable to your installation. Browsing through the pages feels like a sort of Redmond Roulette, because you must fill in any required fields (such as the Name text box on the Customize the Software page) before leaving any given page. If you don't, the Wizard halts you in your tracks with a peremptory message box pointing out your omission. So it's best to deal with the pages in order. You can move from page to page by clicking items in the list box or by clicking the Next button.

    Customize the Software page Enter your name in the Name text box (compulsory). If appropriate, enter the organization in the Organization text box.

    Display Settings page You can use the Colors drop-down list, the Screen Area drop-down list, and the Refresh Frequency drop-down list to specify the colors, screen area, and refresh rate to use instead of accepting the Windows defaults. For custom settings, click the Custom button and specify them in the Custom Display Settings dialog box.

    Time Zone page Select the time zone in the Time Zone drop-down list.

    Providing the Product Key page Enter the product key on this page. (This is compulsory for creating a fully automated answer file.)

    Computer Names page Enter the computer name in the Computer Name text box (compulsory).

    Administrator Password page Enter the password for the Administrator account in the Password text box and the Confirm Password text box. Select the Encrypt Administrator Password in Answer File check box if you want to do just that. To have Windows log the Administrator on automatically, you can select the When the Computer Starts, Automatically Log On As Administrator check box and specify the number of times in the Number of Times to Auto Logon text box. (Autologon can be useful for the first boot, but beyond that, it's a severe security threat.)

CONTINUED ⟶

Networking Components page Select the Typical Settings option button or the Customize Settings option button as appropriate. If you select the latter, customize the settings as discussed in "Specifying Networking Settings" earlier in the chapter.

Workgroup or Domain page Leave the Workgroup option button selected and enter the name of the workgroup in the Workgroup text box.

17. Click the Next button. Windows displays the Windows Setup Manager dialog box shown below telling you that it has created an answer file and inviting you to specify the location for it.

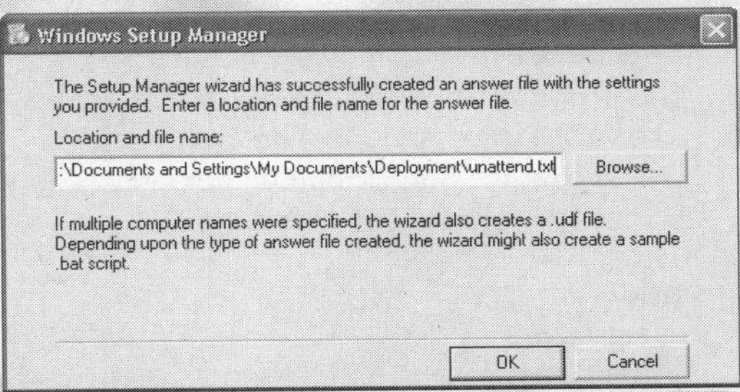

18. Enter the appropriate location and change the filename from its default `UNATTEND.TXT` to `WINNT.SIF`. Click the OK button. Windows XP Setup Manager creates the file and saves it under that name.

19. Choose File ➢ Exit. Windows XP Setup Manager closes itself.

Now you've created the basic file. It's ready to go—but before you run it, you probably want to take a look at the contents. (You might also want to add extra parameters. Consult the Setup Manager Help file for possibilities.) Right-click the file in an Explorer window, choose Open With from the context menu, select Notepad in the Open With dialog box, and click the OK button. Windows opens the file in Notepad. Depending on the options you chose, it should look something like this:

```
;SetupMgrTag
[Data]
    AutoPartition=1
    MsDosInitiated="0"
    UnattendedInstall="Yes"
```

CONTINUED ➡

```
[Unattended]
    UnattendMode=FullUnattended
    OemSkipEula=Yes
    OemPreinstall=No
    TargetPath=\WINDOWS

[GuiUnattended]
    AdminPassword=*
    EncryptedAdminPassword=NO
    OEMSkipRegional=1
    TimeZone=85
    OemSkipWelcome=1

[UserData]
    ProductID=NNNNN-NNNNN-NNNNN-NNNNN-NNNNN
    FullName="Andy Rondolophberger"
    OrgName="Rondolophberger Pharmaceuticals"
    ComputerName=Verwirrung

[Display]
    BitsPerPel=32
    Xresolution=800
    YResolution=600
    Vrefresh=85

[Identification]
    JoinWorkgroup=LAUREL

[Networking]
    InstallDefaultComponents=Yes
```

If you've chosen other options—for example, customizing networking or choosing language settings—you'll see further lines covering them. You can also add other lines as necessary to take other actions, such as specifying that the installation repartition the hard drive or convert the file system to NTFS. You'll find details of the possibilities in the Help files contained in DEPLOY.CAB.

If you make any changes, save the file. Then close it and copy it to a floppy disk. Then boot the computer from the Windows XP CD and put the floppy disk in the floppy drive. Windows installs automatically using the settings you specified.

WHAT'S NEXT?

This chapter has discussed how to install Windows, either as a clean install or as an upgrade to your current version of Windows. You've also learned how to use the Windows Update feature to keep your copy of Windows updated, compatible, and secure, and how to create an answer file to perform an unattended installation.

The next chapter discusses how to get started with Windows XP: logging on and off, switching users, finding out who's logged on, and shutting down Windows.

Chapter 3

Using the Desktop and Getting Help

In the first part of this chapter, I'll discuss how to get started with Windows XP Professional. I'll cover how to log on and log off; how to switch from one user session to another; and how to exit Windows. I'll also discuss how you can find out who else is logged on to the computer when you're working at it; how you can get an idea of which programs the other users are running; and how you can log off another user (or all other users) in order to reclaim the resources they're using.

In the second part of this chapter, I'll discuss how to find the help you need to use Windows XP most effectively. Windows XP includes a greater amount of help than previous versions of Windows and presents that help in a new interface, the Help and Support Center program. I'll describe how to use Help and Support Center and the various areas it offers. I'll also mention other resources that you may need to turn to when you run into less tractable problems.

Adapted from *Mastering Windows XP Professional*
by Mark Minasi

ISBN 0-7821-2981-1 1056 pages $39.99

NOTE

Before we start, here's something you need to know. Windows XP Professional supports three types of users: Computer Administrator users, Limited users, and the Guest user. By default, all named users are set up as Computer Administrator users, which gives them full authority to configure and customize the computer. Limited users, which you create manually, can perform only minimal configuration and customization. The Guest user, an account that's created automatically by Windows, can perform no configuration or customization. In the first part of this chapter, I'll assume you're logging on as a Computer Administrator user, because that's most likely to be the case.

Logging On and Logging Off

Logging on and off in Windows XP works differently from previous versions of Windows. Logging on and off could hardly be easier, but it's important to understand what happens when you log on and off and how logging on and off differ from switching users.

In earlier versions of Windows, only one user at a time could be logged on to a computer running Windows. For a second user to log on, the first user needed to log off. Logging off involved closing all the open programs and files: either the user could close the programs and files manually before logging off, or Windows would close them automatically when the user issued the Log Off command (and confirmed that they wanted to log off).

Once all the programs and files were closed, and all network and Internet connections were closed as well, Windows displayed the Log On to Windows dialog box or the Enter Network Password dialog box, depending on whether the computer was attached to a network. Another user could then log on to Windows, run programs, open files, establish network and Internet connections, and so on.

In Windows XP, multiple users can be logged on at the same time (unless your computer is part of a domain, a topic I'll discuss in the next section), though of course only one user can actually be using the computer. Each of those users who is logged on can have programs running and files open. Windows XP lets you switch quickly between users without closing the programs and files.

Only one user can be *active*—actually using the computer—at any time. (Given that most computers have only one keyboard, mouse, and monitor, this may seem too obvious to mention—but things are very different in

Unix and Linux, in which multiple users can be actively using the same computer at the same time, some locally and some remotely.) A user who is logged on but not active is said to be *disconnected*.

This means that, for example, Jane and Jack can keep their programs open while Ross is using the computer. When Jane logs back on (in the process disconnecting Ross, who perhaps stepped away for a cup of coffee), Windows resumes her session from where she left off, displaying the programs she had running and the files she had open. Windows reestablishes any of Jane's persistent network connections, including any Internet connection that's set to connect automatically.

Being able to leave multiple users up and running is great—up to a point. But it has serious implications for performance and file integrity. The following sections discuss these considerations briefly.

FAST USER SWITCHING, PERFORMANCE, AND FILE INTEGRITY

Having multiple users logged on to Windows at the same time affects performance because each user who's logged on takes up some of the computer's memory. Having a user logged on itself takes up relatively little memory, but each program that the user has running, and each file that they have open, adds to the amount being used.

Windows XP needs a minimum of 64MB of RAM to run at an acceptable speed. For each light user, reckon another 32MB of RAM; for each moderate user, 64MB; and for each heavy user, 128MB. If you have 256MB of RAM, you should be able to have two or three users logged on and running several programs each without running short of memory.

Having multiple users logged on at once can also affect file integrity. For example, what happens when two users try to change the same file at the same time? The short answer is: It depends.

Some programs are smart enough to realize that someone else has a copy of the file open. For example, if you try to open in Word 2002 the same document that another user has open, Word displays the File in Use dialog box to warn you that the document is locked for editing and to offer you ways to work with the document (open a read-only copy; create a local copy and merge your changes later; or receive notification when the original copy is available).

CONTINUED →

Other programs aren't smart enough to spot the problem. For example, WordPad (Windows XP's built-in word-processing program) lets you open a document that another user has open, change it, and save the changes. The other user can then save *their* changes to the same file, which can end up with some of the changes you've made and some that the other user has made. And this is assuming that only two users are editing the document at the same time. For all WordPad knows, half the people in Delaware could be editing the document at the same time and wiping out each other's changes.

If your computer has a modest amount of RAM—say, 64MB, 96MB, or 128MB—or if you're having problems with users opening files at the same time, turn off the Fast User Switching feature. Choose Start ➢ Control Panel to open Control Panel, click the User Accounts link to open the User Account screen, click the Change the Way Users Log On or Off link, clear the Use Fast User Switching check box, and then click Apply Options. When you turn off Fast User Switching, only one user can be logged on to the computer at any given time, and that user must log off before another user can log on. This reduces the amount of memory needed and avoids most problems with shared files.

Logging On

To start using Windows, log on from the Welcome screen. Figure 3.1 shows an example of the Welcome screen, which displays a list of the users who have accounts set up on the computer. Any programs a user has running appear listed under the username, together with the number of e-mail messages waiting for them. If a user is logged on but has no programs running, the Welcome screen displays *Logged on* beneath their name.

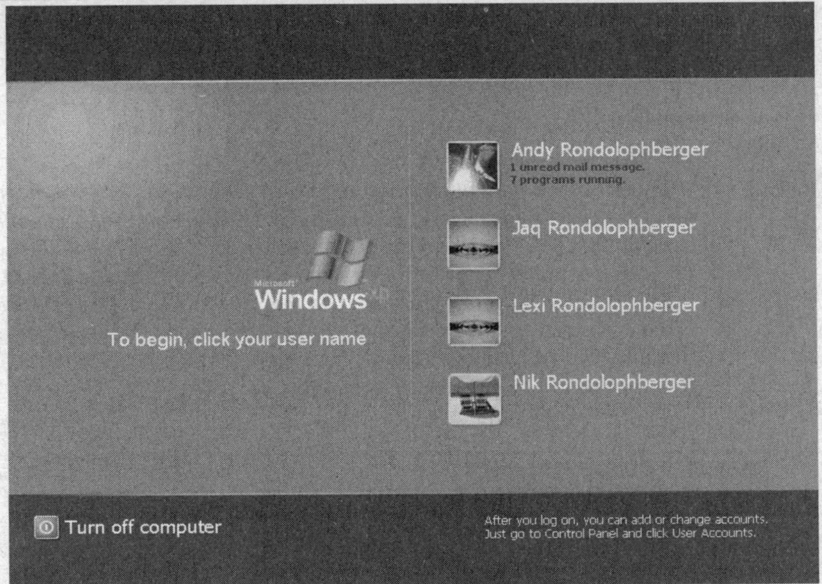

FIGURE 3.1: The Welcome screen lists the users with accounts on this computer, any tasks the user has running, and any unread e-mail messages they have.

By default, user accounts are set up without passwords, so you log on by clicking the username under which you want to log on. (If an administrator has set up Windows to require passwords, you'll need to enter the password for the account as well.)

When it accepts your logon, Windows displays your Desktop with its current settings. (The section "Using the Desktop and Start Menu" a little later in this chapter discusses the basics of the Desktop and Start menu.)

The first time you log on, Windows creates your folders and sets up program shortcuts for you—so the logon process takes a minute or two. Subsequent logons are much quicker.

Logging Off

The counterpart to logging on is (unsurprisingly) logging off. When you log off, Windows closes all the programs and files you've been using. If the files contain unsaved changes, Windows prompts you to save them.

To log off, display the Start menu by clicking the Start button, and click the Log Off button. Windows displays the Log Off Windows dialog box (shown in Figure 3.2). Click the Log Off button to log off.

NOTE

If you leave your computer unattended for a while, the screensaver usually kicks in—unless you have something open that prevents the screensaver from starting (or you've disabled the screensaver). For example, a dialog box open on-screen usually prevents the screensaver from starting. The default setting is for the screensaver to start after 10 minutes and to display the Welcome screen. The screensaver gives you some protection against prying eyes (particularly if you're using passwords for logging on), but it also makes it harder to see who's doing what on the computer.

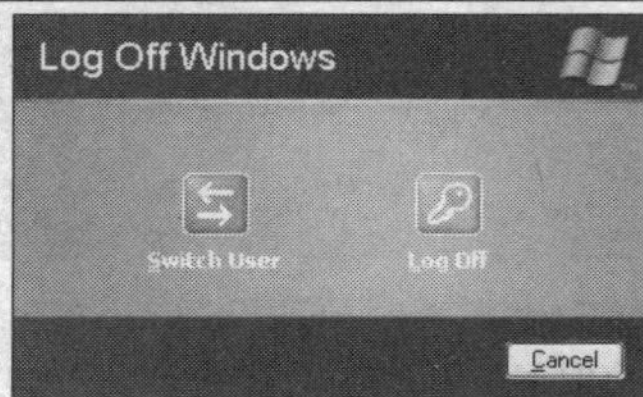

FIGURE 3.2: The Log Off Windows dialog box lets you log off, cancel the command, or switch to another user.

LOGGING ON TO A DOMAIN

If your Windows XP Professional computer is connected to a domain, the computer will boot to a Windows Log On screen when you turn on the computer. You'll need to press Ctrl+Alt+Del to get to the Log On to Windows dialog box. You must supply a valid username and password that has domain access privileges. If you do not have this information, contact your domain administrator.

Before clicking OK, check that the Log On To entry has your domain name listed. If it does not, use the drop-down arrow and select your domain name. If the Log On To entry does not appear, click the Options button. Click OK, and you will log on to the domain. You can only access information in the domain that you have privileges to.

If you want multiuser support, you cannot be joined to a domain. If you were joined to a domain and now are part of a Workgroup and want to enable multiuser support, follow these steps:

1. Choose Start ➢ Control Panel to open Control Panel, and then click the User Accounts link to open the User Accounts screen.
2. Click the Change the Way Users Log On or Off link to open the Select Logon and Logoff Options screen.
3. Click the Use the Welcome Screen check box, and then click the Use Fast User Switching check box.
4. Click Apply Options. Close all open windows, and then restart your system.

Using the Desktop and Start Menu

Once you've logged on successfully, Windows displays the Desktop. Figure 3.3 shows what the Desktop looks like the first time you start Windows and start a couple of programs. Because you can customize the Desktop extensively , your Desktop might not look anything like the Desktop shown in the figure: the wallpaper might be different; the Taskbar could be located at a different side of the screen; or various toolbars might be displayed. About the one unchanging thing about the Desktop is the Start menu button—but even this might not be displayed if someone has chosen to hide the Taskbar (of which the Start button is part).

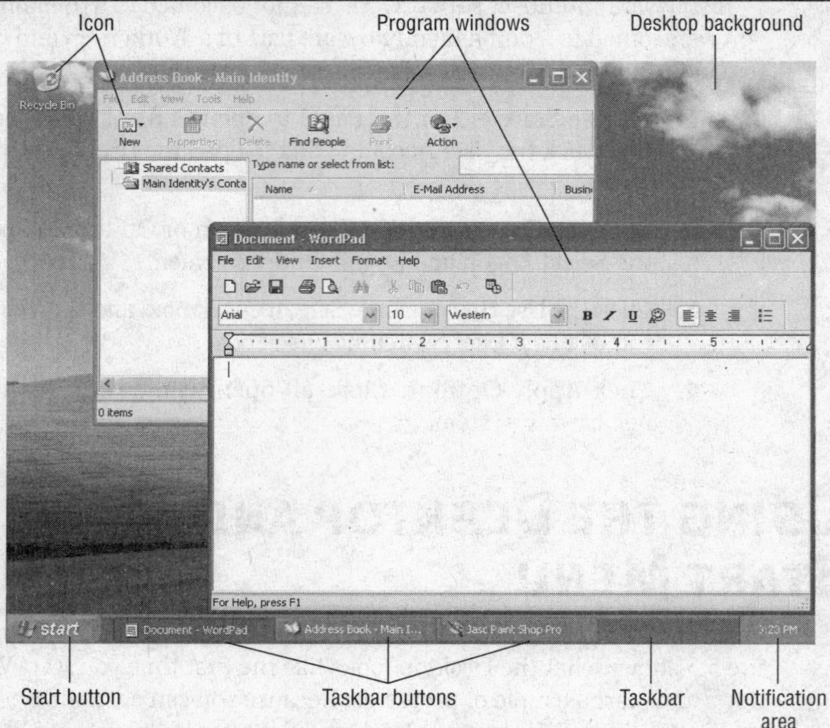

FIGURE 3.3: The components of the Windows Desktop

The following are the basic actions for navigating the Desktop:

- The Desktop contains one or more shortcuts to items. Usually, there's an icon for the Recycle Bin, if nothing else. Double-click an icon to run the program associated with it.
- The Start menu provides access to the full range of programs and features currently installed on Windows. Click the Start button to display the Start menu. Choose one of the items that appears on it, or click the All Programs button to display a cascading menu containing further items.
- The Taskbar gives you quick access to each program that's currently running. The Taskbar displays a button for each active program window. To display that window in front of all other windows, click its button. To minimize the program, click its Taskbar button again.

- The notification area contains items that are useful to have displayed all the time (such as the clock, which is displayed by default), together with information and alerts (which are displayed at appropriate times).
- The Desktop background is a graphic that you can change at will.

Switching to Another User

As you saw in Figure 3.2, the Log Off Windows dialog box also contains a button called Switch User. When you click the Switch User button, Windows keeps your programs running (instead of closing them, as it does when you log off) and displays the Welcome screen so that you can log on as another user or (more likely) other users can log on as themselves.

Using the Connect Command to Switch Users Quickly

Switching users as described above is easy but takes a few clicks. There's a quicker way of switching—by using Task Manager as follows:

1. Right-click open space in the Taskbar and choose Task Manager from the shortcut menu. Windows opens Task Manager.
2. Click the Users tab (shown in Figure 3.4, later in this chapter).
3. Right-click the user that you want to connect as and choose Connect from the shortcut menu. If the user's account has a password, Windows displays the Connect Password Required dialog box. When you enter the password correctly (or if the account has no password), Windows disconnects your session and connects you as the user you selected.

Locking the Computer

To leave your current session running but display the Welcome screen quickly, press Winkey+L. (If you're not using the Welcome screen, Windows displays the Log On to Windows dialog box instead.)

NOTE
If you're connected to a domain, pressing Winkey+L locks the computer.

Microsoft calls this action *locking* the computer, though the term is neither accurate nor helpful with Windows XP's default settings. The computer isn't locked in any useful sense unless all user accounts are protected with effective passwords.

However, if you turn off the Welcome screen and Fast User Switching, Windows manages a semblance of locking. When the current user disconnects their session, Windows displays a blank background topped by the Unlock Computer dialog box, which tells the user that the computer is in use, that it has been locked, and that only the current user or an administrator can unlock it. If you've applied passwords, this is true; if you haven't, anyone can click the OK button in the Unlock Computer dialog box to unlock the computer and log on as the current user.

Checking Which User Is Currently Active

If you're in any doubt as to which user is currently active, display the Start menu (by clicking the Start button or pressing the Winkey) and check the username displayed at the top.

Seeing Who Else Is Logged On to the Computer

As you saw a page or two ago, the Welcome screen displays details of each user logged on to the computer and the number of programs they're running. But if you don't want to display the Welcome screen (and disconnect your session by doing so), you can find out which other users are logged in by using Task Manager as follows:

1. Right-click the Taskbar and choose Task Manager from the shortcut menu. Windows displays Task Manager.
2. Click the Users tab (shown in Figure 3.4), which lists the users and their status.

FIGURE 3.4: The Users tab of Task Manager shows you which other users are logged on to the computer. You can send them messages, switch to their sessions, or log them off forcibly.

NOTE

Limited users and the Guest user can't see which other users are logged on or which processes they're running. As a result, Limited users and the Guest user can't switch directly to another user's session by using Task Manager, though they can disconnect their own session or log themselves off by using Task Manager.

Seeing Which Programs the Other Users Are Running

It's not easy to see exactly which programs the other users of the computer are running unless you know the names of the executable files for the programs, but you can get an idea by using the Processes tab of Task Manager. This tab also shows you how much memory each program is using, which helps you establish whether—or why—your computer is running short of memory.

Follow these steps to start Task Manager and display its Processes tab:

1. Right-click the Taskbar and choose Task Manager from the shortcut menu to open Task Manager.
2. Click the Processes tab, which lists the processes you're running.
3. Select the Show Processes from All Users check box. (This check box is cleared by default.) Task Manager adds to the list all the processes that the other users are running as well. Figure 3.5 shows an example of the Processes tab. You can sort the list of processes by any column by clicking the column heading. In the figure, the processes are sorted by the User Name column so that it's easy to see which process belongs to which user.

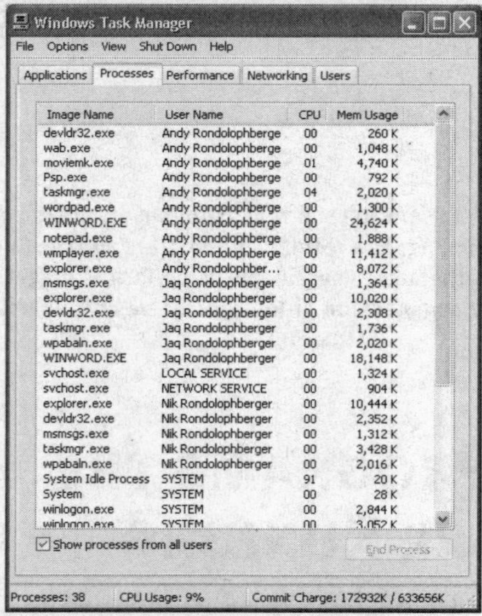

FIGURE 3.5: Use the Processes tab of Task Manager to see which programs the other users are running.

As you can see in the figure, three of the Rondolophbergers are running programs, and between them they're using quite a chunk of memory: the Commit Charge counter in the lower-right corner of the Processes tab shows that 172932K (about 169MB) out of 633656K (about 619MB) of memory has been used up. In the list, you can see some of the principal offenders: copies of WINWORD.EXE (Microsoft Word) that Andy and Jaq are running (24,624K and 18,148K, respectively), several instances of EXPLORER.EXE, and some programs with unpronounceable names such as DEVLDR32.EXE and WPABALN.EXE.

Some of the other names are readily identifiable. For example, WMPLAYER.EXE is the executable for Windows Media Player, as you'd expect, and TASKMGR.EXE is the executable for Task Manager itself. You don't need to memorize the mapping of each executable filename to its program, but if you look at Task Manager now and then, you'll learn to scan the list of processes and see which is running. This will help you decide whether you should go ahead and log another user off Windows (as described in the next section) or whether doing so will trash their work and ruin their life.

WHICH NAME CORRESPONDS TO WHICH PROGRAM?

To find out which program corresponds to each executable file, display the Applications tab of Task Manager. Right-click a program and choose Go to Process from the shortcut menu. Task Manager displays the Processes tab and selects the process for that program.

That's easy enough—but there are many more processes running than programs. Try closing all the programs listed on the Applications tab of Task Manager, and you'll see that there's still a goodly list of processes left. Try stopping any obvious services that you can temporarily dispense with, and see if an associated process disappears. For instance, try closing your Internet connection or stopping your PC Cards. Did either of those actions lose you a process? Then you have an idea of what that process does.

If you're desperate to find out which function or service an executable runs, try searching for the executable. The folder that contains the executable may give you a clue as to the program, or there may be a comment on the executable that reveals its purpose. Then again, the executable may prove to be one of the mysterious system files stored in the Windows folder or the Windows\System32 folder. If the latter is the case, figure it's something unknowable and leave it alone.

While you're looking at Task Manager, there are a couple of other things you might as well know.

First, you can also see in the figure that it's not just the Rondolophbergers who are using memory like there was no tomorrow—Windows also has a number of processes open on its own account. The LOCAL SERVICE account is running `SVCHOST.EXE` (service host), as is the NETWORK SERVICE account. The SYSTEM account is running a dozen or more processes, of which you can see only the top few in the figure. Of these, the first, the System Idle Process, is consuming 91 percent of the processor cycles. (This is actually good news. When the System Idle Process is taking up most of the processor cycles like this, the computer is idling along—goofing off until the user does something that presses it into action.)

Second, you may have noticed that the numbers in the Mem Usage column don't add up to anything like the 172932K listed as being committed (even though you can't see the whole column). That's because that committed figure is both physical memory (RAM) used and virtual memory (hard disk space being used to simulate more RAM). If you want to see how much virtual memory each process is taking up, follow these steps:

1. In Task Manager, choose View ➢ Select Columns to open the Select Columns dialog box (shown in Figure 3.6).

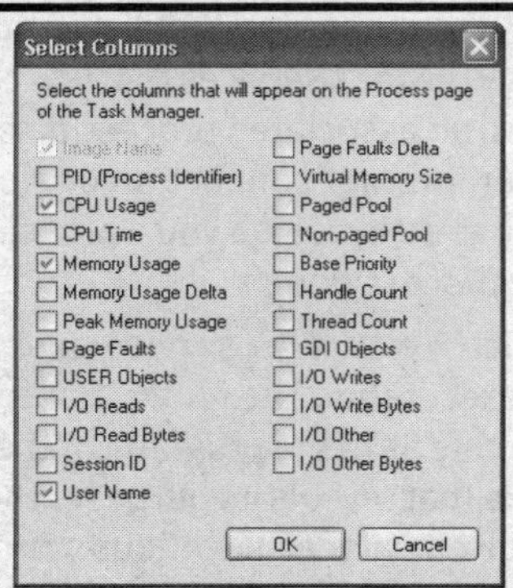

FIGURE 3.6: Use the Select Columns dialog box to add further columns of information to Task Manager's Processes tab.

2. Select the Virtual Memory Size check box.
   - Also select the check boxes for any other information you want to see in Task Manager. Many of the items here are somewhat arcane, but you might want to look at CPU Time or Peak Memory Usage.
3. Click the OK button. Task Manager closes the Select Columns dialog box and adds the columns you chose to the Processes tab.

Figure 3.7 shows the Processes tab of Task Manager with the Virtual Memory Size column added and the processes sorted by that column. Notice that the two copies of Word have very heavy memory usage indeed (when you add the Mem Usage column and the VM Size column). SVCHOST.EXE also shows itself as a heavyweight, using a little over 11MB of virtual memory in addition to its 10MB of RAM.

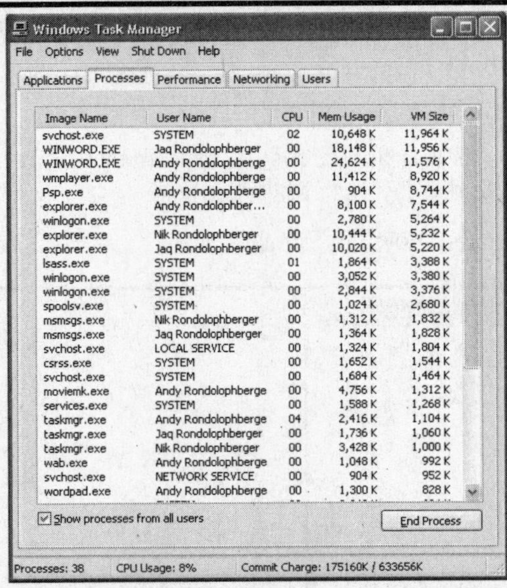

Image Name	User Name	CPU	Mem Usage	VM Size
svchost.exe	SYSTEM	02	10,648 K	11,964 K
WINWORD.EXE	Jaq Rondolophberger	00	18,148 K	11,956 K
WINWORD.EXE	Andy Rondolophberge	00	24,624 K	11,576 K
wmplayer.exe	Andy Rondolophberge	00	11,412 K	8,920 K
Psp.exe	Andy Rondolophberge	00	904 K	8,744 K
explorer.exe	Andy Rondolophber...	00	8,100 K	7,544 K
winlogon.exe	SYSTEM	00	2,780 K	5,264 K
explorer.exe	Nik Rondolophberger	00	10,444 K	5,232 K
explorer.exe	Jaq Rondolophberger	00	10,020 K	5,220 K
lsass.exe	SYSTEM	01	1,864 K	3,388 K
winlogon.exe	SYSTEM	00	3,052 K	3,380 K
winlogon.exe	SYSTEM	00	2,844 K	3,376 K
spoolsv.exe	SYSTEM	00	1,024 K	2,680 K
msmsgs.exe	Nik Rondolophberger	00	1,312 K	1,832 K
msmsgs.exe	Jaq Rondolophberger	00	1,364 K	1,828 K
svchost.exe	LOCAL SERVICE	00	1,324 K	1,804 K
csrss.exe	SYSTEM	00	1,652 K	1,544 K
svchost.exe	SYSTEM	00	1,684 K	1,464 K
moviemk.exe	Andy Rondolophberge	00	4,756 K	1,312 K
services.exe	SYSTEM	00	1,588 K	1,268 K
taskmgr.exe	Andy Rondolophberge	04	2,416 K	1,104 K
taskmgr.exe	Jaq Rondolophberger	00	1,736 K	1,060 K
taskmgr.exe	Nik Rondolophberger	00	3,428 K	1,000 K
wab.exe	Andy Rondolophberge	00	1,048 K	992 K
svchost.exe	NETWORK SERVICE	00	904 K	952 K
wordpad.exe	Andy Rondolophberge	00	1,300 K	828 K

FIGURE 3.7: If you want to see virtual memory usage, add the Virtual Memory Size (VM Size) column to the Processes tab in Task Manager.

Logging Another User Off

If necessary, any Computer Administrator user can log another user off the computer.

Logging someone else off isn't usually a great idea, because while you can use Task Manager to see which processes they're running (as described in the previous section), you can't see whether they have any unsaved work in them. If you don't use passwords to log on to Windows, it's much better to log on as the other user and close the programs and documents manually. Then log off (as the other user) and log back on as yourself. If you do use passwords, you'll need to know the other user's password to log on as them, which kinda defeats the point of having passwords in the first place.

That said, you may need to log another user off if they are running enough programs to affect the computer's performance or if they have open a single-user program or a document that you need to use. If you do so, you may want to send them a message as described in the next section so that they know what's happened.

To log another user off, follow these steps:

1. Right-click the Taskbar and choose Task Manager from the shortcut menu to display Task Manager.
2. Click the Users tab (shown in Figure 3.8).

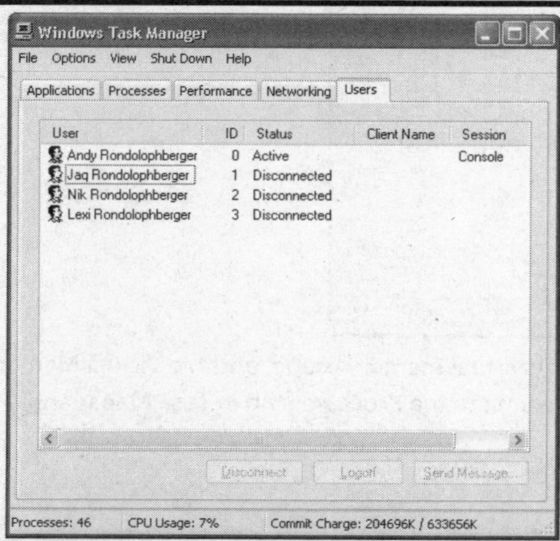

FIGURE 3.8: From the Users tab of Windows Task Manager, you can log another user off the computer.

3. Select the user and click the Logoff button. (Alternatively, right-click the user and choose Log Off from the shortcut menu.) Windows displays the Windows Task Manager dialog box (shown in Figure 3.9), asking if you want to log the selected user off.

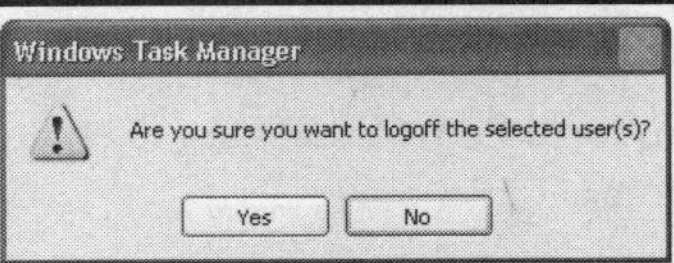

FIGURE 3.9: You can log another user off the computer—but be aware that doing so will cost them any unsaved work.

4. Click the Yes button. The other user's session is toast–as is any unsaved work they had open.

Sending a Message to Another User

You can send a message to another user logged in to this computer. Because the other user can't be using the computer at the same time as you, this feature is not useful for real-time communication–it's not exactly instant messaging–but it can be useful for making sure a family member or a colleague gets a message the next time they use the computer. (For example, you might ask them not to shut down the computer because you're still using it.) It's also useful for notifying another user that you've had to terminate a program that they were using.

To send a message to another user, follow these steps:

1. Right-click the Taskbar and choose Task Manager from the shortcut menu to display Windows Task Manager.
2. Click the Users tab.
3. Right-click the user and choose Send Message from the shortcut menu. Windows displays the Send Message dialog box (shown in Figure 3.10).

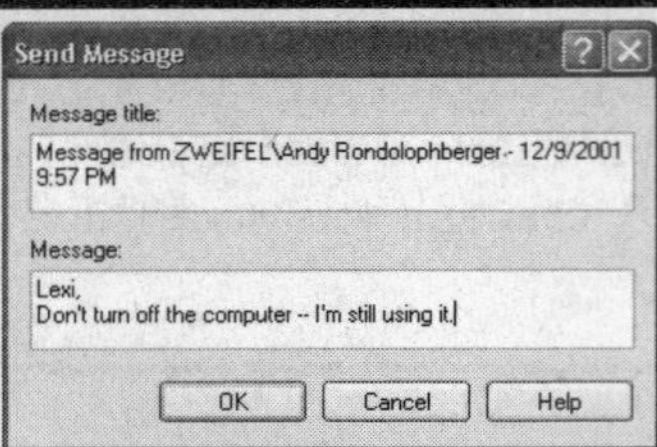

FIGURE 3.10: Use the Send Message dialog box to send a message to another user logged on to this computer.

4. Enter the message title in the Message Title text box and the message in the Message text box.
   - To start a new line, press Ctrl+Enter. (Pressing the Enter key on its own registers a click on the OK button, sending the message.)
   - To type a tab, press Ctrl+Tab. (Pressing the Tab key on its own moves the focus to the next control.)
5. Click the OK button to send the message.

The next time the user logs on to Windows, they receive the message as a screen pop. Figure 3.11 shows an example.

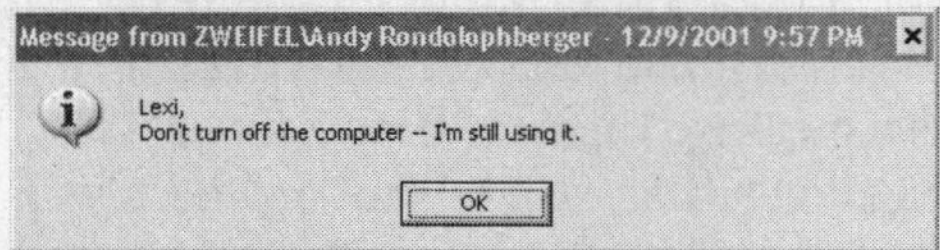

FIGURE 3.11: When you send a message, the user receives a screen pop like this when they start using the computer.

USING THE WINKEY

Windows XP provides a number of keyboard combinations for the Winkey, the key (or keys) with the Windows logo on the keyboard. If you're comfortable leaving your hands on the keyboard, these combinations are doubly convenient, because not only can you avoid reaching for the mouse, but you can also display with a single keystroke a number of windows and dialog boxes that lie several commands deep in the Windows interface.

Table 3.1 lists the Winkey combinations.

TABLE 3.1: Winkey Combinations

Winkey Combination	What It Does
Winkey	Toggles the display of the Start menu
Winkey+Break	Displays the System Properties dialog box
Winkey+Tab	Moves the focus to the next button in the Taskbar
Winkey+Shift+Tab	Moves the focus to the previous button in the Taskbar
Winkey+B	Moves the focus to the notification area
Winkey+D	Displays the Desktop
Winkey+E	Opens an Explorer window showing My Computer
Winkey+F	Opens a Search Results window and activates Search Companion
Winkey+Ctrl+F	Opens a Search Results window, activates Search Companion, and starts a Search for Computer
Winkey+F1	Opens a Help and Support Center window
Winkey+M	Issues a Minimize All Windows command
Winkey+Shift+M	Issues an Undo Minimize All command
Winkey+R	Displays the Run dialog box
Winkey+U	Displays Utility Manager
Winkey+L	Locks the computer

Shutting Down Windows

You can shut down Windows in several ways:

- By clicking the Turn Off Computer button at the bottom of the default Start menu or by choosing Start ➢ Turn Off Computer from the classic Start menu. (If you're connected to a domain, Turn Off Computer becomes Shut Down.)

- By clicking the Turn Off Computer button on the Welcome screen and then clicking the Turn Off button on the Turn Off Computer screen (shown in Figure 3.12).

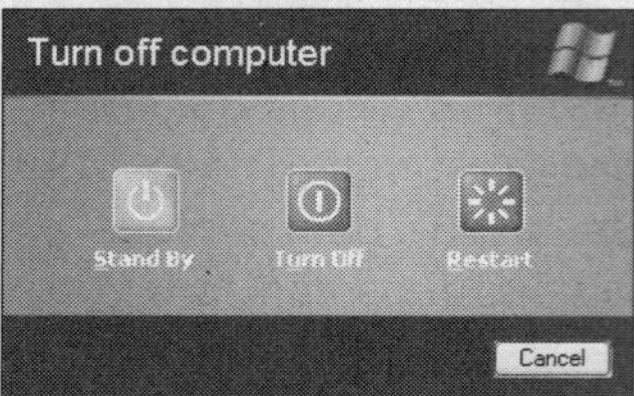

FIGURE 3.12: To turn off the computer, click the Turn Off button on the Turn Off Computer screen.

- By choosing Shut Down ➢ Turn Off from Windows Task Manager.
- By pressing Alt+F4 with the Desktop active and then clicking the Turn Off button on the Turn Off Computer screen.

From the Turn Off Computer screen, you can also click the Hibernate button to make your computer hibernate or the Restart button to restart the computer and Windows. If your computer doesn't support hibernation, the Hibernate button doesn't appear on the Turn Off Computer screen.

POWERING DOWN YOUR COMPUTER WHEN WINDOWS HAS CRASHED

If Windows won't shut down because it has crashed, you'll need to shut it down the hard way. To do so, press the power button on the computer. On ACPI-compliant computers, you may need to hold the power button down for four seconds or more to shut the system down—short presses of the power button may have no effect.

On some computers, a short press of the power button may make Windows display the Turn Off Computer screen so that you can specify whether to hibernate, turn off the computer, or restart it. Under normal circumstances, catching the power signal like this is pretty smart, helping to dissuade users from powering down the computer without exiting Windows first. But if Windows has crashed, you won't be able to do anything from the Turn Off Computer screen.

HELP AND SUPPORT CENTER

Help and Support Center is the latest in Microsoft's efforts to provide help resources powerful enough to silence the ringing of the phones on its costly support lines. Windows XP's Help and Support Center builds on the improvements introduced in the Help and Support Center in Windows Me, which introduced a Web-style interface to replace the old-style Help-file interface in earlier versions of Windows, by integrating many more external resources. For example, you can now search the Microsoft Knowledge Base, an online database of questions and answers, directly from Help and Support Center instead of having to access it separately by using Internet Explorer. And many hardware manufacturers are now providing product-support information that's accessible through Help and Support Center.

Starting Help and Support Center

Choose Start ➢ Help and Support to open Help and Support Center at the Home page. You should see something like Figure 3.13, except that it will contain some updated information. (Your hardware manufacturer may also have customized Help and Support Center by adding content to it or by adapting its interface.)

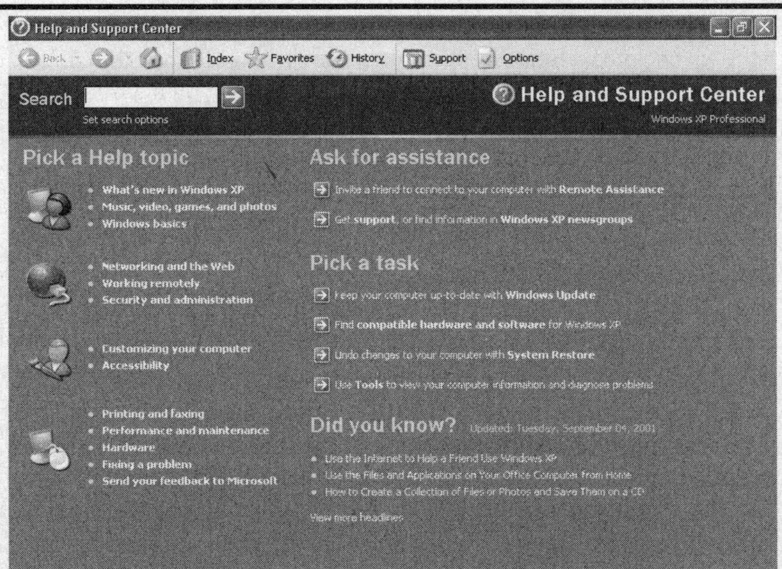

FIGURE 3.13: The Home page in Help and Support Center provides links to the many different areas of Help and Support Center.

As you can see in Figure 3.13, the Help and Support Center window has a toolbar (at the top, starting with the Back button) for primary navigation rather than a menu bar. This toolbar is called the *navigation bar*. Below the navigation bar appears the Search bar.

TIP

You can open multiple Help and Support Center windows at once, which can be a help when you're searching for different pieces of help information or navigating different routes in search of the same piece of information.

Finding Your Way around Help and Support Center

Help and Support Center has access to a large amount of information in Help files that Windows installs on your hard drive, together with troubleshooters for stepping you through the process of finding solutions to common problems and links for running Windows programs (such as Remote Assistance and the System Configuration Utility) that may help you solve or eliminate problems. But Help and Support Center's strongest feature is that it also provides a gateway to information resources on the Web and Internet.

Because of the amount of information and resources that Help and Support Center offers, you may find that it takes you a while to get the hang of navigating around Help and Support Center. This section highlights the main ways of finding the information you need: searching, browsing, using the History feature, and using the Index.

Searching for Help

If you don't see an immediately appropriate link on the Help and Support Center Home page, the easiest way to find information on a particular topic is to search for it.

To search, enter the search term or terms in the Search text box and click the Start Searching button or press Enter. Help and Support Center displays the Search Results pane on the left side and adds a toolbar containing four buttons (Add to Favorites, Change View, Print, and Locate in Contents) under the right side of the Search bar.

The Search Results list box breaks up the results into three categories:

Suggested Topics Suggested topics are keyword matches—one or more of your search terms match a keyword in each of these topics. These topics are further broken into subcategories such as Pick a Task and Overviews, Articles, and Tutorials.

Full-Text Search Matches Full-text matches are topics that contain one or more of your search terms in the body text of the help topic rather than in the keywords.

Microsoft Knowledge Base These results are from the Microsoft Knowledge Base (see the next sidebar). Use them to glean extra or extraneous information beyond that offered by the topics listed in the Suggested Topics and Full-Text Search Matches lists.

To display a category, click its heading. Then click a search result to display it in the right pane, as in the example in Figure 3.14. By default, Windows highlights the word or words you searched for, as in the figure. If there are one or two instances this can be a help, but if there are many instances, this highlighting appears as more of a defacement than an enhancement. But you can get rid of it, as described after the sidebar.

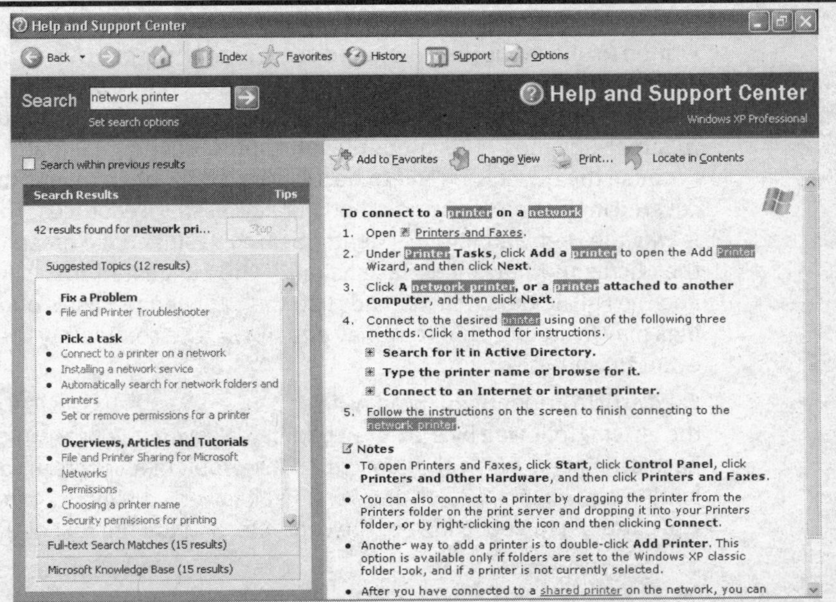

FIGURE 3.14: Click a search result in the Search Results pane to display the page in the right pane.

NOTE

You can also start searching for help from Search Companion by clicking the Information in Help and Support Center link. There's no advantage to starting to search this way unless you happen to have Search Companion displayed when you want help.

MAKING THE MOST OF THE MICROSOFT KNOWLEDGE BASE

The Microsoft Knowledge Base is an online repository of knowledge and wisdom accumulated by Microsoft about its products. Given that the Knowledge Base is one of the main tools that Microsoft's support engineers use for troubleshooting customer problems with Windows, it's a great resource for searching for solutions to problems that Windows' local help resources don't know about.

The disadvantage to the Knowledge Base, and perhaps the reason it's not more heavily emphasized in Microsoft's battery of help solutions, is the way it's arranged and the necessarily scattershot nature of its coverage. The Knowledge Base consists of a large number of answers that Microsoft's support engineers and other experts have written to questions that frustrated users and developers have submitted. The answers vary greatly in length, depending on the complexity of the problem and user level, ranging from beginner topics to super-advanced (developer-level) topics. Coverage is patchy, because the questions tend to be answered only when they're not covered in the Help files and other more accessible resources. This is why the Help and Support Center Search Results pane presents the Microsoft Knowledge Base list after the Suggested Topics list and the Full-Text Search Matches list: the Knowledge Base's offerings may be helpful, but they may equally well be completely irrelevant to your needs.

Each article is identified by an Article ID number, which consists of the letter *Q* followed by a six-digit number (for example, Q201950). Each article has a title that describes the problem it covers, information on which products and versions it covers, a summary that you can scan to get an idea of the contents, and the full text of the

CONTINUED →

article. Beyond this, each article is tagged with keywords describing the main areas of its content. By searching for keywords, you can avoid passing references to words you might have included in the search, thus producing a more focused set of results.

For power use, you may get better results by searching the Knowledge Base directly by using Internet Explorer or another browser, because the Knowledge Base's Web interface offers extra options that Help and Support Center does not, such as searching for what's new in the last few days on a particular product and being able to display either titles and excerpts from hits found or just titles. To search the Knowledge Base directly, point your browser at `search.support.microsoft.com/kb/c.asp`.

If you know the number of a particular query, enter it in the Search text box. For example, if you read newsgroups on Microsoft-related subjects, you'll often see references to particular queries (or, more accurately, to the *answers* to particular queries) mentioned as the place to find a fix for a given problem.

You can also use the Article ID to retrieve the article by e-mail by sending a message to `mshelp@microsoft.com` with the Article ID number in the Subject line.

If you don't know the Article ID but think you can locate it by searching article titles, you can get an index of Knowledge Base articles by e-mail by sending a message to `mshelp@microsoft.com` with the word "Index" in the Subject line.

Setting Search Options

Help and Support Center lets you specify how you want it to search. To set search options, take the following steps:

1. Click the Options button on the navigation bar. Help and Support Center displays the Options screen.
2. In the Options list in the left pane, click the Set Search Options link. Help and Support Center displays the Set Search Options screen (shown in Figure 3.15).

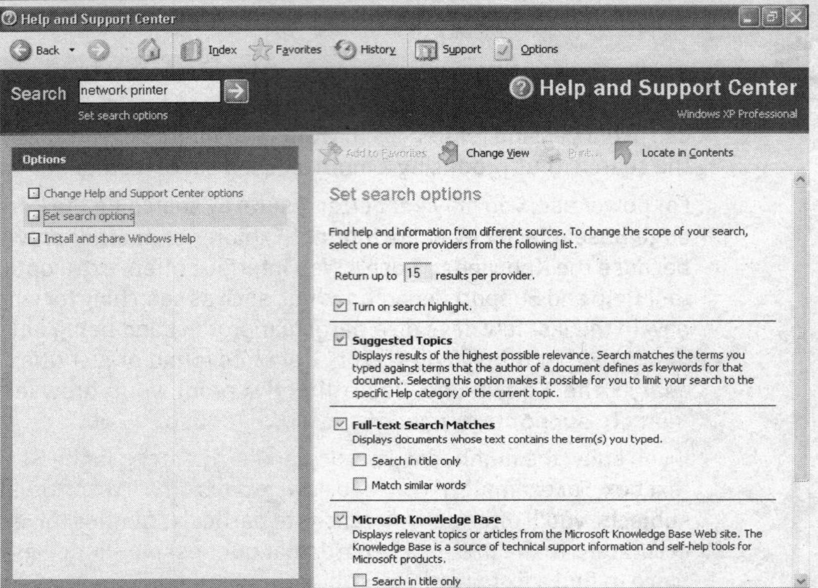

FIGURE 3.15: Choose search options on the Set Search Options screen in Help and Support Center.

3. In the Return Up to *NN* Results per Provider text box, enter the number of search results you want Help and Support Center to get at once from each source of help. The default setting is 15, but you may want to increase this number if you find 15 doesn't give you the information you need. The disadvantage to returning more search results is that it takes longer to download those that come across your Internet connection.

4. Clear the Turn On Search Highlight check box if you don't want Help and Support Center to highlight your search terms in each result it displays.

5. If you don't want to use the Suggested Topics category, clear the Suggested Topics check box. (Usually, this category is well worth using, but in some circumstances you might want to set up Help and Support Center to search only the Knowledge Base.)

6. If you don't want to use full-text searching, clear the Full-Text Search Matches check box. If you do use full-text searching, you can refine it by selecting the Search in Title Only check box to limit full-text searches to the titles of documents instead of including their body text, or the Match Similar Words check box to have full-text searching include matches with words it thinks are similar to (instead of identical to) your search terms.

7. Clear the Microsoft Knowledge Base check box if you don't want to search the Knowledge Base. You might want to avoid searching the Knowledge Base if you find its suggestions too esoteric or if you're working offline. If you continue to search the Knowledge Base, you can set the following search options to target the results:
   - Select the Search in Title Only check box if you want to limit searches to the titles of documents instead of including their body text.
   - In the Select a Product or Topic drop-down list, select the product or topic to search for.
   - In the Search For drop-down list, choose the search method you want by selecting the All of the Words item, the Any of the Words item, the The Exact Phrase item, or the The Boolean Phrase item. (A *Boolean phrase* is one that uses terms such as AND, OR, or NOT—for example, "Internet NOT Explorer" to search for documents that contain *Internet* but do not contain *Explorer*.)

Setting Help and Support Center Options

While you're setting search options, your eye will probably be caught by the Change Help and Support Center Options link in the Options pane on the Set Search Options screen. These are the options you can set:

Show Favorites on the Navigation Bar check box Leave this check box selected (as it is by default) to have Help and Support Center display the Favorites button on the toolbar. Clear this check box to remove the Favorites button.

Show History on the Navigation Bar check box Leave this check box selected (as it is by default) to have Help and Support Center display the History button on the toolbar. Clear this check box to remove the History button.

Font Size Used for Help Content list Select the Small option button, the Medium option button, or the Large option button to set a font size you find comfortable.

Options for Icons in the Navigation Bar list Specify whether Help and Support Center should display text on the navigation bar buttons by selecting the Show All Text Labels option button, the Show Only Default Text Labels option button, or the Do Not Show Text Labels option button.

Browsing for Help

As you saw in Figure 3.13, Help and Support Center provides a list of a dozen or so *help topics* on the left side of its Home page. You can browse any of these help topics by clicking its link. Figure 3.16 shows an example of a help topic. Click one of the links in the topic area to display the links or information available.

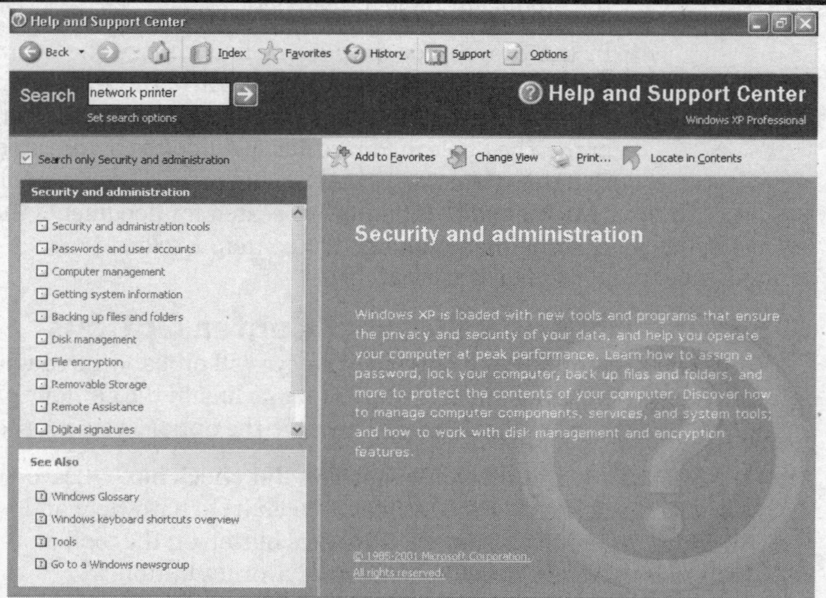

FIGURE 3.16: Follow the links in the Pick a Help Topic list to reach help topic areas.

Similarly, Help and Support Center provides a list of key support topics on the right side of its Home page. The Ask for Assistance list provides links to Remote Assistance, Support (from Microsoft), and Windows XP Newsgroups. The Pick a Task list includes links to tools such as Windows Update and System Restore, the Tools area of Help and Support Center for help-specific tools, and Help and Support Center's features for finding XP-compatible hardware and software.

Support Page

The Support page (shown in Figure 3.17 with Remote Assistance information displayed) offers a variety of support tools, some of the items that actually provide support (such as Remote Assistance–accessed via the Ask a Friend to Help link–and Microsoft Online Support) and some that are just links to Windows utilities (such as My Computer Information and System Configuration Utility).

Windows Update Page

The Windows Update page provides an alternative method of accessing Windows Update. (You can also access Windows Update from the Start menu.)

Compatible Hardware and Software Page

The Compatible Hardware and Software page (shown in Figure 3.18) provides a mechanism for searching for information on whether particular products are compatible with Windows XP. To open the Compatible Hardware and Software page, click Find Compatible Hardware and Software for Windows XP in the Pick a Task section.

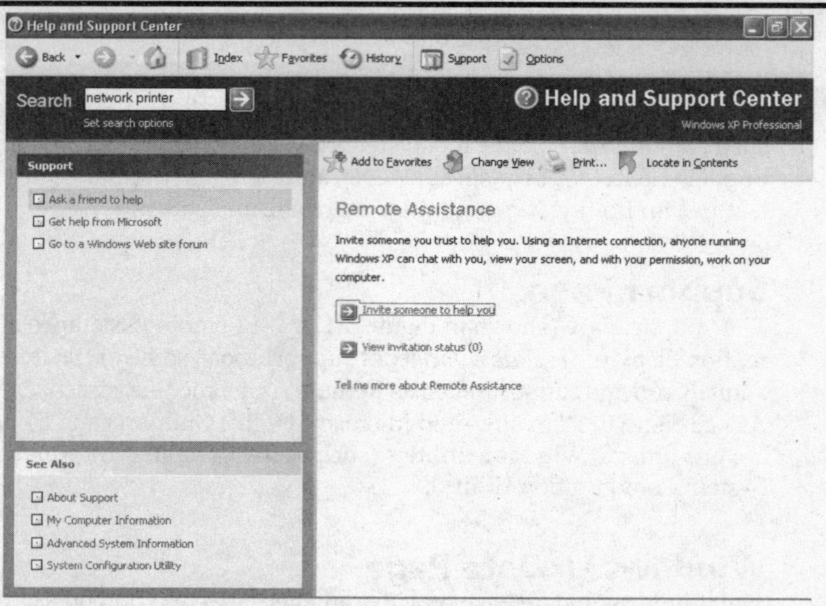

FIGURE 3.17: The Support area contains tools and links to Windows utilities.

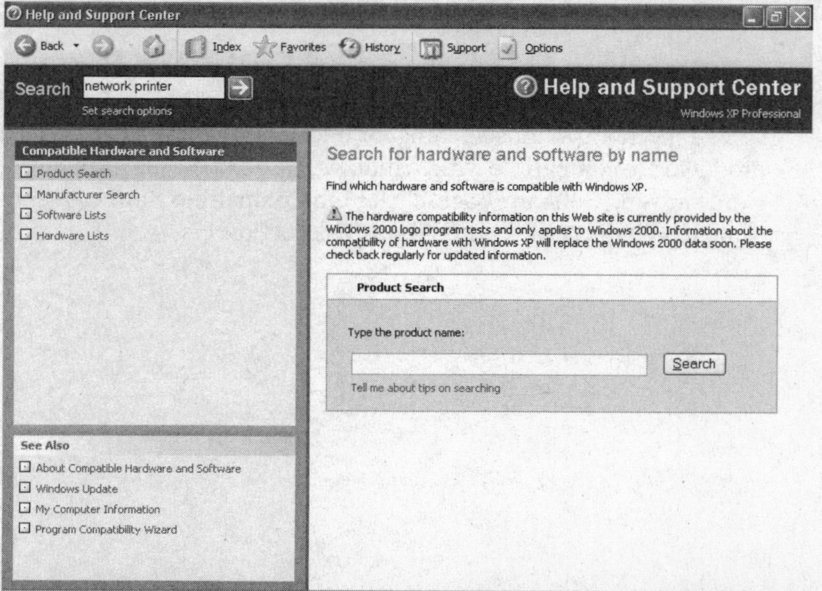

FIGURE 3.18: Use the Compatible Hardware and Software page to search for compatibility information for a specific product.

Tools Page

To access the Tools page, in Help and Support Center click the Use Tools to View Your Computer Information and Diagnose Problems in the Pick a Task section. The Tools page (shown in Figure 3.19 with the Advanced System Information screen displayed) contains the Tools Center, which provides access to a number of tools for configuring and troubleshooting Windows. You'll notice that some of these tools have already popped up on other Help and Support Center pages you've seen so far. This illustrates the large number of redundant paths deliberately built into Help and Support Center to make it easier for you to find the information and tools you need to solve a problem.

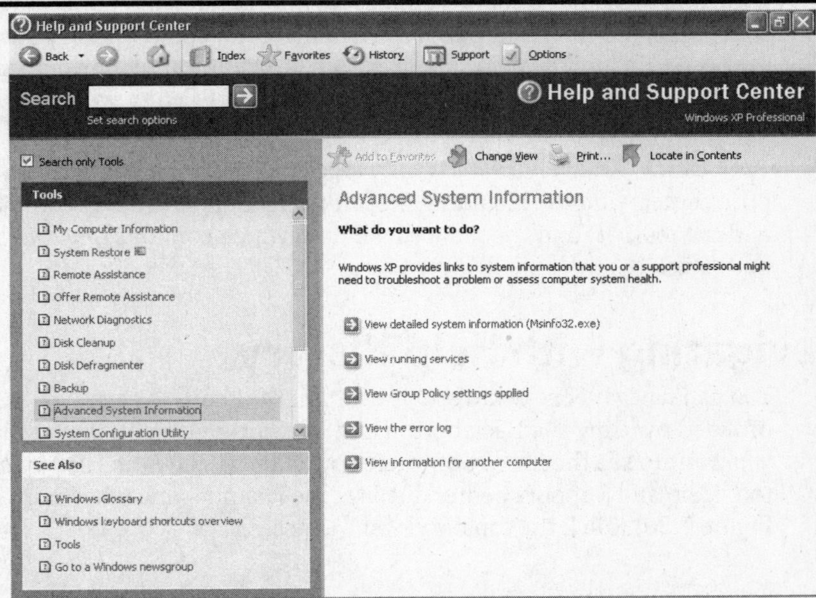

FIGURE 3.19: The Tools page provides links to a large handful of system tools.

Creating and Using Favorites in Help

You can create favorites in Help and Support Center so that you can access pages of information quickly whenever you need to.

To add the current page to your favorites, click the Add to Favorites button. Help and Support Center adds the favorite to your Favorites list and displays a message box telling you that it is doing so.

To access a favorite, click the Favorites button on the toolbar. Help and Support Center displays the Favorites pane. Select the favorite you want to display and click the Display button.

To rename a favorite, click it in the Favorites pane, and then click the Rename button. Help and Support Center displays an edit box around the favorite's name. Type the new name and press the Enter key.

To delete a favorite, select it in the Favorites pane and click the Remove button.

Using Views

Designed to display a serious amount of information and options at the same time, the Help and Support Center window can threaten visual overload or simply swamp a small screen. To help you retain your sanity and your screen real estate, the Help and Support Center window has a reduced view as well.

Click the Change View button to toggle between the full Help and Support Center window (including the left navigation pane, the Search bar, and the toolbar) and the reduced window, which contains only the content page.

Navigating with Help History

You can navigate backward and forward in the chain of pages you've browsed by using the Back button and Forward button on the toolbar. If you want to see the history of where you've been, click the History button. Help and Support Center displays the History pane (shown in Figure 3.20). Click the topic you want to access.

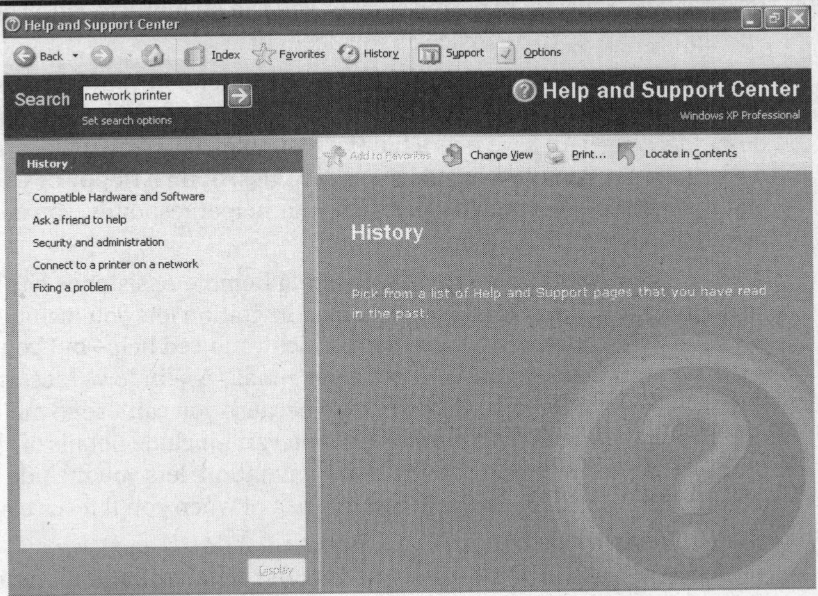

FIGURE 3.20: Use the History pane to return to topics you've visited recently.

Printing Help Information

It goes without saying that you can print help information if you want a hard copy of it handy: To print the current topic, click the Print button, and then click the Print button in the Print dialog box that Help and Support Center displays.

But it's worth pointing out that, instead of printing just an individual screen at a time, you can print a whole section of help by selecting the Print All Linked Documents check box on the Options tab of the Print dialog box. You can also select the Print Table of Links check box if you want to print a table of linked pages.

Using Remote Assistance

Remote Assistance lets you permit a designated helper to connect to your computer, see what's going on, and help you out of trouble. The helper—a friend or an administrator; whomever you choose—can control the computer directly if you give them permission, or you can simply chat with them and apply such of their advice as you deem fit.

To use Remote Assistance, both your computer and your helper's must be running Windows XP. You send an invitation via e-mail or via Windows Messenger, or save it as a file (for example, to a network location designated for Remote Assistance request files, or on a floppy or CD that you then pop in the snail mail). When your helper responds, you decide whether to accept their help.

Each of the three methods of requesting Remote Assistance has its advantages and disadvantages. An e-mail invitation lets you include details of the Windows problem with which you need help—but you don't know when the recipient will check their e-mail. A Windows Messenger invitation will be received immediately (because you can't send an invitation to someone who isn't online), but you can't include details of the problem. A file invitation, like an e-mail invitation, lets you include details of the problem, but you have no idea of when you'll receive a response to it (if ever).

On the other end of the wire, you can offer Help via Remote Assistance. All you need is for someone to send you an invitation.

Security Considerations

Like all remote-control technologies, Remote Assistance has serious security implications that you need to consider before using it.

If you give another person control of your computer, they can take actions almost as freely as if they were seated in front of the computer. You can watch these actions, and you can take back control of the computer at any time, but you may already be too late: it takes less than a second to delete a key file, and little longer to plant a virus or other form of malware.

Even if you *don't* give your helper control and instead simply chat, keep your wits about you when deciding which of their suggestions to implement. Malicious or ill-informed suggestions can do plenty of damage if you apply them without thinking. Never take any actions that could compromise your security or destroy your data. Above all, treat any incoming files with the greatest of suspicion and virus-check them using an up-to-date antivirus program before using them.

One particular problem is that you can't tell that the person at the other computer is who they claim to be. For this reason alone, you should always protect your Remote Assistance connections with a strong password known only to the person from whom you're requesting help. That way, if someone else is at their computer or has identity-jacked them, they won't be able to respond to the Remote Assistance invitation you send.

Enabling Remote Assistance

Remote Assistance is enabled by default. To find out if Remote Assistance is enabled on your computer, follow these steps:

1. Display the System Properties dialog box (for example, by pressing Winkey+Break or clicking the System link on the Performance and Maintenance screen of Control Panel).
2. Click the Remote tab:

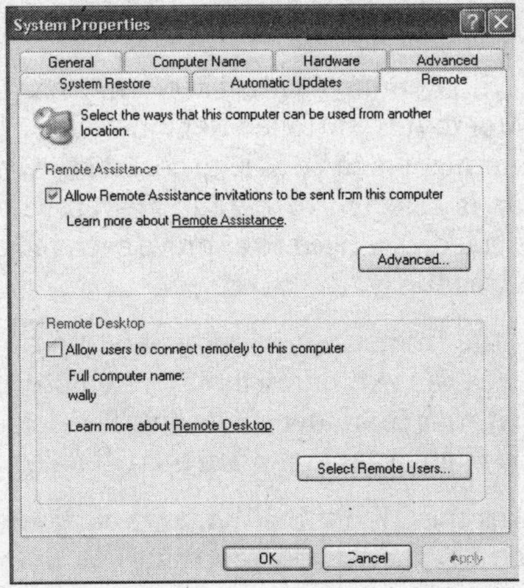

3. Check the status of the Allow Remote Assistance Invitations to Be Sent from This Computer check box. If this check box isn't selected, select it.
4. Click the OK button. Windows closes the System Properties dialog box.

Setting Limits for Remote Assistance

To set limits for Remote Assistance, follow these steps:

1. In the Remote Assistance section of the Remote tab, click the Advanced button to open the Remote Assistance Settings dialog box:

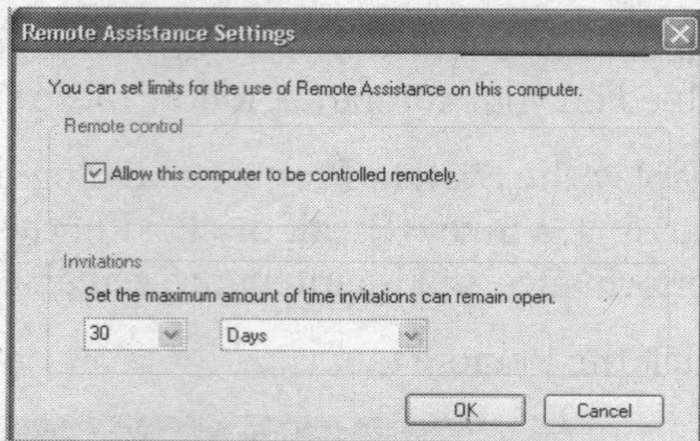

2. In the Remote Control section, clear the Allow This Computer to Be Controlled Remotely check box if you don't want your helpers to be able to control the computer. (This check box is selected by default.) Even when this check box is selected, you need to approve each request for control of the PC manually.
3. In the Invitations section, use the two drop-down lists to specify an expiration limit for Remote Assistance invitations that your computer sends out. The default setting is 30 days; you might want to shorten this period considerably for security.
4. Click the OK button. Windows closes the Remote Assistance Settings dialog box, returning you to the System Properties dialog box.
5. Click the OK button. Windows closes the System Properties dialog box.

You're now ready to start sending out invitations for Remote Assistance.

Sending a Remote Assistance Invitation via E-Mail

To send a Remote Assistance invitation as an e-mail message via your existing e-mail account, follow these steps:

1. Choose Start ➢ All Programs ➢ Remote Assistance. Windows opens a Help and Support Center window to the Remote Assistance topic.
2. Click the Invite Someone to Help You link. Help and Support Center displays the Pick How You Want to Contact Your Assistant screen of Remote Assistance (shown in Figure 3.21).
   - ▶ The first time you go through these steps, Help and Support Center displays a screen bearing Important Notes. If you want to skip this page in the future, leave the Don't Show This Page Again check box selected (as it is by default) and click the Continue button.

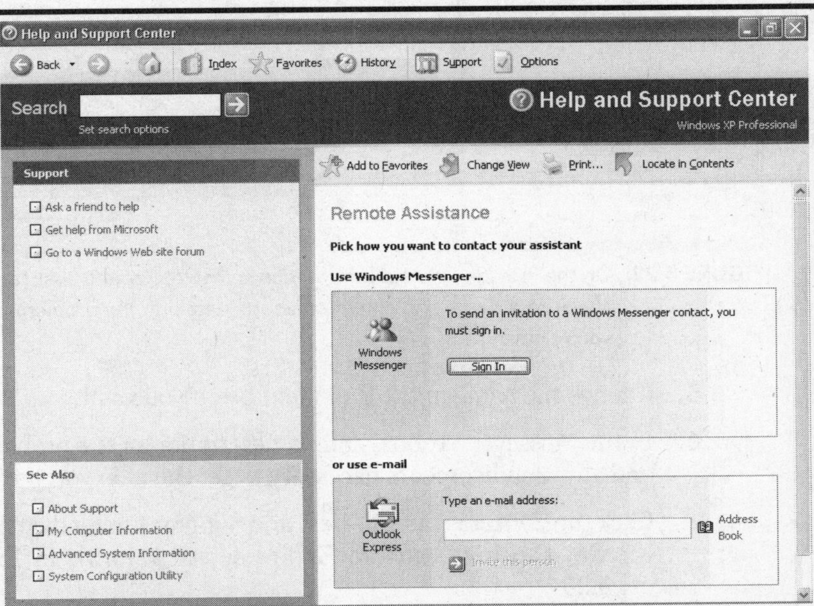

FIGURE 3.21: On the Pick How You Want to Contact Your Assistant screen of Remote Assistance, specify which type of Remote Assistance invitation to send.

3. In the Or Use E-mail area, enter your putative assistant's e-mail address in the Type an E-mail Address text box. Either type in the address or click the Address Book button and use Address Book to specify the address.

4. Click the Invite This Person link. Help and Support Center displays the Provide Contact Information screen (shown in Figure 3.22).

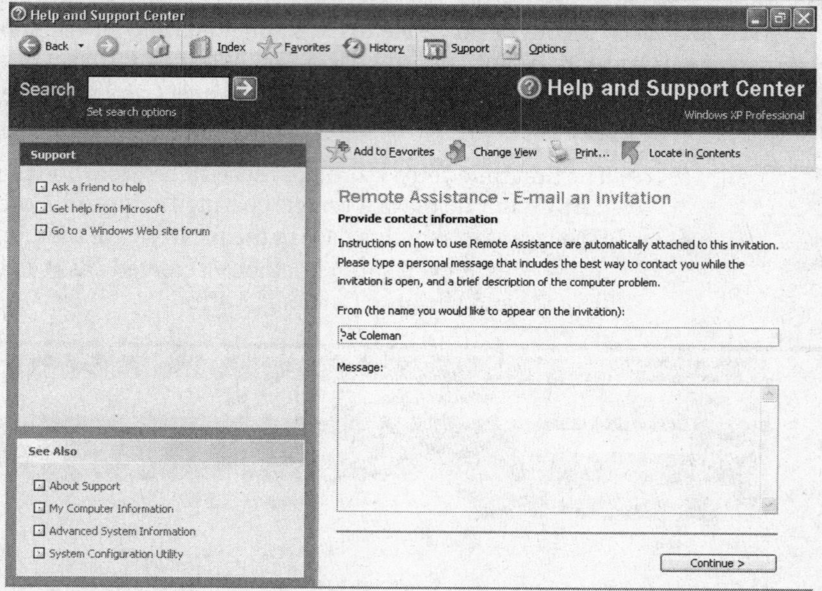

FIGURE 3.22: On the Provide Contact Information screen of Remote Assistance, check your name and enter a message detailing the problem you're having.

5. Change the name in the From text box if you want.

6. In the Message text box, enter a description of the problem and any blandishments necessary to get the help you want.

7. Click the Continue button. Help and Support Center displays the Set the Invitation to Expire screen (shown in Figure 3.23).

8. In the Set the Invitation to Expire area, specify the time limit for the recipient to accept the invitation. Choose a number in the first drop-down list and a time period—Minutes, Hours, or Days—in the second drop-down list.

9. To set a password, make sure the Require the Recipient to Use a Password check box is selected, and then enter the password in the Type Password text box and the Confirm Password text box.

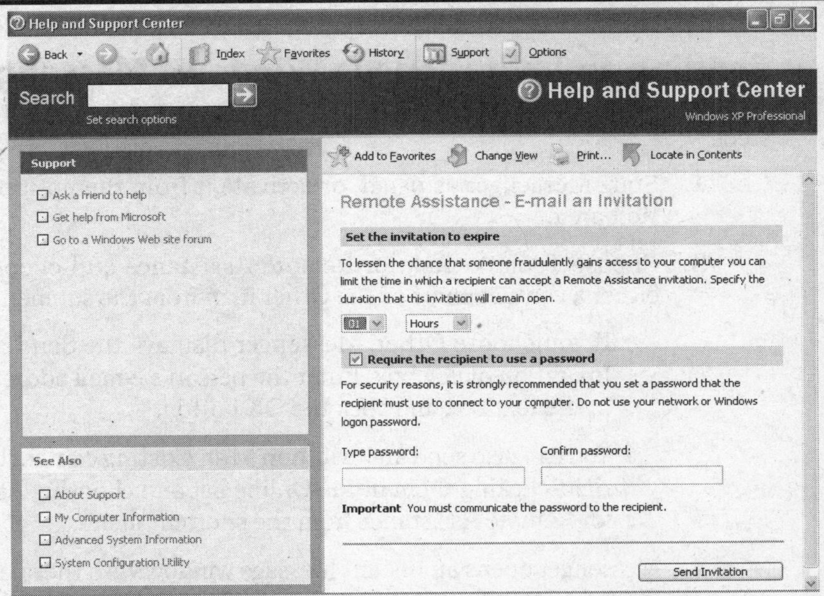

FIGURE 3.23: On the Set the Invitation to Expire screen of Remote Assistance, set the expiration period for the invitation and enter a password.

10. Click the Send Invitation button. Help and Support Center creates a file named `rcBuddy.MsRcIncident` containing the invitation and sends it via your default e-mail client with a message explaining how to use it. Help and Support Center then displays a screen telling you that the invitation has been sent successfully.

    - If Help and Support Center can't send the file—for example, if your ISP's mail server is down—it invites you to save the file and send it manually.

- If you've set Outlook Express to warn you if other programs attempt to send mail in your nlook Express will display an Outlook Express dialog box, warning you that a program (Help and Support Center) is trying to send a message. CLick the Send button.

Sending an Invitation via Windows Messenger

To send an invitation via your existing Messenger account, follow these steps:

1. Start Messenger as usual, or activate it from the notification area.
2. Choose Tools ➢ Ask for Remote Assistance and choose either a contact name or the Other item from the submenu.
   - If you choose Other, Messenger displays the Send an Invitation dialog box. Enter the person's e-mail address in the text box and click the OK button.
   - You can also send an invitation to an existing contact by right-clicking them in the Online list and choosing Ask for Remote Assistance from the shortcut menu.
3. Messenger opens an Instant Message window with the specified user and displays a note saying that you've invited the user to start Remote Assistance.
   - To cancel the invitation, click the Cancel link in the Instant Message window, or press Alt+Q.
4. Wait for a response, then proceed as described in "Receiving Remote Assistance," later in this chapter.

Saving an Invitation As a File

Saving an invitation as a file works in essentially the same way as sending an invitation as an e-mail message, except that instead of specifying an e-mail address, you click the Save Invitation As a File link, create the invitation, and then specify a filename and location in the Save File dialog box. For example, your company might designate a network folder as a drop-box for Remote Assistance requests. Administrators would then examine the contents of the folder and respond to the requests accordingly.

Alternatively, you could save the file to a floppy disk or other mobile medium and mail it to a helper.

Viewing the Status of Your Invitations

To view the status of the Remote Assistance invitations you've sent (or saved), display the Remote Assistance screen in Help and Support Center.

Click the View Invitation Status link. Windows displays the View or Change Your Invitation screen of Remote Assistance. Figure 3.24 shows an example.

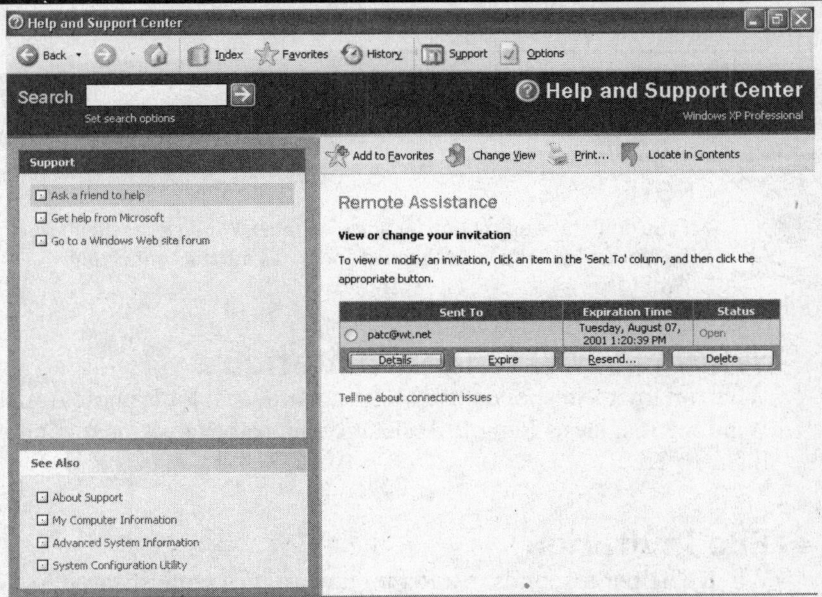

FIGURE 3.24: Viewing the status of invitations you've sent

From here, you can view the details of an invitation by clicking the Details button, kill an open invitation by clicking the Expire button, resend an invitation by clicking the Resend button, or delete an invitation by clicking the Delete button.

Receiving Remote Assistance

The following sections describe what happens when you receive a response to your Remote Assistance request.

E-Mail Invitation

When a helper responds to an e-mail invitation, Windows displays a Remote Assistance dialog box such as that shown in Figure 3.25, telling you that the person has accepted the invitation and asking if you want to let them view your screen and chat with you. Click the Yes button to start the Remote Assistance session.

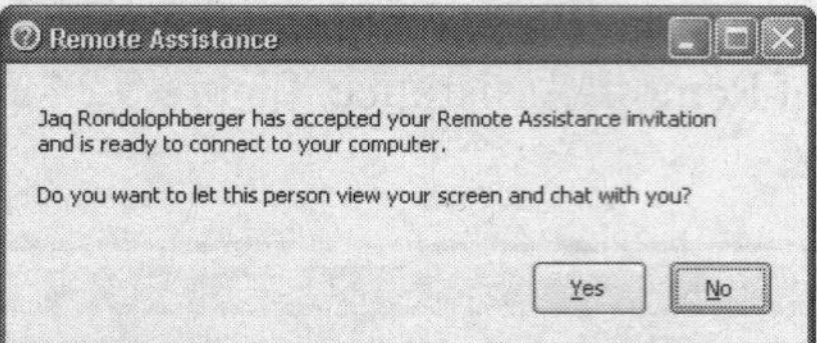

FIGURE 3.25: Remote Assistance dialog box indicating an accepted invitation

NOTE

If you don't take any action for a few minutes, Windows assumes you're not in the market for Remote Assistance and times out the connection.

Windows Messenger Invitation

When an invitee responds to a Messenger request for Remote Assistance, Windows displays a Remote Assistance dialog box such as that shown in Figure 3.25.

File Invitation

When a helper responds to a Remote Assistance request saved in a file, Windows displays a Remote Assistance window telling you that the person has accepted the invitation and asking if you want to let them view your screen and chat with you. Click the Yes button to start the Remote Assistance session.

Receiving Assistance

Once the Remote Assistance session is established, Remote Assistance displays the Remote Assistance window shown in Figure 3.26, which provides a chat pane and control buttons.

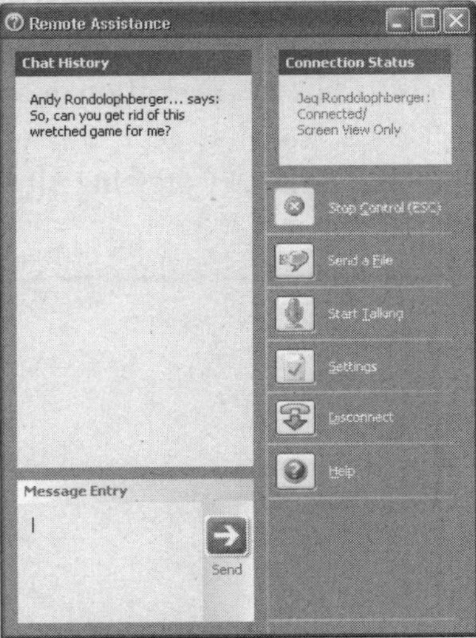

FIGURE 3.26: During a Remote Assistance session, this Remote Assistance window provides a chat pane and control buttons.

Chatting with Your Helper

- Type a message in the Message Entry text box and press the Enter key or click the Send button to send it.
- To start voice transmission, click the Start Talking button. Your helper then sees a dialog box asking if they want to use a voice connection. If they click the Yes button, Remote Assistance establishes the voice connection. Talk as usual, and then click the Stop Talking button when you want to stop using the voice connection.

NOTE

The first time you use the talk feature, Remote Assistance runs the Audio and Video Tuning Wizard if you haven't run it before.

- To choose voice settings, click the Settings button. Windows displays a Remote Assistance Settings dialog box. Choose the Standard Quality option button or the High Quality option button as appropriate. Alternatively, click the Audio Tuning Wizard button (if it's available) to run the Audio and Video Tuning Wizard to optimize your speaker and microphone settings. Close the Remote Assistance Settings dialog box when you've finished.

Giving Your Helper Control of Your Computer If your helper requests control of your computer, Windows displays the Remote Assistance dialog box (shown in Figure 3.27). Click the Yes button or the No button as appropriate.

You can regain control by pressing the Esc key, by pressing Alt+C, or by clicking the Stop Control button.

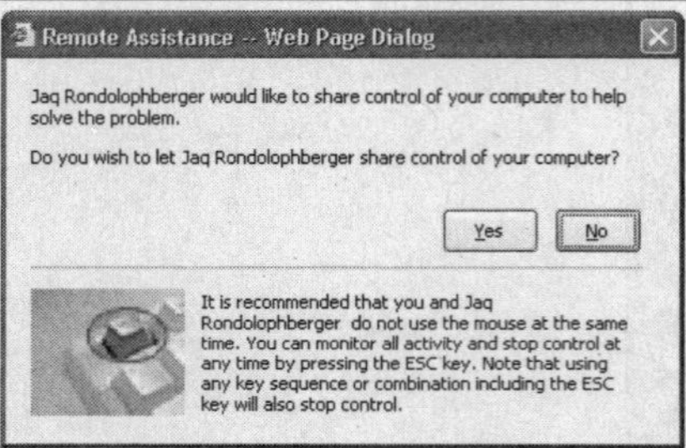

FIGURE 3.27: When your helper requests control of the computer, decide whether you trust them or not.

Disconnecting Your Helper To disconnect your helper, click the Disconnect button. Remote Assistance closes the connection and restores your Desktop to its full complement of colors (if you chose to optimize performance for your helper).

When your helper disconnects themselves, Windows displays a Remote Assistance dialog box telling you so. Click the OK button to close this dialog box, then close the Help and Support Center window.

Responding to a Remote Assistance Invitation

This section discusses how to respond to a Remote Assistance invitation that someone sends you. As you'd expect, the specifics vary depending on whether it's an e-mail invitation, a Messenger invitation, or a file invitation.

E-Mail Invitation

When someone sends you a Remote Assistance invitation via e-mail, you receive an e-mail message with the subject line YOU HAVE RECEIVED A REMOTE ASSISTANCE INVITATION FROM and the username. The message comes with explanatory text, augmenting whatever message text the requester entered, and an attached file with a name such as `rcBuddy.MsRcIncident`.

Open the file by double-clicking it. Alternatively, in Outlook Express, click the Attachment icon, select the file from the drop-down menu, select the Open It button in the Open Attachment Warning dialog box, and click the OK button. Windows displays a Remote Assistance window such as that shown in Figure 3.28, giving the details of the Remote Assistance invitation: who it's from and when it expires.

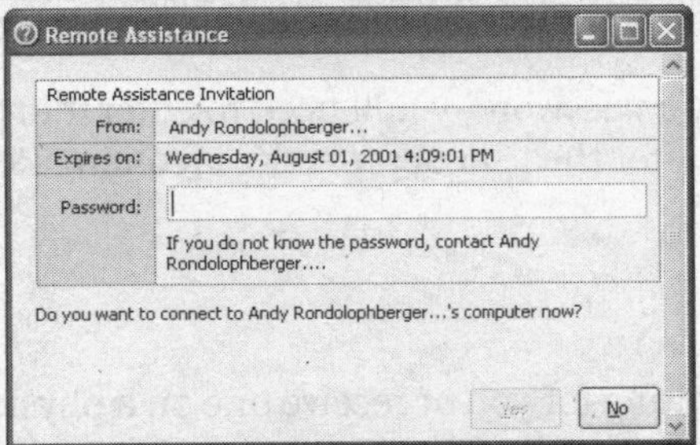

FIGURE 3.28: Double-click the file you receive to open the Remote Assistance invitation.

Enter the password (if the window is displaying a Password text box) and click the Yes button to start the help session. Windows tries to contact the remote computer.

Windows Messenger Invitation

When someone sends you a Remote Assistance invitation via Messenger, you see a Conversation window such as that shown in Figure 3.29. Click the Accept link (or press Alt+T) to accept it or click the Decline link (or press Alt+D) to decline it.

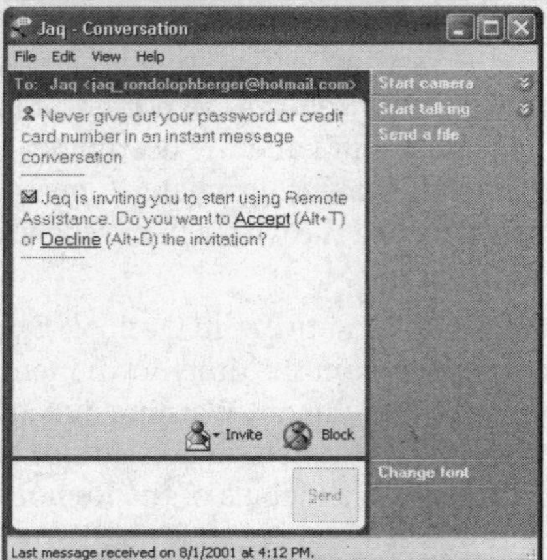

FIGURE 3.29: Receiving a Remote Assistance invitation in Messenger

If the user chose to specify a password, you'll need to enter it in a Help and Support Center window after the user accepts the incoming Remote Assistance connection.

File Invitation

If you find a file invitation waiting for you or receive one on a physical medium, double-click the file to open it. The rest of the procedure is the same as for an e-mail invitation, discussed in the section before last.

Providing Remote Assistance

If Windows is able to contact the remote computer, and if the user accepts the Remote Assistance connection, Windows displays the Remote Assistance window, which features a chat pane, a view panel that shows the user's Desktop, and assorted command buttons.

Chatting with the User To chat with the user via text, click the Show Chat button to display the chat pane if it's not currently displayed. Type a message in the Message Entry text box and press the Enter key or click the Send button to send it.

To hide the chat pane so that you can see more of the remote screen, click the Hide button.

To chat via voice, click the Start Talking button. Remote Assistance displays a dialog box asking the person at the other end whether they want to use voice. If they click the Yes button, Remote Assistance activates the audio hardware. Click the Stop Talking button to stop using voice to chat.

Scaling the Display You can scale the remote display to fit the area available on your screen by clicking the Scale to Window button, and restore it to its actual size by clicking the Actual Size button. Depending on the resolution you and the remote user have set, scaling the display may make the fonts illegible, but viewing the whole screen at once may make it easier for you to see what's happening on the computer than viewing only a partial screen and having to scroll to its outer reaches.

Taking Control of the Remote Computer To request control of the remote computer, click the Take Control button. Windows displays a Remote Assistance dialog box on the remote screen asking the user if they want to give you control. If they click the Yes button, you get a Remote Assistance dialog box telling you so. When you dismiss this dialog box, you have control of the computer and can take any action with it as if you were working directly on it. To release control, click the Release Control button or press the Esc key.

WARNING

Avoid pressing the Esc key when taking keyboard actions on the remote computer. Even combinations that use the Esc key will release control.

Transferring Files to and from the Remote Computer To transfer a file to the remote computer, click the Send a File button. Windows displays a Remote Assistance dialog box. Use the Browse button to locate the file, and then click the Send File button to send it. The remote user then gets to decide whether to keep the file and in which folder to save it. (If you have control of the computer, you can make these decisions.)

To transfer a file from the remote computer to your computer, have the user click the Send a File button in their Remote Assistance window. Alternatively, if you have control of the computer, you can do this yourself.

Disconnecting from the Remote Computer To disconnect from the remote computer, click the Disconnect button. Then close the Remote Assistance Services window manually. Unless you expect you'll need to reconnect to the remote computer to help the user further during the time remaining before the Remote Assistance invitation expires, delete the invitation file before you forget.

If the person you're helping disconnects the connection, Windows displays a Remote Assistance dialog box telling you so.

Microsoft Online Support (Get Help from Microsoft)

Microsoft Online Support lets you automatically collect information on a problem you're having and submit it to Microsoft electronically. A Microsoft technician then sends a solution, which appears as a pop-up in your notification area. You can read the response in the Help and Support Center window and apply the wisdom it contains to fix the problem.

Microsoft Online Support lets you avoid both long waits on hold and the difficulty of explaining complex problems and system configuration over the phone.

To use Microsoft Online Support, you need a Microsoft Passport or a Hotmail account. If you don't have one, Help and Support Center walks you through the process of getting one.

To connect to Microsoft Online Support, click the Get Help from Microsoft link in the Support pane and follow through the steps the Help and Support Center presents. For obvious reasons, your computer needs a working Internet connection to use this feature.

Windows Newsgroups (Go to a Windows Web Site Forum)

The Windows Newsgroups are an assortment of Windows-related online newsgroups that you can access through a Web-based front end. Though these newsgroups are run under the auspices of Microsoft, they suffer to some extent from the problems of noise and irrelevance that characterize public newsgroups. (See Chapter 14 for a discussion of newsgroups and how to use Outlook Express to access them.)

To access the Windows Newsgroups, take the following steps:

1. Display the Support page of Help and Support Center.

2. In the Support pane, click the Go to a Windows Web Site Forum link. Help and Support Center displays the Windows Newsgroups screen.
3. Click the Go to Windows Newsgroups link. Help and Support Center activates or launches Internet Explorer (or your default browser) and displays the Windows XP Newsgroups home page, which lists the newsgroups.
4. Click one of the newsgroup links. Internet Explorer activates or launches Outlook Express (or your default newsreader) and opens that newsgroup in it.

Using the Troubleshooters

Windows XP includes a number of *troubleshooters* for troubleshooting common problems with hardware and software configuration. Help and Support Center provides a central starting point for running these tools, though Windows also offers you the chance to run the appropriate troubleshooter when it detects that you've run into a configuration problem.

To run one of the troubleshooters, follow these steps:

1. From the Help and Support Center Home page, click the Fixing a Problem link. Help and Support Center displays the Fixing a Problem screen.
2. In the Fixing a Problem list, click a link to display a list of troubleshooters for that problem.
3. Click a Troubleshooter, and then follow the onscreen instructions. Figure 3.30 shows the Printing Troubleshooter.

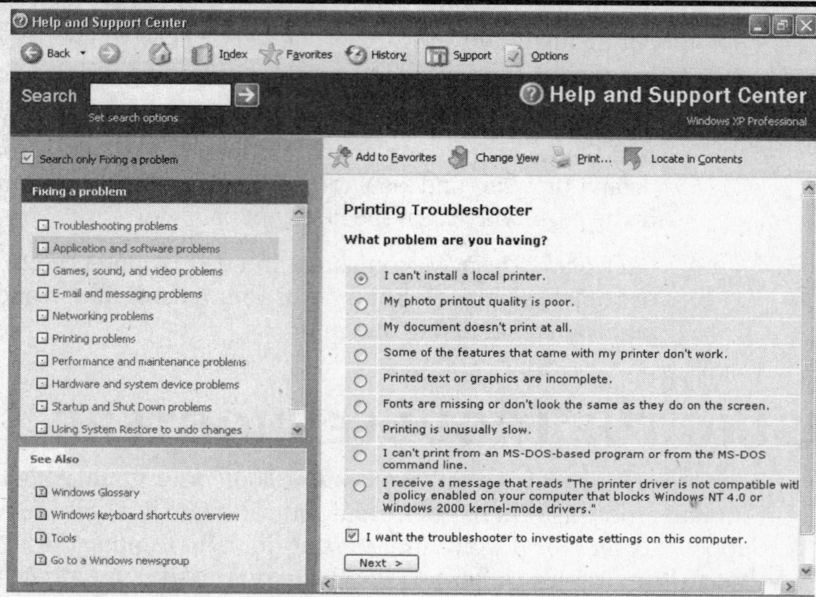

FIGURE 3.30: Windows XP includes troubleshooters that attempt to walk you through the steps of solving a problem.

Finding Help on the Internet and Web

If you can't find the information you need through Help and Support Center, try the Internet and the Web.

Help on the Web

With earlier versions of Windows, the first port of call when looking for help on the Web was the Microsoft Web site, which offered all sorts of resources from the latest patches and drivers to the Knowledge Base. But now that Help and Support Center both seamlessly searches the Microsoft Web site and provides links to some hardware and software manufacturers' offerings, and Windows Update can automatically download and prompt you to install updates and patches to Windows, there's less reason to access the Microsoft Web site manually unless you need, say, the extra search capabilities that the Knowledge Base Web site offers.

To find information from hardware and software manufacturers not partnered closely enough with Microsoft to rate inclusion in Help and Support Center's repertoire, to download the latest drivers, or to find other sources of information, the Web can be either more or less valuable, depending on your luck and your persistence in searching.

Chapter 13 discusses how to surf the Web with Internet Explorer.

Help in Newsgroups

Another good source of information and help are the many computer-related public newsgroups (such as the `comp.sys` hierarchy) and the Microsoft public newsgroups (in the `microsoft.public` hierarchy).

Chapter 14 discusses how to use Outlook Express to read news.

What's Next?

When a new version of Windows is released, the question always arises about how to install and use new and existing applications. In the next chapter, Guy Hart-Davis walks you through the steps to take care of these issues and also shows you how to remove applications that you no longer need.

Chapter 4

Installing, Removing, and Running Programs

However wonderful the features built into Windows XP—and some of them *are* pretty wonderful; some less so; see the rest of the book for details—they're not the be-all and end-all of computing. The programs bundled with Windows XP let you perform a few basic tasks, from creating simple documents to playing music and video to creating simple video movies of your own. But sooner or later, you're going to want to install a third-party program and run it so that you can carry on with your business and your life.

On the assumption that this is probably going to happen sooner rather than later, this chapter discusses how to install, configure, remove, and run programs—and how to shut them down when they fail to respond to conventional stimuli.

Revised and adapted from *Mastering Windows XP Home Edition* by Guy Hart-Davis

ISBN 0-7821-2980-3 1024 pages $39.99

The chapter uses various programs as examples, ranging from the latest (and supposedly greatest) programs specially designed for Windows XP to Windows 9*x* programs to DOS programs that are still only just starting to suspect that graphical environments exist. The odds are overwhelmingly against these programs being the ones you want to use with your copy of Windows XP, but these programs provide examples of many of the issues you'll encounter with installing, running, and removing programs.

NOTE

If you performed an in-place upgrade of your previous version of Windows to Windows XP, the installation processes should have configured all your programs for use already, so you shouldn't need to reinstall them. However, if you have old programs that you find don't run properly on Windows XP, you may need to run them in Compatibility mode. If so, turn to the section "Running Programs in Compatibility Mode," later in this chapter.

Good News on Compatibility

If you've used any of the versions of Windows NT, or if you've used Windows 2000, you'll know that program compatibility has been a major issue for the NT code base. In order to make NT stable and crash-proof, the designers made heavy sacrifices in compatibility. Many Windows 9*x* programs flat out wouldn't run on NT. Games and other programs that tried to access hardware directly were particularly problematic: Windows 9*x* lets a program access hardware directly, whereas NT's Hardware Abstraction Layer (HAL) forces all hardware requests to be brokered by the operating system.

In Windows 2000 Professional, Microsoft greatly increased the number of programs that would run on the NT code base—but some Windows 9*x* programs still wouldn't run, and many DOS-based games wouldn't run either. Direct hardware access was still a problem, because the HAL was still there. Briefly, if the program could run in protected mode, letting the HAL handle the communications with the hardware, it would usually run, though it might've run a bit more slowly than on other versions of Windows (or on DOS). If the program insisted on trying to communicate with the hardware directly, HAL gave it grief. (Fill in your own *2001* pun here: "I'm sorry, DOOM, I'm afraid I can't do that," and so on.)

On this front, Windows XP brings very welcome good news: XP is able to run most 32-bit Windows programs without problems. It can also run many 16-bit Windows programs. And it can run a number of DOS programs. Most of this happens transparently: You install the program by running its setup routine or installation routine as usual; you run the program as usual; and that's that. Behind the scenes, Windows XP provides more flexibility in providing the program with the type of environment it needs. On the surface, all is serene.

That's for many programs—perhaps most programs. But some programs don't run properly like this. For some, you need to explicitly use Windows XP's Compatibility mode to fool the program into thinking that it's running on the version of Windows that it expects. Windows XP then mimics the environment of that version of Windows for that program, sustaining the illusion that things are to the program's liking. For example, if a program expects Windows 95 and won't run without it, Compatibility mode tells the program that it's running on Windows 95 and tries to prevent it from finding out the truth. Usually the program then runs fine, though you may notice some loss of performance as Windows XP mollycoddles the program.

NOTE

If you're familiar with the Mac, you might be wondering how Windows XP's Compatibility mode compares with Mac OS X and its Classic technology for running programs that won't run on OS X. Basically, there are similarities between Compatibility mode and Classic, but Compatibility mode is both less gruesome conceptually and far lighter on the memory. Classic essentially loads a hefty chunk of System 9.1 (on top of OS X, which isn't exactly svelte itself) and uses it to run the program, whereas Windows XP essentially dupes the program into a false sense of security by giving it the cues it expects. This duping requires a bit more memory and system resources, but nothing like the overhead that the Mac needs to run a program in Classic mode. But then Windows XP is less of a drastic change from its predecessors than OS X, which is essentially mutated Unix with a new graphical interface.

EXPERT KNOWLEDGE: 16-BIT PROGRAMS AND 32-BIT PROGRAMS

Okay, time out. What *is* a 16-bit program, and what's a 32-bit program? Where does the number of bits come from, and what does it mean?

A layperson's answer to the first question might be that 16-bit programs are programs designed to run on 16-bit versions of Windows (for example, Windows 3.1) and 32-bit programs are programs designed to run on 32-bit versions of Windows (Windows 9*x*, Windows NT, Windows 2000, and Windows XP).

Actually, it's not quite that simple. To get a fraction more technical, 16-bit programs are written to the Win16 application programming interface (API), and 32-bit programs are written to the Win32 API. The APIs are sets of rules that tell programmers how they can access the functionality that an operating system exposes to them and how a program should behave so that it gets along with the operating system and other programs running on it.

Normally, 32-bit programs *are* written for 32-bit operating systems, and 16-bit programs *are* (or, you might hope, *were*) written for 16-bit operating systems (which have largely gone the way of the dodo). But by using the Win32s extensions—a 32-bit operating system extension that sat on top of the 16-bit Windows 3.1 operating environment (which in turn sat on top of the 16-bit DOS operating system)—you could run a 32-bit program on Windows 3.1. So some 32-bit programs were written for a 16-bit operating system. And because 32-bit operating systems can normally run 16-bit programs, many 16-bit programs are used to this day, running more or less happily in virtual machines on 32-bit operating systems. The 32-bit operating system may have to perform a process called *thunking*, essentially gearing down to run a 16-bit program. Thunking typically involves some overhead and a slight loss of performance. But if the 16-bit program ran at an acceptable speed on Windows 3.1 with, say, a 486 processor, it should run at a decent speed on even a modest Celeron or Duron processor, even with any thunking needed.

CONTINUED →

Just as 32 valves are better than 16 (for making a satisfactory engine growl if not for reaching the speed limit ahead of that pickup in the next lane at the traffic signal), 32 bits are better than 16. The advantage of 32 bits is that you can move more information at once—*much* more information. 32 bits can represent a range of more than 4 billion integer values (4,294,967,296, to be precise), whereas 16 bits can represent only 65,536 integer values. 64 bits can represent correspondingly more than 32 bits, and 64-bit PC operating systems are on their way. In fact, Windows XP Professional and .NET Server will have 64-bit versions for the forthcoming 64-bit Itanium processor from Intel.

That still hasn't answered the second question: Where does the number of bits come from, and what does it mean? The bit-ness of a program essentially comes from the *word size* of the computer it's running on. The word size is the biggest number that the computer can handle in one operation. 286 systems, those fire-breathing speed-demons of the mid-1980s, used a 16-bit word size, enabling them to handle much more data at once than the (exhaust-breathing) 8-bit systems that preceded them. 386 systems upped the ante to a 32-bit word size, at which it has stayed for several generations of chips: Even Pentium IV and Athlon systems use 32-bit words. The Itanium processor will have a 64-bit word size, enabling it to handle impressively large chunks of data in a single operation.

When you're installing programs on Windows XP, you seldom need to worry about how many bits they're going to use, because Windows XP handles any necessary transitions between 32-bit and 16-bit code seamlessly. You *do* sometimes have to worry about *where* you install older programs so that all users of the computer can use them—but more on this a little later in the chapter.

Once you've set up Compatibility mode for a program, it runs in Compatibility mode each time, so you shouldn't need to tweak it any further unless some of its features misbehave.

Compatibility mode is very impressive, and it's great when it works. But some ancient programs (particularly DOS programs) may never work, even with Compatibility mode. In these cases, your choices of course of action are approximately (a) give up on the program, (b) dual-boot your system with the version of Windows with which the program was last known to work, or (c) use emulation software such as VMWare to run on top of Windows XP a session of the version of Windows with which the program works.

Programs You Shouldn't Even *Try* to Run on Windows XP

No matter how impressive Windows XP's compatibility with programs designed for earlier versions of Windows (or for DOS), there are some types of programs you should never try to run on Windows XP. These include the following:

Operating systems Obviously, you can't install DOS, an earlier version of Windows, or another operating system or operating environment on top of Windows XP—at least, not without using some kind of PC-emulation software (such as VMWare).

Old antivirus programs Antivirus programs designed for previous versions of Windows don't know how to deal with Windows XP. You may be able to update the program. More likely, you'll need to get a whole new version.

Old troubleshooting and cleanup utilities Most troubleshooting and cleanup utilities designed for earlier versions of Windows will give XP nothing but grief. So will disk utilities (for example, Norton Utilities) designed for earlier versions. As with the antivirus programs, these utilities don't know how Windows XP works—in fact, most of them assume that Windows works in a completely different way. So despite Windows XP's ability to restore your system after bad software goes on the rampage, it's a mistake to let old troubleshooting and cleanup utilities loose on your system in the first place. Where you still need the added functionality to supplement Windows XP's capabilities, invest in a new utility specifically designed for Windows XP.

Some potential offenders are smart enough to figure out the problem and quit on their own. Figure 4.1 shows the Incorrect Operating System dialog box that an old version of Network Associates' VirusScan displays if you try to install it on Windows XP without using Compatibility mode.

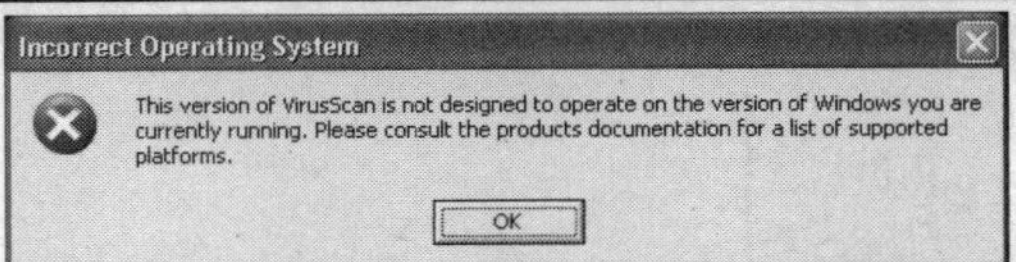

FIGURE 4.1: This old version of VirusScan is smart enough to refuse to be installed on Windows XP.

Multiuser Considerations

As you saw earlier in the book, Windows XP offers strong multiuser capabilities. From the start, Windows XP encourages you to set up your computer for multiple different users to use, allowing each their own custom settings. Moreover, multiple users can be logged on to the computer at the same time (though only one user can be active); other users can be running programs in the background (as it were) while the current user is working away unaware of them.

Windows XP's multiuser capabilities raise some issues for programs and files, as discussed in the next section.

Who Can Install Programs?

First, you'll remember that Windows XP supports three types of users: Computer Administrator users, Limited users, and the Guest user. Only Computer Administrator users can install and remove programs. Limited users and the Guest user cannot install or remove programs.

If a Limited user or the Guest user tries to install a program, Windows displays the Install Program As Other User dialog box (shown in Figure 4.2), telling them that they'll probably need administrator rights to do so. The user can specify a valid Computer Administrator username in the User Name text box and the appropriate password in the Password text box in order to proceed with administrative privileges.

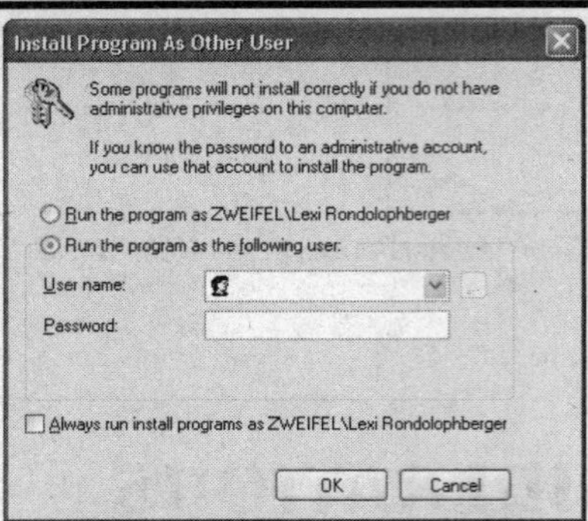

FIGURE 4.2: To install or uninstall a program, you need to have Computer Administrator rights. If you don't, Windows stops you in your tracks with a warning such as this one.

If the user tries to continue with the installation without supplying Computer Administrator credentials, they usually run into an error message and abrupt termination of the setup routine. Figure 4.3 shows a couple of examples from Microsoft Office under different circumstances.

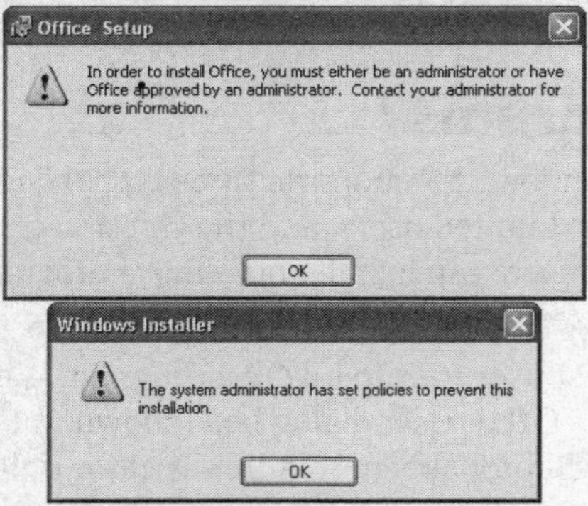

FIGURE 4.3: The Microsoft Office installation grinds to a halt if the user doesn't supply Computer Administrator credentials.

Figure 4.4 shows an example from a program that would prefer to remain nameless.

FIGURE 4.4: Perhaps the ultimate tight-lipped error message. Again, this signified that the installation had crashed because of a lack of permissions.

Who Is the Program Available To?

In some operating systems, you can install a program for some users but not for others. By contrast, Windows XP by default makes any program you install available to all users of the computer—provided that the program's setup routine does things in the right way. For example, if you install Office XP, the setup routine automatically creates shortcuts for all users to use the programs, so the next time any user logs on, they'll have a swath of new programs that they can use from the Start menu.

Office XP of course knows all about Windows XP, because they're both Microsoft products and they're roughly the same vintage. Eudora Pro 4.2, on the other hand, is a couple of years old at this writing and hasn't heard of Windows XP. But it installs fine and is available to all users after installation, because its setup routine was (presumably) constructed along Microsoft's guidelines.

If the program's setup routine is deficient, you may need to install the program to an explicitly shared location or create shortcuts for it manually. For example, if you install Lotus SmartSuite Millennium Edition on Windows XP by using its setup routine, the user who installs SmartSuite gets the full set of shortcuts for it (plus a slew of shortcuts clogging the notification area, plus the indescribably wretched SmartCenter program-launcher and general menace). Other users get none of these—except for shortcuts to Net-It Now! Starter Edition, little-known Web-publishing companion software that was included with SmartSuite. This isn't useful, helpful, or even amusing.

TIP

Windows expects all programs to be installed into the `\Program Files\` folder. Putting them there seems to help make them available for all users, though it's not a guarantee of success. Putting them in another folder is usually not a good idea, though if you need to make small programs easily accessible to all users, you might be tempted to put them in the `\Documents and Settings\All Users\` folder.

What Happens When Multiple Users Open the Same File at the Same Time?

Problems arise with some programs when different users have the same file open. For example, multiple users can open the same WordPad file at the same time, and each can save their changes into (or through) the other's changes. The result is pretty horrible.

Of course, some files are *designed* to be accessed by multiple users at the same time. For example, most database files are designed so that they can routinely be accessed by dozens, hundreds, or even thousands of users at the same time. The program prevents any *record* from being accessed by more than one user at a time. Some database programs prevent users from accessing records adjacent to any record being accessed by another user, to avoid the problems that can occur when records are added to or deleted from the database, either of which actions changes the numbering of records. But as long as each user is (virtually) cordoned off from all other users in the recordset, all is well. Similarly, Excel lets you explicitly share workbooks with other users.

At the risk of generalizing absurdly, more complex (or perhaps more smartly designed) programs use some form of locking mechanism so that they can tell when another user has a file open. This locking mechanism can consist of flags on the file in question, but often it's implemented as a separate file that's created when the file is opened and is deleted when the file is safely closed. You can see this easily enough with Word, which creates a locking file in the same folder as the document you've opened (or just saved, in the case of a new document) *and* sets a flag on the document. The locking file replaces the first two characters of the file's name with the characters `~$`, so that a document named `PENGUINS.DOC` would generate a locking file named `~$ENGUINS.DOC`. (Before you ask what happens with two-character filenames—if the file's name is six characters or fewer, Word *adds* the `~$` to the beginning of the filename. Seven characters, it replaces the first character. Eight characters, it replaces the first two.) If you open the locking file in a text editor (such as Notepad), you'll see that it contains the name of the current user (several times over, with variations in the spacing), some extended characters, and a variety of spaces.

NOTE

Word's locking files are hidden, so you won't see them in Explorer or in common dialog boxes unless you've selected the Show Hidden Files and Folders option button in the Advanced Settings list box on the View tab of the Folder Options dialog box (choose Tools ➢ Folder Options) in Explorer.

When you go to open a file, Word takes a quick look through the folder that contains the file to see if there's a locking file for it. If there is, it displays the File in Use dialog box to let you know about the problem and offer you options for proceeding. When you close the file that was open, Word deletes the locking file. But if you delete the locking file while the file is open, Word still knows that the file is open, because the flag is still set on the file, locking file or no.

As you might imagine, any program that doesn't use a locking mechanism so that it can tell when its files are open is going to have problems with multiple users accessing the same file. Very generally speaking, the less complex the program, the less likely it is to check that a file is open, and the more likely you are to have a problem with multiple users opening a file at the same time.

This problem also arises with files that can be opened with two or more different programs that are available on the computer. For example, if you use WordPad to open a Word document, it opens the document without any locking. You can then open the same document in Word while it's still open in WordPad. Word then locks the document, and you won't be able to save changes to the original file from WordPad.

What Happens When Multiple Users Run the Same Program at the Same Time?

By and large, having two or more users open the same document file at the same time (in the same program or in different programs) is more of a problem than having two or more users run the same program at the same time.

The brief answer to this question is as follows:

- Some programs are designed to be used by multiple users at once, so they don't cause problems.
- Some programs are too dumb to notice that they're being used by multiple users at once, so each session is happy enough. Some of these programs are designed to run multiple instances for any given user anyway, so they're in good shape to run multiple instances for multiple users.
- Some programs notice there's a problem with multiple sessions and deal with it gracefully.
- Some programs notice there's a problem and sulk conspicuously.

With most programs, the problem comes not with the executable files and libraries (DLLs) but with the settings files. Windows XP handles the executables and libraries, running each in a separate memory space and segregating each user's programs from all other users' programs. But if a program is designed to use a central settings file rather than to implement a separate settings file for each user, the settings file can cause problems. If the program locks the settings file when the first user runs the program, the settings file won't be available when the second user runs the program. The same goes if the settings information is stored in a central location in the Registry.

Perhaps the easiest way around this is to use a separate settings file for each user, or to keep separate Registry entries. As you'd imagine, that's what the Microsoft Office programs do. For example, if you're familiar with Word, you probably know that it stores a lot of information in the global template, which is saved in the file `NORMAL.DOT`. The global template is always loaded when you're running Word, so Word maintains a separate global template for each user. This way, it avoids problems when users in separate sessions of the same installation of Word change their settings at the same time.

Problems also arise when separate instances of a program try to use the same hardware resources on the computer at the same time—for example, the COM ports, the audio output, or the microphone input—or the same set of data files.

How a program handles a problem gracefully depends on what the program does and what the problem is. In a program that can manage only one instance running on the computer at the same time, when you start a new instance in another user session, you'll typically see a warning dialog box that lets you choose to either cancel running the new instance of the program or forcibly terminate the other user's session of the program.

As you'd expect, some programs are smarter than others. In particular, it shouldn't come as a shattering surprise to learn that current Microsoft programs are much more aware of Windows XP's multiuser functionality than earlier Microsoft programs or programs from other software companies.

For example, Windows Media Player lets you switch user while you're still playing music or video, or copying a CD. The music (or video) continues to run even while the Welcome screen is displayed. If you then log back on as the same user, Windows Media Player simply keeps going without interruption. Only when you log on as another user does Windows Media Player stop playing the music or video (or copying the CD). And—perhaps more important—it exits the instance that was playing or copying for the other user, freeing up the sound and video circuitry together with whatever system resources it was using. (Before you ask—Windows Media Player quits when you switch to another user even if it wasn't playing.)

TIP

If you're experiencing problems with programs that can't run multiple instances successfully at the same time, or with shared documents being opened by multiple users at once, turn off Fast User Switching. All these problems should disappear in a quick puff of logic.

Installing a Program

After all that buildup, you're probably raring to install a program. You can do this in a couple of ways. The more formal way is to use the Add/Remove Programs window. The less formal way is to run the setup program manually.

Whichever method you choose, if the program you want to install is on a CD, DVD, or other removable medium, load it into the appropriate drive on your computer. If the program is on a network drive, establish a connection to that drive.

If you have Autoplay enabled, the setup routine may start automatically when you insert the CD or other medium in its drive. Cancel out of the setup routine if you want to use the Add/Remove Programs window for the installation. Alternatively, use the manual installation method described in the section after next.

Installing a Program Using the Add/Remove Programs Window

The Add/Remove Programs window provides the more formal way of installing a program. This way has no particular advantages over the next method except that, because Windows explicitly manages the process, it should have no excuse for professing ignorance of the program after you've installed it.

1. Choose Start ➢ Control Panel. Windows displays Control Panel.
2. Click the Add or Remove Programs link. Windows displays the Add or Remove Programs window.
3. Click the Add New Programs button in the left-hand column of the window. Windows displays the Add New Programs page of the window (shown in Figure 4.5).

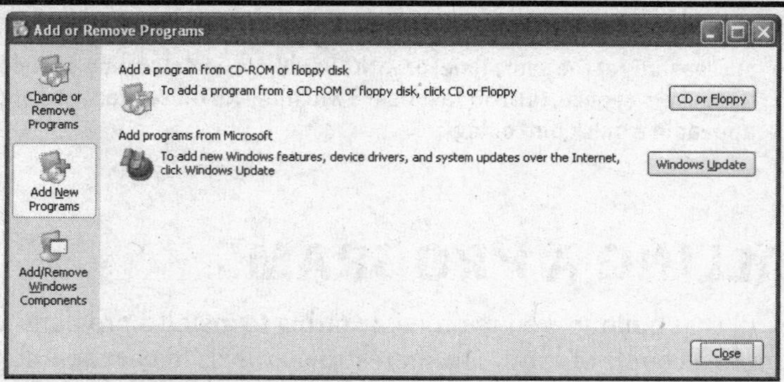

FIGURE 4.5: The formal way to install a new program is to use the Add New Programs page of the Add or Remove Programs window.

4. Click the CD or Floppy button, even if the program you want to install is on a removable disk, on a network drive, or on your hard drive. Windows displays the Install Program from Floppy Disk or CD-ROM page of the Add Programs Wizard.

5. If the program is on a CD or a floppy, and you haven't inserted the disk already, do so now.

6. Click the Next button. Windows searches your floppy drives and CD drives for a SETUP.EXE file and displays the Run Installation Program dialog box (shown in Figure 4.6). If Windows found a SETUP.EXE file, it lists it in the Open text box and invites you to make sure it's the correct file; if it didn't (as in the figure), it suggests you browse to find the file manually.

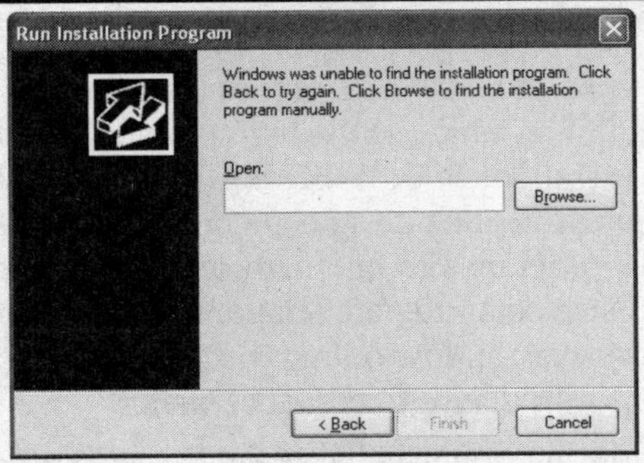

FIGURE 4.6: If Windows doesn't find a setup file in your floppy drive or CD drive, the Run Installation Program dialog box lets you choose the file manually.

7. If Windows didn't find a SETUP.EXE file, or if it found the wrong one (which can happen easily enough if you have multiple CD drives and install software frequently), click the Browse button. Windows displays the Browse dialog box. Navigate to the folder that contains the setup file, select it, and click the Open button. Windows closes the Browse dialog box and enters the program's path and filename in the Open text box.

TIP

If the setup program has a name other than SETUP.EXE, *NN*SETUP.EXE, INSTALL.EXE, or another widely used name or name variation for setup programs, Windows may not list it in the Browse dialog box. Select the Programs entry in the Files of Type drop-down list in the Browse dialog box to make Windows list all executable files in the folder. If the setup program isn't an executable file (unlikely but possible), select the All Files entry in the Files of Type drop-down list.

8. Click the Finish button. Windows closes the Run Installation Program dialog box and starts the program's setup routine.

What happens next depends on the whims of the setup routine's programmers or (more commonly) on which of the two commonly used Windows installers they used—InstallShield or WISE. Suffice it to say that the usual steps for installing a program include agreeing to its license agreement, choosing which of the program's components to install, selecting a Start menu folder (often still called a Program Group, in an embarrassing hangover from Windows 3.*x* days), and twiddling your thumbs (or taking a break). For some programs, you'll have to reboot as well.

At the end of the setup routine, you usually get a message box telling you that setup completed successfully. When you dismiss this message box, Windows returns you to the Add or Remove Programs window, from which you can add further programs or simply click the Close button.

NOTE

You might be tempted to use the Change or Remove Programs page of the Add or Remove Programs window to see how much space the program you just installed is taking up—but don't bother, because the Change or Remove Programs page doesn't list the new program until you close the Add or Remove Programs window and reopen it.

You may see some amusing messages when installing old programs. Figure 4.7 shows an example: a Windows 95 Detected dialog box from the setup routine for PhotoWorks 2.01. PhotoWorks identifies Windows XP as Windows 95, tells you that Windows 95 is still in beta, and warns you that PhotoWorks may not work properly because of that. (After this gaffe, PhotoWorks figured out that Windows XP didn't need Win32s, the 32-bit subsystem for Windows 3.1*x*; installed itself correctly; and then ran without problems.)

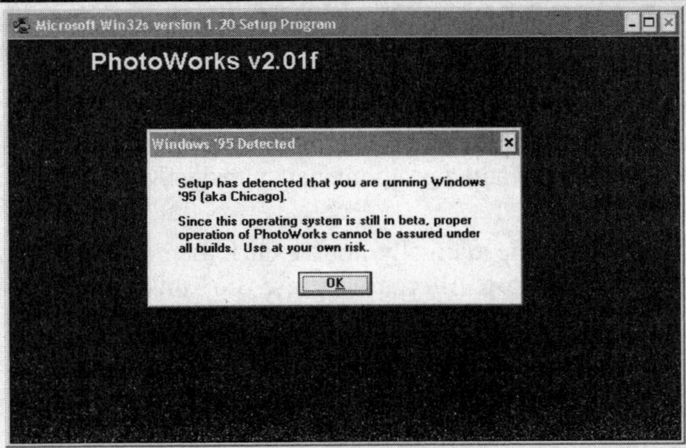

FIGURE 4.7: The PhotoWorks 2.01 setup routine identifies Windows XP as Windows 95—and warns you that it's still in beta.

If Windows knows about a problem with an application you're installing, it displays a dialog box warning you of the problem. Figure 4.8 shows an example in which Windows has detected an issue with Lotus Approach 9.*x*. (If you're using Autoplay, Windows performs such a check before even starting the setup routine for the software.) Click the Continue button, the Cancel button, or the Details button as appropriate.

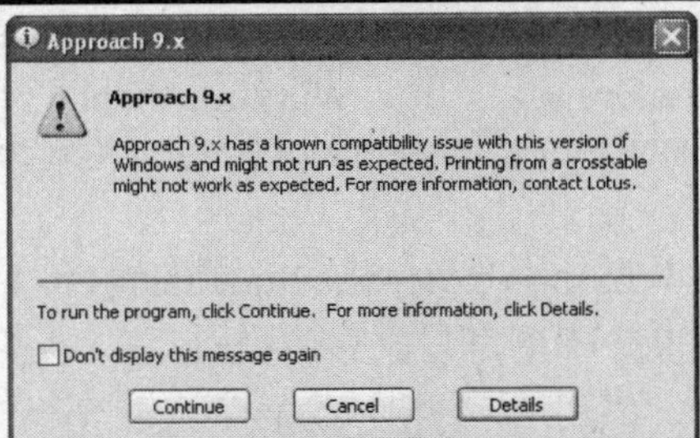

FIGURE 4.8: Windows alerts you to any known issues with software that you're about to install.

Installing a Program by Running Its Setup Routine Manually

If you don't like jumping through hoops unnecessarily, you may want to forsake using the Add or Remove Programs window for installing programs, because you can add a program just as easily by running its setup routine manually.

To run a setup routine manually, double-click its file in an Explorer window or on the Desktop. Alternatively, use the Run dialog box as follows:

1. Choose Start ➢ Run or press Winkey+R. Windows displays the Run dialog box (shown in Figure 4.9).

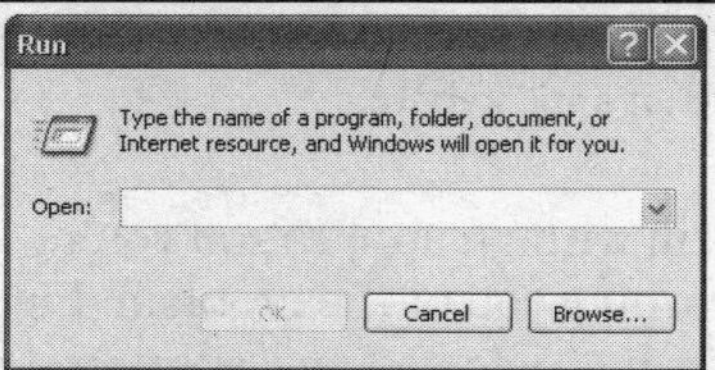

FIGURE 4.9: You can also run a setup routine directly from an Explorer window or from the Run dialog box.

2. In the Open text box, enter the path and filename of the setup program. Either type in the path and filename or browse to it. (Click the Browse button. Windows displays the Browse dialog box. Navigate to and select the file, then click the Open button.)
3. Click the OK button. Windows closes the Run dialog box and starts running the setup program.

Removing a Program

Removing a program is usually even easier than installing a program, because you don't usually have to have the setup medium (CD, floppy, or whatever) and you have to make even fewer decisions.

Follow these steps to remove a program:

1. Choose Start ➢ Control Panel. Windows displays Control Panel.
2. Click the Add or Remove Programs link. Windows displays the Add or Remove Programs window.
3. If the Change or Remove Programs page of the window isn't displayed, click its tab. Windows displays the page.
4. In the Currently Installed Programs list box, select the entry for the program you want to remove. The Add or Remove Programs window displays information about the program—its size (the approximate amount of space it's taking up on disk), a rough description of how often you've used it over the last 30 days (Frequently, Occasionally, or Rarely), and the date you used it last—together with a Change/Remove button. Figure 4.10 shows these details.

   ▶ If you have a lot of programs installed, use the Sort By drop-down list to sort the programs. You can sort by Name, Size, Frequency of Use, and Date Last Used. Obviously enough, the Name category is useful for finding programs by name. The Size category is good for determining which programs are hogging disk space when you need to free some up in a hurry. And the Frequency of Use category and Date Last Used category are useful for rooting out the programs you installed on a whim and have used hardly at all.

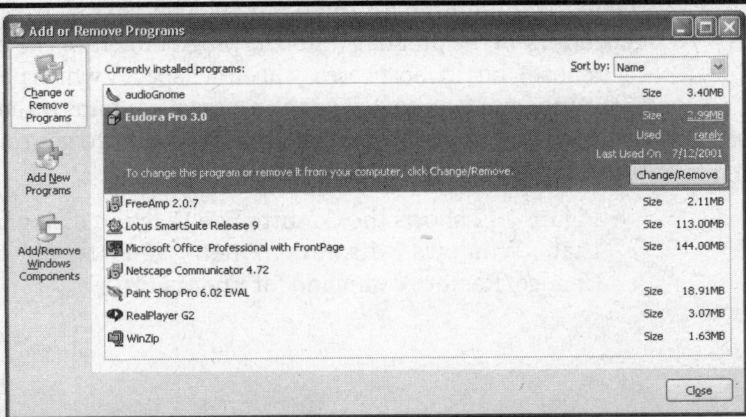

FIGURE 4.10: Use the Change or Remove Programs page of the Add or Remove Programs dialog box to uninstall a 32-bit program.

5. Click the Change/Remove button. Windows checks to see if other users are using the computer (because they might be using the program that you're about to remove). If any other user is logged on, Windows displays the Warning dialog box shown in Figure 4.11.

    - At this point, you can click the Switch User button to display the Welcome screen, then log on as each user from there and log them off. But usually you'll find it easier to use the Users page of Task Manager to either switch to the other users or simply log them off.
    - When you're ready, click the Continue button if the Warning dialog box is still displayed. (If it's not, click the Change/Remove button in the Add or Remove Programs dialog box instead.)

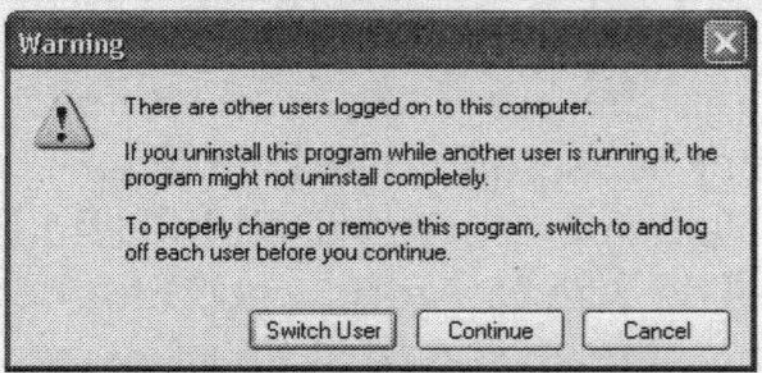

FIGURE 4.11: Before letting you uninstall a program, Windows warns you if other users are logged on to the computer.

6. Once you've cleared the Warning hurdle, Windows invokes the uninstall routine for the program. The next steps vary depending on the program (or on its programmers or the tool they chose), but in most cases, you either specify which parts of the program to uninstall (if the program contains discrete components) or simply confirm that you want to get rid of the program:

    - Figure 4.12 shows the Confirm File Deletion dialog box that Windows displays when you issue the Change/Remove command for Eudora Pro.

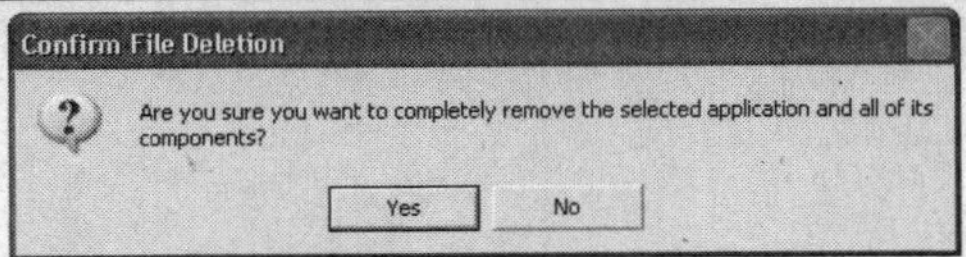

FIGURE 4.12: Windows invokes the program's uninstall routine. In this case, Eudora Pro offers no partial uninstall and so treats the uninstall as a deletion.

- Figure 4.13 shows the Select Lotus SmartSuite Applications dialog box, which lets you specify which SmartSuite programs to uninstall or uninstall the lot.

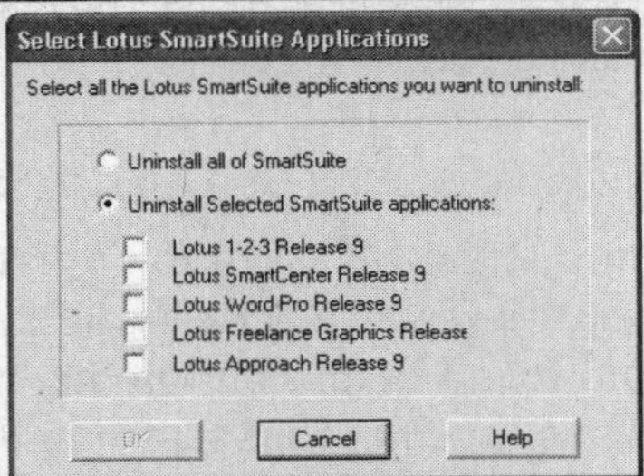

FIGURE 4.13: Windows invokes the program's uninstall routine, which lets you specify which components to uninstall (as in the case with Lotus SmartSuite here) or confirm the uninstallation.

7. Choose uninstall options and click the appropriate button. You'll then typically see something like Figure 4.14, in which unInstallShield (InstallShield's evil twin) is removing Eudora Pro.

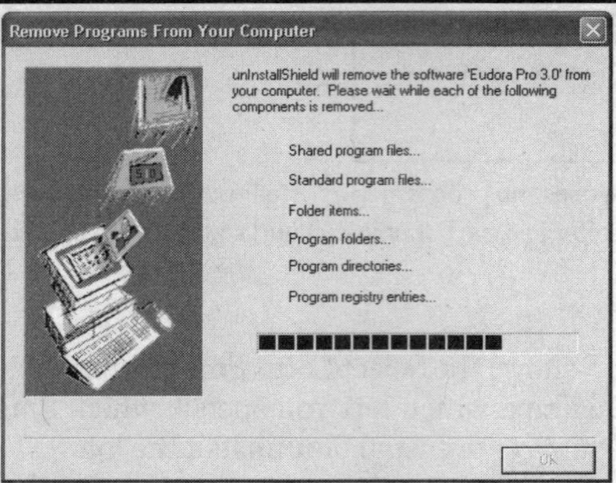

FIGURE 4.14: Here's an example of what you see when uninstalling a program. Here, unInstallShield is removing Eudora Pro.

8. If the uninstall routine tells you that it was unable to remove some parts of the program that you've asked to uninstall completely, it usually lets you know which parts are left. For example, unInstallShield provides a Details button that you can click to display a dialog box such as that shown in Figure 4.15. In this case, it's easy enough to delete these folders manually by using Explorer.

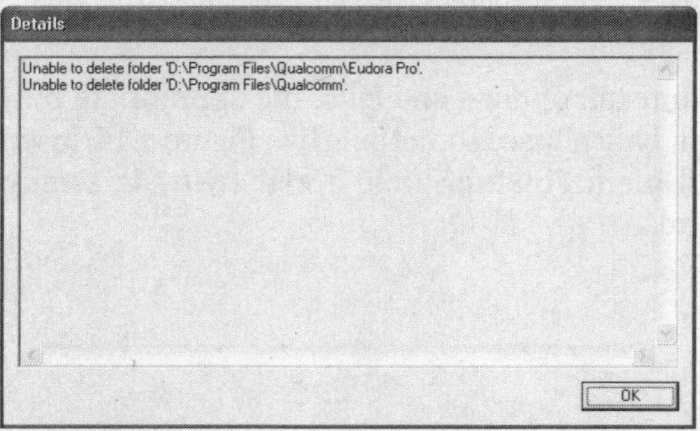

FIGURE 4.15: If unInstallShield can't remove all the components of a program, it provides details in the Details dialog box.

TROUBLESHOOTING: UNINSTALLING 16-BIT WINDOWS PROGRAMS AND DOS PROGRAMS

Windows' Add or Remove Programs feature tracks all 32-bit programs installed on the computer, and it's able to track many 16-bit programs as well. But some 16-bit Windows programs and most DOS programs don't show up in the Add or Remove Programs dialog box, so you can't remove them that way.

The preferred way of removing a program that doesn't show up in the Add or Remove Programs window is to run its uninstall routine manually. Some Windows programs add a shortcut to their uninstall routine to the program folder (or, in Windows XP, to the Start menu submenu) that contains their other shortcuts. If there's no shortcut, you'll need to dig through the folder that contains the program to see if it has one. The file might be an EXE file, but it might also be a BAT (batch) file.

If the program doesn't have an uninstall routine, you'll need to remove it manually. (If you've only just installed the program, you *could* use the System Restore feature to return your system to its state before you installed the program—but usually you'll have made other changes to your computer since installing the program.) This usually means deleting the folder (or folders) that contains the program and removing any references to it that you can find.

There are two problems with removing a program manually like this. First, you don't necessarily know where the program has put all its files. This is usually more of a problem with Windows programs, which (following Microsoft's own recommendations) often put shared files into the `\Windows\` folder or one of its subfolders, than with DOS programs (which probably don't know that the `\Windows\` folder exists, and certainly don't care about it even if they do know). So if you simply delete the folder or folders the program created, it may leave detritus in other folders. (This is why uninstall routines exist, of course.)

The second problem is that the program may also have added commands to configuration files of their era (such as `AUTOEXEC.BAT` or `WIN.INI`) that will cause errors when you've deleted its files. You'll need to discover these additions manually (usually when you get an error message) and delete them or comment them out manually. Because Windows XP uses these configuration files only for compatibility, these errors are likely to cause you annoyance rather than grief—unlike in the old days, when a command for a missing program could make Windows 3.1 refuse to load.

Running Programs

In Windows, you can start a program in any of several ways. If you've used a previous version of Windows, you'll probably be familiar with these ways. They break down into two categories: starting a program directly by opening it and starting a program indirectly by opening a file whose file type is associated with the program.

You can start a program directly in any of the following ways:

- Click its shortcut on the Start menu (or on the All Programs submenu, or on one of its submenus).
- Double-click a shortcut on the Desktop or in an Explorer window.
- Click a shortcut on the Quick Launch toolbar or another Desktop toolbar.
- Choose Start ➢ Run. Windows displays the Run dialog box. Enter the name of the program in the Open text box, either by typing or by browsing for it. (Click the Browse button. Windows displays the Browse dialog box. Navigate to and select the file, then click the Open button.) Then click the OK button.

NOTE

Using the Run dialog box seems a clumsy way of running a program, but it's useful for running Windows utilities for which Windows doesn't provide a Start menu entry (for example, the Registry Editor, discussed in Part V) and for running programs for which you don't want to create a shortcut but whose path and filename you can type (or otherwise enter) without undue effort.

- Double-click the icon or listing for the program in an Explorer window (or on the Desktop). You can also use the Search feature to locate the program you want to run.

Almost all setup routines create shortcuts to their programs automatically. Usually, the setup routine puts a shortcut on the Start menu or in a subfolder of the Start menu. Some setup routines place a shortcut directly on the Desktop; some consult you first; others don't. Some setup routines offer to also put a shortcut in the notification area; other setup routines do so without consulting you; while others yet are civilized enough to respect Microsoft's guidelines for notification-area use—that the notification area should be used for warnings and information rather than loaded with shortcuts for every program in sight.

Running Programs in Compatibility Mode

If a program won't run normally on Windows XP, try running it in Compatibility mode. As mentioned earlier in the chapter, Compatibility mode lets you tell Windows XP to emulate Windows 95, Windows 98, Windows NT 4, or Windows 2000 so that a program thinks it's running on the operating system it knows and likes.

TIP

Often, you'll need to run the program's setup routine in Compatibility mode to get the program to install in the first place. Then run the program itself in Compatibility mode as well.

Windows XP comes with the Microsoft AppCompat database of compatibility problems known about programs. AppCompat is automatically updated by the Windows Update, which gives you another incentive to accept Windows Update's offers to download every update available—at least until your computer's hardware and all your software are working as perfectly as you could wish.

NOTE

You can set Compatibility mode only on files on local drives. You can't set Compatibility mode on a program located on a network drive. But you can create a shortcut on a local drive to a program located elsewhere and then specify Compatibility mode for the shortcut.

Windows provides two ways of setting up a program to run in Compatibility mode. The first way is formal and cumbersome, but it lets you test whether the Compatibility mode you choose works for the program. The second way is much quicker, but you run the risk of getting a program comprehensively hung if Compatibility mode doesn't work.

Let's take it from the top.

The Formal Way of Setting Compatibility Mode

Here's the formal way to run a program in Compatibility mode:

1. Choose Start ➢ All Programs ➢ Accessories ➢ Program Compatibility Wizard. Windows displays a Help and Support Center window and starts the Program Compatibility Wizard in it.

2. Read the information and cautions on the Welcome to the Program Compatibility Wizard screen and click the Next button. Windows displays the How Do You Want to Locate the Program That You Would Like to Run with Compatibility Settings? screen (shown in Figure 4.16).

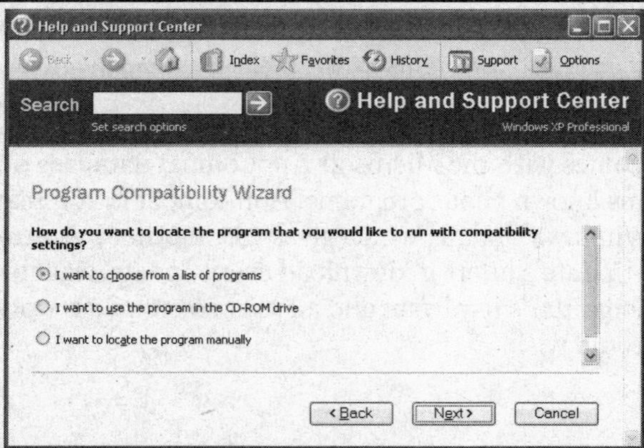

FIGURE 4.16: On the How Do You Want to Locate the Program That You Would Like to Run with Compatibility Settings? screen in Help and Support Center, choose how to select the program you want to run in Compatibility mode.

3. Use one of the following three ways to locate the program:

   - To set Compatibility mode for a program that's already installed, select the I Want to Choose from a List of Programs option button and click the Next button. The Wizard scans your hard drive and displays a list of programs

(Figure 4.17 shows an example). Select the program and click the Next button.

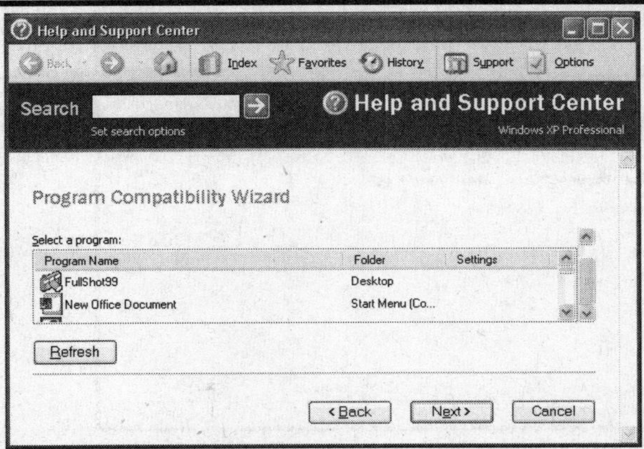

FIGURE 4.17: Select a program from the list that the Program Compatibility Wizard assembles.

- To set Compatibility mode for a program you're installing from CD, insert the CD, select the I Want to Use the Program in the CD-ROM Drive option button, and click the Next button.
- To set Compatibility mode for a program that isn't installed and whose installation medium isn't on CD, or if you're just feeling ornery, select the I Want to Locate the Program Manually option button and click the Next button. The Wizard displays the Which Program Do You Want to Run with Compatibility Settings? screen (shown in Figure 4.18). Enter the path in the text box, either by typing or by clicking the Browse button and using the resulting Please Select Application dialog box (a common Open dialog box) to select the program. Click the Next button.

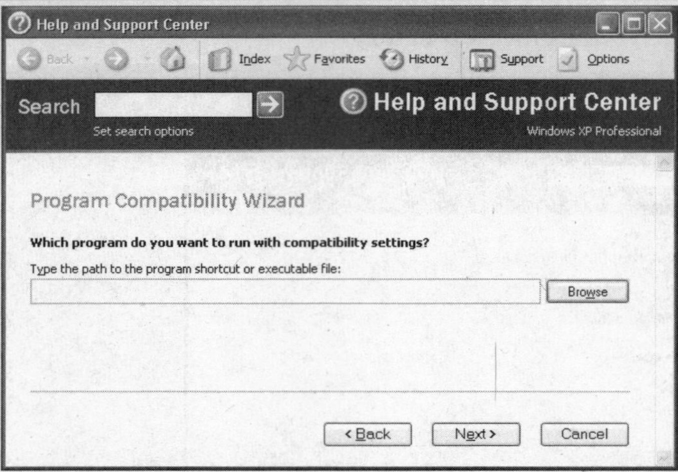

FIGURE 4.18: If necessary, or if you prefer, you can identify the program manually on the Which Program Do You Want to Run with Compatibility Settings? screen of the Program Compatibility Wizard.

4. The Wizard displays the Select a Compatibility Mode for the Program screen (shown in Figure 4.19).

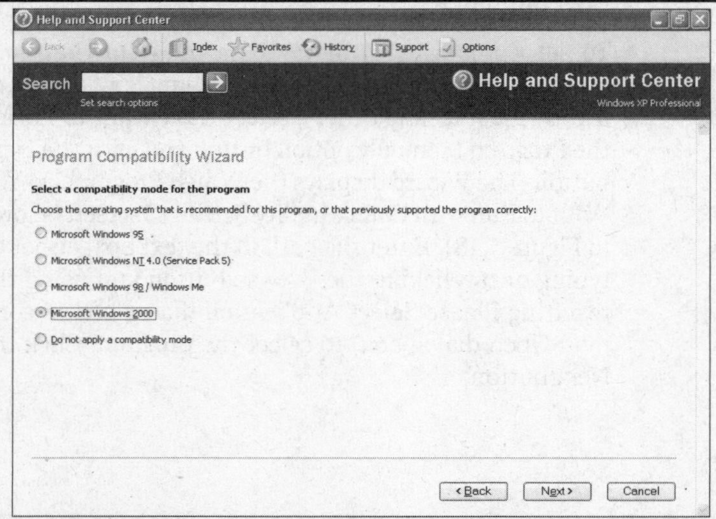

FIGURE 4.19: On the Select a Compatibility Mode for the Program screen of the Program Compatibility Wizard, select the Compatibility mode you want to use.

5. Select the option button for the operating system you think the program needs: Windows 95, Windows NT 4.0 (Service Pack 5), Windows 98/Windows Me, or Windows 2000.

6. Click the Next button. The Wizard displays the Select Display Settings for the Program screen (shown in Figure 4.20).

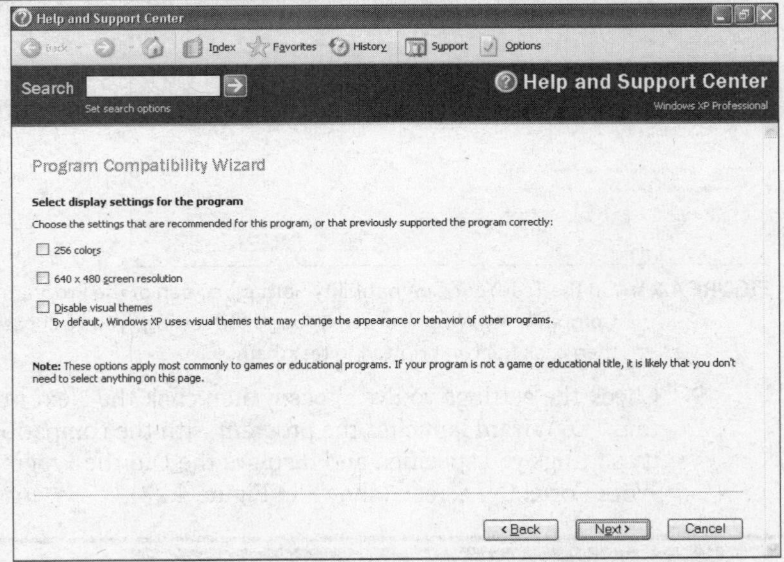

FIGURE 4.20: On the Select Display Settings for the Program screen of the Program Compatibility Wizard, you can apply limitations to the display settings used for the program.

7. If you know the program needs display limitations, select the 256 Colors check box, the 640×480 Screen Resolution check box, or the Disable Visual Themes check box.

   - For most programs, you don't need to select any of these display limitations.

8. Click the Next button. The Wizard displays the Test Your Compatibility Settings screen (shown in Figure 4.21).

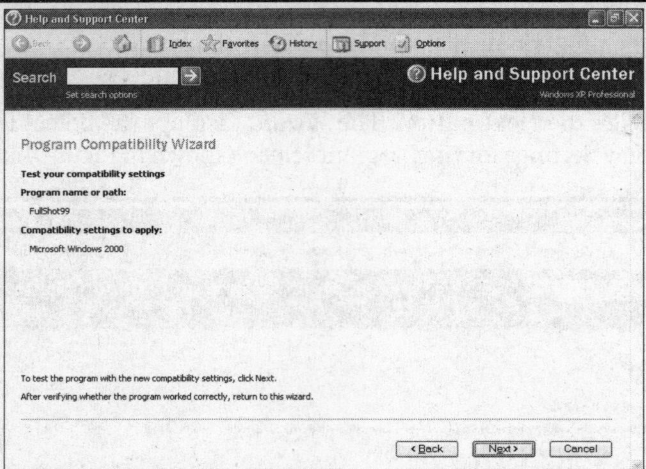

FIGURE 4.21: On the Test Your Compatibility Settings screen of the Program Compatibility Wizard, check through the settings you've chosen, then click the Next button to test them.

9. Check the settings you've chosen, then click the Next button. The Wizard launches the program with the compatibility settings you specified and displays the Did the Program Work Correctly? screen (shown in Figure 4.22).

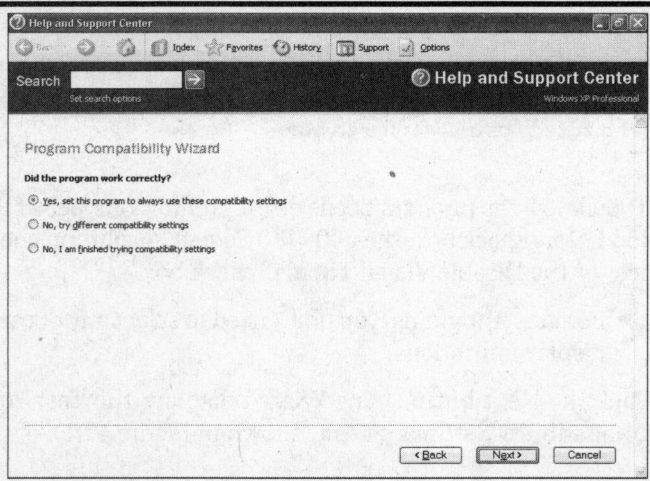

FIGURE 4.22: On the Did the Program Work Correctly? screen, tell the Program Compatibility Wizard whether the program launched correctly with the computer settings.

10. Choose the appropriate option button:

   - If the program ran okay, select the Yes, Set This Program to Always Use These Compatibility Settings option button, and click Next. The Wizard displays the Program Compatibility Data screen (shown in Figure 4.23), on which you can choose whether to send Microsoft information on the program, the settings you chose, and whether they solved the problem.

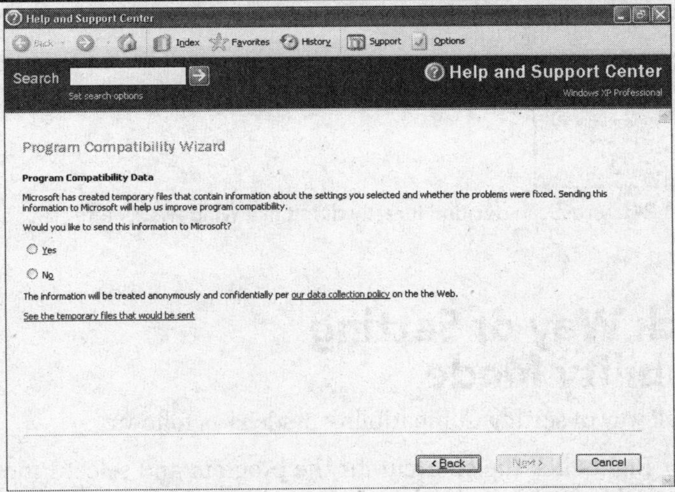

FIGURE 4.23: On the Program Compatibility Data screen of the Program Compatibility Wizard, you can choose whether to send Microsoft information on a program that you couldn't get to work.

   - If the program didn't run correctly, but you want to try other settings, select the No, Try Different Compatibility Settings option button. Click the Next button. The Wizard returns to the Select a Compatibility Mode for the Program screen. Return to step 5 and try again.
   - When no compatibility settings seem to work, select the No, I Am Finished Trying Compatibility Settings option button. Click the Next button. The Wizard displays the Program Compatibility Data screen (discussed above). In this case, you have more incentive for sending Microsoft information, as it may help them fix the problem with this program in the future.

11. Choose the Yes button or the No button as appropriate.
12. Click the Next button. If you chose the Yes button, the Wizard sends the compatibility data. Either way, it displays the Completing the Program Compatibility Wizard page.
13. Click the Finish button. The Wizard closes itself.

Remember that old version of VirusScan from earlier in the chapter that didn't want to install on Windows XP? It was happy to install in Compatibility mode for Windows 95—but parts of it wouldn't run on Windows XP (see Figure 4.24).

FIGURE 4.24: VirusScan decided it really didn't like Windows XP after all.

The Quick Way of Setting Compatibility Mode

The quick way of setting Compatibility mode is as follows:

1. Right-click the shortcut for the program and select Properties from the shortcut menu. Windows displays the Properties dialog box for the shortcut.
2. Click the Compatibility tab. Figure 4.25 shows an example of this tab.

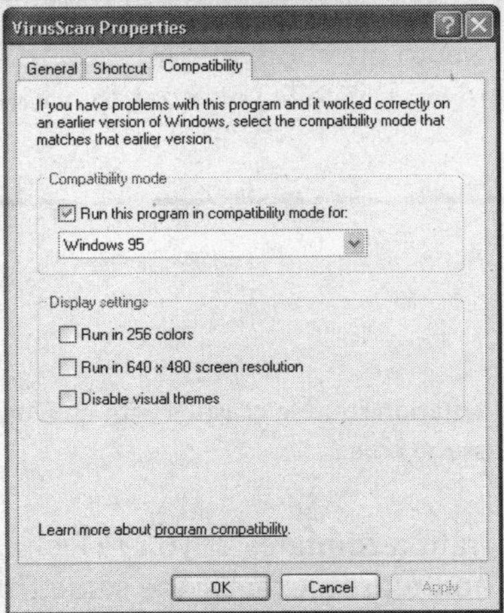

FIGURE 4.25: You can also choose Compatibility mode settings on the Compatibility tab of the Properties dialog box for the shortcut.

3. Select the Run This Program in Compatibility Mode For check box if it's not already selected.
4. In the drop-down list, select the mode you want to use.
5. In the Display Settings group box, select the Run in 256 Colors check box, the Run in 640×480 Screen Resolution check box, or the Disable Visual Themes check box as necessary. (Again, for most programs, you won't need to set these options.)
6. Click the OK button. Windows applies your choice and closes the Properties dialog box.

Even with Compatibility Mode, Some Programs Don't Work

Some programs plain don't work even when you use Compatibility mode. For example, Lotus SmartSuite 96 won't install on Windows XP, no matter whether you try to run it from the CD or copy its files to a local drive and use Compatibility mode. When you run the SmartSuite 96 installation routine on Windows XP, you get to specify the program folder and the type of installation (typical, minimal, custom). Then the installation crashes with the Output message box shown in Figure 4.26. This message box mentions an overflow (trying to put more information in a memory register than will fit), but beyond that, it tells you next to nothing useful.

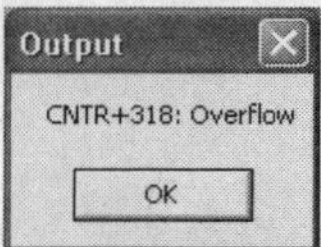

FIGURE 4.26: Lotus SmartSuite 96's installation routine crashes with an Output CNTR+318: Overflow message box.

After this message box, the program terminates. If you're feeling determined, and you lather, rinse, and repeat, exactly the same thing happens over.

NOTE

Microsoft may have fixed this problem with SmartSuite 96 by the time you read this book. But given that Lotus used to be a major competitor of Microsoft's in the programs field, and that IBM (which owns Lotus) used to make OS/2, and that this version of SmartSuite is a good five years out of date, they may not have gotten around to bothering.

Making Programs Run at Startup

If you want a program to start every time you log on to Windows, place a shortcut to it in your Startup folder. Starting programs automatically like this can save you a few seconds each time you start Windows if you always need to use the same programs.

Your Startup folder is the `\Documents and Settings\`*`Username`*`\Start Menu\Programs\Startup\` folder. Navigating to this folder usually takes nearly as long as placing in it the shortcuts you want.

TIP

To make a program start automatically each time any user of your computer logs on to Windows, place a shortcut to the program in the Startup folder for All Users. As you'd guess, this folder is the `\Documents and Settings\`*`All Users`*`\Start Menu\Programs\Startup\` folder.

To prevent a program from running at startup, obviously enough, you remove its shortcut from the Startup folder.

Specifying the Size at Which a Program Runs

By default, most programs start in a "normal" window—one that's not maximized and not minimized. If you'd like the program to start up maximized or minimized, right-click its shortcut and choose Properties from the shortcut menu. In the Properties dialog box that Windows displays, choose Maximized or Minimized in the Run drop-down list on the Shortcut tab, and click the OK button.

You can do this for any shortcut to a program or to a file—so if you want, you can have shortcuts open different-sized windows for files of the same file type.

EXPERT KNOWLEDGE: RUNNING A PROGRAM AS ANOTHER USER

Sometimes you may need to run a program under a user account other than the user as which you're currently logged on to Windows. For example, your current user account might not have permission to access the file or folder you want to manipulate with the program, but you have access to another account that does have permission for that file or folder.

To run a program as another user, create a shortcut to it and set the advanced property called Run with Different Credentials. When you open that shortcut, Windows displays the Run As dialog box, in which you can specify the user account under which you want to run the program.

Killing a Program That's Not Responding

Programs run pretty well on Windows XP—but not all programs run well all the time. Sooner or later, a program will hang or crash on you.

When this happens, first, make sure the program doesn't have an open dialog box that you can't see. When you're working with multiple programs, you can easily get an open dialog box stuck behind another open window. If the dialog box is *application modal*, it prevents you from doing anything else in the program until you dismiss it. (Dialog boxes can also be *system modal*, in which case they prevent you from doing anything else on your computer until you deal with them.)

Minimize all other open windows (right-click the Taskbar and choose Show the Desktop from the shortcut menu), and see if the dialog box appears. If not, you'll probably have the program that's not responding still displayed on your screen, probably with only some parts of the window correctly drawn. For example, typically the areas of the program that were covered by other programs or windows will not be redrawn (or not redrawn correctly).

Next, try using Alt+Tab to switch to the program and bring out from behind it any dialog box that's hiding. Chances are that this won't work either, but it's worth a try. If the dialog box appears, deal with it as usual, and the program should come back to life.

If that didn't work, try using Task Manager to switch to the program:

1. Right-click the Taskbar and choose Task Manager from the shortcut menu. Windows displays Task Manager.
2. If the Applications tab isn't displayed, click the Applications tab. The Applications tab (shown in Figure 4.27) lists each running program and its status. The status can be either Running (all is well with the program, as far as Windows is concerned) or Not Responding (Windows believes that the program is not responding to conventional stimuli).
3. Select the program that's not responding.
4. Click the Switch To button. Task Manager attempts to switch to the program, and minimizes itself in the process.

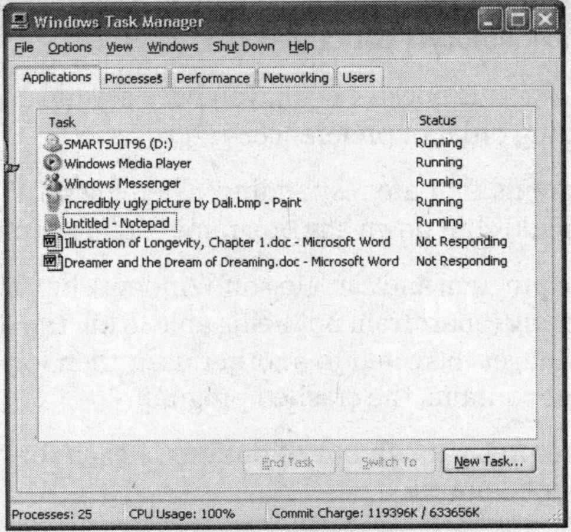

FIGURE 4.27: The Applications tab of Task Manager lists all running programs and their status: Running or Not Responding.

If that didn't work either, it's probably time to kill the program. Take the following steps:

1. Restore Task Manager by clicking its button on the Taskbar.
2. Decide whether the program has hung or crashed. (See the nearby sidebar "*Not Responding* Status Isn't Always Terminal" for advice on determining whether the program is still viable.)
3. Select the task in the Task list.
4. Click the End Task button. Windows displays the End Program dialog box (shown in Figure 4.28).

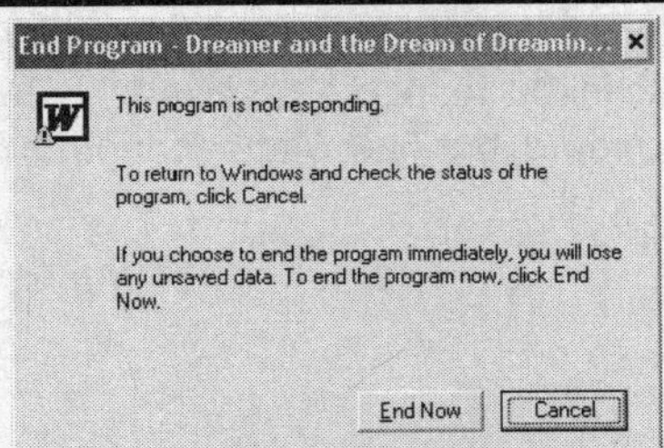

FIGURE 4.28: To terminate the program, click the End Now button in the End Program dialog box.

5. Click the End Now button. Windows terminates the program and frees up the memory it contained.

If killing the program like this doesn't work, you have several options. Here they are, in descending order of preference:

- Close all other programs that are responding. Then log off Windows. Doing this should shut down any programs you're running.
- If you can't close the program and can't log off Windows, but Task Manager is still working (apart from not being able to kill the program), use Task Manager to switch to another user, then log off the user session that contains the crashed program.
- At this point, you're pretty much out of options. Reach for the Reset button on your computer.

EXPERT KNOWLEDGE: *NOT RESPONDING* STATUS ISN'T ALWAYS TERMINAL

When you see a program listed as having Not Responding status on the Applications page of Task Manager, you may be tempted to kill it off right away. But you'd do better to stay your hand for a minute or two. Why? Because Not Responding status doesn't necessarily mean that a program has hung or crashed:

- First, Not Responding may mean nothing more than that a program is responding more slowly than Windows expects; if you give it a few seconds, or perhaps a few minutes, it may start responding normally again. If your computer seems unresponsive overall, back off and give it a few minutes to sort itself out.
- Second (and often related to the first point), Not Responding may mean that Windows is struggling to allocate enough memory to the program; this often causes the program to run slowly. Task Manager is a little harsh in this respect—it's Windows' fault that the program isn't responding, but Task Manager points the finger at the program.

CONTINUED →

- Third, VBA-enabled programs (for example, Microsoft Word and Microsoft PowerPoint) are often listed as Not Responding when they're running a VBA routine or macro. In this case, Not Responding means only that VBA temporarily has control over the program. When VBA releases control of the program—in other words, when the routine ends—Task Manager lists the program as Running again. (If the program shouldn't be running a macro, try pressing Ctrl+Break to stop it.)

WHAT'S NEXT?

This chapter has discussed how to install programs, how to run them—using Compatibility mode if necessary—and how to remove them when you tire of them. It's also touched on the types of programs you shouldn't even try to install on Windows XP, and it's shown you how to use Task Manager to kill a program that's crashed.

The next chapter discusses how to manage files, folders, and disks in Windows XP Professional.

Chapter 5

Managing Files, Folders, and Disks

Files are the basis of almost all computing. Whatever you do—whether it's running a program, typing a memo, or optimizing system performance—you are working with a file. Folders and disks contain and organize those files. This chapter focuses on file, folder, and disk management in Windows XP.

File Management Overview

Files are necessary because computer memory is volatile—that is, whatever it contains is erased when you shut down the PC. In that way, memory is like a worktable that gets cleared off at the end of each workday and its contents discarded. When you save something as a file, you store it on a *disk*, where it is safe until you need it again. You can think of a disk as a file cabinet in which you store files for safekeeping.

Revised and adapted from *Windows XP Home Edition Simply Visual* by Faithe Wempen

ISBN 0-7821-2982-X 448 pages $24.99

A computer has at least one hard disk, which is inside the case and cannot be removed easily. In addition, most computers have at least one type of removable *drive*, such as a floppy-disk drive, a Zip drive, or a CD-ROM drive.

Because a disk can potentially hold hundreds or even thousands of files, *folders* are used to help keep them organized. If a disk is like a file cabinet, a folder is like a drawer in the cabinet or like an expandable cardboard folder within a drawer. (The latter is actually a more apt analogy because computer folders are not fixed in size, but expand or contract to hold whatever you place in them.)

Folders can contain other folders—a folder can be the *parent folder* of one folder and the *child folder* of another. This arrangement allows you to create sophisticated file-organization systems. For example, you might have a Projects folder, and within that folder, you could have some word processing files that pertain to all projects in general, plus several child folders for your specific projects. Within each of those individual child folders, you could have more files that pertain generally to that project, plus more child folders for files dealing with certain aspects of the project.

In Windows, all these abstract concepts such as file, folder, and disk take on a visual appearance. You can see and work with icons that represent specific files, folders, and drives on your system. You use a program called Windows Explorer to view and manipulate the files, folders, and drives on your system.

NOTE

Windows Explorer is an atypical program in that its name doesn't appear in the title bar. Instead, the name of the folder being browsed appears there.

For example, on the right side of the following figure, the contents of the D: drive appear. Folders are represented by an icon that looks like a paper folder, along with the folder's name. Files are listed with their name, but the icon depends on the type of file. Notice in this figure that the D: drive contains a number of folders, and at the very bottom of the list is a single file called Log, with an icon that looks like a notepad.

Most files on your hard disk were placed there when Windows or one of your applications was installed, and they don't require any special handling. The primary reason you will want to work with the file system is to manage the data files you create using various applications such as your word processor. You might need to move, copy, or delete those files, check on a file's name, protect a file from changes, or perform some other operation.

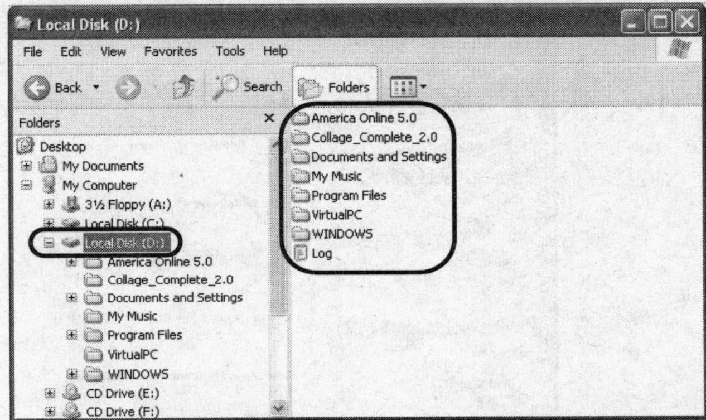

The following sections explain how to open a file management window and display the contents of a folder in which a particular file resides. Then the latter part of the chapter explains how to do things to the files themselves.

Opening a File Management Window

NOTE

In earlier versions of Windows, there was a sharp distinction between My Computer and Windows Explorer because only Windows Explorer could contain a folder list. In Windows XP, however, you can switch between the folder list and the System Tasks pane by simply clicking the Folders button on the toolbar.

You can open a file management window in two main ways, and each results in a slightly different default display, or view:

My Computer Displays an overview of all the disks on your PC, from which you can begin browsing for a specific disk or folder. It includes a System Tasks pane to the left of the listing instead of a folder list.

Windows Explorer Displays the contents of the My Documents folder (on the same disk that Windows is installed on) by default. This display includes the folder list, for easy navigation to some other folder or disk.

Both displays are "file management windows" in a generic sense because they help you manage your files. Throughout this book, if the instructions say to start in My Computer or Windows Explorer, you should open that particular window; if the instructions say simply to use a file management window, you can start in either one.

In both displays, when the folder list is turned off, the System Tasks pane appears; it goes away when you turn the folder list back on (by clicking the Folders button on the toolbar). This System Tasks pane contains shortcuts to popular activities such as moving, copying, and deleting, and you'll see it in use later in this chapter.

Opening the My Computer Window

NOTE

In earlier versions of Windows, a My Computer icon on the desktop opened My Computer; it didn't appear on the Start menu. If you miss the convenience of that icon, you can create a shortcut to My Computer on the desktop.

When you want to start looking for a particular folder at a bird's-eye level of your system—with all the available drives to choose from—My Computer is the best place to start. To open My Computer, choose Start ➢ My Computer.

NOTE

In other words, click Start and then click My Computer.

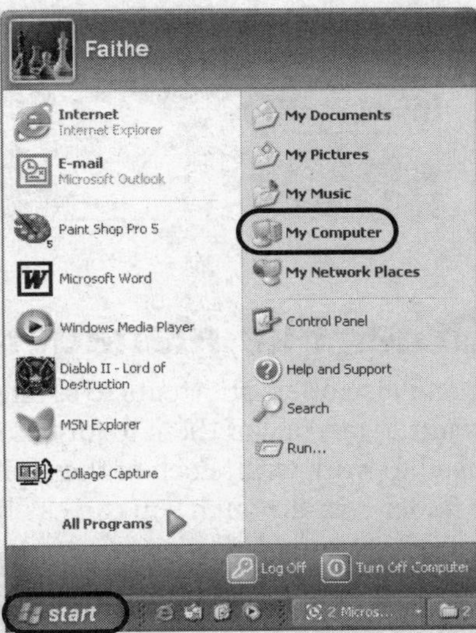

Opening the Windows Explorer Window

NOTE

Windows Explorer is a little bit more trouble to open than My Computer, because you have to wade through several menu levels to get to it. However, if you find yourself using Windows Explorer frequently, you can create a shortcut to it on your desktop or in the Quick Launch toolbar, for quicker access.

When you start with Windows Explorer, the folder list appears automatically. The contents of the My Documents folder also appears by default. To open Windows Explorer, choose Start ➢ All Programs ➢ Accessories ➢ Windows Explorer.

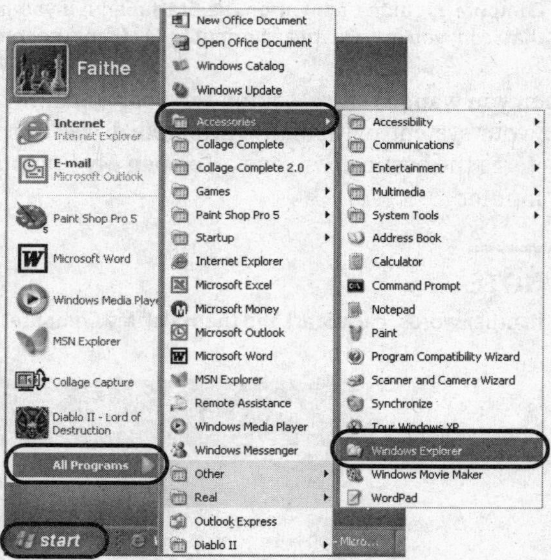

Opening Other File Management Windows

The Start menu also offers shortcuts to several special-purpose folders; you might want to use one of them to jump to a particular folder that you know you need to work with. Each of these shortcuts opens the folder *without* the folder list, although you can easily display it if you want it.

My Documents Opens the My Documents folder, which most business applications use to store data files.

My Pictures Opens the My Pictures folder, which is a child folder of My Documents and is used primarily to store pictures acquired from scanners and digital cameras.

My Music Opens the My Music folder, also a child folder of My Documents. It's used to store music clips for Windows Media Player; some other music programs might utilize it as well.

My Network Places Opens the My Network Places folder, which enables you to browse your local area network for access to other computers and shared resources. If you don't have a network, you won't see this option on the menu.

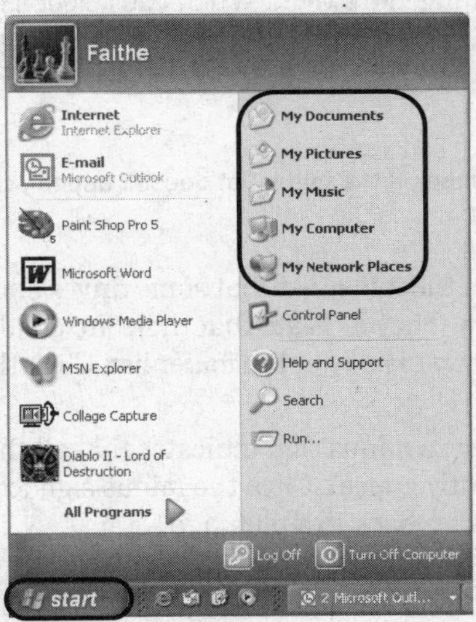

NAVIGATING BETWEEN FOLDERS

Once you've opened a file management window (either through My Computer or Windows Explorer), you can choose which drive's or folder's content you want to display. This process of navigating between folders is a very important skill that you'll use over and over as you work with Windows.

Selecting from the Folder List

NOTE

Some people don't like to leave the folder list displayed because it takes up so much room on-screen; they prefer to close it and leave that space for the display of the chosen folder's contents. In upcoming sections, you'll learn ways to navigate between folders that don't involve the folder list.

One of the easiest ways to switch to a different folder is to select it from the folder list (sometimes called a folder tree, because its branches look something like a tree). When you select a folder on the list, its contents appear in the right pane of the file management window.

TIP

Remember, if the folder list doesn't appear, click the Folders button on the toolbar.

Notice on the folder list that some drives and folders have plus signs next to them. They indicate that there are child folders beneath that don't currently display in the folder list. Click the plus sign to expand the list.

Conversely, a minus sign indicates that all the child folders for that folder currently appear. Click the minus sign to collapse the list and to change the sign back to a plus sign.

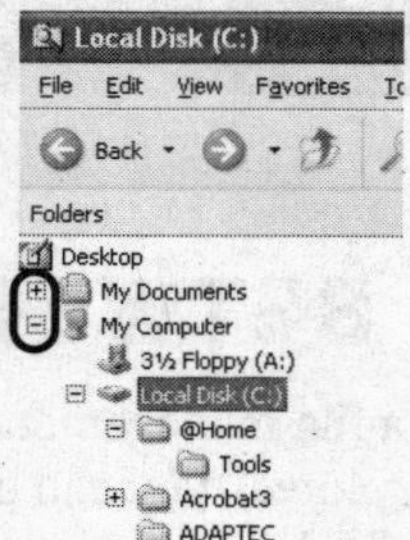

Moving Up and Down in the Folder System

Think of the folder list as a branching root system, in which you start off with the disk at the top (the granddaddy parent folder) and then child folders within that disk, and then further child folders within some of the folders, and so on. Moving "up" in the system means moving closer to the top, or toward the *root folder*. Moving "down" means moving into a child folder within the current folder.

You have already seen in the preceding section that you can move freely between folders using the folder list. But if the folder list isn't displayed, you'll need a different method. (You might even prefer the alternative method to the folder-list method.)

Moving to a Child Folder of the Current Folder

To move down into a child folder, display the folder or disk containing the folder you want, and then double-click the icon for that folder. In this example, I'll double-click the Helpnote folder to view its contents.

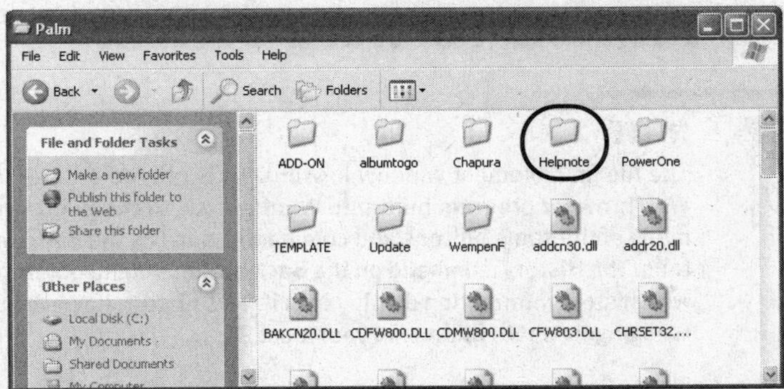

The folder's contents now appear in the right pane. Notice that the title bar of the screen now displays the name of the folder.

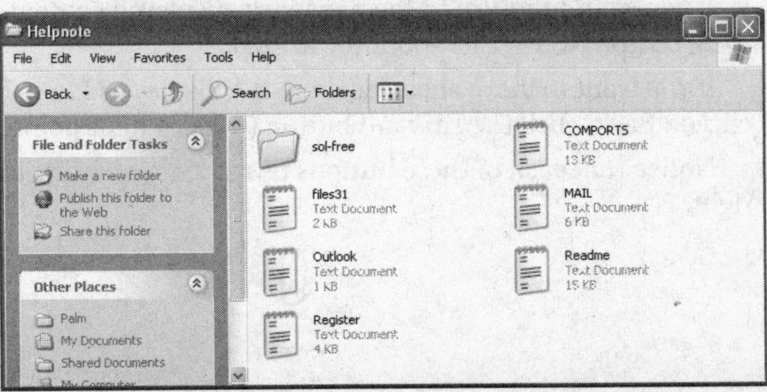

Moving Up One Level to the Parent Folder

NOTE

In some earlier versions of Windows, such as Windows 95, whenever you double-clicked a folder to display its contents, by default it opened in a new window instead of replacing the contents in the existing one. If you want to duplicate this behavior in Windows XP, choose Tools ➢ Folder Options ➢ Open Each Folder in Its Own Window, and click OK. However, if you do this, the steps in the rest of this chapter may not match what happens on your screen.

To move back up to the parent folder of the currently displayed one, click the Up button in the toolbar (it has a green arrow over a yellow folder). The contents of the parent folder now appear in the right pane.

Using Back and Forward Buttons

NOTE

The file management window in Windows is related to Internet Explorer, the Web browser program built into Windows XP, to the point where they share many of the same buttons and commands, such as the Back and Forward buttons. The History command on the Back button's menu opens the Explorer bar with history information displayed in it. This history, however, pertains only to Web pages, not to folders on your local PC.

When you display a different disk's or folder's contents, whatever contents were previously displayed in the right pane are replaced by the new display.

If you want to return to the previously displayed contents, click the Back button (it has a left-pointing arrow).

If you want to move ahead again to the display as it was before you clicked Back, click the Forward button (it has a right-pointing arrow).

Notice that each of these buttons has a down-pointing arrow to its right.

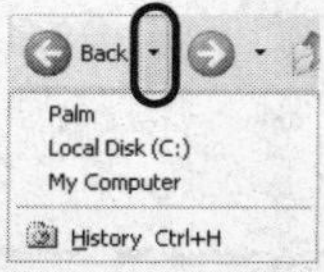

Clicking that down arrow opens a list of all the locations that have displayed since you opened the window, and you can choose the one you want rather than having to click Back or Forward repeatedly until your desired location appears.

MANIPULATING FILES AND FOLDERS

Now that you know how to display the desired folder, it's time to learn what you can actually *do* with the contents of that folder and why you might want to do it.

NOTE

When you perform an action on a folder, everything within it (files and child folders) is also affected. For example, if you copy a folder to another disk, everything in that folder gets copied too.

Selecting Files and Folders

As I mentioned earlier, the primary reason that most people open a file management window is to do something to a data file they've created in some program. For example, you might want to delete a letter you created using your word processor or to copy it onto a floppy disk.

Before you can act on a file or folder, however, you must *select* it. No matter what the activity, it's always a two-part equation, like a subject-verb sentence: First you select what you want to act on (the subject); then you select the activity (the verb).

To select a single file or folder, simply click it. To deselect it, click somewhere else (away from it). A selected file appears in white letters with a dark background, the opposite of unselected ones. In the following figure, I've selected the "chapter 3" file.

NOTE

In the default Windows XP color scheme, that dark background is blue, but yours might be different depending on the appearance options you've chosen.

You can select multiple files and/or folders and act on them as a group. For example, if you needed to delete 10 different files in the same folder, you could select them all and then issue the Delete command once. (You can't select multiple files or folders in different locations at once.)

If all the files/folders you want to select are contiguous (that is, listed one right after another), you can select them like this:

1. Click the first file or folder you want to select (for example, the AR folder in the next figure).
2. Hold down the Shift key, and click the last file or folder in the group (G0303 in the figure). That file and all the files in between become selected.
3. Release the Shift key. You can now perform the task, and all the selected files or folders will be affected.

NOTE

Is "contiguous" determined by rows or by columns? It depends on the view. In Icons and Thumbnails views, contiguous runs by rows, from left to right and then down to the next row. In List view, contiguous runs by columns, from top to bottom and then to the next column. In single-column views such as Details and Tiles, it's a nonissue. The figure shown here is in Icons view.

If the files are noncontiguous, use this method instead:

1. Click the first file or folder you want.
2. While holding down the Ctrl key, click each additional file you want to select.
3. Release the Ctrl key. Any action you perform now will affect all the selected files or folders.

You can also select files and folders located in a cluster in the window (but not necessarily contiguous in the strict sense) by enclosing them in a "box." To do so, follow these steps:

1. Point to an area above and to the left of the first file you want to include (M0301 in the following figure).
2. Hold down the left mouse button and drag down and to the right, creating a box around your targeted files.
3. Release the mouse button. Any files that fell within the box you drew are selected.

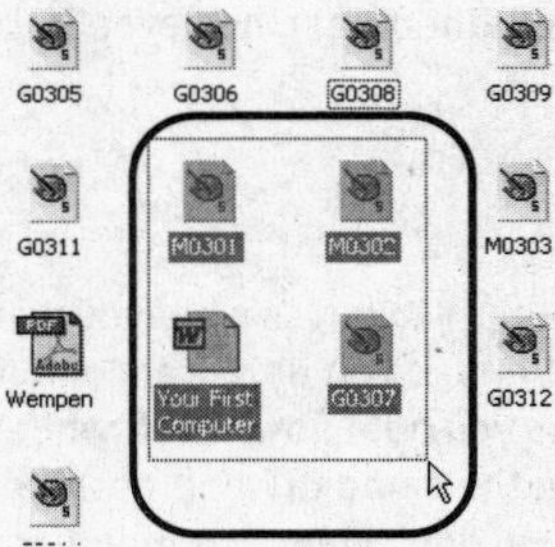

Moving and Copying Files and Folders

Now that you know the various ways to select files and folders, it's time to learn what actions you can take with them. Two very common actions are moving and copying. You might want to copy a file to a floppy disk to share with a friend, for example, or move some infrequently used data files to a secondary hard disk to free up space on your primary disk.

You have a couple of options for moving and copying: You can use the drag-and-drop method with the mouse, or you can use menu commands. I'll show you both methods in the following sections.

Moving Files and Folders

To move a file using the drag-and-drop technique, do the following:

1. If the folder list doesn't appear, click the Folders button to display it.
2. Display the folder containing the file(s) or folder(s) to be moved.
3. In the folder list, make sure the destination folder's or drive's name is visible (but don't click it to select it). If necessary, click a plus sign to expand the folder list and make the destination visible.
4. Select the file(s) or folder(s) to be moved.

WARNING

Don't move program files or folders—that is, files or folders needed to run particular programs. Most programs will not work anymore if you move their files. Your safest bet is to move only the data files you have created yourself. You can *copy* any files without fear, however.

NOTE

Windows attempts to guess what you want to do based on the source and destination locations. If you drag from one drive to another, it assumes you want to copy unless you hold down Shift while dragging. If you drag from one folder to another on the same drive, it assumes you want to move unless you hold down Ctrl. If you don't want to remember all that, just get in the habit of always holding down Shift when moving and always holding down Ctrl when copying.

5. If you are moving from one disk to another, hold down the Shift key. (Otherwise, Windows will copy rather than move.)
6. Drag the selection to the destination folder or drive on the folder list. For example, in the following figure, I'm dragging the folder named LOD_108 to the A: drive. Then release the Shift key.

NOTE

If there is a plus sign on the mouse pointer as you drag, you are copying rather than moving; press Esc and try again. If there is no plus sign, you are moving.

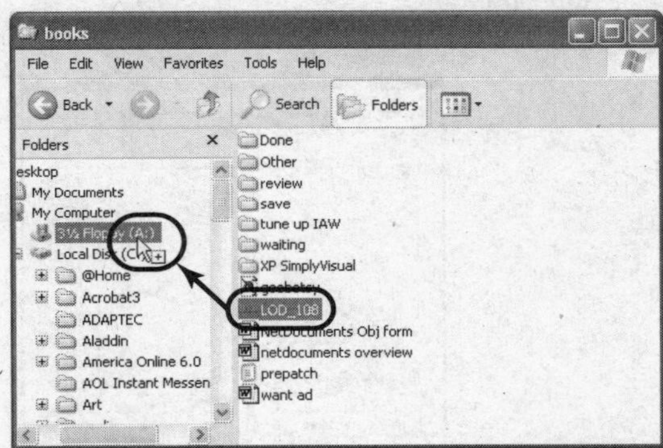

Another way to move a file is to use the Move to Folder command on the Edit menu. This method has the advantage of not requiring the folder list to be visible.

1. Select the file(s) or folder(s) you want to move and then choose Edit ➢ Move to Folder.

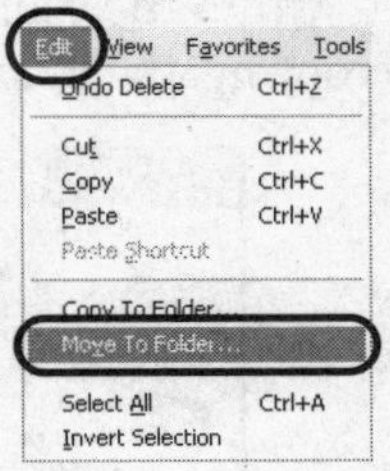

TIP

The Make New Folder button lets you create a new folder on the fly. To use it, be sure to first select the drive or folder that you want as the parent for the new folder. Then click Make New Folder, type a name for the new folder, and click OK. Then click Move to complete the move. You'll learn other ways to create new folders later in this chapter.

2. In the Move Items dialog box, click the plus signs next to drives and folders until the destination location appears, and then select it. (In this example, I want to move the file to the ADAPTEC folder.)

3. Click Move.

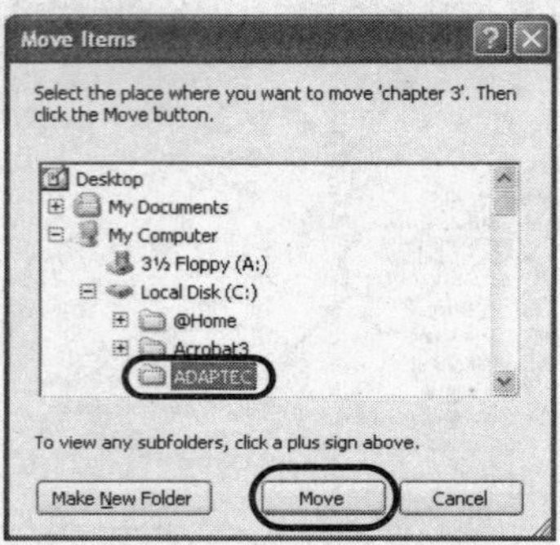

Copying Files and Folders

Copying works almost exactly the same as moving, except for a few minor details.

When you copy with drag-and-drop, you must hold down Ctrl as you drag if you are copying within the same drive; otherwise a plain drag-and-drop will move. While copying, the mouse pointer shows a plus sign, like so:

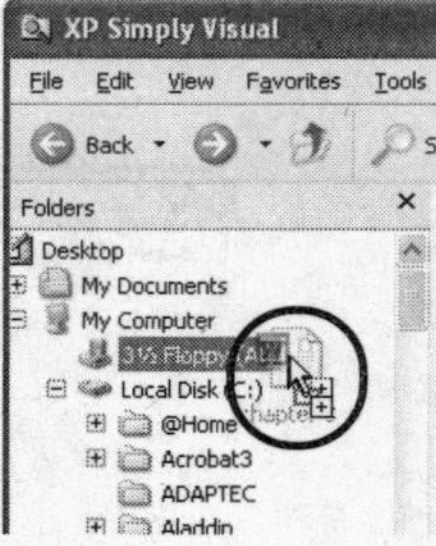

You can also copy using the Copy to Folder command on the Edit menu, which works just like the Move to Folder command you just learned about.

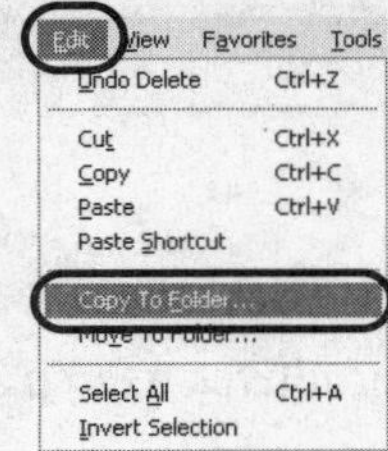

Deleting Files and Folders

NOTE

When you delete a file or folder, it isn't destroyed immediately; instead, it is moved to the Recycle Bin. You can get it back later by fishing it out of the Recycle Bin, as you'll learn later in this chapter.

You will probably want to delete old data files that you no longer have any use for, to save space on your hard disk and to make it easier to locate the data files you currently need.

To delete one or more files or folders:

1. Select the file(s) and/or folder(s) you want to delete.
2. Press the Delete key.

NOTE

As an alternative to deleting old files, you might consider moving them to a floppy disk for archival purposes or creating a writeable CD containing those files. You'll learn about writeable CDs in Chapter 20.

TIP

To delete the selection permanently without sending it to the Recycle Bin, hold down the Shift key as you press the Delete key in step 2.

3. In the confirmation box that appears, click Yes.

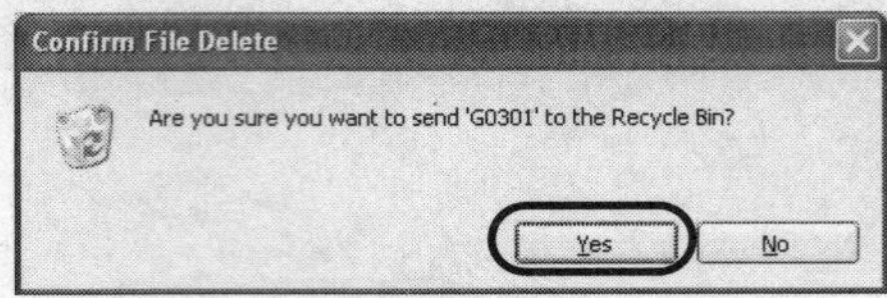

There are many alternatives to step 2. Here are some of them:

- You can right-click your selection and choose Delete from the shortcut menu that appears.
- You can click Throw Away This File from the System Tasks pane.
- You can choose File ➢ Delete.

Renaming Files and Folders

Many people, when they start out in computing, give their data files rather generic names, such as Letter1, Memo99, and so on. They don't realize that over time, they will probably write dozens of letters, and it will be difficult to remember which letter is which.

You can rename a file easily in Windows, to give it a better or more descriptive name than the one you originally assigned.

WARNING

Don't rename files or folders needed to run a program, or the program might not work anymore. Rename only data files and folders that you have created yourself.

NOTE

You can rename only individual files and folders; you cannot rename them as a group. The Rename command isn't available when multiple files or folders are selected.

To rename a file or folder:

1. Select the file or folder.
2. Press the F2 key. The name becomes selected.

TIP

Instead of pressing F2 in step 2, you can select File ➢ Rename, or you can right-click the file and then click Rename from the shortcut menu.

3. Type a new name.
4. Press Enter.

Do you need to type the *file extension* when renaming? Well, it depends. By default, file extensions are hidden for known file types; so if the file's original name doesn't show a file extension, you don't have to type one when you rename the file. In fact, if you do type one, the file's actual name ends up with two extensions, like `MyFile.doc.doc`.

However, in Chapter 6, you'll learn how to set file extensions to display in file management windows. If you rename a file with a displayed extension, you must retype the period and the extension when you type the new name; otherwise, the file will lack an extension, and Windows won't be able to determine its file type.

Creating New Folders

As you saw earlier, you can create new folders on the fly while moving or copying files with the Move to Folder or Copy to Folder command. You can also create new folders at any other time, for any purpose.

For example, suppose you want to organize your documents in the My Documents folder into separate child folders for each of your projects. You could create a folder for each project, and then move each document file that concerns that project into its folder.

To create a new folder:

1. Display the folder that should be the parent folder for the new one.

2. Choose File ➢ New ➢ Folder. A new folder appears with the name New Folder. The name is highlighted, and ready to be typed over with a new name.

TIP

Instead of choosing File ➢ New ➢ Folder in step 2, you can right-click the background of the current folder display and then choose New ➢ Folder from the shortcut menu.

3. Type the name for the new folder and then press Enter.

SEARCHING FOR FILES AND FOLDERS

It's easy to forget in which folder you have stored a particular file, but Windows makes the process of finding lost files painless. Here's what you do:

1. Choose Start ➢ Search.

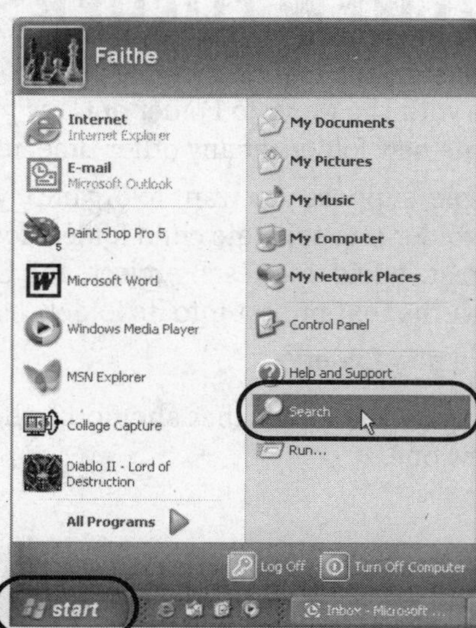

A Search Results window appears, with a Search Companion pane at the left.

2. Click the category that best represents what you want to search for. These search categories restrict your search to files with certain extensions. If you don't want that restriction, choose All Files and Folders as the category.

The Search Companion pane then changes to show additional controls.

NOTE

Each of the specifications in steps 3 through 6 is optional; you can use any combination of them to build your search criteria. The more specific your criteria are, the fewer files will be returned. At any point, you can skip to step 7 to run the search.

3. (Optional) In the Part or All of the File Name text box, type the filename if you know it or any portion of it that you do know.

To represent unknown parts of the name, you can use *wildcard* characters. For example, if you know only that it begins with W, you would use W*. Or, if you know it begins with W and contains exactly six letters, you could use W?????.

4. (Optional) If you remember that the filename contains a certain word or phrase, type it in the A Word or Phrase in the File text box.

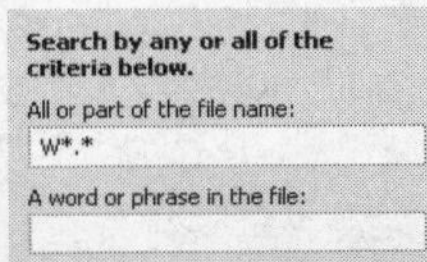

5. (Optional) If you don't want to search all hard drives on your system, open the Look In drop-down list and select a single drive that you want to search, such as the C: drive in this example.

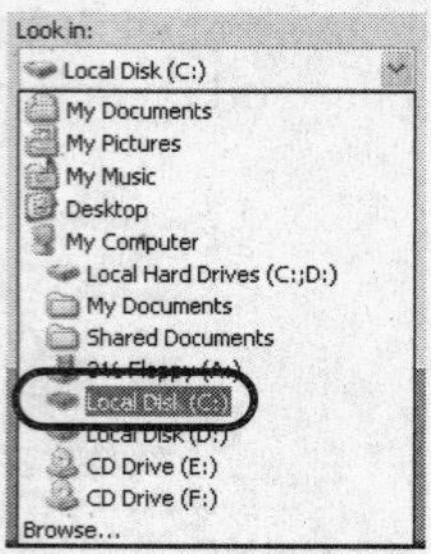

NOTE

You can also click Browse from the Look In drop-down list and pinpoint a specific folder from which to start the search. That way, your search results will reflect only that folder and its subfolders.

6. (Optional) To set any other criteria for the search, click one of the other buttons to display additional controls, and make your selections. Here, for example, I have chosen When Was It Modified? and filled in some date criteria.

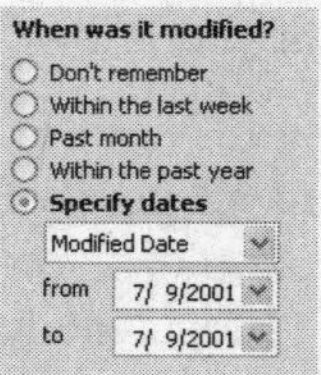

7. Click the Search button to begin the search.

Any files that match all the specifications appear on a list in the right pane.

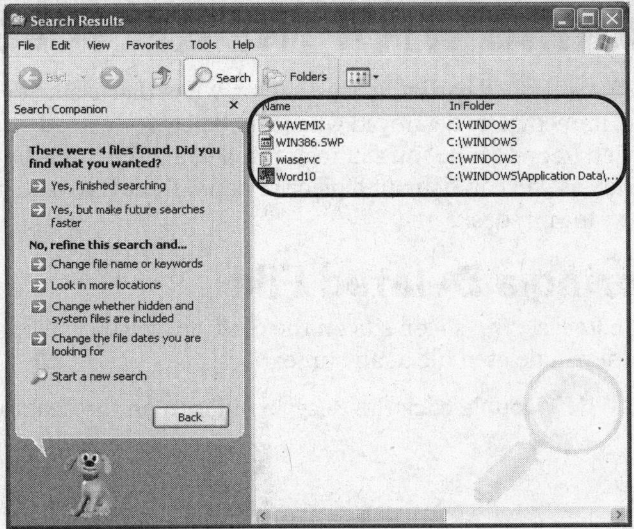

Working with Search Results

As you can see in the preceding figure, the Search Companion makes it easy to refine your initial search after you see the results. Just follow the prompts in the Search Companion pane if you need to make changes.

Let's assume for the moment, though, that the file you were searching for *did* appear in the search results. What can you do with it now?

Locate it. Make a note of the location listed in the In Folder column. Now you know where the file is stored, and you can find it later in Windows Explorer or through whatever program you used to create it.

Open it. You can double-click the file to open it in the program you used to create it. (You can open a file this way from any file management window, not just from a search.)

Move, copy, rename, or delete it. The same file management operations that you learned earlier in this chapter can be employed in the Search Results window.

Working with the Recycle Bin

As I mentioned earlier in the chapter, when discussing deleting, a file is not immediately destroyed when you delete it. Instead, it goes to a folder called Recycle Bin. You can restore a deleted file from the Recycle Bin much as you can fish out a piece of paper from the wastepaper basket next to your desk.

Restoring a Deleted File

The Recycle Bin's icon sits on the desktop, so you can open it and retrieve a deleted file at any time:

1. Double-click the Recycle Bin icon on the desktop.

The Recycle Bin window opens.

2. Select the file you want to restore. (In the following figure, I've selected Introduction.)
3. In the Recycle Bin Tasks pane, click Restore This Item. (Notice the name change here; this pane is usually called System Tasks.)

NOTE

There are many alternatives to step 3. You can choose File ➢ Restore, right-click the file and choose Restore from the shortcut menu, or drag the file out of the Recycle Bin window and into some other file management window or onto the desktop.

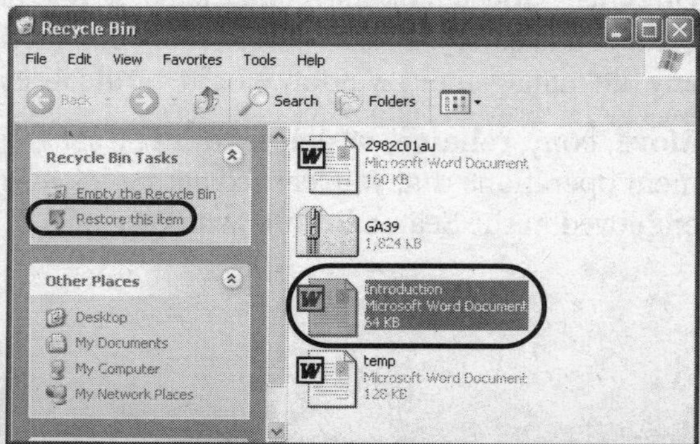

Emptying the Recycle Bin

If you are certain you don't want any of the files in the Recycle Bin, you can empty it to free up the hard-disk space that those files are occupying. If there are only a few small files, the difference might be negligible; but when the Recycle Bin contains many large files and your hard-disk space is running short, emptying the bin is a worthwhile proposition.

TIP

If you are trying to delete some files to free up hard-disk space for some other purpose, keep in mind that the space is not actually freed until the Recycle Bin is emptied.

You need not open the Recycle Bin window in order to empty the bin; simply do the following:

1. Right-click the Recycle Bin icon on the desktop and then choose Empty Recycle Bin.

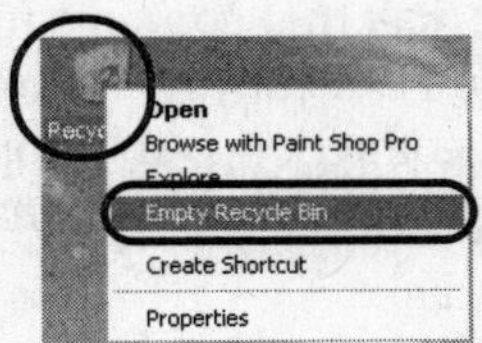

2. A confirmation message appears. Click Yes.

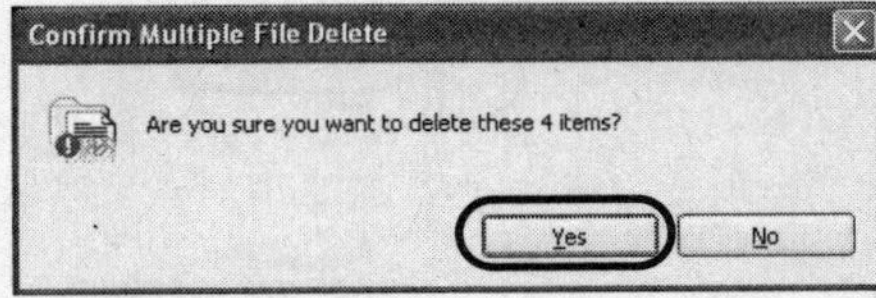

You can also empty the Recycle Bin while its window is open.

1. With no files selected in the Recycle Bin window, click Empty the Recycle Bin in the Recycle Bin Tasks pane.

NOTE

Instead of the clicking in step 1, you can choose File ➢ Empty Recycle Bin. If you do that, you don't need to worry about making sure no files are selected beforehand.

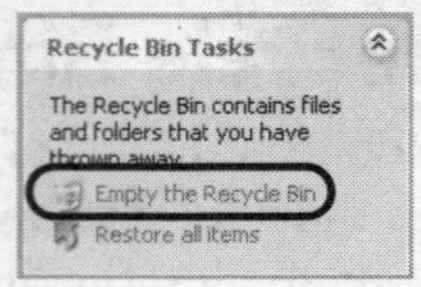

2. Click Yes to confirm.

Formatting Disks

Formatting a disk creates an organizational structure called a file allocation table, or FAT, that makes it possible for files and folders to be stored on the disk. You can format both hard and floppy disks. For information about formatting disks, see Chapter 32.

Copying a Floppy Disk

If you have a floppy disk that contains important data, you might want to make a copy of it. You can copy its contents to your hard disk and then to another floppy, but going floppy-to-floppy is faster. You can make the copy using a single floppy drive, by swapping the disks out as prompted.

To copy a floppy disk:

1. In My Computer, right-click the floppy drive and then choose Copy Disk.

2. In the Copy Disk dialog box, click Start.

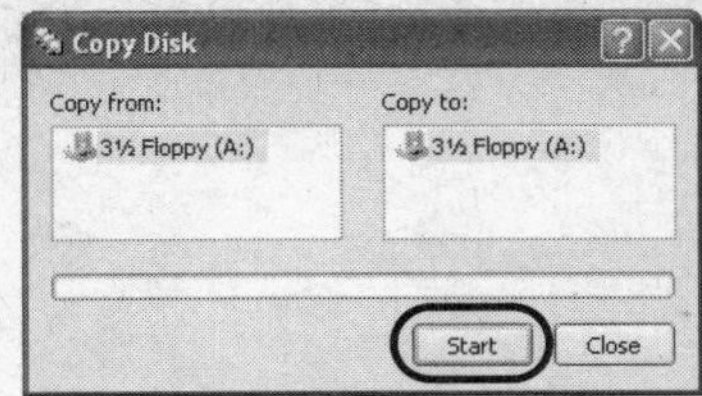

3. Insert the disk to be copied and then click OK. Then wait for the disk to be copied into your computer's memory.

4. When prompted, insert the disk to contain the copy and then click OK.

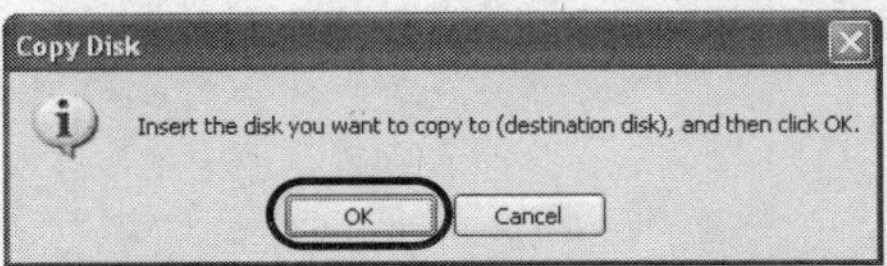

5. When a Copy Completed Successfully message appears, click Close.

What's Next?

As you know, in Windows XP Professional, there is almost always more than one way to perform any task. This chapter has looked at several ways to manage files, folders, and disks. The next chapter continues the topic by discussing the ways in which you can change the appearance of files and folders and by further describing how you can manipulate files and folders.

Chapter 6

Setting File Management Options

Windows XP is extremely flexible—it lets you customize almost every aspect of its operation, from how it looks to how it behaves. One of the areas you can customize is the file management window, which you worked with in Chapter 5. This chapter picks up where Chapter 5 left off in describing file management. As you'll see in this chapter, you can make a wide array of choices about how files and folders appear and how you manipulate them.

Revised and adapted from *Windows XP Home Edition Simply Visual* by Faithe Wempen

ISBN 0-7821-2982-X 448 pages $24.99

Choosing How Files Are Displayed

Back in Chapter 5, you may have seen some file listings that didn't look exactly the way they did on your own screen. That's because you have a choice of how you want the file listings to appear. In the following sections, you'll learn how to change their appearance.

Some file settings affect only the window you are working with at the moment or only the folder currently displayed; other settings affect all file management windows globally. In this chapter, we'll start out with the more temporary settings and work our way to the global settings at the end.

Selecting a View

In most file management windows, you can choose from five views, ranging from very large icons to very small ones, and from very little detail to lots of detail. Each view has its own usefulness. Before I describe each of the views, however, I'll tell you how to change your view from within any folder.

To change the view, open the View menu and then click the view you want: Thumbnails, Tiles, Icons, List, or Details.

Windows saves your view preference for that folder, and the next time you display its contents, the files will appear in your chosen view. However, the setting doesn't affect any other folders, so if you change to a different folder, you must set the view again.

Here are brief descriptions and illustrations of the five views:

Thumbnails view If the file is a graphic in a supported format, a miniature (that is, "thumbnail") version of the picture appears in place of the icon. Or, if the item is a folder that contains files in supported formats, tiny versions of the first few files appear on the folder icon's face.

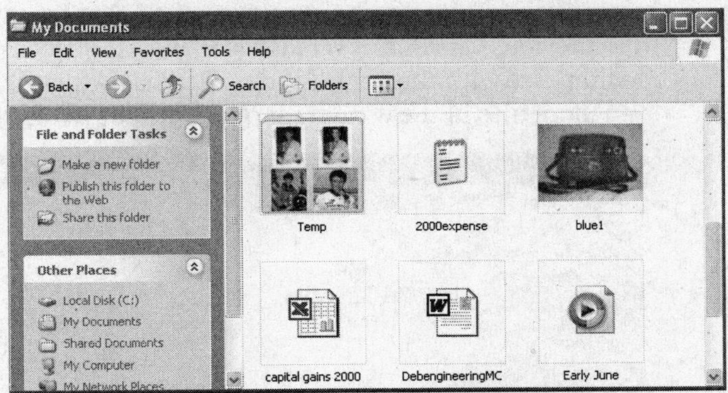

Tiles view The filename appears to the right of the icon, along with the file type (if known) and the file size.

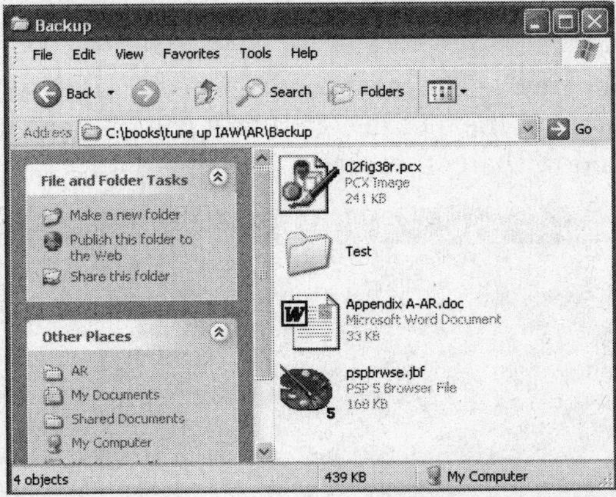

NOTE

Recall from Chapter 5 that a file's extension is a three-character code after the filename that tells Windows the file's type. For example, you might have `Config.bak` and `Config.sys` in the same folder; the `.bak` extension indicates that `Config.bak` is a backup copy.

Icons view This view is the same as the Large Icons view from previous versions of Windows. It shows the icons at a medium size with the name (and no details) beneath, and it fits even more files in the window at once without scrolling.

List view The most compact view, List view displays the names of the files in columns; it can fit many more files in a window than other views.

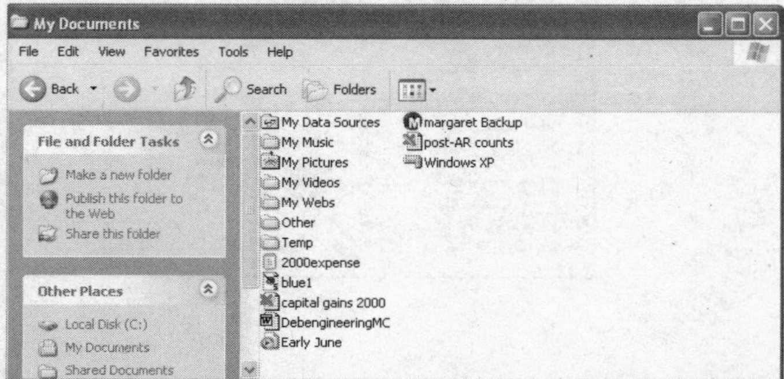

Details view This view is like List view except that the filenames appear in a single column and there are additional columns containing other information such as file size and date last modified. You can sort by any of the columns by clicking its heading.

Changing the Displayed Details

In Details view, certain details about the files appear in columns. You can change which details appear there:

1. Choose View ➢ Choose Details.

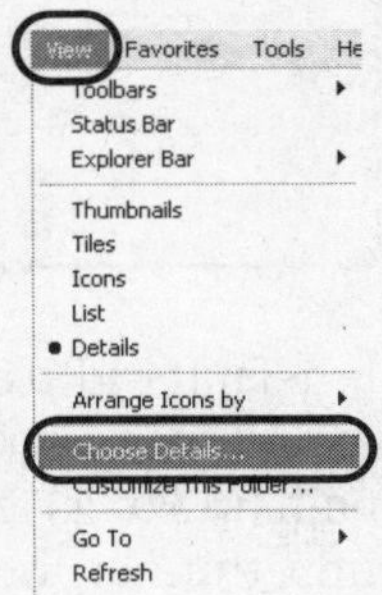

TIP

If you select a lot of details, you will probably need to scroll to the right to see all the details unless your file management window is very large or even maximized.

2. You should now see the Choose Details dialog box. Select or deselect the details you want to appear. To do so, you can either click the check box next to a detail or click its name and then click the Show or Hide button.

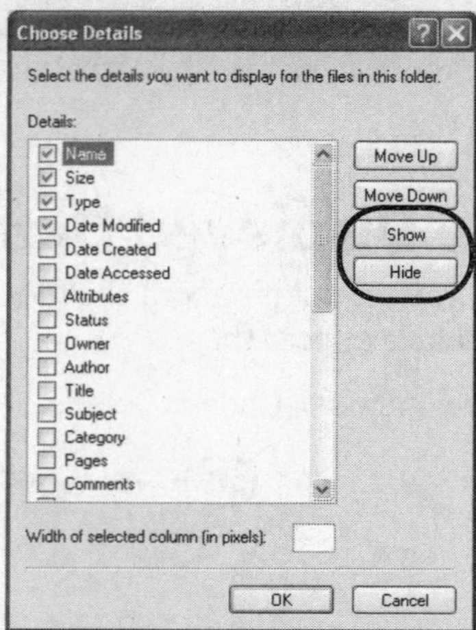

3. To change the default width of a particular column, select its title in the list and then change the number in the Width of Selected Column (in *Pixels*) text box. Decrease the number to make a column thinner; increase it to make the column wider.

4. To rearrange the column order, click a detail and then click Move Up or Move Down.

5. Click OK to close the dialog box.

Changing File Sort Order

When you are trying to locate a certain file or folder in a long list, you might want to sort the listing by a particular criterion. Some examples: If you are looking for all your Excel files, you can sort by file type; or if you are looking for a file that begins with a certain letter, you can sort by filename. And if you are looking for a file you worked on earlier today, you can sort by date.

To change the sort order:

1. Choose View ➢ Arrange Icons By.

2. In the submenu that appears, click the way you want the icons arranged (such as Size in this example).

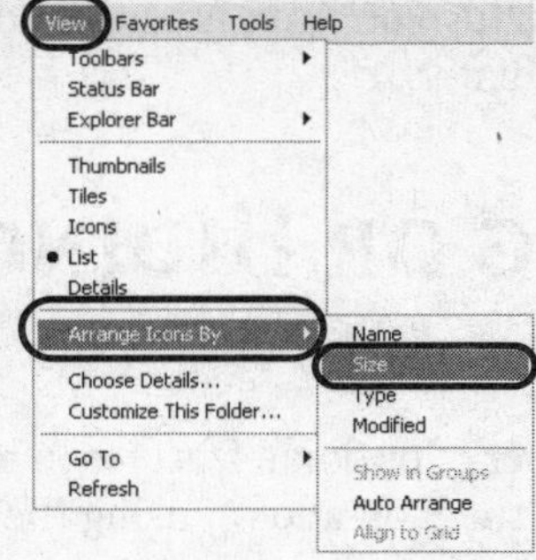

The files re-sort themselves to match the order you specified. Folders appear first, followed by files.

The Show in Groups option on the submenu creates a heading for each sort category. (Shown in the following figure are the headings for Type.) If you sort by Name, the first letter of each name is a category. If you sort by Modified date, the divisions are based on the last access to the file, such as This Year and Last Year. Each sort option has its own grouping method.

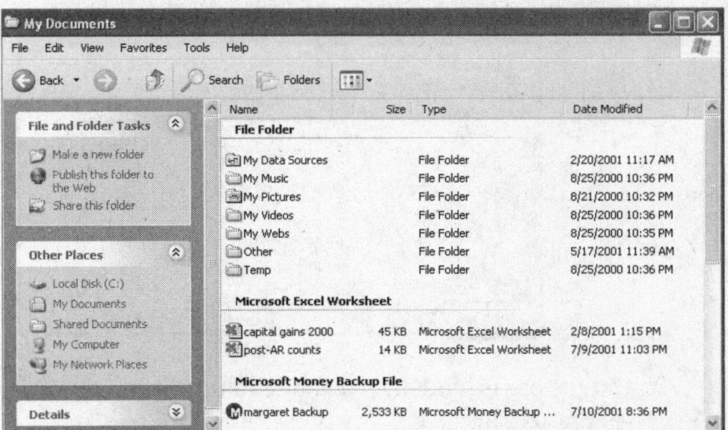

The Auto Arrange option sets the display to automatically re-sort the list whenever it becomes out of order. For example, when you create a new folder within the current folder, that new folder is placed, by default, at the bottom of the window. When you close and reopen the window, the new folder gets sorted in with the others; but until you do so, or until you refresh the display or change the sort method, the folder remains at the bottom. If you turn on Auto Arrange, however, it snaps into its appropriate spot immediately.

Displaying or Hiding Window Controls

There are a number of optional features in a file management window, and you can turn them on and off using the View menu. These settings apply to the window for as long as it is open, no matter which folder's contents you are viewing; but when you close the window, the settings are not retained.

Displaying or Hiding the Status Bar

The status bar, when displayed, appears at the bottom of the window and provides information about whatever is selected. For example, when you select a group of files, the status bar reports the total number of files selected and the disk space they collectively occupy.

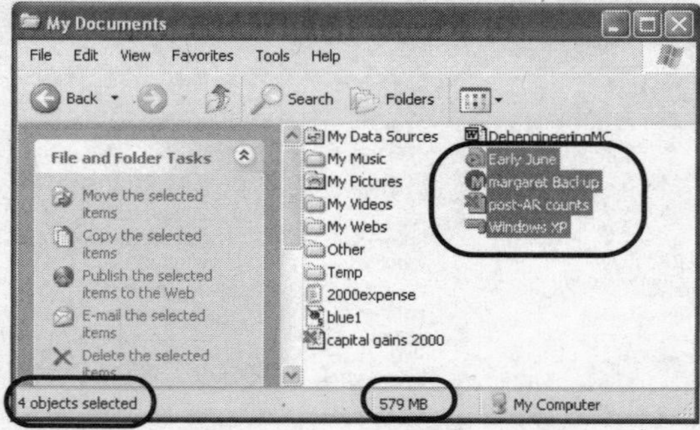

The status bar is hidden by default. To turn it on (or off again), choose View ➢ Status Bar.

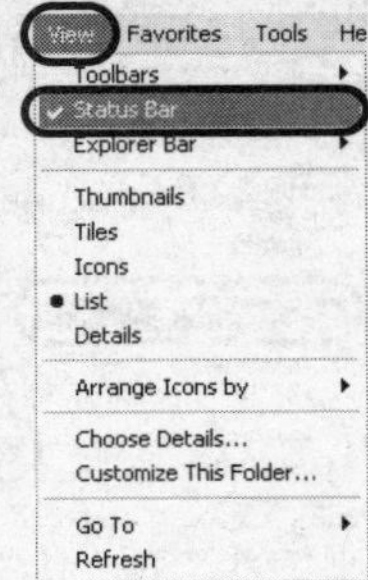

Controlling the Explorer Bar

The Explorer bar is an extra pane that sometimes appears in a file management window to help with certain tasks. For example, the Folders list that you worked with in Chapter 5 when managing files appeared in the Explorer bar. The Folders list is only one of several displays that can appear in that space.

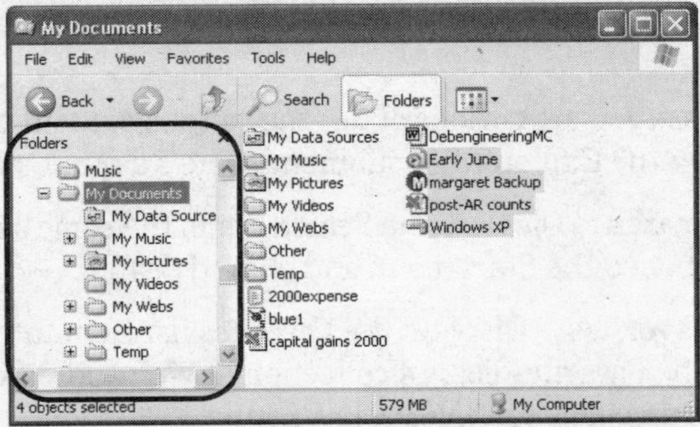

Other displays that can appear in the Explorer bar include the Search pane, which you can use to search your hard disk for misplaced files (covered in Chapter 5), and a History list that displays the names of Web pages you have visited recently using Internet Explorer.

Since, in most cases, content appears in the Explorer bar as part of some other activity, such as searching or Web browsing, you will seldom need to turn on the Explorer bar manually and select content to appear in it.

But if you do want to change the content of the Explorer bar, simply choose View ➢ Explorer Bar and then click the content that you want to appear in it (such as Folders in this example). The Explorer bar opens at the left side of the file management window, with the chosen content displayed.

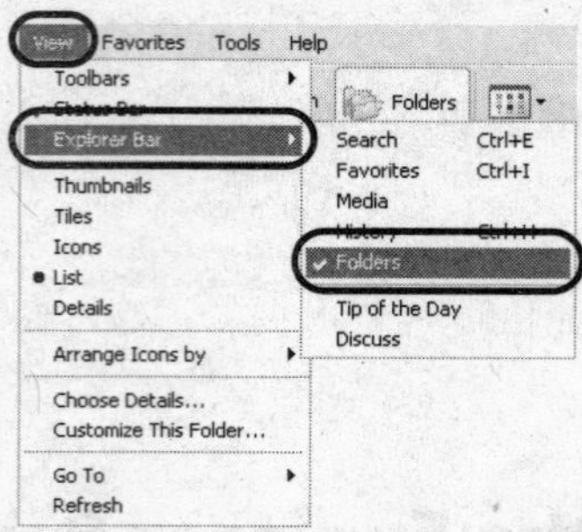

Unlike other optional window features, you don't turn the Explorer bar off by reselecting it from the menu. Instead, you click the Close (X) button in the bar's top-right corner to close it, as you would close a separate window.

In case you are curious about the various content choices you can make on the Explorer Bar submenu, here's a quick summary of them:

Search Displays the Search pane, the same as if you had opened the Start menu and clicked Search.

Favorites Displays the Favorites list from Internet Explorer. The Favorites list is a collection of Web addresses you create yourself, as you'll learn in Chapter 13.

Media Displays a media player, which you can use to control media clips. For example, if you display the contents of a folder that contains audio clips, you can select one of them and then use the controls in the Media pane to play it. This is different from the stand-alone Windows Media Player, which you'll learn about in Chapter 18.

History Displays the History list from Internet Explorer. The History list is a log of the Web sites you have visited recently.

Folders Displays the Folders list that you are already familiar with from Chapter 5.

The remaining two options on the Explorer Bar submenu don't control the Explorer bar content per se, but rather an additional pane at the bottom of the window:

Tip of the Day Displays helpful hints for using Windows XP.

Discuss Displays a toolbar of buttons that are useful when working with newsgroups or other online discussions.

Setting Folder Options

Folder options apply to all folders, not just the selected one, and they apply permanently, not just as long as the current file management window is open. These are global settings that you adjust once and then don't have to change again (unless you change your mind about your preferences, of course).

To change folder options, open the Folder Options dialog box from any file management window:

1. Choose Tools ➢ Folder Options.

2. In the Folder Options dialog box, change the folder settings as desired:

   Tasks You can choose whether to show the File and Folder Tasks pane (the blue-framed pane that contains shortcuts to common tasks and that appears when the Explorer bar is not present) or whether to use Windows classic folders instead, which does not include the pane.

   Browse Folders The default is Open Each Folder in the Same Window. When you double-click a folder to open it, its contents replace the previous contents in the same window. This prevents a lot of windows from opening that you will need to close later, thereby saving you time. Alternatively, you can select Open Each Folder in Its Own Window.

TIP

Opening each folder in its own window was the default in Windows 95, so you might want that setting if you've upgraded from Windows 95 recently and want to feel more at home in Windows XP.

Click Items As Follows The default here is Double-Click to Open an Item (Single-Click to Select). The alternative, Single-Click to Open an Item (Point to Select), makes Windows work more like a Web page.

3. Click OK to accept your changes.

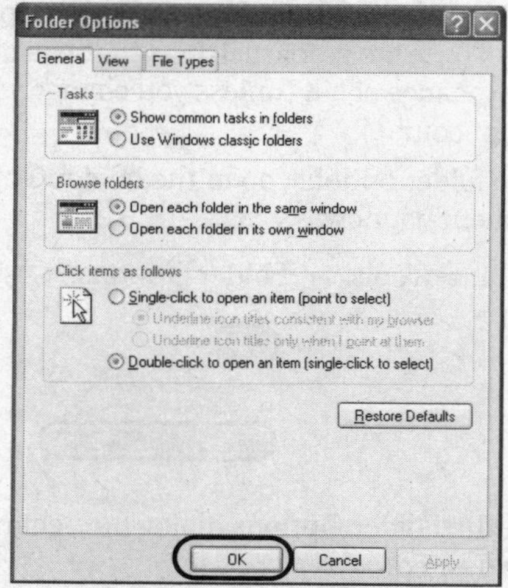

Setting Folder Viewing Options

The final options you'll learn about in this chapter deal with file management in a very global way. They are options that affect all displays in which filenames appear. This can include the Save and Open dialog boxes in applications, for example, and your e-mail program when you are selecting file attachments for e-mail.

To control the way files and folders are displayed in a global way:

1. Choose Tools ➢ Folder Options.

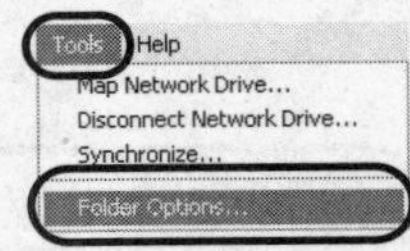

2. Click the View tab.

3. In the Advanced Settings pane, under Files and Folders, select or deselect any of the check boxes as desired. Here are a few of the most common settings:

   Hidden Files and Folders The default is Do Not Show Hidden Files and Folders. If you choose Show Hidden Files and Folders instead, any files or folders that have the Hidden attribute will appear in file listings, but they will appear slightly dim or faded to indicate that they are hidden.

TIP

To set a file or folder to have the Hidden attribute, right-click it, choose Properties, and then mark the Hidden check box in its Properties box.

   Hide Extensions for Known File Types This option is turned on by default. More experienced Windows users might want to turn it off so that they can see the file extensions; this can help distinguish between listed files that have the same name but different extensions.

TIP

You'll need to scroll down in the Folder Options dialog box to access some of the options listed here.

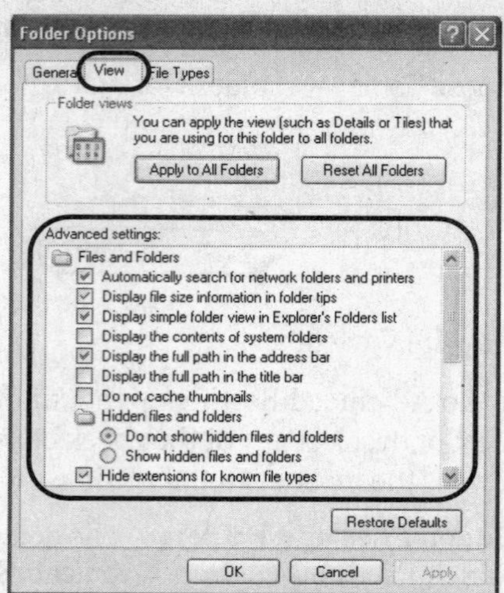

Remember Each Folder's View Settings Also on by default, this setting is what makes it possible for Windows to reopen a folder using the same view settings as you were using the last time you closed it.

Restore Previous Folder Windows at Logon This option is off by default, but you might want to turn it on. If you shut down Windows with file management windows open, those same windows will reopen at startup if you mark this check box.

Show Control Panel in My Computer This setting is also off by default. Earlier versions of Windows included a Control Panel icon in the My Computer window. Mark this option to have that happen in Windows XP as well.

4. Click OK to close the dialog box.

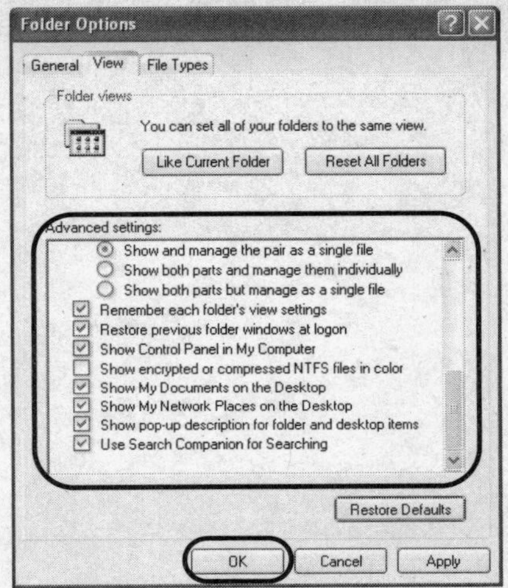

WHAT'S NEXT?

In Windows XP Professional, items such as a modem, a file, a printer, and so on, are known as objects, and each object has settings, or properties, associated with it. The next chapter explores how to access these properties (often by right-clicking) and, in some cases, how to change them.

Chapter 7

Setting Object Properties

All objects in Windows XP Professional—from modems, folders, files, and shortcuts to other computers on the network—have properties, or settings, that affect how the object looks and, oftentimes, how the object operates. In this chapter, we'll take a look at some of these properties, but first we'll look at one way to access these properties, and that is through right-clicking an object. We'll also look at how you can use a right-click to get stuff done faster. We'll then take a look at Property dialog boxes and file properties. We'll examine how to compress and encrypt files and folders in Windows XP Professional and then close this chapter with a look at folder properties and the settings you will find associated with My Computer.

Revised and adapted from *Windows XP Professional: In Record Time* by Peter Dyson and Pat Coleman

ISBN 0-7821-2450-X   496 pages $29.99

RIGHT-CLICKING IN WINDOWS XP PROFESSIONAL

Right-clicking an object in Windows XP Professional displays a shortcut menu that contains options relating to the type of object you are working with. Sometimes the same options are available from the conventional menus, but using a right-click can be faster and more convenient.

NOTE

For this discussion, we are assuming that you have not switched the mouse button functions by changing the settings in Control Panel. If you have, you will have to switch this discussion too. And if you don't use a mouse but use some other type of pointing device, such as a trackball, you'll have to find the equivalent right-click button; consult the Help files that come with the pointing device for more information.

You can right-click in many places in the Windows XP Professional interface, and you can right-click inside many of today's applications too. For example, Microsoft Word, Excel, and the other Office XP applications all support context-sensitive right-clicking, as do many of the Windows XP Professional accessory programs and system utilities. When you right-click a spreadsheet cell, the options contained in the shortcut menu will be different from those in the shortcut menu that is displayed when you right-click text or a graphic in Word.

The thing to remember is that right-clicking can do no harm; so if you don't know whether an item will open a shortcut menu, try it and see. If it does, the menu will open; if it doesn't, nothing will happen. Just remember that you can close any Windows XP Professional shortcut menu by clicking somewhere else or by pressing the Esc key on the keyboard. Many of these menus will also have some standard entries, such as Cut, Copy, Paste, Open, Print, and Rename.

TIP

Many of today's keyboards have a right-click or menu key located between the Windows key and the right-hand Ctrl key; you can press it to trigger a right-click for the currently highlighted object. If you are a touch typist, using this key will be faster than moving your hand to the mouse, moving the mouse pointer, and clicking the right button.

Here's a quick review of what happens when you right-click certain common objects:

- Right-click the Desktop to display a menu you can use to customize your Desktop.
- Right-click the Start button to open a menu that contains Open, Explore, and Search options, as well as two entries relating to users.
- Right-click a blank part of the Taskbar to open a menu you can use to manage any windows open on the Desktop, run the Task Manager, or look at the Taskbar properties. We'll be looking at properties in more detail later in this chapter.
- Right-click a program icon on the Taskbar. This opens the application's System menu, just as if you had right-clicked the application window's title bar or clicked the System button. Use the selections it contains to resize the application window or to close the application.
- Right-click a file and the menu contains lots of options, including opening the file with its associated application program. Depending on the file type, you will also see Open With, which allows you to specify the program you want to use to open this file.
- Right-click a folder and the menu you see is very similar to the one for a file. If you choose Open, you will see the contents of the folder.
- Right-click a printer in the Printers folder to set a printer as the default printer or, if you are on a network, to print offline.

For example, if you right-click My Computer on the Start menu, you'll see this menu:

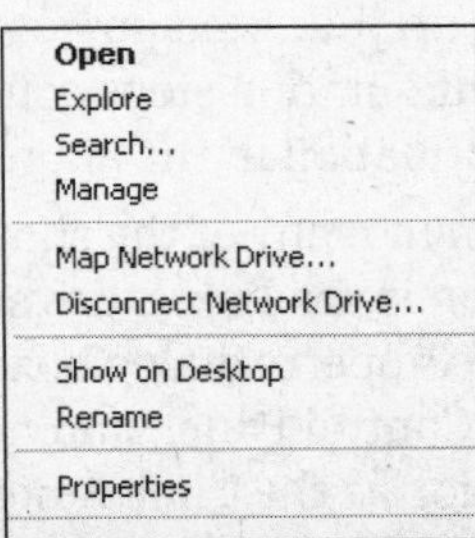

And if you right-click the Taskbar, this is what you'll see:

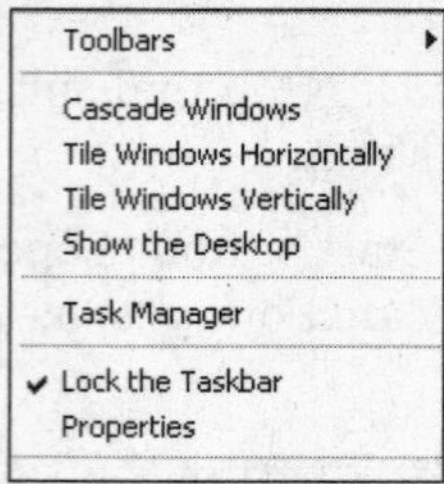

Many Windows XP Professional objects, such as My Network Places, My Computer, printers, and folders, have the shortcut menu item Explore, which opens the item in an Explorer two-pane format, with the object in the left pane of the window and its contents in the right pane. The contents will vary according to the object and can include other computers on the network, disk drives, files, folders, and even print jobs being processed by your printer. In addition, some applications will add their own entries to a shortcut menu, entries that are specific to that application.

TIP

Certain items, such as hard disks, have a Sharing and Security selection in their shortcut menus, so you can specify how each item is shared with other users on the network.

USING PROPERTY DIALOG BOXES

XPObject properties are collected together and displayed on one or more tabs in a special dialog box called a Property dialog box. When you install a new printer or set up your modem, for instance, the Wizard that walks you through the configuration steps collects all the information together and places that information in the appropriate Property dialog box.

The very last item in many of the shortcut menus that we looked at in the preceding section is the Properties selection, which gives you fast and easy access to these Property dialog boxes. You can also get to an item's properties through Control Panel, and many dialog boxes have a Properties button that performs the same function. Once a Property dialog box is open, you can not only display the current settings but can also change them. Some Property dialog boxes have a single tab with just a few settings, while others may have multiple tabs; it all depends on the complexity of the object you are working with.

TIP

To open an object's Property dialog box from the keyboard, highlight the object, and press Alt+Enter.

Changing File Properties

Right-click a document file and choose Properties to open the file's Properties dialog box, as Figure 7.1 shows. The document file in Figure 7.1 is a Microsoft Office document created by Word, and you'll see that there are several tabs, because Word keeps its property information in several locations; files created by other applications may display a dialog box with just a single tab.

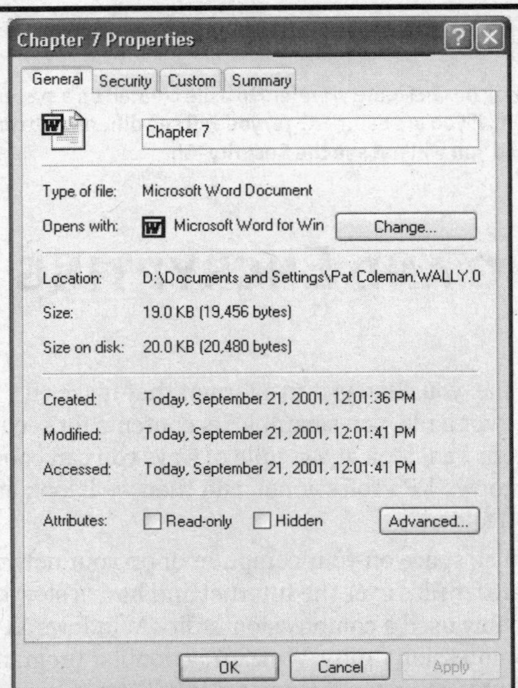

FIGURE 7.1: A Property dialog box for a Word document file

The information shown on the General tab includes the document type and the name of the application associated with this file type, its location and size, as well as the create, last modified, and last accessed dates. This tab also includes two attribute check boxes:

Read-Only Set this attribute to prevent anyone from doing anything to this file other than reading it.

Hidden Check this box to hide the file. It will function as normal, but you won't be able to see it in the Explorer or other programs.

Clicking the Advanced button opens the Advanced Security Settings dialog box, which you use to establish special permissions for a document. You can also set permissions using the Security tab. Chapter 25 discusses security in Windows XP Professional.

The Custom tab lets you create your own properties to attach to this file, and the Summary tab details the document title, subject, author, and other details, such as page and character count and the revision number.

NOTE

The Properties dialog box in Figure 7.1 refers to a file created on a system using the NTFS file system. If you are using FAT32, you will see different attributes on the General tab, and you will not see the Security tab.

Compressing and Encrypting Files

When you compress a file, you change it to a format that makes it smaller. When you encrypt a file, you scramble its contents for security purposes. In this section, we'll look at a couple of ways you can compress files and folders in Windows XP Professional, and then we'll look at how to compress a file and a folder.

If you have limited disk space on your computer or on your network, or if you often need to transfer files over the Internet and have a slow connection, you have probably used a compression utility. Windows XP Professional includes a compression utility, WinZip7, a popular program that has been widely distributed in previous versions. When you compress, or "zip," a file or a folder in Windows XP Professional, that file or folder can be uncompressed, or "unzipped," by almost any other compression utility.

Compressing a file or a folder is fast and easy. You simply right-click the file or folder in an Explorer-type window, choose Send To on the shortcut menu, and click Compressed Folder on the submenu. A compressed copy of the file or folder is placed in the folder that contains the original file. You can compress other files or folders by simply dragging them to the compressed folder. When you then move the file or folder out of the compressed folder, it is uncompressed. You can also uncompress a file or folder by simply double-clicking it.

A compressed folder has a zipper on it:

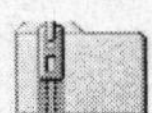

You can also compress files, folders, and disks in another way. In the General tab of the object's Properties dialog box, click the Advanced button to open the Advanced Attributes dialog box, which is shown in Figure 7.2. The attributes shown here are only available with NTFS. They are not available if you are using FAT32; the Advanced button will not even be present.

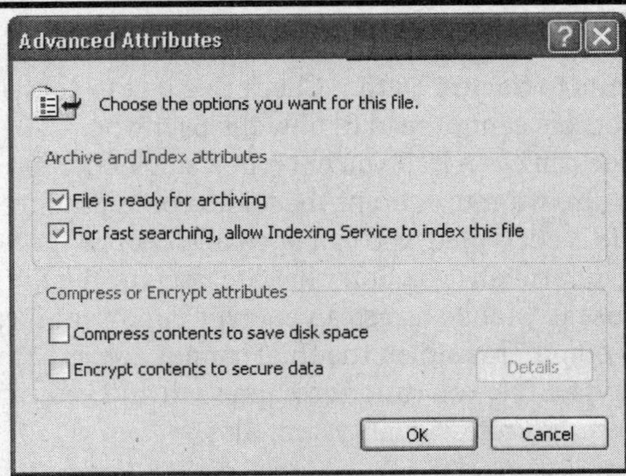

FIGURE 7.2: The Advanced Attributes dialog box

At the top of the Advanced Attributes dialog box, you will see two check boxes:

File Is Ready for Archiving Specifies whether the file has been changed or modified since it was last backed up.

For Fast Searching, Allow Indexing Service to Index This File Specifies whether the contents of the file should be indexed to allow for faster searching. Once the contents are indexed, you can search for text within the file as well as for properties, such as the create date or other attributes.

At the bottom of the Advanced Attributes dialog box, you will see two more check boxes:

Compress Contents to Save Disk Space Check this box to compress the file so that it occupies less space on your hard disk. Files are compressed by about one-third, so a 200MB file shrinks down to 135MB. This is a great way to keep large files that you only need to access occasionally. The next time you use the file, it is automatically uncompressed; you don't have to do anything special. There are certain types of files that you shouldn't compress, however. For example, most multimedia and graphics files are already stored using their own compression scheme, and there is no point in compressing a database file since the added overhead of decompressing the file for each transaction you run could seriously affect performance. If you compress a file, you cannot encrypt it.

Encrypt Contents to Secure Data Check this box to encrypt the file so that others cannot read it; only the user who encrypted the file can open it. If you encrypt a single file, you are asked if you also want to encrypt the folder containing the file. Once the file is encrypted, you can open and change the file just as you would normally; you don't have to decrypt the file before you can use it. Mobile users can encrypt important files so that if their computer is stolen the thief cannot access those files. If you encrypt a file, you cannot compress it, and you can't encrypt Windows XP Professional system files.

The Windows XP Professional Encrypting File System (EFS) forms the basis for encrypting files on NTFS hard disks. Before you rush off and encrypt all your files though, here are some operational points to consider:

- If you are part of a network, remember that encrypted files cannot be shared, and files opened over the network will be decrypted before they are transmitted.
- When you move or copy an encrypted file to a non-NTFS disk, the file is decrypted.

- Any user with Delete permission can delete an encrypted file or folder, so encryption is not protection against accidental deletion.
- Use Cut and Paste to move a file into an encrypted folder; if you use drag-and-drop, the file will not automatically be encrypted.
- If you use applications that create temporary files, such as Microsoft Word, encrypt at the folder level so that these temporary files are encrypted automatically. If you just encrypt a single important document, the Word temporary files will not be encrypted. You should also encrypt the Temp folder on your hard disk for this same reason.

CHANGING FOLDER PROPERTIES

Many of the properties we looked at in the last section also apply to folders. Figure 7.3 shows the Properties dialog box for a My Pictures folder.

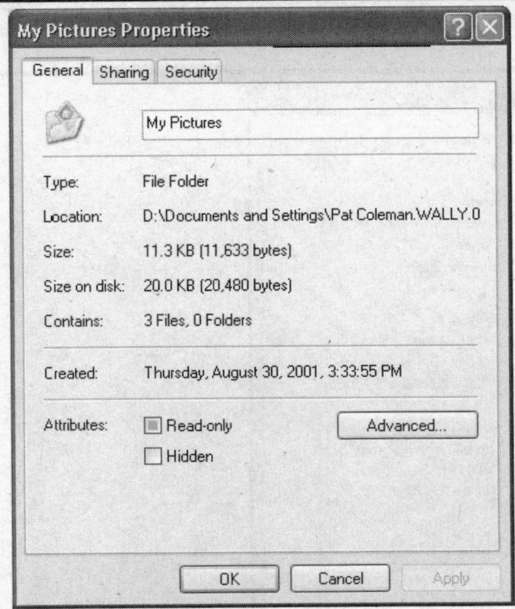

FIGURE 7.3: The Properties dialog box for a My Pictures folder

To change folder properties, right-click the folder, select Properties, choose the General tab, and then click the Advanced button to open the Advanced Attributes dialog box for this folder, where you can compress or encrypt the folder. Again, as with files, these are mutually exclusive choices, you must choose one or the other. When you apply compression or encryption at the folder level, you are asked if you want the change to apply to all subfolders as well.

TIP

You can also encrypt or decrypt a file or folder from the command prompt using the `cipher` command. Type `Cipher /?` at a command prompt for more information.

SYSTEM PROPERTIES

The System Properties dialog box gives you access to some of the most important sets of properties in Windows XP Professional. Right-click My Computer on the Start menu, and choose Properties to open the dialog box shown in Figure 7.4. If necessary, click the General tab to bring it to the front.

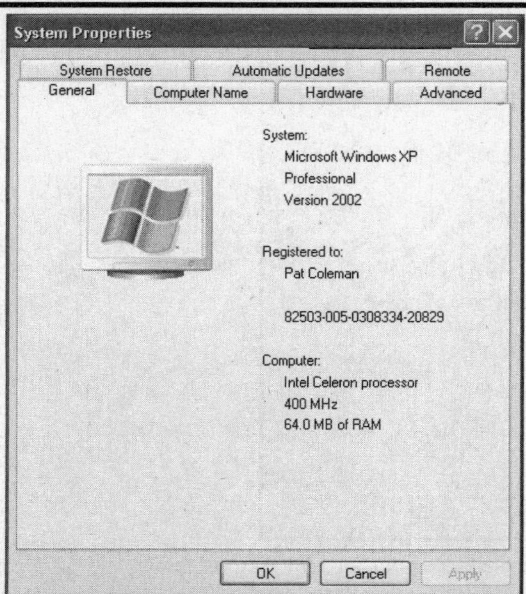

FIGURE 7.4: The System Properties dialog box open at the General tab

The General tab lists detailed information about your computer, including the processor and the amount of memory installed. When someone asks you a technical question about your system, this is likely the place to find the answer.

The Computer Name tab details the information that identifies your computer to others on the network. Click Network ID to start the Network Identification Wizard, which guides you through making any changes, or click Change to open the Computer Name Changes dialog box and change the name of your computer or to change your workgroup or domain membership; consult your system administrator before making any changes here.

The Hardware tab gives you access to the Add Hardware Wizard, which is used to install hardware components, and the Device Manager, which is used to adjust hardware configuration. Click the Hardware Profiles button to open the Hardware Profiles dialog box, in which you can create different hardware configurations. You can create additional profiles to enable or disable certain hardware devices on your system. Once you have two or more hardware profiles, you will be prompted to choose one of them when Windows XP Professional starts. You can also create different hardware profiles for different users.

The Advanced tab, shown in Figure 7.5, contains three sets of options: Performance, User Profiles, and Startup and Recovery.

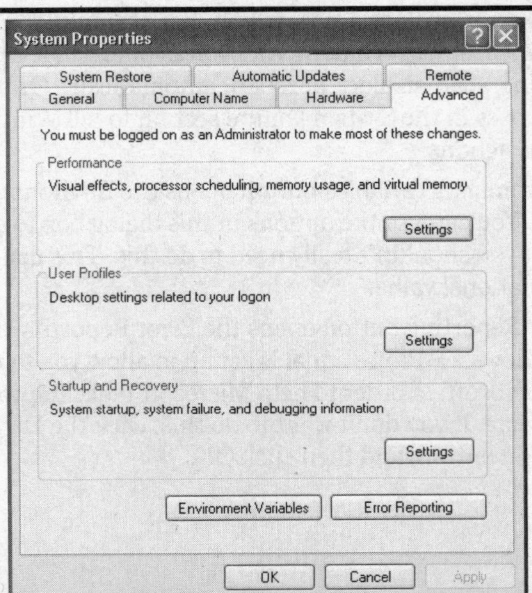

FIGURE 7.5: The System Properties dialog box open at the Advanced tab

In the Performance section, click the Settings button to open the Performance Options dialog box. You use the options in the Visual Effects tab in this dialog box to tell Windows whether you want to optimize the system for performance or speed. In the Advanced tab, you can select options that control how your computer responds to applications versus background system services, allowing you to set the system responsiveness and look at and change the computer's virtual memory settings. It's best to leave these alone and let Windows XP Professional manage virtual memory automatically, unless you really know what you are doing.

In the User Profiles section, click the Settings button to open the User Profiles dialog box. Here, you establish different Desktop configurations, which can be associated with different users. You can also create a roaming profile that provides your Desktop appearance to every computer on your network, so, no matter where you log on to the network, you will always have your own configuration available.

In the Startup and Recovery section, click the Settings button to open the Startup and Recovery dialog box. You use the options in this dialog box to choose an operating system to load on restart, assuming that you installed Windows XP Professional as a dual-boot system. You can also specify what you want Windows XP Professional to do when it encounters a serious system error, such as a system halt. For example, you can specify that if the system stops, Windows XP Professional will log the event to the system log, send an alert, or reboot automatically. Or you can select all the check boxes in the System Failure section to tell Windows to take all three of these actions.

Clicking the Environment Variables button opens the Environment Variables dialog box. You can use the options in this dialog box to adjust system variables, but you shouldn't really need to do this. This dialog box is primarily of informational value.

Clicking the Error Reporting button opens the Error Reporting dialog box. By default, Windows XP Professional is set up to allow you to report software errors to Microsoft, in order to help Microsoft make improvements to future software. If you don't want to do this, click the Disable Error Reporting option button, and then click OK.

What's Next?

As was the case with previous versions of Windows, you can adjust many features of Windows XP Professional to conform to the way you like to work with your computer. In the next chapter, Faithe Wempen shows you how to change the appearance of the screen.

Chapter 8

Adjusting Screen Appearance

Everyone has different tastes, so why should one Windows look-and-feel suffice for all? In this chapter, you will learn how to make the Windows desktop look radically different, with colors, wallpapers, icons, screen-resolution changes, and more. You'll also learn how to customize the taskbar so that it takes up more or less space on-screen or appears in a different location.

Changing the Display Mode

The display mode is actually a combination of three distinct settings: resolution, color depth, and refresh rate. The following sections explain those settings and how to adjust them.

Revised and adapted from *Windows XP Home Edition Simply Visual* by Faithe Wempen

ISBN 0-7821-2982-X 448 pages $24.99

Changing the Resolution and Color Depth

The *resolution* is the number of pixels that make up the display. The more pixels (dots) per inch, the finer the level of detail, and the smaller everything will appear on-screen. For example, at a high resolution such as 1280×1024, all the icons on the desktop will appear very tiny (see the next figure), while at a low resolution, such as 800×600 (second figure), they will appear much larger. Reason? An icon, a menu, a character of text, and so on is a precise number of pixels in size. When the pixels are closer together, the object looks smaller. The Windows desktop, on the other hand, always expands to fill the entire available screen space; it doesn't have a fixed size.

NOTE

In earlier versions of Windows, the lowest resolution was 640×480, but in Windows XP, the lowest resolution for most video cards is 800×600.

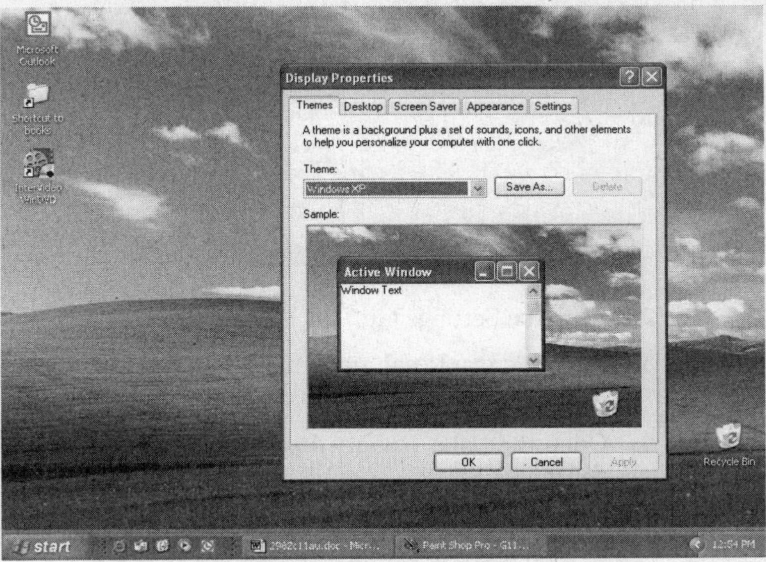

You might want to increase the resolution if you would like to see more detail on-screen at once without scrolling. For example, at a higher resolution, you can see greater portions of Web pages at once and more cells in a spreadsheet. Or, if you have limited vision, you might want to decrease the resolution so that everything appears larger.

Color depth is the number of colors to choose from for each pixel. The higher the color depth, the more unique colors you can display at once on-screen, and thus the better your photographs and graphics will look.

Color depth is measured in bits. For example, 4-bit color depth provides 16 color choices because 16 combinations are possible with a 4-digit binary number (2 to the 4th power). There are 8 bits in a byte, so 4-bit color requires half a byte for each pixel. In an 800×600 display, that would be 800×600 (480K) divided by 2, or 240K. That's not much—most video cards come with at least 4MB these days. Higher resolutions add up quickly, however. For example, 1024×768 in 32-bit color would require about 2.51MB.

Windows XP's default is to use a high color depth (32-bit), which results in the best-quality display. If, however, you are playing a game that requires some other color depth, or if you are concerned about sluggish system performance, you might decrease the color depth to see if that helps.

To adjust the resolution and color depth:

1. Right-click the desktop and then choose Properties to open the Display Properties dialog box.

2. Click the Settings tab.
3. Under Screen Resolution, drag the slider to the left or right to change the resolution.
4. Open the Color Quality drop-down list and choose a color depth.
5. Click OK.

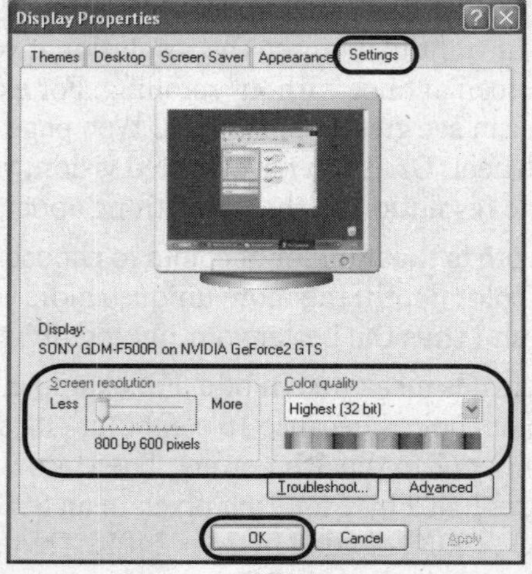

6. If this is the first time you have chosen this resolution or color depth, a dialog box appears asking you to confirm that the new display mode works. Click Yes within 15 seconds, or the display will revert to the previous resolution setting.

Changing the Refresh Rate

The *refresh rate* is the speed at which each pixel's color is refreshed by the laser inside the monitor. Each pixel's color starts decaying immediately after the laser hits it, so the laser must repaint the entire screen many times per second, pixel by pixel. The more times per second this happens, the higher the refresh rate and the less flicker you see in the display. Flicker is caused by pixels starting to decay to black before the laser gets around to hitting them again. The refresh rate is limited by the monitor's capability.

To change the refresh rate, do the following:

1. Right-click the desktop and then choose Properties.

2. In the Display Properties dialog box, click the Settings tab and then click the Advanced button. A properties box for the monitor and video card appears.

NOTE

The Hide Modes That This Monitor Cannot Display check box, when active, prevents you from selecting a higher refresh rate than the driver for your monitor thinks it can handle. Leave this marked. An exception might be appropriate if Windows hasn't correctly identified your monitor and you know your monitor is capable of a higher refresh rate than the current driver will allow.

3. Click the Monitor tab; then open the Screen Refresh Rate drop-down list and choose a refresh rate. To eliminate noticeable flicker, set the refresh rate to at least 85Hz if your monitor is capable of it.
4. Click OK. Your monitor changes its refresh rate.

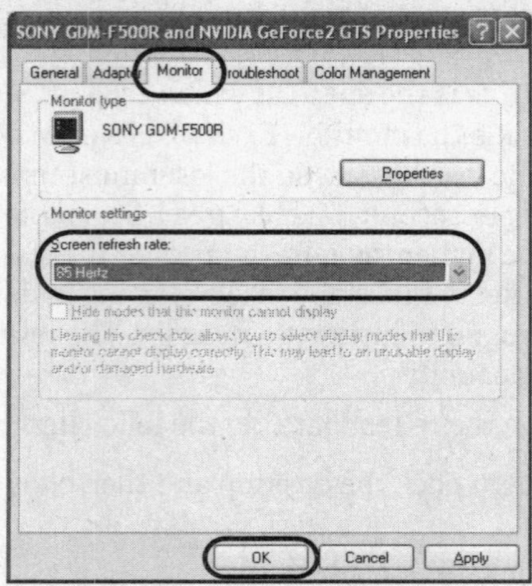

5. If this is the first time you have changed to this refresh rate, a confirmation box appears. Click Yes.
6. Click OK to close the Display Properties box.

Changing the Desktop Appearance

Customizing the Windows desktop is a favorite activity with almost everyone. Windows XP makes it easy to express your own personal flair by the background, font, and color choices you make for the on-screen display. In the following sections, you will learn about several of the adjustments you can make to change how Windows looks.

Working with Desktop Themes

A *desktop theme* is a combination of font, background image, and color choices, plus, in some cases, sounds and icons. Applying a theme to your desktop is a time-saver because you don't have to adjust individual appearance settings, and you also get the benefit of preselected color combinations and other choices designed to look good together.

NOTE

If there's something about a theme you don't like—the colors, the desktop background, and so forth—don't worry. You will learn to change it later in this chapter.

Windows XP has a new look-and-feel compared with earlier Windows versions, and one reason is that it has a new theme called Windows XP applied by default. If you prefer the classic Windows appearance, you can change to the Windows Classic theme. You can also choose any of several other themes.

To change the theme:

1. Right-click the desktop and then choose Properties.

2. In the Display Properties dialog box, click the Themes tab (if it doesn't already appear).
3. Open the Theme drop-down list and choose the theme you want. A sample of it appears in the Sample pane.

TIP

If you have an active Internet connection, you can choose More Themes Online to open a Web browser window that enables you to download additional themes from Microsoft's Web site.

4. Click OK.

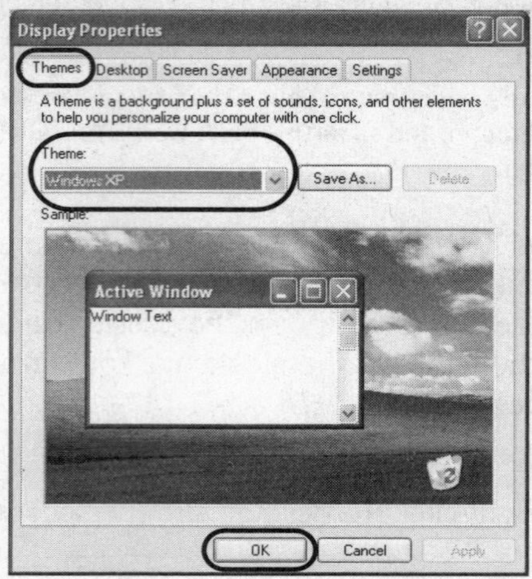

Notice the Save As button in the dialog box. If you have modified the appearance so that the settings for a particular theme are no longer fully in effect, the word *modified* will appear next to the current theme name. If you see that, you can click Save As to save the modified settings under a new theme name.

The Delete button enables you to delete the themes you have created; it is inactive unless one of your custom themes is selected.

Changing the Desktop Background

The background is the big flat area on which all the icons sit. By default, it contains *wallpaper* of a grassy hill and blue sky. You can choose a different wallpaper, or turn off wallpaper altogether and use a solid color as the background.

To change the desktop background:

1. Right-click the desktop and then choose Properties.

2. In the Display Properties dialog box, click the Desktop tab.
3. Click the name of a graphic on the Background list. A sample appears. Or click None from the list to remove the wallpaper altogether.
4. Open the Position list and choose Stretch, Tile, or Center.

   Stretch enlarges a single copy of the image to fill the available space.

   Tile fills the available space with multiple copies of the image at its default size.

   Center places a single copy of the image at its default size in the center of the desktop and allows whatever color you select in step 5 to appear around the edges.

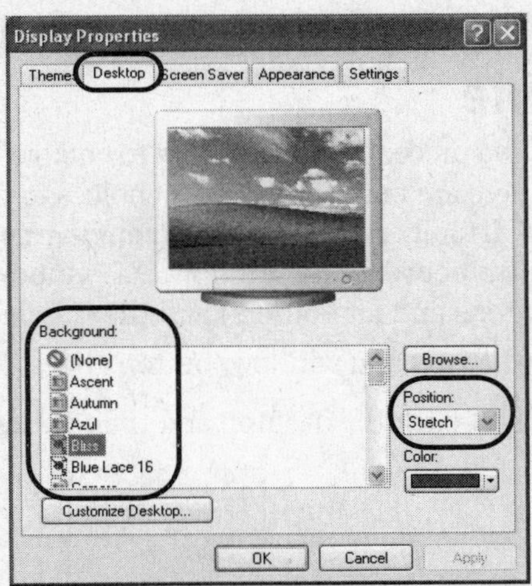

5. If you chose None in step 3, or if you chose Center in step 4, click the Color button to open a palette from which to choose a solid background color.

NOTE

The Customize Desktop button enables you to change which icons appear on the desktop. You'll learn more about it in the upcoming section "Changing Desktop Icon Appearance."

Rather than choose a color from the palette, you can click Other to open a dialog box containing a larger assortment of colors from which to choose.

6. Click OK.

Changing Screen Colors and Window/ Button Style

You saw in the preceding section how to change the desktop background color, but there are many other color choices to be made. You can change the color of virtually every screen element you see. You can also switch back and forth between the Windows XP window and button style (the big blue buttons and fat borders) and the classic Windows style.

To change colors and window/button style:

1. Right-click the desktop and then choose Properties.

2. In the Display Properties dialog box, click the Appearance tab.
3. Open the Windows and Buttons list and choose either Windows XP Style or Windows Classic Style.
4. Open the Color Scheme list and choose a different color scheme if desired.

NOTE

The color schemes are completely different for the Windows XP style and the Windows classic style. Classic style has many more to choose from.

5. Open the Font Size list and select a font size. The available font sizes depend on your choice in step 4. The Windows Standard color scheme, for example, has Normal, Large Fonts, and Extra Large Fonts to choose from; some other color schemes have only Normal.

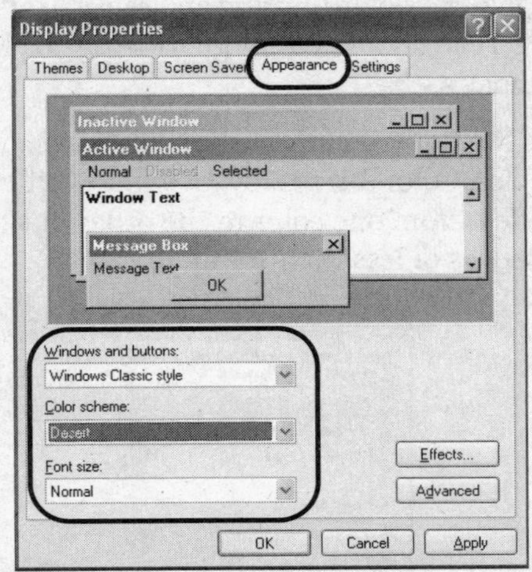

TIP

You can click the Effects button to open the Effects dialog box. There you can fine-tune some appearance settings for Windows, such as showing shadows under menus, making menus fade in and out, and enlarging the icons on the desktop.

6. If you are satisfied with the colors you've selected, click OK, and you're done. Otherwise, click Advanced to adjust colors for individual parts of the screen and go on to step 7.

7. In the Advanced Appearance box, open the Item list and select the item you want to recolor or change the settings for. You can also click an item in the sample area above if you don't know its name.

NOTE

The available items depend on the item you choose. For example, here I've selected Active Title Bar, and all the options are available. If you choose an item, such as Desktop, that doesn't contain text, the Font controls won't be available. Different aspects are also customizable depending on whether you are using Windows XP style or Windows classic style buttons and menus.

8. If the Size box next to Item is available, select a size. The measurements are in pixels.
9. Click the Color 1 button and select a different color if desired. You can choose Other for a dialog box that offers more color choices.
10. If the Color 2 button is available, click it and select a second color. Color 2 is mostly for window title bars; it allows a fade effect from one color to the other. It's not available in color depths of less than 16-bit.

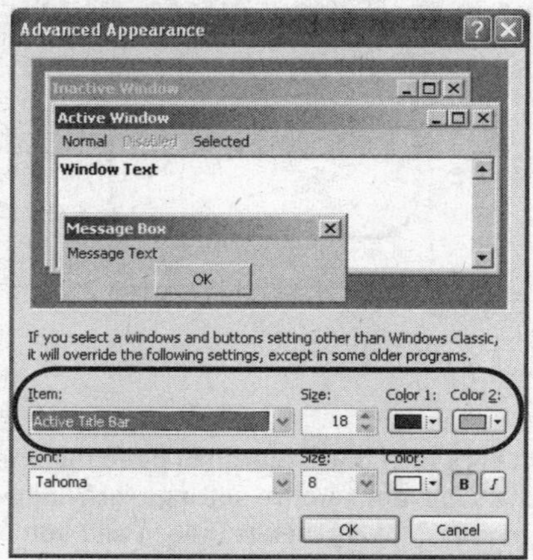

11. If the Font list is available, open it and choose a font. Font is available only for items that contain text.
12. If the Size box next to Font is available, enter a font size. Font size is measured in points. A point is 1/72 of an inch.
13. If the Color box next to Font is available, click it and choose a text color.

14. If the B and I buttons are available, click them to toggle Bold and Italic on and off if desired.

15. Go back to step 7 to customize some other screen item, or click OK if you're finished.

16. Click OK to close the Display Properties box.

Changing Desktop Icon Appearance

By default, the Windows desktop is fairly empty; there are very few system icons on it. One that *does* appear by default is the Recycle Bin.

If you have worked with other versions of Windows, however, you may be accustomed to extra shortcuts for Internet Explorer, My Computer, My Documents, and My Network Places. You can place these icons back on the desktop in Windows XP with a few simple mouse clicks. You can also change the icons used for these shortcuts.

To modify the desktop icon configuration:

1. Right-click the desktop and then choose Properties.

2. In the Display Properties dialog box, click the Desktop tab and then click Customize Desktop.

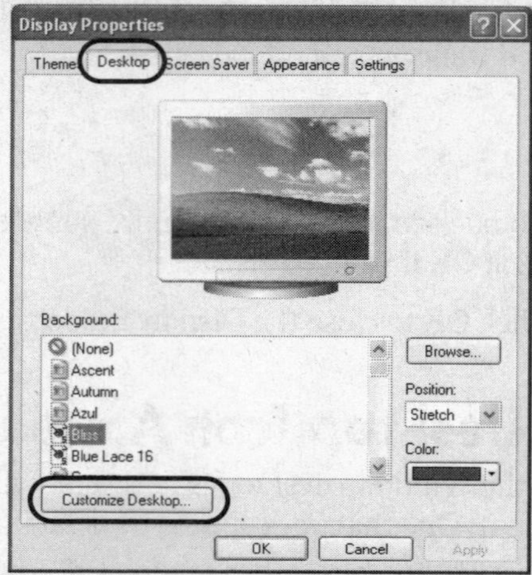

3. In the Desktop Items dialog box, under Desktop Icons, mark the check boxes for any shortcuts you want to appear on the desktop.

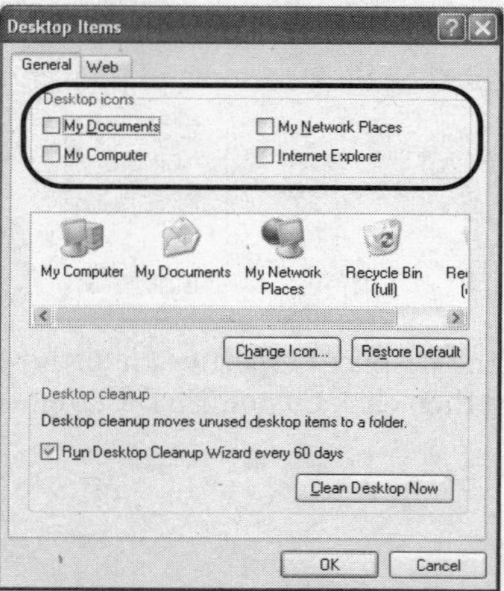

4. If you want to change the icon used for a particular shortcut, do the following:

   a. Click the icon you want to change and then click Change Icon.

b. In the Change Icon dialog box, click the alternative icon to use. Or, to browse in a different location for an icon, click Browse and choose a different *icon file*.

c. After selecting an icon, click OK.

d. Repeat steps a through c for any other icons you want to change.

5. Click OK to close the Display Properties box.

Choosing a Screensaver

If you often leave your computer turned on and unattended for long periods of time, you might want to use a *screensaver*, or set the monitor to turn itself off completely after a specified period of inactivity. The latter, in particular, can reduce your electric bill, especially if you have a large monitor.

To set up a screensaver, follow these steps:

1. Right-click the desktop and then choose Properties.

2. In the Display Properties dialog box, click the Screen Saver tab. Then open the Screen Saver drop-down list and choose a screensaver. A sample of it appears in the preview area.
3. In the Wait box, enter the number of minutes of idle time before the screensaver activates.
4. (Optional) If you want users to have to type the currently logged-in user's password when the screensaver deactivates, mark the On Resume, Password Protect check box.

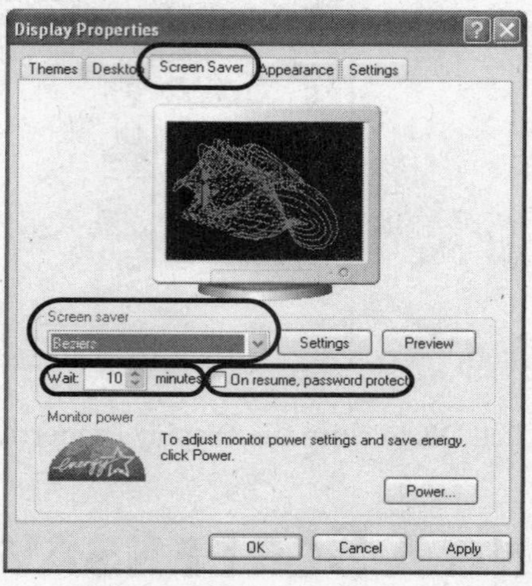

TIP

The Preview button previews the chosen screensaver in full-screen view, not just in the preview area. To exit from the full-screen preview, move the mouse or press a key.

5. (Optional) To change the settings for the chosen screensaver, click the Settings button. Then make any changes in the dialog box that appears and click OK. The settings for each

screensaver are different; here are the settings for Bezier, for example:

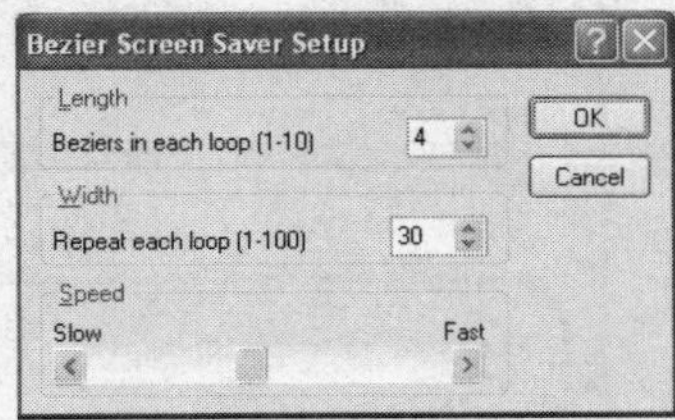

6. If you don't need to change the monitor's automatic shutoff setting, click OK, and you're done. Otherwise, click the Power button.

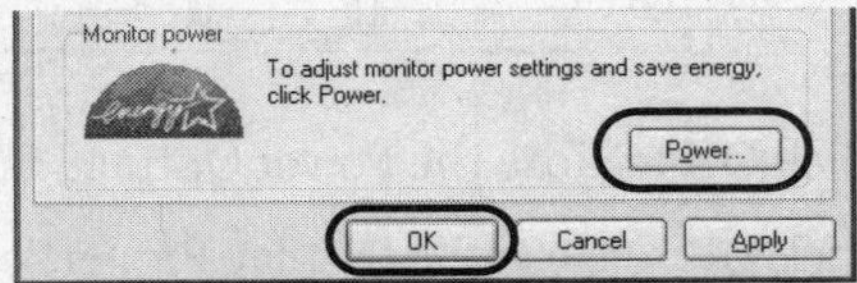

NOTE

There are many more options you can set for power management than are covered here. Experiment with the settings in the Power Options Properties dialog box on your own. You might want to create additional power management schemes, for example, or set up the PC to go into a standby mode when you press the power button.

7. In the Power Options Properties dialog box, open the Turn Off Monitor drop-down list and select a number of minutes of idle time that should elapse before the monitor shuts off.

8. (Optional) If you want your hard disks to stop spinning after a certain interval of inactivity, open the Turn Off Hard Disks drop-down list and select a number of minutes. Most people leave this set to Never for a desktop PC.

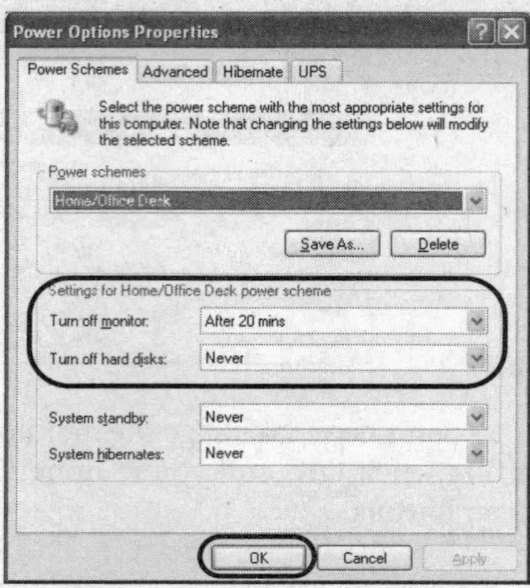

9. Click OK to close the Power Options Properties dialog box.
10. Click OK to close the Display Properties dialog box.

Changing How the Taskbar Looks and Operates

You have already learned about a few small ways to customize the taskbar, such as adding the Quick Launch toolbar to it. In this final section of the chapter, you'll find out about some other taskbar options that affect the way it looks and behaves.

Setting Taskbar Properties

Like most other on-screen items, the taskbar has its own set of properties you can adjust for it. To check them out and make changes if desired, do the following:

1. Right-click the taskbar and then choose Properties.

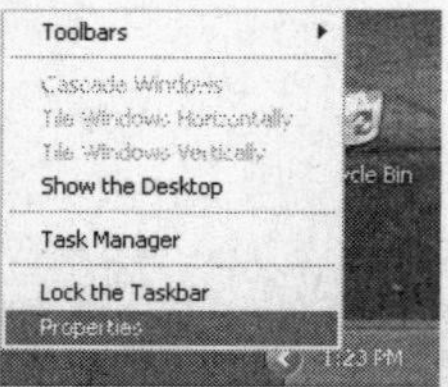

2. In the Taskbar and Start Menu Properties dialog box, mark or clear the check boxes for any of the following settings:

   Lock the taskbar. When this is selected, no changes to the taskbar are allowed. When cleared, you can make changes.

   Auto-hide the taskbar. When selected, the taskbar appears as a very thin line at the bottom of the screen until you move your mouse into its area; then it springs open. This can save screen space.

NOTE

You may have noticed the term *notification area* in this dialog box. It's the current name for what used to be called the system tray or the status area.

   Keep the taskbar on top of other windows. When selected, the taskbar is always visible, no matter what other windows are open. When cleared, the taskbar is like other windows, in that a window can be placed on top of it, obscuring it.

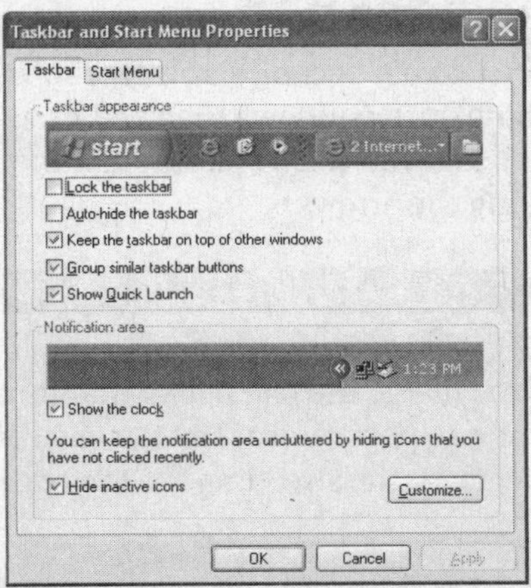

   Group similar taskbar buttons. When marked, if two or more of the same sort of window are open (such as two Word documents or two file management windows), they show up as a single button on the taskbar. Click it to see a menu showing all the open windows in that category.

When the check box is cleared, each window has its own taskbar button.

Show Quick Launch. When marked, the Quick Launch toolbar appears on the taskbar. When cleared, it does not.

Show the clock. When marked, the clock appears at the right end of the taskbar.

Hide inactive icons. When marked, the notification area displays only recently accessed icons, along with a left-pointing arrow button; you can click the button to see the rest of the icons.

Resizing the Taskbar

By default, the taskbar occupies a single row at the bottom of the screen. If there are more open windows than will fit, up and down arrows appear on the taskbar, and you can scroll through the "pages" of open window icons by clicking the arrows.

You can also enlarge the taskbar so that it has multiple rows. To do so, position the mouse pointer over the top edge of the taskbar and drag upward. To decrease the size, drag the top edge back down.

What's Next?

In addition to modifying the appearance of the screen, you can customize settings such as the date and time, and you can customize the keyboard and mouse and the audio and system sounds. The next chapter shows you how to adjust all of these items.

Chapter 9

Customizing System Settings

In Chapter 8 you learned some ways to make Windows XP look different. Now it's time to learn how to make Windows act and sound different too. In this chapter, you will learn how to change the date and time, adjust keyboard and mouse performance, and change audio and system sounds.

Setting the Date and Time

Have you ever wondered how your computer always seems to know the date and time? It's because of timekeeping circuitry built into the motherboard. A small battery on the motherboard keeps this clock powered even when you turn off the computer.

Revised and adapted from *Windows XP Home Edition Simply Visual* by Faithe Wempen

ISBN 0-7821-2982-X 448 pages $24.99

NOTE

Windows XP comes with a feature that will automatically synchronize the time on your computer with a time server on the Internet once a week. You'll see how to turn it on or off in these steps.

If you move to a different time zone, or if your computer's clock starts losing time (which can happen if the battery needs changing), you can adjust the date and time setting through Windows.

To change the date or time:

1. Double-click the clock on the taskbar.

The Date and Time Properties dialog box appears.

2. If the date shown on the Date & Time tab is incorrect, click the correct date on the calendar. To see a different month or year, open the Month or Year drop-down list and make another selection.

3. If the time shown is incorrect, enter a new time in the text box below the clock.

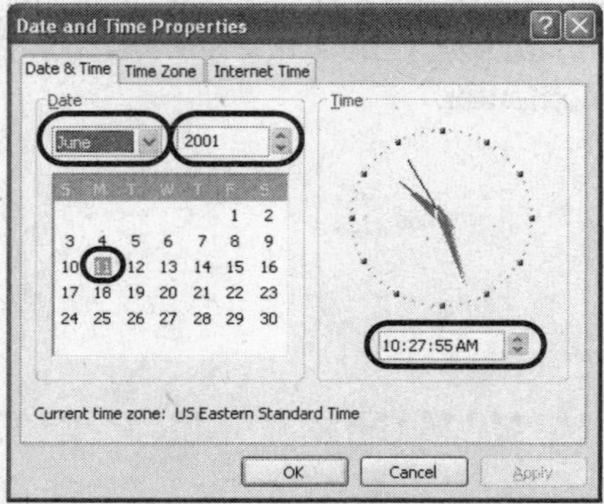

4. If you have changed time zones, click the Time Zone tab. Then select your time zone from the drop-down list.

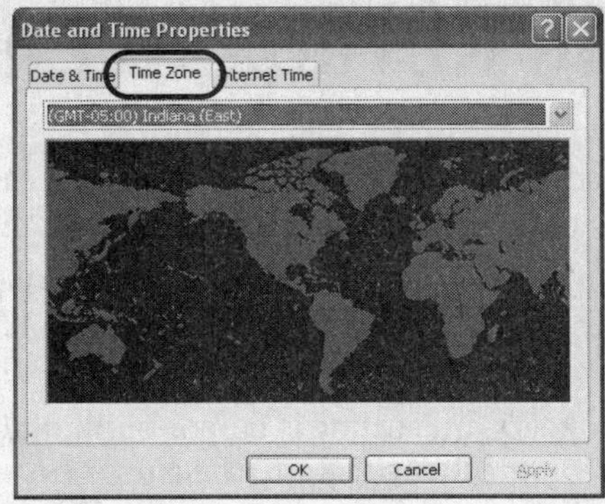

5. To check the time against a *time server* on the Internet, click the Internet Time tab and then click Update Now. If one server doesn't work, try choosing another one from the list of servers and clicking Update Now again.

6. If you don't want to use the time server automatically in the future, clear the Automatically Synchronize with an Internet Time Server check box.

TIP

You might turn off automatic synchronization if your computer isn't connected to the Internet full-time. That way, you can manually use Update Now whenever you happen to be connected instead of worrying about trying to be connected when the next update is scheduled.

7. Click OK.

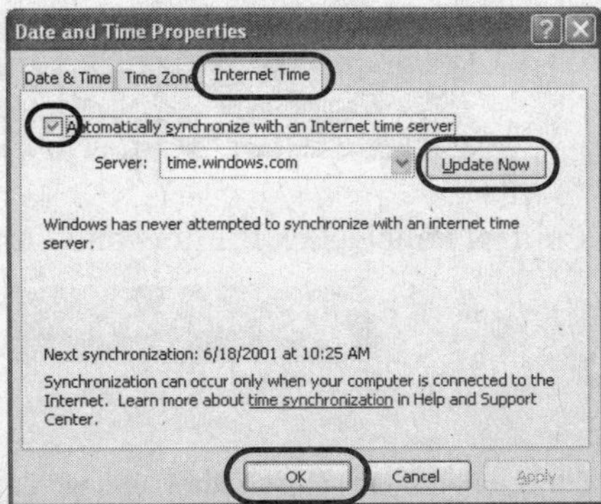

Changing Keyboard Properties

The keyboard works pretty well right out of the box; you don't need to do anything special to make it work. However, you can make a few fine-tuning adjustments to its performance to make typing more convenient.

Two of the keyboard settings you can adjust have to do with *key repeat*. You can set the repeat delay (the amount of time before a key starts repeating) and the repeat rate (the speed at which repeating occurs once it starts).

The other keyboard setting is cursor blink rate. When you type in a word processor or other program, the cursor (usually a vertical line) blinks to make it easier for you to locate it. The cursor blink rate controls the speed of the blinking.

To set keyboard properties:

1. Choose Start ➢ Control Panel.

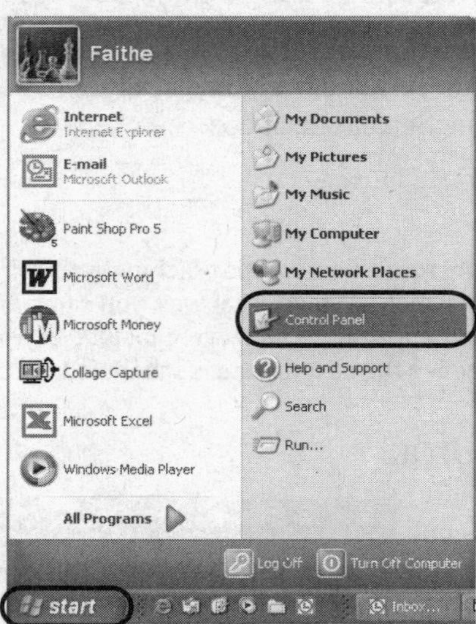

2. In Control Panel, click Printers and Other Hardware.

NOTE

If your Control Panel is in classic view, you won't see Printers and Other Hardware. Double-click Keyboard and skip to step 4.

3. In the Printers and Other Hardware window, click Keyboard.

4. In the Keyboard Properties dialog box, click the Speed tab if it isn't already selected.
5. Drag the sliders to adjust repeat delay and repeat rate. To test the settings, click inside the text box and then hold down a key.

NOTE

Both the keyboard and the mouse have a Hardware tab in their Properties boxes, but most people won't need to use it. It contains options for installing a different device driver, in case Windows has detected your keyboard or mouse incorrectly (not likely) or in case you have a custom driver that you want to install.

6. Drag the Cursor Blink Rate slider to adjust the blink rate.
7. Click OK to close the Keyboard Properties box.

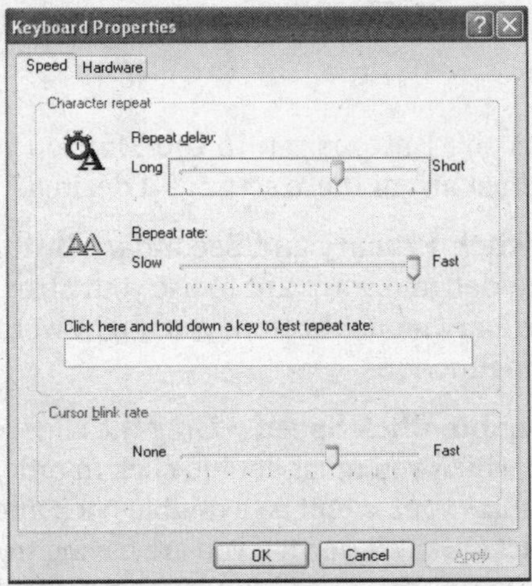

8. Close Control Panel.

Adjusting Mouse Operation

Since you use your mouse for almost all activity in Windows, it's imperative that the mouse operate the way you want it to. Fortunately, almost every aspect of mouse operation is customizable. You can change the range of cursor motion, the size of the cursor, and many other factors.

To explore mouse settings, and possibly make some changes, do the following:

1. Choose Start ➢ Control Panel.
2. Click Printers and Other Hardware.

NOTE

If Control Panel is in classic view, double-click Mouse instead of following steps 2 and 3.

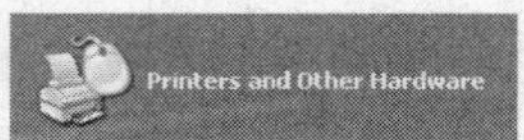

3. In the Printers and Other Hardware window, click Mouse.

4. On the Buttons tab in the Mouse Properties dialog box, adjust any of these settings if desired:

   Switch Primary and Secondary Buttons If you are left-handed and you want to use your strongest finger for the primary mouse button, you might want to switch the button functions.

   Double-Click Speed Drag the slider to adjust the speed at which you must double-click in order for Windows to recognize your intent as a double-click and not two single clicks. Slow it down if you are having trouble double-clicking fast enough; speed it up if you are accidentally double-clicking frequently. Test the new setting by double-clicking the folder to the right of the slider.

TIP

Sybex's Website, www.sybex.com, includes a bonus chapter, "Using the Accessibility Tools," for *Windows XP Home Edition Simply Visual*. This chapter covers many more accessibility features that are useful to people with physical disabilities, limited vision, or limited hearing.. On the Home page, type the book's ISBN code, 2982, in the Search box and then click Go. On the search results page, click the book's title to go to the page for the book.

ClickLock This setting turns the mouse button into a toggle, like the Caps Lock key, so that you don't have to hold it down when you want to drag. It's useful for people with limited mobility or dexterity—but irritating for almost everyone else.

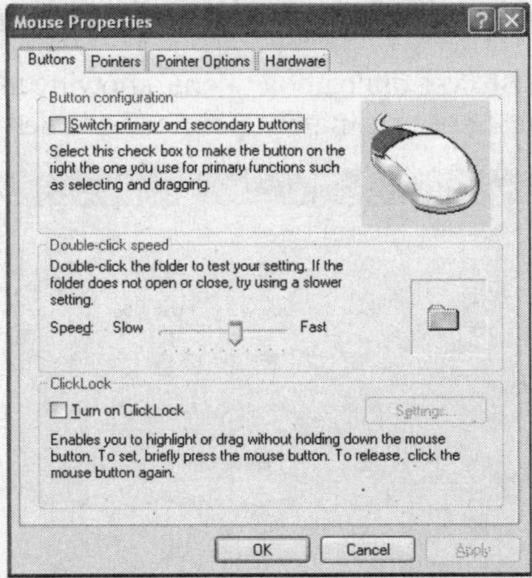

5. Click the Pointers tab; then open the Scheme drop-down list and select a different *pointer scheme* if desired.
6. To enable or disable the *pointer shadow*, click the Enable Pointer Shadow check box.
7. (Optional) If you want to customize the chosen pointer scheme, click an individual pointer on the list and then click Browse.

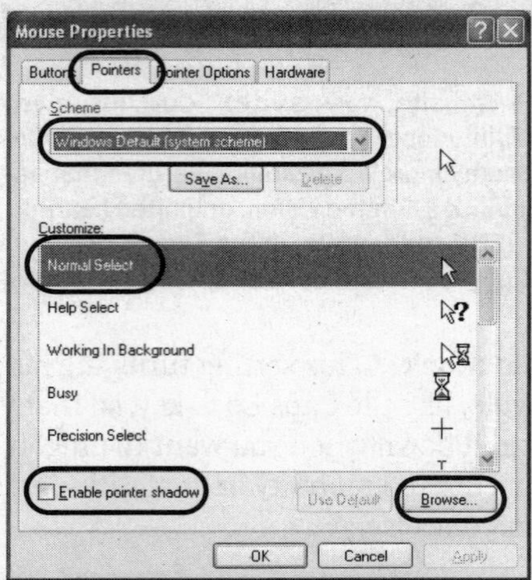

A Browse dialog box opens, showing all the available pointers. Select a different pointer and click Open.

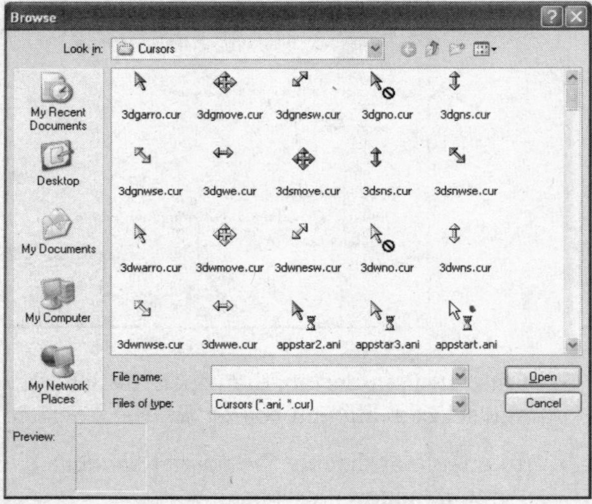

8. Click the Pointer Options tab and then adjust any of these settings as desired:

   Pointer Speed Drag the slider to change the mouse sensitivity—that is, the distance that the mouse pointer moves on-screen in relation to the distance that you physically move the mouse.

Enhance Pointer Precision Turn this feature on to enable some minor improvements to pointer movement; turn it off on a slower computer to improve performance.

Snap To Turn on to make the mouse pointer automatically jump to the default command button in a dialog box whenever one is open, making it easier for you to click that button.

Display Pointer Trails Turn on to make a "trail" appear behind the pointer when you move it—similar to exhaust fumes from a car. The trail can help you find the mouse on-screen more easily if you have limited vision.

Hide Pointer While Typing When this is enabled, the mouse pointer disappears when you are typing in a program such as a word processor, to avoid confusion between the mouse pointer and the cursor. When you move the mouse, the cursor pops back into view.

Show Location of Pointer When this is enabled, you can press the Ctrl key to make a radiating circle flash around the pointer. This is good for people with limited vision or those who tend to "lose" the pointer on-screen, but who don't like the pointer trails feature.

9. Click OK to accept your new settings.

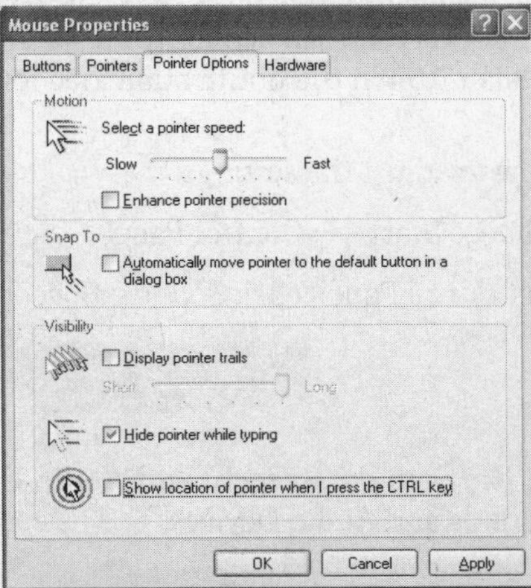

Setting Sound and Audio Properties

Sound and audio properties control how sound comes out of your PC. Most PCs have a sound card, or sound support built into the motherboard. You plug speakers into the sound card or into a built-in speaker jack on the PC, and Windows sends forth sounds and music from the sound card. It's all pretty straightforward, unless you have more than one sound card or some special speaker configuration. In that case, you might need to adjust the sound and audio properties for best performance with your system.

NOTE

Why might someone have more than one sound card? Primarily so that they can have more than one set of speakers plugged in simultaneously, each doing its own thing. People who use a computer to record their own music might find this especially useful. For example, with two sound cards, you could have external speakers playing an audio CD while an electronic keyboard plugged into another sound card feeds music into some headphones and records only the keyboard track to disk.

Even though you probably won't need to adjust your sound and audio settings, it's a good idea to check them out anyway just for your own education. There are also a few little tweaks and secrets hidden in these properties that everyone can benefit from, such as the ability to show or hide the speaker icon in the notification area for quick volume adjustments.

Here's how to adjust the settings:

1. Choose Start ➢ Control Panel.
2. In Control Panel, click Sounds, Speech, and Audio Devices.

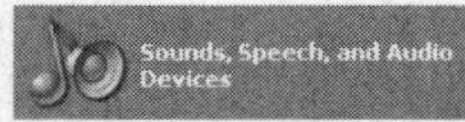

3. In the Sounds, Speech, and Audio Devices window, click Sounds and Audio Devices.

4. On the Volume tab of the Sounds and Audio Devices Properties dialog box, change any of the following settings as desired:

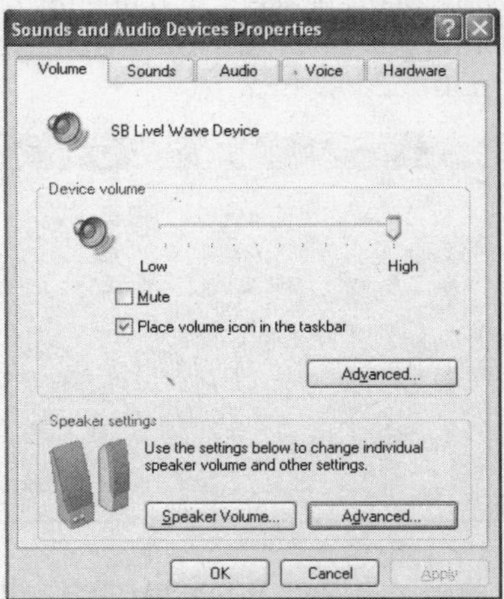

Device Volume Drag the slider to adjust the overall system volume.

Mute Mark this check box to temporarily disable all sounds from the speakers.

Place Volume Icon in the Taskbar Select or deselect to add or remove a shortcut for adjusting the volume in the notification area (next to the clock). This icon is a little speaker. Double-clicking that icon in the notification area will open the full Play Control dialog box; single-clicking it will open a single Volume slider like this:

Advanced (in Device Volume Section) Click this button to open the Play Control dialog box, through which you can adjust the volume for individual devices such as the microphone, speakers, and line in. This is the same dialog box that you get when you double-click the speaker icon in the notification area.

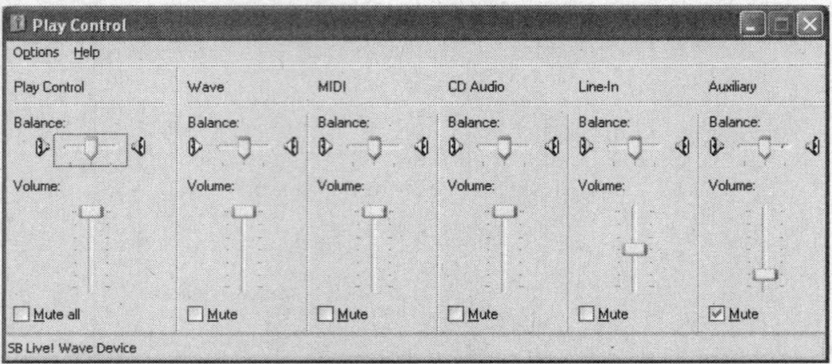

Speaker Volume Click to open a dialog box in which you can adjust the volume for right and left speakers separately.

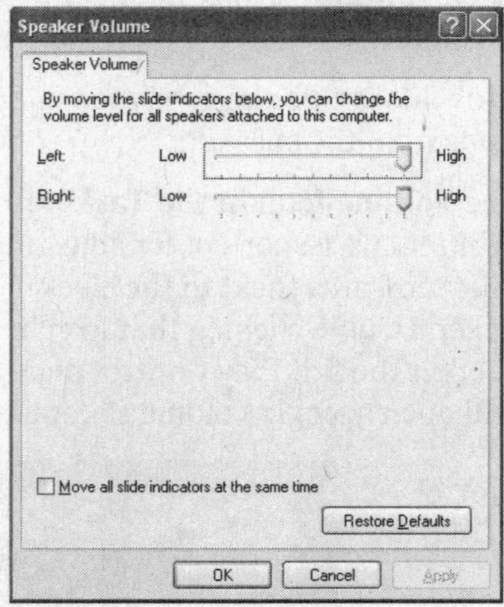

Advanced (in Speaker Settings section) Click to open an Advanced Audio Properties dialog box, where you can choose a speaker configuration that takes advantage of any extra speaker features you have, such as a woofer or Surround Sound.

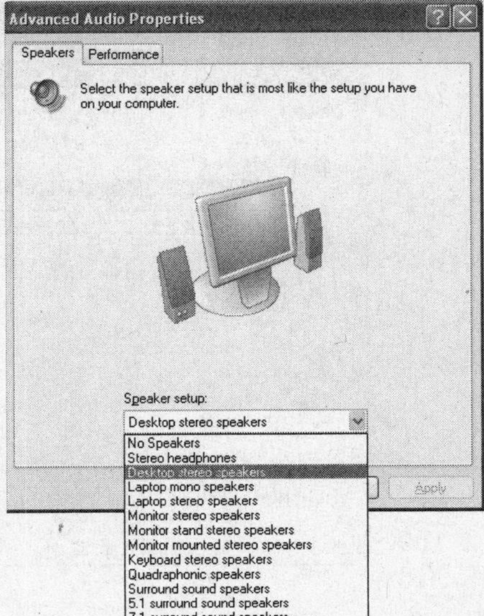

5. Click the Audio tab and then make any changes needed to the following controls:

   In the Sound Playback section, if you have more than one sound card, choose the one you want to use as the default. The Volume and Advanced buttons in this section are the same as those on the Volume tab.

   In the Sound Recording section, if you have more than one sound recording device, select the default one. Normally, this would be the same as your default playback device—your sound card. However, if you have more than one sound card, you might use one for playback and another for recording.

   In the MIDI Music Playback section, select the default device to use for *MIDI music*. If you aren't sure, leave it set for the default.

NOTE

You will learn in the next section how to select system sounds on the Sounds tab of this dialog box.

6. Click OK to close the Sounds and Audio Devices Properties box.

7. Close Control Panel.

Assigning Sounds to Events

You may have noticed that in your day-to-day Windows activities, sounds play at certain times. For example, there's a startup sound, a shutdown sound, a sound when an error occurs, a sound when you receive new e-mail, and so on. You can control these sounds, either by selecting a different *sound scheme* or by assigning individual sounds to *program events*.

To change your system sounds:

1. Repeat steps 1 through 3 of the preceding procedure to reopen the Sounds and Audio Devices Properties dialog box.
2. Click the Sounds tab; then open the Sound Scheme drop-down list and select a scheme. (Or, to turn off all sounds, choose No Sounds. This removes sound assignments for all system events.)

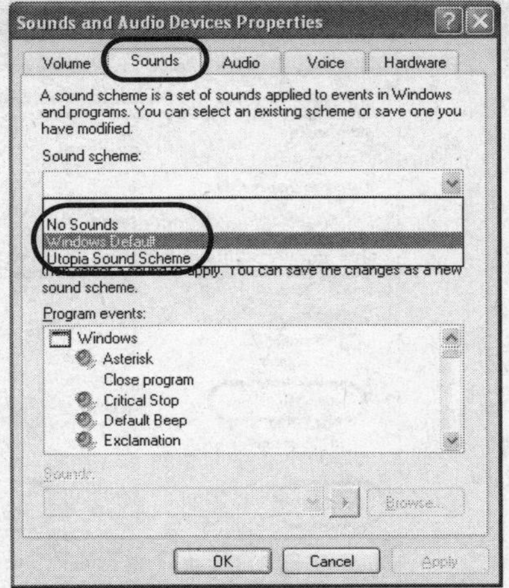

3. If any sound changes have been made since you last selected a scheme, a warning box appears. Click No to decline to save your current settings, or click Yes to save them. (If you choose Yes, enter a name for the new scheme and then click OK.)

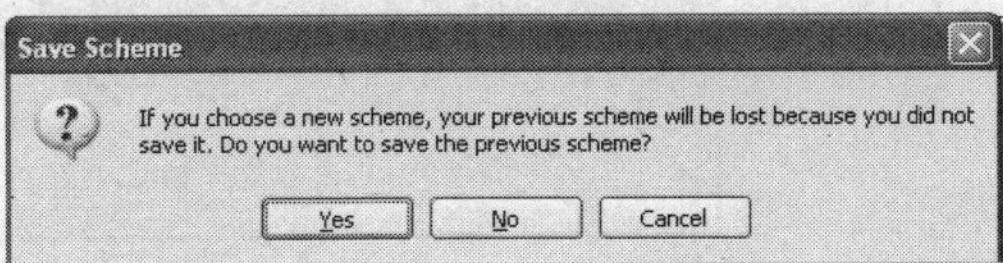

4. To change an individual program event's sound, select the event in the Program Events section and then choose a sound from the Sounds drop-down list. Or, to assign a sound that isn't on that list, click Browse, locate and select the sound file, and click OK.

   To preview a sound, click the Play Sound button. (This button has a right-pointing arrow and is at the bottom left of the screen.

5. Repeat step 4 for each program event you want to change.

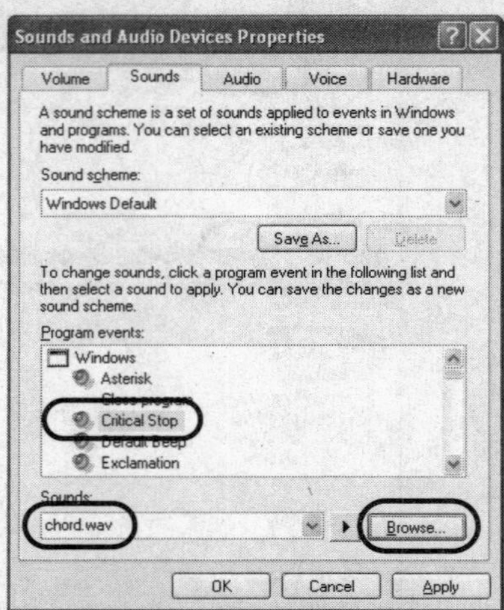

6. (Optional) If you want to save your changes as a new scheme, click Save As. The Save Scheme As dialog box opens.
7. Type a name for the new scheme and then click OK.

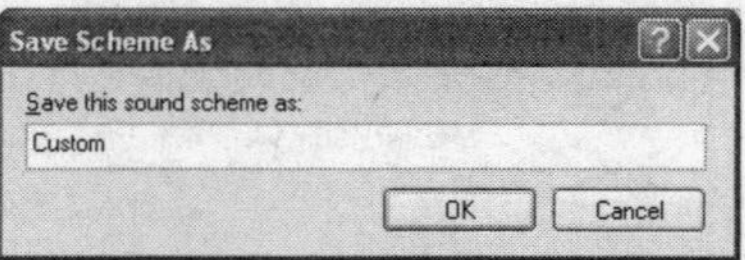

8. Click OK to close the Sounds and Audio Devices Properties box.
9. Close Control Panel.

You can change many more Windows settings than this chapter has explored. You might want to go through Control Panel on your own, icon-by-icon, and see what's available. For example, if you have a game controller, you can calibrate it using the Game Controllers Properties in Control Panel.

What's Next?

The next chapter looks at a task that most of us need to take care every day—printing. It discusses how to install a local printer, how to install a network printer, how to manage the printing process, and how to print from a Windows application.

Chapter 10

Printers and Printing

We have a friend who is bound and determined to have a paperless office. He's on the road a lot and has office space at corporate headquarters and at home. Two things really set off this Type-A guy, however: not being able to get on e-mail and not being able to print. No matter how much we may strive to work electronically, Hewlett-Packard and the rest of the printer manufacturers are thriving.

Installing and using printers becomes easier and easier with each new generation of equipment, which, by the way, continues to decrease in cost and size and increase in output speed and number of features. In addition, each new version of Windows includes tools that make installing a printer easier and faster. In this chapter, we will go step by step through the process of installing both a network and a local printer, and then we'll discuss how to establish the settings that are most appropriate for how and what you print.

Revised and adapted from *Windows 2000 Professional: In Record Time* by Peter Dyson and Pat Coleman

ISBN 0-7821-2450-X 496 pages $29.99

TIP

When you buy or acquire a new printer, put the manual somewhere where you can find it. Each printer or series of printers has idiosyncrasies, such as how you change the cartridge and the type of cartridge to use, and you'll need to follow the manufacturer's advice about these things.

Installing Printer Drivers

If you have upgraded to Windows XP Professional from an earlier Windows version, you may not need to install your printer. The Setup program probably recognized it automatically, as it did your keyboard, mouse, monitor, and so on. To check, choose Start ➢ Printers and Faxes and see if it's listed. In Figure 10.1, for example, two printers appear. If your printer is already installed, you can skip to the "Printing Documents" section later in this chapter.

FIGURE 10.1: Use the Printers and Faxes folder to add, remove, and configure printers.

NOTE

If you don't see Printers and Faxes on the Start menu, look for it in Control Panel under Printers and Other Hardware. If you would like Printers and Faxes to appear on the Start menu in the future, right-click the Taskbar and choose Properties, click the Start Menu tab, and click the Customize button next to Start Menu. Then click the Advanced tab and place a checkmark next to Printers and Faxes on the Start Menu Items list.

If your printer does not already appear in the Printers and Faxes window, you'll need to install a driver for it. You can do this by running the Setup program that came with the printer or by using Windows XP's Add Printer Wizard.

You can install either a local or a network printer in Windows XP. A *local* printer is one that is physically attached to your computer by a cable. A *network* printer is a printer that is attached to another computer on your network. Figure 10.1 shows one of each.

To install either a local printer or a network printer, you use the Printers and Faxes folder. Let's start by looking at how to install a local printer.

Installing a Local Printer Driver

To add a new printer to your system, first be sure that the printer cable is securely connected to both the printer and to your computer. Also, be sure you've followed any setup instructions that came with the printer such as removing packing tape or padding.

Almost all printers come with a Setup disk, and if you have that disk available, it's better to run that Setup utility than to install the printer through the Add Printer Wizard in Windows. That's because extra printing utilities might be included on the Setup disk, and you'll want to take advantage of those utilities.

However, if you do not have a Setup disk for the printer, or if you have a driver disk that does not contain a Setup program you can run, you can do the following:

1. Turn on the printer.
2. From the Printers and Faxes folder, click Add a Printer (in the Printer Tasks area at the left) to start the Add Printer Wizard.
3. At the Welcome screen, click Next to open the Local or Network Printer screen.

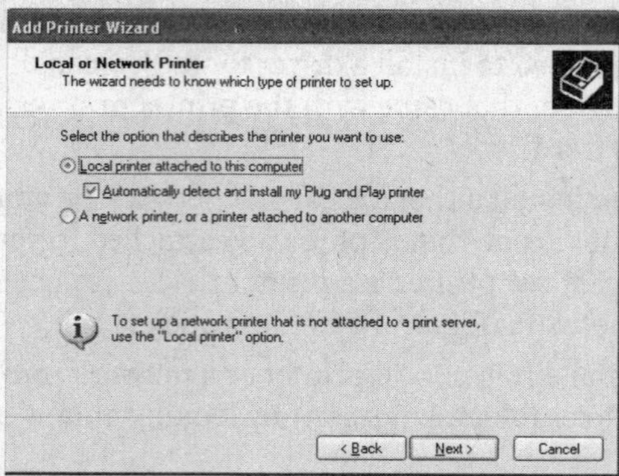

4. Click Local Printer Attached to This Computer.
5. If you want Windows XP Professional to find and install your printer, leave the Automatically Detect and Install My Plug and Play Printer check box checked. Otherwise, click this check box to clear it.
6. Click Next. The Wizard searches for any Plug-and-Play printers, and if it finds one, you see the New Printer Detection screen:

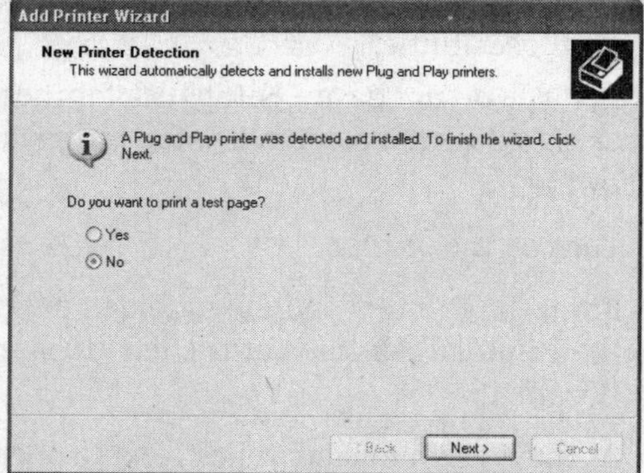

Click Next and skip to step 12. If the Wizard could not find a Plug-and-Play printer that was not already installed, you'll see the following message instead. Click Next and go to step 7.

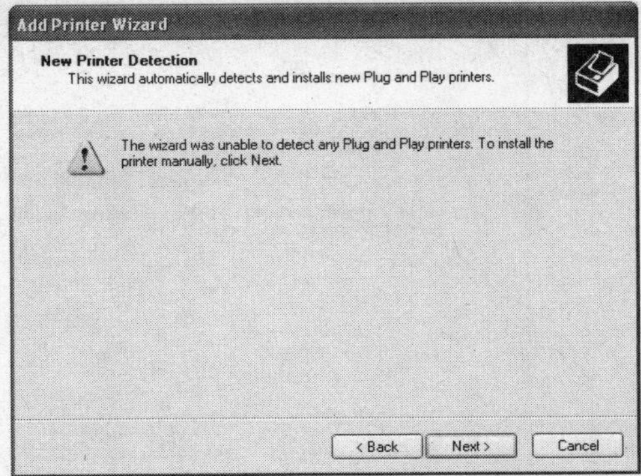

TIP

If you allow Windows to detect the printer automatically, you don't have the opportunity to enter details about the printer such as name and network sharing preferences. You can configure these details for the printer later, however, by right-clicking the printer's icon and choosing Properties.

NOTE

If you want to install more than one driver for the same printer, you must install the second driver manually, as explained in steps 7 through 11. Windows will detect the printer only if a driver is not already installed for it. For example, if you have a PostScript printer and you want to install both a PostScript and a non-PostScript driver for it, Windows will probably detect it initially as a non-PostScript printer. You can re-run the Add Printer Wizard to set up the PostScript driver later. PostScript drivers usually have (PS) after the printer name, and non-PostScript drivers have (MS). You might want two different drivers for the same printer if there are certain features available only in one mode or the other, for example, or if you need to print to a file and have compatibility with someone else's printer.

7. In the Select a Printer Port screen (shown below), select the printer port to use (most likely, LPT1, which is selected by default), and click Next.

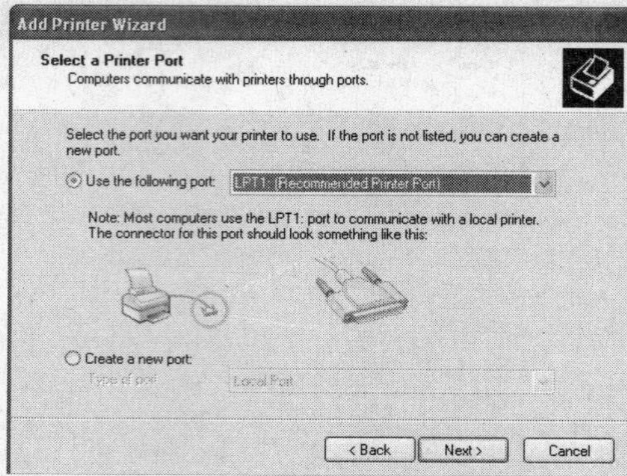

8. Select the manufacturer and model of your printer, and click Next to open the Name Your Printer screen:

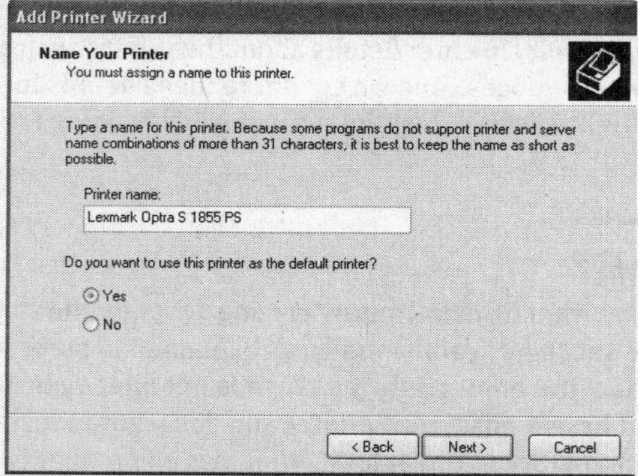

NOTE

If you don't see your printer listed and you have the CD or floppy disk that came with your printer, click Have Disk. If you don't see your printer listed and no disk came with your printer, visit the printer manufacturer's Web site to see whether a driver is available for download.

The driver selected in Figure 10.2 is *digitally signed*. That means it has been certified to work with Windows XP and has not been altered since its creation. If you use an unsigned driver, such as one for a previous version of Windows, it might work perfectly, or it might cause problems. Try to use signed drivers whenever possible.

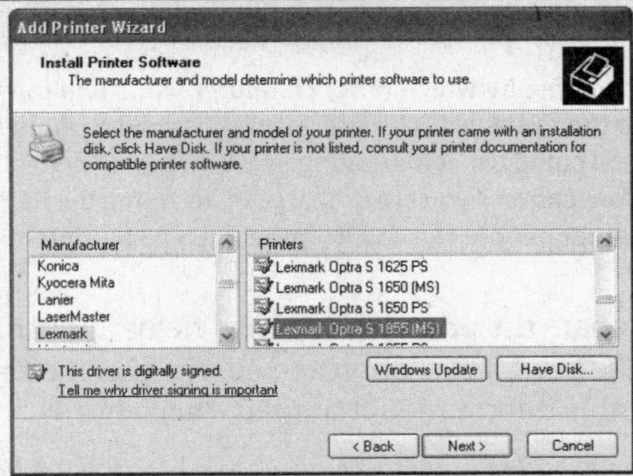

FIGURE 10.2: Use digitally signed drivers when possible.

9. Supply a name for your printer, choose whether you want this printer to be the default printer (the one that Windows and applications automatically print to), and then click Next to open the Printer Sharing screen:

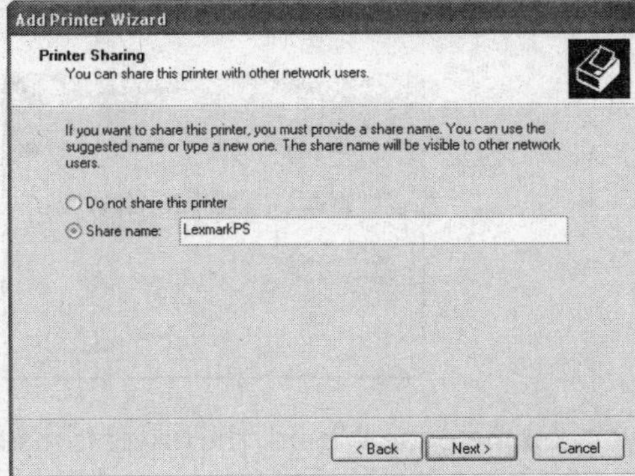

10. If you're on a network and you want others to be able to use your printer, choose Share As, and provide a share name. Otherwise, click Do Not Share This Printer. Then click Next.

NOTE

The Share name is the name by which other computer users will identify the printer. It need not be the same as the printer's actual model or manufacturer name. For example, you could call it Marketing or Production. Try to stick with a consistent naming convention if you are in charge of inventing the names for a group of printers, so other people can easily figure out which printer is which.

11. If you chose to share the printer, additional fields appear for you to specify the printer's location and enter any comments about it. Enter this information if desired; then click Next.
12. If you want to print a test page (always a good idea), click Yes. Otherwise click No to skip the test print. Then click Next.
13. Click Finish.
14. If you chose to print a test page, a message such as the following appears letting you know that it's in progress. If it printed all right, click OK; otherwise click Troubleshoot and see "What to Do If Your Test Page Doesn't Print" section below.

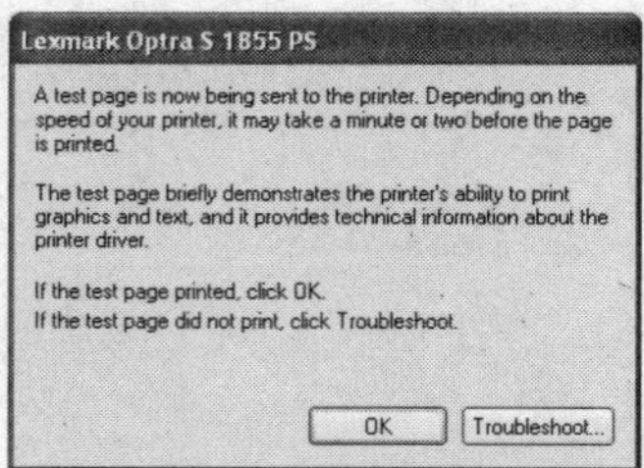

After you complete the Wizard, the driver is installed for the printer, and an icon for it appears in the Printers and Faxes folder.

What to Do If Your Test Page Doesn't Print

Most of the time, installing a printer is a straightforward process, but if your test page didn't print or didn't print correctly, the first thing to do is click Troubleshoot in the dialog box that asks about this. You'll be presented with a list of troubleshooting steps. See Figure 10.3. You can also access this same Print Troubleshooter directly by choosing Start ➢ Help and Support ➢ Printing and Faxing ➢ Fixing a Printing Problem ➢ Printing Troubleshooter.

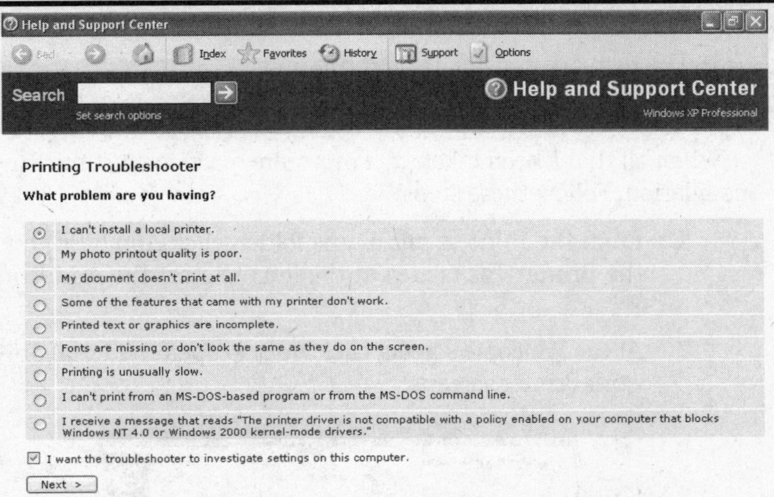

FIGURE 10.3: The Printing Troubleshooter, part of the Help and Support Center, walks you step by step through the troubleshooting process.

If you work through these steps and you still can't print, try downloading an updated driver from the printer manufacturer's Web site. Sometimes Windows XP balks at drivers written for earlier Windows versions. While you're online, you might also make sure your printer is on the Hardware Compatibility List, which you'll find at `www.microsoft.com/hcl`. Printers on this list are guaranteed to be compatible with the versions of Windows listed for them.

Installing a Network Printer Driver

As mentioned earlier, a network printer is a printer that is not physically attached to your own computer. It might be attached to someone else's computer on your network or to a server, or it might be directly connected to the network via its own networking interface.

In order to print to a network printer, you must install its driver on your PC. But before you can do that, the following things need to have already taken place:

- The printer must already be installed as a local printer on some other computer in the network, or the printer must be directly connected to the network with its own network interface.

- The printer must be set up to be shared.
- The network must be up and running.
- The printer must be turned on.

When all that's been taken care of, you're ready to start the driver installation. Follow these steps:

1. From the Printers and Faxes folder, click Add a Printer (in the Printer Tasks area at the left) to start the Add Printer Wizard.
2. At the Welcome screen, click Next to open the Local or Network Printer screen:

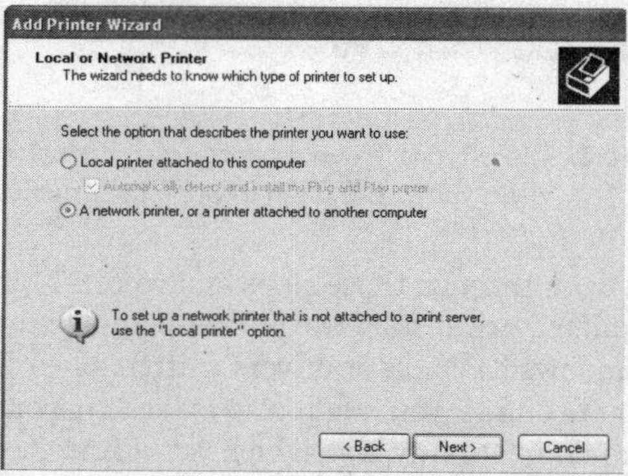

3. Select A Network Printer, Or a Printer Attached to Another Computer, and click Next to open the Specify a Printer screen:

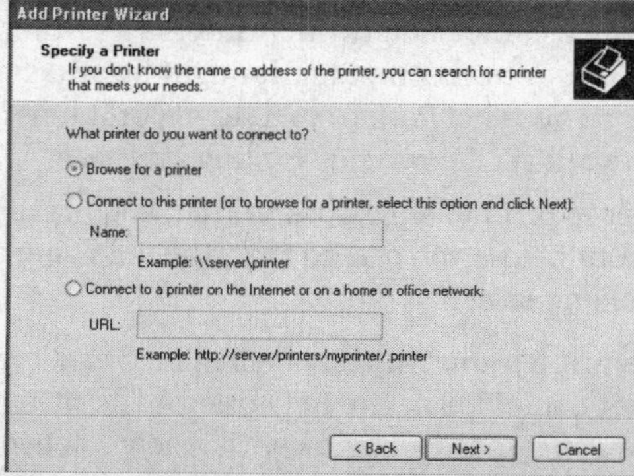

4. If you know the exact path and name for the printer, click Connect To This Printer and then type the path and name. Then click Next and skip to step 7.
5. If you don't know the exact name, leave Browse for a Printer marked and click Next to open the Browse for a Printer screen:

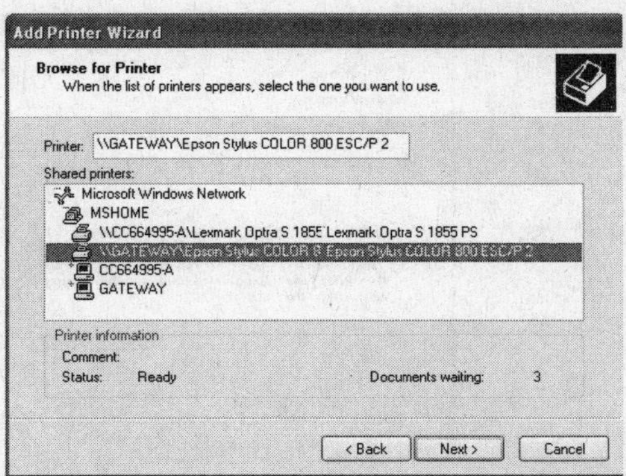

6. Select the printer you want to install. Click a plus sign next to a computer or workgroup name to expand it if needed to locate the printer you want. Then click Next.
7. Click Yes or No to choose whether this printer should be your default printer. Then click Next.

TIP

You can set a different printer as the default printer at any time by right-clicking its icon in the Printers and Faxes folder and choosing Set As Default Printer.

8. Click Finish.

SHARING A PRINTER

Before you can install and use a network printer, that printer must be shared. That means if you want to share your printer with others, you must set it up to be shared. You saw in the "Installing a Local Printer Driver" section earlier in the chapter how to share the printer while you are installing it, but you can also change its sharing settings at any time later.

To share a printer or to change its sharing settings, follow these steps:

1. In the Printers and Faxes folder, right-click the printer and choose Sharing from the shortcut menu to open the Properties dialog box for that printer at the Sharing tab:

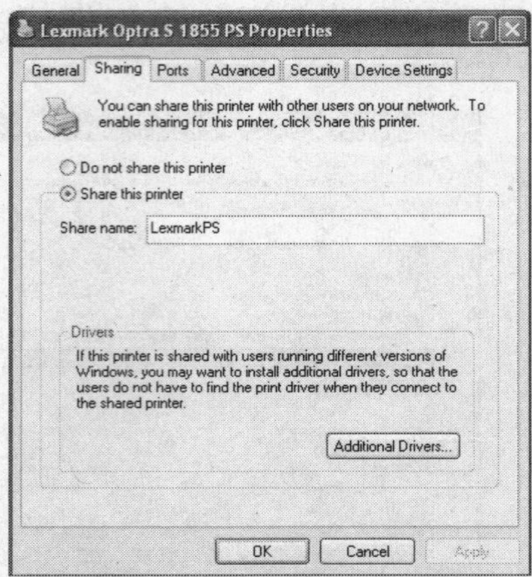

NOTE

To display the Security tab if you are not on a domain, in Control Panel or any Explorer-like window, choose Tools ➢ Folder Options to open the Folder Options dialog box. Click the View tab, and in the Advanced Settings list, clear the check mark from the Use Simple File Sharing (Recommended) item. We'll discuss the options on the Security tab later in this chapter.

2. Click the Share This Printer option button.
3. Accept the Share Name that is generated, or enter a new one.
4. Click the General tab if you want to enter or change a comment about this printer or its location.

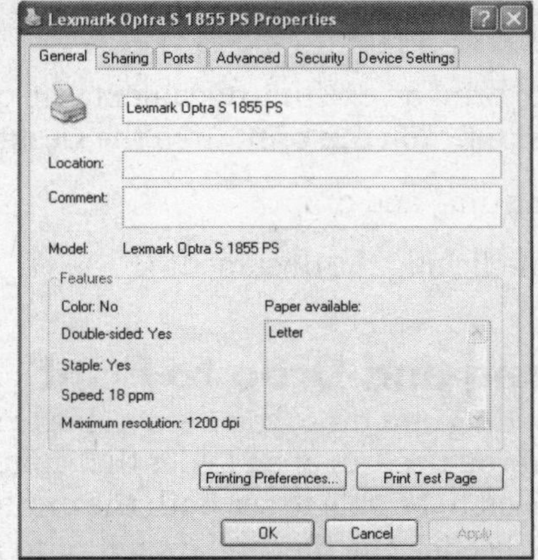

5. Click OK.

The icon of this printer in the Printers folder will now have a hand under it to indicate that it is shared.

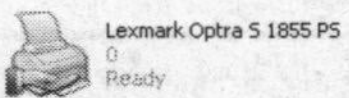

PRINTING DOCUMENTS

After you install a printer driver, either local or network, you're ready to print, and you can do so either from the desktop or from an application.

Regardless of where you print from, Windows XP is actually handling the process. Its print spooler program accepts the document and holds it on disk or in memory until the printer is free, and then sends it to the printer for processing.

TIP

To bypass the print spooler in Windows and send documents directly to the printer, right-click the printer and choose Properties to open the Properties dialog box for that printer. Click the Advanced tab, and select the Print Directly to the Printer option button. Doing so can slow Windows performance during printing, however, so you would not want to do this except when troubleshooting problems with the print spooler.

Printing from the Desktop

If you want to print an existing document, the quickest way is to print from the Desktop. You can print from the Desktop in a couple of ways:

- By using drag-and-drop
- By right-clicking the document

Using Drag-and-Drop to Print

To print with drag-and-drop, you need a shortcut to your printer on the Desktop, and you need an open folder that contains the file. In other words, you need to be able to see both the printer icon and the filename or icon. Simply click the file, and drag it onto the printer icon. Windows XP Professional opens the file in the program in which the document was created or in the program you've associated with the file by using the Open With command, and then it prints the file. For example, in Figure 10.4, a Word document from the open folder is poised to be dragged to the printer shortcut on the desktop.

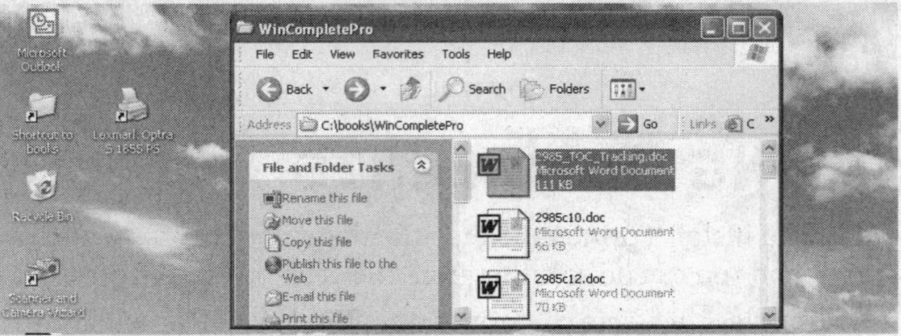

FIGURE 10.4: Printing with drag-and-drop

When you print in this manner, you use the default print settings, which we'll look at in the upcoming "Printing from an Application" section. The entire file is printed, only one copy is printed, the printed output is in portrait orientation (vertical), and the default paper tray is used. You have no opportunity to modify these settings with this method.

Right-Clicking to Print

To print using the right-click method in Windows, open a folder that contains the file you want to print, right-click the file, and select Print from the shortcut menu. In a flash, the program associated with the file opens, and the document prints. Just as when you drag-and-drop to print, the default settings are used.

Printing from an Application

If you want more control over how your document is printed, such as the orientation of the paper, the number of copies, and so on, you'll want to print from the application. You can usually print in a couple of ways in an application:

- By clicking the Print button on the toolbar (the graphic that looks like a printer)
- By choosing File ➢ Print

If you click the Print button, usually the document is immediately spooled to the printer, and you have no opportunity to specify the number of copies, exactly what you want to print, and so on.

Choosing File ➢ Print opens the Print dialog box. It's different in every program, but all have certain elements in common. Figure 10.5 shows the Print dialog box from Microsoft Word 2002. You can use the program's Print dialog box to specify the options that control what is printed and how.

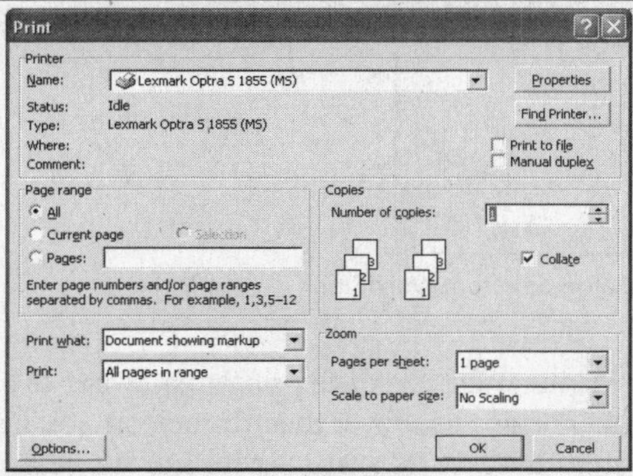

FIGURE 10.5: The Print dialog box from Word 2002.

NOTE

The steps are the same whether you are printing on a local printer or a network printer.

Let's walk through the steps to print a document from WordPad, one of the applications that comes with Windows XP Professional. Follow these steps:

1. Choose Start ➢ All Programs ➢ Accessories ➢ WordPad.
2. Open an existing document, or create a new one.
3. Choose File ➢ Save As, and save the document if it is new (it's usually prudent to save before you print).
4. Choose File ➢ Print to open the Print dialog box, as shown in Figure 10.6. Notice how it differs from the Print dialog box from Word in Figure 10.5.

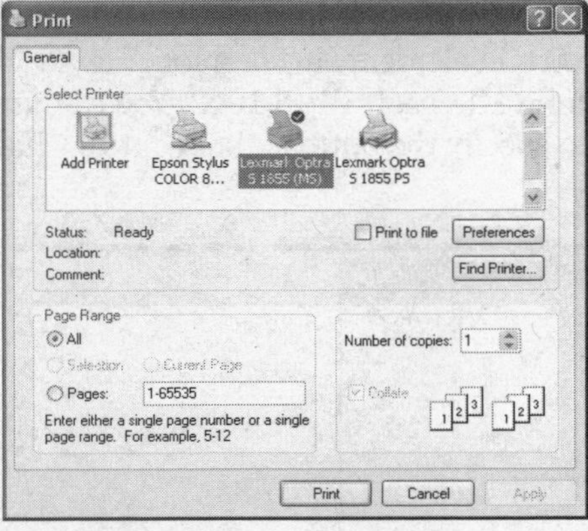

FIGURE 10.6: The Print dialog box from WordPad.

5. In the Select Printer area, click the printer you want to use. If you place the mouse cursor over the printer icon, you'll see a ScreenTip that displays its status–whether it's ready to print or if documents are waiting in the print queue.

NOTE

Look back to Figure 10.6 for a moment; in that version of the Print dialog box, you would select the printer from the Name drop-down list instead.

6. In the Page Range area, choose whether to print the entire file, only a selection, the current page, or selected pages. To print a selection, you need to select the desired part of the document first and then open the Print dialog box.
7. In the Number of Copies box, select the copies to print. When you print more than one copy, they are collated by default. If, for some reason, you don't want them collated, clear the Collate check box.
8. Click the Preferences button to open the Printing Preferences dialog box for the chosen printer:

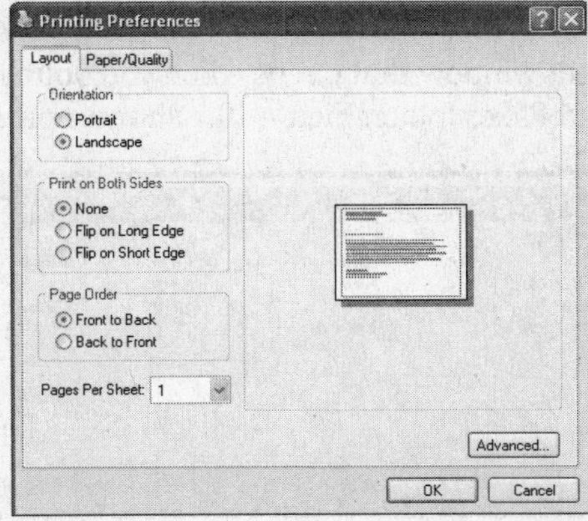

9. If you want the document to print in Landscape mode (horizontally), click Landscape. (You will need to change this setting back to Portrait the next time you print if you don't want Landscape mode permanently.)
10. If you want to select a certain paper tray or feeder, click the Paper/Quality tab, and choose a different one from the Paper Source drop-down list.
11. Click OK to close the Printing Preferences box.
12. Click Print.

The preceding steps showed printing from WordPad, but if you print from some other program you might have additional printing options as well. For example, if you'll look back to Figure 10.5 again, you'll notice an Options button in the bottom left corner of the Print dialog box. This allows you to adjust program-specific settings for Word, such as printing field codes. Most users will not need to set any of the options found here.

Managing the Printing Process

If you've ever meant to print a short paragraph from a file but forgot to click the Selection option and ended up printing an 80-page document instead, you know how important it is to be able to stop the printing process. And if you've ever sent something to the printer and then waited and waited in vain for the document to print, you know you need a way to find out what's going on.

To halt printing, to check the status of a document you've sent to the printer, or to clear all documents out of the print queue, you use the print management window that opens when you double-click the printer in the Printers and Faxes folder. Figure 10.7 shows a print management window.

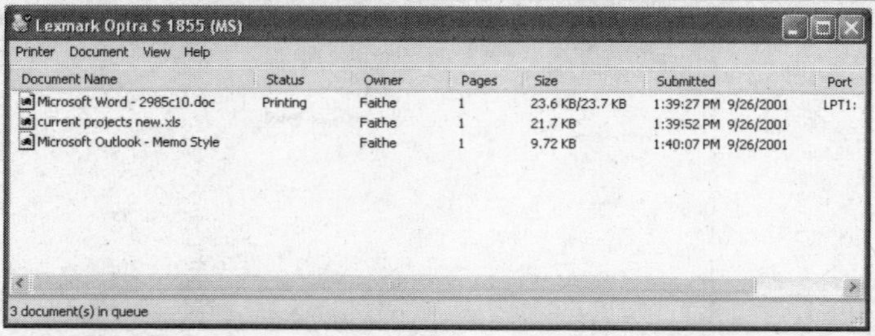

FIGURE 10.7: Status information is displayed in a print management window.

The columns in this window are:

Document Name The name of the document.

Status Whether the document is printing, paused, or being deleted.

Owner The name of the person who sent the document to the printer.

Pages The number of pages in the print job.

Size The size of the print job in kilobytes.

Submitted The date and time the document was sent to the printer.

Port The printer port being used.

Once you know what's happening or about to happen in the print queue, you can take charge of it:

- To cancel the printing of a document, right-click the document in the print queue and choose Cancel from the shortcut menu, or click the document and press the Delete key.
- To cancel the printing of all documents in the print queue, choose Printer ➢ Cancel All Documents.
- To temporarily halt the printing of a single document, right-click the document, and choose Pause. You can use Pause to make a certain document wait while another one goes ahead of it in the queue.
- To resume the printing of a document you have paused, right-click the document, and choose Resume.

NOTE

When you choose Pause or Cancel, the printing probably won't stop right away. Whatever has already been spooled to the printer's buffer must print before the printing stops.

Managing Printer Drivers

Each printer driver in the Printers and Faxes folder represents a "printer" to which you can print. As you've already learned earlier in the chapter, there can be more than one driver per physical printer. You can have different driver icons for the same printer, each with its own settings.

Setting the Default Printer

To set a different printer as the default, right-click the printer, and choose Set As Default Printer from the shortcut menu. To create a shortcut to this printer on the Desktop, right-click the printer icon, and choose Create Shortcut from the shortcut menu.

Renaming and Deleting Print Drivers

Printer icons can also be renamed like other files; right-click one and choose Rename and then type a new name. This does not affect the name by which the printer is shared on the network, if it is shared; you must change that through the printer's Properties dialog box. (Right-click the icon, choose Properties to open the Properties dialog box, and then change the name on the Sharing tab.)

If you decide you don't want a certain printer driver anymore, you can delete it just as you delete any other file from a file management window. Select it and press the Delete key, or right-click it and choose Delete. Depending on the printer, you might see a message asking whether you want to delete some leftover files that were used only for this printer; click Yes if you don't plan to reinstall this printer later, or click No if you do.

Customizing the Printer's Properties

All objects in Windows XP have *properties* (settings) that affect how the object looks and behaves. A print driver's properties control how the printer works. Different settings are available for different types of printers, but most printers enable you to select the following:

- The paper source
- The print quality
- Whether the printer will be shared
- When the printer will be available
- Whether documents will be spooled to the printer or printed directly

To open a printer's Properties box, right-click its icon and choose Properties. Figure 10.8 shows the properties for a PostScript-type laser printer; Figure 10.9 shows the properties for a color inkjet printer.

NOTE

The available settings also depend on whether you are looking at the properties for a local printer or a network printer. Some settings can be modified only by a user working at the PC to which the printer is directly connected and/or only if that user has the appropriate network permission.

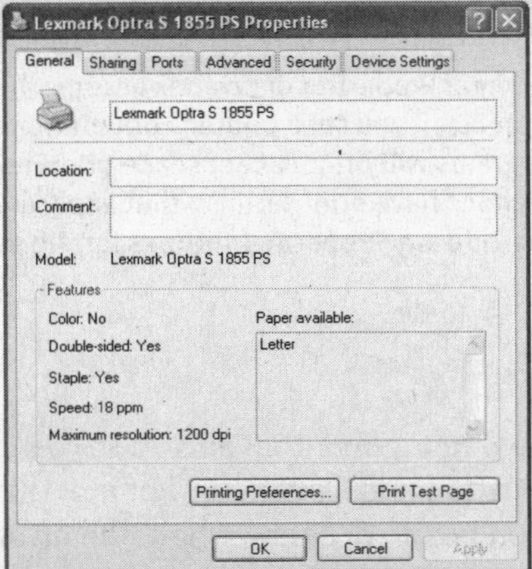

FIGURE 10.8: The Properties dialog box for a laser printer

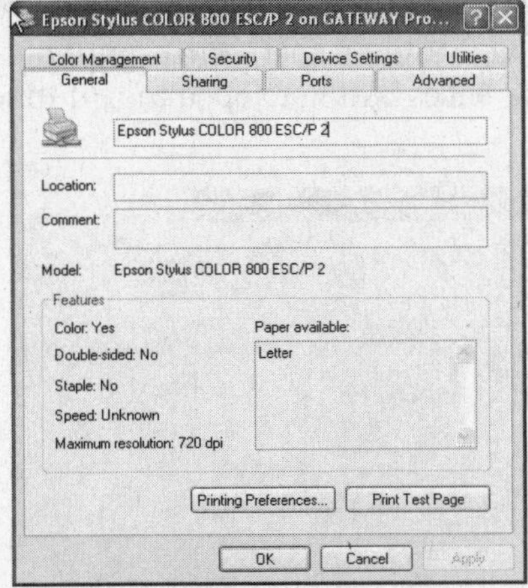

FIGURE 10.9: The Properties dialog box for an inkjet printer. Notice its tabs are different from those in Figure 10.8.

In this section, we'll look at each of the tabs in the printer Properties dialog box and describe some of their typical settings.

NOTE

The settings you specify in the printer Properties dialog box become the default settings for that printer. For example, if you set a printer's orientation to Landscape, all documents in all programs will print in Landscape orientation until you change it again. Some programs have print settings that apply only to the individual document; these override any Properties settings for the printer.

The General Tab

On the General tab, which is shown in Figures 10.8 and 10.9, you can change only a couple of fields: Location and Comment. For a network printer, you might use the Location box to describe where the printer is situated (for example, third-floor printer room), and you can use the Comments box to say something pertinent about the printer (for instance, "Legal-size paper only").

You can print a test page from the General tab by clicking Print Test Page.

To specify layout (portrait or landscape), paper source, print quality, and color, click the Printing Preferences button to open the Printing Preferences dialog box.

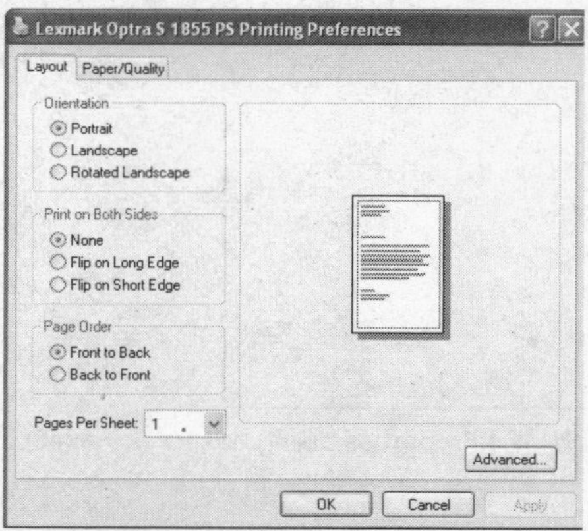

In this dialog box, click the Advanced button to open the Advanced Options dialog box, which contains a description of a number of printer features and in which you can also change the paper size.

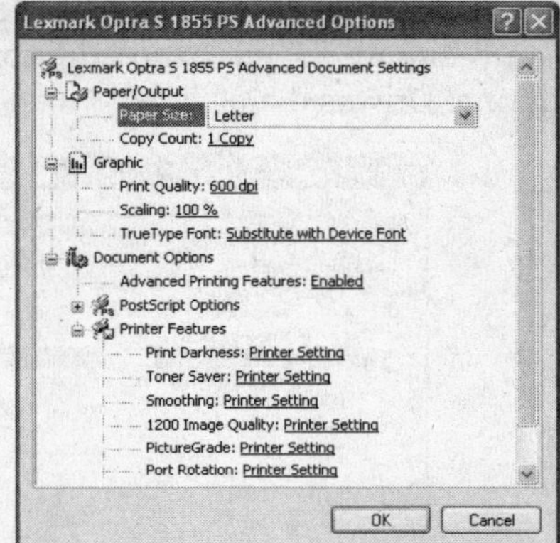

The Sharing Tab

If you want to share your printer with other users on your network, click the Sharing tab, which is shown in Figure 10.10. As mentioned earlier in the "Installing a Network Printer" section, you can click the Share This Printer option button, and then enter a name for the printer.

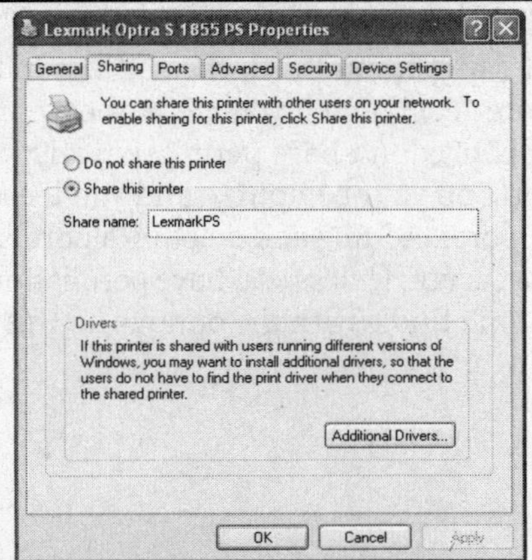

FIGURE 10.10: The Sharing tab

If you will be sharing this printer with people running versions of Windows other than Windows XP, click the Additional Drivers button to open the Additional Drivers dialog box:

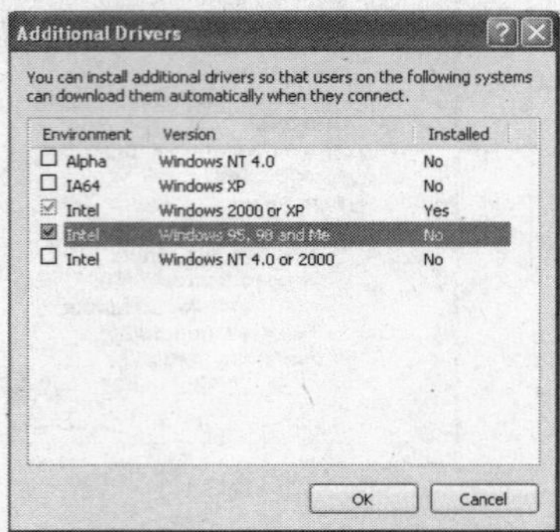

You'll see a list of systems. Click a system so that users on that system can automatically download the driver when they connect to your printer. (You will be prompted for your Windows XP Professional CD-ROM, and perhaps the printer setup disk for the printer as well.)

The Ports Tab

You normally don't need to be messing around with the settings in the Ports tab, which is shown in Figure 10.11, and if you are on a corporate network, you shouldn't. (You probably don't have permission anyway.) On this tab, you'll see a list of ports on your computer, and you'll see buttons to add, delete, and configure ports. Adding and deleting a port is relatively easy; retrieving a deleted port is not. Unless you have permission *and* know exactly what you're doing, don't fiddle with the options on this page.

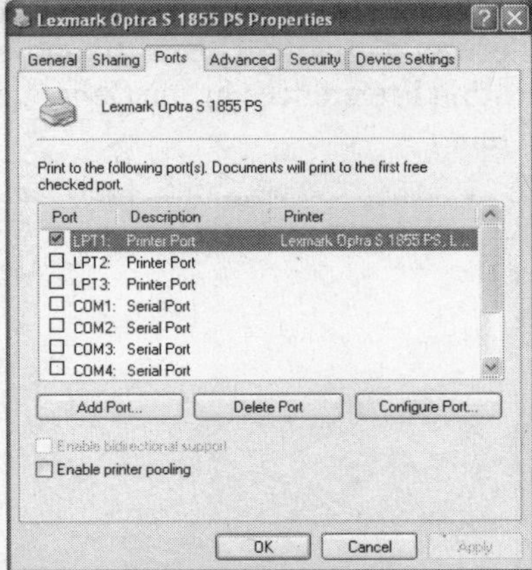

FIGURE 10.11: The Ports tab

The Advanced Tab

You can use the Advanced tab to set a number of options such as the following:

- When the printer is available for use. This is useful if you share the printer and don't want others to tie it up during certain hours.
- The default priority of the printing document (1 is the lowest; 99 is the highest). It's a good idea to leave this set to 1; you can then set a higher priority for certain documents to allow them priority status in the queue.
- The printer driver associated with the printer
- Whether documents will be spooled or sent directly to the printer
- To check for mismatched documents (a document whose setup doesn't match the printer setup)
- To store printed documents so that they can be printed from the print queue rather than being spooled again
- Whether to use advanced printing features. This is enabled by default. This means that certain features such as page order and pages per sheet are available, depending on your printer.

Clicking Printer Defaults displays the dialog box in which you can specify the layout, paper size, and printing quality. This is the same dialog box you see when you click Printing Preferences in the General tab. Figure 10.12 shows the Advanced tab.

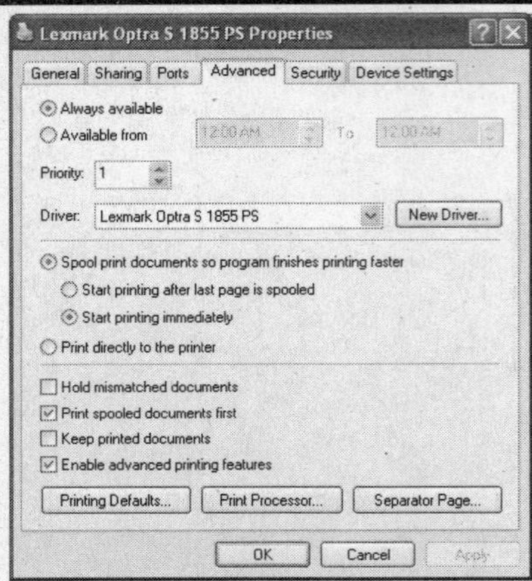

FIGURE 10.12: The Advanced tab

One other handy option on the Advanced tab is the Separator Page button. A separator page identifies the beginning of a document. When several print jobs are being sent to a network printer, a separator page makes it easy for users to locate their particular documents. To specify a separator page, follow these steps:

1. Click Separator Page to open the Separator Page dialog box:

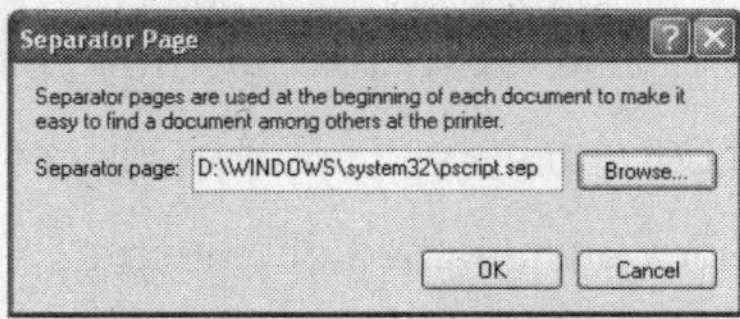

2. In the Separator Page box, enter a filename for the page you want to use, or click Browse to locate one. You'll find some already-existing separator pages in the System 32 folder. They have a .sep extension.
3. Click OK.

The Security Tab

On the Security tab, shown in Figure 10.13, you can assign printer permissions to individuals and groups. This can be handy if you want certain people to be able to take full control over the printer but other people only to be able to print.

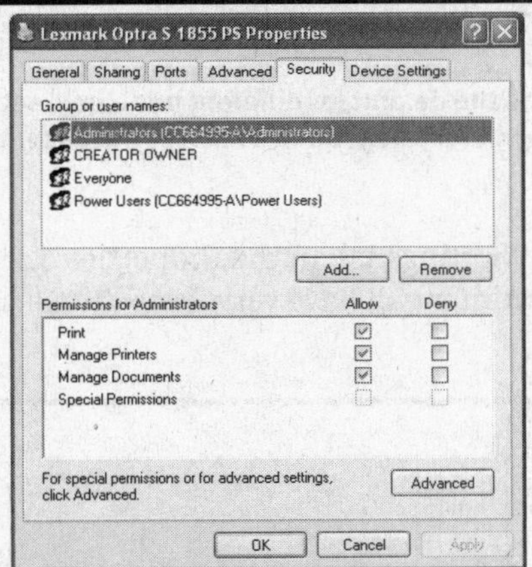

FIGURE 10.13: The Security tab

TIP

As mentioned earlier, unless you are connected to a network domain, the Security tab does not appear by default. However, it can be useful for users on all types of networks, not just domains. To make it appear, open any file management window and choose Tools ➢ Folder Options to open the Folder Options dialog box. Click the View tab, and in the Advanced Settings list, clear the check mark from the Use Simple File Sharing (Recommended) item. The next time you open a printer's Properties, the Security tab will appear.

To assign permissions to an existing group, click the group name in the Group or User Names section and then mark or clear check boxes in the Permissions For section.

You can also add individuals or groups with the Add button, or delete them with the Delete button. (You'll find more information on creating users and groups and assigning permissions in Chapter 25.)

The Device Settings Tab

Most printers have a Device Settings tab, but some have more options than others. The most significant setting here is the paper tray; you can specify which tray to pull from by default if the printer contains more than one.

TIP

If you want a different tray to be the default for different print jobs, set up two instances of the printer driver with different names and set the paper tray differently for each one.

Figure 10.14 shows the Device Settings tab in the Properties dialog box for a laser printer; an inkjet printer will have very few settings, if the tab appears at all.

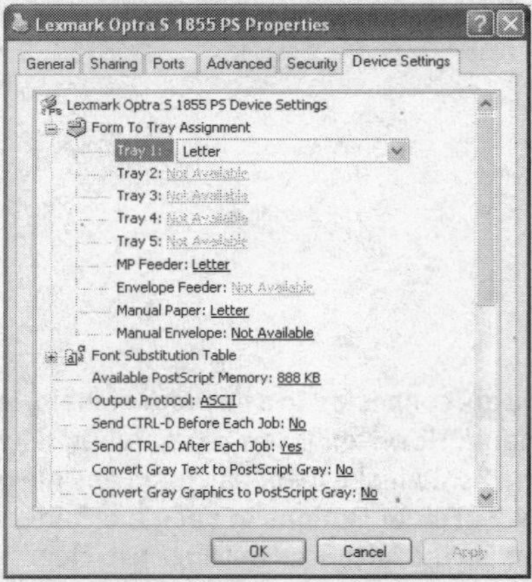

FIGURE 10.14: The Device Settings tab for a laser printer

The Color Management Tab

For a color printer, you'll see the Color Management tab. When you install a new scanner, printer, or monitor, Windows XP Professional automatically installs a color profile that is used when colors are scanned, printed, or displayed. For most desktop systems, this profile is sufficient and is selected by default in the Color Management tab. Graphic artists and those doing complicated color desktop publishing, however, may want to specify a color profile in order to better control the color quality on the printer, scanner, or monitor. To add a color profile, click the Add button, and then select a profile from the list in the Add Profile Association dialog box.

Other Tabs

Depending on the printer, you might have a Utilities or Services tab. Such a tab typically contains links or buttons that run printer utilities such as head cleaning for an inkjet printer. There might also be a Graphics tab on which you can adjust the fineness of the graphic imaging and the method used for converting solid-color inks to shades (*dithering*).

Understanding Fonts

Before we complete our discussion of printers and printing, we need to take a quick look at fonts. In Windows XP Professional, a font is the name of a typeface, and a font can have size, which is usually described in points (one point equals 1/72 of an inch), and a style, such as bold or italic. Most fonts are TrueType or OpenType fonts. These fonts are designed specifically to work with Windows (and Macintosh) systems and have many advantages. They're identified by a TT or an O symbol, respectively.

TIP

For end-user purposes, there is little difference between TrueType and OpenType. OpenType is an improved and updated version of TrueType.

Some fonts are not TrueType fonts, however, and they are identified with a capital A symbol. Such fonts are usually not scalable, so you should avoid using them when it is practical to do so.

To see the fonts installed on your system, choose Start ➢ Control Panel ➢ Appearance and Themes. In the See Also bar, click the ➢ Fonts link. Figure 10.15 shows the Fonts folder that opens.

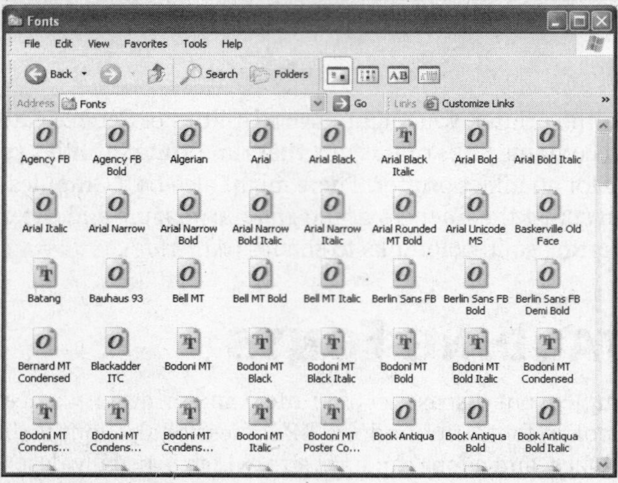

FIGURE 10.15: The Fonts folder

To see what an individual font looks like at several sizes, double-click a font. Figure 10.16 shows representative sizes of the Comic Sans MS font and displays some information about this font. To see printed output of a particular font, simply click the Print button, which is shown in Figure 10.16.

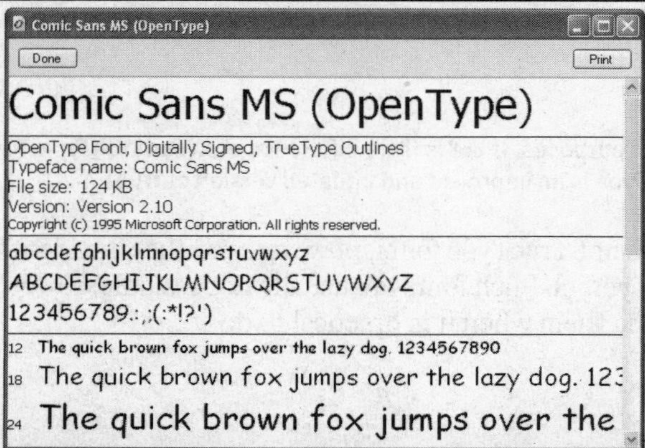

FIGURE 10.16: A sample of what's available in the Comic Sans MS font

TIP

If you are overwhelmed by the number and type of fonts shown in the Fonts folder, choose View ➢ Hide Variations (Bold, Italic, etc.).

With hundreds of fonts on a typical system, it's sometimes difficult to know what font to choose for a task. One way to analyze the fonts on your system is to sort them by similarity. You can then see at a glance whether you have several virtually identical fonts and then delete some of them.

To see a list of fonts that are similar to a certain font, follow these steps:

1. In the Fonts folder, choose View ➢ List Fonts by Similarity.
2. In the List Fonts by Similarity To drop-down list, select a font.

You'll see a list of font names, in order from the most similar to the least similar.

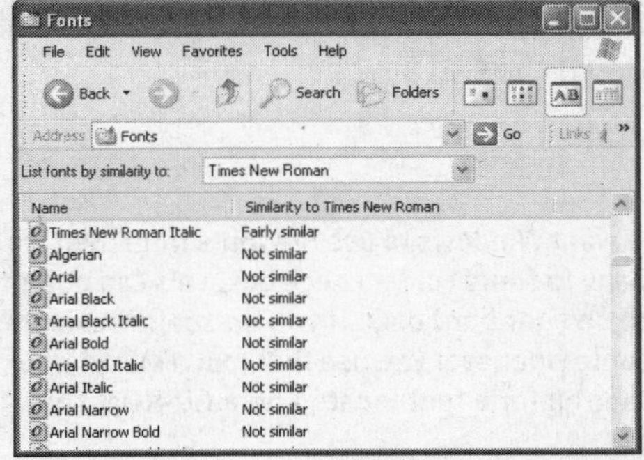

Although Windows XP Professional comes with a great many fonts installed, you may well want to install other fonts for particular purposes. Some programs, such as Office XP, come with extra fonts and install them automatically during setup. You might also acquire fonts from other sources that require manual installation.

Follow these steps to manually install a font:

1. In the Fonts folder, choose File ➢ Install New Font to open the Add Fonts dialog box:

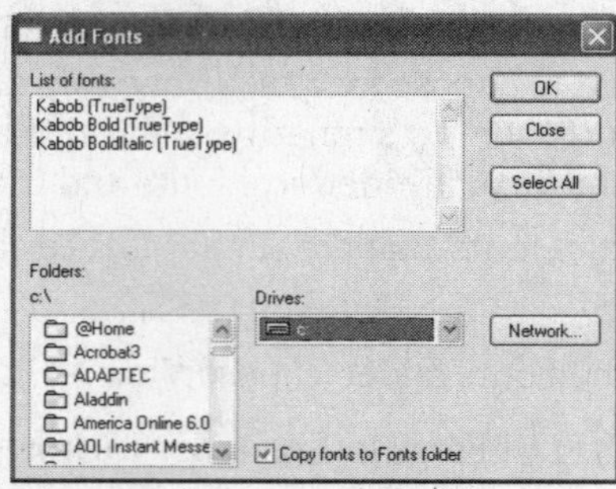

2. Select the drive and the folder containing the font.
3. Select the font(s) to install. To choose more than one, hold down the Ctrl key.

TIP

If you want Windows to use the fonts from their current location instead, clear the Copy to Fonts Folder check box. This can potentially save a little bit of disk space on your hard disk. If you do so, however, the current location must be available whenever you use that font. For example, you would not want to use this option for a font located on a CD-ROM that you were borrowing from a friend.

4. Click OK.

By default, fonts are installed into the \Windows\Fonts folder on the same drive as Windows itself.

WHAT'S NEXT?

The ability to share data between applications is not new with Windows XP Professional, but it is an important feature of the operating system. In the next chapter, Peter Dyson and Pat Coleman will explain how to share data and discuss what's happening under the Windows hood that makes such a feature possible.

Chapter 11

Sharing Information between Applications

Unless you are brand-new to the Windows environment, you have probably used the Cut, Copy, and Paste commands, and you may have even embedded and linked objects—all without knowing you were using object linking and embedding (OLE). In this chapter, we'll quickly go over the steps for these tasks and take a look at the underlying structure that makes OLE work.

You will probably find that a couple of the topics in this chapter are new to you if you have previously used a version of Windows 9*x*. In Windows XP Professional, the ClipBook Viewer has replaced the Clipboard Viewer, and it includes some features that were not previously available in Clipboard Viewer. (The ClipBook Viewer, however, has been around in previous versions of NT and Windows 2000 Professional.)

Adapted and revised from *Windows 2000 Professional: In Record Time* by Peter Dyson and Pat Coleman

ISBN 0-7821-2450-X   496 pages $29.99

The idea of sharing information has always been central to the development of the Windows family of operating systems, and, of course, it is the heart and soul of the Internet. In this skill, we'll start with the basics and then give you some information about OLE.

USING THE CLIPBOARD

The Clipboard is an area in memory that serves as the temporary storehouse for an item that you cut or copy. When you paste an item, a copy stays on the Clipboard until you cut or copy another item, close Windows XP Professional, or intentionally clear the Clipboard. Thus, you can paste the same item multiple times.

How much you can store on the Clipboard depends on the available memory. You don't normally need to be concerned about this unless you are cutting and pasting very large files such as graphics, video, and sound.

NOTE

When you cut an item, you actually remove it from the source document and place it in the destination document. When you copy an item, it remains in the source document, and a duplicate is placed in the destination document.

Windows XP Professional includes the ClipBook Viewer, a utility that you can use to save and share items that you place on the Clipboard. After we look at the various ways you can use the Clipboard in Windows applications, we'll take a look at the ClipBook Viewer.

Copying, Cutting, and Pasting in Windows Applications

You can cut, copy, and paste as follows:

- Within a document
- Between documents in the same application
- Between documents in different applications
- Between applications in different versions of Windows

- Between applications running on other computers on a local network
- Between a site on the Web and an application on your local drive or a network drive

Regardless of the source and destination, the process is the same. Here are the steps:

1. Open the source document, and select what you want to cut or copy.
2. Choose Edit ➢ Cut (or press Ctrl+X) or Edit ➢ Copy (or press Ctrl+C). The item is now stored on the Clipboard.
3. Open the destination document, and place the insertion point where you want the item.
4. Choose Edit ➢ Paste (or press Ctrl+V).

You choose Edit ➢ Paste Special if you want to link or embed an object within a document, and we'll look at that in the "Understanding OLE" section, later in this chapter.

Figure11.1 show a selection that's being copied from the Sybex Web site, and Figure 11.2 shows that selection copied into WordPad.

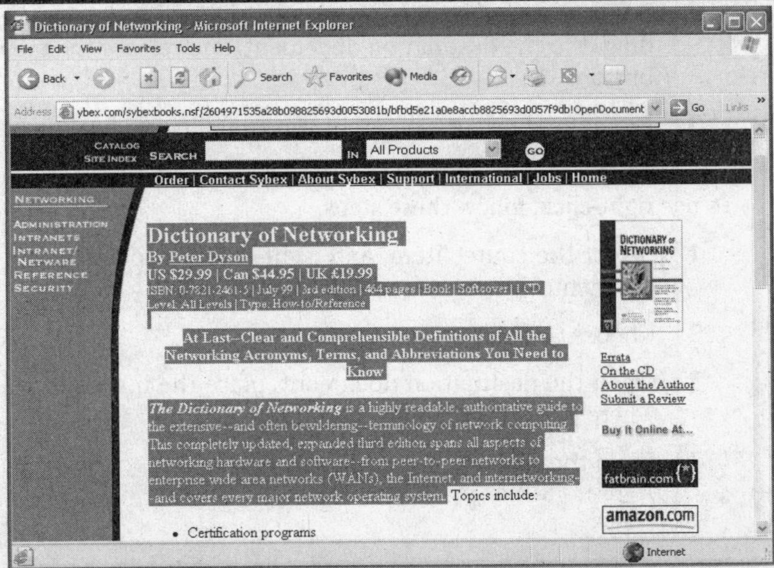

FIGURE 11.1: Copying a selection from a Web page

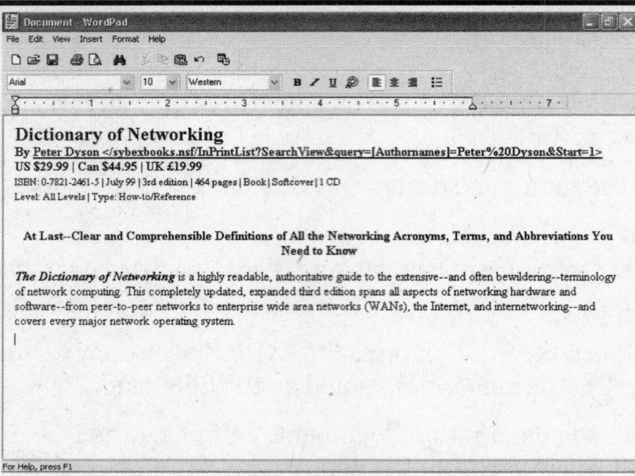

FIGURE11.2: Pasting the selection into WordPad

You can also use drag-and-drop to cut, copy, and paste, and you can right-click a selection to use the shortcut menu for these tasks. To use drag-and-drop, follow these steps:

1. Open both the source document and the destination document so that both are visible on the Desktop.
2. Select what you want to cut or copy, right-click the selection, drag it to the destination document, and release the mouse button.
3. From the shortcut menu that appears, choose Move Here, or choose Copy Here.

To use right-click, follow these steps:

1. Select the source item, and right-click to open the shortcut menu.
2. Choose Cut or Copy.
3. Open the destination document, place the insertion point where you want the item, and right-click.
4. From the shortcut menu, choose Paste.

NOTE

See the section "Working with the ClipBook Viewer," later in this chapter, for information on how to clear the Clipboard.

Capturing Screens with the Clipboard

If you ever create documentation, training materials, or promotional materials about software, you may find it quite handy to capture screens with the Clipboard. If you do a lot of this, you'll want to use a professional program such as Collage or FullShot, especially if you need to edit the image. You can, however, capture a full screen or a window and save it using the Clipboard. Follow these steps:

1. Open the window or screen that you want to capture.
2. Press Alt+Print Screen to capture the entire screen, or press Ctrl+Alt+Print Screen to capture only the open window.
3. To save the image as a file, choose Start ➢ Programs ➢ Accessories ➢ Paint.
4. In Paint, press Ctrl+V to open the image.
5. Choose File ➢ Save As to open the Save As dialog box.
6. Select a folder in which to save the file, enter a name for the file in the File Name box, and choose the type in which you want to save it from the drop-down Save As Type box.
7. Click Save.

The file is now saved as a separate document, and you can insert it in your document. For example, to insert the screen capture into a Microsoft Word document, follow these steps:

1. Open the destination document in Word.
2. Choose Insert ➢ Picture ➢ From File to open the Insert Picture dialog box.
3. Select the file, and click Insert.

You can now save the image as part of the destination document. If you do so, the image will reside both in that document and as a separate file in the folder where you originally saved it.

You can also copy the image from the Clipboard directly into a destination document if you want. In that case, the image is not saved as a separate file but as part of the document in which you place it.

Figure 11.3 shows a screen capture inserted in a Word document.

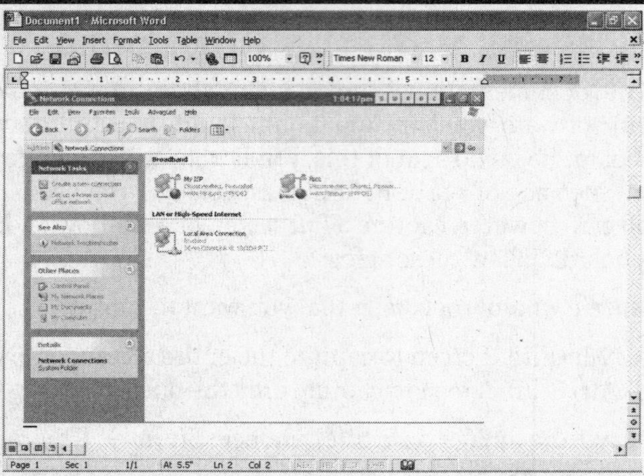

FIGURE 11.3: Even if you don't have a professional program, you can easily capture screens using the Clipboard.

WORKING WITH THE CLIPBOOK VIEWER

As we mentioned in the introduction to this chapter, the Clipboard Viewer in previous versions of Windows *9x* has been replaced with the ClipBook Viewer. Using the ClipBook Viewer provides several advantages over the Clipboard Viewer:

- You can save what is on the Clipboard as a page and reuse it at a later time. In fact, you can save as many as 127 pages.
- You can give a page a descriptive name of as many as 47 characters.
- You can share pages with others on your network.

Starting the ClipBook Viewer

To start the ClipBook Viewer, follow these steps:

1. Choose Start ➢ Run to open the Run dialog box.
2. In the Open box, type **`clipbrd`**, and click OK.

You'll see the screen shown in Figure 11.4.

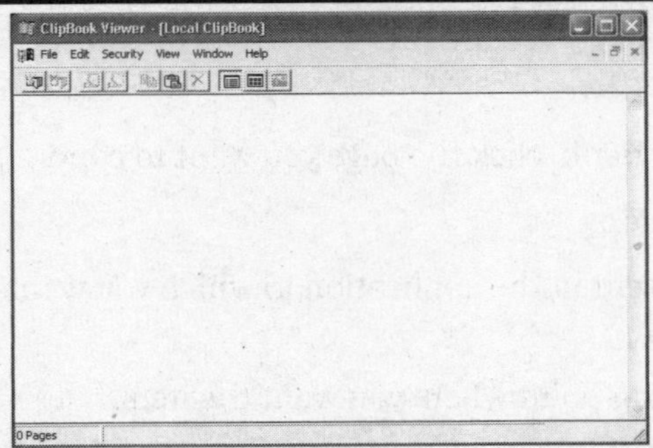

FIGURE 11.4: The ClipBook Viewer

Pasting an Item into the ClipBook

To use the ClipBook, you paste items from the Clipboard into pages. Here are the steps:

1. Cut or copy something to the Clipboard.
2. Open the ClipBook Viewer.
3. Choose Edit ➢ Paste to open the Paste dialog box:

4. In the Page Name box, enter a name for the page, and click OK.

You'll now see the item in Thumbnail view in the Local ClipBook. You can also view it on the Clipboard. To change the view, choose View ➢ Table of Contents to display an alphabetic list of your pages. To display the contents of a page, choose View ➢ Full Page.

Copying an Item from the ClipBook

To copy an item from the ClipBook into an application, follow these steps:

1. Open ClipBook Viewer.
2. In the Local ClipBook, click the page you want to copy.
3. Choose Edit ➢ Copy.
4. Open the document in the application to which you want to copy the item.
5. Place the insertion point where you want the item.
6. Choose Edit ➢ Paste.

Sharing ClipBook Pages

If you are on a local area network, you can share ClipBook pages with other users who also have ClipBook Viewer installed. Follow these steps:

1. In the Local ClipBook, click the page you want to share.
2. Choose File ➢ Share to open the Share ClipBook Page dialog box.
3. To start the program in which the page was created when a user inserted the page in a document, click the Start Application on Connect check box. To run the program minimized, also click the Run Minimized check box.
4. If you want to ensure that users can't edit or delete the page, click the Permissions button to open the ClipBook Page Permissions dialog box.
5. After you set the permissions, click OK twice.

Clearing the Clipboard

To clear the contents of the Clipboard, follow these steps:

1. Open the ClipBook Viewer.
2. Click the Clipboard window.
3. Choose Edit ➢ Delete, and then click Yes.

Understanding OLE

When you use the Clipboard to insert an item from a document in one application into a document in another application, you are inserting a static element. For example, if you insert an Excel worksheet or a portion of a worksheet into a Word document, the worksheet is not updated in Word when you update it in Excel. In addition, you cannot edit the worksheet in Word.

Most of the time, this is probably what you want. However, in some cases it is really helpful to insert a copy of a document that changes whenever it's edited in the originating application; it can also be useful to be able to edit the source document right inside the destination document. For example, you are working on a report that contains the next quarter's budget, which is in a state of flux. The report is created in Word, and the budget worksheet is being created in Excel. You have a couple of choices here:

- Insert a new copy of the worksheet every time it is updated.
- Insert a link to the worksheet so that changes to it are reflected in the Word document.

Obviously, the most efficient choice is to link to the worksheet. The technology that makes this possible is OLE (object linking and embedding), which has been available in the Windows family of operating systems since Windows 3.1. OLE allows you to create *compound* documents that contain linked or embedded *objects*.

A compound document is simply one that consists of portions created in different applications. For example, our report might contain text created in Word, the budget worksheet created in Excel, and a company logo created in Paint. An object is the portion of the document from a different application that you either link or embed, and it can be text, graphics, sound, or video.

To use OLE, all the programs involved must support it. How can you tell if this is the case? If the Paste Special item is not present on the Edit menu, the program does not support linking and embedding. You'll see why this is important in the next section.

Before we get down to the nuts and bolts of linking and embedding, though, we need to define both these terms and explain the differences between them. When you link an object to a document, the document contains only a link to the object. To change the object, you edit the original file. Any such changes are reflected in the linked object.

When you embed an object in a document, the document contains a copy of the object. Any changes made to the original object are not reflected in the document unless the embedded object is updated. Embedding an object is rather similar to inserting a static element via the Clipboard; the difference is that you can click an embedded object to edit it in the application in which it was created.

Whether you link or embed an object depends on the situation. If it's important for the document to be current at all times, link the object. Otherwise, you can embed the object. Now, let's walk through the steps for doing both and take a look at how you edit an object.

Embedding Objects

To embed an object, follow these steps:

1. Open the application that contains the information you want to embed, and select the information.
2. Choose Edit ➢ Copy.
3. Open the document that will contain the embedded object.

4. Place the insertion point where you want the object, and then choose Edit ➢ Paste Special to open the Paste Special dialog box:

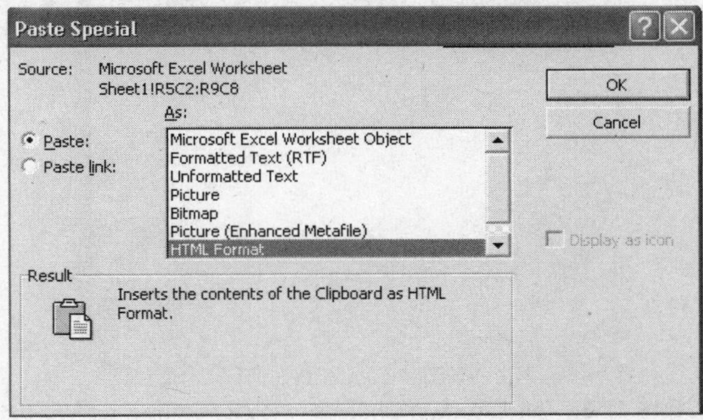

5. Click Paste, and select the format you want to use.
6. Click OK.

To edit an embedded object, follow these steps:

1. Open the document that contains the object.
2. Double-click the object to open it in an editing window that displays the tools and menus of the application in which the object was created.
3. Edit the object, and then click outside it.

Figure 11.5 shows an embedded object ready for editing.

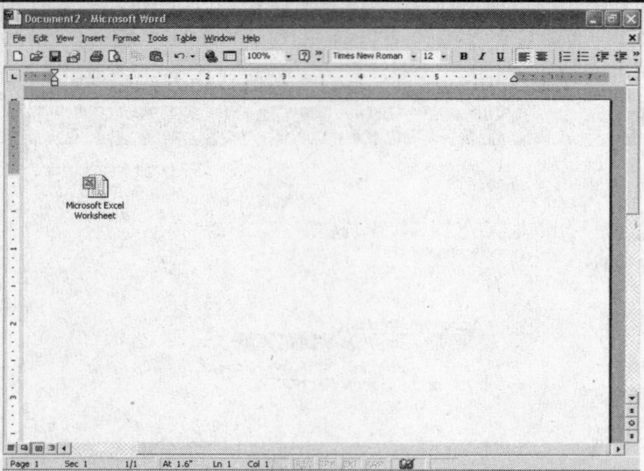

FIGURE 11.5: This Excel worksheet is ready for editing in a Word document.

TIP

To view an embedded object in Word, you need to be in Print Layout view.

Linking Objects

To link an object, follow these steps:

1. Open the application that contains the information you want to link, and select the information.
2. Choose Edit ➢ Copy.
3. Open the document that will contain the embedded object.
4. Choose Edit ➢ Paste Special to open the Paste Special dialog box.
5. Click Paste Link, and select a format for the object.
6. If you want to display a copy of the object in the document, click Float over Text. If you want to display an icon instead, click Display As Icon.
7. Click OK.

Figure 11.6 shows a Word document with an icon that indicates an Excel worksheet is linked to the document.

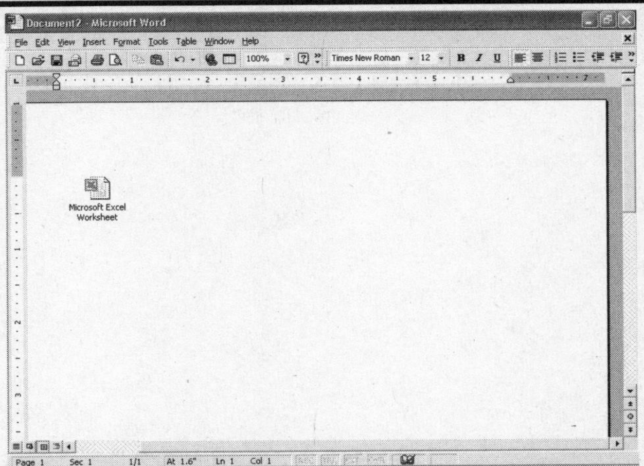

FIGURE 11.6: A Word document with a linked Excel worksheet

To edit a linked object, follow these steps:

1. Open the document that contains the link.
2. Double-click the link (whether it floats on the page or is an icon) to open the originating application and the document that contains the information that was linked and make your changes.
3. Save the file, and then close the application. Changes are reflected in the linked object.

WHAT'S NEXT?

This chapter completes our look at Windows XP Professional essentials. Next we'll turn to the Internet, and we'll begin with a look at how to connect via a modem or broadband connections and then look at the features included with Windows XP Professional that let you connect to the outside world.

PART ii
Communications and the Internet

Chapter 12

Connecting to the Outside World

In recent years, the expansion of the Internet has been nothing short of astonishing; everyone wants to connect. And there have never been more ways of establishing that connection: modems, cable, DSL, and satellite have all become popular connection methods. In this chapter you'll learn how to select and set up your Internet connection method of choice and how to configure Windows to work with the connection through the New Connection Wizard. You'll also learn about HyperTerminal, a modem utility that enables you to connect with non-Internet computer services such as bulletin boards or book catalogs at your local library.

Adapted and revised from *Windows 2000 Professional: In Record Time* by Peter Dyson and Pat Coleman
ISBN 0-7821-2450-X 496 pages $29.99

TYPES OF INTERNET CONNECTIONS

A few years ago, there was only one way that most people could use to connect to the Internet: a regular dial-up modem. Today, however, alternative methods proliferate.

Modem The oldest and slowest way of connecting to the Internet or other online services, but still the mainstay in the industry. You use a modem to dial the telephone number of your Internet service provider, who also has a modem, and the two modems communicate with one another via telephone line. Modems are inexpensive and easy to set up and can be used anywhere there is regular telephone service. The primary drawback is speed; it's limited to 56Kbps.

ISDN Stands for Integrated Subscriber Digital Network. It's a digital type of telephone line, available from the local telephone provider in most areas. ISDN requires the installation of a special phone line, usually carrying a higher than normal monthly charge. It also requires you to work with a service provider that supports ISDN, and you need a special ISDN-type modem. The payback for all this fuss? Increased speed compared with a conventional modem, up to about 120Kbps to 240Kbps versus 56Kbps for a traditional dial-up modem. You must connect and disconnect with ISDN, but dialing is very quick, almost instantaneous. Because the improvement over normal modem performance is modest, and the cost is high, ISDN is not very popular anymore now that cable and DSL have proliferated. However, ISDN is available in more areas than cable or DSL are.

Cable This Internet service bypasses telephone lines altogether, and connects through the same fiber optic cable used for your cable television service. It requires a "cable modem," which is actually not a modem but a terminal adapter that sends and receives data over the attached cable. It also requires a network card in your PC to interface with the terminal adapter. Windows does not know you have a cable Internet connection; all it knows is that it is getting Internet access via a network. Cable Internet is very fast—more than 1Mbps in many cases—and is always on. However, it is available only in residential areas, and not all areas have it yet.

DSL DSL stands for Digital Subscriber Line. It's a way of using regular existing telephone lines to get high-speed Internet access, and it's kind of tricky how it works. A telephone line consists of several channels, most of which are unused when placing and receiving regular calls. DSL uses some of these unused channels on the line to send and receive digital data. You can use a DSL connection at the same time you are talking on the telephone on the same line, because the channels are separate. DSL speed depends on the type of DSL being provided, but it's typically equivalent to cable speed—1 Mbps or so. DSL is available in both residences and businesses, but not all areas offer it yet. DSL is always on, and your computer sees it as a regular network Internet connection.

Satellite In the past, satellite Internet access has been less desirable than cable or DSL because the speedy satellite connection was only one-way. You could receive data quickly via satellite, but for sending data you had to rely on a regular modem. However, recent improvements in satellite service have resulted in an always-on, two-way satellite Internet connection that rivals cable and DSL in speed and convenience. Satellite is a good option for someone living in a remote area that doesn't offer any other high-speed connection type. It requires a special satellite dish, a receiver, and a network card, and your computer sees it as a regular network connection, just like cable and DSL.

For Windows purposes, cable, DSL, and satellite are all identical. Your computer is connected to an external terminal adapter via a network card, and Windows sees only the network card and its ability to provide Internet service. There are differences between the technologies, of course, but Windows doesn't care about that.

Windows does make a distinction between a regular modem and an ISDN, but both require a dial-up connection to the ISP so the differences are minor. You will likely need to run a special setup program that came with an ISDN terminal adapter rather than using Windows' New Modem Wizard, but once the ISDN hardware is set up, it serves much the same functionality as a conventional modem.

When you order cable, DSL, or satellite service, a professional installer typically comes to your house to set it up, or you buy a self-install kit with detailed instructions for the specific technology. Therefore, this chapter won't go into detail about how to set up this hardware. We also won't go into detail about installing IDSN hardware here, since so few people are using it these days and since the steps depend on the brand and model of IDSN equipment.

With a normal modem, however, you might have to do the setup yourself, so the next section will help you check out your modem and install a driver for it if needed.

WORKING WITH A MODEM

Although cable, DSL, and other Internet technologies are wonderful, many people still use regular modem service, for one reason or another. It's cheaper (around $20 a month, as opposed to $40 a month or more for other technologies), and it's widely available even in small towns and rural areas. A modem is also necessary to use a non-Internet dial-up connection with a program such as HyperTerminal, discussed at the end of this chapter.

If you plan to use a modem for Internet access, the following sections are for you; they will help you check your modem, install any drivers needed for it, and configure its properties.

Checking a Modem

If your computer came with a modem pre-installed, it's likely ready to go. But let's check to make sure. To check installed modems, do the following:

1. Choose Start ➢ Control Panel ➢ Printers and Other Hardware ➢ Phone and Modem Options. The Phone and Modem Options dialog box opens.

2. Click the Modems tab. This tab lists all installed modems on the PC.

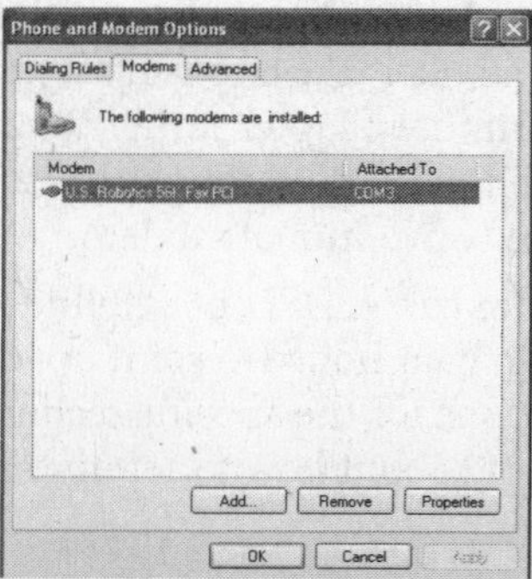

3. Select your modem, and then click Properties to open the Properties dialog box for your modem. If your modem does not appear on the list, skip to the section "Adding a Modem" later in this chapter.
4. Check the Device Status area on the General tab. It should report "This device is working properly." If it does not, click the Troubleshoot button and follow the instructions that appear instead of completing the rest of the steps here.
5. Click the Diagnostics tab, and then click the Query Modem button. Windows sends some test codes to the modem and reports the results after a minute or so. If at least one of the lines in the Response area does not report Success or OK, or if an error message appears instead of results, go back to step 4 and click the Troubleshoot button.

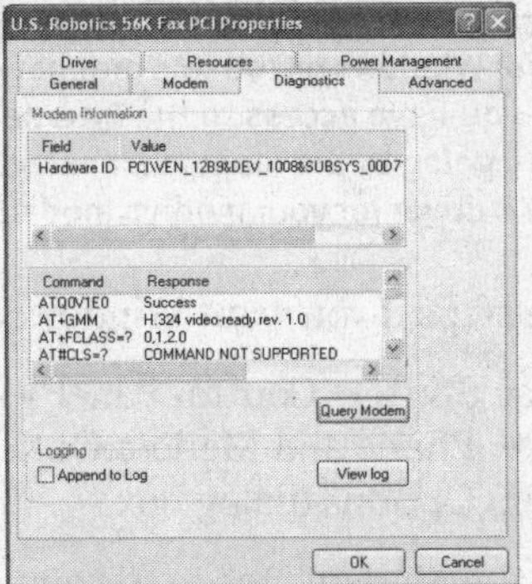

6. Click OK to close the modem's properties, and then OK again to close the Phone and Modem Options box.

Now that you've confirmed that your modem is operational, you're ready to put it to use.

TIP

Most modems have two jacks: one for the line in, and one for a phone out. If all the Windows-based modem tests come back normal but the modem isn't working very well, or isn't working at all, check to make sure you don't have the line and phone wires switched. A staticky phone line can also cause connection problems that Windows will not be able to detect.

Setting Up a Modem in Windows

Almost all modems today are Plug and Play, so you should not have to do anything special to set one up in Windows XP. Just install it, and Windows detects it automatically the next time you turn on your computer. If Windows does not automatically see the modem, try running the Setup program on the disk that came with the modem.

If you don't have a Setup utility for the modem, your next recourse is to ask Windows to look for the modem. You can use the Add New Hardware applet in Control Panel, or you can click the Add button on the Modems tab of the Phone and Modem Options dialog box. The latter is the method explained below.

NOTE

If your modem is old, the Setup disk that came with it might not contain a driver for Windows XP. A driver designed for Windows 2000 might work; one designed for Windows 95/98/Me probably won't. If you can't find a usable driver, and if you have access to the Internet through some other computer or method, try going to the modem manufacturer's Web site and downloading a Windows XP driver for your modem model.

Follow these steps if you want Windows XP to look for your modem:

1. Choose Start ➢ Control Panel ➢ Printers and Other Hardware ➢ Phone and Modem Options to open the Phone and Modem Options dialog box.
2. Click the Modems tab, and then click Add to start the Add Hardware Wizard.
3. Click Next. Windows attempts to find and identify your modem.

NOTE

You might see little tan information bubbles pop up in the lower right corner of your screen while Windows is detecting; you can ignore them.

4. If you see a message that your modem has been set up successfully, click Finish and you're done. Skip the rest of these steps.

If, on the other hand, a message appears that Windows wasn't able to locate the modem, click Next to open the Install New Modem screen:

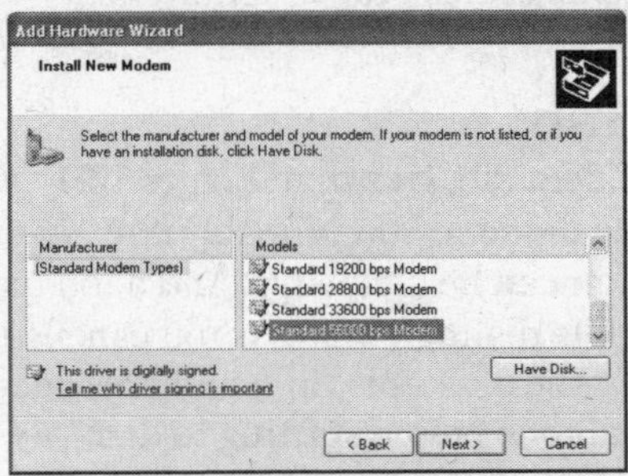

5. A list of modem types appears. These are very general types; Windows XP Professional does not come with drivers for specific models. Click the one that most closely matches your modem, and then click Next to open a list of ports.

Or, if you have a driver disk or a downloaded driver, click Have Disk and then indicate its location.

6. Click the port on which the modem is installed. An external modem will probably be on COM1 or COM2. Then click Next.

WARNING

If you're installing an internal modem, and no ports appear on the list, you're out of luck; this Wizard will not be able to help you. Try physically removing and reinstalling the modem, perhaps in a different slot on the motherboard.

7. Click Finish. A generic driver is installed for the modem.

Using one of these generic drivers will not result in very good modem performance, but it perhaps will let you connect to the Internet or to the modem manufacturer's bulletin board service long enough to download a better driver.

Changing Modem Properties

Most modems work fairly well right out of the box; you do not need to change any properties in order for it to operate correctly. However, there are a few properties you might be interested in changing, and we'll outline them here.

To display the modem's properties, select it on the Modems tab and click the Properties button, just as you did earlier in the chapter when you were checking it for proper operation.

Modem Tab

On the Modem tab, shown in Figure 12.1, you can control the speaker volume for the modem. You probably already know that a too-loud modem speaker can be annoying! And a too-quiet one can prevent you from hearing the dialing progress. You can also set a maximum port speed (usually the default is fine) and choose whether the modem should listen for a dial tone before starting to dial.

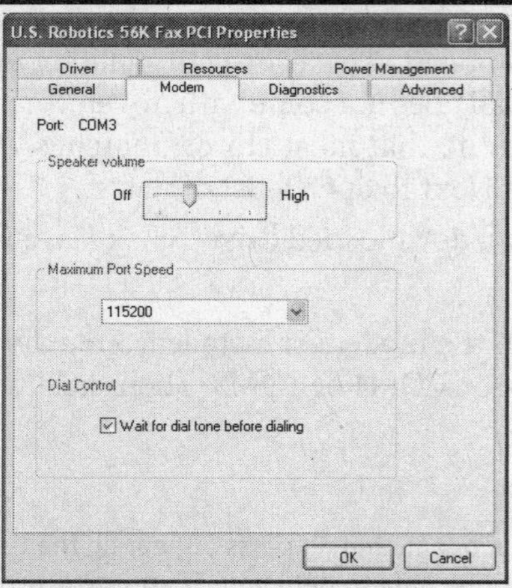

FIGURE 12.1: Adjust modem volume on the Modem tab.

Driver Tab

On the Driver tab (Figure 12.2) you can update the modem driver, should you run across a better one sometime in the future. Clicking the Update Driver button starts a Wizard that lets you change the driver for the modem without uninstalling it. (Some earlier versions of Windows required you to delete the modem and then reinstall it in order to change its driver.) There is also a Roll Back Driver utility, in case you update a driver and then find that you preferred the older one. Simply click the Roll Back Driver button to revert to the driver that was previously installed.

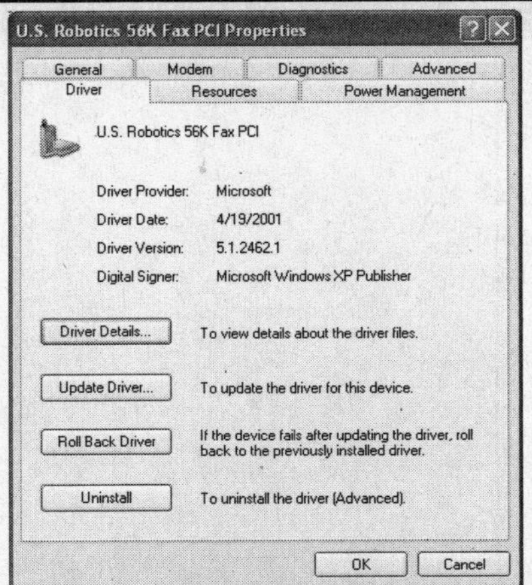

FIGURE 12.2: Control which driver is used for the modem on the Driver tab.

Power Management Tab

Not all modems have this tab. If yours does, you can use it to specify whether the modem should be allowed to wake up the computer from Standby. This option might be useful if you use your PC to receive faxes, for example, and a fax comes in the middle of the night when your computer is in low-power Standby mode.

Advanced Tab

Modems speak a language all their own, based on a set of Hayes commands that include numbers, letters, and symbols. For example, the command AT means Attention and Z means Reset. Windows sends these codes to the modems invisibly, behind the scenes, so you don't have to know the codes.

However, sometimes you might need to send a specific code to the modem, to troubleshoot a problem or overcome a bug in a program, for example. Should you ever need to do this, you can enter that command on the Advanced tab of the modem's Properties dialog box, as shown in Figure 12.3.

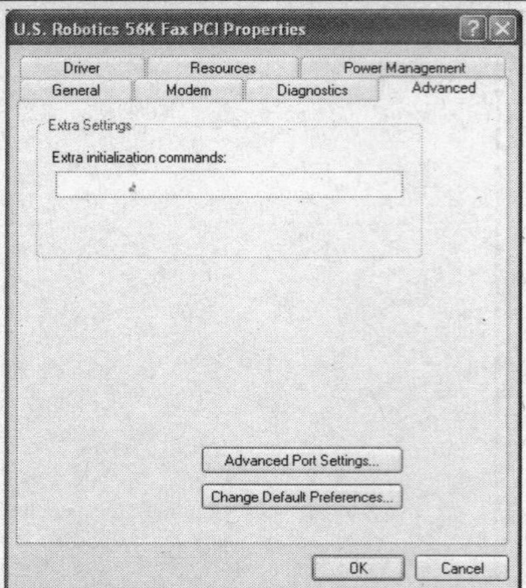

FIGURE 12.3: System-level modem settings are accessed from the Advanced tab.

Another way to troubleshoot certain kinds of modem properties is to adjust the buffer settings for the modem's communication. These have to do with error correction; we won't get into them in detail here. Should you ever need to work with those settings, you'll find them by clicking the Advanced Port Settings button on the Advanced tab.

One more useful thing on the Advanced tab: from here you can set default connection preferences. These preferences include the number of idle minutes before automatic disconnection, the amount of time to wait while establishing a connection before deciding that it has failed, and the type of flow control and data compression in use. To set these, click the Change Default Preferences button.

Setting Up Your Internet Connection

In times past, setting up a connection to the Internet used to be quite a complex operation, but that is no longer the case. The New Connection Wizard walks you through the steps of setting up your Internet connection. All you need is an account with an Internet Service Provider (ISP) and a method of connection, and you're all set. That method can either be a modem or ISDN terminal adapter and phone number to dial, or a full-time Internet connection such as cable or DSL.

NOTE

Some cable and DSL systems require you to log on with a user name and password; others don't. The New Connection Wizard allows for both possibilities.

Starting the New Connection Wizard

The first few steps of the New Connection Wizard are the same no matter what type of connection you are setting up:

1. Start the New Connection Wizard. You can do it in any of these ways:
   - Choose Start ➢ All Programs ➢ Accessories ➢ Communications, and then select New Connection Wizard.
   - Choose Start ➢ Control Panel ➢ Network and Internet Connections ➢ Internet Options to open the Internet Properties dialog box, click the Connections tab, and then click the Setup button.
   - In Internet Explorer, choose Tools ➢ Internet Options to open the Internet Options dialog box, click the Connections tab, and then click the Setup button.
2. At the Welcome screen, click Next to open the Network Connection Type screen. As you can see, the New Connection Wizard has more capabilities than simply setting up Internet access; however, the Internet access portion is what we're concerned with at the moment.

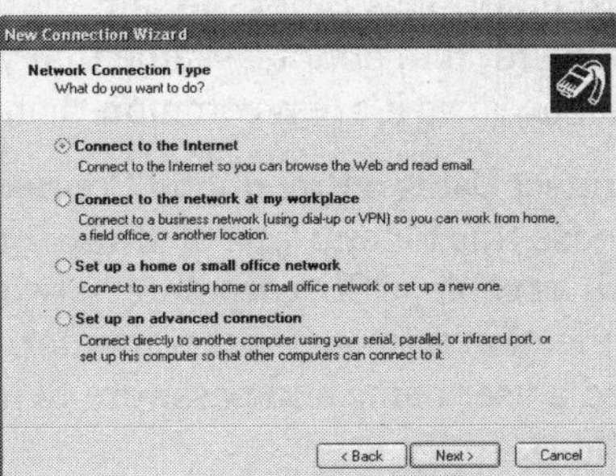

3. Click Connect to the Internet and then click Next.

4. Another list of choices appears:

   Choose from a list of Internet service providers (ISPs) Select this option if you do not already have an ISP account and you have no idea of what's available in your area. If you go with this option, you'll skip the rest of the steps here. Follow the prompts to complete the Wizard, and you'll end up in a folder window with an icon called Refer Me to More Internet Service Providers. Double-click that icon and follow the prompts to choose a provider and sign up. (You'll need a credit card.)

   Set up my connection manually Choose this option if you already have an ISP account and you know the pertinent settings for it, such as your user name and password and the phone number to dial if it's a dial-up connection.

   Use the CD I got from my ISP Choose this option if you already have an ISP account and it came with a setup disk. You'll use that setup disk instead of the steps in this book.

5. Next the Wizard asks how you will connect to the Internet. This step is where the process diverges a bit depending on connection type:

   Connect Using a Dial-Up Modem Choose this option for a modem or for ISDN.

   Connect Using a Broadband Connection That Requires a User Name and Password Choose this option for cable or DSL if you have a user name and password that you must enter. This is not the same as your e-mail address and password. If in doubt, assume that you do *not* have this type, because it's less common than the following one.

   Connect Using a Broadband Connection That Is Always On Choose this for any type of always-on network connection, such as cable, DSL, corporate network, or shared Internet connection from another computer, except if you think you need a user name and password to logon (see the above option).

6. After making your choice, click Next.

7. If you chose Connect Using a Broadband Connection That Is Always On in step 5, click Finish and you're done. Otherwise continue to step 8.
8. Type the ISP's name. This is for your own use; it'll be the name of the connection icon. Then click Next.
9. If you chose Connect Using a Dial-Up Modem in step 5, type the phone number that the modem should dial, and then click Next. You won't see this screen if you are setting up a cable or DSL connection.
10. You are prompted for your name and password. Type your user name and password in the boxes provided.

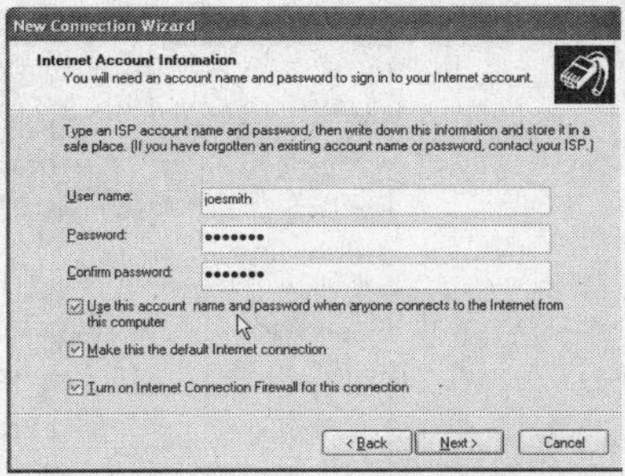

11. Deselect any of the option check boxes desired (we recommend you leave them all marked). Then click Next.
12. Click Finish. The connection is created.

Testing a Dial-Up Internet Connection

If you just set up an always-on Internet connection, you can test it by opening Internet Explorer (choose Start ➢ Internet Explorer). If a Web page appears, you're connected.

Testing a dial-up connection requires an extra step or two. Windows does not automatically establish a dial-up connection after you create it; you must do that manually to check it out. To do so, follow these steps:

1. Choose Start ➢ Connect To and then the connection name.

   Or, if the Connect To command does not appear on the Start menu, choose Start➢All Programs➢Accessories ➢ Network Connections and then double-click the connection icon.

One other alternative: you can choose Start ➢ My Network Places and then click Network Connections.

TIP

If the Connect To command does not appear on your Start menu, you can set it up to do so. Right-click the Start button and choose Properties. Click the Start Menu tab. Click the Customize button next to Start Menu. Click the Advanced tab. On the Start Menu Items list, scroll down to the Network Connections area, and click Display as Connect To Menu.

2. A Connect dialog box appears. Confirm the settings in it, and then click Dial.

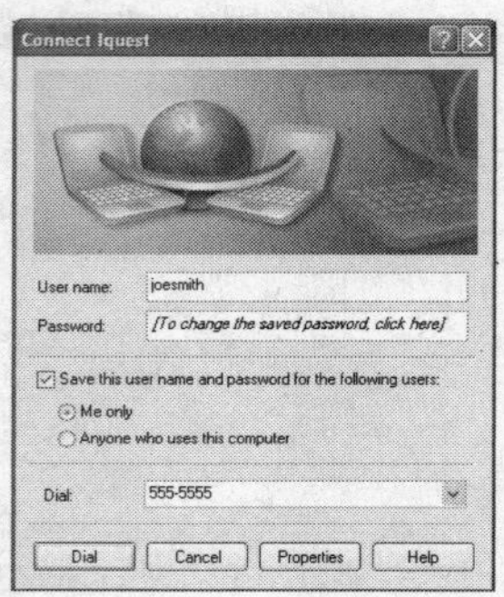

3. If a confirmation message appears telling you that you're now connected, click OK. (You might not see that, depending on your settings.)
4. A dial-up icon appears in your notification area. To disconnect the connection, right-click it and choose Disconnect, or double-click it to open a dialog box and click Disconnect from there.

TIP

To test a non–dial-up Internet connection such as cable or DSL, try opening Internet Explorer. If a Web page appears, your Internet connection is working. See Chapter 13 for more information about Internet Explorer.

Setting Internet Explorer Options

Now that we've configured a connection to an Internet Service Provider, we can take a look at how to configure Internet Explorer so that it works most efficiently; we'll cover the details of actually using Internet Explorer in Chapter 13. You might want to revisit this section once you've read Chapter 13 and you have a better idea of what options you might find useful.

You can access the Internet Options dialog box in either of two ways:

- Choose Start ➢ Control Panel ➢ Network and Internet Connections ➢ Internet Options.
- Choose Tools ➢ Internet Options from within Internet Explorer.

NOTE

If you open Internet Options in Control Panel, the dialog box you see is called Internet Properties. If you open Internet Explorer and choose Tools ➢ Internet Options, this same dialog box is now called Internet Options. The tabs are the same, and the functions these tabs perform are the same; only the dialog box name is different.

This dialog box has six tabs, and in the next few sections, we'll review the most important configuration choices you can make on each of these tabs. We'll start with the General tab.

General Options

The Internet Properties dialog box General tab shown in Figure 12.4 contains these settings:

Home Page Lets you choose which Web page opens each time you connect to the Internet. A home page is the first Web page you see when you start Internet Explorer. Click Use Current to make the current page your home page (if you are online to the Internet), click Use Default to return to the default setting, and click Use Blank to start each Internet session with a blank screen. To use a different Web page as your home page, type the URL in the Address box.

Temporary Internet Files Lets you manage those Web pages that are stored on your hard disk for fast offline access.

Delete Cookies: Removes stored cookies from visits to Web sites. *Cookies* are small files containing identifying information that some Web sites use to track your usage and remember your settings.

Delete Files: Removes all stored pages. You might use this if your hard disk is getting full, for example.

Settings: Opens a dialog box in which you can change how temporary Internet files are stored. You can specify how often stored copies are refreshed, how much hard disk space can be used for storing the files, and where the files are stored. You can also use View Files to open an Explorer window listing the stored Web pages and graphics files, or use View Objects to open an Explorer window listing other Web-related files such as ActiveX controls.

History Lets you control how many days' worth of historical data is retained in Internet Explorer. You can click the History button on the IE toolbar to view your history as far back as the number of days you specify here. This feature can be useful to monitor the Internet viewing habits of your kids, for example, or to help yourself remember a site you want to revisit. If you are running low on hard-disk space, consider reducing this number of days. To delete all the information currently in the History folder, click the Clear History button.

Colors Lets you choose which colors are used as background, links, and text on those Web pages for which the original author did not specify colors. By default, the Use Windows Colors option is selected.

TIP

To change the Windows Colors, right-click the desktop and choose Properties, and then select a color scheme from the Appearance tab, or click the Effects button to choose colors for individual screen elements.

Fonts Lets you specify the font style and text size to use on those Web pages for which the original author did not make a specification.

Languages Lets you choose the character set to use on those Web pages that offer content in more than one language. English is rapidly becoming the most common language in use on the Internet, so you may not use this option often.

Accessibility Lets you choose how certain information is displayed in Internet Explorer, including font styles, colors, and text size. You can also specify that your own style sheet is used.

FIGURE 12.4: The General tab in the Internet Properties dialog box

Security Options

The Security tab shown in Figure 12.5 lets you specify the overall security level for each of four zones. Each zone has its own default security restrictions that tell Internet Explorer how to manage dynamic Web page content such as ActiveX controls and Java applets. The zones are:

Internet Sites you visit that are not in one of the other categories; default security is set to Medium.

Local Intranet Sites you can access on your corporate intranet; default security is set to Medium-Low.

Trusted Sites Web sites you have a high degree of confidence will not send you potentially damaging content; default security is set to Low.

Restricted Sites Sites that you visit but do not trust; default security is set to High.

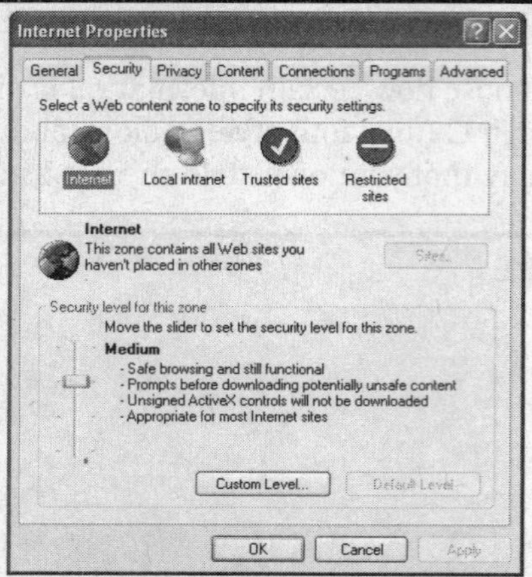

FIGURE 12.5: The Security tab in the Internet Properties dialog box

To change the current security level of a zone, just move the slider to the new security level you want to use:

High Excludes any content capable of damaging your system. Cookies are disabled, and so some Web sites will not work as you might expect. This is the most secure setting.

Medium Opens a warning dialog box in Internet Explorer before running ActiveX or Java applets on your system. This is a moderately secure setting that is good for everyday use.

Medium-Low Same as Medium but without the prompts.

Low Does not issue any warning but runs the ActiveX or Java applet automatically. This is the least secure setting.

Click the Custom Level button to create your own settings in the Security Settings dialog box, which is shown in Figure 12.6. You can individually configure how you want to manage certain categories, such as ActiveX controls and plug-ins, Java applets, scripting, file and font downloads, and user authentication.

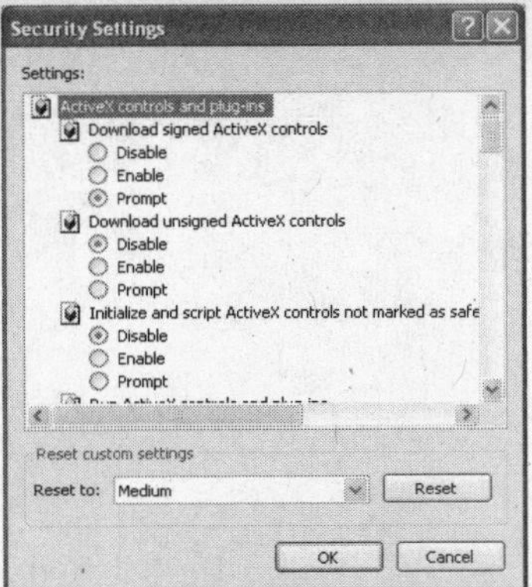

FIGURE 12.6: The Security Settings dialog box

Privacy Options

The Privacy tab, shown in Figure 12.7, enables you to specify how much information about you and your Web surfing habits gets revealed to the hosts of the Web sites you visit.

Many Web sites use cookies to keep tabs on their visitors. A *cookie* is a small text file that's created on your hard disk when you visit a certain Web site. The next time you visit that same site, it looks for the cookie and restores any settings saved in the cookie. Cookies can be helpful to everyone; they enable you to view personalized settings at Web stores, for example, and they enable the stores to collect marketing data. However, some people object to them as an invasion of privacy, so IE enables you to control the types of cookies that will be accepted and how long they will remain.

Drag the slider up or down to change the Privacy setting, just as you did on the Security tab. You can also click the Advanced button to fine-tune the settings.

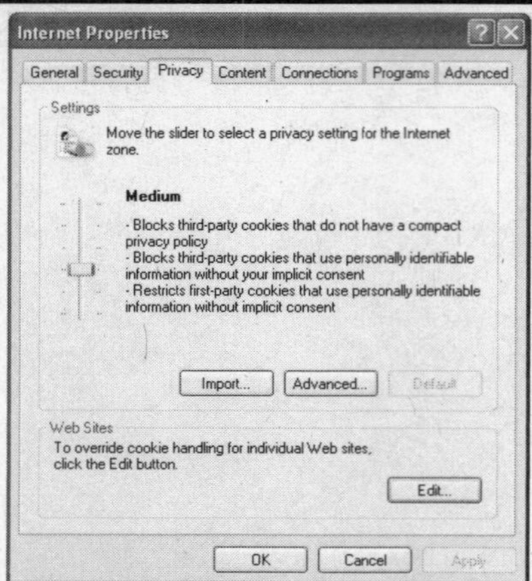

FIGURE 12.7: Adjust Privacy settings on the Privacy tab.

You can override the current Privacy setting for individual Web sites with the Edit button. Click it to display the dialog box shown in Figure 12.8; then enter a Web site and click Allow or Block to always accept or always reject cookies from that site.

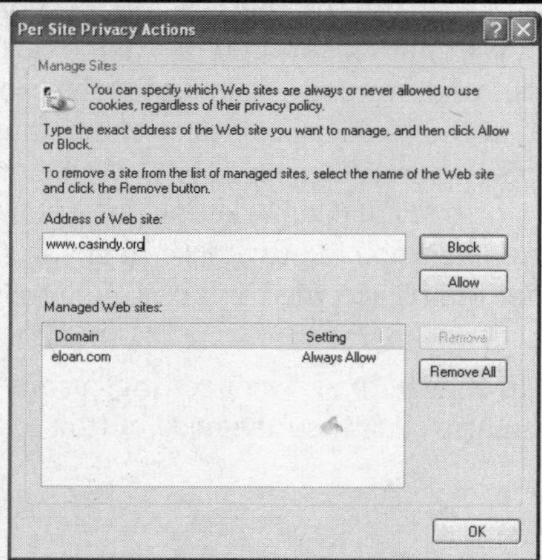

FIGURE 12.8: Override the Privacy settings for individual Web sites here.

Content Options

The Content tab, which is shown in Figure 12.9, contains settings you can use to restrict access to sites and specify how you want to manage digital certificates:

Content Adviser Lets you control access to certain sites on the Internet and is particularly useful if children have access to the computer. Click Enable to enable the feature, and then use the tabs in the Content Advisor dialog box to establish the level of content you will allow users to view:

Ratings Lets you use a set of ratings developed by the Recreational Software Advisory Council (RSAC) for language, nudity, sex, and violence. Select one of these categories, and then adjust the slider to specify the level of content you will allow.

Approved Sites Lets you create lists of sites that are always viewable or always restricted regardless of how they are rated.

General Specifies whether people using this computer can view material that has not been rated; users may see some objectionable material if the Web site has not used the RSAC rating system. You can also opt to have the Supervisor enter a password so that users can view Web pages that may contain objectionable material. You can click the Change Password button to change the Supervisor password; remember that you have to know the current Supervisor password before you can change it.

Advanced Lets you look at or modify the list of organizations providing ratings services.

Certificates Lets you manage digital certificates used with certain client authentication servers. Click Certificates to view the personal digital certificates installed on this system, or click Publishers to designate a particular software publisher as a trustworthy publisher. This means that Windows XP Professional applications can download, install, and use software from these agencies without asking for your permission first.

Personal Information Lets you look at or change the settings for Windows AutoComplete and your own personal profile. Click AutoComplete to change the way that this feature works within Windows XP Professional, or click My Profile to review the information sent to any Web sites that request information about you when you visit their site.

FIGURE 12.9: The Content tab in the Internet Properties dialog box

Connections Options

The Connections tab, which is shown in Figure 12.10, allows you to specify how your system connects to the Internet. Click the Setup button to run the New Connection Wizard and set up a connection to an Internet Service Provider. (See the New Connection Wizard section earlier in this skill for complete details.) If you use a modem, click the Settings button to open the My Connection Settings dialog box, where you can specify all aspects of the phone connection to your ISP.

The option buttons in the center of the Connections tab control whether Windows will automatically connect you to the Internet when needed, will prompt you to connect, or will not connect. If you have a dial-up connection via modem, or a cable or DSL connection that requires you to connect with a user name and password, you will probably want to set this to either Dial Whenever a Network Connection Is Not Present or Always Dial My Default Connection. If you have network access (including cable or DSL), or connect through someone else's computer through connection sharing, set it to Never Dial a Connection. Users with network Internet access can also click the LAN Settings button to fine-tune that connection. But if your connection is currently working, it's best to leave them alone.

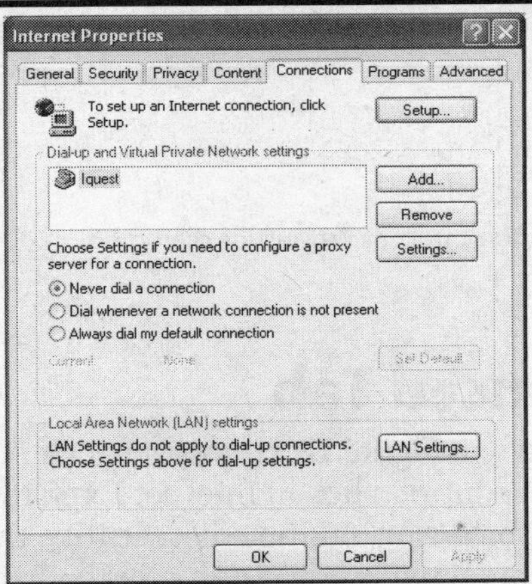

FIGURE 12.10: The Connections tab in the Internet Properties dialog box

Programs Options

The Programs tab, which is shown in Figure 12.11, lets you set your default program choices for HTML editor, e-mail, newsgroup reader, Internet call, calendar, and contact list.

Finally, you can specify that Internet Explorer check to see if it is configured as the default browser on your system each time it starts running.

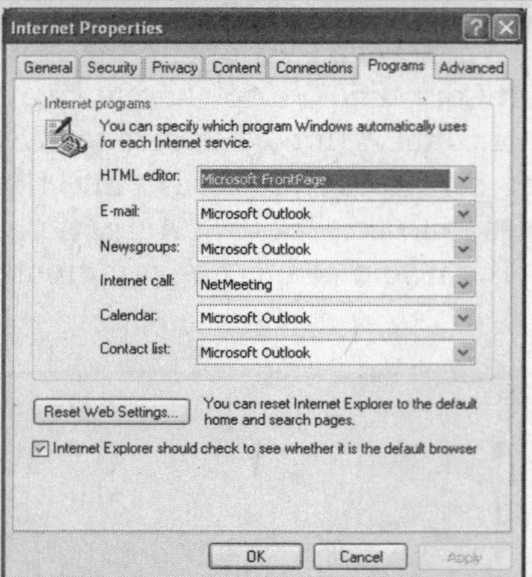

FIGURE 12.11: The Programs tab in the Internet Properties dialog box

Configuring the Advanced Tab

The Advanced tab, which is shown in Figure 12.12, lets you look at or change a number of settings that control much of Internet Explorer's behavior, including accessibility, browsing, multimedia, security, the Java environment, printing and searching, the Internet Explorer toolbar, and how HTTP 1.1 settings are interpreted. Click a check box to turn an option on; clear the check box to turn the option off.

Changes you make here stay in effect until you change them again, until you download an automatic configuration file, or until you click the Restore Defaults button, which returns the settings on the Advanced tab to their original values.

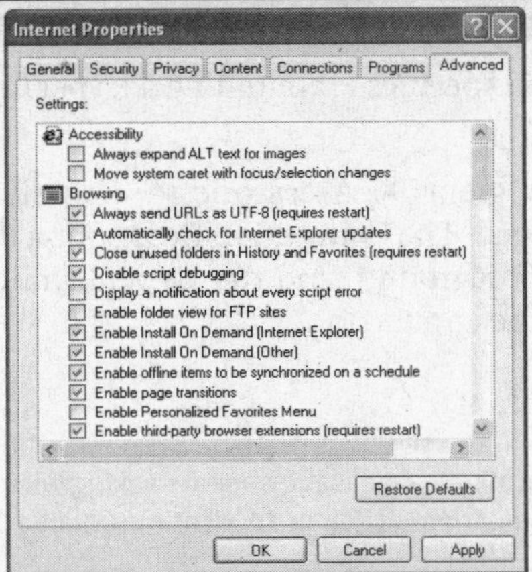

FIGURE 12.12: The Advanced tab in the Internet Properties dialog box

CONNECTING WITH HYPERTERMINAL

HyperTerminal is a utility program you can use to connect to another computer, perhaps one that uses a different operating system such as Unix, or to an information service such as the book catalog at your local library, or to a bulletin board (BBS). You can use this type of connection to download or transfer files.

HyperTerminal is a class of program known as terminal emulation software. In other words, it pretends to be a terminal attached to the remote computer. HyperTerminal is *not* a Web browser and cannot access Web sites on the Internet. (For that particular task, see the description of how to use Internet Explorer in Chapter 13.) Since the Internet is increasingly becoming the de facto standard for online communication, fewer people are using HyperTerminal these days. However, it remains a useful utility for specialized situations, and worthy of brief explanation here.

Creating a New HyperTerminal Connection

To create the phone numbers and specifics for initiating a HyperTerminal connection, follow these steps:

1. Choose Start ➢ All Programs ➢ Accessories ➢ Communications ➢ HyperTerminal. The Connection Description dialog box opens in the foreground, and the HyperTerminal window opens in the background.

NOTE

The first time you run HyperTerminal, a message appears asking whether you want to make HyperTerminal your default Telnet application. Choose Yes.

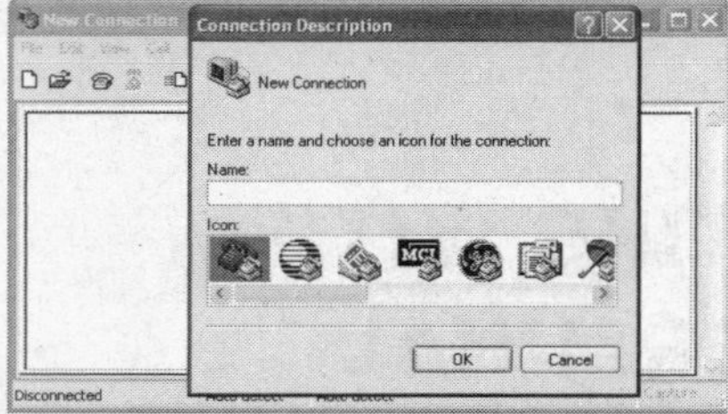

2. In the Name box, enter the descriptive name you want to assign to this connection, and then choose one of the icons from the selection displayed at the bottom of the dialog box.
3. Click OK to open the Connect To dialog box.

4. Verify the country and area code, type the telephone number you want to use with this connection, and confirm your modem type.
5. Click OK to open the Connect dialog box.

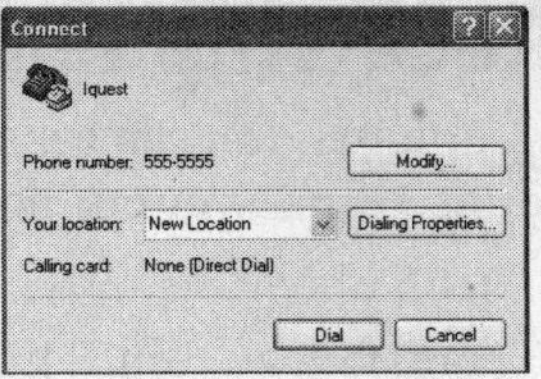

6. Check the phone number for this connection, and if it is incorrect, click Modify to change it. To look at or change any of the settings associated with the phone line or with dialing, click Dialing Properties.
7. When you are ready to make the connection, click Dial. You will be connected to the other computer, and a named window for the connection will open. If you do not want to dial now, click Cancel, and the named window for the connection will be displayed.

The next thing that you see in the window will depend on the service or computer you have connected to; you may be asked to select a terminal type, to enter a password, or to make a selection from a menu. Figure 12.13 shows an example.

When you are finished, use the appropriate command to log off the remote computer before you close the HyperTerminal window.

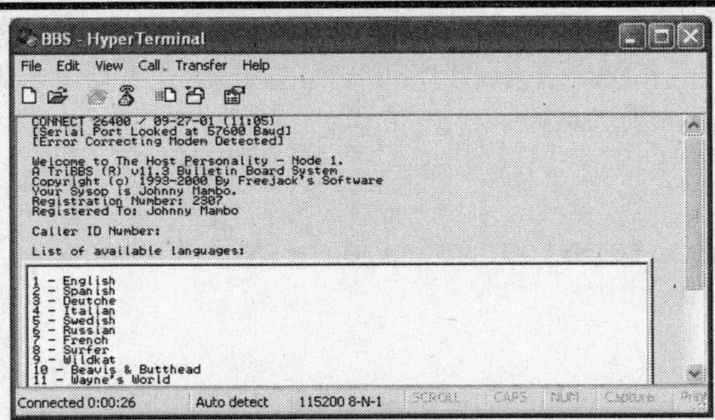

FIGURE 12.13: The main HyperTerminal window when connected to a BBS system

Sending and Receiving Files

While using HyperTerminal, you can send and receive files and capture what you see on your screen to your printer. To send a file, follow these steps:

1. Choose Transfer ➢ Send File to open the Send File dialog box.
2. Enter the name of the file in the Filename box, or click Browse to locate it.
3. In the Protocol box, accept the protocol that HyperTerminal suggests, or click the down arrow to select another protocol from the list.

NOTE

If you know the specific protocol for the system to which you are connected, select that protocol. If you don't know the protocol, stick with Zmodem, which is a generic, commonly used protocol.

4. Click Send.

To receive a file, follow these steps:

1. Choose Transfer ➢ Receive File to open the Receive File dialog box.
2. Indicate where the received file should be stored, and specify the protocol if necessary.
3. Click Receive.

To capture what you see on your screen to the printer, choose Transfer ➢ Capture to Printer.

WHAT'S NEXT?

Now that you know how to set up an Internet connection, it's time to turn to the tools you can use to access information on the Internet. In the remainder of the chapters in this part of the book, we'll look at several of these tools. The next chapter starts by discussing the Web browser that's included with Windows XP Professional, Internet Explorer.

Chapter 13

Web Browsing with Internet Explorer

Obviously, the most important thing about Internet Explorer is not the program itself but all the resources you can access using it. And, to be completely honest about it, Internet Explorer is so easy to use that you hardly need a how-to book, a manual, or even this chapter. If you know how to open any Windows XP Professional program, you know how to open Internet Explorer, and you can start browsing immediately by simply clicking links.

Thus, in this chapter we're going to move briskly through the tasks you most commonly perform with Internet Explorer. As we proceed, we'll point out some new features of version 6 and show you how to expand on what comes naturally.

Adapted and revised from *Windows 2000 Professional: In Record Time* by Peter Dyson and Pat Coleman

ISBN 0-7821-2450-X 496 pages $29.99

STARTING INTERNET EXPLORER

You can start Internet Explorer in several ways, but regardless of the method you use, the MSN start page shown in Figure 13.1 appears by default. Later in this chapter, you'll see how to specify any page you want as your start page. In the next section, we'll identify and discuss the components of the Internet Explorer interface.

FIGURE 13.1: You can retain the page at `www.msn.com` as your start page or select any other page that suits your fancy or interests.

From the Desktop

From the Desktop, you can start Internet Explorer in several ways

- Click the Launch Internet Explorer Browser button on the Quick Launch toolbar. In Windows XP Professional the Quick Launch toolbar does not appear by default. If the Quick Launch toolbar is not visible, right-click the taskbar and choose Toolbars ➢ Quick Launch.
- Double-click the Internet Explorer shortcut on the desktop, if one appears there.

- Choose Start ➢ Internet Explorer.
- Choose Start ➢ All Programs ➢ Internet Explorer.

NOTE

If other Web browsers (such as Netscape Navigator) are installed on your system, one of them may appear at the top of the Start menu instead of Internet Explorer. To change back to Internet Explorer, right-click the taskbar and choose Properties from the shortcut menu to open the Taskbar and Start Menu Properties dialog box. Click the Start Menu tab, and then click the Customize button to open the Customize Start Menu dialog box. On the General tab, open the Internet drop-down list, choose Internet Explorer, and then click OK.

From a Hyperlink

You can also start Internet Explorer from any document in any Windows application that includes a hyperlink if Internet Explorer is your default browser. For example, if you receive an e-mail that includes a URL in the body of the message, simply click the URL to open Internet Explorer at that page. A hyperlink can be text or an image. A text hyperlink is usually underlined and in a color that is different from normal text.

From Windows Explorer

In Windows Explorer, HTML files are indicated by the Internet Explorer icon, and when you click such a file, it opens in Internet Explorer.

You can also open any file on your hard drive, a floppy, or your network by choosing File ➢ Open. If it is not an HTML file, it will open in its associated program.

A LOOK BEHIND THE SCENES: VIEWING HTML PAGES

HTML is the abbreviation for HyperText Markup Language, the programming language that is used to create Web pages. HTML uses tags to tell the browser how to display the page on the screen. Tags are enclosed in angle brackets, and most come in pairs. For example, the <H1> tag defines a first-level heading, like this:

```
<H1>This is a level 1 heading.</H1>
```

CONTINUED ➞

An HTML file is really just a plain text file that can be created with a text editor such as Notepad or with a program such as Microsoft FrontPage. To view the HTML behind any page you open in Internet Explorer, choose View ➢ Source. The file is displayed in Notepad and looks similar to the following example.

www.sybex[1] - Notepad

File Edit Format View Help

```
<HTML>
<!-- Lotus-Domino (Release 5.0.7 - March 21, 2001 on Windows NT/Intel) -->
<HEAD>
<TITLE>Sybex, Inc. -- Quality Computer Books &amp; Software</TITLE><META NAME="keywords" CONTENT=
<SCRIPT LANGUAGE="JavaScript">
<!--
function DoSearch(){
chosen = document.forms[1].SearchIn.options.selectedIndex;
chtxt = document.forms[1].SearchIn.options[chosen].value
chentry = document.forms[1].SearchIn.options[chosen].text
qtext = document.forms[1].Query.value
if (qtext == "") {
searchline = "/sybexbooks.nsf/" + chtxt + "?openview"
} else {
searchline = "/sybexbooks.nsf/" + chtxt + "?Searchview"
}

document.forms[1].action = searchline
document.forms[1].submit()

//chosen = document.forms[1].SearchIn.options.selectedIndex;
//chtxt = document.forms[1].SearchIn.options[chosen].value
//searchline = "/sybexbooks.nsf/" + chtxt + "?Searchview"
//document.forms[1].action = searchline
//document.forms[1].submit()
}

<!--

function MM_findObj(n, d) { //v3.0
  var p,i,x;  if(!d) d=document; if((p=n.indexOf("?"))>0&&parent.frames.length) {
    d=parent.frames[n.substring(p+1)].document; n=n.substring(0,p);}
  if(!(x=d[n])&&d.all) x=d.all[n]; for (i=0;!x&&i<d.forms.length;i++) x=d.forms[i][n];
  for(i=0;!x&&d.layers&&i<d.layers.length;i++) x=MM_findObj(n,d.layers[i].document); return x;
}

function MM_swapImage() { //v3.0
  var i,j=0,x,a=MM_swapImage.arguments; document.MM_sr=new Array; for(i=0;i<(a.length-2);i+=3)
   if ((x=MM_findObj(a[i]))!=null){document.MM_sr[j++]=x; if(!x.oSrc) x.oSrc=x.src; x.src=a[i+2];
}
```

To return to Internet Explorer and the page displayed in the browser, click the Close button in Notepad.

Looking at source code is a great way to get introduced to HTML. If you're interested in learning more about HTML and creating Web pages, check out the following Sybex titles: *Mastering Microsoft FrontPage 2002 Premium Edition*, and *Mastering HTML 4*, Second Edition.

GETTING HELP

You have at your fingertips several ways to get help with Internet Explorer. For starters, choose Help ➢ Contents and Index. Click the Search tab, and enter a word or phrase to search for a topic. If you want to search the Web for help, choose Help ➢ Online Support. This displays the Microsoft Product Support Services page at `support.microsoft.com/directory/`.

If you're new to Internet Explorer but have used Netscape Navigator, choose Help ➢ For Netscape Users to access a list of tips and corresponding terminology.

TIP

The Help ➢ Tip of the Day command toggles on/off a tip pane at the bottom of the IE window containing helpful hints for using the program most effectively. Since the tip pane takes up space onscreen, most people prefer to leave it turned off.

A Quick Tour of Internet Explorer

The Internet Explorer window has much in common with other Windows application windows: vertical and horizontal scrollbars display as necessary, you can size various portions of the window by clicking and dragging, and you can display a ScreenTip by placing the mouse cursor over an item. In the upper-right corner are the Minimize, Restore, and Close buttons.

In this section, we'll look briefly at the components of the Internet Explorer window, and in later sections we'll look at some specific components that you can use to enrich and supplement your browsing experience. Figure 13.2 is your components road map.

Here is a general description of each component:

Title bar Displays the name of the current Web page or other file that is displayed in the Internet Explorer window.

Menu bar Contains a set of menus, some of which contain the same items that appear on that menu in other Windows programs.

Standard toolbar Contains several buttons that correspond to items on the Menu bar, as well as navigation buttons such as Back, Forward, and Home.

Address bar Contains a drop-down box in which you can enter or select the resource you want to access. Click the Go button or press Enter to go to the specified page or other resource.

Links bar Contains a short list of preselected hyperlinks. You can add to this list by dragging hyperlinks onto it.

NOTE

By default the Links bar appears as shown in Figure 13.2, on the same line as the Address Bar, with only its name visible. You can view its content by clicking the ···»··· button at the right, or drag it down onto a separate row. If it won't drag, choose View ➢ Toolbars, and if a check mark appears next to Lock the Toolbars, click it to remove the check mark.

Activity Indicator Is animated when Internet Explorer is sending or receiving data.

Main window Displays the resource—Web page, document file, image, and so on—that you most recently accessed.

Status bar Displays information about the current state of Internet Explorer.

- When you choose a menu command, the status bar displays a description of what it does.
- When you point to a hyperlink, the status bar displays its URL.
- When you click a hyperlink to open another page, the status bar displays a series of messages related to the progress of that process.

NOTE

The status bar might not appear by default, depending on your system. If the status bar does not appear, choose View ➢ Status Bar to display it.

Security zone Appears on the status bar, and displays the security zone currently active. For information about Internet Security and selecting security zones, see Chapter 12.

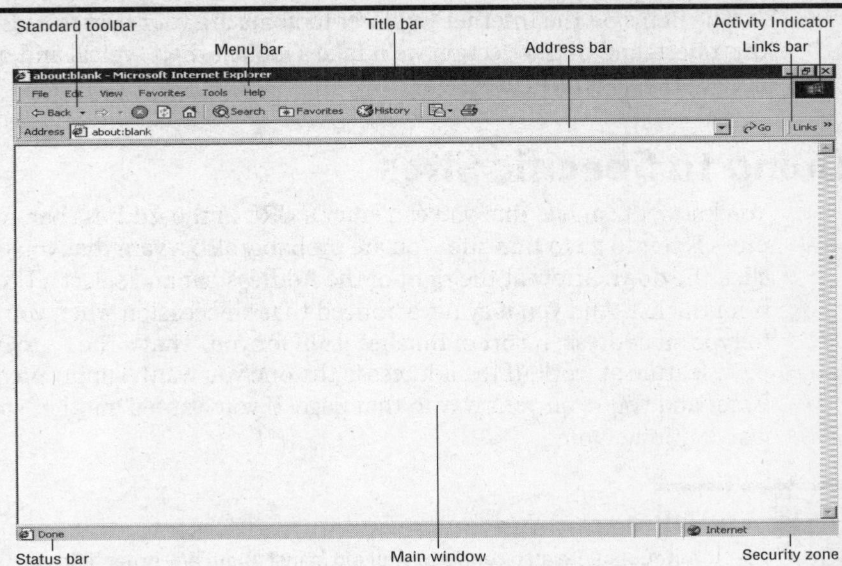

FIGURE 13.2: Many Internet Explorer window components are similar to those in other Windows applications.

NOTE

Figure 13.2 shows a blank page, to keep things simple while you learn about the parts of the window. You can start IE with a blank page every time if you wish. Choose Tools ➢ Internet Options, and on the General tab, click the Use Blank button. To quickly display a blank page as a one-time occurrence, type `about:blank` in the Address bar and press Enter.

MOVING AROUND THE WEB

To even begin to describe what you'll find on the Web these days is an exercise in futility. What was suspect a year ago is commonplace today, and what appears today to be well in the future may be up and running tomorrow. You can buy and sell almost any commodity, search the world's vast storehouse of information, play blackjack, chat with somebody on another continent, witness the birth of a baby, locate a lost relative, book a cruise, scout new business opportunities—the list is indeed endless. And, as the saying goes, one thing leads to another.

Part ii

The items on the Internet Explorer toolbars are your best friends in this quest, and in this section we'll take a look at their typical and not-necessarily-so-typical uses.

Going to Specific Sites

You know, of course, that you can enter a URL in the Address bar and press Enter to go to that site. You are probably also aware that you can click the down arrow at the right of the Address bar and select a URL from the list. And you may have noticed that on occasion when you start to type an address, it sort of finishes itself for you. That's the AutoComplete feature at work. If the address is the one you want, simply press Enter and you're on your way to that page. If you wanted another site, just continue typing.

TIP

AutoComplete also comes to your aid in just about any other field you fill in on a Web page—stock quotes, search queries, passwords, and so on. You can often click a drop-down list and make a selection. This information is encrypted and stored on your computer and is not accessible to Web sites, so you needn't be concerned about security when you use AutoComplete. To adjust AutoComplete settings, choose Tools ➢ Internet Options and click the AutoComplete button on the Content tab.

Internet Explorer assumes that when you enter a URL in the Address bar you want to go to a Web page or some other HTML document. Therefore, whether you enter `http://www.sybex.com` or `www.sybex.com`, you'll reach the Sybex Web site.

If you want to access another type of resource, such as an FTP archive, a Telnet host, or a Gopher server, you'll need to enter the full URL, for example, `ftp://ftp.archive.edu`.

TIP

If you want to edit only part of an address that's already displayed in the Address bar, place the cursor in the Address bar, hold down Ctrl, and press the right or left arrow to jump forward or backward to the next separator character (\\\.,? or +).

You can also run a program from the Address bar. Simply type its path (for example, `C:\Program Files\FrontPage.exe`), and press Enter. To find a file using the Address bar, enter the drive letter (for example, **D:**), and press Enter. Internet Explorer opens a window similar to that shown in Figure 13.3.

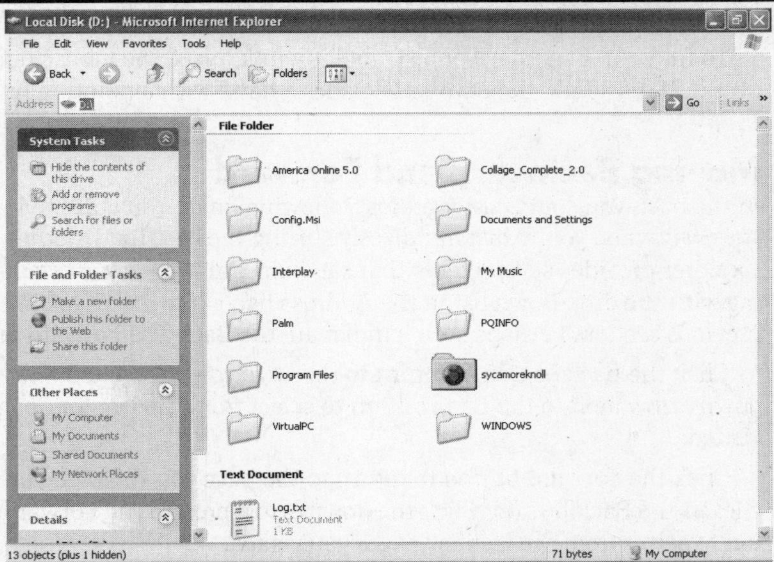

FIGURE 13.3: Browsing for a file with Internet Explorer

In addition, you can search from the Address bar. Enter the word or phrase you want to find, and press Enter. We'll look at searching in detail later in this chapter in the section "Finding Exactly What You Want on the Internet."

Using and Managing Links

The term *link* is short for hyperlink, which is a term, a phrase, an image, or a symbol that forms a connection with another resource that can reside on your local computer, your local network, or the Internet. You may also hear these connections referred to as hot links, hypertext links, or hypermedia. They all mean the same thing, and clicking one takes you to that resource. Links are the heart and soul of the Internet, and in the incipient days of browser development gave rise to ponderous discussions about the linear structure of books, film, and speech versus the nonlinear format of the World Wide Web.

Today, we seldom discuss links; we just take them for granted and click. In Internet Explorer, textual links are underlined and are usually in a different color from normal text. After you click such a link to jump to that resource and then return to the page on which the link resides, the link will be in yet another color, indicating that you've "visited" it.

To find out if an image or a symbol is a link, place the mouse pointer over it. If it's a link, the pointer becomes a hand with a pointing finger.

Moving Backward and Forward

In the past, you could easily get lost following links. You still can lose your way when you're just mindlessly surfing the Net, but Internet Explorer provides several tools that can help you retrace your steps, starting with the drop-down list in the Address bar, as we discussed in the previous section. Perhaps even handier are the Back and Forward buttons.

Click the Back button to return to the page you just visited. Click the down arrow next to the Back button to select from the last four pages you visited.

Click the Forward button to return to the page you visited before you clicked the Back button. Click the down arrow next to the Forward button to select from the last few pages you visited.

Adding Your Own Links to the Links Bar

Another way to keep track of links that you follow and want to revisit is to add them to the Links bar. When you first install Windows XP Professional, the Links bar contains the following:

- Customize Links, which takes you to a Microsoft page that gives you information on how to add, remove, and rearrange items on the Links bar
- Free Hotmail, which takes you to a page where you can sign up for a Hotmail e-mail account
- Windows, which takes you to the Microsoft Windows site
- Windows Media, which takes you to a page at the Microsoft Web site devoted to multimedia (videos, music, and so on)

NOTE

Remember, by default the Links bar shares a line with the Address bar. You can drag the Links bar to its own line so that more of its buttons are visible onscreen, or click the » button at the right end to see its buttons in drop-down list format. You might need to unlock the toolbars first.

To add a link, drag it from the Web page to the Links bar; to remove, right-click it, and choose Delete from the shortcut menu. To rearrange items on the Links bar, click the item, and then drag it to a new location.

Another quick and easy way to keep track of pages you want to revisit is to add them to your Favorites list, and we'll look at how to do that in the following section.

Keeping Track of Your Favorite Sites

As we've mentioned, Internet Explorer provides several devices you can use to prevent getting lost in cyberspace, and a particularly handy one is the Favorites bar. To open it, click the Favorites button on the Standard toolbar to open the Favorites list in an Explorer bar pane to the left of the main window, or choose Favorites from the Menu bar to view the Favorites list in menu form. Figure 13.4 shows the Favorites list in the Explorer bar, and Figure 13.5 shows the Favorites menu.

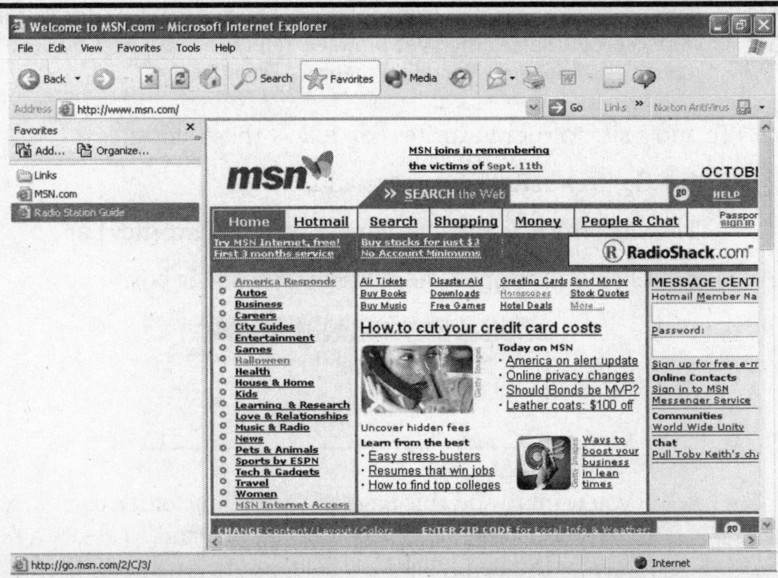

FIGURE 13.4: Click the Favorites button to open the Favorites bar.

FIGURE 13.5: Choose the Favorites menu to see this drop-down list.

Adding a Site to Your Favorites List

Clicking a Favorites item takes you to that resource. Initially you'll see the following items on the Favorites menu or in the Favorites bar:

- Links, which opens a menu containing the same items as are on the Links bar
- MSN.com, which takes you to the msn.com home page
- Radio Station Guide, which takes you to a page where you can click a button to hear a radio webcast from stations such as the BBC and CNN

NOTE

On some Web pages, you will see a suggestion that you "bookmark" this page. Netscape and some other Web browsers refer to a list of sites that you want to revisit as a bookmark list rather than as a Favorites list.

To add a site to your Favorites list, follow these steps:

1. Go to the site you want to add.
2. Click the Favorites button to open the Favorites bar.
3. Click Add to open the Add Favorite dialog box:

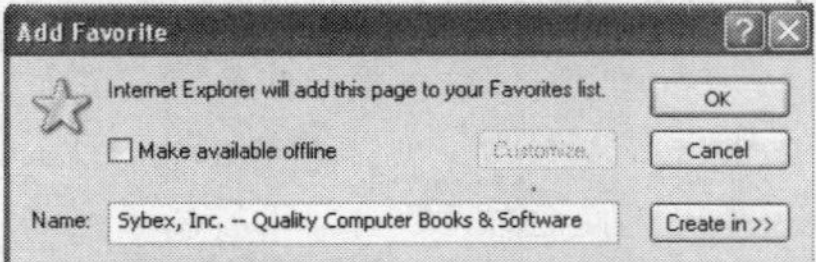

4. If you want to add this page to an existing folder, click Create In, select a folder, and click OK. If you want to create a new folder for this item, click New Folder, enter a name for the folder, and click OK.

5. In the Add Favorite dialog box, Internet Explorer provides a name for this Favorite site. To give the site another name in your Favorites list, replace the default name with the name you want.
6. Click OK.

NOTE

Each user's Favorites are stored separately, so if you log on as a different user, your favorites won't follow you. Instead you'll see the default Favorites list shown earlier in Figure 13.5.

You can also add items to your Favorites list in some other ways:

- Right-click a link, and choose Add to Favorites from the shortcut menu.
- Right-click the current page outside a link, and choose Add to Favorites from the shortcut menu to add that page.
- Drag and drop a link on a Web page to the Favorites button on the Standard toolbar.

TIP

If you want really quick access to a Web site, create a shortcut to it on the Desktop. Right-click in an empty area of the page, and choose Create Shortcut. You'll see a message that the shortcut will be placed on your Desktop. Now all you need to do to open Internet Explorer and connect to that page is to double-click the shortcut.

Maintaining Your Favorites List

You'll find out soon enough that your Favorites list will grow quickly, and that over time many of them will no longer be useful to you. Perhaps you bookmarked the agenda for an event that is now long past, for example, or an article about zebras for your child's research paper last semester. Or perhaps you have just lost interest in a particular subject that used to fascinate you.

To keep your list manageable, you need to do some periodic housekeeping, weeding out what you don't want and rearranging or renaming what you do keep so that it is meaningful.

Deleting a site from your Favorites list is simple: right-click it in the list, and choose Delete from the shortcut menu. You might, however, want to get in the habit of following the link before you right-click—just in case the site is more important than you remembered and you want to keep it in the list.

To move an item to another place in the list or to another folder, simply click and drag it. To create a new folder, click Organize to open the Organize Favorites dialog box, and click Create Folder.

To rename an item, right-click it and choose Rename from the shortcut menu. Type the new name, and press Enter.

Returning to Where You Were

Yet another way to keep track of where you've been and to quickly revisit sites of interest is the History list. To display it, click the History button on the Standard toolbar. You'll open the History bar, which will look similar to that in Figure 13.6. Simply click a link to go to that page. Click a folder to see pages in that site that have links in the History list. To specify how many days you want to keep links in the History list, choose Tools ➢ Internet Options, and on the General tab change the number in the Days to Keep Pages in History box.

You can display the items in the History list by date, by site, by most visited, and by the order in which you visited sites today. Click the View down arrow to choose an order. If you want to search for something on the history list, click Search, enter a word or a phrase, and click Search Now.

To delete an item from the History list, right-click it, and choose Delete from the shortcut menu. To clear the History list completely, click the Clear History button on the General tab of the Internet Options dialog box.

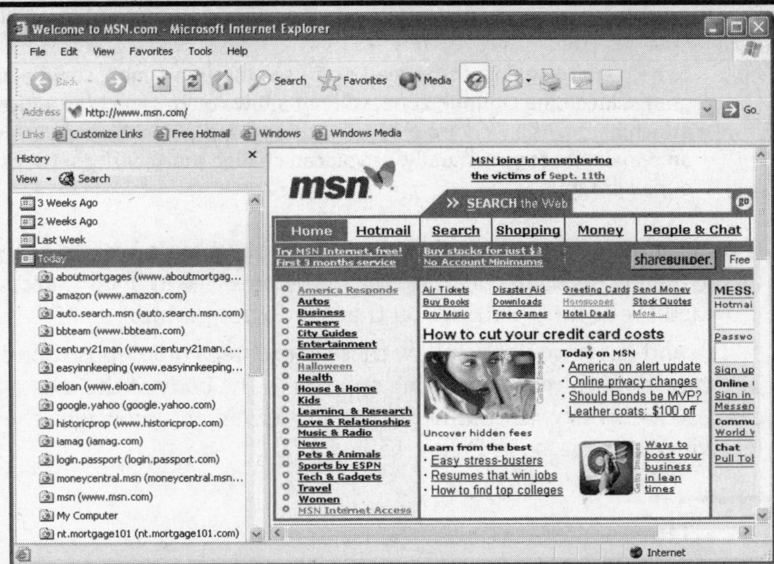

FIGURE 13.6: You can use the History bar to see where you went today and in previous days and weeks.

Reading Mail and News and Sharing Pages

If you hear the new mail beep as you're exploring the Internet, you can quickly open your Inbox in Outlook Express by clicking the Mail button on the Standard toolbar and choosing Read Mail. To check a newsgroup, click the Mail button, and choose Read News. To compose an e-mail message, click the Mail button, and choose New Message to open the New Message window.

Sometimes you might run across a Web page that someone else you know would be interested in. Internet Explorer offers a quick way to mail that link:

1. Display the page.
2. Click the Mail button, and choose Send a Link. The New Message window opens with the link in the body of the message and the site title in the Subject and Attach lines.
3. Address your message, compose your message, and click Send.

NOTE

To help guard against the spread of viruses through e-mail, some e-mail programs, including Outlook 2002, will not allow you to send Web addresses as attachments. As a workaround, you can copy-and-paste the page's address in an e-mail message manually, or you can change the security settings in your e-mail program.

If your recipient is connected to the Internet and has a Web browser, he or she merely needs to click the link in the message to open that page, provided the security settings on that PC do not prohibit it.

To send the page itself, follow these same steps but choose Send Page. The current page you are viewing appears in the body of the message. You can also add your own comments to let the recipient know why they're receiving the page, as in Figure 13.7.

TIP

Sending a page requires less security than sending a link, so it can potentially be used as a workaround in an e-mail program that prohibits sending a link because of its security settings.

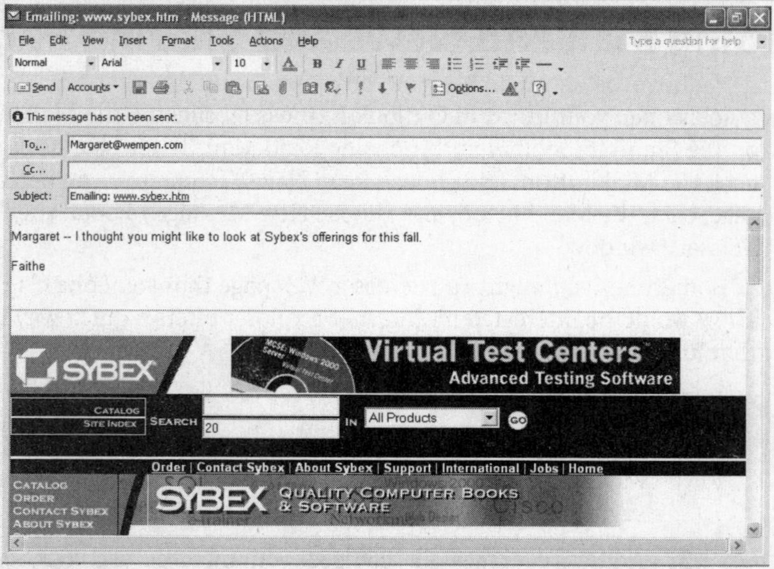

FIGURE 13.7: Sending a Web page in the body of an e-mail message

WARNING

Before you willy-nilly include Web pages in your e-mail, be sure that your recipient's e-mail program can handle HTML messages. For more information about e-mail and HTML, see Chapter 14.

Tuning in a Web Radio Station

You might have noticed that one of the default Favorites items is Radio Station Guide. It takes you to the Windows Media.com site, where you can select from hundreds of online radio stations (see Figure 13.8). The Windows Media Player program that comes with Windows XP Professional is a more feature-rich way of playing these stations, but Internet Explorer can do it too.

TIP

Earlier versions of Internet Explorer included a Radio toolbar, but this feature has been omitted from IE 6.0. Microsoft encourages users to play radio stations through Windows Media Player, which is covered in Chapter 18.

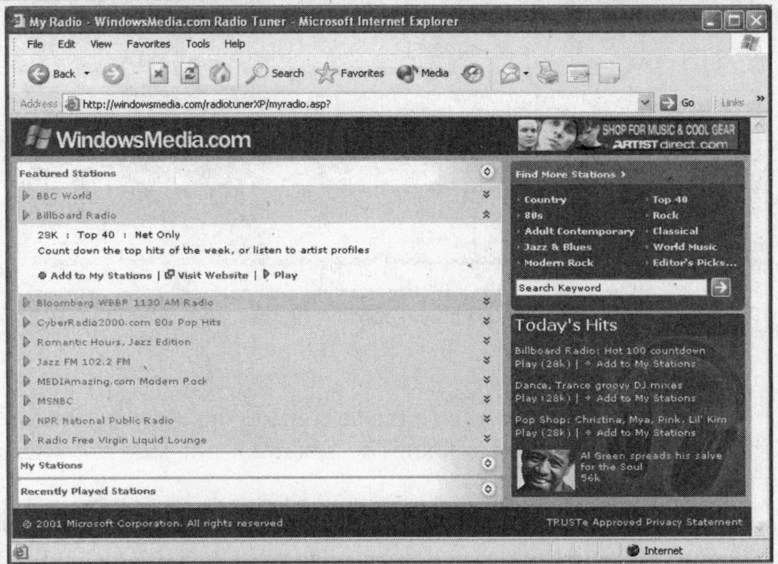

FIGURE 13.8: You can tune in to Internet radio stations through the Windows Media site.

To select a station, choose Favorites ➢ Radio Station Guide to open the WindowsMedia.com site. Click the name of a station to open information about it, and then click the Play hyperlink beneath the name to start listening to it.

Depending on your settings, you might see a message asking whether you want to play the media in Internet Explorer's own window; if you see that, click Yes. Media controls appear in the Explorer bar to the left of the main window, as in Figure 13.9. (If you choose No, the content will play in whatever program is set as the default for that media type.) You can control the broadcast with the buttons there, the same as with any radio or tape player in your home stereo. A Web page for the selected station appears in a separate Internet Explorer window.

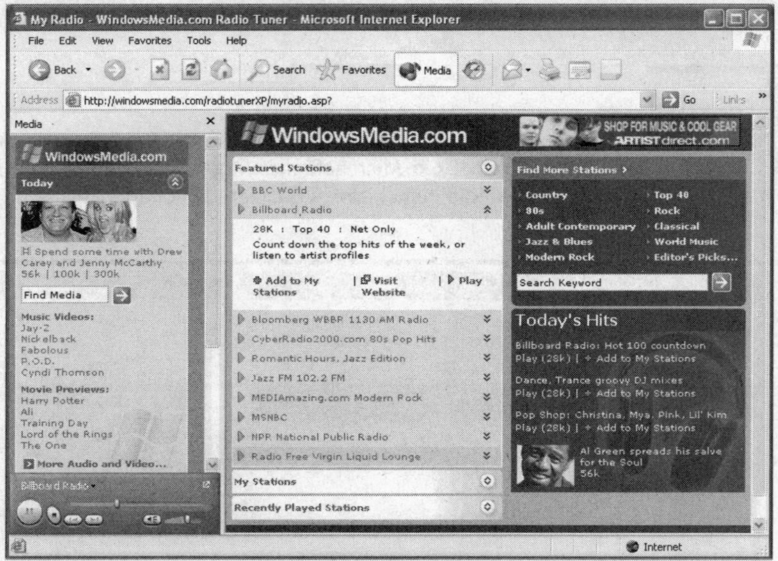

FIGURE 13.9: Use the media player controls in Internet Explorer to listen to a radio station.

To toggle the Explorer pane media controls on/off, click the Media button on the Standard toolbar. The broadcast will continue whether the controls display or not.

The quality of your listening experience will depend on your speakers, your system, and the speed at which you are connected. Generally speaking, the slower your Internet connection, the larger the buffer that must load before the station can begin playing. A buffer is a holding area for incoming data that is ready to be played. It helps prevent choppiness in the broadcast due to Internet traffic slowdowns. People with regular dial-up modem Internet service might experience a several minute delay between selecting a station and hearing it, and there might be occasional broadcast choppiness even with buffering.

Internet Explorer's radio controls are rather primitive; if you are interested in Internet Radio, see Chapter 18 to learn about the more sophisticated controls in Windows Media Player 8. Some multimedia hyperlinks in Internet Explorer open Windows Media Player automatically when you click on them.

Saving and Printing Web Pages

If you always want to see the most current version of a Web page, you probably want to place a link to it on the Links bar or the Favorites list. However, in some cases, you'll want to save it to your local hard drive or to a drive on your network. For example, we recently wanted easy access to a rather long U.S. government document. In this case, the document had been written and distributed over the Internet and was not going to change. Therefore we saved it to our local network so that we could get to it quickly without being connected to the Internet.

Saving the Current Page

In Internet Explorer, you can save the current page in several formats:

- As a complete Web page, including all graphics, frames, and style sheets as separate files.
- As a single-file Web archive including all the information needed to display the page in an e-mail program such as Outlook Express or Outlook.
- As a single text file in HTML format, minus any external files such as graphics.
- As plain text in ASCII format, without any formatting or codes.

To save the current page, follow these steps:

1. Choose File ➢ Save As to open the Save Web Page dialog box:

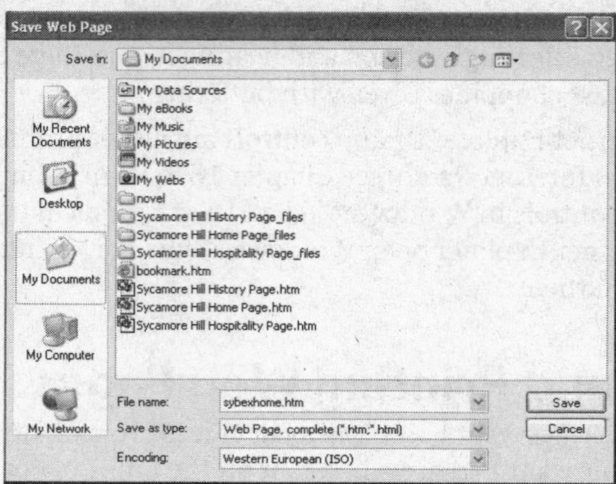

2. Select a folder in which to save the page, and in the File Name box enter a name if you want something different from that which Internet Explorer proposes.

3. In the Save As Type drop-down box, select the format in which you want the page saved. Your choices are:

   - Web Page, complete (*.htm,*.html)
   - Web Archive, single file (*.mht)
   - Web Page, HTML only (*.htm,*.html)
   - Text File (*.txt)

NOTE

If you choose Web Page, complete, a separate folder will be created to hold ancillary files for the page.

4. Click Save.

You can also save a Web page without opening it if its link is displayed. Follow these steps:

1. Right-click the link, and choose Save Target As from the shortcut menu. You'll see a dialog box that shows you that the page is being downloaded.

NOTE

If the Save Target As command is not available, you cannot save the current page using this method; use the File ➢ Save As method instead.

2. In the Save As dialog box, select a folder, and specify a filename.
3. Click Save.

NOTE

When you save a target, the only file type available is Web Page, complete. If you want one of the other file types, you'll need to open the page and follow the steps for saving information on the current page.

Saving Portions of a Page

You can also save only a portion of text from a Web page or an image. To save a portion of text to use in another document, select the text, and then press Ctrl+C. Open the other document, place the insertion point where you want the text, and press Ctrl+V.

To save an image, follow these steps:

1. Right-click the image, and choose Save Picture As from the shortcut menu to open the Save Picture dialog box.
2. Select a folder, a filename, and a type, and click Save.

To save an image as wallpaper, right-click the image and choose Set As Wallpaper from the shortcut menu. To specify how you want the wallpaper displayed, right-click the desktop, choose Properties to open the Display Properties dialog box, click the Desktop tab, and select an option in the Position drop-down box.

WARNING

Every time you right-click an image and choose Set as Wallpaper, the image is saved under the name Internet Explorer Wallpaper. When you do the same to another image on some other Web page, that image replaces whatever image was previously saved under that name. If you want to save an image more permanently, right-click the image, and choose Save Picture As from the shortcut menu.

Printing the Current Page

If you want to quickly print the current page, simply click the Print button on the Standard toolbar. If, however, you want more control over what's printed and how, choose File ➢ Print to open the Print dialog box, as shown in Figure 13.10.

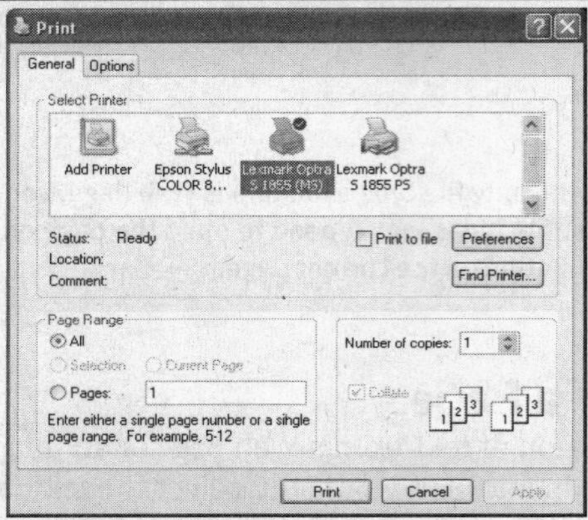

FIGURE 13.10: The Print dialog box, open at the General tab

For the most part, this is your standard Windows Print dialog box. (For details about printers and printing in Windows XP Professional, see Chapter 10.) The difference is the Options tab, which you can use to specify how frames and links are printed. It's shown in Figure 13.11.

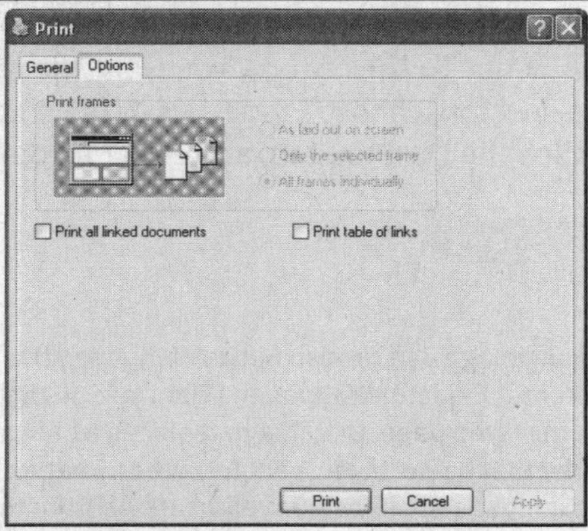

FIGURE 13.11: The Print dialog box in Internet Explorer has an Options tab for determining which content to print.

The Print Frames section on the Options tab lets you specify how a document that contains frames should be printed. Frames are divided-off areas of the page, each with its own content in it. Frames used to be a common design element on Web pages, but nowadays they have fallen out of favor, such that most commercial Web sites do not use them. If the page you are printing does not have frames, the options in the Print Frames area will be unavailable, as in Figure 13.11.

If the Print Frames options are available, you can:

- Select the As Laid Out on Screen option in the Print Frames section to print the Web page exactly as it is displayed on your screen.
- Select the Only the Selected Frame option to print only a frame you have previously selected. (To select a frame, click inside it in an empty space–in other words, not on a link.)
- Select the All Frames Individually option if you want to print each frame on a separate sheet of paper.

In addition, regardless of the frame status of the page, you can:

- Select the Print All Linked Documents option if you want to print the pages that are linked to the current page as well. (Be sure you really want to do this; you could need lots of paper.)
- Select the Print Table of Links option if you want to print a table that lists the links for the page at the end of the document.

When you have all your options selected, click the Print button on any tab to print the document.

To print the target of any link, right-click the link, and choose Print Target from the shortcut menu to open the Print dialog box.

TIP

By default, Windows does not print the background colors and background images of Web pages. First, the printed output could be illegible, and, second, unless you have a rather powerful printer, spooling and printing could be really slow. If, for whatever reason, you want or need to print the background, choose Tools ➢ Internet Options to open the Internet Options dialog box. Click the Advanced tab, scroll down to the Printing section, check the Print Background Colors and Images check box, and click OK.

Working Offline

As we mentioned earlier in this chapter, if you want to view Web pages when you aren't connected to the Internet, and having the most current version possible is not important, you can simply save them to your local hard drive. If having the most current information is important, you can choose to "work offline."

To make the current page available for offline viewing, follow these steps:

1. Right-click in an empty spot on the page and choose Add to Favorites to open the Add Favorite dialog box.
2. Click the Make Available Offline check box.
3. If you want to view only certain content offline, click the Customize button to start the Offline Favorite Wizard. Follow the onscreen instructions. You can also establish a schedule for updating the page using this Wizard. Click Finish when you're done.
4. Before you close your connection to the Internet, choose Tools ➢ Synchronize to ensure that you have the most up-to-date content for the page you want to view offline.

To view pages offline, choose File ➢ Work Offline, and in the Favorites bar select the page you want.

Finding Exactly What You Want on the Internet

The serendipitous experience of clicking and following hyperlinks may suffice while you're polishing off your lunch of tuna sandwich and chips or filling the occasional lazy, rainy afternoon, but most of the time when you connect to the Internet, you have something specific in mind that you want to do or find. Regardless of what you're looking for—information about a topic, an e-mail or a mailing address, a business, a Web page, and so on—the way to find it is to use a search service. *Search service* is a relatively new term for what we referred to in the past as a search engine, a program that can search a file, a database, or the Internet for keywords and retrieve documents in which those keywords are found.

Examples of search services that you may have used include MSN, Yahoo!, Excite, Google, InfoSeek, AltaVista, and Lycos. To search with one of these services, you go to the site (for example, `http://www.yahoo.com`); optionally, select a category, enter a keyword or phrase, and click Search (or some similar button). The default search service used with the Search Companion in Internet Explorer is MSN, but you can search using additional search engines as well.

Let's try a search with the Search Companion built into Internet Explorer 6. Suppose, for example, a customer in London has asked for a quote in euros, but you aren't sure what a euro is. Let's search the Internet for the answer. Follow these steps:

1. In Internet Explorer, click the Search button on the Standard toolbar to open the Search Companion bar:

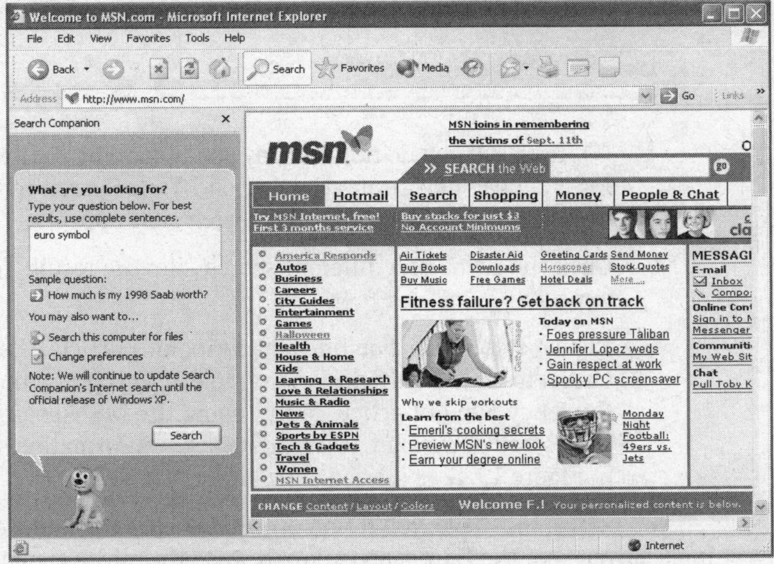

2. In the Type Your Question Below box, type **`euro symbol`**.

3. Click Search. Search results from MSN appear in the main window. (No surprise here; Microsoft owns both MSN and Internet Explorer.)

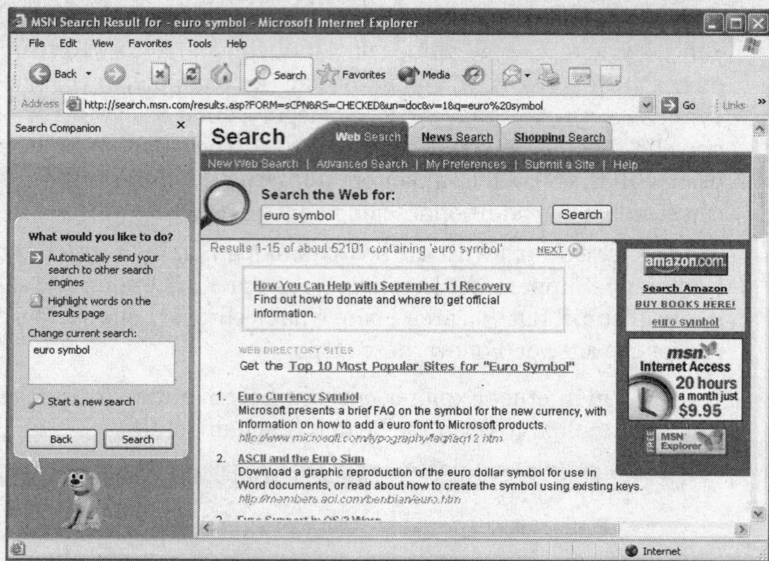

4. (Optional) If you do not find any useful-looking results from MSN, click the Automatically Send Your Search to Other Search Engines. A list of other search sites appears.
5. Click the name of a different search site; the results from it appear.
6. Repeat step 5 until you find a likely looking article title; then click it to read the article. For example, if you choose the Euro Currency Symbol article found using the MSN search and then scroll down a bit, you'll arrive at the information shown in Figure 13.12.

If you peruse this page, you'll find out that euro is the name of the single currency of the European Union. It was officially designated on January 1, 1999, and will be in common use in the form of coins and bills by 2002. In Windows programs, the symbol is available in the Times New Roman, Arial, and Courier New fonts.

TIP

If you want a different search engine to appear by default in the Search Companion, return to the opening screen of the Search Companion (one way is to click the Search button to turn it off and then again to turn it back on) and click Change Preferences. Then click Change Internet Search Behavior and select a different default search engine.

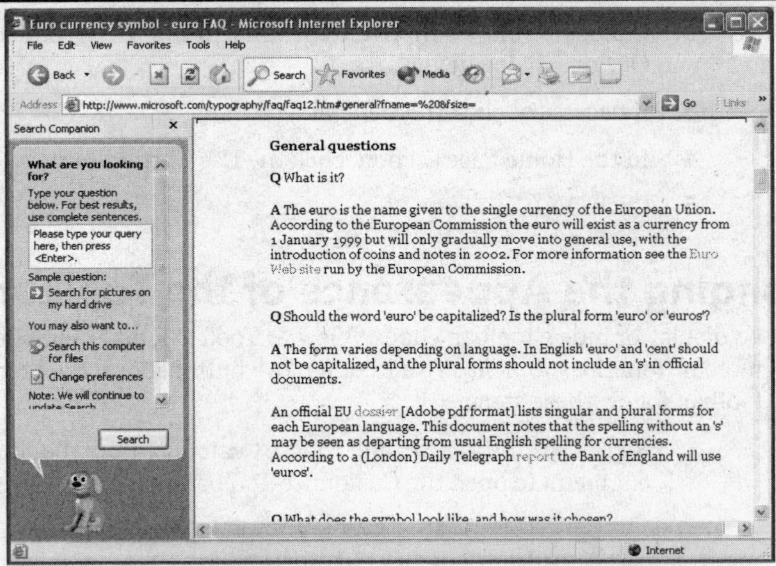

FIGURE 13.12: Everything you need to know about the euro symbol

Customizing Internet Explorer

You can personalize the way you connect to the Internet and the features of Internet Explorer in myriad ways, and to do most of this you use the Internet Options dialog box, which we looked at in detail in Chapter 12. Here we want to touch briefly on a couple of these options again and also look at how you can customize toolbars.

Choosing a Start Page

As we mentioned at the beginning of this chapter, when you first install Windows XP Professional, your start page is set as `www.msn.com`. Until you change this setting, this is the page that will open every time you start Internet Explorer. To establish a start page of your choosing, follow these steps:

1. Open the page you want to use as your start page.
2. Choose Tools ➢ Internet Options to open the Internet Options dialog box.
3. If necessary, click the General tab.
4. In the Home Page section, click the Use Current button.
5. Click OK.

Changing the Appearance of the Toolbars

To display or hide a toolbar, choose View ➢ Toolbars, and then select a toolbar from the submenu. To add or remove buttons from the Standard toolbar, follow these steps:

1. Right-click the toolbar, and choose Customize from the shortcut menu to open the Customize Toolbar dialog box:

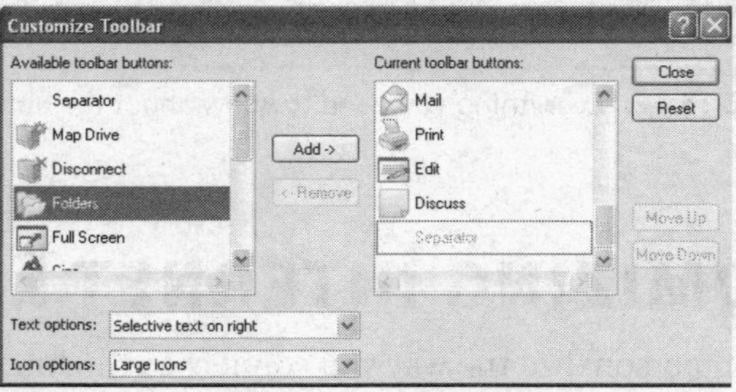

2. To add a button, select it from the pane on the left, and click Add.
3. To delete a button, select it from the pane on the right, and click Remove.
4. To specify whether or where to display button labels, click the Text Options down arrow and select from the list.

5. To specify the icon size, click the Icon Options down arrow.
6. To rearrange the order of the buttons, select a button in the pane on the right, and click Move Up or Move Down.
7. When the toolbar is to your liking, click Close.

TIP

To return to the default arrangement of the toolbar, click the Reset button in the Customize Toolbar dialog box.

To move the menu bar or a toolbar up or down, place the cursor over the left vertical bar of the bar you want to move, and drag it to a new position.

Dealing with Cookies and Temporary Internet Files

As you learned in Chapter 12, a cookie is a file that is stored on your computer by the server of a site that you visit. When you revisit the site, Internet Explorer sends the cookie back to the server, perhaps to identify you so that the server can present to you a customized Web page. A cookie is only a simple data file; it cannot "look" at your hard disk or send any other information back to the server or run other programs on your computer.

A temporary Internet file is a copy of a Web page that you have visited. Both cookies and temporary Internet files are stored in the Temporary Internet Files folder on your computer. To take a look at what's in this folder, follow these steps:

1. In Internet Explorer, choose Tools ➢ Internet Options to open the Internet Options dialog box.
2. If necessary, click the General tab, and then in the Temporary Internet Files section, click the Settings button to open the Settings dialog box.
3. Click the View Files button to open the Temporary Internet Files folder, as shown in Figure 13.13.
4. Scroll to the right as needed to see the details of the files.

NOTE

By default the files are displayed in Details view; you can change to any other view, just as with any other file listing.

5. When you are finished perusing the files, close the folder window. Then return to the Settings dialog box and click Cancel to close it. This returns you to the Internet Options dialog box.

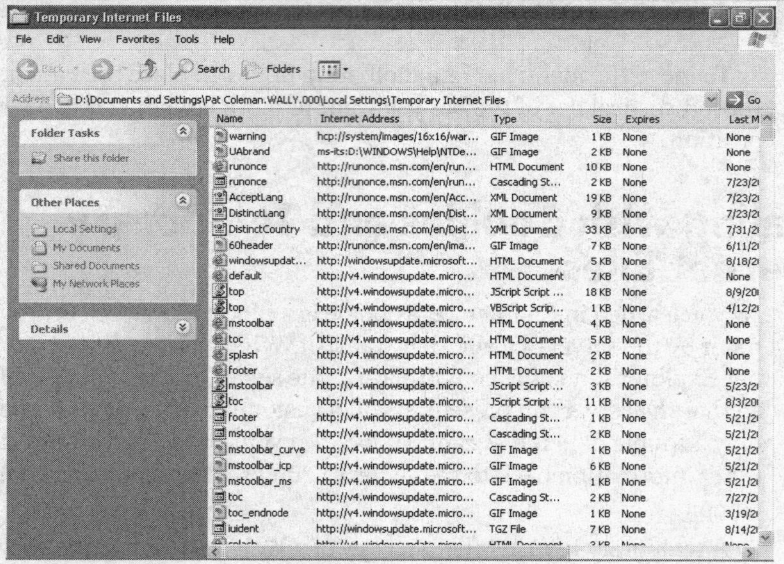

FIGURE 13.13: Cookies and temporary Internet files are stored in the Temporary Internet Files folder.

When you access a Web page, Internet Explorer first checks to see if the page is in your Temporary Internet Files folder. If it is, it checks to see if the page has been updated since being stored, and if not, it loads the page from the Temporary Internet Files folder (also called the *cache*). This is obviously faster than downloading the page from the server.

If you want to save space on your local disk, however, you can empty the Temporary Internet Files folder, either manually or whenever you exit Internet Explorer. To empty the folder manually, in the General tab of the

Internet Options dialog box, click Delete Files. To empty the folder automatically when you close Internet Explorer, follow these steps:

1. In the Internet Options dialog box, click the Advanced tab.
2. Scroll down to the Security section.
3. Click the Empty Temporary Internet Files Folder When Browser Is Closed check box.
4. Click OK.

WHAT'S NEXT?

Although a Web browser is an essential Internet tool, an e-mail program is arguably the most-used Internet tool and, probably, the most-used of all application programs. In the next chapter, we'll look at Outlook Express, the e-mail program that's included with Windows XP Professional.

Chapter 14

Using Outlook Express for E-Mail and News

Of all the features of the Internet, intranets, and local area networks, e-mail is, without question, the most used. Instead of playing phone tag with a colleague at work, you send her e-mail. Millions of extended families stay in touch via e-mail, and an e-mail address has become an expected component of a business card.

Windows XP includes an e-mail program called Outlook Express that you can use to send and receive e-mail, to store and organize received messages, and to store the e-mail addresses of people with whom you correspond. Outlook Express is far from your only choice for e-mail reading; you could choose to use Microsoft Outlook, Eudora, or some other program instead. However, since Outlook Express comes free with Windows XP, this chapter will focus on it.

Adapted and revised from *Windows 2000 Professional: In Record Time* by Peter Dyson and Pat Coleman

ISBN 0-7821-2450-X 496 pages $29.99

In addition to its e-mail capabilities, Outlook Express also manages messages from Internet newsgroups. These are public forums on various topics (over 34,000 of them at this writing) in which people can post messages for everyone to read and respond to. You'll learn about OE's newsgroup features at the end of this chapter.

INTRODUCING OUTLOOK EXPRESS

The quickest way to start Outlook Express is to click the Launch Outlook Express icon on the Quick Launch taskbar, if the Quick Launch taskbar is displayed. You can also start it by choosing Start ➢ All Programs ➢ Outlook Express or, from within Internet Explorer, by choosing Tools ➢ Mail and News and then selecting an item from the submenu.

NOTE

Before you can open and use Outlook Express to send and receive e-mail, you need to configure Outlook Express for your e-mail accounts. See "Setting Up Mail Accounts" later in the chapter.

When you first open Outlook Express, you'll see a screen similar to that shown in Figure 14.1. To return to this screen at any time later, you can click Outlook Express at the top of the Folders list.

NOTE

The very first time you start Outlook Express, the Internet Connection Wizard runs so you can set up a mail account. You can do this now (and skip to the next section in the chapter to learn how to do it), or you can click Cancel and do it later.

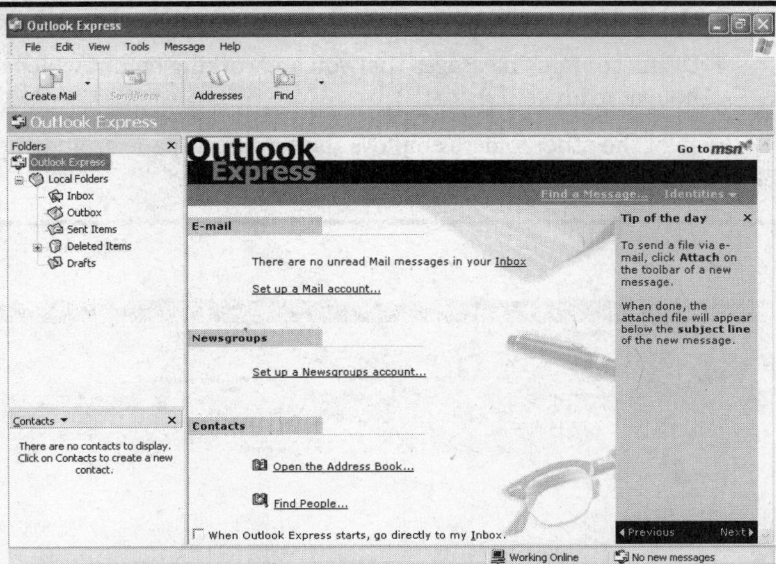

FIGURE 14.1: The opening screen in Outlook Express

To go to the Inbox folder, click the Inbox hyperlink, or click Inbox in the Folders list.

TIP

To go directly to the Inbox when Outlook Express starts up, choose Tools ➢ Options and check the Go directly to my Inbox folder check box.

As you can see in Figure 14.2, the Inbox contains four panes. In the upper left is the Folders list, the same as in Figure 14.1. The Folders List is a tool for organizing messages. Initially, it contains the following folders, although you can create additional folders, as you'll see later in this chapter:

- Inbox contains both newly received messages and messages that you have not yet disposed of in some way.
- Outbox contains messages that are ready to be sent.
- Sent Items contains copies of messages that you have sent (a handy device if you send lots of e-mail).

- Deleted Items contains copies of messages that you have deleted.
- Drafts contains messages that you are working on but which are not yet ready to be sent.

Each of the other folders employs the same four-pane arrangement as the Inbox.

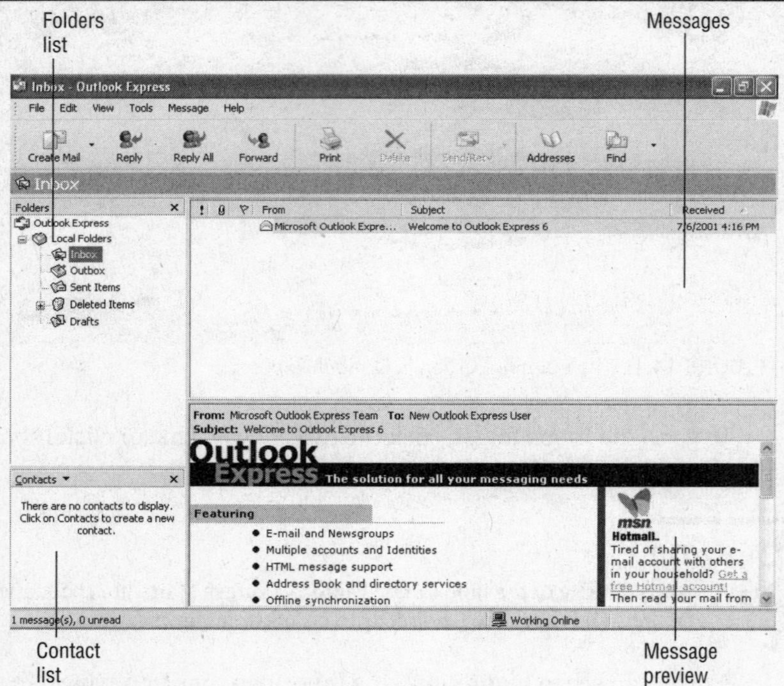

FIGURE 14.2: The Inbox window is divided into four panes.

The Contacts pane contains the names of people in your Address Book. To compose a message to anyone on this list, simply double-click the name. The list is empty in Figure 14.2, as yours will be initially as well. You will add the e-mail addresses of friends and associates as you go.

At the top right is the list of incoming messages. Unread messages, if any, appear in boldface. At the bottom right is the Preview pane, where the currently selected message appears. You can read the entire message in the Preview pane by scrolling down, or you can double-click the message to open it in its own window.

Setting Up Mail Accounts

Almost everyone with Internet access has at least one e-mail account, and many people have several. You probably got an e-mail account free when you signed up for your ISP, for example, and you might also have a Web-based e-mail account from a service like Hotmail, or an additional account from your workplace.

NOTE

One exception: you cannot use Outlook Express to send and receive e-mail from your America Online account, if you have one. AOL requires you to use its own e-mail program built into the AOL software.

Unless someone has pre-configured Outlook Express for you (a distinct possibility if your PC is in a corporate environment), you must set up your e-mail account(s) in Outlook Express before you can send or receive e-mail. It's not difficult to do because a Wizard walks you through the steps.

Before you get started, gather the following information:

- Your e-mail address
- Your e-mail password
- The incoming and outgoing mail server names
- The mail server type

Your e-mail address is probably the same as your Internet sign-on ID (if you have a dial-up connection) with "@" and the name of your service provider tacked on. For example, if your user ID is bob99, and your service provider is nowhere.net, your e-mail address would be bob99@nowhere.net.

Your e-mail password is probably the same as your Internet sign-on password, again if you have a dial-up connection. If you have an always-on connection like cable, DSL, or network, you might have to look up your e-mail password in the startup kit for your Internet service.

Some service providers use the same name for both incoming and outgoing mail servers; others use separate ones. Your ISP should tell you the names of the mail servers, but if you have to guess, try "mail" plus the ISP's name, as in mail.nowhere.net for both incoming and outgoing. If that doesn't work, try "pop" for the incoming (pop.nowhere.net) and "smtp" for the outgoing (smtp.nowhere.net).

Finally, there's the mail server type. Outlook Express can work with several types of e-mail servers: POP3, IMAP, or HTTP. You'll need to know which type yours is in order to set it up. Here are some clues:

- If you have a "regular" Internet e-mail account, it's probably POP3. Another good bet that it's POP3 is if the letters "POP" appear anywhere in the mail server's name, as in pop.nowhere.net.
- If you have a corporate e-mail account through your company's mail server, it might be IMAP or POP. Try IMAP first.
- If you have a Web-based e-mail account such as Hotmail, it's probably HTTP.

Since the steps are slightly different for POP3 and IMAP versus HTTP, we'll cover them separately.

Setting Up a POP3 or IMAP E-Mail Account

Ready to go? Then follow these steps to set up a POP3 or IMAP mail account.

1. In Outlook Express, choose Tools ➢ Accounts to open the Internet Accounts dialog box.
2. Click the Mail tab. Any accounts already set up will appear here. If your account is already here, you can skip the rest of the setup.
3. Click the Add button, and then click Mail. The Internet Connection Wizard opens and asks for your display name. This is the name that you want to appear along with your e-mail address on the mail you send.
4. Type the desired display name, and click Next. It asks for your e-mail address.
5. Type your e-mail address, and click Next. The E-mail Server Names screen appears.

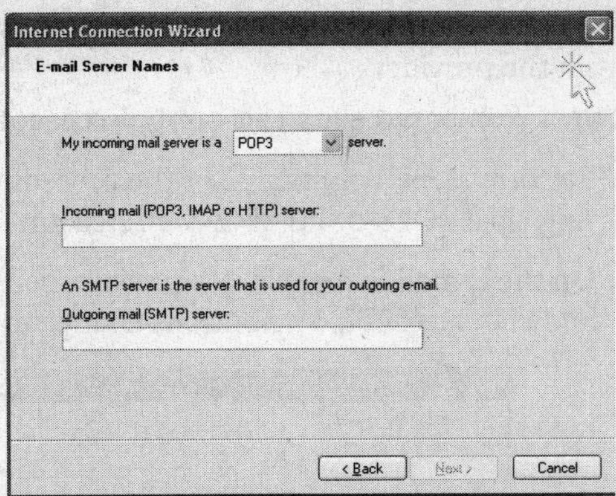

6. Open the drop-down list and choose POP3 or IMAP.
7. Type the names of the incoming and outgoing mail servers in the fields provided. Then click Next.
8. You are prompted for your account name and your password. Type them in the boxes provided. Your account name is probably the same as your e-mail address, or the portion of your e-mail address before the @ sign.
9. If you want Outlook Express to remember your password so you don't have to enter it each time, leave the Remember password check box marked. Otherwise clear it. Then click Next to display a summary screen.

NOTE

Most people should leave the Logon using Secure Password Authentication check box unmarked. If your mail server happens to require this, the ISP or network administrator will inform you.

10. Click Finish. The new account appears in the Internet Accounts dialog box.
11. Click Close to close the Internet Accounts dialog box.

Setting Up a Web-Based E-Mail Account

Outlook Express makes it very easy to set up a Hotmail or an MSN account; setting up a Web-based e-mail account from some other provider is more difficult but still possible if you can get the needed server information from the provider.

To set up a Web-based e-mail account, do the following:

1. Perform steps 1 through 5 of the preceding procedure, "Setting Up a POP3 or IMAP E-Mail Account."
2. On the E-mail Server Names screen, open the drop-down list and choose HTTP. The options change to these:

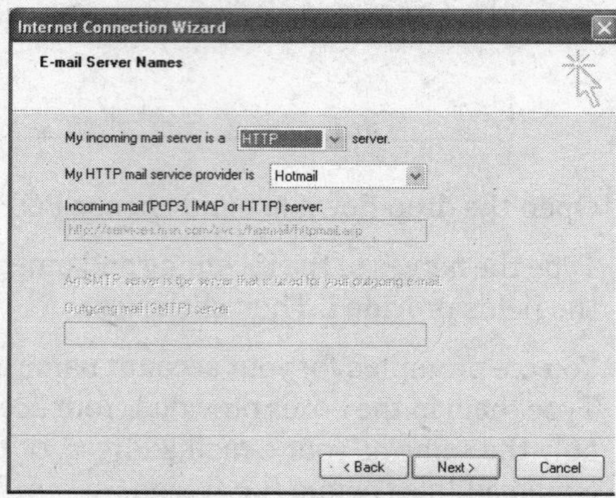

3. Hotmail is the default. If your provider is other than Hotmail, open the My HTTP Mail Service Provider Is drop-down list and choose either MSN or Other.
4. If you chose Other in step 3, the Incoming Mail (POP3, IMAP, or HTTP) Server text box becomes available; type the Web address of the mail server. (If you are not sure what it is, contact Technical Support for the service.)
5. Click Next. You are prompted for your account name and your password.
6. Type your user name and password in the boxes provided. Your account name is probably the same as your e-mail address, or the portion of your e-mail address before the @ sign.
7. If you want Outlook Express to remember your password so you don't have to enter it each time, leave the Remember password check box marked. Otherwise clear it. Then click Next to display a summary screen.

NOTE

Web-based e-mail does not generally require using the Logon using Secure Password Authentication option.

8. Click Finish. The new account appears in the Internet Accounts dialog box.
9. Click Close to close the Internet Accounts dialog box. A message appears asking whether you would like to download the folders from the mail server you added.
10. Click Yes. The folders are downloaded, and appear in the Folders list.

Web-based e-mail accounts appear as separate items on the Folders list, whereas POP3 and IMAP accounts are integrated into the main Inbox. Figure 14.3 shows Outlook Express set up for one POP3 and one HTTP (Hotmail) account.

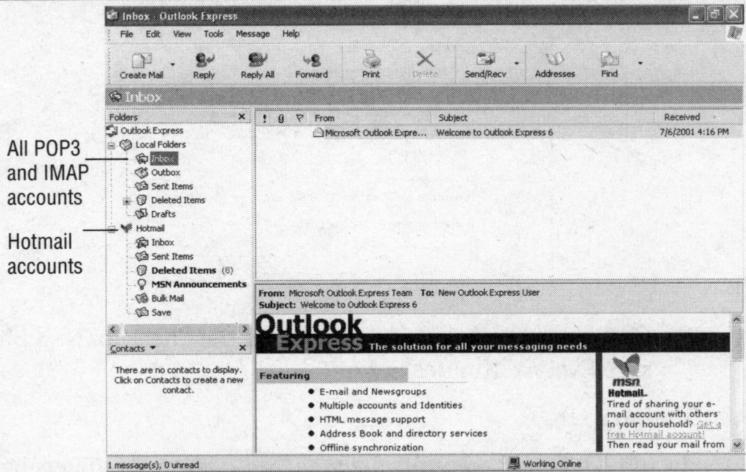

FIGURE 14.3: Outlook Express with a Hotmail account as well as a normal POP3 account configured.

Now that your mail accounts have been set up, you are ready to start receiving, replying to, and creating e-mail.

RECEIVING E-MAIL

If you are connected to the Internet, Outlook Express will automatically check mail servers for new messages and download them when you open Outlook Express. By default, Outlook Express will also check for new mail every 30 minutes, as long as you remain connected.

You can also check for new mail by choosing Tools ➢ Send and Receive ➢ Receive All or by clicking the Send/Recv button on the toolbar in the main window.

To adjust the time interval at which Outlook Express checks for new messages, follow these steps:

1. Choose Tools ➢ Options to open the Options dialog box:

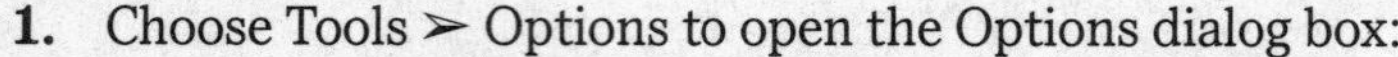

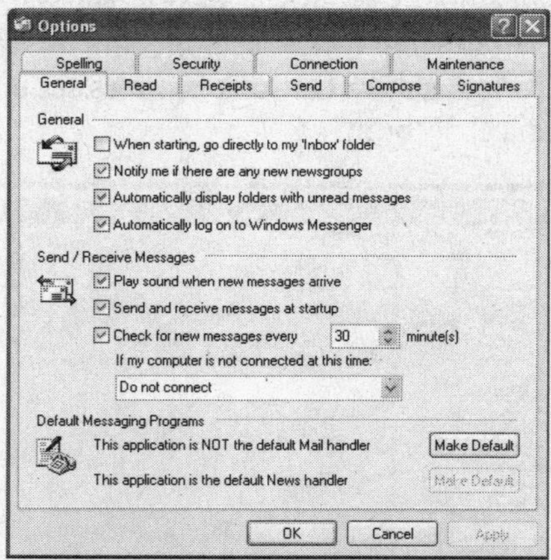

2. Click the up or down arrow to change the Check for New Message Every *x* Minutes option.
3. Click OK.

By default, all e-mail accounts are included in every send/receive operation. To exclude one of them, do the following:

1. Choose Tools ➢ Accounts to open the Internet Accounts dialog box.
2. Click the account on the list, and then click Properties to open the Properties dialog box for that account.

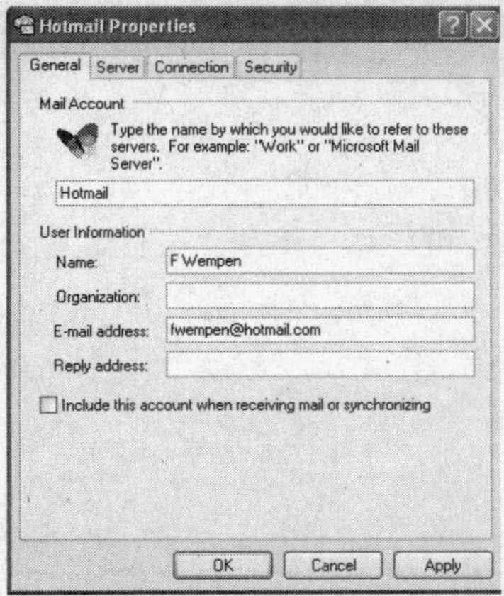

3. Clear the Include This Account When Receiving Mail or Synchronizing check box.
4. Click OK to close the Properties box.
5. Click Close to close the Internet Accounts dialog box.

From that point on, the only way to get new mail from that account is to specify it individually. For example, for an account called Hotmail, you would choose Tools ➢ Send and Receive ➢ Hotmail, or click the down arrow on the Send/Recv button and choose Hotmail from the list of accounts.

Reading and Processing Messages

You can click a message header to display the message in the lower pane. That pane has its own scroll bar for scrolling through the message.

You can also double-click the message to view it in its own window, as shown in Figure 14.4.

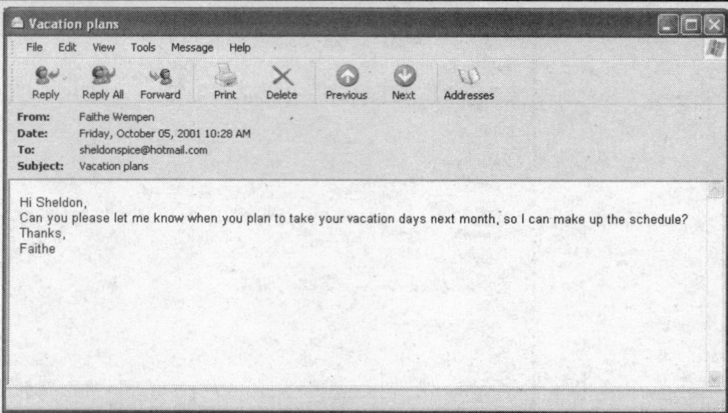

FIGURE 14.4: A received message opened in a separate window. Notice the different buttons on the toolbar.

Printing Messages

For various reasons, it's often handy to have a paper copy of e-mail messages. You can print in a couple of ways:

- To print a message without opening it, select its header, and click the Print icon on the toolbar in the main window.
- To print an open message, click the Print icon on the toolbar in the message window.

Changing a Message's Read Status

If you want to postpone taking action on a particular message, you might find it helpful to return the message to its unread status. That way it continues to appear in bold on the list. To do so, select the header and choose Edit ➢ Mark As Unread. You can go the other way too: on the Edit menu you can also choose Mark As Read to mark an unread message as read, or Mark All Read to mark all messages as read.

Flagging a Message

Another way to make a message stand out is to attach a flag to it. This does not affect its read status, but simply makes it more noticeable. To do so, select the header and choose Message ➢ Flag Message. This places a red flag to the left of the message header, as in Figure 14.5.

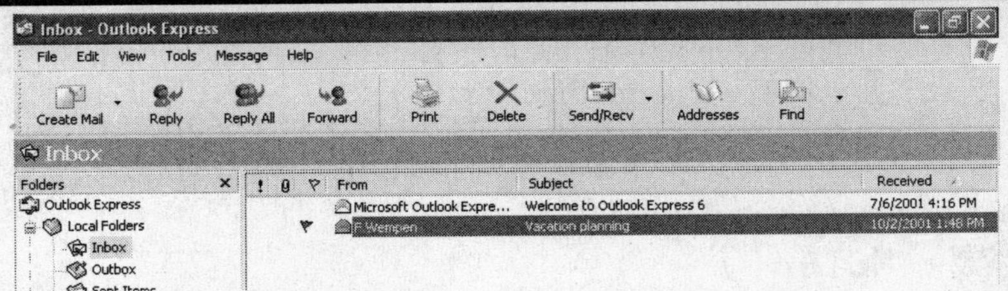

FIGURE 14.5: A message has been flagged for later action.

Moving Messages

You can easily move a message from one folder to another by dragging and dropping it. For example, if you receive a message that you want to modify and send to some else, select the message header and then drag it to the Drafts folder. Open it, revise it, and then send it on its way.

Saving Messages

You can save messages in folders you create in Windows Explorer, and you can save messages in Outlook Express folders. You can also save attachments as files.

Saving Messages in Windows Explorer Folders To save messages in a folder in Windows Explorer, follow these steps:

1. Open the message, or select its header.
2. Choose File ➢ Save As to open the Save Message As dialog box:

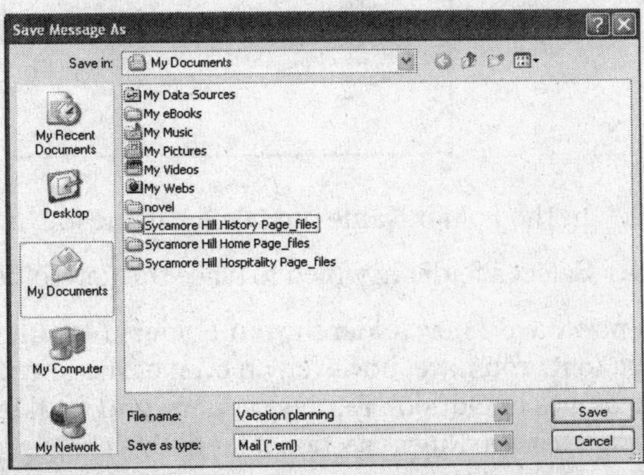

3. Select a folder in which to save the message. Outlook Express places the subject line in the File Name box. You can use this name or type another name.
4. Change the file type if desired, and then click Save.

NOTE

In Windows Explorer, when you double-click a file that has the default .eml extension, it opens in Outlook Express. If you save a message as an HTML file (with an .htm extension), it opens in Internet Explorer.

Saving Messages in Outlook Express Mail Folders As we've mentioned, you can create your own Outlook Express folders to store messages. This enables you to keep messages close at hand without clogging up your Inbox. For example, you might want to create folders for people with whom you regularly correspond, or you might want to create folders for current projects. To create a new folder, follow these steps:

1. Choose File ➢ New ➢ Folder to open the Create Folder dialog box:

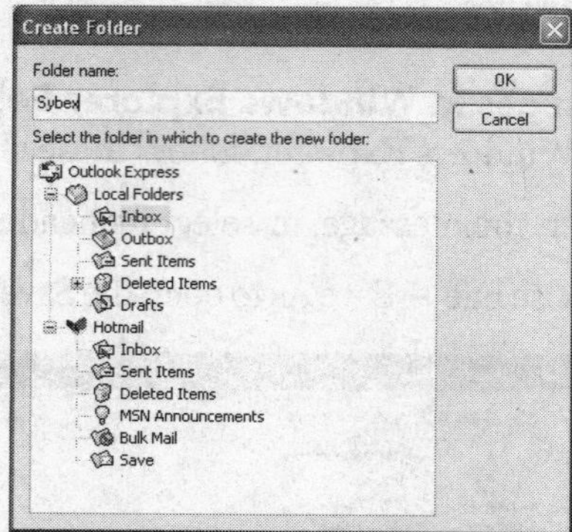

2. In the Folder Name box, type a name for your folder.
3. Select a folder in which to place the new folder, and click OK.

You now have a new folder in your Folders List, and you can drag any message to it. You have, however, an even easier and more efficient way to save messages in Outlook Express folders, and we'll look at that in the "Applying Message Rules" section later in this chapter.

Saving Attachments An attachment is a file that is appended to an e-mail message. You'll know that a message has an attachment if the header is preceded by the paper clip icon. When you open the message, you'll see the filename of the attachment in the Attach line in the header. To open an attachment, double-click its filename.

To save an attachment, follow these steps:

1. Open the message, or select its header, and choose File ➢ Save Attachments to open the Save Attachments dialog box.

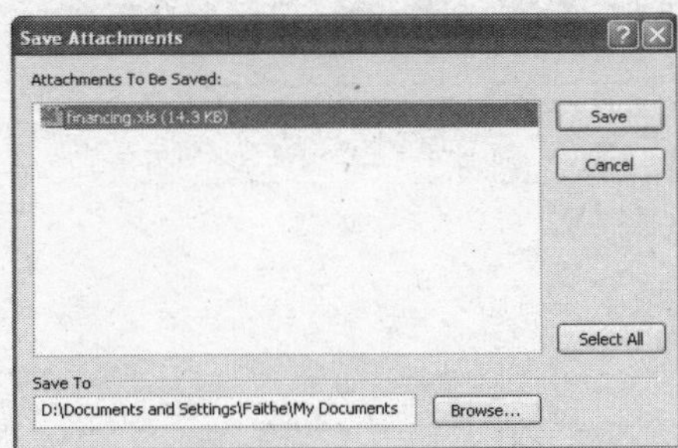

2. Select a folder in which to save the file, and click Save.

We'll discuss how to attach a file to an outgoing message later in this chapter in the "Attaching Files to Messages" section.

Replying to Messages

To reply to a message, open the message or select its header and then click the Reply button on the toolbar. If the message is addressed to multiple recipients and you want to reply to all of them, click the Reply All button. Either way, a reply window opens pre-addressed to the recipients. You simply type your response and click Send.

TIP

Outlook Express automatically places the names of the people you reply to in your Address Book. The name shows up on the Contacts list immediately. To open the Address Book and choose more recipients, click the To button.

- By default, Outlook Express includes the text of the original message in your reply, as in Figure 14.6. According to Internet tradition, this squanders bandwidth, and it's better not to include the original message unless it's really necessary. When is it necessary?

- When you want to be sure that the recipient understands the nature of your reply and the topic to which it is related
- When your message is part of a series of messages that involve some sort of question-and-answer sequence
- When it's important to keep track of who said what when

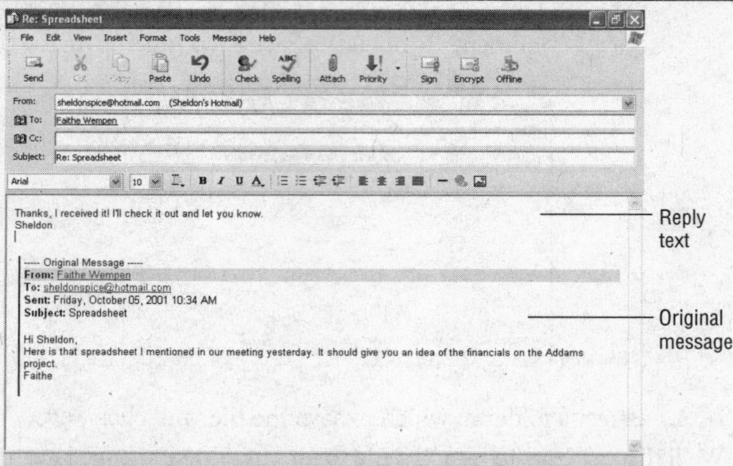

FIGURE 14.6: The reply window quotes the full text of the message to which you are replying.

An alternative is to include only the relevant portions of the original message in your reply. To do so, follow these steps:

1. Open the message, or select its header, and then click the Reply button.
2. The message is now addressed to the original sender, and the original subject line is preceded by Re.
3. In the body of the message, edit the contents so that the portions you want are retained, and then enter your response.
4. Click the Send button.

If you don't want to include the original message in your reply, you can simply open the message, click the Reply button, choose Edit ➢ Select All (or press Ctrl+A), and press Delete.

TIP

If you're rather sure that you almost always don't want to include the original message, choose Tools ➢ Options, and in the Options dialog box, click the Send tab. Clear the Include Message in Reply check box.

Forwarding Messages

Forwarding an e-mail message is much easier than forwarding a letter through the U.S. mail, and it actually works. To forward a message, follow these steps:

1. Open the message.
2. Click the Forward button on the toolbar in the message window.
3. Enter an address in the To field.
4. Add your own comments if you want.

NOTE

Many people enjoy forwarding funny or inspirational writings to friends and family, but for every person who enjoys receiving it, there is another person who thinks it's annoying. Therefore be judicious when forwarding.

Deleting Messages

To delete a message, you can select its header and press Delete (or click the Delete button on the toolbar), or you can open it and then click the Delete button. The message is not yet really deleted, however; Outlook Express has placed it in the Deleted Items folder. There it will sit indefinitely or until you manually delete it from there, as in the following steps:

1. Choose Edit ➢ Empty 'Deleted Items' Folder.
2. When Outlook Express asks if you are sure you want to delete these items, click Yes.

You can set up Outlook Express to automatically empty the Deleted Items folder every time you exit the program. To do so, choose Tools ➢ Options, click the Maintenance tab, and mark the Empty Messages from the Deleted Items Folder on Exit check box.

Creating and Sending Messages

In this section, we'll walk through the steps to create and send a simple text-only message.

NOTE

You can also create messages in HTML (HyperText Markup Language) and include hyperlinks, pictures, colorful formatting, sounds, and so on. We'll look at that in the next section.

To begin a new message, you can click the Create Mail button in the main window to open the New Message window, as shown in Figure 14.7. If the intended recipient appears in the Contacts pane in the main window, you can double-click that person's name to open the New Message window, and the To line will automatically display the recipient's name.

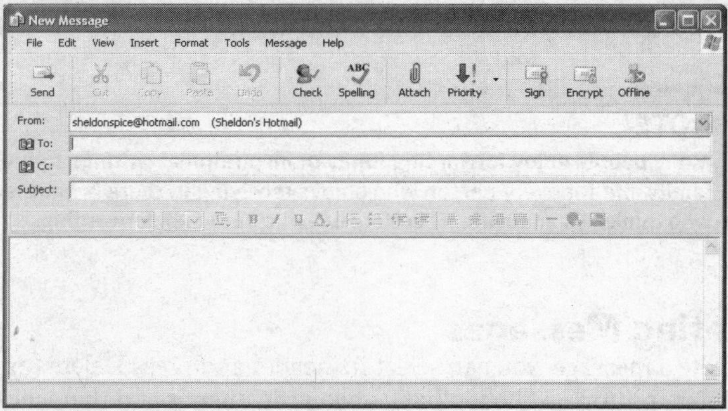

FIGURE 14.7: You create a new message in the New Message window.

TIP

By default, Outlook Express creates messages in plain text (no formatting). However, if someone else has been using your computer, your default might be set differently. If you see a formatting toolbar above the message body area, even if its controls are grayed out (unavailable), choose Format ➢ Plain Text to switch to Plain Text mode before you begin composing your message. To change the default, choose Tools ➢ Options in the main window, click the Compose tab, and click the Plain Text button in the Mail Sending Format area.

Now, follow these steps:

1. If necessary, enter the address of the primary recipient in the To field. If you are sending a message to multiple primary recipients, separate their addresses with semicolons.

   You can click the To button to display your Address Book and choose a name from there if you don't remember the address offhand. Doing so opens the Select Recipients dialog box. Click a name, and then click To-> to move that name to the To column. Repeat to address the message to multiple recipients as needed; then click OK to return to composing the message.

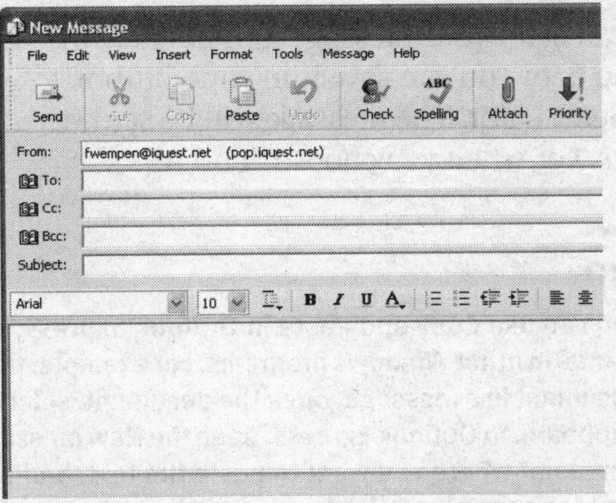

2. Optionally, enter e-mail addresses in the Cc (carbon copy) and Bcc (blind carbon copy) fields. If the Bcc line does not appear, choose View ➢ All Headers to make it appear.

   You can also enter Cc and Bcc recipients in the Select Recipients dialog box. To open it, click the To, Cc, or Bcc button; they all take you to the same place. Then click the name you want and then click Cc-> or Bcc-> to move the name to the corresponding column. Click OK to return to composing.

3. Enter a subject line for your message.

NOTE

If you don't enter a subject line, Outlook Express will ask if you're sure you don't want a subject line. Unless you have a good reason not to do so, enter some text in the subject line. Your recipient will see this text in the header information for the message and will then have a clue as to the nature of your message.

4. Enter the text of your message.
5. If appropriate, establish a priority for your message. Choose Message ➢ Set Priority, and then choose High, Normal, or Low. The default is Normal.
6. Click Send to start your message on its way.

You can send your message immediately by clicking the Send button, as in step 6, or you can save it in your Outbox to send later by choosing File ➢ Send Later. The message will be sent when you choose Send and Receive All or when you choose Send All.

TIP

You can use Copy and Paste in Outlook Express, just as you use those commands in other Windows programs. For example, to include a portion of a Word document in a message, open the document, select the text, and copy it to the Clipboard. In Outlook Express, open the New Message window, place the insertion point where you want to paste the text, and press Ctrl+V. Use this same process to copy portions of e-mail messages to other messages or to documents in other applications.

Creating Formatted E-Mail Messages

In the previous section, we created a plain text message, but, as we mentioned, you can also compose messages in Rich Text (HTML) and include all sorts of neat effects.

WARNING

Before you send a formatted message, be sure that your recipient's e-mail program can display it effectively. When you open the New Message window and choose Format , Rich Text (HTML), the message you compose is essentially a Web page. Newer e-mail programs such as Netscape Messenger and the commercial version of Eudora, Eudora Pro, can read, compose, and send HTML messages, but many others cannot, including America Online and the freeware

version of Eudora. An easy way to find out if your recipient's e-mail program can handle HTML is to send a simple plain text message and ask first.

Let's look at some bells and whistles you can include in Outlook Express e-mail messages. Click the Create Mail icon to open the New Message window, and be sure that the Rich Text (HTML) option is selected. (Open the View menu, and if there is no dot next to Rich Text (HTML), click it to select it.) You'll see the screen shown in Figure 14.8. Notice the Formatting toolbar, which contains many of the same tools you see and use in your Windows word processor. You'll also see the Font and Font Size drop-down list boxes that are present in your word processor.

TIP

If the toolbar appears grayed out (unavailable), click in the message body area and it will become active.

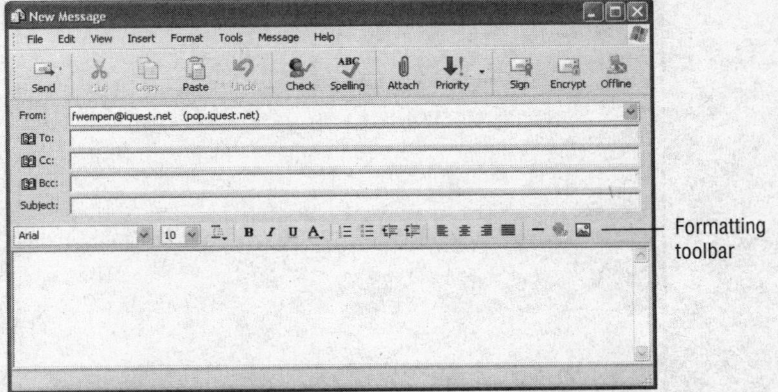

FIGURE 14.8: You can use the Formatting toolbar when creating a message in HTML.

- As you create your message, just pretend that you're using a word processor and use the Formatting tools to apply emphasis to your message. All the usual design rules apply, including the following:
- Don't use a lot of different fonts.
- Remember, typing in all capital letters in e-mail is tantamount to shouting.

- Don't place a lot of text in italics. It's hard to read on the screen.
- Save boldface for what's really important.

To insert a horizontal line that spans the message window, choose Insert ➢ Horizontal Line.

To apply HTML styles such as Definition Term or Definition, click the Paragraph Style button on the Formatting toolbar.

USING STATIONERY

In addition to formatting, you have another way to add some class or some comedy to your e-mail messages: stationery. In the New Message window, choose Message ➢ New Using, and then choose a predesigned format from the list in the submenu, or click Select Stationery to open the Select Stationery dialog box and select from a larger list. Here's one example of what you'll find:

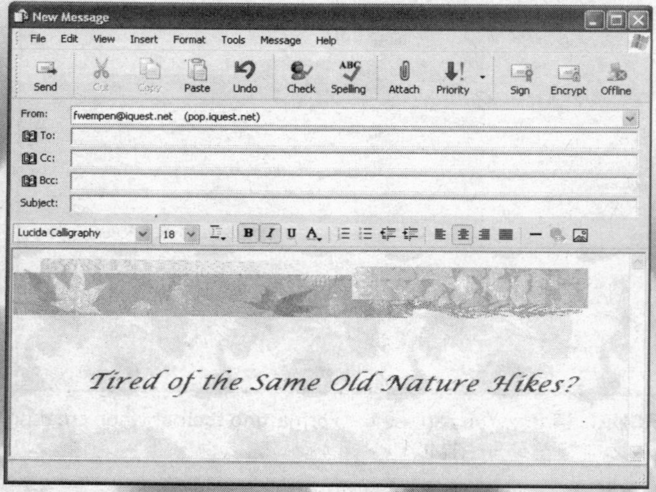

To customize stationery, click Create New in the Select Stationery dialog box to start the Stationery Setup Wizard. Follow the onscreen instructions.

Adding Pictures to Messages

- You can insert a picture in a message in two ways:
- As a piece of art
- As a background over which you can type text

To insert a picture as a piece of art that you can size and move, follow these steps:

1. In the New Message window, choose Insert ➢ Picture to open the Picture dialog box.
2. Enter the filename of the picture in the Picture Source text box, or click the Browse button to locate it.
3. Optionally, in the Alternate Text box, enter some text that will display if the recipient's e-mail program cannot display the picture, and specify layout and spacing options if you want. (You can also size and move the picture with the mouse once you place it in the message.)
4. Click OK.

To insert a picture as background, follow these steps:

1. In the New Message window, choose Format ➢ Background ➢ Picture to open the Background Picture dialog box.
2. Enter the filename of the picture, or click Browse to select a predesigned stationery background or locate another file.
3. Click Open, and then click OK to insert the background.

Adding a Background Color or Sound to Messages

To apply a color to the background of your message, choose Format ➢ Background ➢ Color, and select a color from the drop-down list. Now type something. Can you see it on the screen? If not, you have probably chosen a dark background and your font is also a dark color—most likely black if you haven't changed it from the default.

To make your text visible, click the Font Color button, and select a lighter color from the drop-down list.

To add a background sound, follow these steps:

1. In the New Message window, choose Format ➢ Background ➢ Sound to open the Background Sound dialog box.
2. Enter the filename of the sound, or click Browse to locate a sound file.
3. Specify the number of times you want the sound to play or whether you want it to play continuously. (In our opinion, a sound that plays continuously while the recipient is reading the message is far more likely to annoy than to entertain.)
4. Click OK.

Including Hyperlinks in Messages

- When you insert a hyperlink in a message, the recipient can go directly to the resource simply by clicking the hyperlink. You can insert a hyperlink in three ways:
- Simply type it in the message body. Be sure to include the entire URL. When you press the spacebar or the Enter key after typing the address, it will become underlined, indicating it is a hyperlink.
- In the New Message window, choose Insert ➢ Hyperlink to open the Hyperlink dialog box, and then enter the URL in the text box.
- In Internet Explorer, choose Tools ➢ Mail and News ➢ Send a Link to open the New Message window. The URL of the current page is automatically inserted in the message body in Outlook Express. (This works only if Outlook Express is your default e-mail program.)

Adding a Signature to Messages

We know people who never sign their e-mail messages. After all, their name is in the From line in the message header. We also know people who append elaborate signatures, touting their accomplishments or advertising their businesses. We usually just sign our first name at the bottom of messages, but what you do depends on your personal style or whether you're sending business or personal correspondence.

To create a signature that's automatically added to all your outgoing messages, follow these steps:

1. Choose Tools ➢ Options to open the Options dialog box.
2. Click the Signatures tab.
3. Click New. A new signature appears in the Signatures box (by default it's called Signature #1) and the insertion point moves to the Text box in the Edit Signature area.

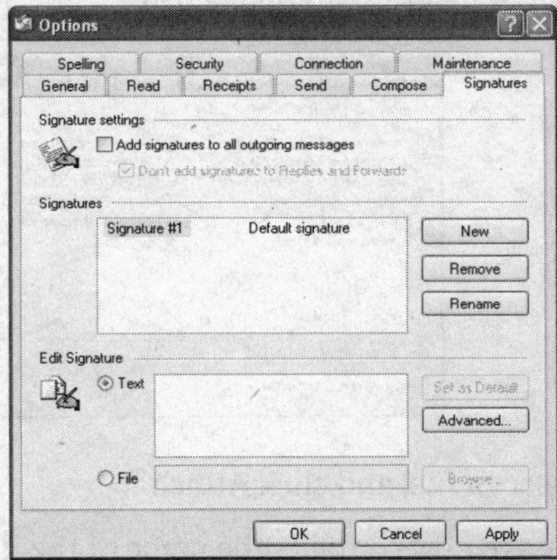

4. To create a text signature, enter the content in the Text box.
5. If you want to use a file you've already created as your signature, click the File option button, and enter the filename, or click Browse to locate it.
6. If you have multiple e-mail accounts, click the Advanced button to open the Advanced Signature Settings dialog box, and specify which accounts should use this signature.
7. Click the Add Signatures to All Outgoing Messages check box, and click OK.

If you don't want the signature automatically appended to all outgoing messages, leave the Add Signatures to All Outgoing Messages check box unselected. Then, to add this signature to a message, choose Insert ➢ Signature in the New Message window.

Attaching Files to Messages

In Outlook Express, sending a file or multiple files along with your message is painless and simple. Follow these steps:

1. In the New Message window, choose Insert ➢ File Attachment or click the Attach button on the toolbar to open the Insert Attachment dialog box:

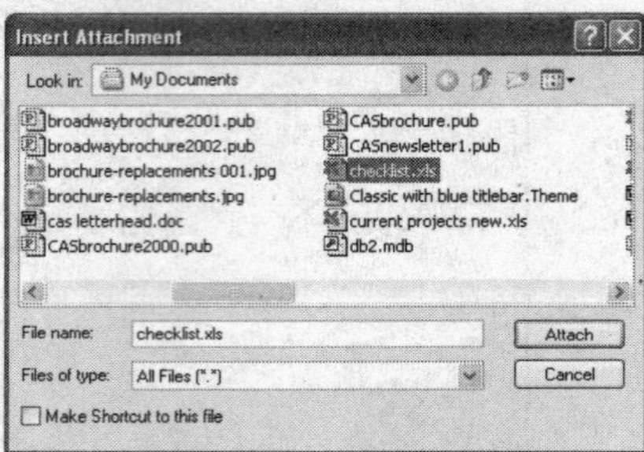

2. Select a file, and click Attach.

Your message now contains the name of the file in the Attach line.

TIP

If the file is large or if you know that the recipient has a slow connection, you'll want to compress it first. To compress a file in Windows XP, right-click it in Windows Explorer and choose Send To ➢ Compressed Folder. This creates a file with a .zip extension that contains a compressed version of the file. The original is not affected. If the recipient has Windows XP, he or she can access the compressed file by double-clicking it. Recipients using other operating systems might need an unzipping utility such as WinZip. Such utilities can be downloaded for free from shareware sites all over the Internet.

Applying Message Rules

Using the Rules Editor, you can specify where messages go after they are downloaded, block unwanted messages, and, in general, manage incoming messages more efficiently—especially if you deal with a lot of e-mail. In this section, we'll give you a couple of examples that illustrate the possibilities, but, as you will see, there are lots of possibilities, and you'll need to apply the options that make the most sense for your situation.

Let's start by establishing a rule that sends all mail from a particular person to that person's Outlook Express folder. Follow these steps:

1. In the main Outlook Express window, choose Tools ➢ Message Rules ➢ Mail to open the New Mail Rule dialog box:

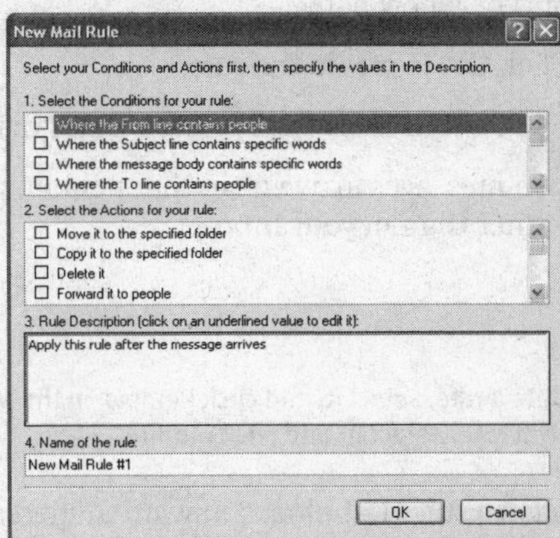

2. In the Select the Conditions for Your Rule section, click the Where the From Line Contains People check box.

3. In the Select the Actions for Your Rule section, click the Move It to the Specified Folder check box.

4. In the Rule Description section, click contains people to open the Select People dialog box:

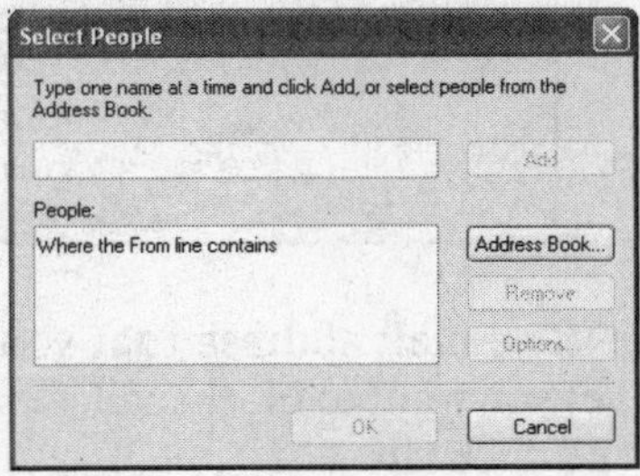

5. Enter a name, or select a name from your Address Book, and click OK.

6. Click specified to open the Move dialog box.

7. Select the folder where you want this person's messages to go, and click OK. If you need to create a folder, click New Folder.
8. Accept the name of the rule that Outlook Express proposes, or type a new name.
9. Click OK to create the rule.
10. Click OK to close the Message Rules dialog box.

Now, when messages arrive from that person, you'll find them in his or her folder rather than in your Inbox.

TIP

To delete a rule, select it, and click Remove in the Message Rules dialog box. To modify a rule, select it, and click Modify.

To establish a rule that blocks unwanted messages, follow these steps:

1. In the main Outlook Express window, choose Tools ➢ Message Rules ➢ Blocked Senders List to open the Message Rules dialog box at the Blocked Senders tab.
2. Click Add to open the Add Sender dialog box:

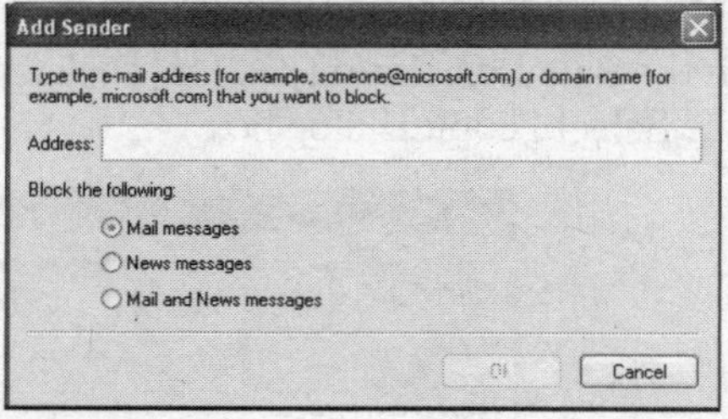

3. Enter the e-mail address that you want to block, specify whether you want to block mail, news, or both from this person, and click OK.
4. Click OK again in the Message Rules dialog box.

Mail from that address will now go immediately to the Deleted Items folder. News from that person will simply not be displayed. (More on news in the last part of this chapter.) To change or delete this rule, open the Message Rules box, select the address, and click Modify or Remove.

Adding and Managing Identities

Windows XP's multiple-user feature makes it easy for several people to share a PC, each with his or her own settings and privacy. For example, when a different user logs into Windows XP, Outlook Express starts from scratch with no mail accounts set up. That way each user can manage his or her mail independently.

If you don't want to go to the trouble of setting up multiple user accounts but still want some mail privacy between individuals, Outlook Express's Identities feature will fit the bill. When you switch to a different identity, different mail settings apply.

NOTE

You can also set up Identities in Address Book by choosing Start ➢ Programs ➢ Accessories ➢ Address Book.

To set up other identities in Outlook Express, follow these steps:

1. In the main Outlook Express window, choose File ➢ Identities ➢ Add New Identity to open the New Identity dialog box:

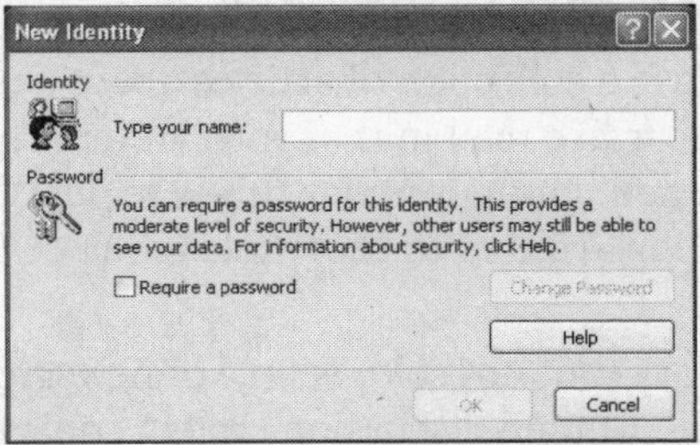

2. Enter the name of the identity you want to establish. If you want to establish identities for the members of your family, for example, you could simply enter a person's first name.
3. If you want to password protect this identify, click the Require a Password check box. Enter the password twice—once in the New Password box and again in the Confirm New Password box. Click OK twice.
4. Outlook Express asks if you want to switch to this new identity now. If you do, click Yes; otherwise, click No.

NOTE

If you choose Yes and Outlook Express immediately terminates, restart the computer (choose Start ➢ Shutdown ➢ Restart) and then reopen Outlook Express and then switch to the new identity with File ➢ Switch Identity.

5. In the Manage Identities dialog box, click New if you want to set up another identity; otherwise, click Close.

The first time you log on as a new identity, the Internet Connection Wizard will run to help the new identity set up a mail account.

To switch from one identity to another, choose File ➢ Switch Identity to open the Switch Identities dialog box. Select the identity, and click OK. To log off from an identity, choose File ➢ Identities ➢ Logoff *identity*.

To delete an identity, select the identity in the Manage Identities dialog box, and click Remove.

Reading Newsgroups with Outlook Express

A newsgroup is a collection of articles about a particular subject. A newsgroup is similar to e-mail in that you can reply to what someone else has written (the newsgroup term for this is to *post*), and you can send a question or a response either to the whole group or to individuals within the group.

The primary (but not sole) source of newsgroups is Usenet, which is a worldwide distributed discussion system consisting of newsgroups with names that are classified hierarchically by subject. In a newsgroup name, each component is separated from the next by a period. For example, `rec.crafts.metalworking` is a recreational group devoted to the craft of metalworking. The leftmost portion represents the largest hierarchical category, and the name gets more specific from left to right. Table 14.1 lists the major top-level newsgroup categories and explains the topics each discusses. Currently, there are thousands and thousands of newsgroups on every conceivable topic. For an extensive listing of them, go to `sunsite.unc.edu/usenet-i/hier-s/master.html`.

Table 14.1: The Major Newsgroups

Newsgroup	What It Discusses
Alt	Newsgroups outside the main structure outlined below
Comp	Computer science and related topics, including operating systems, hardware, artificial intelligence, and graphics
Misc	Anything that does not fit into one of the other categories
News	Information on Usenet and newsgroups
Rec	Recreational activities, such as hobbies, the arts, movies, and books
Sci	Scientific topics, such as math, physics, and biology
Soc	Social issues and cultures
Talk	Controversial subjects, such as gun control, abortion, religion, and politics

You access newsgroups by accessing the server on which they are stored. Not all servers store the same newsgroups. The network administrator or the owner of the site determines what to store. Almost all news servers "expire" articles after a few days or, at most, a few weeks because of the tremendous volume. Although they might be archived at the site, these articles are no longer available to be viewed by users.

WARNING

Most newsgroups are uncensored. (Some groups have a moderator who approves every post, but the vast majority do not.) You can find just about anything at any time anywhere. Nobody has authority over newsgroups as a whole. If you find certain groups, certain articles, or certain people offensive, don't go there, or use the Rules Editor that we talked about earlier to prevent certain articles from even being displayed. But, remember, anarchy reigns in newsgroups, and you never know what you might stumble upon in the least likely places.

Setting Up a Newsgroups Account

Before you can read newsgroups, you must set up a newsgroups account. Before you start, get the name of your news server from your ISP, and then follow these steps:

1. In the main Outlook Express window, select the Outlook Express folder, and, in the pane on the right, click Set Up a Newsgroups Account to start the Internet Connection Wizard.
2. Supply the information that the Wizard requests, and click Finish when you are done.

You'll now see a folder in the Folders list for your news server.

Connecting to Newsgroups

The next task is to download the list of newsgroups from your server. When Outlook Express asks if you want to do this, click Yes. This may take a while if you have a slow connection, but notice the incrementing number of newsgroups in the Downloading Newsgroups dialog box. In the process of writing this section, we downloaded a list of more than 34,000 newsgroups.

TIP

Only the names of the newsgroups are downloaded to your computer; their contents remain on the news server. Each time you connect to the news server, a message will let you know when new newsgroups are available and will offer to update your list. To completely re-download the entire list (for example, to remove groups that no longer exist), click Reset List.

When the list has finished downloading, you'll see the Newsgroup Subscriptions dialog box.

Finding a Newsgroup of Interest

- You can select a newsgroup to read in two ways:
- You can scroll through the list (this will take a lot of time).
- You can search on a term.

Just for the sake of doing it, scroll the list a bit. As you can see, it's in alphabetic order by hierarchical categories. If you don't see anything right away that strikes your fancy, you can perform a search. Enter a term in the Display Newsgroups Which Contain text box, and then don't do anything! In a second, you'll see a list of newsgroups that contain articles about your topic. For example, in Figure 14.9 we have typed **dogs** as the term to look for.

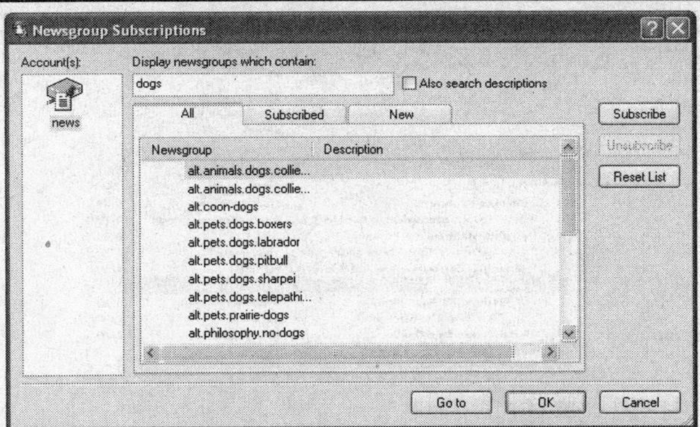

FIGURE 14.9: Use this dialog box to search for and subscribe to newsgroups.

SUBSCRIBING TO A NEWSGROUP

Subscribing to a newsgroup doesn't involve a fee or any other transaction. Subscribing means simply creating a subfolder for a particular newsgroup in your news folder. Then, instead of selecting it from the Newsgroup Subscriptions dialog box, you can simply click the newsgroup's folder to see the list of articles in it.

You can browse a group whether or not you have subscribed to it. To browse it without subscribing, select it and click Go To.

If you know you want to subscribe to a group, click Subscribe, or double-click it. Subscribing is as simple that, so you don't have to be too choosy about the groups you subscribe to. Subscribe to lots of them, and then sort them out later! To unsubscribe to a newsgroup, right-click its folder, and choose Unsubscribe.

Reading a Newsgroup

To display the message headers in a newsgroup, click it in the Newsgroup Subscriptions dialog box and then click Go To. Or, if you have subscribed to the group, it appears in your Folders list under the mail server, and you can simply click its name there to go to it.

To read an article, simply click its header to display the message in the lower pane. Figure 14.10 shows an article being read in a newsgroup.

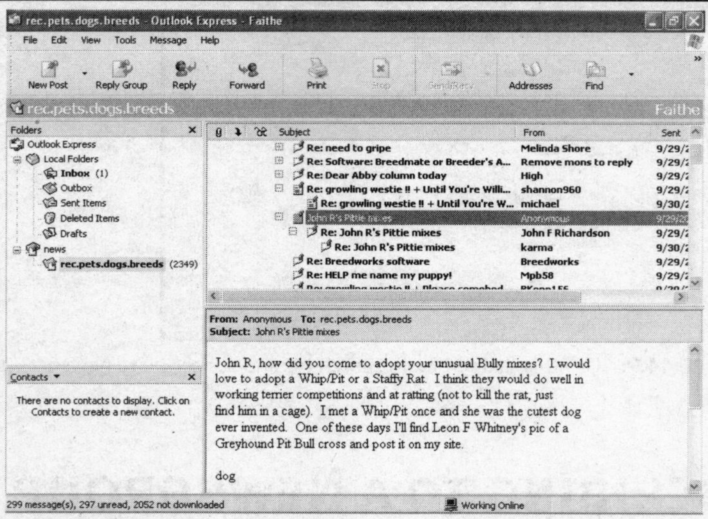

FIGURE 14.10: Reading an article in the rec.pets.dogs.breeds newsgroup

Outlook Express is a threaded newsreader in that it groups messages that respond to a subject line. If you see a plus sign to the left of a newsgroup header, you can click the plus sign to display a list of related messages. The more up-to-date term for threads is *conversation.* Figure 14.10 shows an expanded conversation.

NOTE

Newsgroup articles are grouped by conversations by default, but you can also organize your e-mail messages by conversations. With your Inbox selected, choose View ➢ Current View ➢ Group Messages by Conversation.

To read the articles from another newsgroup or to search for another newsgroup, double-click your main news folder, and then click Newsgroups to open the Newsgroup Subscriptions dialog box. Or, if the other newsgroup has been subscribed to, click its name on the Folders list.

Posting to a Newsgroup

Replying to a newsgroup article or sending a message to a newsgroup is known as posting. You post to a newsgroup in much the same way that you compose and send e-mail. To send an original message to a newsgroup, open the newsgroup, and click the New Post button. The New Message window will open with the group's name in the To line.

To reply to an individual article, click the Reply button, and to reply to the entire newsgroup, click the Reply Group button.

WARNING

Do not use your real e-mail address when posting to a public newsgroup unless you want to get a lot of unsolicited junk e-mail. Get a free Web-based e-mail account from a service such as Hotmail and use it for all your newsgroup activity.

Customizing Outlook Express

Throughout this chapter, we've mentioned from time to time ways that you can specify how Outlook Express handles certain features, such as signatures. In most cases, you do this through the Options dialog box (shown in Figure 14.11), which you open by choosing Tools ➢ Options. Here's a quick rundown of what to use each tab for in the Options dialog box:

General Use this tab to specify settings for how Outlook Express starts and for sending and receiving messages.

Read Use this tab to set options for reading news and mail. For example, you specify a maximum number of news article headers to download at one time.

Receipts Use this tab if you want to verify that your message has been read by the recipient.

Send Use this tab to set, among other things, the format (HTML or Plain Text) in which you will send all messages and the format you'll use to reply to messages. You can also specify whether copies of sent messages will be stored and whether you want Outlook Express to put the names and addresses of people you reply to in your Address Book.

Compose Use this tab to specify the font and font size for mail messages and news articles that you create and to select stationery fonts for HTML messages.

Signatures For details about how to use this tab, see the section "Adding a Signature to Messages."

Spelling Checks the spelling of your message. You will have this tab only if you have Microsoft Word, Excel, or PowerPoint 95 or 97 installed.

Security Use this tab to specify your desired Internet Security zone and to get a digital ID.

Connection Use this tab to specify how Outlook Express handles your dial-up connection.

Maintenance Use this tab to specify what Outlook Express does with deleted items and to clean up downloaded messages, as well as to specify that all server commands are stored for troubleshooting purposes.

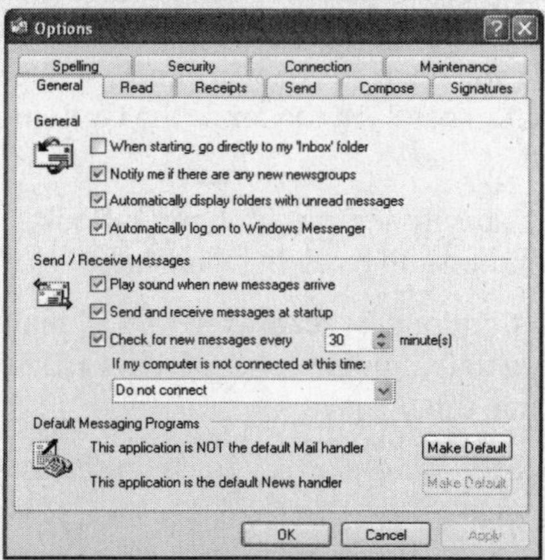

FIGURE 14.11: You use the Options dialog box to customize Outlook Express for the way you work.

WHAT'S NEXT?

In addition to Internet Explorer and Outlook Express, Windows XP Professional includes a number of other tools that you can use to communicate over the Internet. In the next chapter, we'll look at some of those tools.

Chapter 15

Using the Communications Programs

You may never have an occasion to use the programs I'm going to discuss in this chapter, but I'm including information about them so that you'll know they exist, what each is best suited for, and how to access them when the need arises.

Adapted from *Mastering Windows XP Professional*
by Mark Minasi
ISBN 0-7821-2981-1 1056 pages $39.99

Communicating and Sharing with NetMeeting

NetMeeting is an application that you can use to do the following:

- Chat with someone over the Internet, via voice or by typing on the screen
- Audio conference
- Videoconference
- Share applications
- Collaborate on documents
- Transfer files
- Draw on the Whiteboard

Obviously, you need the proper equipment to do some of these, and, as we look at the individual features of NetMeeting, I'll point that out.

Installing NetMeeting

NetMeeting was included with several previous versions of Windows. As of this writing, it is not on any menu in Windows XP Professional, but you can install it by doing the following:

1. Choose Start ➢ Help and Support to open Help and Support Center.
2. In the Search box, type **NetMeeting**, and press Enter.
3. In the Search Results bar, click the What's New in Other Areas of Windows XP Professional link.
4. In the pane on the right, click the plus sign (+) next to NetMeeting, and then click the Using NetMeeting link.
5. In the Using NetMeeting pane, click the NetMeeting link.

6. In the Using NetMeeting screen, click the NetMeeting link to open it. You'll see the following screen, which presents an overview of NetMeeting:

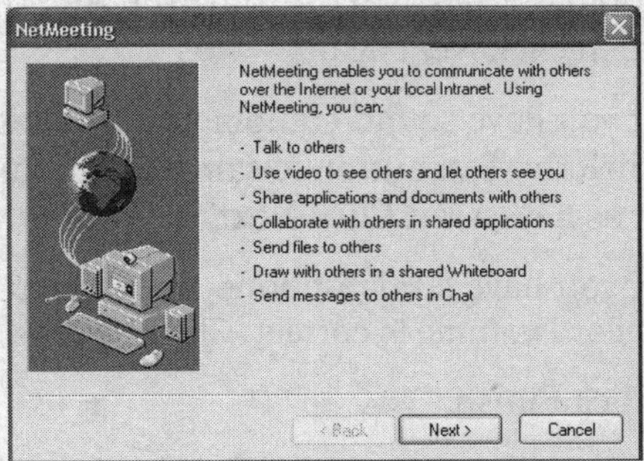

Take a look at it and click Next.

7. Click Next to open a screen in which you enter at least your first name, your last name, and your e-mail address, and then click Next.

8. If you want to log on to a directory server whenever you start NetMeeting, click Log on to a Directory Server When NetMeeting Starts. If you don't want your name to appear in the directory listing for that server, click Do Not List My Name in the Directory. Click Next.

NOTE

Directory servers are maintained by organizations or companies and provide a list of people who are logged on to the server and have chosen to display their names. If you are connected to the Internet and log on to a directory server, you can click a name in the list to connect to that person. We'll look at exactly how this works later in this chapter and also talk about why you might or might not want to display your name.

9. In the next screen, specify your modem speed or connection mode, and then click Next.

10. If you want quick access to NetMeeting, leave the options selected in this screen so that you display a shortcut to NetMeeting on your Desktop and an icon on the Quick Launch toolbar. Click Next to start the Audio Tuning Wizard, and then click Next again.
11. If you have sound equipment (speakers and a sound card), click the Test button to sample the volume, and then change it as necessary. Click Next.
12. If you have a microphone, speak into it to ensure that the record volume is correct. Click Next.
13. Click Finish.

You're now ready to start using NetMeeting, which is shown in Figure 15.1. You'll see a NetMeeting icon on your desktop. Click it to start NetMeeting.

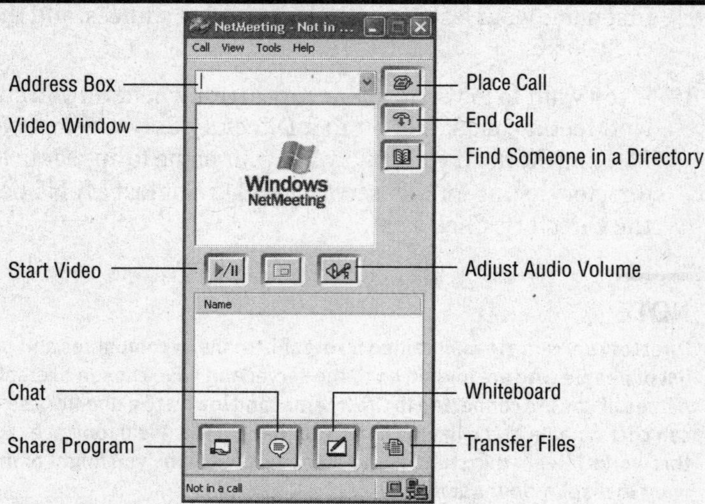

FIGURE 15.1: The opening NetMeeting window

Making a Call

You can place a call in NetMeeting in the following ways:

- By connecting directly to an Internet directory server or to another computer using that computer's name or address.
- By using a gateway on your network to connect to a telephone or videoconferencing system.
- By using a gatekeeper, which is a computer on your network that locates and connects to people, computers, and gateways.

When you make a call in any of these ways, the person you call does not have to be running NetMeeting.

When you make the connection, you can communicate in several ways, depending on your equipment:

- If both people have microphones, sound cards, and speakers, you can talk just as you would over the telephone.
- If both people have microphones, sound cards, speakers, video cards, and video cameras, you can talk and be seen on the screen.
- If you don't have any of this equipment or just prefer it, you can communicate via the Chat application.

NOTE

You can see video even if you don't have a camera, and you can hear another person who is using a microphone if you have speakers. Video runs in the Video window.

To make a call, follow these steps:

1. In the Address box, enter one of the following:
    - An e-mail address
    - A computer name
    - A telephone number
    - An IP (Internet Protocol) address.
2. Click the Place Call button.

If NetMeeting cannot determine how to place the call, it displays the Place a Call dialog box, as shown in Figure 15.2. In the Using box, select the type of connection you are trying to make, and then click Call.

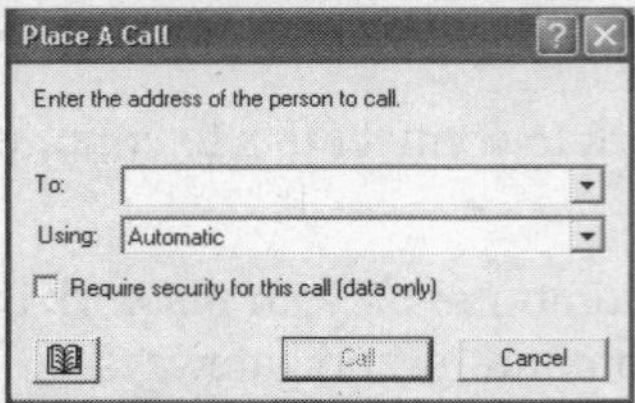

FIGURE 15.2: The Place a Call dialog box

FINDING AN IP ADDRESS

An IP address is a unique number that identifies your computer on the Internet; for example, `209.254.117.155`. The first three parts of this number refer to your ISP (Internet Service Provider), and the last three digits refer to your computer. Unless you have a permanent connection to the Internet such as your ISP has, each time you log on you are assigned a different IP address. As I've mentioned, using an IP address is one way to connect through NetMeeting with others who are on the Internet.

To find out what your current IP address is, follow these steps:

1. Choose Start ➢ All Programs ➢ Accessories ➢ Command Prompt to open the Command Prompt window.
2. At the prompt, type **`ipconfig`** and press Enter.

Now you can share your IP address with someone who wants to call you. I've done this via e-mail before, and it works great. If the person you want to call is not running Windows XP Professional or Windows 2000 Professional, but Windows *9x* instead, they can type **`winipcfg`** to find out their IP address. Remember, though, every time you disconnect from the Internet or lose your connection, you lose that IP address. You'll get another one when you connect again.

Using the Chat Application

If you've visited chat rooms on the Web, you know how to use chat. What you type appears on the screen for you and others to see. Figure 15.3 shows the Chat window. To open Chat, click the Chat button in the main NetMeeting window.

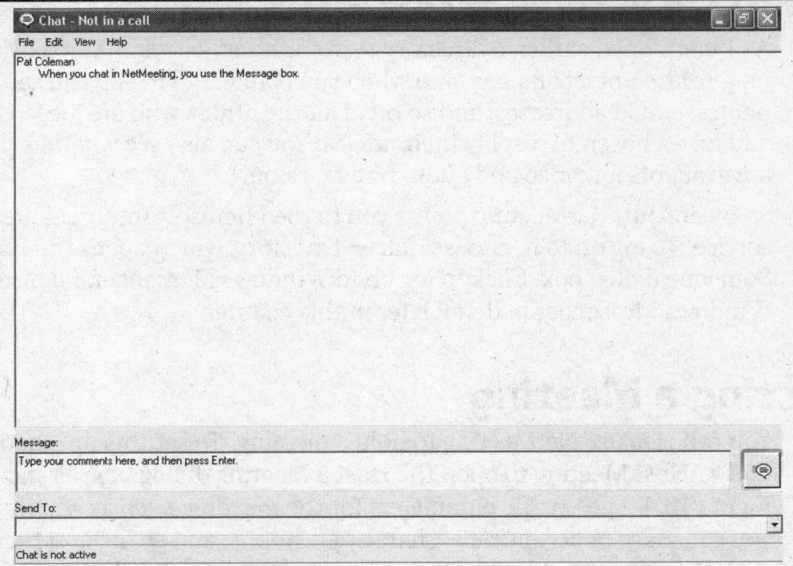

FIGURE 15.3: Chatting in NetMeeting

To use Chat, you need to know only the following:

- Click in the Message box, type, and press Enter to send your words of wisdom.
- If the session involves more than one person, click the down arrow in the Send To box to specify whether to send your chat lines to an individual or to the whole group.
- To save the contents of a Chat session, choose File ➢ Save As.
- To end a session, close the Chat window.

TIP

To customize the format of the Chat window, such as the fonts used and the display of information, choose View ➢ Options.

Using Directory Servers

As I mentioned earlier, a directory server is a service maintained by an organization or a company, and when you connect to it, you can see the names, e-mail addresses, and so on of all the others who are logged on and have chosen to display their names. You can also see whether they are available for video and audio transmission.

By default, NetMeeting points you to the Microsoft Internet Directory service. To log on to it, choose Call ➢ Directory, which opens the Find Someone dialog box. Click to log on to Windows Messenger. I'll discuss Windows Messenger in detail later in this chapter.

Hosting a Meeting

You can also use NetMeeting to hold a meeting. To set this up, choose Call ➢ Host Meeting to open the Host a Meeting dialog box, as shown in Figure 15.4. Specify the parameters for the meeting, such as whether only you can place or accept calls, share applications, and so on, and then click OK. Now others can call you or you can call others. The meeting lasts until you end it (or until you or the others lose their connections).

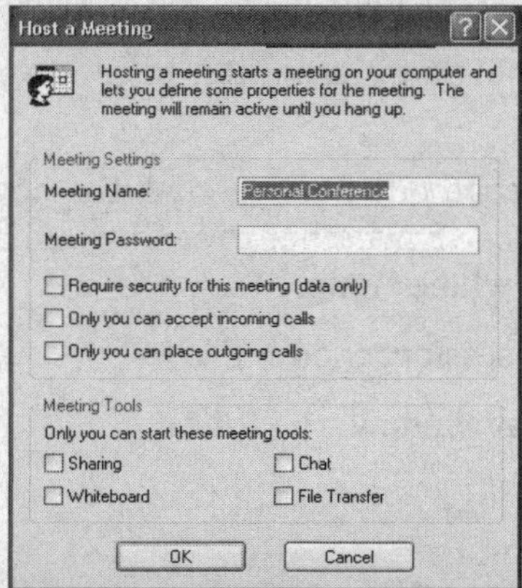

FIGURE 15.4: Setting the guidelines for a meeting

Using Video

When you are receiving or sending video, images are displayed in the video window. To set up video transmissions, choose Tools ➢ Options to open the Options dialog box, and click the Video tab, which is shown in Figure 15.5. You can specify when to send and receive video, the size of the image, its quality (do you want speed or clarity?), and the properties of your camera.

FIGURE 15.5: Setting up video transmission

Sharing Applications

While you are in a call or in a meeting, you can share documents and applications. To do so, open the program you want to share, and then click the Share Program button to open the Sharing dialog box. Specify the program to share and who will control it, and then click Close. Others will now be able to see and interact with you and your application.

NOTE

To share the Whiteboard, click the Whiteboard button in the main NetMeeting window.

USING WINDOWS MESSENGER

Instant messaging (IM) is hot because it's a great way to keep in touch with people. The big advantage to IM is that the communication—the conversation, if you will—takes place in real time. If someone is online, you can communicate with them. Like other IM software, Windows Messenger (hereafter called Messenger) notifies you when your contacts come online (and notifies your contacts when *you* go online), so you know who's available to chat. The disadvantage to IM, of course, is that the person or people with whom you're communicating need to be online at the same time as you. If they're not online (or are pretending not to be online), you can't communicate with them.

Starting Messenger

To start Messenger, choose Start ➢ All Programs ➢ Windows Messenger. Alternatively, if Messenger is displaying an icon in the notification area, double-click it.

If you haven't added a .NET Passport to your Windows XP user account, Messenger displays a Click Here to Sign In link in its window. Clicking this link starts the .NET Passport Wizard, which guides you through the process of adding an existing .NET Passport to Windows XP or getting a new .NET Passport and adding that to Windows. Once you've done that, Messenger signs you in.

Once you've started Messenger, it displays an icon in your notification area. Click this icon to display a menu of actions you can take with Messenger.

When Messenger appears on your screen, chances are that it tells you that you don't have anyone in your contacts list and suggests you click the Add button to start adding contacts. (If you've just set Messenger up, your lack of contacts should be no surprise.) Figure 15.6 shows Messenger with a modest number of contacts added. As you can see in the figure, Messenger tells you the number of new messages you have in your Hotmail account (if you have one).

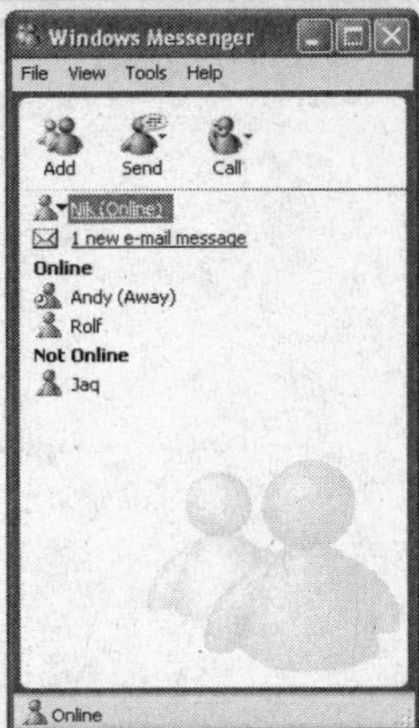

FIGURE 15.6: Messenger with a number of contacts added

You're probably itching to add some contacts and get on with messaging. But before you do that, configure Messenger by choosing options as described in the next section.

Configuring Messenger

Messenger comes with a raft of configuration options. You don't need to set all of them at once—this section covers them all in case you want to—but you should know about them before using Messenger. At the very least, you should edit your public profile so that you know what information other people can access about you.

Choose Tools ➢ Options to display the Options dialog box, and then configure your choice of the options described in the following sections.

Personal Tab Options

The Personal tab of the Options dialog box (shown in Figure 15.7) contains a couple of important settings and a couple of trivial ones.

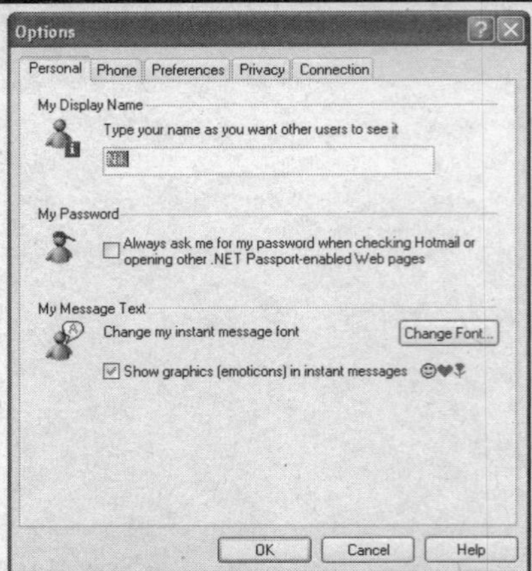

FIGURE 15.7: On the Personal tab of the Options dialog box, set your display name and edit your Passport public profile.

My Display Name text box Enter the name you want Messenger to display for you.

Always Ask Me for My Password When Checking Hotmail or Opening Other .NET Passport-Enabled Web Pages check box Select this check box (which is cleared by default) if you want to enter your Passport password manually each time it's required by a Web site. Entering the password manually improves your security, but you may find yourself needing to enter the password too often for speedy or comfortable browsing.

Change Font button Use this button and the resulting Set My Message Font dialog box to specify the font you want to use in IM windows.

Show Graphics (Emoticons) in Instant Messages check box Clear this check box (which is selected by default) if you want to prevent Messenger from displaying emoticons (for example, ☺).

Phone Tab Options

The Phone tab of the Options dialog box (shown in Figure 15.8) lets you specify your country or region code and your home, work, and mobile phone numbers.

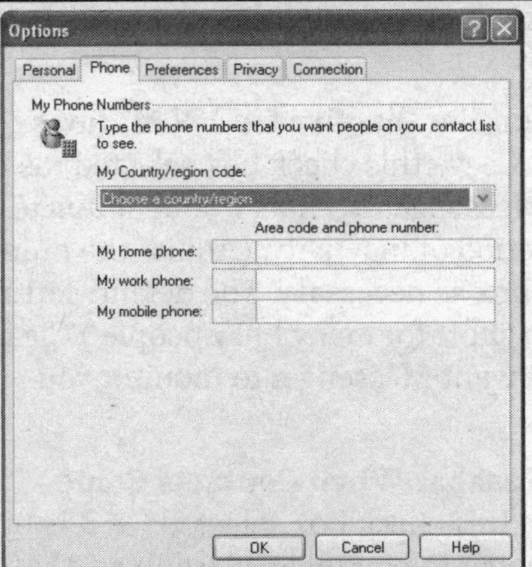

FIGURE 15.8: On the Phone tab of the Options dialog box, specify your country or region code and enter the phone numbers you want Messenger to know.

Preferences Tab Options

The Preferences tab of the Options dialog box (shown in Figure 15.9) contains a slew of options that affect Messenger's behavior:

Run This Program When Windows Starts check box Leave this check box selected (as it is by default) if you want Windows to launch Messenger every time you log on to Windows. Clear this check box if you prefer to run Messenger manually when you need it.

Allow This Program to Run in the Background check box Leave this check box selected (as it is by default) if you want Messenger to be able to run in the background and lurk in your notification area when you're not actively using it. Keeping Messenger running in the background lets you know instantly when one of your contacts comes online or sends you a message, but it also means that you need to keep your Internet connection open all the time. If you don't want Messenger to run in the background, clear this check box, and Messenger will exit when you close its window.

Show Me As "Away" When I'm Inactive for *NN* Minutes check box and text box Leave this check box selected (as it is by default) if you want Messenger to change your status to Away after the specified period of inactivity. (Adjust the number of minutes in the text box as necessary. The default setting is 10 minutes, which is too short for many busy people.) Clear this check box if you don't want Messenger to monitor you in this way.

Display Alerts Near the Taskbar When Contacts Come Online check box Leave this check box selected (as it is by default) if you want Messenger to pop up an alert above the notification area when one of your contacts comes online.

Display Alerts Near the Taskbar When an Instant Message Is Received check box Leave this check box selected (as it is by default) if you want Messenger to pop up an alert above the notification area when you receive an instant message.

Play Sound When Contacts Sign in or Send a Message check box Leave this check box selected (as it is by default) if you want Messenger to play a sound when contacts of yours sign in or send you a message. This audio alert is especially useful if you turn off the two visual alerts. If you use this option, you can click the Sounds button to customize the sounds displayed. Windows displays the Sound and Audio Devices Properties dialog box. In the Program Events list box on the Sounds page, scroll down to the Windows Messenger category, and assigns sounds that you like to the Contact Online event (when a contact signs in), the New Alert event (when Messenger displays an alert), the New Mail event, and the New Message event. Then click the OK button. Windows closes the Sound and Audio Devices Properties dialog box.

File Transfer text box Specify the folder in which you want Messenger to put files that you receive from your contacts. The default setting is your `My Documents\My Received Files` folder.

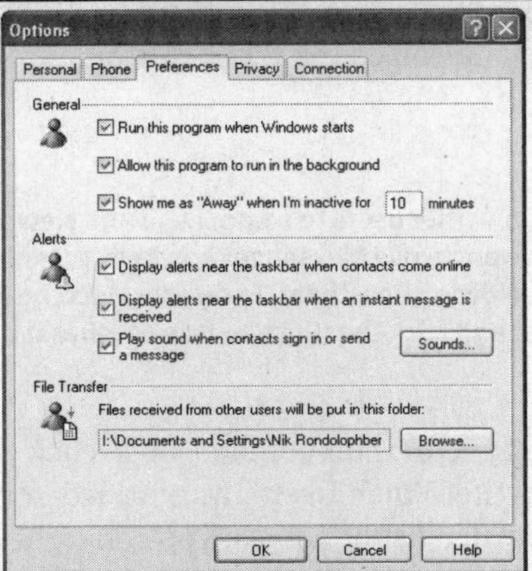

FIGURE 15.9: On the Preferences tab of the Options dialog box, customize Messenger's behavior.

Privacy Tab Options

The Privacy tab of the Options dialog box (shown in Figure 15.10) is where you maintain your Allow List (people who can see your online status and can send you messages) and your Block List (people who can do neither).

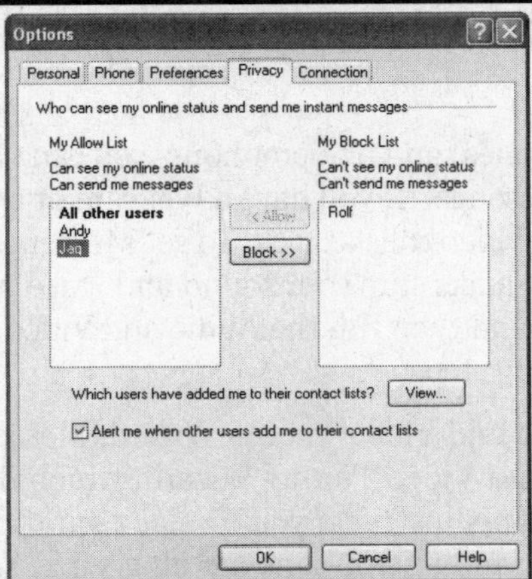

FIGURE 15.10: Use the Privacy tab of the Options dialog box to keep your Allow List and your Block List up-to-date.

To move a contact from one list to another, select them in the appropriate list box and click the Allow button or the Block button.

TIP

By default, Messenger allows all other users to contact you and view your status until you block them. If you want to use Messenger privately, consider blocking all other users until you decide to allow them. To do so, select the All Other Users item in the My Allow List and click the Block button to move it to the My Block List.

To see which users have added you to their contacts lists, click the View button. Messenger displays the Which Users Have Added You? dialog box, which provides an unadorned list of names. You can right-click a name and choose Add to Contacts from the shortcut menu to add the person to your list of contacts, or choose Properties from the shortcut menu to display a Properties dialog box giving information about the person.

Connection Tab Options

On the Connection tab of the Options dialog box, you can specify proxy server settings if you connect to the Internet through a proxy server (for example, through a company network). If not, leave these settings alone.

Running the Audio and Video Tuning Wizard

If you have speakers (or headphones) and a microphone, you can use them to make voice calls via Messenger. If you have a Webcam or another live video camera, you can make video calls as well. To set Messenger up for making voice and video calls, make sure your sound and video hardware is plugged in and working, and then run the Audio and Video Tuning Wizard by taking the following steps:

1. Choose Tools ➢ Audio and Video Tuning Wizard. Messenger starts the Audio and Video Tuning Wizard, which displays its first screen. This instructs you to make sure that your camera, speakers, and microphone are plugged in and turned on, and to close any other programs that might be using them.

2. Click the Next button. The Wizard displays its second screen (shown in Figure 15.11).

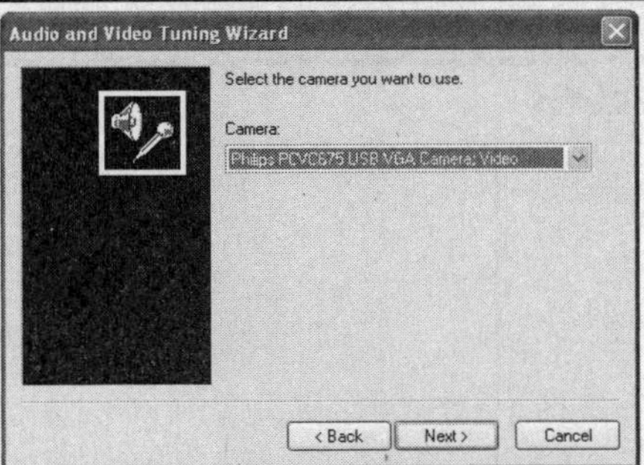

FIGURE 15.11: On the second screen of the Audio and Video Tuning Wizard, choose the video camera to use for video calls.

3. In the Camera drop-down list, select the video camera to use.
4. Click the Next button. The Wizard grabs the video feed from the camera and displays it on its third screen (shown in Figure 15.12).

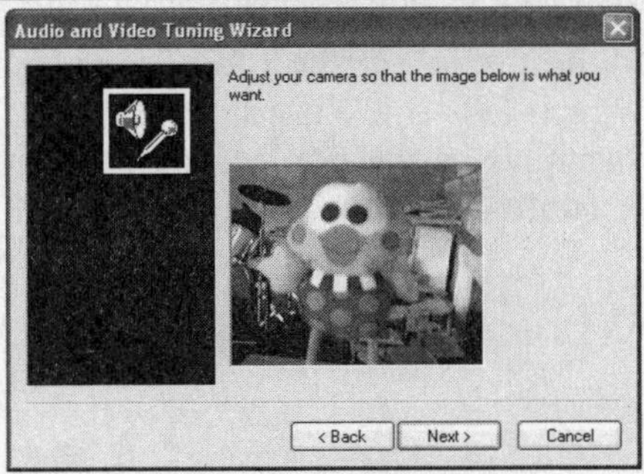

FIGURE 15.12: On the third screen of the Audio and Video Tuning Wizard, adjust your video camera to show the image you want.

5. Adjust the picture until it shows what you want it to.
6. Click the Next button. The Wizard displays its fourth screen with tips on positioning your microphone and speakers.

7. Move your microphone or your speakers if necessary.
8. Click the Next button. The Wizard displays its fifth screen (shown in Figure 15.13).

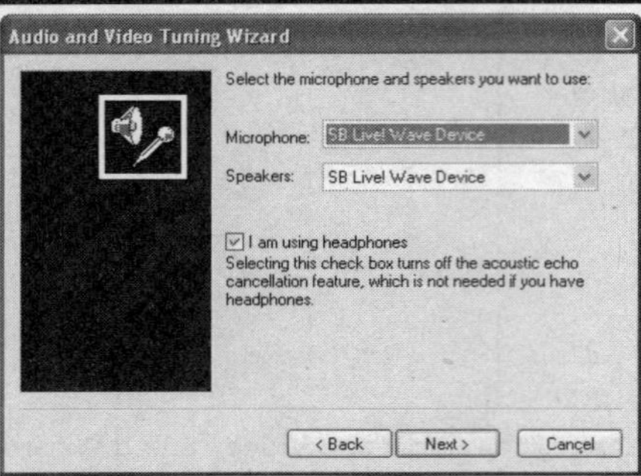

FIGURE 15.13: On the fifth screen of the Audio and Video Tuning Wizard, choose which microphone and speakers to use.

9. In the Microphone drop-down list, select the microphone to use.
10. In the Speakers drop-down list, select the output device (for example, a sound card) connected to the speakers.
11. If you're using headphones, select the I Am Using Headphones check box, which tells the Wizard to turn off echo cancellation. (With headphones, you don't need this because the echoes should be confined to your head.)
12. Click the Next button. The Wizard displays its sixth screen (shown in Figure 15.14).

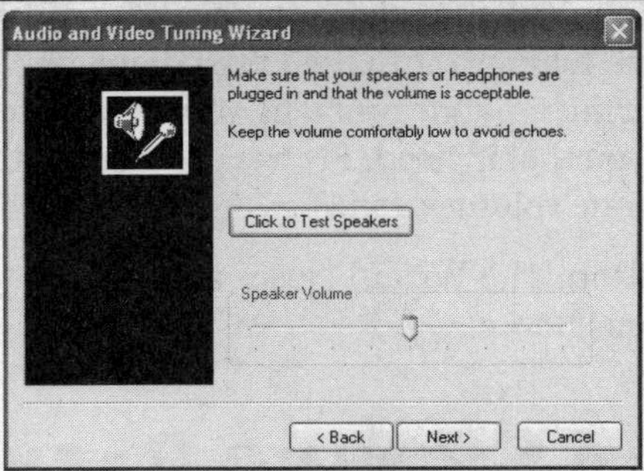

FIGURE 15.14: On the sixth screen of the Audio and Video Tuning Wizard, test your speakers or headphones.

13. Click the Click to Test Speakers button to play a sound for a volume check. Drag the Speaker Volume slider to adjust the volume as necessary. Click the Stop button (which replaces the Click to Test Speakers button) to stop the sound.
14. Click the Next button. The Wizard displays its seventh screen (shown in Figure 15.15).

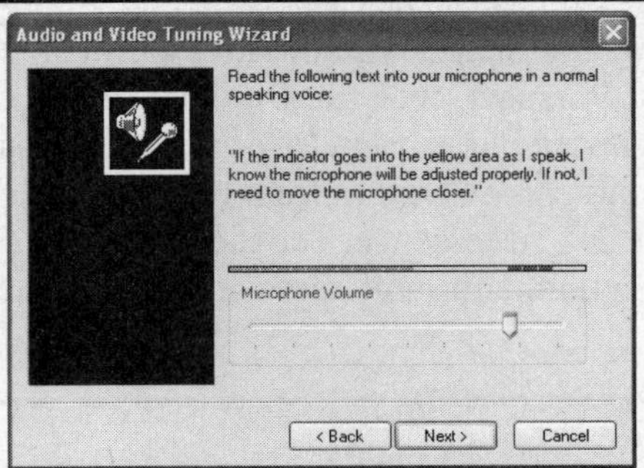

FIGURE 15.15: On the seventh screen of the Audio and Video Tuning Wizard, set your microphone volume.

15. Speak into your microphone for 20 to 30 seconds at normal volume. (If you want, read the sample text shown, but it's instructive rather than magical, so declaim poetry or curse fluently if you prefer.) The Audio and Video Tuning Wizard adjusts the Microphone Volume slider to an appropriate level.

16. Click the Next button. You should see the eighth and final screen of the Wizard, telling you that you've completed the Wizard. (If you had a microphone problem, you'll see instead a dialog box telling you that instead. Fix the problem and try setting the microphone volume again.)

17. Click the Finish button. The Wizard closes and applies the settings it helped you choose.

Signing Out and Signing Back In

Messenger automatically signs you in when you start it. But you can sign out manually, leaving Messenger running, by choosing File ➢ Sign Out.

NOTE

The first time you sign out, if you have things going on, Messenger displays a dialog box explaining that signing out will close all your conversations and stop any file transfers. Click the OK button to proceed. After that, Messenger doesn't give you any warning when you sign out.

To sign back in as the same user, click the Click Here to Sign in As Username link in the Windows Messenger window. Messenger signs you in. To sign in using a different Passport, click the Or, Click Here To Sign In As Someone Else link, or choose File ➢ Sign In, or click the Messenger icon in the notification area and choose Sign In from the menu it displays. Messenger displays the .NET Messenger Service dialog box (shown in Figure 15.16). Enter your sign-in name and password, and then click the OK button.

FIGURE 15.16: Signing back in to Messenger Service

ADDING A CONTACT

You can add a contact to your list of contacts in several ways: by using their e-mail address or Passport sign-in name; by searching for them in a directory; by adding them when they contact you; or by reciprocating when they add you as a contact.

Adding a Contact by E-Mail Address or Passport Sign-In

If you know a contact's e-mail address or Passport sign-in name, you can add them to your contacts list as follows:

1. Click the Add button in the Messenger window (or choose File ➢ Add a Contact). Messenger displays the How Do You Want to Add a Contact? screen of the Add a Contact Wizard (shown in Figure 15.17).
2. Leave the By E-mail Address or Sign-In Name option button selected, as it is by default.
3. Click the Next button. Messenger displays the Please Type Your Contact's Complete E-mail Address screen.

FIGURE 15.17: On the How Do You Want to Add a Contact? screen of the Add a Contact Wizard, specify whether to add a contact by e-mail address or Passport sign-in name or to search for them.

4. Enter the e-mail address and click the Next button. Messenger searches for a matching user. If it finds one, it displays a Success screen telling you that it has added the contact to your list. If Messenger doesn't find a match, it offers to send a message to the user inviting them to try Messenger. Take up this request if you like.

Adding a Contact by Searching for Them

You can also add a contact to your contacts list by searching for them:

1. Click the Add button in the Messenger window (or choose File ➢ Add a Contact). Messenger displays the How Do You Want to Add a Contact? screen of the Add a Contact Wizard.
2. Select the Search for a Contact option button.
3. Click the Next button. Messenger displays the Type Your Contact's First and Last Name screen (shown in Figure 15.18).

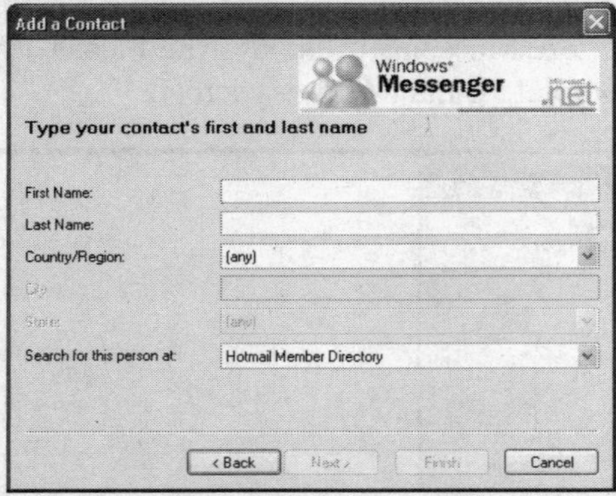

FIGURE 15.18: To add a contact to your list in Messenger, you can search for them by name.

4. Enter the person's first name and last name. If you're sure of their country or region, specify that in the Country/Region drop-down list.
   - By default, Messenger searches in the Hotmail Member Directory. You may be able to choose another search

location, such as your Address Book, in the Search for This Person At drop-down list.

5. Click the Next button. Messenger displays a Search Results screen showing possible matches.
6. Select the right person and click the Next button. Messenger then walks you through the process of having the .NET service send an e-mail to the person and tell them how to install Messenger and contact you. You can add your own message to this e-mail, but Messenger won't give you the person's e-mail address so that you can contact them directly.

Adding a Contact When Someone Adds You to Their Contacts List

You can also add a contact quickly by adding a person who adds you to *their* contacts list (unless you've configured Messenger not to notify you when this happens).

When someone adds you to their contacts list, Messenger displays the Windows Messenger dialog box shown in Figure 15.19, asking whether you want to allow this person or block them. Select the Allow This Person to See When You Are Online and Contact You option button or the Block This Person from Seeing When You Are Online and Contacting You option button as appropriate. If you want to add the person to your contacts list, leave the Add This Person to My Contact List check box selected. If not, clear it. Then click the OK button. Messenger closes the dialog box and takes the actions you specified.

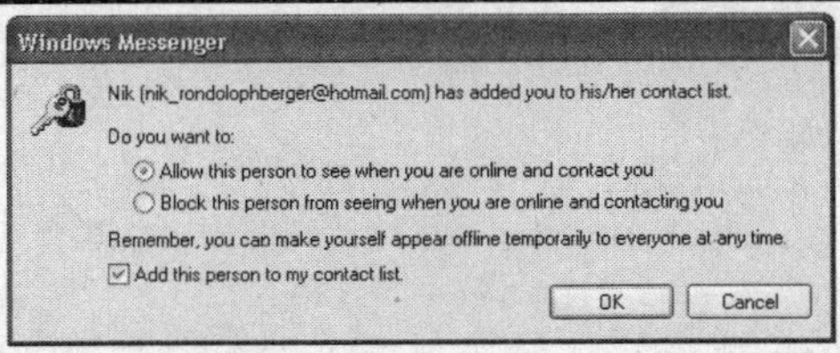

FIGURE 15.19: Messenger displays this Windows Messenger dialog box when someone adds you to their contacts list. Specify whether to allow the contact or block them.

Removing a Contact from Your Contacts List

To remove a contact from your contacts list, select their entry and press the Delete key (or choose File ➢ Delete Contact). Alternatively, right-click the contact and choose Delete Contact from the shortcut menu. Messenger deletes the contact without confirmation.

Chatting

To chat with a Messenger user, double-click the user's entry in the Online list, or right-click the user's entry in the Online list and choose Send an Instant Message from the shortcut menu.

Messenger opens a Conversation window of chat with the user. Figure 15.20 shows an example. Type a message into the text box and press the Enter key (or click the Send button) to send it.

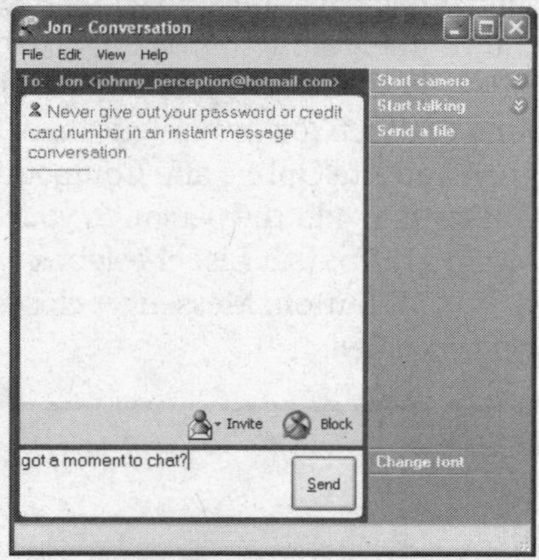

FIGURE 15.20: Starting a conversation in Messenger

The other user receives a screen pop-up (of which Figure 15.21 shows an example) telling them that you've sent them a message and a minimized Conversation window. The user can display the Conversation window by clicking the screen pop-up (if they're quick enough to catch it before it disappears) or by clicking the Conversation window's button on the Taskbar.

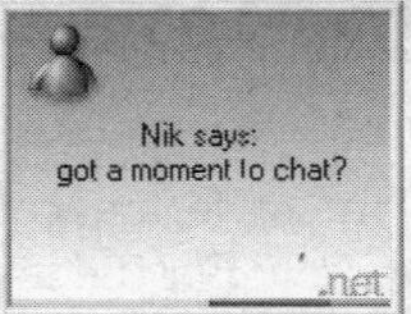

FIGURE 15.21: Messenger displays a screen pop-up like this when someone sends you a message.

Figure 15.22 shows a chat getting started in a Conversation window. Note the readout at the bottom that tells you that the other protagonist in the chat is typing a message. This alert helps you avoid sending overlapping messages and having the conversations spiral off into multiple threads.

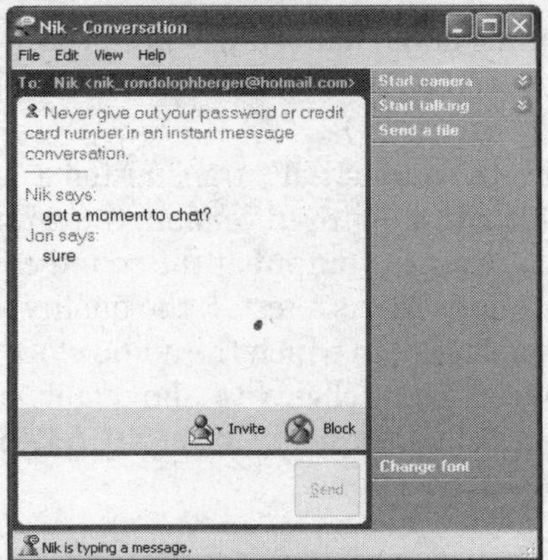

FIGURE 15.22: Chatting in a Conversation window. The readout at the bottom warns the user that the other participant is typing a message.

Adding More People to a Conversation

To add a third or fourth person to your current conversation, choose File ➢ Invite ➢ To Join This Conversation. From the submenu, select one of your contacts from the context menu. Alternatively, select the Other item, specify the user's e-mail address in the Invite to This Conversation dialog box, and click the OK button. Messenger adds the user to the conversation if they're online.

Setting Font, Style, and Color for Text You Send

If you want to be distinctive, you can change the font, style, and color for text you send to others and that you see on your screen. For the text you see in the Messenger windows, you can change the size as well. (You can't change the size of the text that others see, and they can't change the size that you see.)

To set the font, style, color, and size, choose Edit ➢ Change Font. Messenger displays the Change My Message Font dialog box. Choose settings you like and click the OK button to apply them.

Adding Voice to a Conversation

If both participants have functioning audio hardware, you can add voice to a Messenger conversation between two people. (You can't use voice in a conversation that has three or four people.)

As usual for Internet telephony, the audio that's transmitted is converted from its (spoken) analog form to a digitized version, transmitted digitally, and then converted back to analog output at the sound card, headphones, or speakers on the other end. As a result, the quality tends to suffer compared to a regular phone call, in which the audio stays analog the whole way. That said, you can get intelligible audio quality over a connection as slow as 21.6Kbps, acceptable quality in the 40–53Kbps range, and good quality over faster connections.

NOTE

If you haven't run the Audio and Video Tuning Wizard, Messenger runs it the first time you click the Talk button.

To add voice to your current conversation, click the Start Talking heading in the right pane in the Conversation window. Messenger displays a Speakers volume control and a Microphone Mute check box (shown in Figure 15.23) and notifies the person you're chatting with that you want to have a voice conversation. They get to accept this or decline it. If they accept, Messenger establishes the connection.

To hang up the voice portion of the call, click the Stop Talking heading.

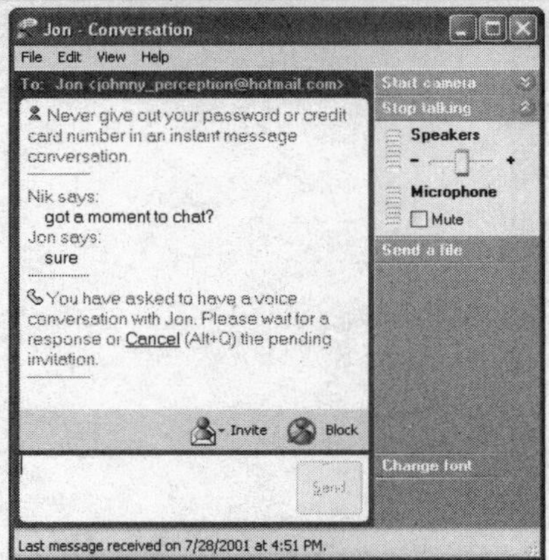

FIGURE 15.23: When you add voice to a Messenger conversation, the Conversation window displays a Speakers volume control and a Microphone Mute control.

Adding Video to a Conversation

If one or both participants have video hardware installed, you can add video to a Messenger conversation between two people. (As with voice, you can't use video in a conversation that has three or four people.)

To add video to a conversation, click the Start Camera heading. Messenger displays a camera panel on your computer with a picture-in-picture picture of the video you're sending, and invites your victim to take part in the video conversation. If they accept, they receive a larger version of the picture. Figure 15.24 shows a conversation with incoming video.

To toggle your picture-in-picture picture on and off, click the Options button and choose Show My Video As Picture-in-Picture from the menu.

To stop transmitting or receiving video, click the Stop Camera heading.

FIGURE 15.24: You can also add video to a Messenger conversation.

Blocking and Unblocking Users

To block somebody from chatting with you, take one of the following actions:

- In a Conversation window with the person you want to block, click the Block button or choose File ➢ Block.
- In a Conversation window with multiple people, click the Block button and choose the person from the pop-up menu, or choose File ➢ Block and choose the person from the submenu.
- From the Windows Messenger window, right-click the person and choose Block from the context menu.

When you block a user from a Conversation window, Messenger displays the Windows Messenger dialog box shown in Figure 15.25 telling you that the blocked user will not be able to contact you or see your online status. When you unblock a user, Messenger displays a similar dialog box telling you that the other user *will* be able to do these things. In either case, you get an OK button to proceed with the blocking or unblocking, a Cancel button to cancel it, and a Don't Show Me This Message Again check box that you can select to prevent Messenger from telling you what you already know.

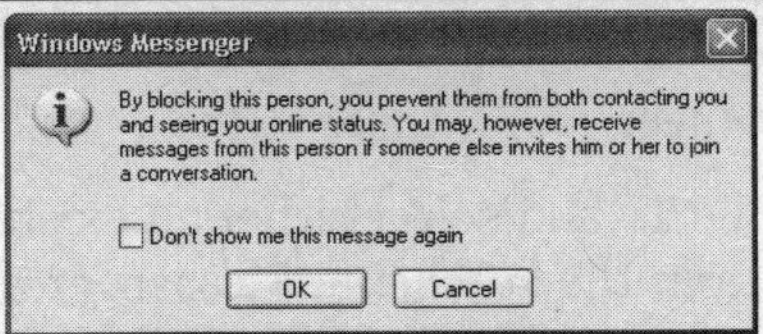

FIGURE 15.25: When you block a user, Messenger displays a dialog box to make sure you understand the consequences of your action. Select the Don't Show Me This Message Again check box to prevent Messenger from displaying this dialog box again.

To unblock a user, take one of the following actions:

- In a Conversation window, choose File ➢ Unblock.
- In a Conversation window with multiple participants, choose File ➢ Block and select the blocked user from the submenu.
- In the Windows Messenger window, right-click the blocked user and choose Unblock from the shortcut menu.

Changing Your Status

To let people know what you're up to, you can change the status that Messenger displays for you. To do so, click your icon in the Windows Messenger window and choose Online, Busy, Be Right Back, Away, On the Phone, Out to Lunch, or Appear Offline from the pop-up menu. You can also set your status by choosing File ➢ My Status and selecting the status from the submenu.

Transferring Files

Messenger provides an easy way to transfer files quickly to other Messenger users who are currently online.

Sending a File

To send a file to someone via Messenger, follow these steps:

1. Choose File ➢ Send a File To and select either an existing user or the Other item from the submenu. Messenger displays the Send a File dialog box, which is an Open dialog box in disguise.
   - If you select the Other item, Messenger displays the Send a File dialog box (shown in Figure 15.26). Enter the person's e-mail address, select the service in the Service drop-down list (if applicable), and click the OK button.

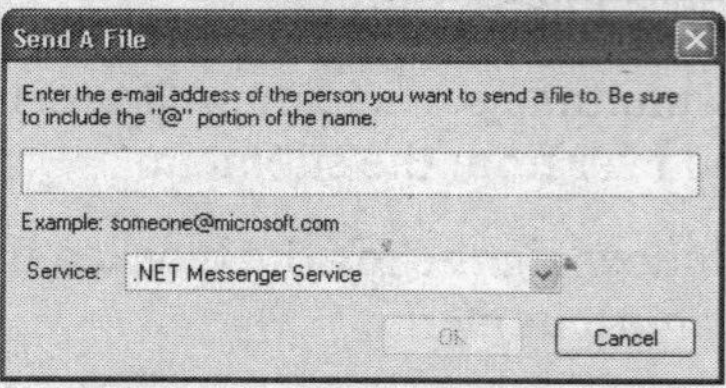

FIGURE 15.26: Use the Send a File dialog box to send a file to a Messenger user who isn't one of your contacts.

   - To send a file to a user you're chatting with in a Conversation window, click the Send a File heading or choose File ➢ Send a File. You don't need to identify the user because Messenger knows it already. (If you're chatting with multiple people, Messenger displays the Send a File submenu listing the people in the conversation.)
2. Navigate to the file, select it, and click the Open button. Messenger contacts the user, asking them if they want to accept or decline the file.
   - You can cancel the transfer by pressing Alt+Q or clicking the Cancel link.
3. If the user accepts the file, Messenger displays a progress readout in the Conversation window. When the file transfer is complete, Messenger lets you know that too. Figure 15.27 shows an example of a successful file-transfer session.

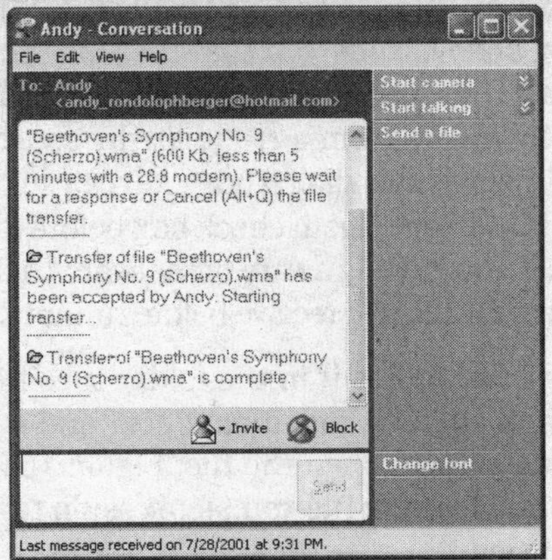

FIGURE 15.27: Messenger keeps you informed at each step of sending a file.

NOTE

If the user does not accept the transfer, or if it fails, Messenger tells you that the user declined the file or the file could not be sent.

Receiving a File

Receiving a file via Messenger is even easier than sending one. Here's what happens:

1. If you're using pop-ups, Messenger displays a pop-up telling you that someone is trying to send you a file. (Messenger identifies the user and the file by name.)
2. Click the pop-up to display the Conversation window. (If you're already in a messaging session with this user, you'll go directly to this step.)
3. To accept the file, click the Accept link (or press Alt+T). To decline the file, click the Decline link (or press Alt+D).

4. If you choose to accept the file, Messenger displays a Windows Messenger dialog box warning you that files may contain harmful viruses or scripts and advising you to make sure that the file you're receiving is from a trustworthy source. Click the OK button to dismiss this dialog box. You can select the Don't Show Me This Message Again check box before dismissing the dialog box if you're fully aware of malware tricks and you carefully check every file you receive before running it.
5. Messenger transfers the file, stores it in the folder specified on the Preferences tab of the Options dialog box, and displays a link that you can click to open the file. Figure 15.28 shows the anatomy of a successful file-transfer session from the recipient's point of view.

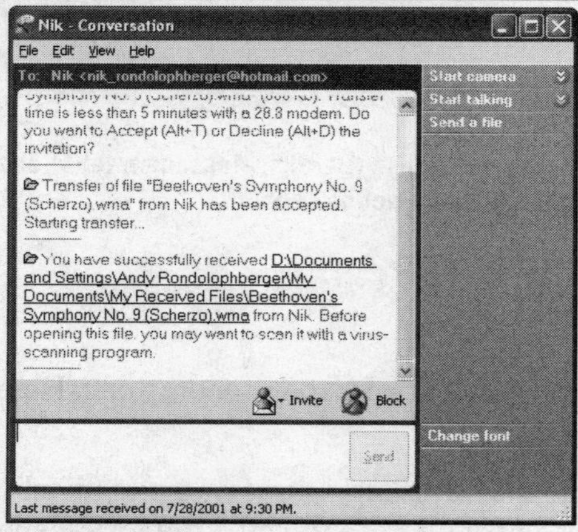

FIGURE 15.28: Likewise, Messenger keeps you well informed when you're receiving a file.

To access your received files folder, choose File ➢ Open Received Files.

Using Remote Desktop Connection

Remote Desktop Connection lets you connect via a dial-up connection, a local area network connection, or across the Internet and take control of somebody's computer (or your own).

Remote Desktop Connection is designed to let you access and control one computer (say, your work computer) from another computer (say, your home computer or your laptop). It's great for catching up with the office when you're at home, or for grabbing the files that you forgot to load on your laptop before you dived into the taxi for the airport.

Remote Desktop Connection Terminology and Basics

Remote Desktop Connection terminology is a little confusing. Here are the terms:

- The *home computer* is the computer on which you're working. The home computer needs to have Remote Desktop Connection installed. Remote Desktop Connection is installed by default in Windows XP Professional.
- The *remote computer* is the computer that you're accessing from the home computer. The remote computer needs to have Remote Desktop installed. Remote Desktop is separate from Remote Desktop Connection and is included in Windows XP Professional and the (forthcoming, at this writing) versions of Windows .NET Server. Remote Desktop is not included in Windows XP Home.

So the typical scenario is for the home computer to be running Windows XP Home and the remote computer to be running Windows XP Professional. You can also access one Windows XP Professional computer from another Windows XP Professional computer.

NOTE

You can access more than one remote computer at a time from the same home computer. However, unless you have impressive bandwidth, this results in slow sessions.

In order for you to connect to another computer via Remote Desktop Connection any active session (whether local or connected via Remote Desktop Connection) on that computer needs to be disconnected. You get a warning about this, but the other user doesn't. If you choose to proceed, the remote computer displays the Welcome screen while your Remote Desktop Connection session is going on. There's no easy way for anyone looking at that computer to tell that you're remotely connected to it.

If a user comes back and starts using the remote computer while your Remote Desktop Connection session is going on, your session will be terminated—with a warning on their side, this time, but not on yours. Frankly, this could be more elegant.

In lay terms, Remote Desktop Connection works as follows:

- Keystrokes and mouse clicks are transmitted from the home computer to the remote computer via the display protocol. The remote computer registers these keystrokes and clicks as if they came from the keyboard attached to it.
- Programs run on the remote computer as usual. (Programs aren't run across the wire—that would be desperately slow.)
- Screen display information is passed to the home computer, again via the display protocol. This information appears on the display as if it came from the video adapter (only rather more slowly, and usually in a window).

Sound can be passed to the home computer as well, so that you can hear what's happening at the remote computer. Transferring sound like this enhances the impression of controlling the remote computer, but sound takes so much bandwidth that transferring it isn't a good idea on slow connections. The default Remote Desktop Connection setting is to transfer sound, but you may well want to switch it off.

Setting the Remote Computer to Accept Incoming Connections

The first step in getting Remote Desktop Connection to work is to set the remote computer to accept incoming connections. Remember that this is the computer that's remote from you and that's running Windows XP Professional (or .NET Server).

To set your computer to accept incoming connections, follow these steps:

1. Click the Start button, right-click My Computer, and choose Properties from the shortcut menu to open the System Properties dialog box.
2. Click the Remote tab, which is shown in Figure 15.29.

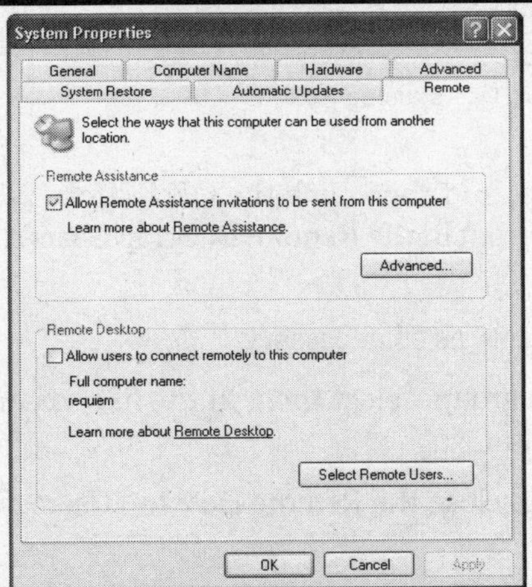

FIGURE 15.29: The Remote tab of the System Properties dialog box

3. To allow users to connect to your computer, select the Allow Users to Connect Remotely to This Computer check box.
4. To specify which users can connect via Remote Desktop Connection, click the Select Remote Users button to open the Remote Desktop Users dialog box (shown in Figure 15.30). The list box shows any users currently allowed to connect to the computer. Below the list box is a note indicating that you (identified by your username) already have access—as you should have.
5. To add users, click the Add button. Windows displays the Select Users dialog box.

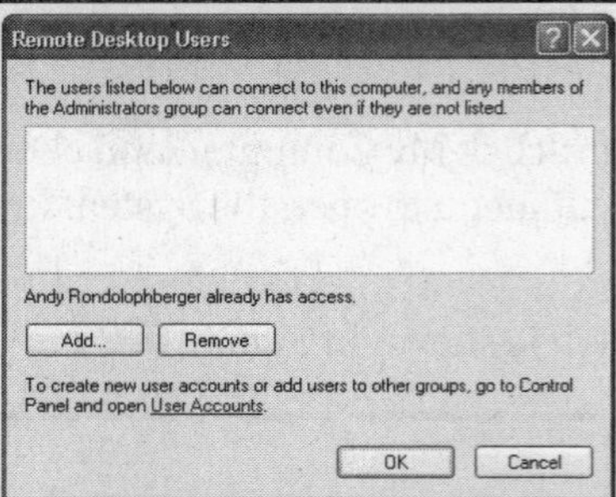

FIGURE 15.30: The Remote Desktop Users dialog box

6. Select a user or group, and then click the OK button. Windows adds them to the list in the Remote Desktop Users dialog box.
7. Add further users or groups as necessary.
8. To remove a user or a group, select them in the list box and click the Remove button.
9. Click the OK button to close the Remote Desktop Users dialog box.
10. Click the OK button in the System Properties dialog box. Windows closes the dialog box and applies your changes.

That's the remote computer all set. Leave it up and running and return to the home computer.

Choosing Settings for Remote Desktop Connection

Next, choose settings for Remote Desktop Connection on the home computer. Remote Desktop Connection has a modestly large number of settings, but many of them are set-and-forget. Even better, you can save sets of settings so that you can quickly apply them for accessing different remote computers (or the same remote computer under different circumstances, such as when the cable modem is working and when it's flaked out on you).

To choose settings for Remote Desktop Connection, follow these steps:

1. Choose Start ➢ All Programs ➢ Accessories ➢ Communications ➢ Remote Desktop Connection. Windows starts Remote Desktop Connection and displays the Remote Desktop Connection window in its reduced state (shown in Figure 15.31).
2. Click the Options button. Windows displays the rest of the Remote Desktop Connection window.

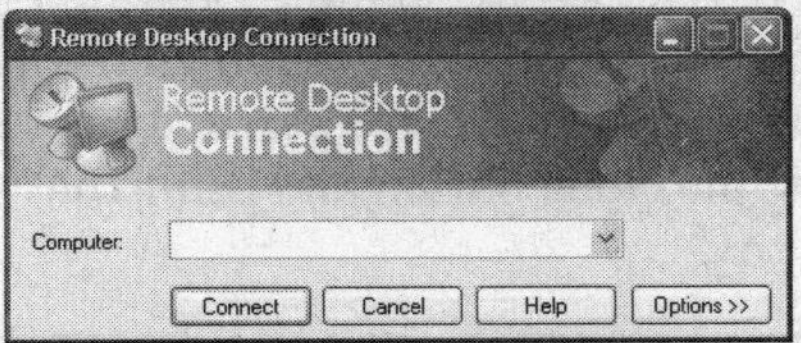

FIGURE 15.31: The Remote Desktop Connection window appears first in its reduced state.

3. The General tab of the Remote Desktop Connection window (shown in Figure 15.32) offers these options:

   Computer drop-down list Enter the name or the IP address of the computer to which you want to connect; or select it from the drop-down list; or click the Browse for More item from the drop-down list to display the Browse for Computers dialog box, and then select the computer in that.

   User Name text box Enter the username under which you want to connect to the remote computer. Windows enters your username by default.

   Password text box If you want to store your password (for the remote computer) for the connection, enter it in this text box and select the Save My Password check box. If you don't enter your password here, you get to enter it when logging on to the remote computer.

   Domain text box If the remote computer is part of a domain, enter the domain name here. If the computer is part of a workgroup, you can leave this text box blank.

Save My Password check box Select this check box if you want to save your password with the rest of the Remote Desktop Connection information. This can save you time and effort, but it compromises your security a bit.

Connection Settings section Once you've chosen settings for a connection, you can save the connection information by clicking the Save As button and specifying a name for the connection in the Save As dialog box that Windows displays. Remote Desktop Connection connections are saved as files of the file type Remote Desktop File, which by default is linked to the RDP extension, in the `My Documents\Remote Desktops` folder. You can open saved connections by clicking the Open button and using the resulting Open dialog box.

FIGURE 15.32: The General tab of the expanded Remote Desktop Connection window

NOTE

You'll see a file named `DEFAULT.RDP` in the `My Documents\Remote Desktops` folder. Windows automatically saves your latest Remote Desktop Connection configuration under this name when you click the Connect button. But by explicitly saving your settings under a name of your choice, you can easily maintain different configurations for different Remote Desktop Connection settings.

4. The Display tab of the Remote Desktop Connection window (shown in Figure 15.33) offers three display options:

   Remote Desktop Size section Drag the slider to specify the screen size you want to use for the remote Desktop. The default setting is Full Screen, but you may want to use a smaller size so that you can more easily access your Desktop on the home computer. When you display the remote Desktop full screen, it takes over the whole of the local Desktop, so that you can't see your local Desktop. (To get to your local Desktop, you use the connection bar, discussed in a moment or two.)

   Colors section In the drop-down list, select the color depth to use for the connection. Choose a low color depth (for example, 256 colors) if you're connecting over a low-speed connection. This choice will be overridden by the display setting on the remote computer if you ask for more colors than the remote computer is using.

   Display the Connection Bar When in Full Screen Mode check box Leave this check box selected (as it is by default) if you want Windows to display the connection bar when the remote Desktop is displayed full screen. The connection bar provides Minimize, Restore/Maximize, and Close buttons for the remote Desktop. (When the remote Desktop is displayed in a window, that window has the control buttons, so the connection bar isn't necessary.)

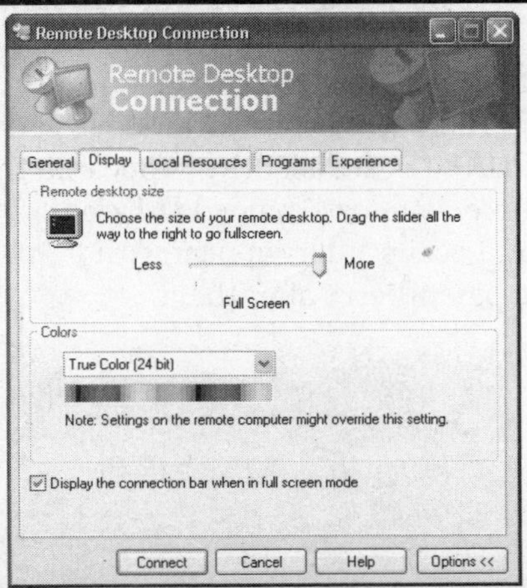

FIGURE 15.33: Choose display settings on the Display tab of the Remote Desktop Connection window.

5. The Local Resources tab of the Remote Desktop Connection window (shown in Figure 15.34) offers the following options:

   Remote Computer Sound section In the drop-down list, specify what you want Windows to do with sounds that would normally be generated at the remote Desktop. The default setting is Bring to This Computer, which transfers the sounds to the home computer and plays them there. This setting helps sustain the illusion that you're working directly on the remote Desktop, but it's heavy on bandwidth, so don't use it over low-speed connections. Instead, choose the Do Not Play setting or the Leave at Remote Computer setting. The Leave at Remote Computer setting plays the sounds at the remote computer and is best reserved for occasions when you need to frighten somebody remotely or pretend to be in your office.

   Keyboard section In the drop-down list, specify how you want Windows to handle Windows key combinations that you press (for example, Alt+Tab or Ctrl+Alt+Delete). Select the On the Local Computer item, the On the Remote Computer item, or the In Full Screen Mode Only item (the default) as suits your needs.

   Local Devices section Leave the Disk Drives check box, the Printers check box, and the Serial Ports check box selected (as they are by default) if you want these devices on your home computer to be available from the remote computer. This means that you can save documents from the remote computer to local drives, print them on your local printer, or transfer them via devices attached to serial ports (for example, a PDA). Local disk drives appear in the Other category in Explorer windows, named *Driveletter on COMPUTERNAME*. Local printers appear with *from COMPUTERNAME* in parentheses after them.

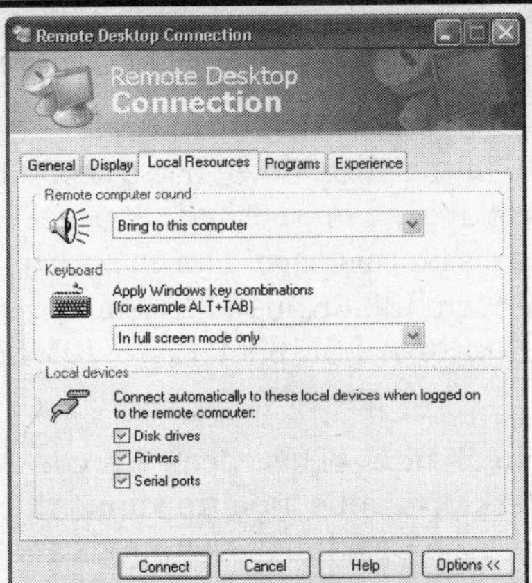

FIGURE 15.34: On the Local Resources tab of the Remote Desktop Connection window, specify how Windows should handle sound, keyboard shortcuts, and devices on the home computer.

6. The Programs tab of the Remote Desktop Connection window (shown in Figure 15.35) lets you specify that Windows run a designated program when you connect via Remote Desktop Connection. Select the Start the Following Program on Connection check box, then enter the program path and name in the Program Path and File Name text box. If you need to specify the folder in which the program should start, enter that in the Start in the Following Folder text box.

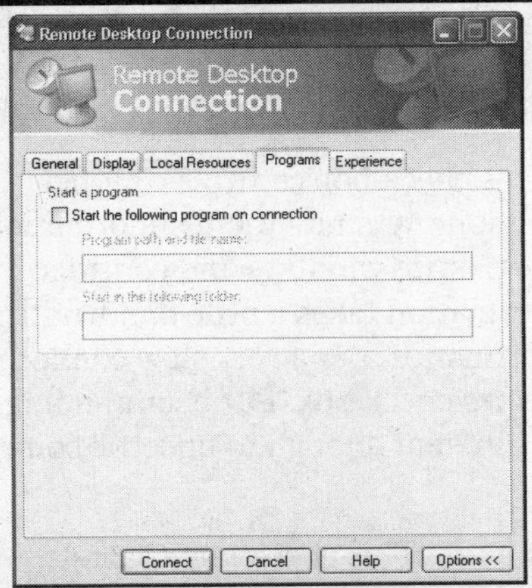

FIGURE 15.35: If you need to have a program run on the remote Desktop when you connect, specify it on the Programs tab of the Remote Desktop Connection window.

7. The Experience tab of the Remote Desktop Connection window (shown in Figure 15.36) contains the following options:

   Choose Your Connection Speed to Optimize Performance drop-down list In this drop-down list, select one of the four listed speeds to apply a preselected set of settings to the five check boxes on this page. The choices in the drop-down list are Modem (28.8Kbps), Modem (56Kbps), Broadband (128Kbps–1.5Mbps), LAN (10Mbps or Higher), and Custom.

   Desktop Background check box This check box controls whether Remote Desktop Connection transmits the Desktop background. Because Desktop backgrounds are graphical, transmitting them is sensible only at LAN speeds. (If you clear this check box, Remote Desktop Connection uses a blank Desktop background.)

   Show Contents of Window While Dragging check box This check box controls whether Remote Desktop Connection transmits the contents of a window while you're dragging it, or only the window frame. Don't use this option over a modem connection, because the performance penalty outweighs any benefit you may derive from it.

   Menu and Window Animation check box This check box controls whether Remote Desktop Connection transmits menu and window animations (for example, zooming a window you're maximizing or minimizing). Don't use this option over a modem connection—it's a waste of bandwidth.

   Themes check box This check box controls whether Remote Desktop Connection transmits theme information or uses "classic" Windows–style windows and controls. Transmitting theme information takes a little bandwidth, so you can improve performance over a very slow connection by clearing the Themes check box. But bear in mind that Windows will look different enough to unsettle some inexperienced users.

   Bitmap Caching check box This check box controls whether Remote Desktop Connection uses bitmap caching to improve performance by reducing the amount of data that needs to be sent across the network in order to display the screen remotely. Caching could prove a security threat, so you *might* want to turn it off for security reasons. But in most cases, you're better off using it.

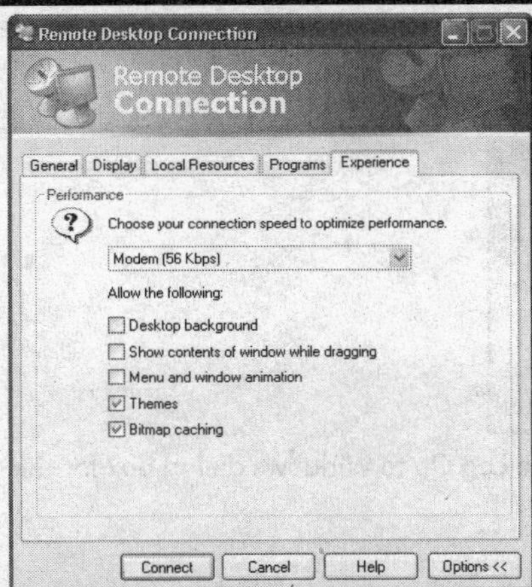

FIGURE 15.36: On the Experience tab of the Remote Desktop Connection window, you can customize which graphical information Remote Desktop Connection transmits in order to balance performance against looks.

8. If you want to save the settings you've chosen under a particular name so that you can reload them at will, click the Save As button on the General tab of the Remote Desktop Connection window.

Connecting via Remote Desktop Connection

Once you've chosen settings as outlined in the previous section, you're ready to connect. If you're connecting via the Internet (rather than a local network) and you have a dial-up connection, make sure it's up and running.

Click the Connect button in the General tab of the Remote Desktop Connection window. Windows attempts to establish a connection to the computer you specified.

If Windows is able to connect to the computer, and you didn't specify your username or password in the Remote Desktop Connection window, it displays the Log On to Windows dialog box (shown in Figure 15.37). Enter your username and password and click the OK button to log in. Windows then displays the remote Desktop. (If you chose to provide your password on the General tab of the Remote Desktop Connection window, you shouldn't need to enter it again.)

FIGURE 15.37: Windows displays the Log On to Windows dialog box for the remote computer.

If you left a user session active on the computer, Remote Desktop Connection drops you straight into it—likewise if you left a user session disconnected and no other user session is active. But if another user *is* active on the remote computer when you submit a successful logon and password, Windows displays the Logon Message dialog box shown in Figure 15.38 to warn you that logging on will disconnect the user's session. Click the Yes button if you want to proceed. Click the No button to withdraw stealthily.

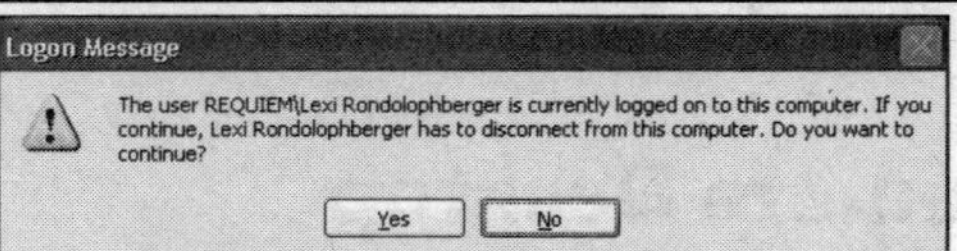

FIGURE 15.38: Windows displays the Logon Message dialog box when you're about to bump a user off the remote computer by logging on.

If you click the Yes button, the active user gets a Request for Connection dialog box such as that shown in Figure 15.39, which tells them that you (it specifies your name) are trying to connect to the computer, warns them that they'll be disconnected if you do connect, and asks if they want to allow the connection.

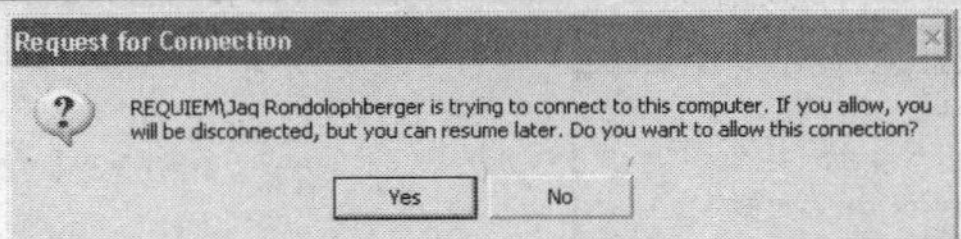

FIGURE 15.39: Windows displays the Request for Connection dialog box to tell the active user of your incoming session.

The active user then gets to click the Yes button or the No button as appropriate to their needs and inclinations. If Windows doesn't get an answer within 30 seconds or so, it figures they're not there, disconnects their session, and lets you in.

If the active user clicks the Yes button in the Request for Connection dialog box, Windows logs them off immediately and logs you on. But if the active user clicks the No button, you get a Logon Message dialog box such as that shown in Figure 15.40, telling you that they didn't allow you to connect. Windows displays this Logon Message dialog box for a few seconds, and then closes it automatically, returning you to the Remote Desktop Connection window.

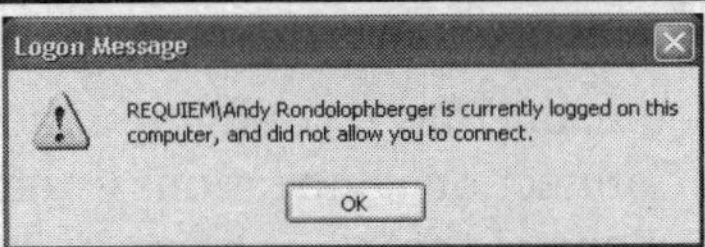

FIGURE 15.40: Windows displays this Logon Message dialog box when the active user decides not to let you interrupt their session on the computer.

If Windows is unable to establish the connection with the remote computer, it displays one of its Remote Desktop Disconnected dialog boxes to make you aware of the problem. Figure 15.41 shows two examples of the Remote Desktop Disconnected dialog box.

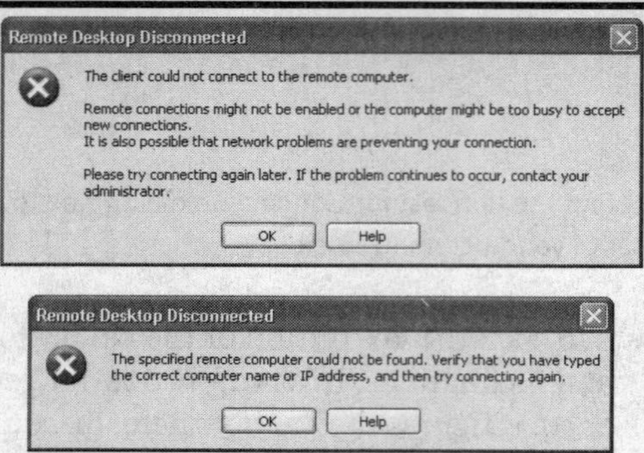

FIGURE 15.41: If Windows is unable to connect, you'll see a Remote Desktop Disconnected dialog box.

The first example of the Remote Desktop Disconnected dialog box tells you that the client couldn't connect to the remote computer and suggests that you try again later. The second example tells you that the remote computer couldn't be found and suggests checking that the computer name or IP address are correct. This should indeed be your first move—but if that doesn't work, that's about all you can do. If the remote computer has been shut down (or has crashed); or if its network or Internet connection has gone south; or if someone has reconfigured the computer not to accept Remote Desktop Connection connections or has revoked your permission to connect—if any of these has happened, you're straight out of luck, and no amount of retyping the computer name or IP address will make an iota of difference.

Working via Remote Desktop Connection

Once you've reached the remote Desktop, you can work more or less as if you were sitting at the computer. The few differences worth mentioning are discussed briefly in this section.

Using Cut, Copy, and Paste between the Local and Remote Computers

You can use Cut, Copy, and Paste commands to transfer information between the local computer and the remote computer. For example, you could copy some text from a program on the local computer and paste it into a program on the remote computer.

Copying from Remote Drives to Local Drives

You can copy from remote drives to local drives by working in Explorer. The drives on your local computer appear in Explorer windows on the remote computer marked as *Driveletter on COMPUTERNAME*. The drives on the remote computer appear as regular drives. You can copy and move files from one drive to another as you would with local drives.

Printing to a Local Printer

You can print to a local printer from the remote Desktop by selecting the local printer in the Print dialog box just as you would any other printer.

Printer settings are communicated to the remote Desktop when you access it. If you add a local printer during the remote session, the remote Desktop won't be able to see it. To make the printer show up on the remote Desktop, log off the remote session and log back on.

Returning to Your Local Desktop

If you chose to display the connection bar, it hovers briefly at the top of the screen, then slides upward to vanish like a docked toolbar with its Auto-Hide property enabled. To pin the connection bar in position, click the pin icon at its left end. (To unpin it, click the pin icon again.) To display the connection bar when it has hidden itself, move the mouse pointer to the top edge of the screen, just as you would do to display a docked toolbar hidden there.

The connection bar provides a Minimize button, a Restore/Maximize button, and a Close button. Use the Minimize button and the Restore button to reduce the remote Desktop from full screen to an icon or a partial screen so that you can access your local Desktop. Maximize the remote Desktop window to return to full-screen mode when you want to work with it again. Use the Close button as discussed in the next section to disconnect your remote session.

Disconnecting the Remote Session

You can disconnect the remote session in either of the two following ways:

- On the remote Desktop, choose Start ➢ Disconnect. Windows displays the Disconnect Windows dialog box (shown in Figure 15.42). Click the Disconnect button.

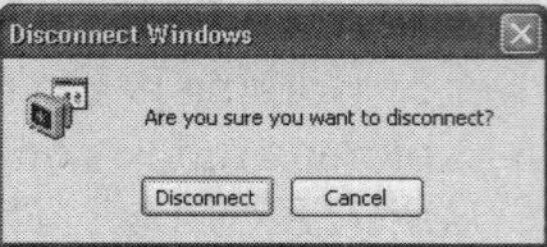

FIGURE 15.42: You can disconnect the remote session by issuing a Start ➢ Disconnect command and clicking the Disconnect button in the Disconnect Windows dialog box.

- Click the Close button on the connection bar (if the remote Desktop is displayed full screen) or on the Remote Desktop window (if the remote Desktop is not displayed full screen). Windows displays the Disconnect Windows Session dialog box (shown in Figure 15.44). Click the OK button.

Windows disconnects the remote session but leaves the programs running for the time being. You can then log on again and pick up where you left off.

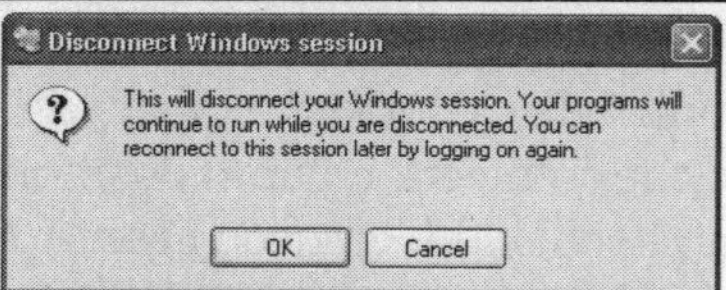

FIGURE 15.43: The Disconnect Windows Session dialog box appears when you click the Close button on the connection bar. Click the OK button to end your remote session while leaving the programs running.

Logging Off the Remote Session

To log off and end your user session, click the Start button on the remote Desktop and choose Log Off from the Start menu. Windows displays the Log Off Windows dialog box (shown in Figure 15.44). Click the Log Off button.

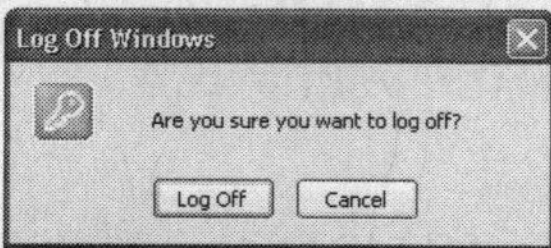

FIGURE 15.44: To log off from the remote computer, choose Start ➢ Log Off and click the Log Off button in the Log Off Windows dialog box.

When someone else bumps you off the remote Desktop (by logging on locally or remotely), Windows displays the Remote Desktop Disconnected dialog box shown in Figure 15.45, telling you that the remote session "was ended by means of an administration tool."

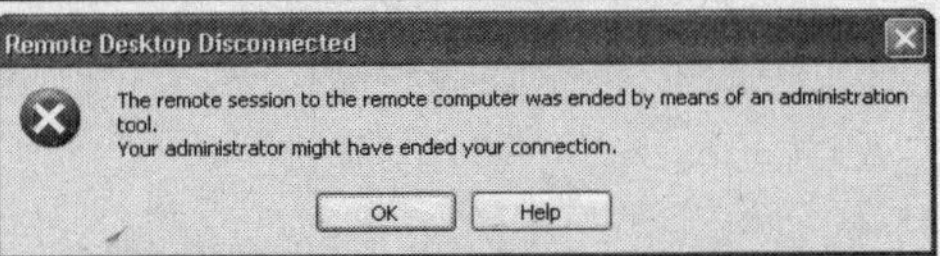

FIGURE 15.45: This Remote Desktop Disconnected dialog box appears when you log off and when someone logs you off the remote computer.

If the network connection between the home computer and the remote computer is broken, the home computer displays a Remote Desktop Disconnected dialog box such as that shown in Figure 15.46.

FIGURE 15.46: This Remote Desktop Disconnected dialog box indicates that the network connection between the home computer and the remote computer was broken.

WHAT'S NEXT?

The next chapter looks at yet another communications program that's included with Windows XP Professional, Fax Services.

Chapter 16

Using Fax Services

Windows XP Professional provides strong fax features—not as strong as those you might need for a corporate network, but strong enough for most home or home-office networks.

Sending Faxes in Windows

Despite the best efforts of Internet fax services that aim to take the telephone and the paper out of faxing, regular, station-to-station, paper faxing remains an essential part of daily office life, especially in home offices that need to share paper-based documents with their clients. But you can save time and effort (not to mention paper) by sending and receiving faxes directly from your computer—and you can keep incoming faxes away from inquisitive eyes around your house or office. If you don't have a fax machine, you shouldn't even need to buy one.

Revised and adapted from *Mastering Windows XP Home Edition* by Guy Hart-Davis

ISBN 0-7821-2980-3 1024 pages $39.99

Sending faxes in Windows isn't difficult, though Windows' faxing components are annoyingly piecemeal instead of being integrated into a single, slick interface. These are the Windows faxing components and what they do:

- Fax Services is the umbrella term for Windows' faxing components. The next four items are essentially manifestations of different aspects of Fax Services, which itself lurks mostly unseen in the background.
- The Fax Configuration Wizard is a user-friendly utility for configuring faxes. As long as you want to use the same settings for all your faxes, the Fax Configuration Wizard is pretty much a one-stop configuration solution.
- The Send Fax Wizard walks you through the steps of sending a fax. The most convenient way to invoke the Send Fax Wizard is by issuing a Print command for the document you want to fax.
- Fax Console is a program for manipulating the faxes you send and receive. It has an Inbox and an Outbox, an Incoming folder, and a Sent Items folder. It also offers features for configuring how Fax Services handles incoming and outgoing faxes.
- Fax Cover Page Editor is a program for creating custom cover pages for your faxes. It's not exciting (but then, neither are most cover pages), but it's effective.

To get faxing in Windows, you'll probably want to take these steps in approximately this order:

1. Install Fax Services by running the Windows Component Wizard. (For reasons best known to Microsoft, Fax Services isn't included in default installations.)
2. Configure Fax Services.
3. Send a few faxes, and use Fax Console to see what happened to them.
4. Receive a fax or two.

Let's take it from the top.

Installing Fax Services

To install Fax Services, make sure you've got your Windows CD (or that you know where your installation source files are). Then follow these steps:

1. Choose Start ➢ Control Panel. Windows displays Control Panel.
2. Click the Add or Remove Programs link. Windows displays the Add or Remove Programs window.
3. Click the Add/Remove Windows Components button. Windows displays the Windows Components Wizard dialog box (shown in Figure 16.1).

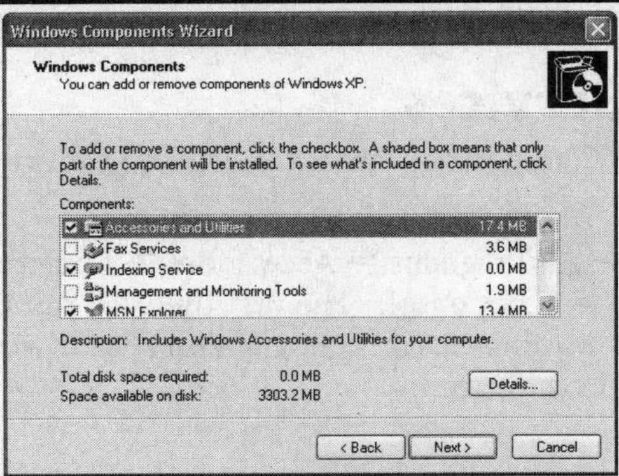

FIGURE 16.1: In order to send faxes, use the Windows Components Wizard to install Fax Services.

4. Select the Fax Services check box. If other check boxes are already selected, leave them be unless you want to uninstall the component in question. (An already selected check box indicates that the component is already installed, not that you're about to install it.)
5. Click the Next button. You'll see the Windows Components Wizard: Configuring Components page as Windows configures things.

6. If Windows displays the Insert Disk dialog box demanding your Windows CD, insert it. Alternatively, identify the hard disk or network location in which Windows can find the Windows installation files. (If the CD is already in the drive, or if the installation source files are still where they used to be, Windows finds them automatically and doesn't prompt you.)
7. When the Wizard finishes, click the Finish button. The Wizard closes itself, returning you to the Add or Remove Programs window.
8. Click the Close button. Windows closes the Add or Remove Programs window.

That's the first step: You've got Fax Services installed. Now you need to configure it.

Configuring Fax Services

Windows provides a Fax Configuration Wizard to help you configure Fax Services. Take the following steps:

1. Choose Start ➢ All Programs ➢ Accessories ➢ Communications ➢ Fax ➢ Fax Console. The first time you run Fax Console, Windows runs the Fax Configuration Wizard, which displays its Welcome screen.

NOTE

If your computer doesn't currently have a fax/modem installed, Windows prompts you to install one. If you click the Yes button, it starts the Add New Hardware Wizard, which displays its Install New Modem page. Install the modem as described in Chapter 33.

2. Click the Next button. The Wizard displays the Sender Information page (shown in Figure 16.2).

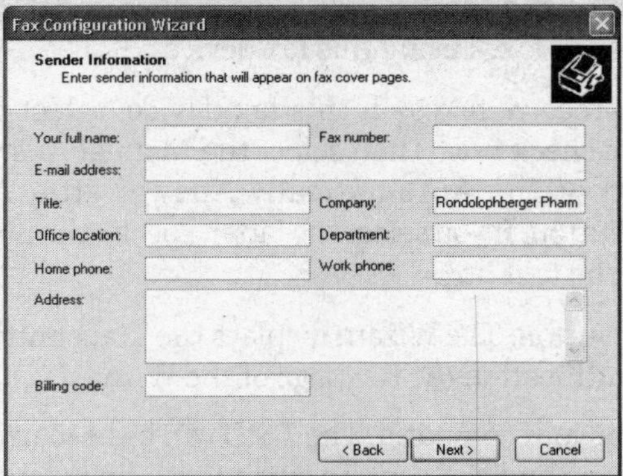

FIGURE 16.2: The Fax Configuration Wizard walks you through configuring Fax Services and entering user information.

3. Enter your fax information: name, fax number, e-mail address, phone numbers, and so on.
4. Click the Next button. The Wizard displays the Select Device for Sending or Receiving Faxes page of the Wizard (shown in Figure 16.3).

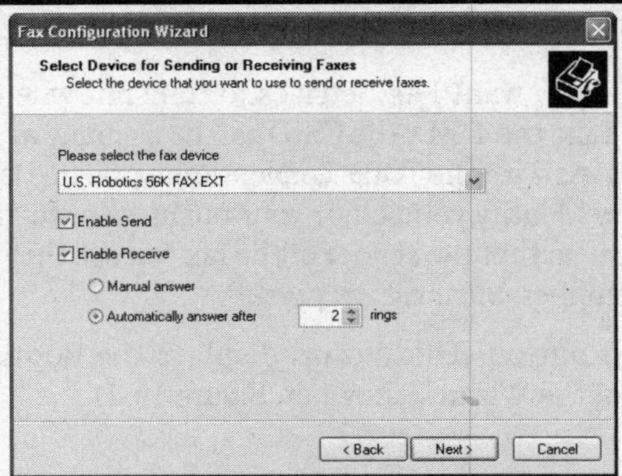

FIGURE 16.3: On the Select Device for Sending or Receiving Faxes page, tell Fax Services which device to use for sending faxes.

5. In the Please Select the Fax Device drop-down list, choose the fax device (for example, a modem) to use for sending faxes.

6. Leave the Enable Send check box selected (as it is by default) if you want to send faxes using this fax device.

7. If you want to receive faxes on this fax device, select the Enable Receive check box. Then select the Manual Answer option button or the Automatically Answer after *NN* Rings option button. If you select the latter, specify the number of rings in the text box.

8. Click the Next button. The Wizard displays the Transmitting Subscriber Identification (TSID) page of the Wizard.

9. Enter a TSID for your computer. The TSID can be as many as 20 characters long and can contain any information you can fit into them. Conventional practice is to use the TSID to identify yourself or your business or to give your incoming fax phone number.

10. Click the Next button. The Wizard displays the Called Subscriber Identification (CSID) page of the Wizard.

NOTE

If you didn't select the Enable Receive check box, you get to skip this step and the next step.

11. Enter the CSID you want Fax Services to transmit when it answers a fax. Like the TSID, the CSID can be as many as 20 characters long. As with the TSID, conventional practice is to use the CSID to identify yourself or your business or to give your fax number so that the sender of the fax can see they've got the right number, business, or person.

12. Click the Next button. The Wizard displays the Routing Options page of the Wizard (shown in Figure 16.4).

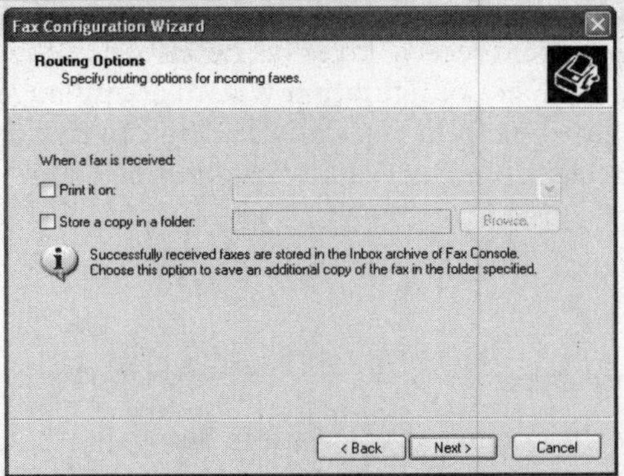

FIGURE 16.4: On the Routing Options page, specify whether Fax Services should print the fax or save it to a folder.

13. By default, Fax Services stores incoming faxes in Fax Console's Inbox. Specify if you want Fax Services to print the fax or save it to another folder as well as the Inbox:

    - To print the fax, select the Print It On check box and select a printer in the drop-down list. (Remember that automatically printing every fax you receive on a shared printer removes the privacy advantages of receiving a fax via computer.) If you don't have a printer set up for this computer, the Print It On check box isn't available.

    - To save the fax to a folder, select the Store a Copy in a Folder check box and use the Browse button and the resulting Browse for Folder dialog box to identify the folder.

14. Click the Next button. The Wizard displays the Completing the Fax Configuration Wizard page, which contains a summary of the options you chose. Check the configuration summary. To change anything, use the Back button to navigate to the appropriate page of the Wizard. When all looks to be right, click the Finish button. The Wizard closes itself, applies the settings you chose, and opens Fax Console.

Once you've used the Fax Configuration Wizard to configure faxing, you should be all set to send and receive faxes (as described in the next sections). You can rerun the Fax Configuration Wizard at any stage by choosing Tools ➢ Configure Fax from Fax Console. You can also change the fax settings more directly from Fax Console as described later in this chapter.

Sending a Fax

To send a fax, follow these steps:

1. Create or open the document you want to fax.
2. Issue a Print command as usual. (For example, press Ctrl+P.)
3. In the Print dialog box, select the Fax item for the fax you want to use.
4. If necessary, choose preferences for the fax. Click the Properties button. Windows displays the Fax Preference tab of the Fax Preferences dialog box. In this dialog box, you can specify a different page size or orientation, but more often you'll want to change the setting in the Image Quality drop-down list. The standard setting is Normal (200×200 dpi). To send documents faster but with a more grainy effect, choose Draft (200×100 dpi).
5. Click the OK button in the Print dialog box. Windows starts the Send Fax Wizard, which displays the Welcome to the Send Fax Wizard page.
6. Click the Next button. The Wizard displays the Recipient Information page of the Send Fax Wizard (shown in Figure 16.5).

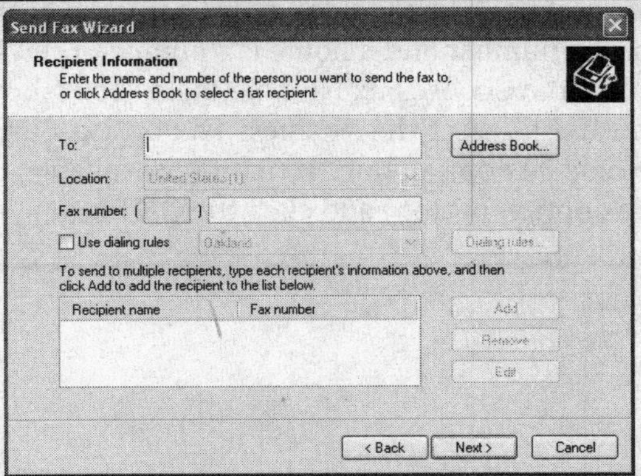

FIGURE 16.5: Specify the recipient or recipients of the fax on the Recipient Information page of the Send Fax Wizard.

7. Enter the name of the recipient (or recipients) in the To text box.

   - If the recipient doesn't have an entry in Address Book and you don't want to add them, enter their name or company in the To text box, and enter the fax number in the Fax Number text box. By default, Fax Services dials the number as you entered it. If you want to use dialing rules (having Windows add any country, region, area, or long-distance codes the number needs based on your location), select the Use Dialing Rules check box and use the Location drop-down list to specify your location.
   - To select a recipient from Address Book, click the Address Book button. In the Address Book dialog box, select the recipient from the appropriate contacts list. Click the To button to add the recipient to the Message Recipients list box. Click the OK button.
   - If the recipient's Address Book entry contains no fax number, the Wizard discards the recipient and displays a Send Fax Wizard message box telling you it has done so. If this happens, open Address Book and add the missing fax number, then select the recipient again from the Send Fax Wizard.

- If the recipient's Address Book entry contains both a business fax number and a home fax number, the Wizard displays the Choose Fax Number dialog box (shown in Figure 16.6). Select the Business Fax option button or the Home Fax option button (or, if it's available, the Other Fax option button) and click the OK button.

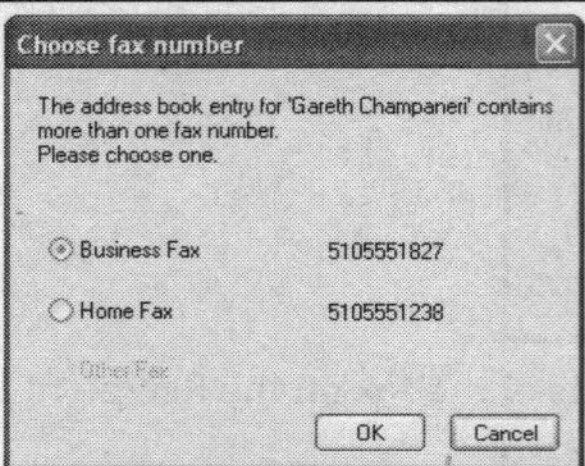

FIGURE 16.6: If the recipient has both business and home fax numbers, the Wizard displays the Choose Fax Number dialog box so that you can select the appropriate number.

- To change the fax number for a recipient you've entered by using Address Book, select the recipient in the list box and click the Edit button. The Wizard displays the Check Fax Number dialog box (shown in Figure 16.7), in which you can change the information as necessary.

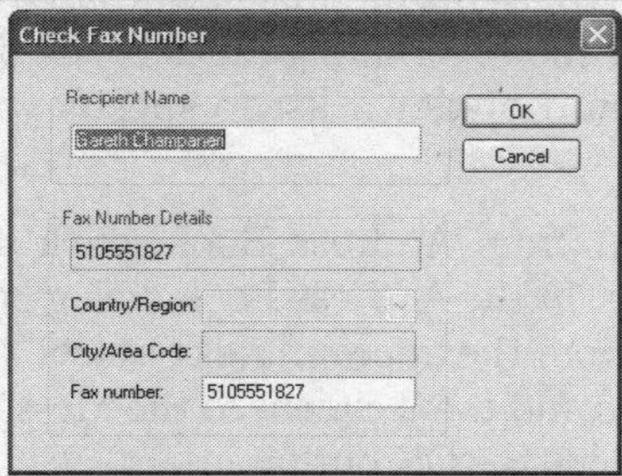

FIGURE 16.7: Use the Check Fax Number dialog box to change a fax number you've entered from Address Book.

8. When you've finished adding recipients, click the Next button. The Wizard displays the Preparing the Cover Page page (shown in Figure 16.8).

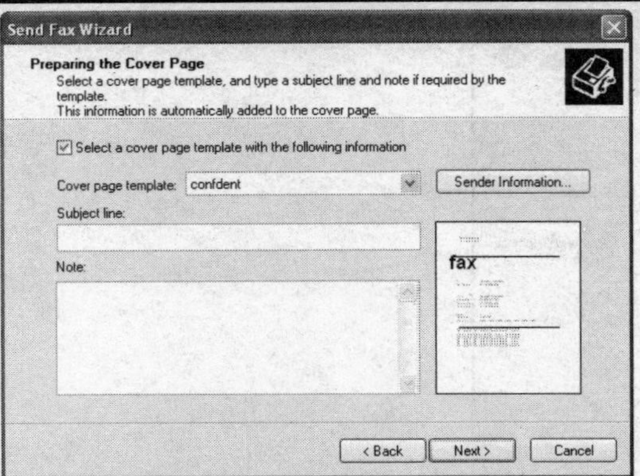

FIGURE 16.8: Use the options on the Preparing the Cover Page page of the Wizard to specify the type of cover page to include (if any).

9. To include a cover page, select the Select a Cover Page Template with the Following Information check box. (If you don't want to include a cover page, leave this check box cleared.) Then specify the information to use:

   - The first time you send a fax from this installation of Fax Services for this user identity, it's a good idea to check the sender information that Fax Services is planning to supply to the recipient. Click the Sender Information button. The Wizard displays the Sender Information dialog box (shown in Figure 16.9). Check that the information is appropriate. Modify it if necessary. To enter a temporary change for this fax but not store the change for future use, select the Use the Information for This Transmission Only check box.

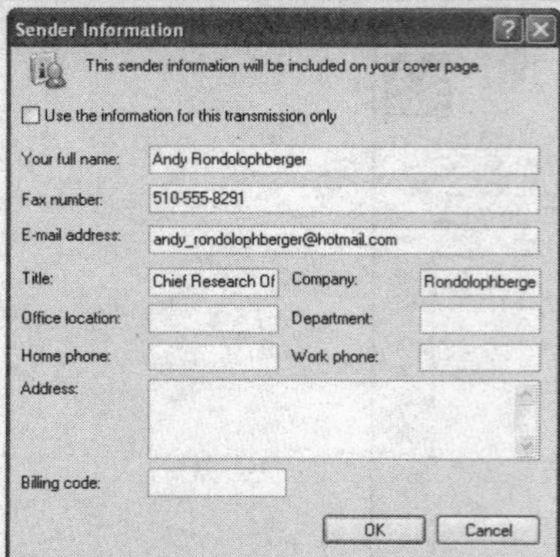

FIGURE 16.9: Check your sender information in the Sender Information dialog box before sending a fax.

- In the Cover Page Template drop-down list, choose the template to use. The preview box on the right side of the Wizard shows an approximation of how the template looks.
- Enter the subject for the fax in the Subject Line text box and any note in the Note text box.

10. Click the Next button. The Wizard displays its Schedule page (shown in Figure 16.10).

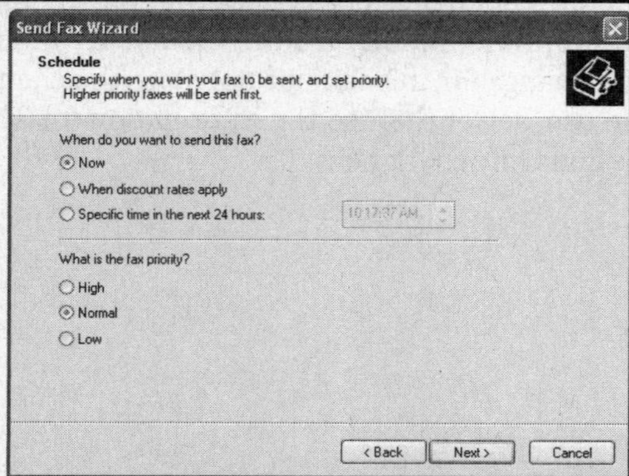

FIGURE 16.10: On the Schedule page of the Send Fax Wizard, specify the fax priority and when you want to send the fax.

11. In the When Do You Want to Send This Fax? list, select the appropriate option button. The default setting is the Now option button. Select the When Discount Rates Apply option button if you want Windows to wait until it thinks telephone rates will be discounted (for example, in the evening). Select the Specific Time in the Next 24 Hours option button and enter a time in the text box if you want the fax to be sent at a particular time. (For example, you might choose to send a fax so that it arrived early in the morning but outside the recipient's sleeping hours.)

NOTE

Looking at the Schedule page of the Send Fax Wizard, you may find yourself wondering where the Wizard gets its knowledge of when discount rates apply. Does it (for example) have a hotline to the decision-makers at your local telco? Or does it apply some standardized information that might be wholly wrong for your location? In fact, it does neither. You specify the discount times in Fax Console, as discussed a little later in the chapter.

12. In the What Is the Fax Priority? list, select the High option button, the Normal option button, or the Low option button as appropriate. High-priority faxes get sent before low-priority ones if they're due to be sent at the same time. Usually priorities become important only when you stack up faxes for later transmission.

13. Click the Next button. The Send Fax Wizard displays the Completing the Send Fax Wizard page (shown in Figure 16.11), which lists the choices you've made.

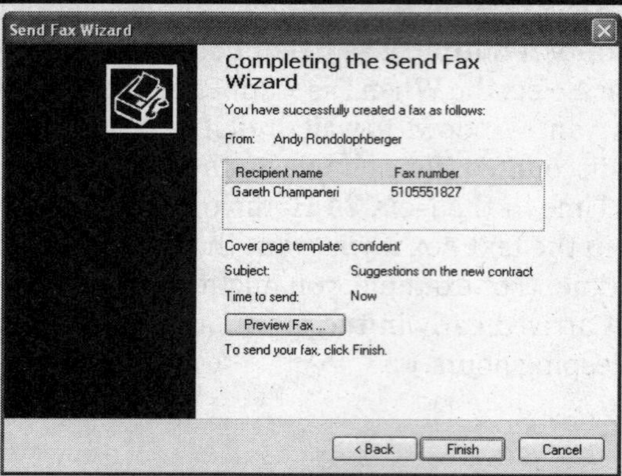

FIGURE 16.11: Review your choices on the Completing the Send Fax Wizard page.

14. Review the details of the fax. To look at how the fax will appear, click the Preview Fax button. Use the Back button to adjust any details. When you're ready, click the Finish button. The Send Fax Wizard closes and either starts sending the fax or queues it for transmission, depending on the options you chose.

If you chose to send the fax immediately, Fax Services displays the Fax Monitor dialog box (shown in Figure 16.12 at its expanded size) so that you can see what's happening. Click the More button and the Less button (which replace each other as appropriate) to toggle between the small and expanded sizes of this dialog box. Click the Disconnect button to disconnect the current connection, the Answer Now button (not shown in the figure) to answer an incoming fax call manually, the Clear List button to clear the list of fax events, or the Hide button to hide the Fax Monitor dialog box.

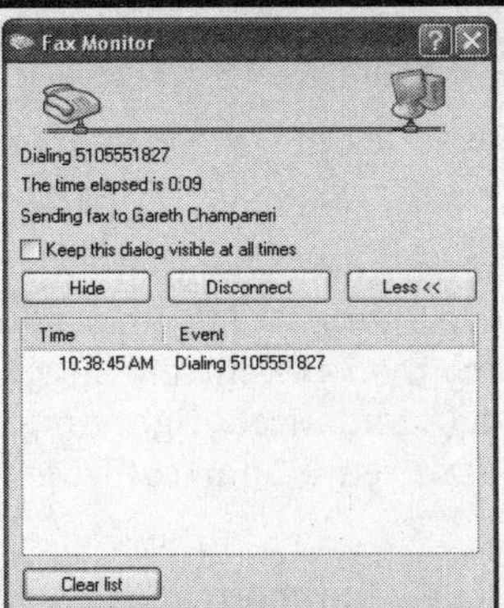

FIGURE 16.12: The Fax Monitor dialog box lets you see what's happening on your fax modem.

If you're sending a lot of faxes, you may want to select the Keep This Dialog Visible at All Times check box to make Fax Services display the Fax Monitor dialog box all the time, whether it's sending faxes or not. You can also display the Fax Monitor dialog box at any time by choosing Tools ➢ Fax Monitor from Fax Console.

EXPERT KNOWLEDGE: FAXING AN EXISTING DOCUMENT FROM THE SEND TO MENU

When you're faxing a document you've just created, or that you've opened to review or edit before faxing it, starting the Send Fax Wizard from the Print dialog box is convenient. But if you want to fax an existing document, you can save time by faxing it from the Send To menu.

To create an entry for Fax Services on the Send To menu, follow these steps:

1. Open an Explorer window to the SendTo folder. You'll find it under `\Documents and Settings\`*`Username`*`\`. If you haven't already turned on the display of hidden files in Explorer, you'll need to do so (choose Tools ➢ Folder Options, click the View tab, select the Show Hidden Files and Folders option button, and click the OK button).

CONTINUED ➞

2. Choose Start ➢ Printers and Faxes to open the Printers and Faxes folder.
3. Drag the Fax icon from the Printers and Faxes folder to the SendTo folder. Windows displays a Shortcut dialog box telling you that you cannot move or copy the Fax item and suggesting you create a shortcut instead. (Alternatively, right-drag the Fax icon to the folder and choose Create Shortcut from the context menu.)
4. Click the Yes button. Windows creates the shortcut and names it `Shortcut to Fax` (or whatever your fax was named).
5. Rename the shortcut if you want. (For example, you might want to rename it **Fax**.)

Once you've done this, you'll be able to right-click a document and choose Send To ➢ Fax from the shortcut menu to start the Send Fax Wizard.

Managing Faxes from Fax Console

If you've been following along through the chapter, you probably have Fax Console open by now. If not, choose Start ➢ All Programs ➢ Accessories ➢ Communications ➢ Fax ➢ Fax Console. Windows opens Fax Console (shown in Figure 16.13).

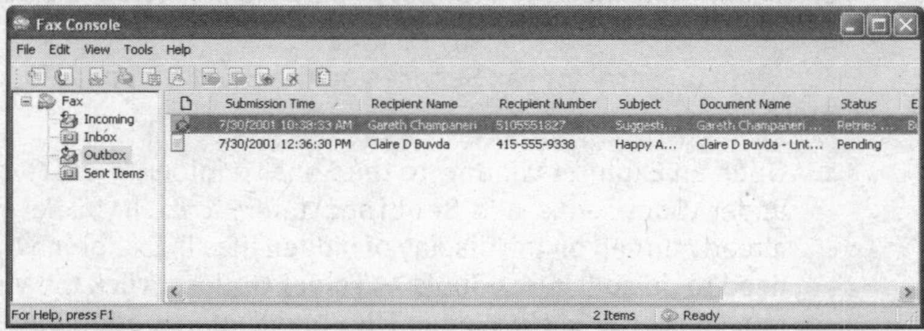

FIGURE 16.13: Use Fax Console to monitor the state of your faxes and to pause or delete outgoing faxes.

As you can see in the figure, Fax Console is a regular Microsoft Management Console snap-in. The left list box shows the fax printer (which may represent one fax device, two, or more), and under it four folders: an Incoming folder, an Inbox folder, an Outbox folder, and a Sent Items folder.

Fax Console supports a variety of actions, most of which you can take either from the shortcut menu for a fax or from the toolbar. Figure 16.14 shows the toolbar with labels.

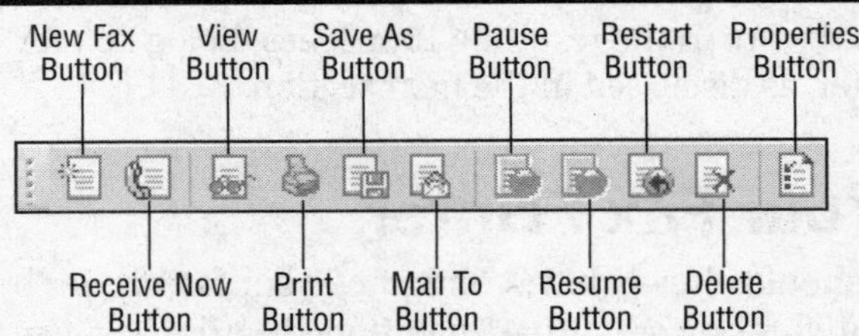

FIGURE 16.14: The Fax Console toolbar

These are the key actions that you may want to take from Fax Console:

View a fax you've received Display the Inbox and double-click the fax, select the fax and click the View button, or right-click the fax and choose View from the shortcut menu. Fax Console opens the fax in Windows Picture and Fax Viewer.

Print a fax you've received Display the Inbox, select the fax, and click the Print button, or right-click the fax and choose Print from the shortcut menu.

Pause an outgoing fax Display the Outbox, select the fax, and click the Pause button, or right-click the fax and choose Pause from the shortcut menu.

Resume an outgoing fax Display the Outbox, select the fax, and click the Resume button, or right-click the fax and choose Resume from the shortcut menu.

Delete an outgoing fax Display the Outbox, select the fax, and click the Delete button. Alternatively, select the fax and press the Delete key, or right-click the fax and choose Delete from the shortcut menu.

Update your sender information Choose Tools ➢ Sender Information and work in the Sender Information dialog box.

Add a personal cover page to a fax Choose Tools ➢ Personal Cover Pages. Fax Console displays the Personal Cover Pages dialog box.

Display the Fax Monitor dialog box Choose Tools ➢ Fax Monitor.

Configure your fax printer Choose Tools ➢ Fax Printer Configuration and work in the resulting Properties dialog box for the fax printer, as discussed in the next section.

Configuring Your Fax Printer

By this time, you should already have configured your fax printer by using the Fax Configuration Wizard. As mentioned earlier, you can rerun the Fax Configuration Wizard at any time from Fax Console by choosing Tools ➢ Configure Fax. But you can also set the same properties, and others, by working directly in the Properties dialog box for the fax printer. To do so, choose Tools ➢ Fax Printer Configuration from Fax Console.

The following sections discuss the options in the Properties dialog box for a fax printer.

General Tab Options

The General tab of the Properties dialog box for a fax printer (shown in Figure 16.15) contains the following options:

Name text box (Actually, *unnamed* text box would be more appropriate.) In this text box, enter the name by which you want to refer to the fax. The default name is *Fax*, which is succinct but uninformative.

Location text box If you feel the need, enter details of the location of the fax in this text box. Making this notation is especially important if you share the fax.)

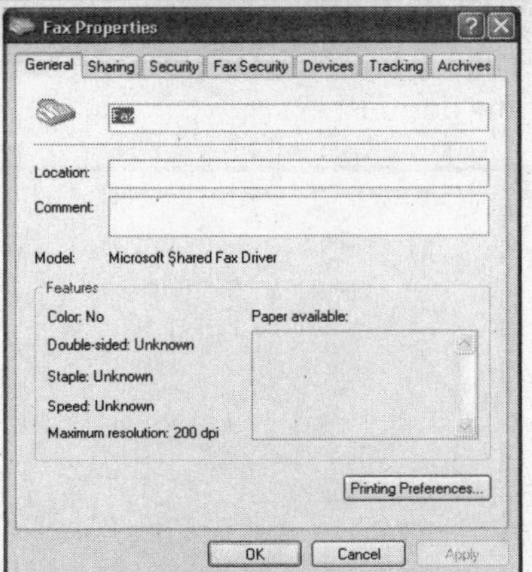

FIGURE 16.15: The General tab of the Properties dialog box for a fax printer

Comment text box Enter any comment about the fax printer in this text box. For example, you might note which phone line it uses.

Features group box This group box summarizes known information about the fax. This group box is mostly designed for printers, and for many fax modems the only relevant information is Maximum Resolution.

Sharing Tab Options

If you want to share your fax with other users on your network, set that option on the Sharing tab.

Security Tab Options

You use this tab to set general printer permissions. Click the Fax Security tab to set specific fax printer options, and then on the Fax Security tab, click the Advanced button to set permissions for a shared fax.

NOTE

For information about sharing and security, see Chapters 24 and 25.

Devices Tab Options

The Devices tab of the Properties dialog box for a fax printer (shown in Figure 16.16) contains the following options:

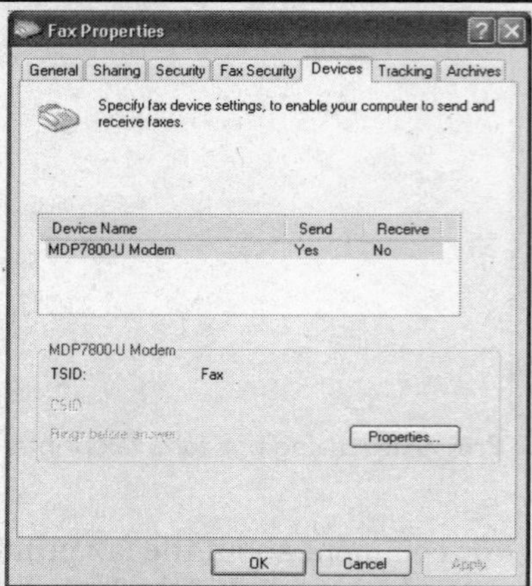

FIGURE 16.16: The Devices page of the Properties dialog box for a fax printer

Device Name list box This list box lists the fax devices installed on your computer and their current Send and Receive settings. To toggle the Send setting or the Receive setting, right-click the fax device and choose Send ➢ Enable, Send ➢ Disable, Receive ➢ Enable, or Receive ➢ Disable from the shortcut menu.

Device section This section lists the TSID, CSID, and Rings before Answer setting for the fax device selected in the Device Name list box.

To change the properties for a device, right-click it in the Device Name list box and choose Properties from the shortcut menu to open the Properties dialog box for the device. Then choose settings as discussed in the following sections.

Send Tab Options The Send tab of the Properties dialog box for a fax device (shown in Figure 16.17) contains the following options:

Enable Device to Send check box Select this check box to enable sending on the fax device. Clear this check box to disable sending. (For example, you might choose to use one fax device for outgoing faxes only and another for receiving faxes.)

TSID text box You can change your TSID in this text box.

Include Banner check box Leave this check box selected (as it is by default) to have Fax Services include a banner of information along the top edge of the faxes you send.

Number of Retries text box Specify the number of retries in this text box. You can set any value from 0 to 99.

Retry After text box Specify the retry interval (in minutes) in this text box.

Discount Rate Start text box and Discount Rate Stop text box Use these text boxes to specify the times that Fax Services should treat as discount rates. (As mentioned earlier in the chapter, you can schedule faxes for transmission at discount-rate times.)

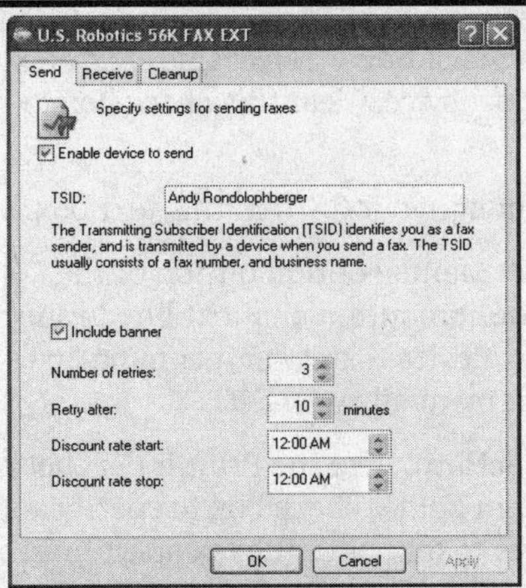

FIGURE 16.17: The Send page of the Properties dialog box for a fax device

Receive Tab Options The Receive tab of the Properties dialog box for a fax device (shown in Figure 16.18) contains the following options:

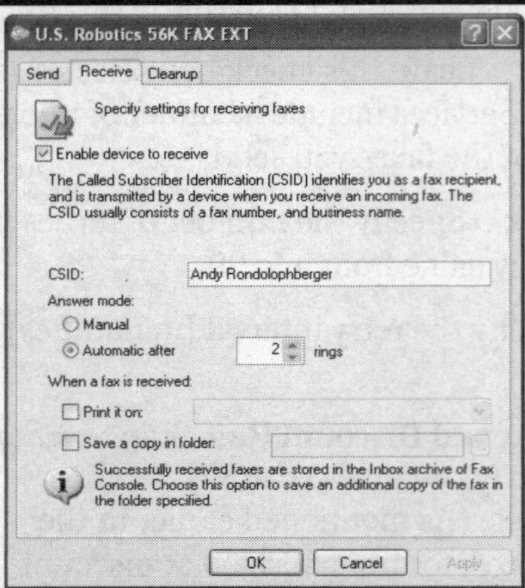

FIGURE 16.18: The Receive tab of the Properties dialog box for a fax device

Enable Device to Receive check box Select this check box to enable receiving on the fax device. Clear this check box to disable receiving.

CSID text box You can change your CSID in this text box.

Answer Mode list Use the Manual option button or the Automatic after *NN* Rings option button and text box to specify whether you want the fax device to answer incoming faxes automatically or to engage it manually yourself.

When a Fax Is Received section Use the Print It On check box and/or the Save a Copy in Folder check box to specify any action you want Fax Services to take with the fax apart from placing it in the Inbox. (See step 13 in "Configuring Fax Services" earlier in this chapter for more information.)

Cleanup Tab Options The Cleanup tab of the Properties dialog box for a fax device (shown in Figure 16.19) contains the Automatically Delete Failed Faxes after *NN* Days check box and text box. If you want Fax Services to dispose of failed faxes, select this check box (which is cleared by default) and specify their stay of execution.

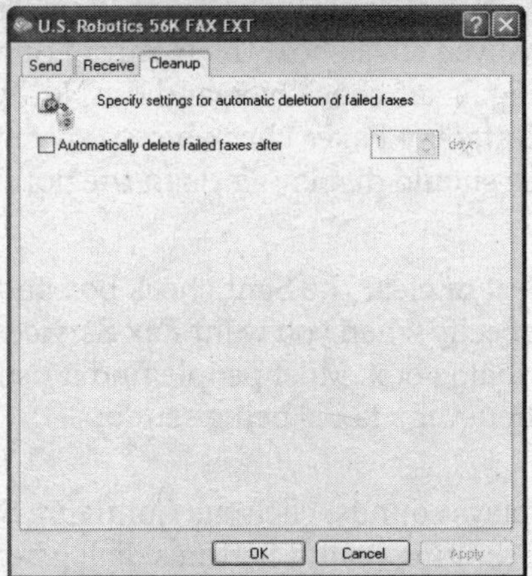

FIGURE 16.19: The Cleanup tab of the Properties dialog box for a fax device

Tracking Page Options

The Tracking tab of the Properties dialog box for a fax printer (shown in Figure 16.20) contains the following options:

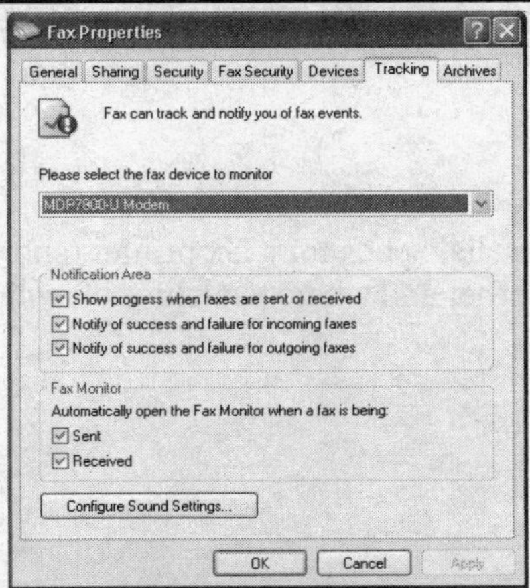

FIGURE 16.20: The Tracking tab of the Properties dialog box for a fax printer

Please Select the Fax Device to Monitor drop-down list
Select the fax device for which you want to set tracking options.

Notification Area section Select or clear the Show Progress when Faxes Are Sent or Received check box, the Notify of Success and Failure for Incoming Faxes check box, and the Notify of Success and Failure for Outgoing Faxes check box to specify for which items Fax Services should display alerts in the notification area.

Fax Monitor section Select or clear the Sent check box and the Received check box to specify when you want Fax Services to display the Fax Monitor dialog box. Most people find it useful to see this dialog box whenever a fax is being sent or received.

To specify when Fax Services plays sounds, click the Configure Sound Settings button and work in the resulting Sound Settings dialog box (shown in Figure 16.21).

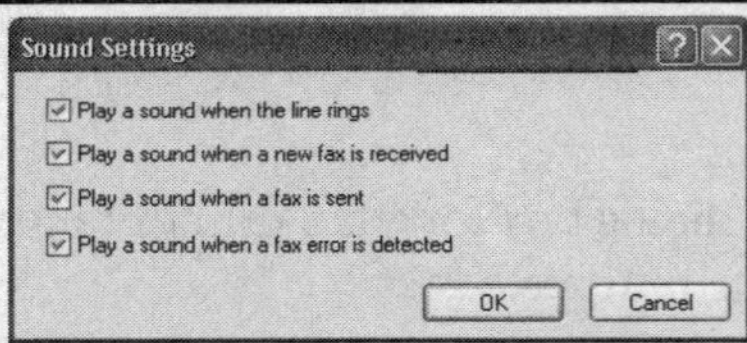

FIGURE 16.21: Use the Sound Settings dialog box to specify when Fax Services should play sounds.

Archives Tab Options

The Archives tab of the Properties dialog box for a fax printer (shown in Figure 16.22) lets you specify whether and where to archive incoming faxes and successfully sent faxes.

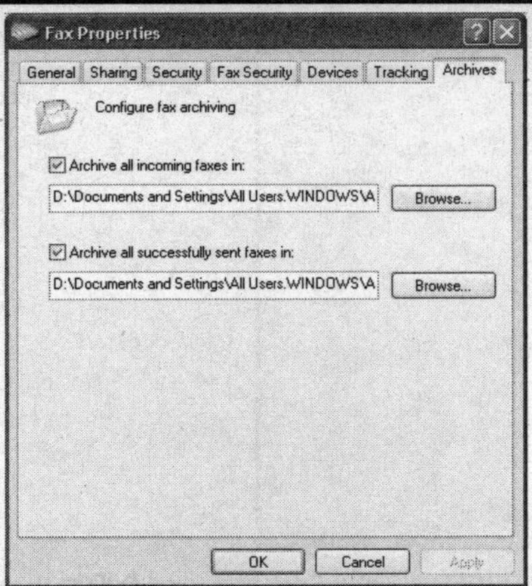

FIGURE 16.22: The Archives tab of the Properties dialog box for a fax printer

When you've finished choosing options, click the OK button. Fax Console closes the Properties dialog box and applies your choices.

Creating Custom Cover Pages with Fax Cover Page Editor

Instead of using Fax Services' canned cover pages, you can use custom cover pages that you create by using Fax Cover Page Editor. (You can also tweak the canned cover pages to suit your needs, or create new cover pages based on them.) Fax cover pages consist of text and graphics in your choice of layout (with some constraints) and use the COV extension.

Start Fax Cover Page Editor by choosing Start ➢ All Programs ➢ Accessories ➢ Communications ➢ Fax ➢ Fax Cover Page Editor. Alternatively, if you have Fax Console open, you can start Fax Cover Page Editor by choosing Tools ➢ Personal Cover Pages, then clicking the New button in the Personal Cover Pages dialog box that Fax Console displays. In either case, you'll see the window shown in Figure 16.23.

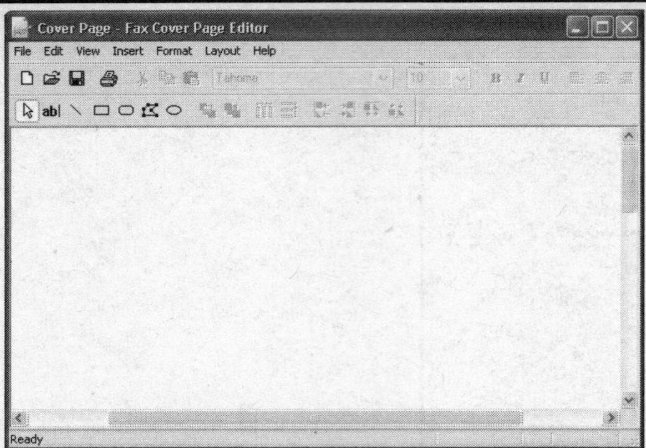

FIGURE 16.23: Use Fax Cover Page Editor to create custom cover pages for your faxes.

Fax Cover Page Editor offers a lot of features that we don't have the space to cover in depth here. But these are the basic steps to follow to put together a cover page:

1. To create a new page, press Ctrl+N or choose File ➢ New.
2. If necessary, adjust the paper size or orientation in the Page Setup dialog box (choose File ➢ Page Setup).
3. If you want to use the grid to help you position items more precisely and evenly, display it: Choose View ➢ Grid Lines.
4. Insert the fields for the text on the cover page by using the Insert menu. For example, choose Insert ➢ Recipient ➢ Name to insert the field for the recipient's name and Insert ➢ Sender ➢ Fax Number to insert the field for the sender's fax number.
5. Arrange the fields by using the commands on the Layout menu:
   - To select one of the items on a cover page, click it. Alternatively, press the Tab key to move from the selected item to the next. Press Shift+Tab to select the previous item.
   - You can select multiple items in a couple of ways. Either select the first item, hold down the Ctrl key, and then

select the remaining items. Or click outside one corner of the group and drag the selection border until it extends around the items.

- To align selected objects, choose Layout ➢ Align Objects and choose Left, Right, Top, or Bottom from the submenu.
- To space selected objects evenly, choose Layout ➢ Space Evenly ➢ Across or Layout ➢ Space Evenly ➢ Down.
- To change the order in which items are stacked on top of each other, select an object and choose Layout ➢ Bring to Front or Layout ➢ Send to Back.

TIP

To copy an item (except the Note field), select it, hold down the Ctrl key and the Shift key, and drag it to where you want the copy to appear.

6. Change the font of a selected field by choosing Format ➢ Font and working in the Font dialog box. Alternatively, use the toolbar buttons.
7. Change the alignment of text in a selected field by choosing Format ➢ Align Text and selecting Left, Center, or Right from the submenu.
8. Change lines and shading by choosing Format ➢ Line, Fill and Color and working in the Line, Fill and Color dialog box. (Before you ask–your color choices are limited to black, white, and shades of gray.)
9. Add any decorative elements (such as shapes or lines) by using the buttons on the Drawing toolbar.
10. Use Print Preview (choose File ➢ Print Preview) to make sure your cover page looks the way you want it to.

11. Save the cover page by choosing File ➢ Save and specifying the name and location in the Save As dialog box.

    - If you want the cover page to be available to all users of this computer, save it in the `\Documents and Settings\All Users\Application Data\Microsoft\Windows NT\MSFax\Common CoverPages\` folder. (You'll need to have selected the Show Hidden Files and Folders option button on the View tab of the Folder Options dialog box from Explorer to get to this folder.)
    - If you want the Personal Cover Pages dialog box to list this cover page automatically, save it in the `\Fax\Personal Cover Pages\` folder under your `\My Documents\` folder.
    - Otherwise, save the cover page in any folder that suits you and add it to the Personal Cover Pages list as described in the next section.

Adding an Existing Cover Page to the Personal Cover Pages Dialog Box

For most purposes, it's easiest to keep your personal cover pages where Microsoft wants you to keep them—in the `\Fax\Personal Cover Pages\` folder under your `\My Documents\` folder. But you can also keep them in other folders if you prefer.

If you do, you can add cover pages to the list in the Personal Cover Pages dialog box as follows:

1. From Fax Console, choose Tools ➢ Personal Cover Pages. Windows displays the Personal Cover Pages dialog box (shown in Figure 16.24).

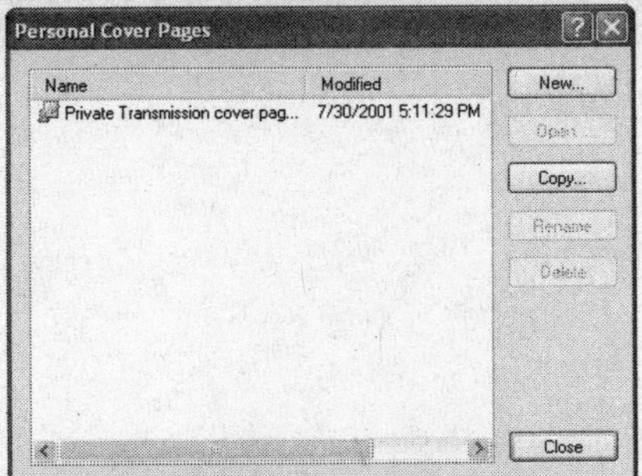

FIGURE 16.24: Use the Personal Cover Pages dialog box to manage your personal cover pages.

2. Click the Copy button. Windows displays the Copy Cover Page to List of Personal Cover Pages dialog box, which is a common Open dialog box by another name.
3. Navigate to and select the cover page file.
4. Click the Open button. Windows closes the dialog box and copies the cover page to the Personal Cover Pages dialog box.

What's Next?

This chapter concludes the part of this book that deals with communications and the Internet. We now turn to Part III, Multimedia in Windows XP, and begin by looking at how to work with photos and still images.

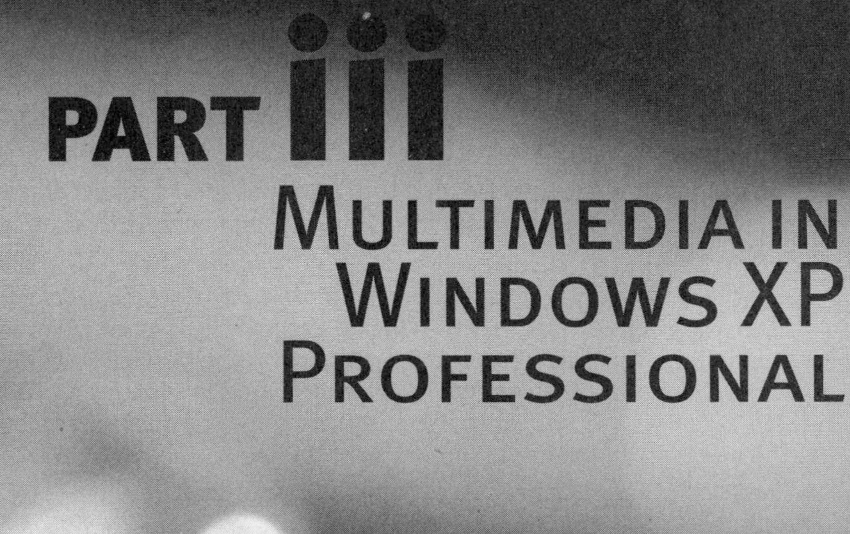

PART iii

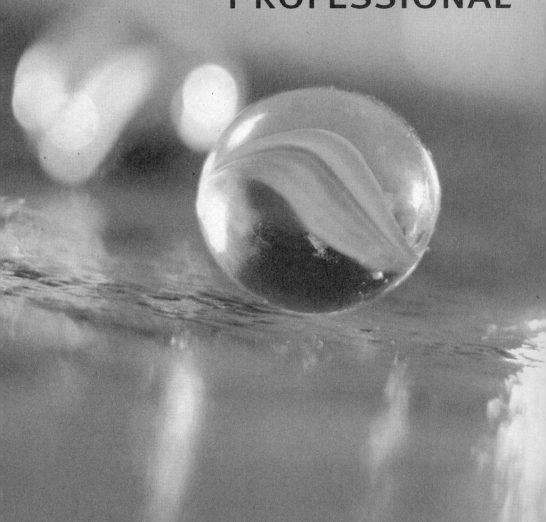

Multimedia in Windows XP Professional

Chapter 17

Working with Photographs and Still Images

Windows XP provides unprecedented support for digital images. From setting up your scanner or camera to producing high-quality prints, Windows guides you every step of the way with easy-to-follow wizards. In this chapter, you will find out how to set up scanners and cameras, how to use them to acquire digital images, and how to print those images yourself or use a professional printing service to do it.

Revised and adapted from *Windows XP Home Edition Simply Visual* by Faithe Wempen

ISBN 0-7821-2982-X 448 pages $24.99

Setting Up a New Scanner or Digital Camera

NOTE

When selecting a scanner or digital camera for use in Windows XP, you will have best results with a model that's on the hardware compatibility list (HCL) for Windows XP. Microsoft publishes this list online at `www.microsoft.com/hcl`. This is a list of devices that various versions of Windows support.

Setting up a scanner or *digital* camera in Windows XP is very easy. Simply connect your scanner or camera to your computer, as described in the instructions that come with it. Windows automatically detects the device, and a bubble appears over the notification area letting you know. Most scanners and digital cameras come with a Setup CD, but you probably won't need it.

Windows XP will work with almost any brand and model of scanner or camera, but Windows may not directly support it. What's the difference? With directly supported models, Windows uses its own drivers and its own interface, so no matter what brand and model you have, the procedures for using the device are the same. If a model is not supported, Windows can't operate it directly, so you must install the interface software that came with the device. This is not a big hardship; you will simply be using the device in the same way that people with earlier versions of Windows use it, rather than in the Windows XP way.

Does Windows Recognize Your Scanner or Camera?

To check to see whether the needed drivers for your scanner or camera are installed in Windows, do the following:

1. Choose Start ➢ Control Panel.

NOTE

If Control Panel doesn't have a Printers and Other Hardware option, the panel might be in classic view. You can either switch to category view by clicking Switch to Category View and then return to step 2, or simply double-click the Scanners and Cameras icon and skip to step 4.

2. In Control Panel, click Printers and Other Hardware.

3. Click Scanners and Cameras.

4. Look for your scanner or camera on the list that appears. If you see it, Windows sees it too.

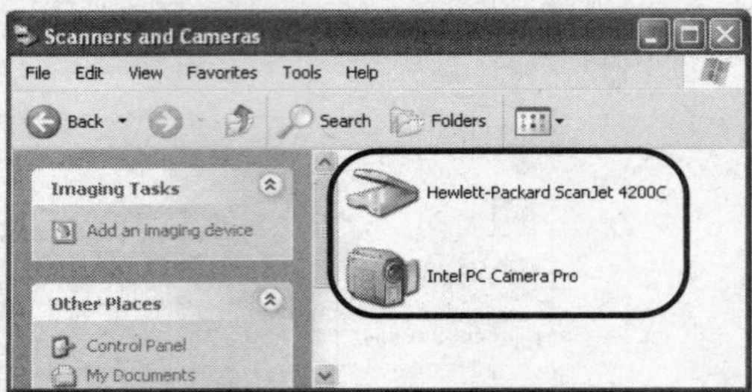

Running the Scanner and Camera Installation Wizard

NOTE

The Scanner and Camera Installation Wizard works well with models on the HCL, but might not work with unsupported models. If it fails to get your device up and running, try the Setup software that came with the device. You can also check the device manufacturer's Web site to see whether an updated driver or Setup program might be available for Windows XP.

If Windows doesn't see your scanner or camera immediately, you might try giving it a little shove in the right direction. Scanners and cameras with USB (Universal Serial Bus) interfaces are usually detected right away, but models that use other interfaces such as a parallel port might not be.

1. Start at the Scanners and Cameras window. To get there, perform steps 1 through 3 of the preceding procedure.
2. Click Add an Imaging Device in the Imaging Tasks pane.

3. The Scanner and Camera Installation Wizard opens. Click Next to continue.

4. Select the manufacturer and model from the list and then click Next, or, if you have a Setup disk that came with the device, insert it and click Have Disk.

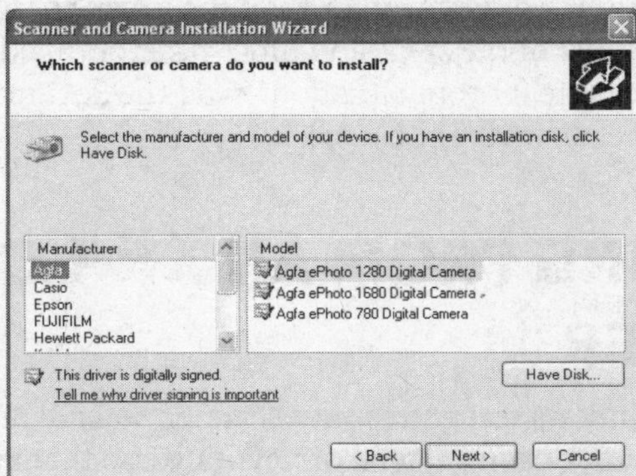

5. Select the port to which the device is connected, or leave Automatic Port Detection chosen if you don't know or if the port doesn't appear on the list. Then click Next.

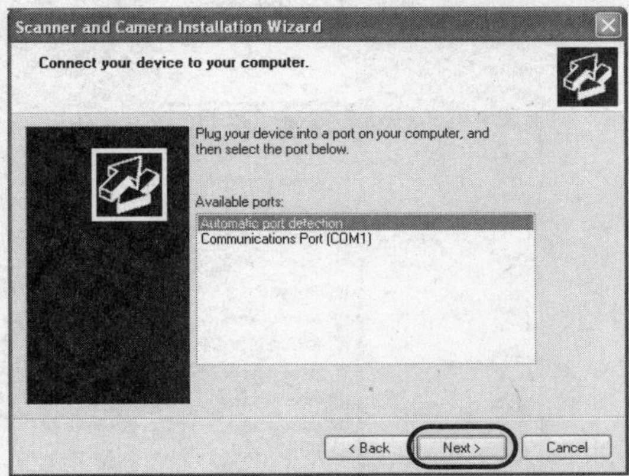

6. Type a name for the device, or leave the default name. Then click Next.

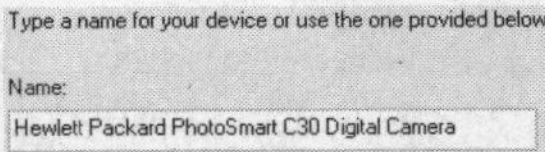

7. Click Finish. Windows installs the drivers for the device and sets it up to appear in the Scanners and Cameras window.

If the preceding steps didn't get your device up and running, try inserting the Setup CD that came with the device and running the Setup program. The disadvantage of this method is that the device will use the manufacturer's drivers, rather than the drives that Windows supplies, so the remainder of the steps and procedures outlined in this chapter may not be accurate for your situation. Read the documentation and online help that came with the device.

SCANNING FROM AN XP-COMPATIBLE SCANNER

When Windows recognizes your scanner, you are ready to scan. You can scan photos, drawings, text, or anything else that appears on paper. The only limitation is that the item to be scanned must fit in your scanner.

1. Choose Start ➢ All Programs ➢ Accessories ➢ Scanner and Camera Wizard.

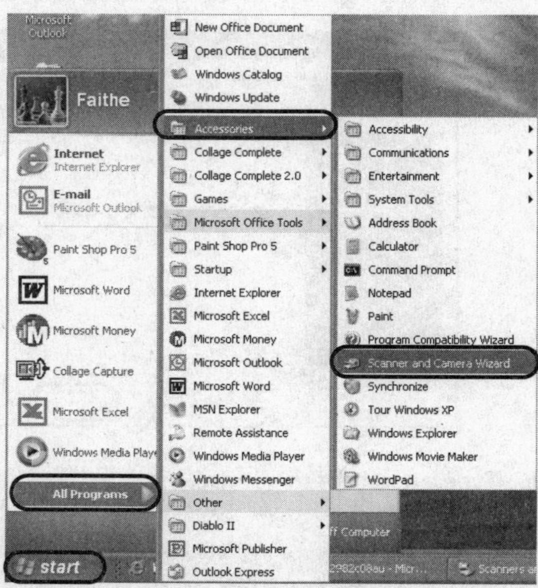

TIP

As an alternative to steps 1 and 2, you can start in the Scanners and Cameras window (from Control Panel) and double-click the device you want.

2. If you have more than one scanner or camera, a box appears, in which you choose which device you want to work with. Click the desired device and then click OK.

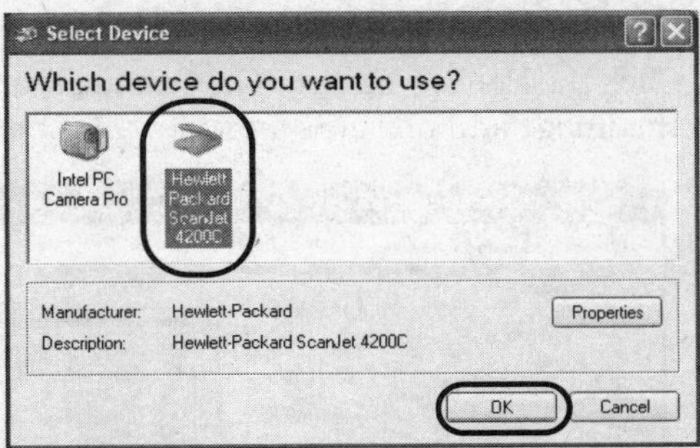

3. The Scanner and Camera Wizard opens. Click Next to continue.

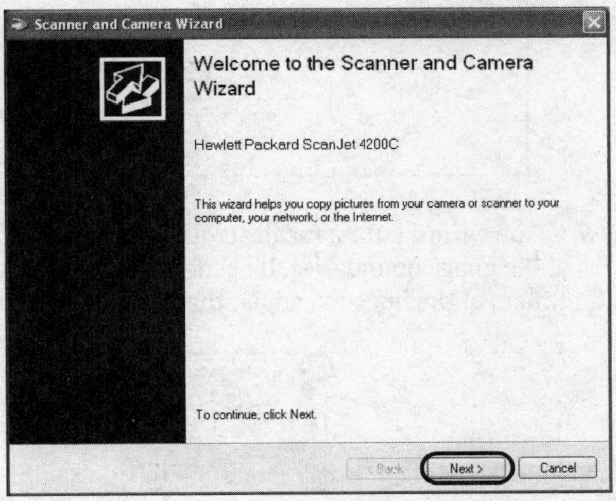

4. Place the item to be scanned in the scanner, if you haven't done so yet.

5. On the Choose Scanning Preferences screen, select the type of picture you want to scan: Color Picture, Grayscale Picture, or Custom.

NOTE

If you choose Custom, you can click the Custom Settings button and fine-tune the scanner settings, but most people won't need to do that because the default settings work well in most cases.

6. Click the Preview button. The scanner scans a quick pass over the image and presents a preview of it on-screen.

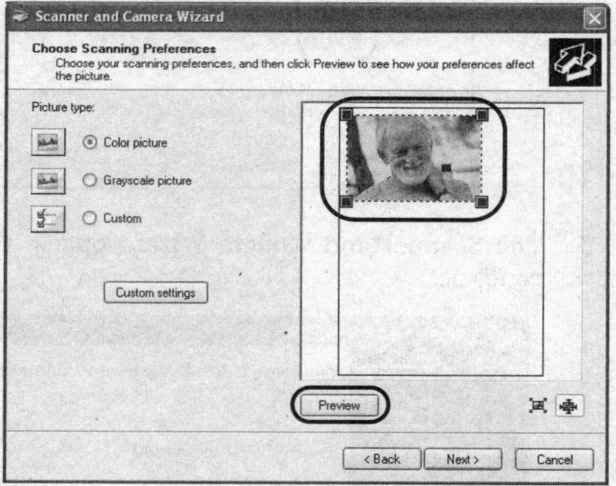

7. The wizard automatically crops based on what it thinks are the image boundaries. If needed, drag the squares in the corners of the image to adjust the area to be scanned.

8. Click Next to continue.

9. Type a name for the picture. The default name is "Picture" or whatever name you last used, but you will probably want a different name.

10. Open the Select a File Format drop-down list and choose a graphics format in which to save. You can choose JPG, BMP, TIF, or PNG.

TIP

JPG is best for use on Web pages, while TIF is popular with commercial print publications. BMP is good for creating images to use as background wallpaper in Windows.

11. If you want to store the picture somewhere other than the default location (in a subfolder with the name you provided in step 9, inside the My Pictures folder), enter it in the Choose a Place to Save... text box, or click Browse to locate it.

12. Click Next to continue, and wait for the scanning to take place.

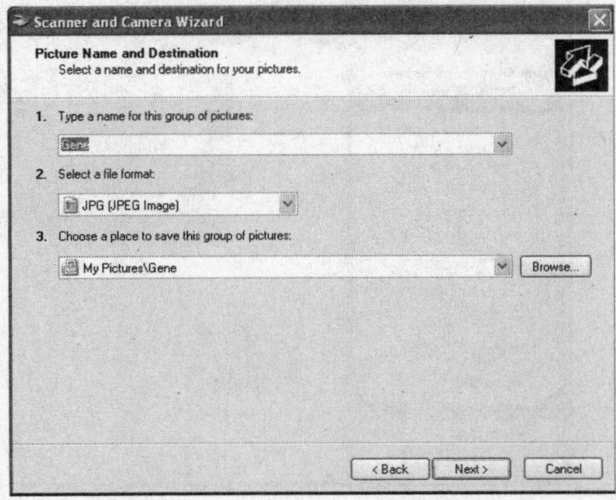

13. After the picture has been scanned, you have the option of copying it to the Internet or ordering a print through a photo service. For now, decline both of these; leave the default Nothing chosen and click Next.

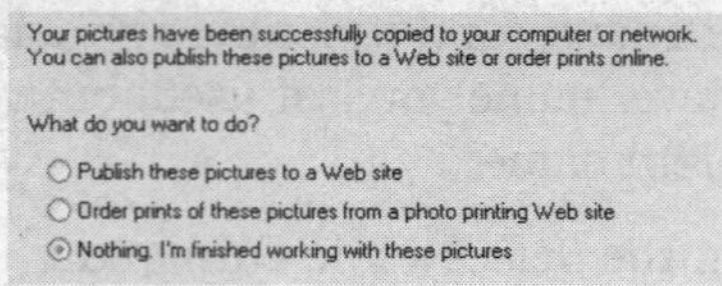

Your pictures have been successfully copied to your computer or network.
You can also publish these pictures to a Web site or order prints online.
What do you want to do?
Publish these pictures to a Web site
Order prints of these pictures from a photo printing Web site
Nothing. I'm finished working with these pictures

14. On the final screen of the wizard, click Finish.

NOTE

The view shown here is called Filmstrip view. A special view for displaying pictures, it's available on the View menu in graphics-display windows such as My Pictures.

A file management window opens, showing the subfolder of My Pictures that you created in the wizard. You can use the links in the shortcut pane to rename it, copy it, or perform any other listed activity. If you want to print, see "Printing a Photo" later in this chapter for some guidance.

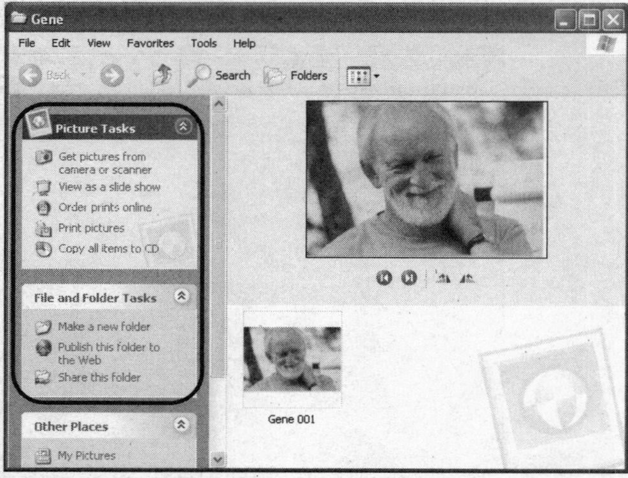

Transferring Pictures from a Digital Camera

A digital camera is like a regular camera except instead of recording images on film, it records them as computer data. There are two main kinds of digital cameras—those that are permanently connected to your PC and those that you can take out into the world and use, and then hook up to your PC for image transfer.

Depending on the type of camera you have and its features, the procedure for transferring pictures to your PC may be a little different from the steps that follow. These steps are for a connected camera, but they point out where a go-anywhere type of camera would be different.

1. Perform steps 1 through 3 of the preceding procedure ("Scanning from an XP-Compatible Scanner").

   The next few steps are for connected cameras only. They show how to take pictures. With a go-anywhere camera, the pictures have already been taken, so you might not have this capability. If your pictures have already been taken, skip to step 5.

2. A preview appears, showing what your camera is "seeing" at the moment. Position the camera so that the desired image appears in the preview.
3. Click the Take Picture button.

4. Reposition the camera and take more pictures if desired. Here, three pictures have been taken.

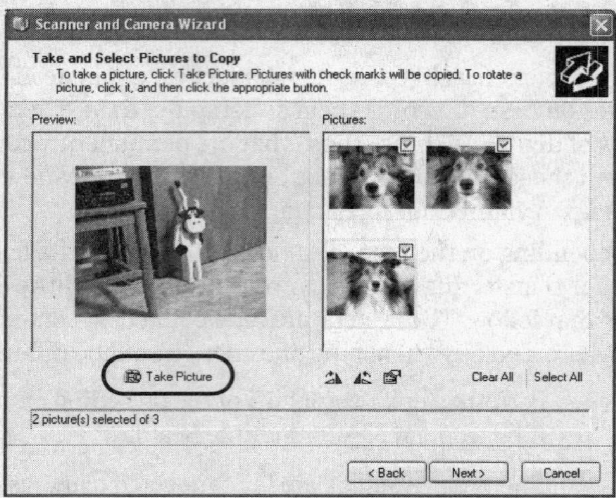

The rest of this procedure applies equally to all types of cameras.

TIP

Note the Rotate Clockwise and Rotate Counterclockwise buttons below the pictures. Click one of these if you need to turn the selected picture 90 degrees.

5. The pictures currently stored in the camera appear. By default, all pictures have a check mark in their upper-right corner, indicating that they will be saved. If you don't want to save one of the pictures, click its check mark to toggle it off. In the next figure, the third picture has been deselected.

6. Click Next to continue.

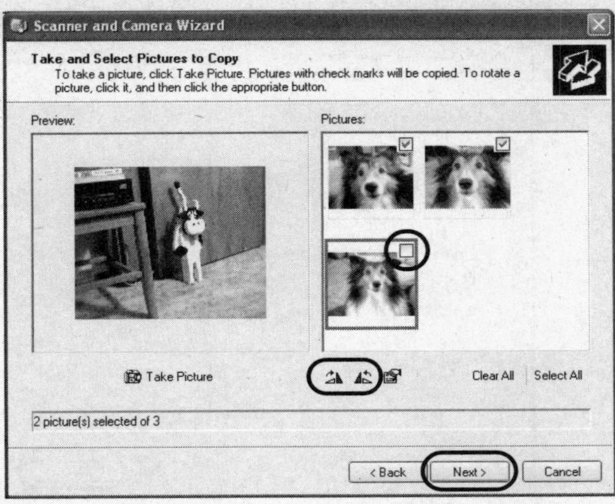

7. In the first text box on the Picture Name and Destination screen, type a name to use as a prefix for the picture names. Each picture will have the name you type plus a number. For example, if you type Camera, the first picture will be named Camera01, the second Camera02, and so on.

8. If desired, select a different save location in the Choose a Place to Save... box. By default, the location is a subfolder with the same name that you typed in step 7, inside the My Pictures folder.

9. (Optional) If you want to remove the pictures from the camera after you save them to your hard disk, mark the Delete Pictures from My Device after Copying Them check box.

10. Click Next to continue.

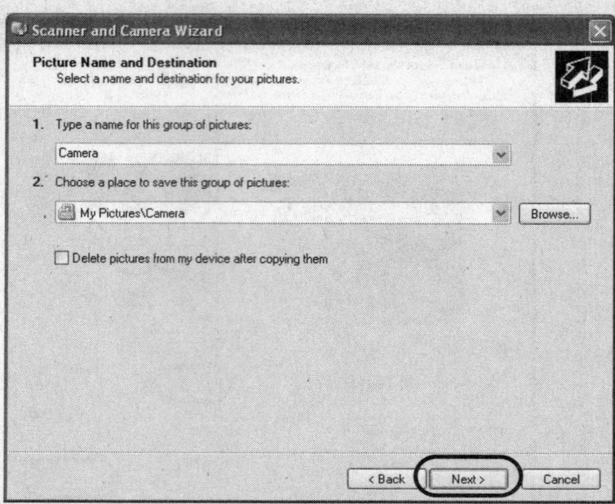
Scanner and Camera Wizard
Picture Name and Destination
Select a name and destination for your pictures.
1. Type a name for this group of pictures:
Camera
2. Choose a place to save this group of pictures:
My Pictures\Camera
Browse...
Delete pictures from my device after copying them
< Back
Next >
Cancel

The files are copied to your computer, and deleted from the camera if you chose that option.

11. As with the scanner, you can choose whether to copy the pictures to the Internet, order prints online, or do nothing. Leave Nothing selected and click Next.

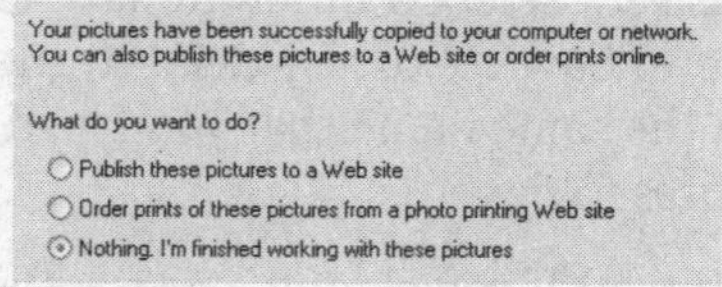
Your pictures have been successfully copied to your computer or network.
You can also publish these pictures to a Web site or order prints online.
What do you want to do?
Publish these pictures to a Web site
Order prints of these pictures from a photo printing Web site
Nothing. I'm finished working with these pictures

12. On the final screen of the wizard, click Finish.

13. The new folder opens with the pictures displayed.

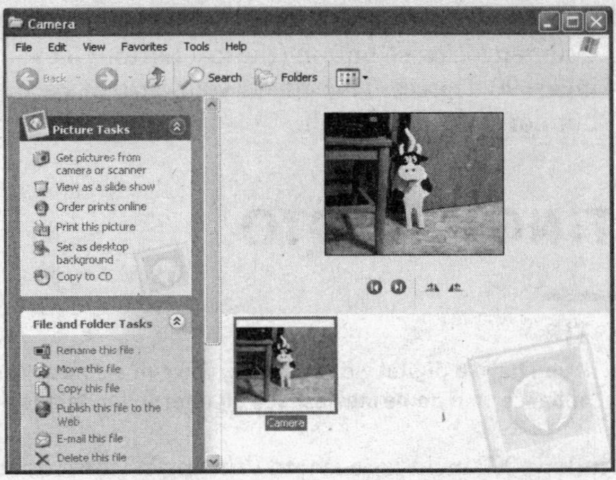

From here, you can use the links in the left pane to rename the pictures, copy them, or perform any other listed activity. The pictures are regular files, just like any others you learned to work with in Chapter 5. If you want to print, see "Printing a Photo" later in this chapter for some guidance.

VIEWING IMAGES

TIP

If you are interested in editing your pictures, I strongly recommend that you buy a graphics management program such as Paint Shop Pro. Windows XP's default graphics program is Paint, but Paint is very simple and lacks features such as cropping and converting to grayscale that you might find useful for editing and manipulating images.

Whether you acquire an image from a scanner or from a camera, the end of the procedure leaves you in a file management window in Filmstrip view, with the image displayed in a preview area. If you don't see a preview, choose View ➢ Filmstrip. You can use the buttons below the image preview to manipulate it:

The Previous Image button (the one with the left arrow) and the Next Image button (the one with the right arrow) let you switch to other images in the same folder, if there are any. You won't use them while working with a single image.

The Rotate Clockwise button (the third button) and the Rotate Counterclockwise button (the last button) let you turn the image 90 degrees. This affects your current view of the picture, but not the picture itself.

PRINTING A PHOTO

TIP

If you have a digital video camera, you can also use Windows XP to edit and enhance your home movies. See Chapter 19 for details.

Windows XP includes a Photo Printing Wizard that can help you get the best possible print of your pictures.

NOTE

Selecting File ➢ Print prints a single copy of the picture on your default printer with default settings. It bypasses the Photo Printing Wizard.

1. In the folder containing the pictures, select all the pictures that you want to print. You can print multiple pictures as a batch.

NOTE

Notice that when you select multiple pictures, none of them appear in the preview area.

2. Under Picture Tasks, click Print This Picture (or Print the Selected Pictures, if you selected more than one).

3. The Photo Printing Wizard opens. Click Next to continue.

4. If you selected more than one picture in step 1, the selected pictures appear. If you have changed your mind about printing a particular picture, clear its check box to deselect it. Then click Next.

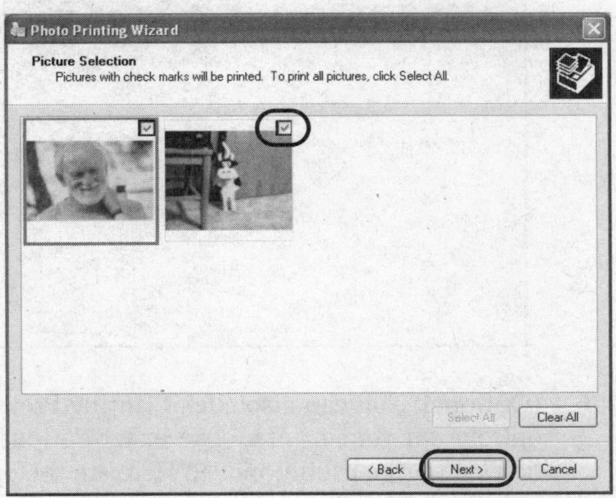

NOTE

The Install Printer button is a shortcut to the Printers folder for adding a new printer to your system. You learned about adding printers in Chapter 10.

5. If you have more than one printer, open the What Printer Do You Want to Use? drop-down list and select the desired printer. For example, you might have a black-and-white laser printer and a color ink-jet printer.

TIP

Notice that I have the option of choosing a paper type from the Media drop-down list. For best photo printing results, use some photo paper for your ink-jet printer. It's a glossy, nonporous paper that makes prints that look almost as good as those developed in a real photo lab.

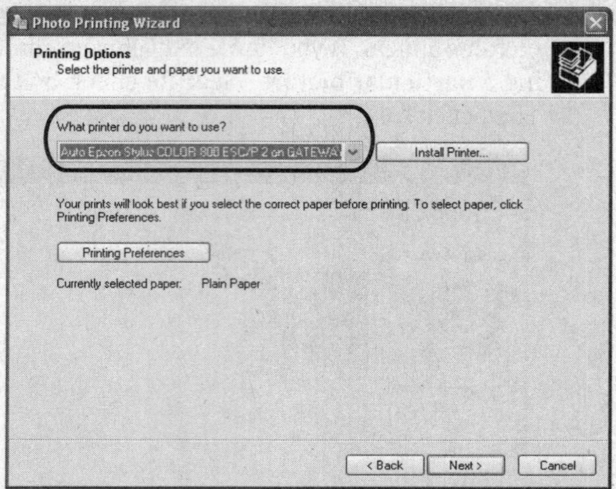

6. (Optional) You can also click Printing Preferences to set options for your printer. The exact options that appear depend on the printer model. Here are the options for my printer:

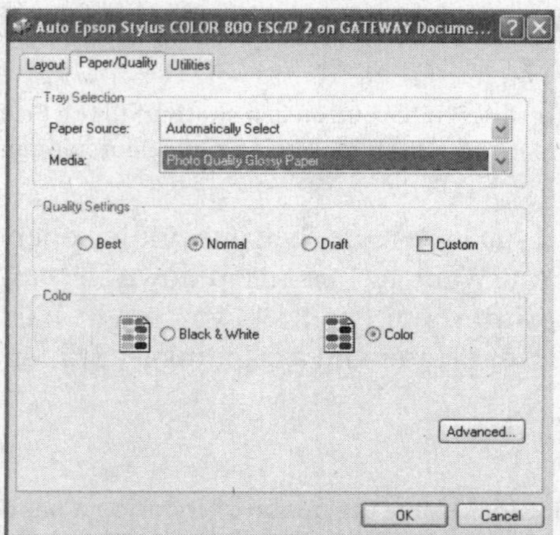

7. On the Printing Options screen, click Next to continue.

TIP

Remember how in grade school, you used to order a certain number of wallet-sized photos, a certain number of 5×7s, and so on? Well, now you can print all the sheets you want of those various sizes by selecting different layouts.

8. On the Layout Selection screen, choose a layout. Many layouts are available, with different numbers and sizes of prints. Then click Next.

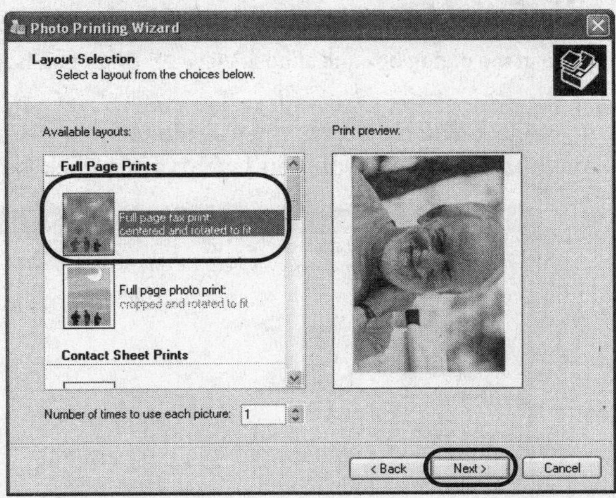

The photos print.

9. Click Finish to close the wizard.

Ordering Photo Prints Online

If your printer doesn't give you the quality of photo printing you want, you might try one of the online printing services. They specialize in printing digital photographs on professional-quality photo printers. Their prices are comparable to those for conventional film developing.

Windows XP has a built-in link to these services. From the file management window for the photos, follow these steps:

1. Select the photos you want to order prints of.
2. In the Picture Tasks pane, click Order Prints Online.

3. The Online Print Ordering Wizard opens. Click Next.

NOTE

If you don't see thumbnail images of the available pictures, right-click a blank area in the dialog box and choose View ➢ Thumbnails.

4. Select which pictures you want to order by clearing the check box next to any you don't want. Then click Next.

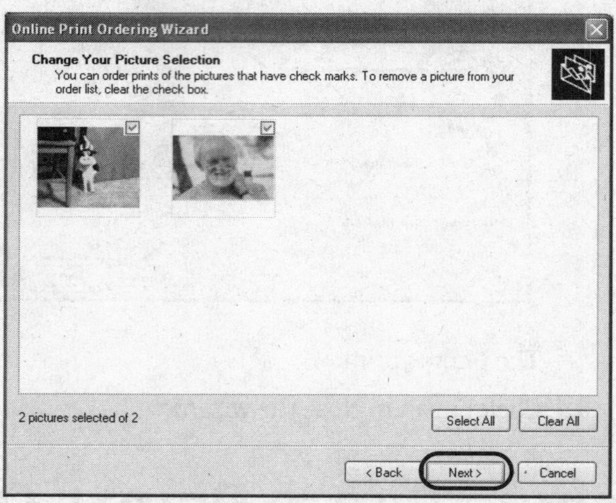

5. Select the company you want to use.

   At this writing, only three are available; by the time you read this, there may be others.

6. Click Next to continue.

   The steps at this point diverge depending on the company you picked. For example, here's what you see if you chose Picture It! On MSN.

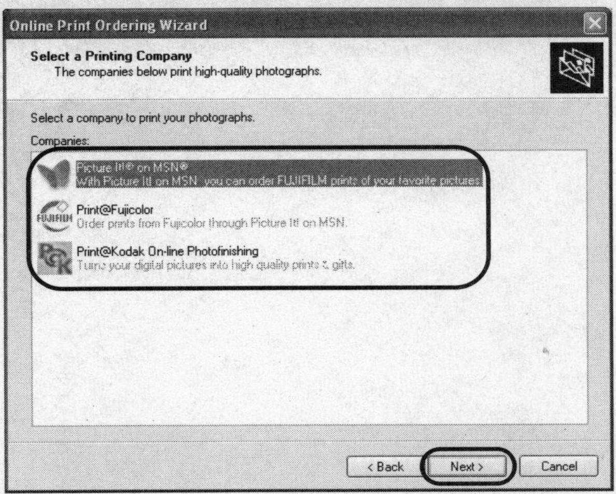

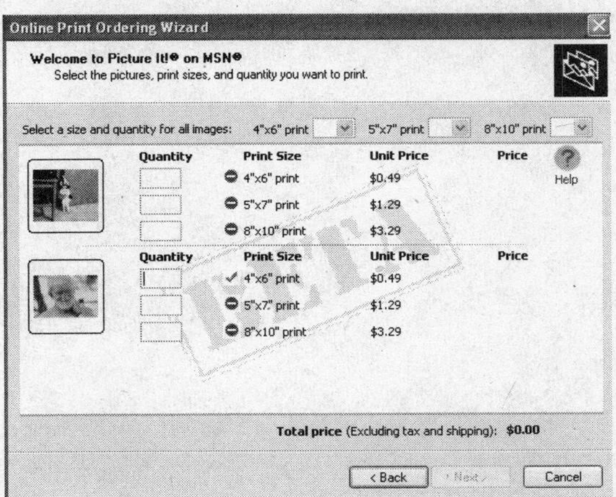

7. Continue following the on-screen prompts to create and place your order.

WHAT'S NEXT?

A feature that is much improved in Windows XP Professional is Windows Media Player. You can use it to play music and videos, and the next chapter looks at this topic in detail.

Chapter 18

Playing Music and Videos

Windows XP has richer, more robust multimedia capabilities than any previous version, including a new and improved version of Windows Media Player for playing sound, music, video clips, and DVD movies. In this chapter, you'll learn the ins and outs of this fun and versatile program.

Introducing Windows Media Player

Media Player 8 is a multipurpose audio and video player in Windows XP. It's similar to Media Player 7, which came with Windows Me. Earlier versions of Windows also had a program called Media Player, but it was simple and plain—nothing like the powerhouse program that you see in Windows XP.

Revised and adapted from *Windows XP Home Edition Simply Visual* by Faithe Wempen

ISBN 0-7821-2982-X 448 pages $24.99

With Media Player 8, you can:

- Play media clips, including videos, music, and sound effects, in any of dozens of different formats.
- With an Internet connection, explore an online Media Guide section that provides free sound and video clips that you can download from your favorite artists.
- With an Internet connection, listen to hundreds of Internet radio stations. Some of these are online broadcasts of your favorite stations around the world; others are Internet-only stations.
- Play audio CDs on your computer, using features such as track selection, random play, and so on.
- Copy songs from your audio CDs to your hard disk so that you can listen to them while you work without inserting the CDs.
- Organize your sound clips from various sources into custom playlists, creating your own "mixes."

To start Media Player, choose Start ➢ All Programs ➢ Windows Media Player.

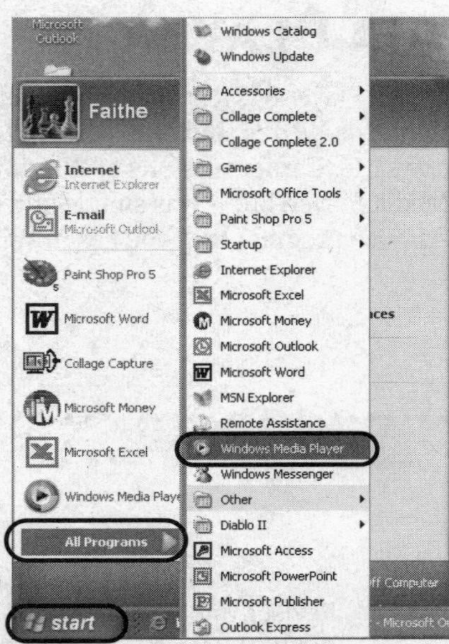

In the preceding figure, since Windows Media Player was also on the top-level menu (because I recently used it), I could have also selected it from there.

TIP

If you have the Quick Launch toolbar displayed, you can also start Windows Media Player by clicking the player's icon there. The icon is a right arrow inside a multicolored circle.

Using the Media Guide

Windows Media Player has several tabs to the left of the main work area. You can click a tab to bring a certain page to the front, as you would in a multi-tabbed dialog box. Let's start with the Media Guide tab. You can skip this section if you aren't connected to the Internet.

You can click any of the links on the Media Guide tab to listen to or watch clips from the featured artists. You can also browse a huge library of material from your favorite artists by clicking Videos/Downloads in the navigation bar at the left.

The format and content available on the Media Guide tab varies greatly over time—even from day to day—because it's actually a Web site that you're accessing, rather than a fixed program.

Playing Internet Radio Stations

Imagine if you could listen to almost any radio station, anywhere in the world, with no static and no antenna problems. That's what Internet radio is like! You'll be amazed at the quality and variety of programming available.

Playing a Featured Station

The Radio Tuner tab includes a Featured Stations list of popular stations. To listen to one of those stations:

1. Click the Radio Tuner tab in Media Player.
2. Click one of the stations on the Featured Stations list. Some details about the station appear below its name.
3. Click Play. The station begins playing.

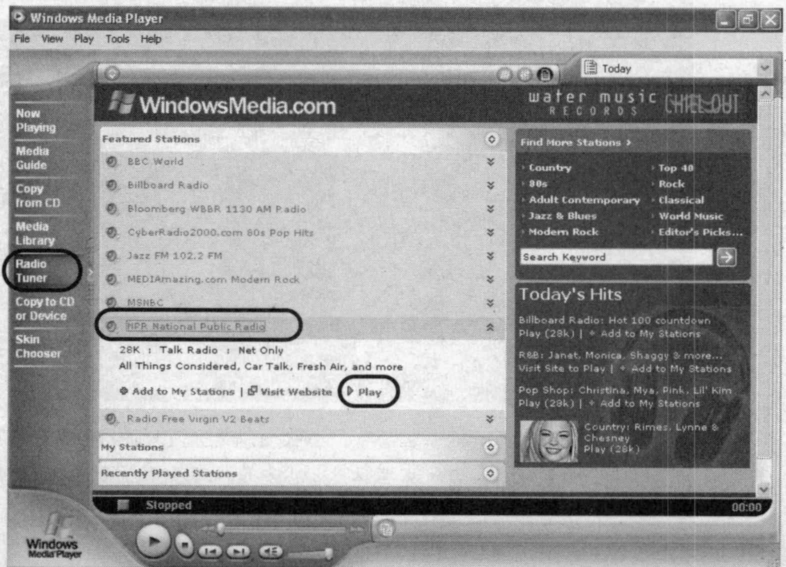

NOTE

Why does a station take so long to load? It's because Internet radio is a streaming audio format. The music is transmitted to your PC just in time for it to be played. On a slow PC, the least little delay can result in a choppy playback, so Media Player creates a buffer—a storage area for several seconds of incoming data. That way, if there is a delay in transmission, the music continues to play out of the buffer while your PC catches up, and there is no interruption. The slower your Internet connection, the longer it takes to fill the buffer initially.

If you have a slow Internet connection, it might take several minutes before the station begins to play. You might also experience some pauses or choppiness in the play. Broadband Internet users should not experience these problems.

If you need some silence, click either Pause or Stop at the bottom of the Media Player window. Pause stops the broadcast temporarily, but picks up where you left off when you click Pause again. Stop stops the station entirely.

NOTE

What's the difference between Pause and Stop when it comes to radio? It depends on how the station is broadcast. If you're listening to a station that broadcasts "live," there is no difference. But if you're listening to a station that broadcasts from prerecording and you click Stop, the recording will start from the beginning when you click Play to start it again. With Pause, though, it will stop at the current spot and restart from that same spot when you click Pause again to "unpause" the broadcast.

To mute the volume while allowing the station to continue to play, click the Mute button. To adjust the volume, drag the Volume slider to the right or left.

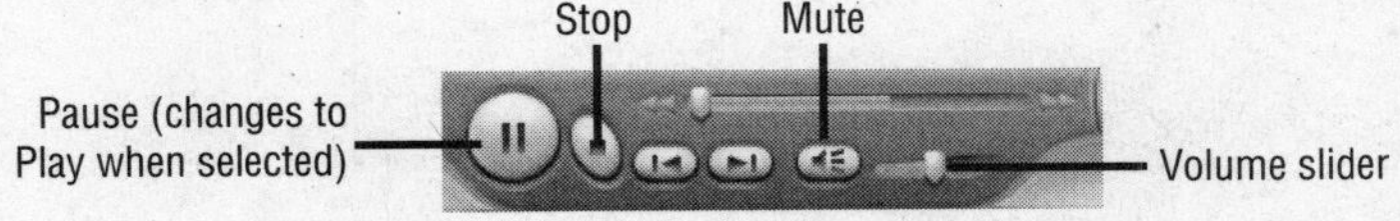

To choose a different station, click it from the station list and then click Play.

You can also see the My Stations list or the Recently Played Stations list by clicking its name. At first, you won't have any stations on either of these lists. When you choose a station to play, it's automatically added to

Part iii

the Recently Played Stations list. You'll learn how to add stations to the My Stations list later in this chapter.

Finding a Station

You can search for a specific station from a list of hundreds all over the world. If you know the station's call letters or location, you can search by that criterion; you can also browse stations by genre. To find a station:

1. Click Find More Stations.

2. (Optional) If you want to limit your search to a certain type of station, open the Browse by Genre list and choose a genre, such as 80s or Latin.

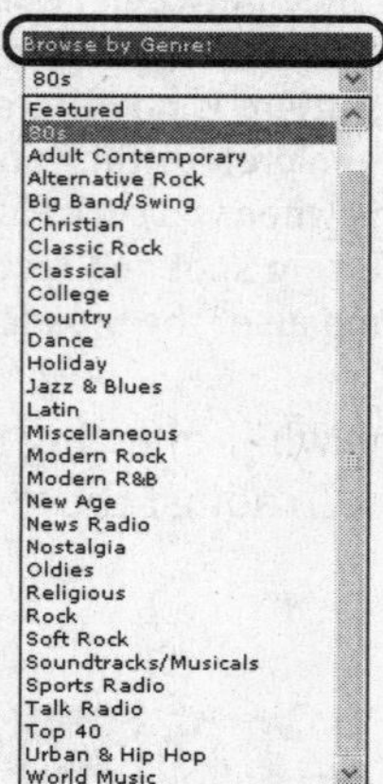

3. (Optional) If you want to further limit the list of stations, do one of the following:
   - To find a station with a certain word in its name or description, enter a word in the Search Keyword box and then click the arrow button next to it.

- To look for stations in a certain area, enter a zip code in the Zip Code box and then click the arrow button next to it.

A list of stations appears.

4. When you find a station you want to try, click it and then click Play. (Here I've selected 1000% Disco.) The station begins playing.

Bookmarking Your Favorite Stations

As on a car radio, you can create presets for your favorite Internet stations. Media Player comes with a list of presets called "Featured Stations," which you see when you click the Radio Tuner tab. You can't edit this list (it contains stations that have paid a fee to Microsoft), but you can create your own list of favorite stations by doing the following:

1. Find a station, as in the preceding section, and click it.
2. Click Add to My Stations.

To play one of the stations on your My Stations list:

1. Click Return to My Stations.

2. If your My Stations list doesn't already appear, click My Stations to see your list.

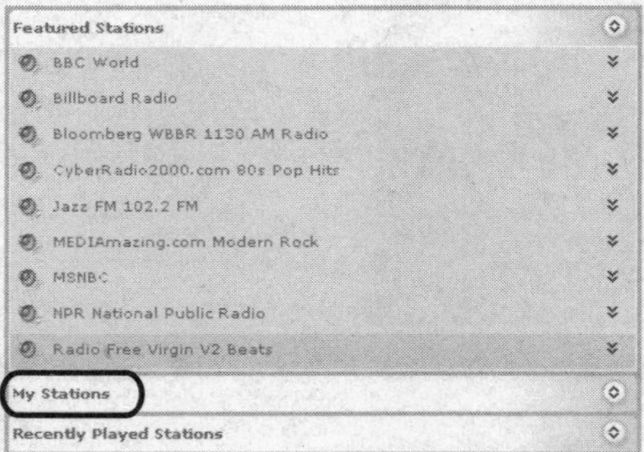

Playing an Audio CD

NOTE

Some audio CDs have computer programs on them as well as music, and inserting such a CD runs the program rather than playing the music. In that case, Media Player won't start automatically; you must exit from the CD's own program and then start Media Player manually.

When you insert an audio CD in your CD-ROM drive, Media Player launches itself and begins playing the CD.

NOTE

To prevent a CD from playing automatically when you insert it, hold down Shift as you insert it.

The Now Playing tab appears by default as the CD starts playing. While the CD plays, you can change to any tab in Media Player. The CD will continue to play.

Customizing the Now Playing Tab

Here's what the Now Playing tab looks like when a CD is playing:

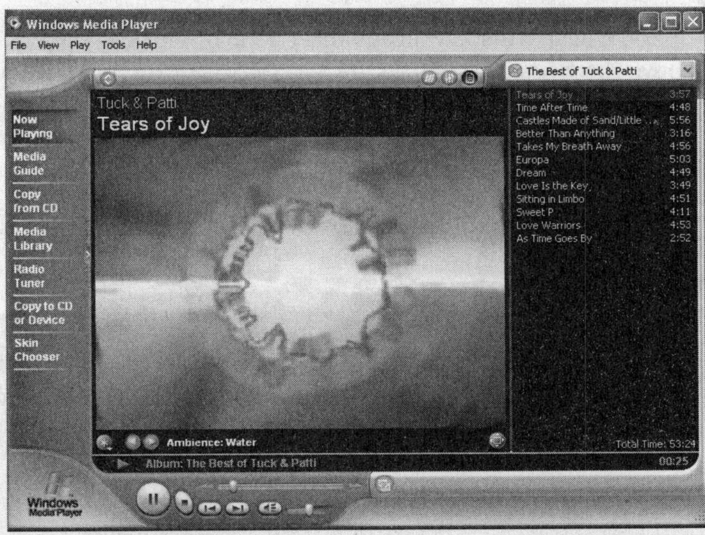

In the center is the *visualization* pane. (A visualization is patterns, colors, or other moving images that react to the music.)

You can click the right- and left-arrow buttons under the current visualization to change it. Click the asterisk button under the pane to choose a different visualization category.

TIP

Choose Tools ➢ Download Visualizations to get more visualizations from the Microsoft Web site.

You can also display an equalizer pane by clicking the Equalizer button above the visualization area. Its controls help you fine-tune the audio output. The buttons and sliders on it work just like those on a regular stereo.

TIP

Remember, to display a description of what any button does, simply point to it.

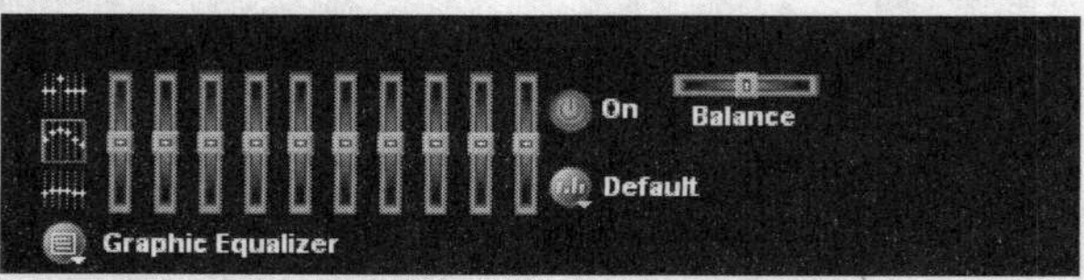

You can click the Graphic Equalizer button in the equalizer pane to change what appears there; instead of an equalizer, for example, you could have captions or SRS WOW effects.

The playlist, if turned on, appears on the right side of the Now Playing tab, reporting the track names and times. You can jump to a particular song on the CD by double-clicking its name on the playlist.

You can turn the playlist display on or off by clicking the Playlist button at the top of the screen.

The third button at the top of the screen is the Shuffle button. Like Shuffle on a regular CD player, it plays the tracks in random order rather than chronologically.

Using the Player Controls

The player controls appear at the bottom of the screen. (They appear in all views, not just Now Playing, but this is a good time to discuss them.) They work just like those on a regular CD player or cassette tape deck. You can pause, stop, fast-forward, rewind, and so on. The big slider above the other player control buttons is Seek; you can drag it to skip forward or backward in the track that's currently playing.

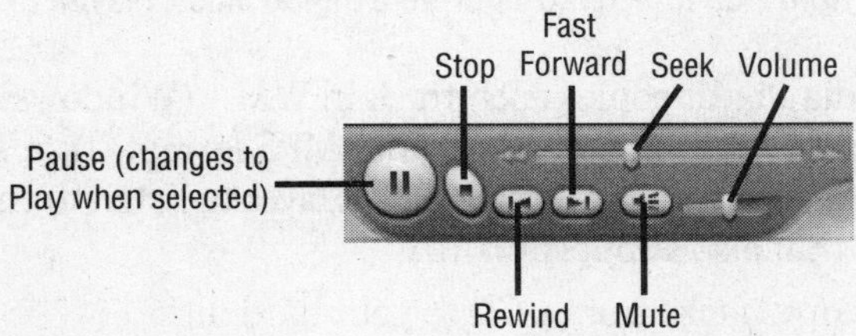

Selecting Which Tracks to Play

If there's a particular track you don't want to hear, right-click its name and choose Disable Selected Tracks from the shortcut menu. Its name will then appear in gray lettering instead of white, indicating that it's disabled.

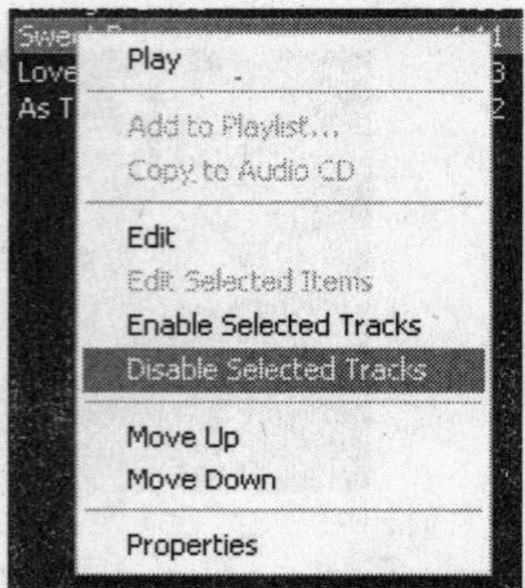

To rearrange the order of tracks in the playlist, right-click a track and then choose Move Up or Move Down to change its position in the playlist.

Copying CD Tracks to Your Hard Disk

Now, let's move on to the Copy from CD tab. From here, you can see detailed information about each track on the CD, and copy tracks to your hard disk for later listening when you no longer have the disc in your drive.

NOTE

Later in this chapter, I'll show you how to transfer tracks from your hard disk or from a CD directly to a portable digital music player.

Media Player copies each track in WMA (Windows Media Audio) format, rather than the more popular MP3 format. That shouldn't be a problem as long as you use Media Player to listen to the tracks or another player that also supports WMA.

To copy tracks from a CD to your hard disk:

1. On the Copy from CD tab, clear the check box for any tracks that you don't want to copy.
2. Click the Copy Music button.

NOTE

By choosing not to protect the content, you enable the copied tracks to be played on other computers; that way, you can copy the tracks onto a disk and take them to some other computer for listening. This is legal as long as you, the original owner, retain the tracks, but it's illegal to share copyrighted tracks with others.

The first time you use the Copy Music feature, you might see a security dialog box. Mark the Do Not Protect Content check box and then click OK.

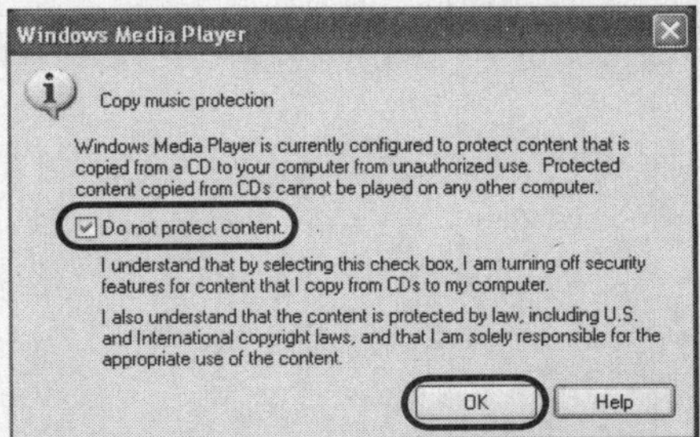

When the tracks have been copied, they show up on the Media Library tab, which you'll learn about in "Playing a Clip" later in this chapter.

Working with the Media Library

Now, let's head over to the Media Library tab, where you can manage all your various types of music clips in one place. I've saved this tab for last because it can be the most complex, especially if you have music from lots of sources.

NOTE

If you want to copy tracks to your hard disk in MP3 format rather than WMA, Windows Media Player can do it. Choose Tools ➢ Options, click the Copy Music tab, open the File Format drop-down list, and select MP3. Then click OK. This dialog box contains many other program options that you might want to explore on your own.

NOTE

In this chapter, I'll show you mostly audio clips in the Media Library, but you can also add video clips to it, in the same way as audio clips.

The Media Library has a folder list, just like the one in Windows Explorer. In the following figure, I've expanded all the branches of the list so that you can see what's there. So far, the only clips I have are the four tracks I copied from the CD in the preceding section. You can see them categorized in various ways on the folder list: by Artist, by Genre, and by Album. All Audio, which is selected here, shows, in the right pane, a master list of all clips in the library.

Playing a Clip

To play a clip, double-click it as usual, or click it and then click the Play button at the bottom of the window. If it's an audio clip, it simply plays and the Media Library remains on-screen. If it's a video clip, it switches to the Now Playing tab so that you can see the video as well as hear it.

Removing a Clip from the Library

To remove a clip from the Media Library, select it and press Delete, or right-click it and choose Delete from Library from the shortcut menu. This removes the clip from the Windows Media Player library only; the clip remains on your hard disk.

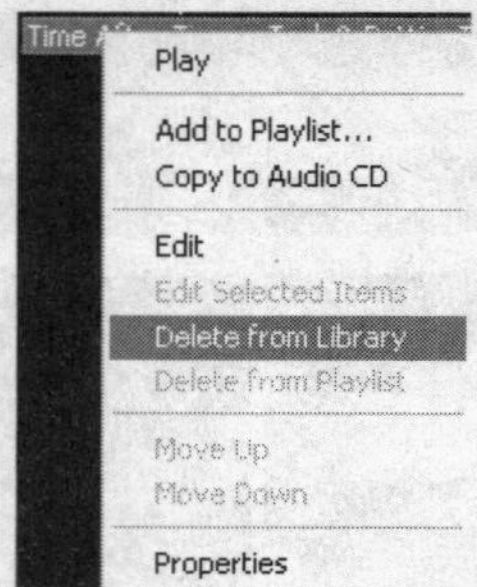

Adding Clips to the Library

As you saw earlier, copying tracks to your hard disk from a CD is one way to get clips into your Media Library. Another way is to download clips from the Internet and then add them to the Media Library like this:

1. Choose File ➢ Add to Media Library ➢ Add File.

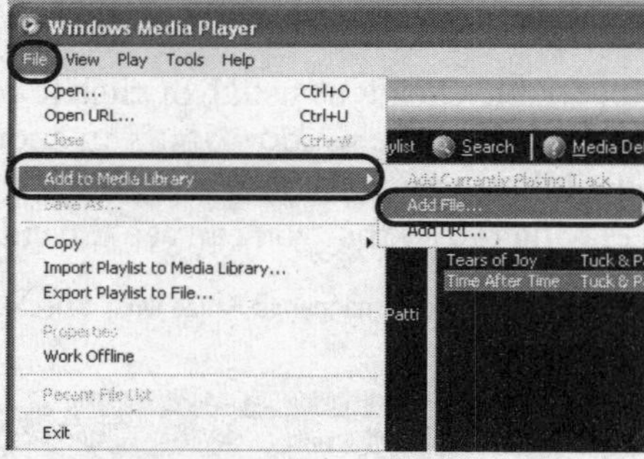

2. In the Open dialog box that appears, locate and select the file you want to add.

NOTE

Depending on how the file was created, it might not have all the information that a CD-copied track contains. For example, both the artist name and the song title might appear together in the Artist column, and there might be no genre or album information. You can edit the entry by right-clicking and choosing Edit and then tabbing between the columns.

3. Click Open.

The song is added to your Media Library.

Automatically Adding Many Clips at Once

NOTE

Some games come with sound clips for various sound effects in the game, and these will be added to the Media Library if you go the automatic route described next. You can avoid this by limiting the search to certain folders on your hard disk (the ones where you know your music clips are stored) or by excluding certain file formats from the search, such as WAV, which is the format of many game sound-effects files.

You're probably thinking that adding all your clips to the Media Library is going to be a big chore, right? Wrong. Media Player has a feature that searches your hard disk and adds all the clips it finds automatically.

To search your hard disk for clips to add:

1. Choose Tools ➢ Search for Media Files.

TIP

The Search button near the top of the Windows Media Player window is not the same as the Tools ➢ Search for Media Files command. Instead, it searches by keyword among files that are already in the Media Library.

2. The Search for Media Files dialog box opens. Open the Search on drop-down list and choose the drive on which you want to search, or choose All Drives.

3. If you don't want to search the entire selected drive, fill in a folder name in the Look In box, or click Browse to locate one. This will search the chosen folder and any child folders within it, ignoring the rest of the drive.

4. (Optional) Click the Advanced button, and enter any additional criteria.

   The default settings here are fine for most people. For example, excluding audio clips under 100K is a good idea because such clips are usually sound effects rather than music.

5. When you have selected the search options you want, click Search.

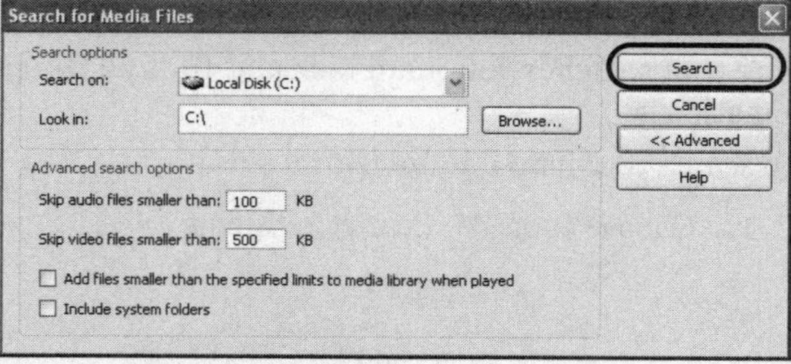

6. When the status appears as Completed, click Close.

7. Click Close again to close the Search box. The found clips now appear in your Media Library.

Copying Music to a Portable Digital Audio Player

If you have a portable digital audio device that Windows Media Player supports, you can copy clips to it from within Media Player.

To get started, connect your portable player to your computer using whatever method it needs (mine uses the USB port) and then turn the device on. The first time you connect it, Windows might go through a process of recognizing and configuring the device.

Then do the following:

1. In the Media Library, display the playlist, album, artist, or other category from which you want to copy clips.
2. Click the Copy to CD or Device tab. The clips you chose to display in step 1 appear in the left pane.

TIP

You can open the Music to Copy drop-down list to choose another playlist, album, artist, or other category if needed.

3. Open the Music on Device drop-down list and choose your portable device. Its current content appears in the right pane. (In the following figure it is empty.)
4. The amount that can fit in your portable player depends on its capacity. If you have more clips selected than will fit, some of them report "May not fit" next to them. Deselect the check boxes of some clips until all selected clips report "Ready to copy."
5. Click Copy Music. The clips are copied to your portable player.

TIP

You can't copy directly from a CD to a portable player; you must first add the tracks from the CD to the Media Library, as you learned earlier, and then transfer them from the Media Library to the portable device.

When a clip has finished copying, "Complete" appears in the Status column and the check mark next to the clip is cleared.

TIP

You can select and deselect track check boxes while other tracks are being copied, so you can change your mind about a track that has not yet been copied.

Creating an Audio CD

Creating an audio CD is just like copying to a portable audio player, thanks to Windows XP's CD-writing technology. Windows Media Player treats a blank, writable CD just like a portable player.

Here's how to create an audio CD from clips in your Media Library:

1. In the Media Library, display the playlist, album, artist, or other category from which you want to make a CD. You will probably want to create a playlist for this purpose.
2. Insert a blank CD into your writable CD-ROM drive. If a file management window opens for it, close that window.
3. In Media Player, click the Copy to CD or Device tab. The clips that you displayed in step 1 appear in the left pane.
4. Open the Music on Device drop-down list and select your writable CD-ROM drive.

5. A music CD can hold about 70 minutes of music. If you have more clips selected than will fit, some of them report "May not fit" next to them. Deselect the check boxes of some clips until all selected clips report "Ready to copy."
6. Click the Copy Music button. The clips are copied to the CD.

WARNING

Avoid using your computer for any other activities while a CD is being created, to avoid errors.

Playing a DVD Movie

Windows XP includes a full-featured DVD player capability, which you can use if you have a DVD drive and *MPEG decoding* capability on your PC. MPEG stands for Moving Picture Experts Group; it's a standard for storing video clips on a DVD drive.

To be able to play a DVD movie on your PC, your PC must have the capability to decode that format of data. That means you must have two things: a DVD-compatible CD-ROM drive and the capability of decoding MPEG-format data in which DVD movies are stored. This decoding capability can come from a separate circuit board in your PC, from a video card that includes MPEG decoding capability, or from special decoding software. Check your computer's manual to see whether you have this capability. Most PCs that come with DVD drives also come with MPEG decoding, but some bargain PCs might not.

To play a DVD movie, simply put it in your DVD drive. It should start playing automatically in Windows Media Player.

If a dialog box like the following one appears, choose Play DVD Video Using Windows Media Player and then click OK.

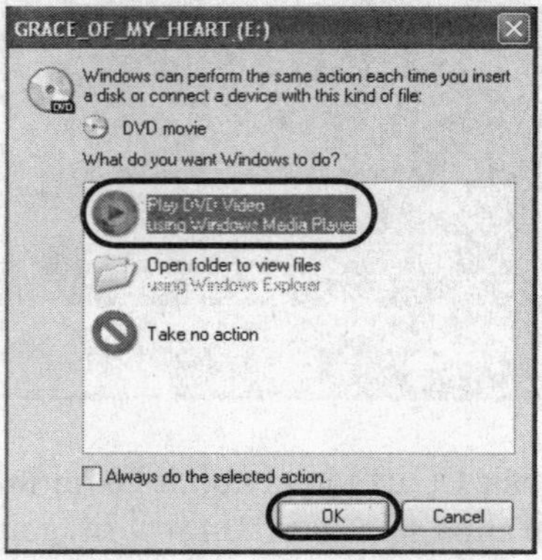

If you think your PC has an MPEG decoder but you see the following message, perhaps you need to install drivers for the decoder. Search the discs that came with your computer and see whether there is a DVD player that you can install. If you install a DVD player, it may not work the same as described here because Windows won't be using Media Player to play the movie, but rather the utility that came with your decoder.

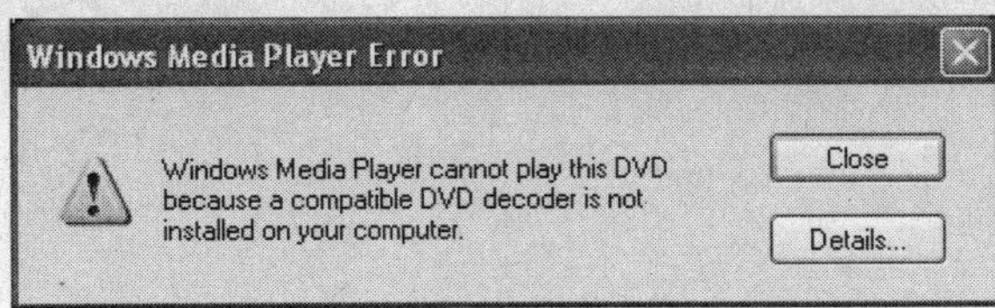

If the movie doesn't start automatically, you can open Windows Media Player, choose Play ➢ DVD or CD Audio, and then select the movie to play.

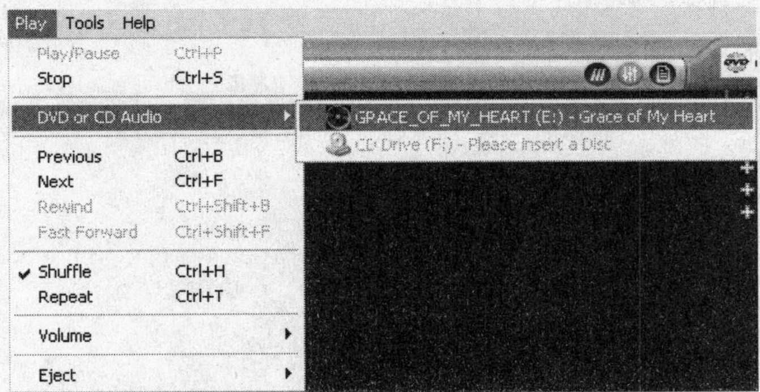

TIP

Some DVDs have special features, such as wide-screen capability. To access the features for the DVD, right-click the display and choose DVD Features; then select a feature from the menu that appears.

Depending on the movie, it may start from the beginning, or you may see an on-screen menu, as shown in the preceding figure. If you do see a menu, you can explore the menu options or simply click Play to get the movie going.

To see the movie display full-screen, click the Full Screen button in the bottom-right corner of the window. To return to a windowed view, press Esc.

WHAT'S NEXT?

Now that you've learned how to play sounds and video, you may be thinking about how to create your own multimedia. The next chapter deals with that topic.

Chapter 19

Creating Your Own Sounds and Videos

With Windows XP, you aren't limited to playing other people's music and videos—you can create your own. Many earlier versions of Windows included Sound Recorder for recording audio with a microphone, but Windows XP also has Windows Movie Maker, which takes audio and video recording and mixing to a new level.

Using Sound Recorder

Let's start by reviewing a venerable Windows accessory: the Sound Recorder. It enables you to record audio, such as your voice or ambient sounds such as rainfall or thunder, much like a portable cassette tape recorder. To do this, you must either have a built-in microphone on your PC (which is often the case with

Revised and adapted from *Windows XP Home Edition Simply Visual* by Faithe Wempen
ISBN 0-7821-2982-X 448 pages 24.99

laptops) or have a microphone attached to the Mic port on your sound card. Sound Recorder will also record any other sounds that your sound card is playing, so you could also use it to record CD music or streaming audio from the Internet–in theory, anyway. (There are better ways to record music from CDs, however, as you saw in Chapter 18.)

Once you have recorded a sound clip, you can attach it to a system event in Windows, you can include it in a Windows Movie Maker show (covered later in this chapter), you can play it as an audio clip in Windows Media Player (Chapter18), or you can use it in a variety of other ways. You can even attach it to an e-mail message and send it to a friend (Chapter 14).

Recording a New Sound Clip

To record a sound clip with Sound Recorder:

1. Choose Start ➢ All Programs ➢ Accessories ➢ Entertainment ➢ Sound Recorder.

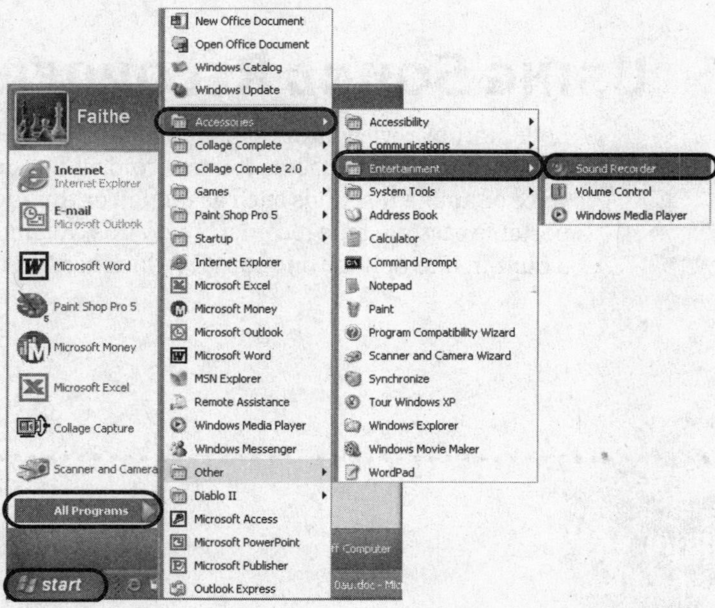

2. Make sure your microphone is plugged into your sound card's Mic port (not applicable on laptops with built-in mikes).

3. Click the Record button in the Sound Recorder window.

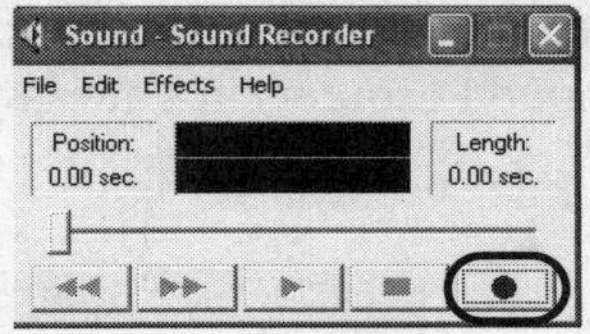

4. Speak, sing, or do whatever it is you want to do into the microphone.

5. When you are finished recording, click the Stop button.

TIP

Remember, to display a description of what any button does, simply point to it.

Playing Back a Recorded Clip

After recording a clip, you will probably want to test it before you save it, to make sure that your microphone worked okay and that the recording level was appropriate.

To play back a recorded clip:

1. Click the Play button in the Sound Recorder window.

2. (Optional) To play a different portion of the recording, drag the slider to the left or right, to skip forward or backward.

3. When the clip finishes playing, it stops automatically. To stop it early, click the Stop button.

If you don't like the clip you've recorded, simply re-record. Whatever you recorded already will be discarded.

Saving a Clip as a File

Once you have recorded a clip you like, you can save it as an audio file on your hard disk. Sound Recorder clips are saved in waveform (WAV) format.

1. Choose File ➢ Save.

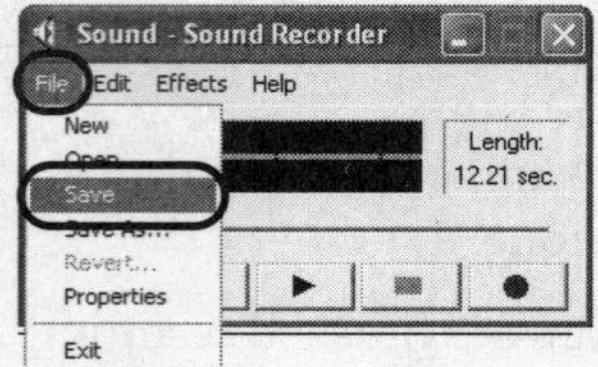

2. In the Save As dialog box, type a name for the clip in the File Name text box.
3. The default save location for sound clips recorded with Sound Recorder is My Documents. Change to a different save location if desired.
4. Click Save. The file is saved.

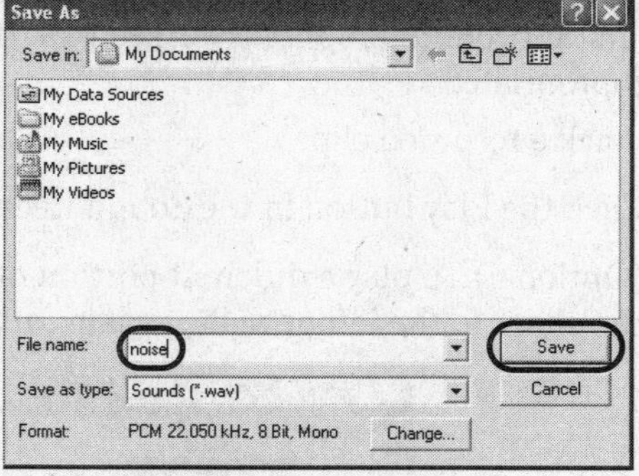

TIP

You can open files to play in Sound Recorder with the File ➢ Open command. You can also double-click sound files in a file management window to play them, but they will play in Windows Media Player rather than in Sound Recorder.

Sound Recorder is very simple—it only records audio. If you would like to record video or edit existing audio or video, try out Windows Movie Maker, which is the subject of the remainder of this chapter.

Introducing Windows Movie Maker

Windows Movie Maker helps you organize multimedia clips—that is, pictures, videos, soundtracks, voice narrations, and so on—into movies that you can play on your computer monitor, store on your hard disk, and e-mail to friends and family.

Suppose, for example, that you have video footage of little Tommy taking his first steps. You can hook up your video camera or VCR to your computer (with the right equipment, of course) and create a digital video clip from that footage. You can then edit that clip and combine it with a soundtrack and voice-over narration.

In order to use video footage, you need a way of getting it into your PC. One way is to buy a video interface device (Dazzle is one brand) that plugs into an open slot on your motherboard or connects to a port on your computer. Its purpose is to translate analog footage, such as from a video camera or VCR, into a digital file on your PC. Another way is to use a digital video camera to record the video directly. Such cameras typically come with their own interface for importing content into your PC, or they work with a FireWire (IEEE 1394) port that you buy and install separately.

A movie need not include video footage, however. If you have a scanner or digital camera, you can import still images from it, and you can also create a movie out of images you've acquired from other sources such as the Internet. A movie with still photos is somewhat like a slide show, with each image remaining on the screen for a few seconds (5 seconds is the default) and then being replaced by the next image.

The music for your movie soundtrack can come from a music clip stored on your hard disk. You can copy one from a CD-ROM, as you learned in Chapter 18, or use a clip that you have downloaded from a Web site.

If you have a sound card and a microphone, you can record voice narration for your movie. This is different from a soundtrack—it plays "on top of" the soundtrack at the same time. You can record your voice using Sound Recorder, as you learned at the beginning of the chapter, but Windows Movie Maker also has a built-in audio recorder that you might find more useful when trying to synchronize narration with video.

Here's a broad overview of the steps for creating a movie. I'll explain each of them in more detail in the remainder of the chapter.

1. Import the content for the movie into Windows Movie Maker collections. These collections are not movie-specific; they can be drawn from again and again.
2. Start a new movie, and arrange the video clips or still photos in the order in which you want them.
3. Add a soundtrack if desired.
4. Record voice narration if desired.
5. Preview your movie and then save it to your hard disk.

STARTING WINDOWS MOVIE MAKER

TIP

If a Welcome window appears, you can explore it to learn more about the program, or click Exit to bypass it.

To start Windows Movie Maker, choose Start ➢ All Programs ➢ Accessories ➢ Windows Movie Maker.

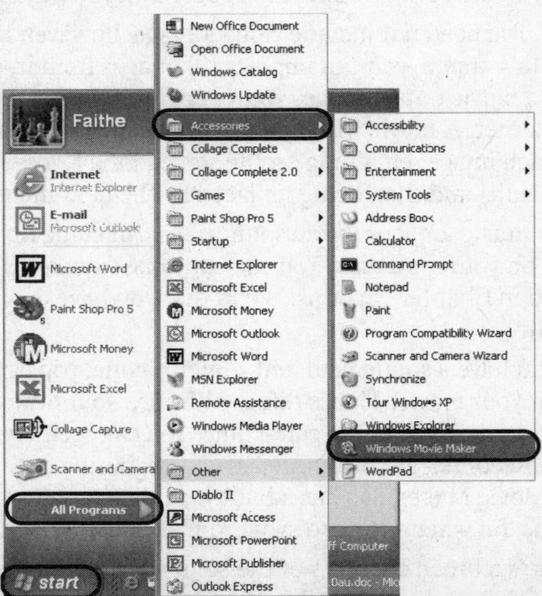

Creating Collections

You can save all your content in the same *collection*, or you can create different collections for each type of content, or for content on particular subjects. Collections are a lot like folders in a file management window.

To create a collection:

1. On the folder list, click the collection into which you want to place the new one. (By default, this is the top-level collection, called My Collections.)
2. Click the New Collection button (or choose File ➢ New ➢ Collection).

3. Type a name for the new collection and then press Enter.

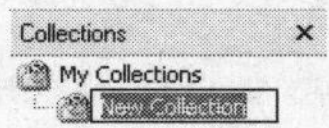

Now, whenever you are recording or importing content, simply make sure the desired collection is selected before you record or import, and the items will be placed in that collection.

WARNING

Before you create more collections, be sure to re-select My Collections. If you create a new collection with some other existing collection selected, the new collection will become subordinate to it, which is probably not what you want.

Recording New Content

You can record new content for your show right from within Windows Movie Maker. The recording process depends on what input devices you have.

Recording from a Video Camera

TIP

Digital video cameras need not be expensive. I'm using a $100 Intel PC Camera Pro that plugs into my USB port, and it works just fine with Windows Movie Maker. Its only drawback is that it must stay attached to the PC in order to function; I can't take it outside to capture footage.

With a digital video camera, you can feed directly into Windows Movie Maker from the camera. You can also take still pictures using your digital video camera, as you saw in Chapter 17.

If you have a regular video camera that records onto tape, you'll need some sort of interface device to connect it to your PC. It might work directly with Movie Maker, or it might require you to use the software that comes with the interface to first save the video to your hard disk. If that's the case, see the upcoming section "Importing Existing Content."

Configuring Your Video Camera

Before you record for the first time, you will want to select your video and audio source and configure the settings for your video camera. To do that:

1. Ensure that your video camera is connected to your PC and that your PC recognizes it. (See Chapter 17.)
2. In Windows Movie Maker, click the Record button (or choose File ➢ Record).
3. In the Record dialog box, open the Record drop-down list and choose what you want to record: Video Only or Video and Audio.

NOTE

If your video camera doesn't have any audio recording capability, as is the case with my Intel PC Camera Pro, Windows Movie Maker will use your computer's microphone to pick up the audio. Make sure your microphone is plugged in and ready.

4. Click the Change Device button.

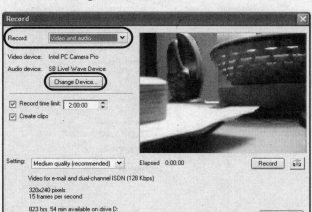

5. In the Change Device dialog box, if your video camera's name doesn't appear in the Video text box, open the drop-down list and select it.

6. If your sound card doesn't appear in the Audio box, open the drop-down list and select it.

7. Click the Configure button to configure the settings for your video camera.

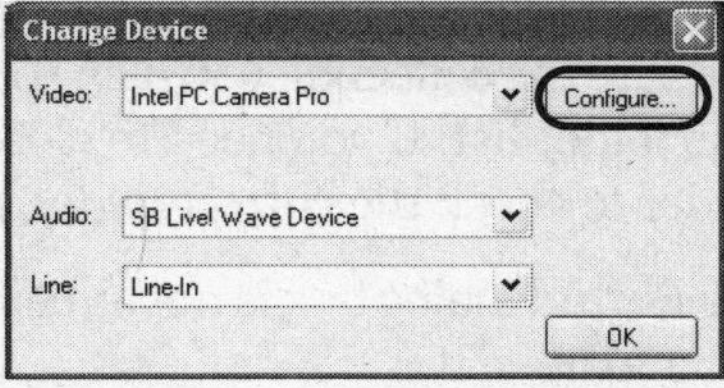

The Properties dialog box appears.

8. The settings for every model of video camera are different; the ones for my camera are shown in the following figure. Make any adjustments to the camera settings and then click OK.

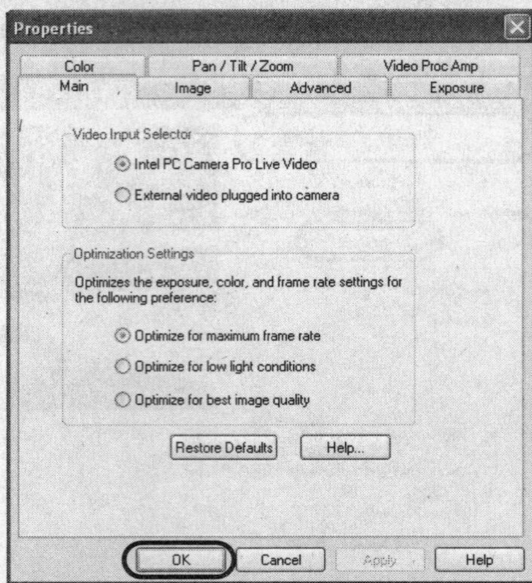

9. Back in the Change Device dialog box, click OK to close it.

From here, you can click Cancel if you are not ready to record yet, or go on to the next section.

Recording a Video Clip

After you initially set the properties for video recording, as you did in the preceding section, you shouldn't have to reset them every time you want to record a video clip. Instead, just do the following:

1. Make sure the collection to which you want to save is selected in the folder list. If you need to close the Record dialog box in order to check the correct folder, click Cancel.
2. If the Record dialog box is not already open, click the Record button to open it.
3. If you want to limit the size of the clip being recorded, make sure the Record Time Limit check box is marked, and enter the time limit in its text box. The default is 2 hours.
4. If you want the video feed broken into separate clips every time it detects a different frame (such as when you turn the camera on or turn off the Pause feature), make sure the Create Clips check box is marked. Otherwise, the entire video feed will be stored in a single clip.

5. The default quality is Medium. If you want a different quality, open the Setting drop-down list and choose one. Higher quality will record more frames per second but will take up more storage space on your hard disk; it will also take longer to transmit when you e-mail the movie to someone later.

6. When you are ready to record, click the Record button. (Or, if you want to take a still photo with the camera instead of recording motion video, click the Take Photo button instead—it's to the right of the Record button—and then skip to step 8.)

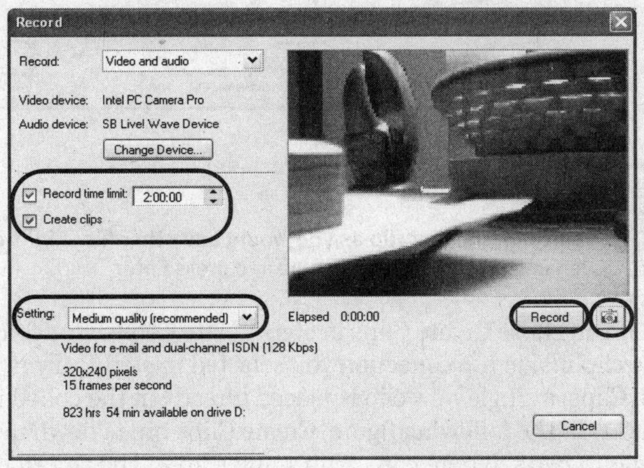

NOTE

Video clips are saved in WMV (Windows Media Video) format; still photos are saved in JPG format.

7. When you are finished recording, click the Stop button.

8. In the Save Windows Media File dialog box, enter a filename in the File Name box. For example, here I'm calling my clip "Office Tour" because I'm recording a video of my office area.

9. Click Save. The clip is saved.

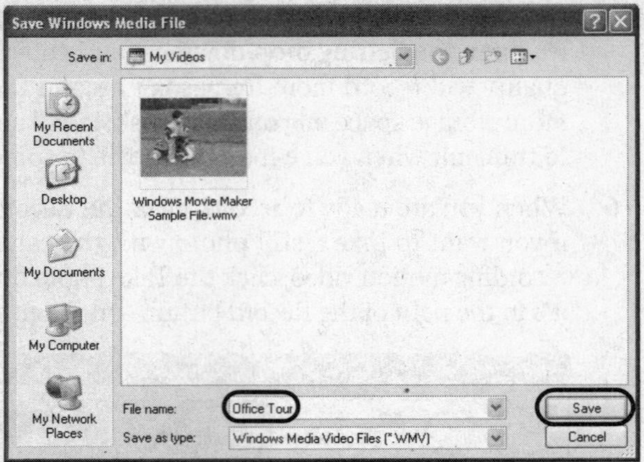

NOTE

You can rename a clip as you would any other file: Right-click it and choose Rename; then type a new name and press Enter.

If you chose Create Clips in step 4, a new collection folder is created for the clip inside the collection you selected in step 1. If you didn't use Create Clips, a single new clip is placed directly in the collection selected in step 1. In the following figure, Create Clips broke down my single recording into two separate clips, Clip 1 and Clip 2. The fact that the video is split isn't a problem, because when you assemble the movie, you can place the clips adjacent to one another so that the movie will appear to be one continuous video piece. Splitting merely adds flexibility to the movie-assembly process.

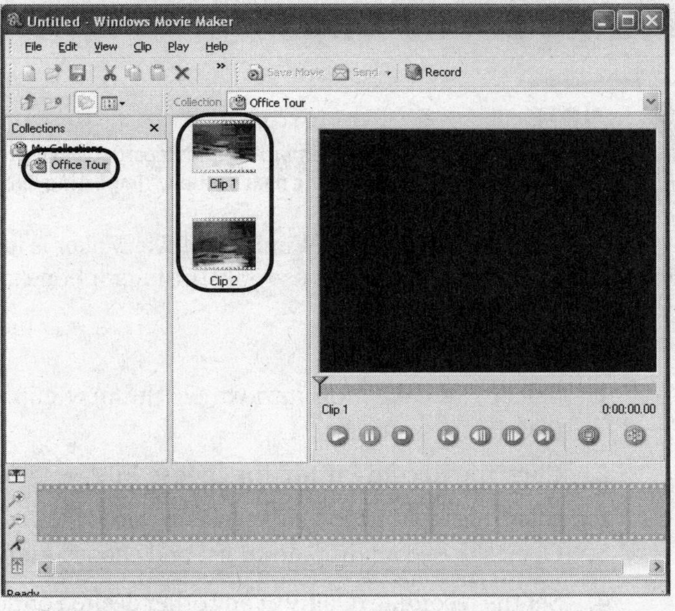

Playing Back a Video Clip

To check out the video clip you recorded, click it and then click the Play button. It plays in the preview pane to the right. Each clip plays separately, even if all the clips were recorded at once. Use the play controls beneath the preview pane to control the clip, just as in Windows Media Player (Chapter 18). You can drag the slider to skip forward or backward in the clip.

Splitting a Video Clip Manually

In addition to using the automatic splits that Windows Movie Maker creates as it records, you can also manually split a video clip into one or more separate clips. To do so, play the clip, and at the desired split point, click the Split button. You can do this with clips you record and also with imported clips from other sources. (See the later section "Importing Existing Content.")

Recording Sound Clips

NOTE

You can also record sound clips with Sound Recorder and then import them into Windows Movie Maker. See the next section, "Importing Existing Content."

Recording a sound clip with Windows Movie Maker is just like recording a video clip, except that you use only the microphone and you set the recording to Audio Only.

To record a sound clip:

1. Select the collection into which the new clip should be placed.
2. Click the Record button (or choose File ➢ Record). The Record dialog box opens.
3. Open the Record drop-down list and choose Audio Only.
4. Set the recording quality or any other desired options, as you did with video.
5. Click the Record button, and begin speaking or making noise into the microphone.

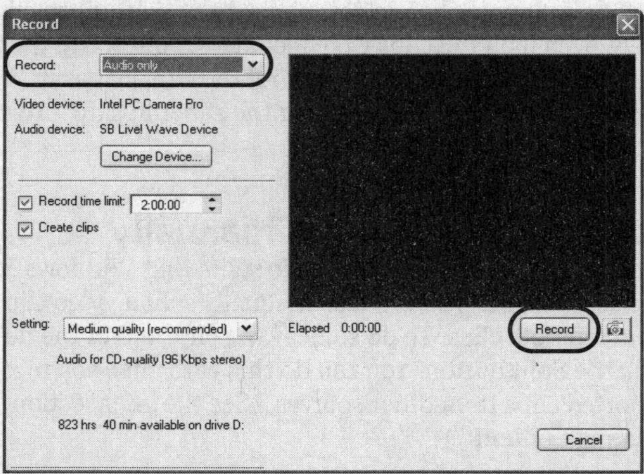

6. Click the Stop button when finished.

7. In the Save Windows Media File dialog box, enter the filename you want to use. The file will be saved in WMA (Windows Media Audio) format.

8. Click Save. The clip is created and placed in the selected collection.

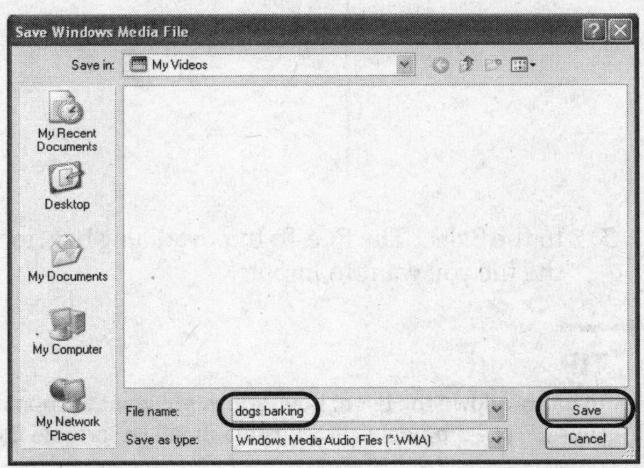

Importing Existing Content

You can import existing videos, music, sounds, still images, and music files into your collections.

Importing existing content is the same regardless of the content's format. Windows Movie Maker accepts content in a wide variety of formats, including all popular digital video formats such as MPEG, WMV, and AVI. It also accepts many sound and graphic file formats.

To import content:

1. Select the collection into which you want to import.

2. Choose File ➢ Import.

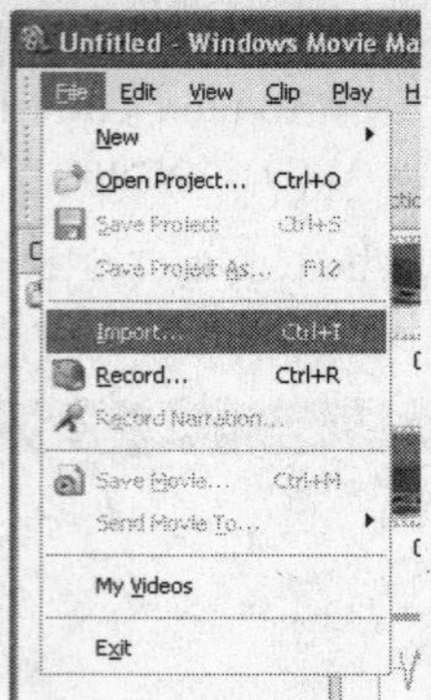

3. In the Select The File To Import dialog box, locate and select the file you want to import.

TIP

To narrow down the list of files, you might want to choose a file type from the Files of Type drop-down list. By default, all importable files are shown.

4. Click Open to import the file.

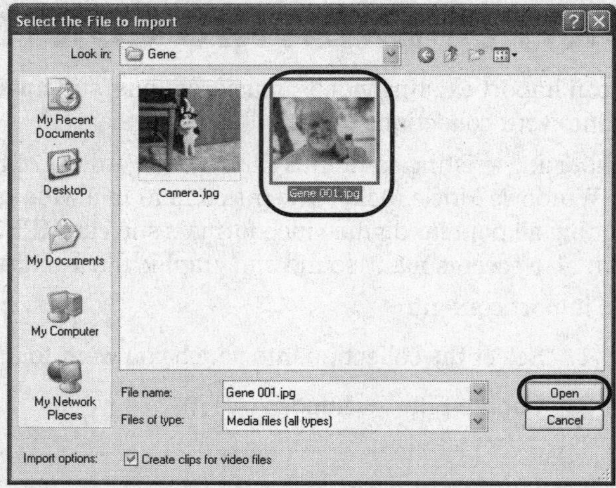

If you find that you accidentally imported the file into the wrong collection, you can easily drag it to another collection, just as you do when managing files in Windows Explorer.

Creating a Movie Project

Now that you have imported or recorded the content for your movie, you are ready to start assembling it in a *project*, which you'll save in Windows Movie Maker.

What's the difference between a movie and a project? Well, when you "publish" the project as a movie, you create a read-only copy that you can never edit again; that's why it's important to save the project as well as the movie. Projects continue to be editable, so you can always make changes and republish the movie whenever you are ready to reflect those changes.

You can assemble a project in any order, but I like to start with the visual images (video clips and still photos) and then add the soundtrack. Finally, as the last step, I add the voice narration.

Starting a New Project

A new, blank project starts when you start Movie Maker, but you can create a new project at any time by doing the following:

1. Click the New Project button (or choose File ➢ New Project).
2. If prompted to save the changes to the existing project, click Yes or No and save (or not) as appropriate.

Understanding Project Views

There are two views of the project: Storyboard and Timeline. *Storyboard view* shows pictures only; each video clip is represented by a picture of the first frame of the video. Each clip takes up the same one-frame space on the storyboard, regardless of its actual length.

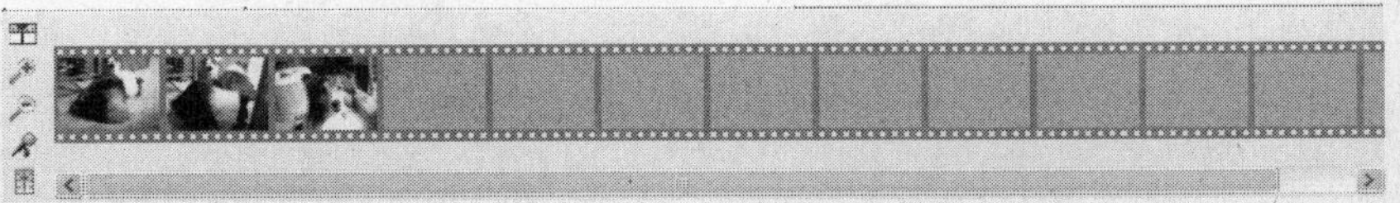

NOTE

You can add audio clips to Timeline view only. If you attempt to drop an audio clip on the storyboard, a message appears, telling you that it is switching to Timeline view; click OK to continue.

Timeline view, in contrast, shows each visual clip's size according to the amount of time it will occupy in the movie. And beneath the pictures runs a soundtrack line indicating what sounds will be heard while the pictures are appearing.

To switch between Storyboard and Timeline views, you can use the View menu or click the buttons to the left of the project area. When in Timeline view, to switch to Storyboard, click the Storyboard button. When in Storyboard view, to switch to Timeline, click the Timeline button.

Adding Clips to the Project

Start your project by dragging pictures or video clips from your various collections into the project timeline or storyboard at the bottom of the screen. Simply drag and drop, as you have learned in file management.

To remove a clip from the project, click it on the timeline or storyboard and then press the Delete key.

To move the clip around on the project, drag it to the left or right.

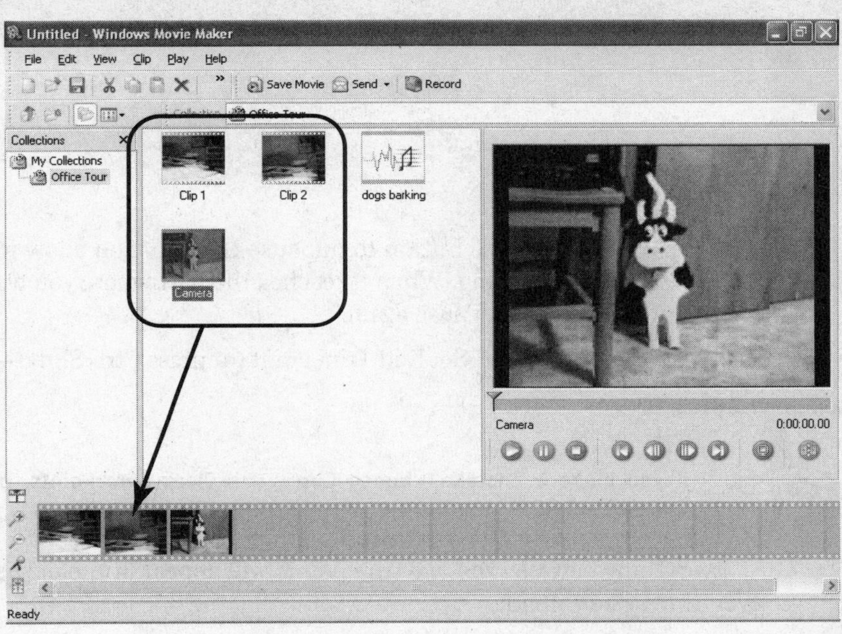

Setting Trim Points for a Video Clip

If you want to use only a portion of a video clip, you have a couple of options. You can split the clip and then use only one of the split portions (see "Splitting a Video Clip Manually" earlier in this chapter), or you can trim the clip. Trimming is active only for the current project, whereas splitting splits the clip in the collection, where it will continue to be split if you use it later in another project.

To set the trim points for a clip, do the following:

1. Add the clip to the project, either on the storyboard or on the timeline.
2. Make sure the clip is selected (again, on the storyboard or the timeline).
3. Click the Play button beneath the preview pane, and when the clip reaches the part where you want it to begin, click the Pause button.
4. Choose Clip ➢ Set Start Trim Point (or press Ctrl+Shift+←).

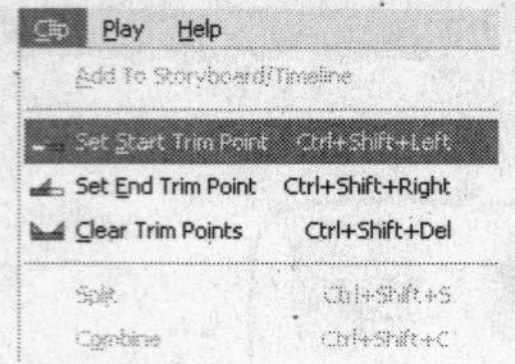

5. Click the Pause button to unpause the clip, and allow it to continue playing. When it reaches the part where you want it to end, click Pause again.
6. Choose Clip ➢ Set End Trim Point (or press Ctrl+Shift+→).

TIP

If you make a mistake, choose Clip ➢ Clear Trim Points, or press Ctrl+Shift+Delete.

Everything between the two trim points will appear in the movie; everything else will not.

Changing the Duration of a Still Image

When you import a photo into a collection, it is assigned a default duration. The original setting is 5 seconds, but you can change the default duration by choosing View ➢ Options and entering a different value in the Default Imported Photo Duration box.

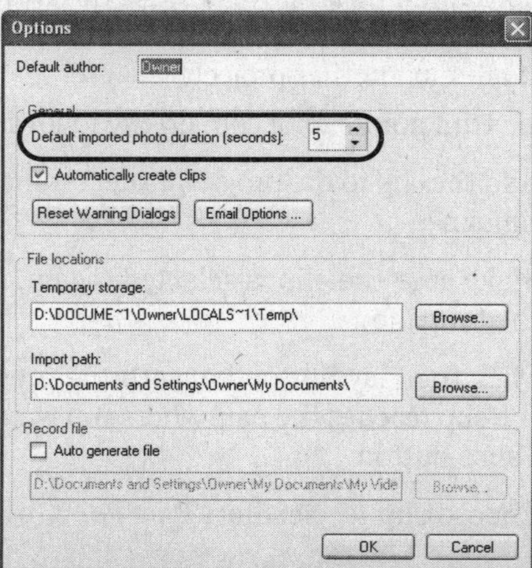

The photo's default duration, however, is always the setting that was in effect when it was imported. So, for example, if you import a photo when the Default Imported Photo Duration is set to 5 seconds, and you later change that setting to 10 seconds, all photos you imported prior to the change will remain with 5-second durations.

You can change a still picture's duration on the timeline in an individual project, however. Do the following:

1. View the project in Timeline view.
2. Click the picture for which you want to change the duration. (Make sure you choose a still photo, not a video clip.) Trim handles (triangles) appear above it.
3. Drag the ending trim handle (the one on the right) to the left to make the picture appear for fewer seconds, or to the right to make it appear longer.

If the picture was not at the end of the project and you increased its duration, the picture to its right may now be partially overlapped or obscured. Select that picture and then drag its beginning trim handle (the one on its left) so that the two pictures don't overlap anymore. Repeat to the end of the project timeline.

Creating Transitions

TIP

Windows Movie Maker doesn't allow you to choose between different transition effects. If that is an important feature to you, and you are working with still images only, try a program like PowerPoint for assembling your presentation.

You saw in the preceding section that it's possible to overlap two objects on the timeline. When you overlap objects, you create a transition effect between them, so that one fades into the other. It's a pretty neat effect and certainly looks better than simply replacing one image with the next.

To create a transition effect, simply make the clips overlap slightly. You already saw how to adjust a clip's trim in the preceding section. Select the clip on the timeline and then drag its left (beginning) handle to the left so that it overlaps with the previous clip slightly.

TIP

As you create transition effects, you might find it helpful to zoom in. Use the plus (+) and minus (–) buttons to the left of the timeline to zoom in or out on the project.

Adding Sound and Narration

Now that the visual part of your movie is assembled, it's time to work on music and narration. If the video you recorded included sound, it will automatically be included with the video footage. In the following sections, you'll learn how to add *additional* sounds and music.

Adding a Musical Soundtrack

To include a soundtrack, add a CD or other music clip to a collection and then drag it onto the timeline. If you are not already in Timeline view, the view switches for you automatically.

You can trim the soundtrack as you trim any other object. Select it; then drag its trim handles, or trim it by playing it and setting start and end trim points as you learned to do for videos earlier.

Recording Narration

After you've finalized the duration of each clip, you're ready to record your narration. You won't want to record it earlier, because if the durations of the clips change, the narration will be off.

To record narration:

1. Prepare your microphone and ensure that it's working.

2. Switch to Timeline view if you aren't already there.

3. Click the Record Narration button to the left of the timeline (or choose File ➢ Record Narration). The Record Narration Track dialog box appears.

4. If the device and line are not correct as shown, click the Change button and select the correct ones. The device should be your sound card, and the line should be the one into which your microphone is plugged (probably Microphone).

5. If you want to mute the video's regular audio track while the narration is speaking, mark the Mute Video Soundtrack check box. Otherwise, the two will play on top of one another.

6. Adjust the recording level using the Record Level slider if desired. Speak into the microphone and use the meter next to the slider as your guide.

7. When you are ready, click Record.

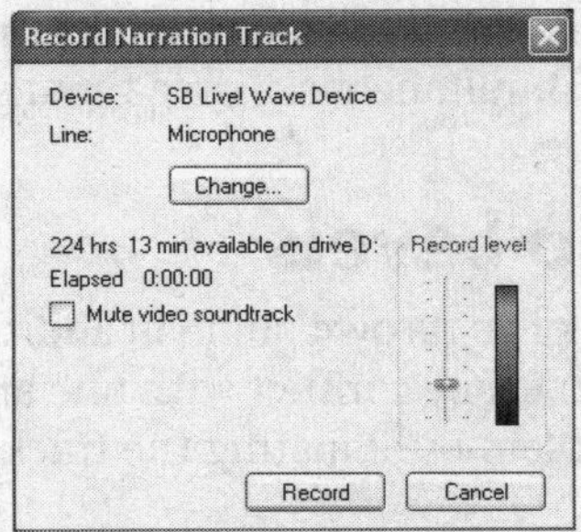

Your movie begins showing in the preview pane, and the Record button becomes a Stop button.

8. Speak into the microphone, narrating as you go along. When you are finished, click Stop.

9. In the Save dialog box that appears, enter a filename for the narration track and then click Save.

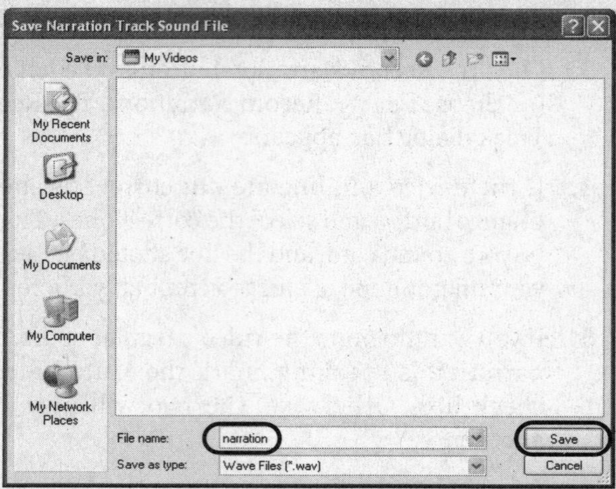

The track is saved in WAV format, like sounds recorded in Sound Recorder.

If you previously assigned a musical soundtrack, you might find that the narration has forced the soundtrack to move over on the timeline. To have them play simultaneously, drag them so that they overlap.

Setting Audio Levels

If the video track has its own audio in addition to the audio tracks you are adding, they can easily conflict with one another unattractively. You can fix this problem by adjusting the tracks so that one or the other is dominant.

To do so:

1. Switch to Timeline view if you aren't already there.
2. Click the Adjust Audio Level button next to the timeline (or choose Edit ➢ Audio Levels).
3. In the Audio Levels dialog box, drag the slider toward Video Track for a louder video track, or toward Audio Track for a louder soundtrack/narration.
4. Click the Close button on the dialog box to close it.

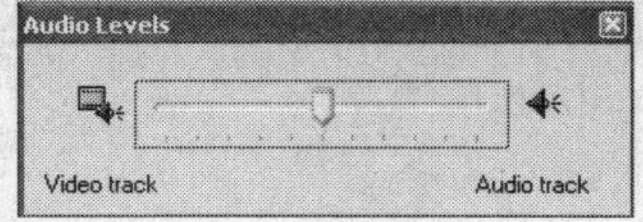

Previewing the Movie

Before you publish the movie (that is, save the project in movie format), you will want to preview it to make sure everything is as you want it to be.

To preview the movie in the preview pane, simply click the Play button while the first clip of the project is selected in the timeline or storyboard.

To view it full-screen, click the Full Screen button beneath the preview pane (or choose Play ➢ Full Screen).

Saving the Movie

Ready to save your project in movie format? First, save your project as a project. Remember, you can't make changes to a published movie, so if you want to change it, you'll need to make the changes to the project and then republish. To save your project, choose File ➢ Save (or click the Save button on the toolbar), and save as you would any other data file in a program.

Now you're ready to publish your movie! To do so:

1. Choose File ➢ Save Movie.

2. In the Save Movie dialog box, choose a quality from the Setting drop-down list. The default is Medium.

3. (Optional) Enter any information desired in the Display Information area.

TIP

If you will be distributing the movie via the Internet, keep the quality at Medium or lower to keep the file size small. If you will be distributing it on a CD or playing the movie on your own PC, and you have plenty of disk space, use a higher quality. You can check the file size in the File Size area of the dialog box.

4. Click OK.

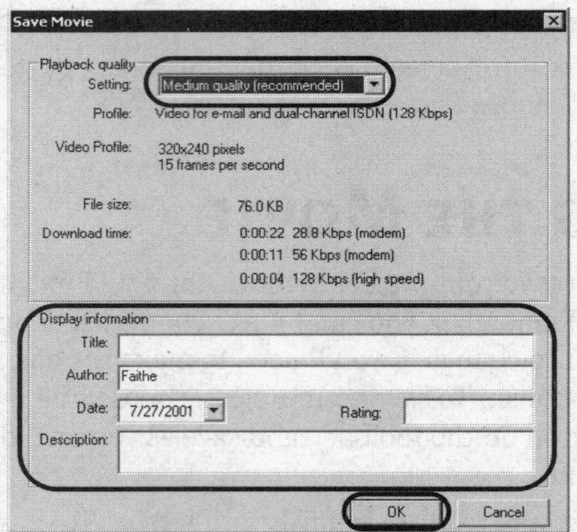

5. In the Save As dialog box, enter a filename for your movie in the File Name text box.
6. Click Save. Your movie is saved.
7. A prompt asks whether you want to watch the movie now. If you click Yes, it will play in Windows Media Player. If you choose No, you return to Windows Movie Maker.

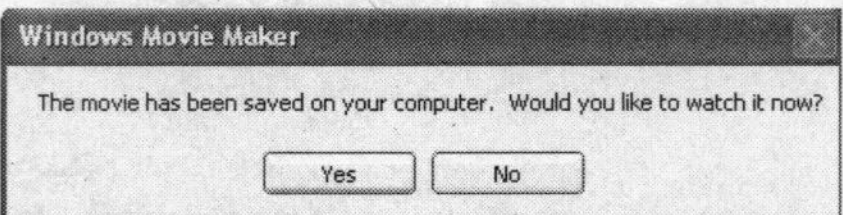

WHAT'S NEXT?

If your computer system includes a writable CD drive, you'll be pleased to know that you can now burn CDs directly from Windows XP. The next chapter walks you through this process in detail.

Chapter 20
Burning CDs

From being an exotic, expensive, and erratically performing technological marvel in the mid-1990s, the recordable CD has progressed to being the most convenient and most cost-effective backup and file-transfer medium for the early 2000s. Recordable CDs now hold up to 700MB of data and can be burned in as little as four minutes. So it should perhaps come as no surprise that Windows XP improves on previous versions of Windows by offering CD-writing capability built into the operating system. This chapter discusses how to use those features, how to choose a CD rewriter drive if you don't have one, and how to choose recordable CD media.

Revised and adapted from *Mastering Windows XP Home Edition* by Guy Hart-Davis

ISBN 0-7821-2980-3 1024 pages $39.99

CD-Recording Basics

To record CDs, you need a CD recorder or a CD rewriter. If you have one, you're all set to record CDs. If you don't have one, see the next sidebar for advice on choosing a CD rewriter.

You also need media–blank recordable CDs or rewritable CDs. The next section discusses those.

EXPERT KNOWLEDGE: CHOOSING A CD REWRITER

Because of its value for backup and file transfer, a CD rewriter is almost indispensable nowadays. Many new PCs—including some high-end laptops—have built-in CD rewriters. If your PC doesn't have a CD rewriter and you want to get one, this sidebar explains what you need to know.

You'll notice that this sidebar discusses CD rewriters rather than CD recorders. That's because CD rewriters have become so ubiquitous and come down so far in price that they've essentially replaced plain old CD recorders. (If you missed CD recorders: The difference between CD recorders and CD rewriters is that CD recorders could write only once to any given disc, whereas CD rewriters can write either once or multiple times to the same disc. If you'd like the acronyms, CD-R discs are *Write Once, Read Multiple* media—*WORM* for short—while CD-RW discs are *Write And Read Multiple* or *WARM* media.)

These are the main considerations for choosing a CD rewriter:

Speed CD rewriter speed is measured by the same rating system as regular old read-only CD drives: 1X, 2X, 4X, and so on. Each X represents 150Kbps (the nominal read rate of the first CD drives), so a 4X drive chugs through 600Kbps, an 8X drive handles 1200Kbps (1.2Mbps), a 12X drive manages 1800Kbps (1.8Mbps), a 16X drive burns 2400Kbps (2.4Mbps), a 20X drive blazes through 3000Kbps (3Mbps), and a 24X drive incinerates 3600Kbps (3.6Mbps).

CD rewriter speed keeps on improving. At this writing, 24X drives are just beginning to appear. These drives can burn a full CD in 4 minutes (other constraints, such as the speed of your system, permitting). 16X drives are more reasonably priced; they can burn a full CD in 5 minutes. 12X drives are starting to look like old

CONTINUED →

technology, though in 2000 they were state of the art; they can burn a full CD in around 6 minutes. 8X drives take about 9 minutes; 6X drives take about 12 minutes; and 4X drives take about 18 minutes.

Those speeds are for the initial writing to the CD. On high-speed drives, the rewriting speeds are typically considerably slower than the writing speeds. For example, a drive might write at 24X but rewrite at 12X, and a 12X drive might rewrite at only 4X. By contrast, slower drives (for example, 4X) may rewrite at the same speed as they write.

CD rewriter speeds are given with the write speed first, the rewrite speed second, and the read speed third. For example, a 24×12×40 drive is one that writes at 24X, rewrites at 12X, and reads at 40X.

As you can see, the higher speed ratings don't translate as directly into a speed gain as the lower speeds do. That's because, no matter how fast the drive is able to burn the CD, there's some overhead in creating the file system on the CD and wrapping up the writing process. So until prices on 24X (or faster) and 16X drives come down, there's little advantage in buying them over buying 12X drives.

CD rewriters almost invariably read data at a faster rate than they write it. Some CD recorders now read up to 32X, making them almost as fast as a dedicated CD drive. Even so, unless you're out of drive bays or ports, look to add a CD recorder to your computer rather than replace your existing CD drive with a CD recorder. That way, you'll be able to duplicate a CD (assuming that you have the right to do so) or install Quake at the same time as listening to music.

Internal or external? Generally speaking, an internal drive will cost you less than an external drive, but you'll need to have a drive bay free in your computer. An external drive will usually cost more, will occupy space on your desk, and will need its own power supply. In addition, most external drives are much noisier

CONTINUED ⟶

than internal drives because they contain their own fans. But if your main computer is a notebook, or if you want to be able to move the drive from computer to computer without undue effort, you'll need an external drive.

EIDE drives are all internal. SCSI drives can be internal or external. Because the parallel port, the USB ports, and any FireWire ports are external connections, almost all of these drives are external only. (You can find internal FireWire CD-R drives if you look hard enough.)

EIDE, SCSI, parallel port, USB, or FireWire? If you have a SCSI card in your computer, you'll probably want to get a SCSI CD recorder, because it will typically perform better *and* put much less burden on the processor than an EIDE CD recorder will. SCSI drives are usually more expensive than EIDE drives of the same speed, but if your computer's already got SCSI, the extra cost is probably worth it. If you need to copy CDs, bear in mind that most SCSI CD recorders will copy CDs directly only from other SCSI drives, not from EIDE drives. If you have a SCSI CD recorder and an EIDE CD drive, you'll need to copy the CD to the hard disk and then burn it to CD from there.

If you don't have SCSI and want an internal drive, or if your CD player is EIDE and you want to do a lot of CD-to-CD duplicating, choose EIDE. Before you buy, make sure that you have an EIDE connector available on your computer. If it's already chock-full of drives (most modern machines can take four EIDE devices), you won't be able to add another without sacrificing an existing one.

If you're looking at an external non-SCSI drive, your current choices are a parallel-port drive, a USB drive, or a FireWire drive. Parallel-port drives perform so slowly—2X at best—that they're barely worth using. USB drives using the USB 1.0 standard are only a bit better—they're limited to 4X speeds by the limitations of USB. (USB 2.0 drives, when they arrive, will be much faster.) FireWire drives offer full speed and great convenience, but if your computer doesn't have a FireWire card, you'll need to add one. (You can get FireWire PCI cards for $100 or so and FireWire PC Cards for a few dollars more.)

Recordable CDs and Rewritable CDs

CDs on which you can record data come in two basic types:

CD-R discs CD-R discs, usually referred to as *recordable CDs*, are CDs that you can record data to only once. Once you finish recording data, you cannot change the information on the disc. Regular CD-R discs hold 650MB, the same amount as a standard audio CD. (650MB holds 74 minutes of uncompressed audio.) Extended-capacity CD-R discs hold 700MB, a small increase that's worth having if you don't have to pay extra for it. 700MB holds 80 minutes of uncompressed audio.

CD-RW discs CD-RW discs, usually referred to as *rewritable CDs*, are CDs that you can record data to multiple times. You can record data to the CD in multiple recording sessions until it is full. You can then erase all the data from the CD and use it again. CD-RW discs specify a theoretical safe maximum number of times that you can reuse them, but if you like your data, you'd be wise not to push them that far. CD-RW discs hold 650MB. CD-RW discs are more expensive than CD-R discs.

To simplify (or perhaps complicate) the terminology, Windows uses the term *writable CD* to refer to recordable and rewritable discs. This isn't a standard term, but it now seems destined to become one.

EXPERT KNOWLEDGE: CHOOSING CD-R AND CD-RW MEDIA

When buying CD-R and CD-RW discs, you need to balance economy with quality. Beware of cheapo discs, because they may give you skips and errors—or even lose your precious music or data. If you can, buy a few discs for testing before you buy a quantity that you'll regret if they're not up to snuff.

One way to save some money is to buy CD-R and CD-RW discs without jewel cases. This makes for a good discount, as the jewel cases are relatively expensive to manufacture and bulky to package (and easy to break, as you no doubt know from personal experience). The discs are typically sold on a spindle, which makes for handy storage until you use them—after which you'll have to find safe

CONTINUED ➞

storage for them on your own. (One possibility is a CD wallet, which can be especially handy if you need to take your CDs with you when you travel. If you buy one, make sure it has soft pockets that won't scratch the CDs as you insert them, and sweep out travel grit frequently.)

For the faster drives, you may need to buy CD-R or CD-RW media designed for use in faster drives. For example, at this writing most 24X drives request (or perhaps require) discs rated at 24X, suggesting that regular (and less expensive) discs will have too many errors to use. Your mileage will vary depending on your discs and your drive, but it's worth testing less expensive discs to see how they perform in a fast drive. If the drive ends up burning at 20X instead of 24X, you lose all of 30 seconds. Unless you're holding your breath for the duration of the burning, you're unlikely to notice the difference.

Audio CDs and Data CDs

Broadly speaking, CDs divide into two categories:

Audio CDs Audio CDs contain uncompressed audio in pulse code modulation (PCM) format. (PCM files are essentially WAV files with different header information at the beginning of the file.) They can be read by both audio CD players and CD-ROM drives. Audio CDs don't have names, though pressed audio CDs are identified by an ID number linked to the artist and the work.

Data CDs Data CDs can contain any file type. They can be read by CD-ROM drives but not by audio CD players. Data CDs can have names up to 16 characters long.

WARNING

Because CD-RW discs use a different technology than regular CD-ROMs, they're not as compatible with all CD-ROM drives. If you want to share a CD with someone else, a CD-R disc is a better bet than a CD-RW disc. Likewise, only the most recent audio players can play CD-RW discs, whereas most audio players can play only pressed audio CDs and audio CD-R discs.

Configuring a Recordable CD Drive

Before you try to burn a CD, it's a good idea to check the settings that Windows has chosen for your CD recorder or CD rewriter. You may want to tweak the configuration or change the drive used for holding temporary files when burning a CD on the Desktop.

To configure a recordable CD drive, follow these steps:

1. Choose Start ➢ My Computer. Windows opens an Explorer window showing My Computer.
2. Right-click the CD drive and choose Properties from the shortcut menu. Windows displays the Properties dialog box for the drive.
3. Click the Recording tab, which is shown in Figure 20.1.

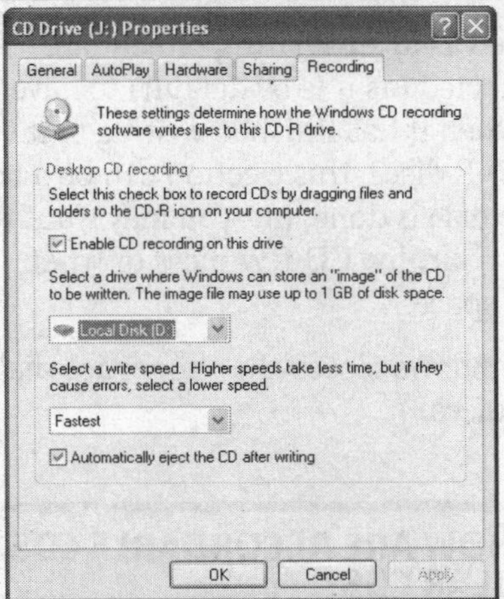

FIGURE 20.1: Check the configuration of your drive on the Recording tab of its Properties dialog box.

4. Choose settings that meet your needs:

   Enable CD Recording on This Drive check box Select this check box to use this drive for recording. Windows lets you use only one drive at a time for recording. This check box is selected by default on the first recordable CD drive on your system and cleared by default on subsequent recordable CD drives.

Select a Drive drop-down list In this drop-down list, select the drive on which Windows should store an *image* of the CD (temporary files containing the data to be written to the CD) when creating the CD. Windows commandeers up to 1GB of space on the drive for a high-capacity CD, so make sure the disc you choose has more than that amount available. (For a standard CD, Windows needs around 700MB of space.)

Select a Write Speed drop-down list In this drop-down list, you can specify the speed that Windows should use when recording a CD. The default setting is Fastest—the highest speed your drive supports. If Fastest doesn't give good results, try the next lower rate. Windows automatically adjusts this speed to match the speed of the current disc, so you may not need to change it manually.

Automatically Eject the CD after Writing check box Leave this check box selected (as it is by default) to have Windows eject the CD when it has finished writing to it. When you're burning CD-R discs, this ejection can be a useful visual signal that the disc is done, but you may want to disable this option when burning CD-RW discs or when using a laptop in a tight space.

5. Click the OK button. Windows closes the Properties dialog box and applies your choices.

EXPERT KNOWLEDGE: HOW ARE RECORDABLE CDS DIFFERENT FROM REGULAR CDS?

If you've looked at CD-R or CD-RW discs, you'll know that most of them look very different from prerecorded audio or data CDs (*pressed* CDs). Depending on their make and type, CD-R and CD-RW discs may have a gold, green, or bluish coating on their data side. Typically, this is a polycarbonate substrate over a reflective layer of 24-carat gold or a silver-colored alloy.

CONTINUED →

Information is transferred to CD-R and CD-RW discs by a different process than for pressed CDs. While pressed CDs are pressed in a mold from a master CD, CD recorders and CD rewriters use a laser to burn the information onto the CD-R or CD-RW media. Pressed CDs use physically raised areas called *lands* and lowered areas called *pits* to store the encoded data. Recordable CDs have a dye layer in which the laser burns marks that have the same reflective properties as the lands and pits. To be pedantic, the laser doesn't actually *burn* anything, but it heats the dye layer to produce the marks. But because the term is not only evocative but also distinguishes from the CD-recording that music artists do, it has stuck: CD recorders and rewriters are widely referred to as *CD burners*, and people speak of *burning a CD*.

Not only do CD-R and CD-RW discs look different from pressed CDs, but they're also less robust. You can damage them more easily with extreme heat and moderate cold, by scratching or gouging them, or by leaving them in direct sunlight. The data is actually stored closer to the label side of the CD than to the business side, so if you're compelled to scratch one side of the CD, go for the business side over the label side.

Burning CDs from Explorer

Burning CDs from Explorer is an easy three-step process:

1. Copy the files to the storage area.
2. Check the files in the storage area to make sure that they're the right files and that there aren't too many of them.
3. Write the files to CD.

Copying the Files to the Storage Area

The first step in burning files (or folders) to CD is to copy them to the storage area. You can do so in several ways, of which these three are usually the easiest:

- Select the files in an Explorer window or in a common dialog box. Then right-click in the selection and choose Send To ➢ CD Drive from the shortcut menu. (Alternatively, choose File ➢ Send To ➢ CD Drive.) This technique is the most convenient when you're working in Explorer or in a common dialog box.
- Drag the files and drop them on the CD drive in an Explorer window or on a shortcut to the CD drive. For example, you could keep a shortcut to the CD drive on your Desktop so that you could quickly drag files and folders to it. This technique is good for copying to CD files or folders that you keep on your Desktop.
- Open an Explorer window to the storage area, and then drag files to it and drop them there. This technique is mostly useful for adding files when you're checking the contents of the storage area. When you insert a blank CD in your CD drive, Windows displays a CD Drive dialog box offering to open a folder to the writable CD folder.

When you take one of these actions, Windows copies the files to the storage area and displays a notification area pop-up telling you that you have files waiting to be written to the CD.

Either click the pop-up or (if it has disappeared) open a My Computer window and double-click the icon for the CD drive. Windows opens an Explorer window showing the storage area, which appears as a list called Files Ready to Be Written to the CD. (For a CD-RW that already contains files, the storage area also contains a list of Files Currently on the CD.) Figure 20.2 shows an example of the storage area. As you can see in the figure, Windows displays a downward-pointing arrow on the icon for each file or folder to indicate that it's a temporary file destined to be burned to CD and then disposed of.

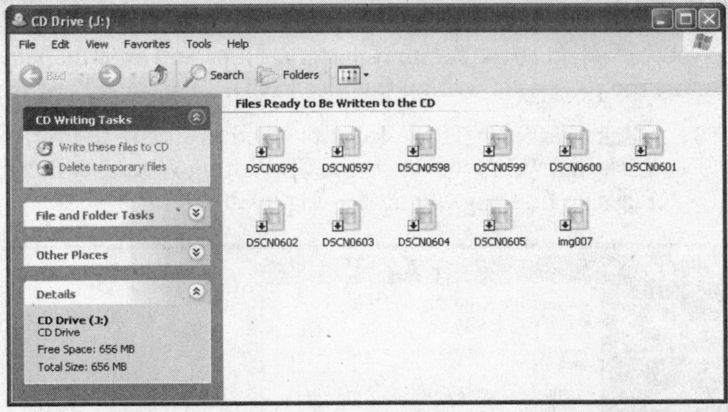

FIGURE 20.2: The storage area holds the copies of files to be burned to the CD. The downward-pointing arrow on each file icon and folder icon indicates that the item is temporary and will be deleted after being burned to CD.

While Windows copies the files, the CD drive will appear to be busy, but it won't actually be writing any information to CD yet.

Checking the Files in the Storage Area

Once you've copied to the storage area all the files that you want to burn to the CD, activate the window that Explorer opened to the storage area and check that the files are all there, that you don't want to remove any of them, and that there aren't too many to fit on the CD. (If you closed the window showing the storage area, you can display the storage area again by opening an Explorer window to My Computer and double-clicking the icon for the CD drive.)

NOTE

By default, the storage area is located in the `\Local Settings\Application Data\Microsoft\CD Burning\` folder under the folder for your account in the `\Documents and Settings\` folder.

To check the size of files in the storage area, select them all (for example, by choosing Edit ➢ Select All), and then right-click and choose Properties from the shortcut menu. Windows displays the Properties dialog box for the files. Check the Size readout on the General tab.

Writing the Files to CD

Once you've looked at the files in the storage area and are satisfied all is well, start the process of writing the files to CD. Take the following steps:

1. Click the Write These Files to CD link in the CD Writing Tasks list. Windows starts the CD Writing Wizard, which displays its first page (shown in Figure 20.3).

FIGURE 20.3: On the first page of the CD Writing Wizard, specify the name for the CD and choose whether the Wizard should close itself when the CD is finished.

2. Enter the name for the CD in the CD Name text box. CD names can be a maximum of 16 characters.
3. If you want the Wizard to close itself when the CD is finished, select the Close the Wizard after the Files Have Been Written check box. If you select this check box, you won't have the option of creating another CD containing the same files, because the Wizard automatically clears the storage area.
4. Click the Next button. The CD Writing Wizard displays the page shown in Figure 20.4 as it burns the CD. The burning goes through three stages: Adding Data to the CD Image, Writing the Data Files to the CD, and Performing Final Steps to Make the CD Ready to Use.

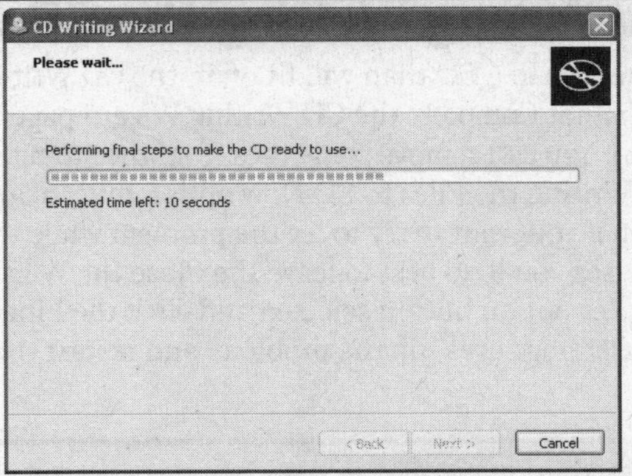

FIGURE 20.4: The CD Writing Wizard shows you its progress in burning the CD.

5. When the Wizard has finished burning the CD, it displays the Completing the CD Writing Wizard page (shown in Figure 20.5) and ejects the CD.

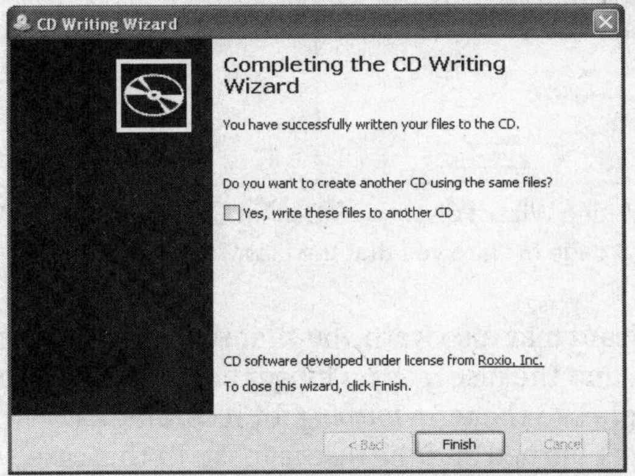

FIGURE 20.5: The CD Writing Wizard displays the Completing the CD Writing Wizard page when it has finished creating the CD.

6. If you want to create another CD containing the same files, select the Yes, Write These Files to Another CD check box.
7. Click the Finish button. The Wizard closes itself and deletes the files from the storage area unless you selected the Yes, Write These Files to Another CD check box.

When Things Go Wrong Writing the CD...

If you try to write more files to a CD than will fit on it, the CD Writing Wizard displays the Cannot Complete the CD Writing Wizard page (shown in Figure 20.6). You can remove some files from the storage area, then select the Retry Writing the Files to CD Now option button, and click the Finish button if you want to try to fix the problem while the CD is open, but in most cases you'll do best to leave the Close the Wizard without Writing the Files option button selected and click the Finish button, then return to the storage area, fix the problem, and restart the writing process.

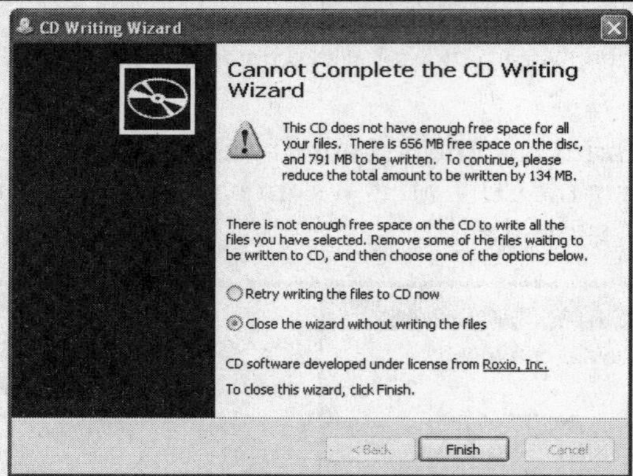

FIGURE 20.6: The CD Writing Wizard displays its Cannot Complete the CD Writing Wizard page to warn you that the files won't fit on the CD.

The CD Writing Wizard may also warn you that there was an error in the recording process, and the disc may no longer be usable. This is the other reason why people like the term *burning* for recording CDs—when things go wrong, you get burned and the disc is toast. In this case, you'll probably want to try writing the files to another CD.

When you've finished creating the CD, test it immediately by opening an Explorer window to its contents and opening some of them. Make sure all is well with the CD before archiving it or sending it on its way.

NOTE

If the CD you create won't read or play properly, it may have suffered recording errors. Try reducing the burning speed by using the Select a Write Speed drop-down list on the Recording tab of the Properties dialog box for the drive.

Clearing the Storage Area

If you end up deciding not to create the CD after all, clear the storage area by deleting the files in it. To do so, click the Delete Temporary Files link in the CD Writing Tasks list. Windows displays the Confirm Delete dialog box (shown in Figure 20.7) to make sure you know the files haven't yet been written to CD. Click the Yes button. Windows deletes the files and removes the Files Ready to Be Written to the CD heading from the Explorer window.

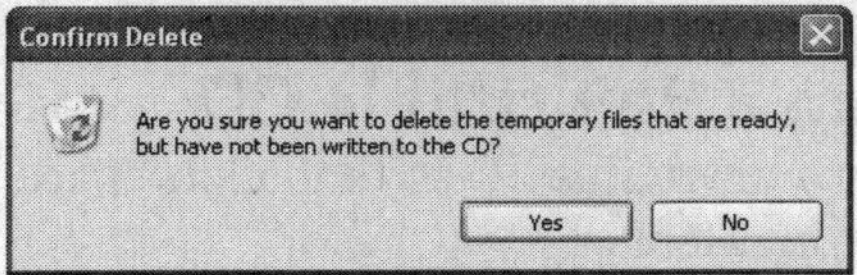

FIGURE 20.7: Windows displays the Confirm Delete dialog box to make sure you want to delete all the files from the storage area.

Working with Rewritable CDs

You record the first set of information to rewritable CDs (CD-RW discs) by using the same procedure as for recordable CDs (CD-R discs). But you can then add further files to them and erase all files from them. The following sections discuss how to take these actions.

Adding Further Files to a Rewritable CD

You can add further files to a rewritable CD by following the same procedure as for initially burning files to it. As mentioned earlier in the chapter, the storage area for a rewritable CD displays a Files Currently on the CD list for a CD-RW that already contains files or folders. Figure 20.8 shows an example of the storage area for a rewritable CD with a file queued for adding to the CD.

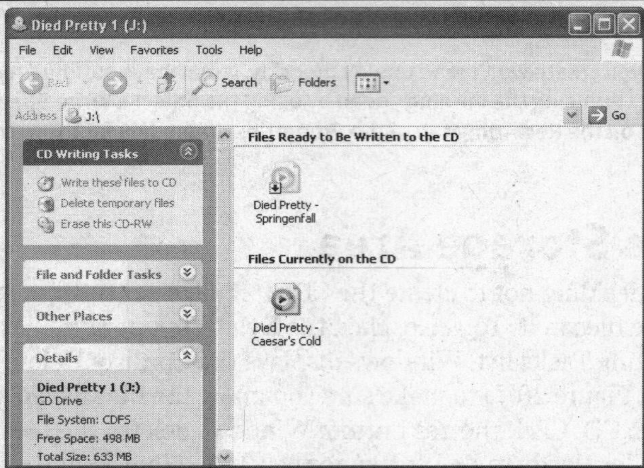

FIGURE 20.8: The storage area for a rewritable CD displays a Files Currently on the CD list.

Erasing All Files from a Rewritable CD

You can erase all the files from a rewritable CD so that all its space is free again. To do so, take the following steps:

1. Open an Explorer window to the CD drive.
2. Click the Erase This CD-RW link in the CD Writing Tasks list. Windows starts the CD Writing Wizard, which displays another Welcome to the CD Writing Wizard page (shown in Figure 20.9)

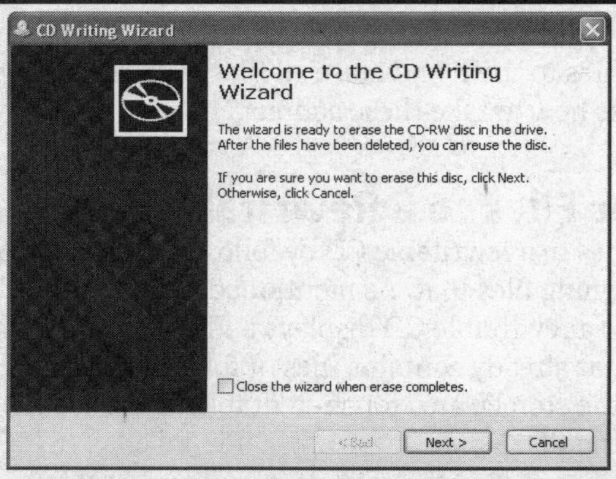

FIGURE 20.9: The CD Writing Wizard walks you through the process of erasing all the files from a CD-RW.

3. If you want the Wizard to close itself after erasing the files, select the Close the Wizard when Erase Completes check box.
4. Click the Next button. The Wizard displays the Erasing the CD page (shown in Figure 20.10) while it erases the files.

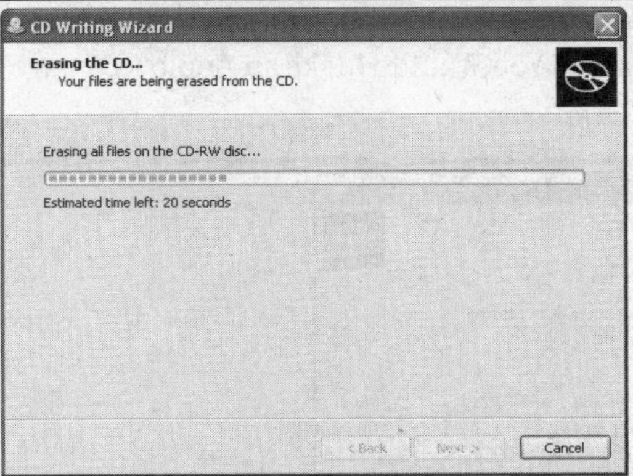

FIGURE 20.10: The CD Writing Wizard displays the Erasing the CD page while it erases the files on the CD-RW.

5. When the Wizard has finished erasing the files on the CD-RW, it displays another Completing the CD Writing Wizard page (shown in Figure 20.11).

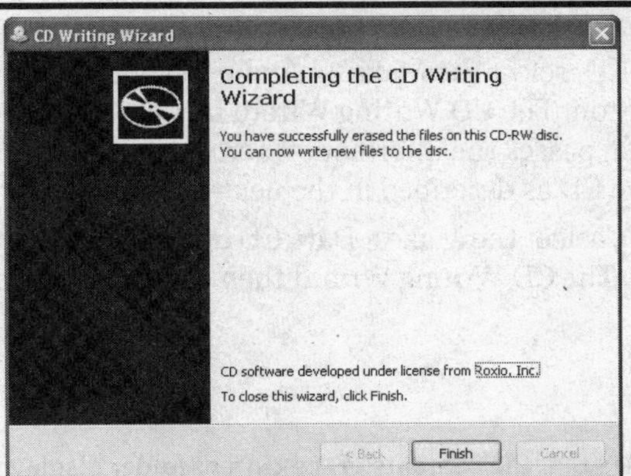

FIGURE 20.11: The Wizard displays this Completing the CD Writing Wizard page when it has finished erasing the files on the CD-RW.

6. Click the Finish button. The Wizard closes itself.

Creating an Audio CD from Explorer

To create an audio CD, you use Windows Media Player, which includes features for creating PCM files from other audio file formats. But you can start the process from Explorer by copying only audio files to the storage area. When you then start the CD Writing Wizard, it displays the Welcome to the CD Writing Wizard page as usual for you to name the CD, but after that it displays the Do You Want to Make an Audio CD? page (shown in Figure 20.12).

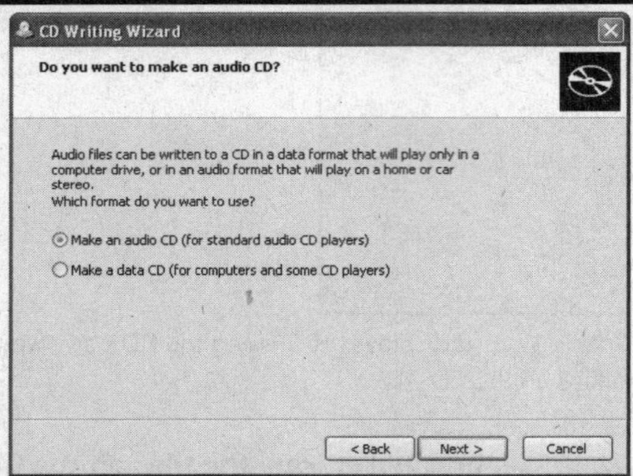

FIGURE 20.12: When the CD Writing Wizard notices that all the files for the CD are audio files, it displays the Do You Want to Make an Audio CD? page.

To create an audio CD, select the Make an Audio CD option button and click the Next button. The CD Writing Wizard launches or activates Windows Media Player, passes the information across to it, and then closes itself. Create the CD as described in the next section.

To create a data CD, select the Make a Data CD option button and click the Next button. The CD Writing Wizard then continues its usual course.

NOTE

If Windows decides that the contents of the current folder displayed in an Explorer window are predominantly music, it displays the Music Tasks list. You can then select a file or folder and click the Copy to Audio CD link. Doing so opens Windows Media Player with the tracks loaded ready for copying to an audio CD.

Burning CDs from Windows Media Player

Windows Media Player includes a feature for burning audio CDs directly from playlists. You can use MP3, WAV, and WMA files to create CDs up to 74 minutes long. (Windows Media Player can't create 80-minute audio CDs.)

TIP

If you want to include tracks in other formats on CDs you burn, convert them to WAV format first. Many sound programs can convert audio files.

Burning a CD from Windows Media Player is even easier than burning a CD from Explorer. That's because the only choice you have to make is which tracks you want to include on the CD: You don't have to name the CD (because it's an audio CD), and you don't have to specify whether it's a data CD or an audio CD (for the same reason).

The only other thing you have to worry about is this: if the tracks have digital licenses, whether the licenses allow the tracks to be copied to CD. If they don't, Windows Media Player will warn you of the problem.

To burn a CD from Windows Media Player, take the following steps:

1. Open the playlist you want to burn to CD, or create a new playlist containing the tracks.
2. Check the number of minutes shown: It must be 74 or fewer, otherwise the burning will grind to a halt when the disc is full. Remove tracks if necessary. (Or add more if you have space left.)
3. Choose File ➢ Copy ➢ Copy to Audio CD. Windows Media Player displays the Copy to CD or Device page and inspects the tracks to make sure that there aren't any license problems. Figure 20.13 shows the Copy to CD or Device page with a playlist queued for writing to CD.

FIGURE 20.13: Windows Media Player ready to write a playlist to CD

4. Click the Copy Music button. Windows begins the copying process, which consists of these three steps:

   Converting Writing out the audio files to uncompressed WAV files. While Windows Media Player converts the tracks, it displays *Converting* and a percentage readout next to the track it's working on.

   Copying to CD Copying the WAV files to the CD. Windows Media Player displays *Copying to CD* and a percentage readout next to each track in turn as it copies the track to the CD.

   Closing the disc When all of the WAV files have been written to the CD, Windows Media Player closes the disc.

5. When Windows Media Player has closed the disc, it ejects the CD. Check the CD manually to make sure that it works (for example, put it back in the drive and try playing it), then label it.

NOTE

You can also launch Windows Media Player and get it ready to burn CDs by selecting music files, right-clicking, and choosing Copy to Audio CD from the shortcut menu. (Alternatively, choose File ➢ Copy to Audio CD.)

Copying a CD

You can make a copy of a CD by using the same techniques as for copying any other files: Copy the files to the storage area, and then write them to CD. Remember that copying CDs of copyrighted works involves copyright issues.

If you have a CD drive (or DVD drive) other than your CD-R or CD-RW drive, you can simply open an Explorer window to My Computer, then drag the icon for the CD and drop it on the icon for the CD-RW drive. Windows copies the files to the storage area. Click the Write to CD link to start the CD Writing Wizard.

If Windows' CD-Writing Capabilities Aren't Enough

Windows offers what might be termed strong but basic features for burning CDs, letting you burn data CDs easily from Explorer and audio CDs even more easily from Windows Media Player. But if you need more advanced CD-burning features (or more bells and whistles), you'll need to buy third-party CD software.

One package you might consider is Easy CD Creator from Roxio, Inc. (You might also consider Easy CD Creator Deluxe, which comes with not only bells and whistles but also gongs such as features for designing CD labels.) Why consider Easy CD Creator in particular? Well, for one thing, you're using Roxio technology already—the CD-burning functionality in Windows is licensed from Roxio. For another, Roxio is a company spun off in 2001 from Adaptec, Inc., a company that has long been one of the major names in CD burning.

What's Next?

This chapter completes our look at multimedia in Windows XP Professional. Part IV discusses one of the most important features of Windows XP: networking. The next chapter begins with an overview of networking architecture.

PART iv

NETWORKING WINDOWS XP PROFESSIONAL

Chapter 21

Understanding the Architecture

Building an operating system is all about choices and trade-offs. Consequently, no single operating system is the best for every user and every need, although I'd argue that Windows XP Professional is in the running. Understanding those choices and trade-offs makes understanding Windows XP Professional easier.

Judging by most books on operating systems, publishers and writers seem to believe that operating system internals are of interest only to programmers. I don't think that point of view is defensible. Support people, power users, and troubleshooters will have a better understanding of the problems and strengths in Windows XP Professional if they are comfortable with terms such as *GDI, user,* and *WOWEXEC*. They've been around since the first version of NT—and remember that XP is just NT version 5.1—but they're still important.

Adapted from *Mastering Windows XP Professional* by Mark Minasi

ISBN 0-7821-2981-1 1056 pages $39.99

In this chapter, I'll take you on a tour of the main components in Windows XP Professional, its client-server structure, and its environment subsystems. We also look at what was, in my opinion, an unwise change in architecture—the decision to move the graphical user interface (GUI) from ring 3 into ring 0. That happened back in the NT 4 days but still affects the robustness of Windows XP Professional and lets you understand the difference between a "blue screen" and a visit from Dr. Watson. Now, if you're not a hardware type and are saying to yourself, "Hmm, I try to answer the phone by the third ring. What's ring 0?" stay tuned; it'll all be clear soon.

Understanding Rings and Things: CPU Privilege Levels

One of the most important concepts related to CPU design and operating system architecture is the notion of *memory protection and privilege*.

A Major Software Problem: Clobbering Memory

Put two programs into a computer, and you'll soon experience the problem of keeping those programs from damaging each other. Even if your computer is running a *multitasking operating system*—that is, an operating system that supports more than one program running at a time—a potential problem lurks. Applications can grow and shrink dynamically, as required by their owners. You start up Microsoft Word, and it may initially ask the operating system for only a couple of megabytes of RAM. But insert a few big graphics, and before you know it, Word is grabbing megabytes by the fistful.

What happens if Word needs four more megabytes, but the operating system has only two more to give it? A well-behaved application would accept the bad news and deal with it. But a buggy application (and unfortunately every application is at least a *little* buggy) might start writing to the memory that it owns and then keep going and going and going, right on past its allotted memory region. In the process, the errant application would overwrite another application's memory, damaging that application. This problem is probably the most common and most troublesome of programming errors, and it's known by many names. Back when I wrote mainframe Fortran for a living, I called it an 0C1 or an 0C4, for the error messages that it generated. Some programmers would say the bad application was "scribbling" all over another application's memory; still others would refer to the application "clobbering" the other application's memory.

Windows 3.1 programs caused this problem all the time. When the Windows 3.1 operating system noticed the problem, it would report a *general protection fault*, or GPF. Windows XP Professional, in contrast, emits one of two error messages: either Dr. Watson or a "crash dump," better known as a "blue screen." (Some folks call it a BSOD, for Blue Screen of Death, but I feel that the "of Death" suffix is a bit over-used at this point.)

Anti-Clobber Features

Now, Dr. Watsons and blue screens aren't necessarily bad things. When the good doctor visits or the screen turns blue, the CPU and the operating system are working together to detect and stop berserk applications before they start destroying other applications. GPFs were a problem in Windows 3.1 because Windows 3.1 didn't use the built-in protection of the CPU chip effectively. As a result, Windows 3.1 was good at sounding the alarm, but not so good at mustering the troops to keep the infidels from the gate; although this isn't a book about Windows 3.1, I explain a bit more about GPFs later.

Applications strayed out of their assigned memory areas so often in Windows 3.1 programs that a company named Numega has made a fair amount of money selling a product called Bounds-Checker that helps you catch a program in the act of stepping out of its allowed memory space. Although Bounds-Checker is one of the truly great debugging applications of our time, Numega should never have *needed* to write it—checking for memory clobbering is the operating system's job, not the job of some third-party utility.

A large portion of the instability in Windows 3.1 can be traced to the system's laissez-faire attitude about how its applications use memory. An example is a word processor scribbling all over a spreadsheet—what's to keep the word processor from scribbling all over the *operating system*?

In the case of Windows 3.1, *nothing* stopped the word processor from scribbling all over the operating system, and that's why Windows 3.1 was so easy to crash. From NT's very beginning, its designers wanted to offer better crash-proofing.

As it turns out, most of today's processors include a built-in feature called the *memory protection model* that makes building an operating system with zero tolerance for memory clobbers fairly simple.

Process Privilege Levels: Kernel and User Mode

Most of today's processors enable you to designate any program running in the processor as either a "kernel mode" application or a "user mode" application. A *kernel mode application* is allowed to, among other things, allocate memory to all other applications. Kernel mode programs are the only programs allowed to modify a very important piece of data in the computer's memory: a table of memory boundaries that defines each application currently running and exactly what memory each application is allowed to access. You'll see that this table of memory boundaries is vitally important.

Here's the sequence of events for allocating memory boundaries:

1. An application asks the operating system (which is a kernel mode program) to load it.
2. The operating system asks the application how much memory it needs.
3. The application tells the operating system its required amount of memory.
4. The operating system loads the application into memory, securing the memory boundaries around the application.

From that point on, whenever the application tries to access memory, the CPU consults a table of application memory boundaries that indicates which RAM goes with which application. Using that information, the CPU can either allow the memory access or declare a *memory access fault*. (I *would* use the term general protection fault, as a memory access fault *is* a GPF, but that term is applied only to Intel processors. Recall that NT was originally designed to run on non-Intel processors, so NT architects tend to use terms that aren't Intel-specific, even though at this point NT *is* Intel-specific, as Microsoft killed Alpha support years ago. In any case, "memory access fault" is the more generic term applying to all processors, so think of it as architecture-independent jargon.)

Only a kernel mode application can modify the table that the CPU consults. The major difference between kernel mode programs and user mode programs is that kernel mode programs define the memory boundaries and user mode programs live in them.

The dichotomy between programs that can define memory boundaries and those that can't is built into the processors that Windows XP Professional currently runs on, the Intel *x*86 and IA64 chips (you know—the Itanium). Although some non-Intel RISC (reduced instruction set computing) chips support only two levels of privilege (kernel mode and user mode), the Intel chips support *four* levels of privilege, which are called *rings.* You'll never see the terms *kernel mode* and *user mode* in an Intel programming manual. Ring 0 applications (Intel-speak for *kernel mode*) can control anything about memory but can also leave some memory control to ring 1 applications. Ring 1 applications, in turn, cannot modify memory protections set by a ring 0 application but can set memory protection on memory that *they* own; ring 1 restrictions must be followed by ring 2 applications. Ring 2 applications get to bully around the last kind, ring 3 applications, and ring 3 applications can't modify any memory and therefore have no one to boss around.

NOTE

Windows XP Professional on Intel computers uses only ring 0 (for kernel mode) and ring 3 (for user mode). Windows XP Professional does not use rings 1 or 2, because many RISC CPUs support only two levels of privilege, and Microsoft wants Windows XP Professional to be able to run on many kinds of CPUs, at least in theory. (As I've said before, currently it's only being implemented on the Intel 32-bit and 64-bit chips.)

Even though the concept of rings took a while to describe, it's a basic and fundamentally important thing to understand about Windows XP Professional—how it protects the memory of one application from all other applications.

You've also got the tools now to understand why Windows 3.1 was so unstable: *all applications lived in ring 0.* Every single device driver, screen saver, application—you name it—had the capability to reallocate the table of memory boundaries anytime one felt like it.

Now you can easily understand an important Windows XP Professional design goal: *don't let the applications get within 10 miles of the kernel mode* (ring 0 on Intel, recall). If an application tries to exceed its allotted memory space, the processor will detect a memory access fault and remove the offending application from memory.

NOTE

An operating system will not protect an application from itself. If an application uses several memory areas and one area overflows into another, Windows XP Professional will probably not detect the overflow unless the application tries to read or write outside of its allotted memory space. That's not an immutable truth, however; a programmer can design a program to take advantage of the built-in memory protection capabilities of Windows XP Professional, but doing so is not a requirement for building an application.

This distinction of kernel mode programs versus user mode programs turned out to be crucial in the design of Windows XP Professional, as you'll see in the rest of this chapter. But in case it's still not clear, think of them this way:

- User mode applications only have the power to access the memory given them by the operating system. They're essentially "penned in" by their memory allocations. So when a user mode application goes awry, it can only damage itself.
- Kernel mode applications have the power to allocate and access any memory in the computer. So when they go crazy, they can damage any program running on the computer.

The relative difference in the amount of damage that kernel mode versus user mode applications can do led Microsoft to the two different responses when the operating system catches an application scribbling over memory that it doesn't own. If it's a user mode application misbehaving, the operating system just kills the application and then calls in Dr. Watson to do an autopsy. Dr. Watson basically stores any relevant information about the application's transgressions in `drwatson.log`. In theory, if you have an application that triggers Dr. Watson errors, that application's vendor should be eager to get your Dr. Watson logs so that the vendor can fix its bugs.

In contrast, by the time that the operating system realizes that a kernel mode application has gone renegade, the operating system really has no idea, nor any way of knowing, how bad things are. Were the passwords compromised? Was the disk driver damaged so that any file writes will actually format the hard disk? The conservative answer is for the operating system to simply say, "I have no idea how corrupted I am, but I know that a severely corrupted operating system is likely to cause damage of some kind...so I'll stop myself before I do any more damage." So XP essentially says, "Computer, activate the self-destruct sequence," shifting the screen from graphical to textual mode, displaying 50 lines of text as white letters on a blue background—hence, the well-known "blue screen"—dumps some information to the screen (and potentially to the hard disk), and stops the system.

Designing Architecture Independence

When Dave Cutler and a bunch of other ex-Digital Equipment Corporation employees started working on NT in its first incarnation back in 1989, they sought to create an operating system that could easily run on just about any microprocessor CPU. That would make for an operating system that was very flexible...but harder to build. Such an operating system, which is designed more generically than one crafted for a single type of CPU, is called an "architecture-independent" CPU. Choosing architecture independence affects the operating system's structure, though, and in this section I'll talk about how XP's architecture-independent childhood has influenced its design.

Architecture Independence in Windows XP Professional: The Big Picture

Back in the late 1980s, you didn't get massive power from Intel's top-of-the-line 486 processor; instead, you got it by plopping 32 MIPS processors on a motherboard. Microsoft has always wanted to keep its premier desktop operating system (NT Workstation, 2000 Professional, and now XP Professional) running basically the same code as its premier *server* operating system (NT Server, 2000 Server, and .NET Server). To feed that need for speed, Microsoft aimed for an operating system that could be quickly re-implemented on any brand-new CPU that was blindingly fast.

Computer manufacturers will always be making a chip that's bigger, faster, and, most important, *newer*. But in the old days, a hardware manufacturer would come out with a nifty new CPU...only to have to wait five years while someone built a full-featured operating system that exploited that chip.

With an architecture-independent operating system, however, those days are gone. Microsoft can re-implement NT for another processor in just a few months. The vital and central importance of architecture independence for Windows XP Professional is that its easily portable structure will, in theory, allow Microsoft to offer a high-quality operating system "first to market" for any new CPU. And in this business, being first often means being the only one in the game.

Minimum CPU Requirements to Be Windows XP Professional–Possible

Well, how architecture-independent *is* Windows XP Professional? Right now, not really very much. But to be a candidate for XPness, a theoretical future CPU must have a few things:

- Data registers that are 32 bits or larger
- Memory address registers that are 32 bits or larger

NOTE

Windows XP Professional needs to be able to allocate a space up to 232 bits, or 4GB. (No, Windows XP Professional doesn't need that much RAM; it's just that the underlying architecture is laid out on a 4GB memory map, as you'll learn later in this chapter.)

- A memory protection model
- At least two levels of privilege for processes so that Windows XP Professional can implement kernel mode and user mode privileges
- The capability to control how any arbitrary process accesses any given block of memory in the following ways:
    - A given process can or cannot read the block of memory.
    - A given process can or cannot write the block of memory.
    - A given process can or cannot execute the block of memory.
- A memory *paging* ability, or CPU support for virtual memory

That looks like a fair number of requirements, but it isn't really. These requirements describe most advanced microprocessors on the market today, as well as larger computers. A Microsoft source once said that they were looking into building NT/370, NT for an IBM mainframe. In theory, that would be possible due to NT's fairly liberal requirements; of course, whether it's *advisable* is a different matter. (Where do you plug in the mouse?)

The Windows XP Professional Baseline: The HAL, the Kernel, and the Drivers

The HAL, the kernel, and the drivers—sounds like a rock band, doesn't it? To keep Windows XP Professional as architecture-independent as possible, Microsoft minimized the amount of the operating system that is hardware-specific. Just three parts of the operating system must change with different computers:

- The hardware abstraction layer, `hal.dll`
- The kernel, `ntoskrnl.exe`
- The device drivers for the computer's specific hardware, such as video drivers, network card drivers, and mouse drivers

Next, we take a brief look at each of these components.

"Open the Drive Bay Door, HAL"

Well, you never have to tell it that, really. The HAL (hardware abstraction layer) exists to smooth out differences *within* the many implementations of a particular microprocessor. For example, the Motorola 68000 was the processor upon which the Apple Macintosh, the Amiga, and the Atari 520 ST were built. They were all desktop microcomputers with GUIs, but any other similarity ends there. Some of the computers made heavy use of interrupts; others used more programmed input/output and direct memory access (DMA). Additionally, a *huge* difference exists between the structure of a PC with one processor and a PC with two or more processors.

The HAL's job is to smooth out those differences, presenting to the operating system a standard-looking set of computer hardware. The HAL is implemented as a file called `hal.dll`. In the 68000 example, the Macintosh, Atari ST520, and Amiga versions would all have the same kernel because they all use the same processor, but they'd need different HALs.

The basic HAL that ships with Windows XP Professional supports two processors, and the HAL that ships with Windows 2000 Server supports as many as four processors. NT can support as many as 32 processors in theory, but you'd need a new HAL to support them. Similarly, if a new peripheral bus were to appear, such as a 256-bit version of PCI, Windows XP

Professional would need only a new HAL and then it would run with no problems.

We Have a Kernel, but Not a General

Unix systems were built in pieces, somewhat similar to the way Windows XP Professional is built today, and the central manager or heart of the operating system was called the *kernel*. That name is used to describe the heart of virtually every operating system, and Windows XP Professional is no exception.

The kernel is mainly a piece of software that schedules tasks on your computer. If several programs all want to run at the same time, the kernel locates the one that has the highest priority and runs that task. The kernel also makes sure that all the processors in a multiprocessor system keep busy.

The kernel also manages all the Windows XP Professional, subsystems, which are the subject of most of the remainder of this chapter. Managing subsystems turns out to be a key concept in understanding the notion of Windows XP Professional borrowing from the microkernel and client-server, see models of operating systems, as you'll see later in this chapter.

They're Called Drivers Because They Can Drive You Crazy

Support for particular pieces of hardware could be built into an operating system–for example, Microsoft could have built support for a Microsoft mouse right into the kernel–but that isn't a particularly good idea. For one thing, if you had a computer that didn't include a Microsoft mouse, the memory required to hold the Microsoft mouse support would be wasted.

Instead, Windows XP Professional, like other operating systems, segregates support for hardware devices into separate software modules called *device drivers*. Although most descriptions of Windows XP Professional do not include device drivers in the hardware-specific part of Windows XP Professional (most just show the HAL and the kernel), these drivers are quite hardware-specific. That fact is worth knowing; support for a particular network card on an Intel system doesn't necessarily mean that it's supported on an Itanium system. (*That's* the part that can drive you crazy.)

Perhaps the other reason that drivers can drive you crazy (and why you care about what they are in the first place) is that they're usually not written by the people who write the operating system. Instead, they're written by somebody at a company that makes a peripheral such as a video board, a mouse, a LAN board, or a SCSI host adapter. These people often don't understand Windows XP Professional all that well, with the result that drivers are often not written very well.

Now, the scary part is that drivers pretty much *must* be kernel mode programs, so a badly written driver can crash your system.

WARNING

In my experience, a bad driver is usually the cause of a Windows XP Professional crash.

More than 90 percent of the Windows XP Professional crashes I've seen were caused either by bad SCSI (Small Computer System Interface) drivers or bad Enhanced Integrated Drive Electronics (EIDE) drivers. Of course, the great strength of Windows XP Professional is that when it dies, it points the finger at who killed it, so at least you can go back to the vendor who wrote the driver and ask the company to fix it. The vendor may not fix the driver, but at least they won't be able to do any finger-pointing at other vendors. The culprit's name is printed in black and white for anyone to see when you run the `dumpexam.exe` program.

"But wait a minute," you cry, "I thought Windows XP Professional was stable." Well, yes, it's stable, but there's no such thing as a bulletproof operating system; as I've already said, designing an operating system involves trade-offs—which is the topic of the next section.

NOTE

Since Windows 2000, desktop NT users have had a pretty neat bulletproofing feature: 2000 and XP will check drivers to see if they are digitally signed. This means that when you download a driver from the Internet, your system can check to see that the driver is actually from the vendor that it claims to be from, rather than a damaged or perhaps maliciously modified driver. By default, XP checks that a file is *digitally signed*, and if it's not, XP asks if you actually want to load the driver. But you can use `secpol.msc` to tell XP to either absolutely *require* signed drivers or to ignore driver signatures.

Designing Robustness

I've made much of how the structure of Windows XP Professional lends it a stability that most of us haven't seen in desktop operating systems, but I haven't really gone too much into the details. I'll do that now.

A Basic Layered Operating System

Most PC operating systems are *layered* operating systems, meaning that they consist of a bunch of pieces of software stacked one atop the other. The pieces tied most closely to the hardware are always represented at the bottom and application software is always at the top. Sandwiched between the applications that users want to run and the hardware on which they want to run, the applications are the intermediary programs that communicate between the two. Figure 21.1 depicts a basic representation of a layered operating system.

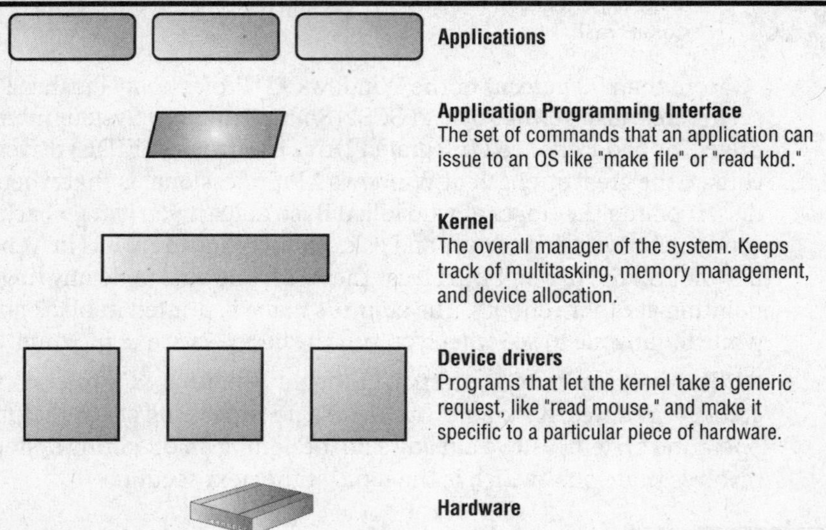

Applications
Application Programming Interface
The set of commands that an application can issue to an OS like "make file" or "read kbd."
Kernel
The overall manager of the system. Keeps track of multitasking, memory management, and device allocation.
Device drivers
Programs that let the kernel take a generic request, like "read mouse," and make it specific to a particular piece of hardware.
Hardware

FIGURE 21.1: The structure of a typical layered operating system, the very basis of more advanced architectures

To a certain extent, the layered structure in Figure 21.1 also represents the design of DOS, OS/2, Windows 3.1, and Windows 9*x*.

At the lowest level of software are the device drivers, which manipulate the system hardware. The APIs, or *application programming interfaces*, are the doorway to the operating system as far as the applications are concerned. If an application wants to create a file, read a keystroke, or paint the screen blue, it must go through the operating system, and it must access the operating system through the APIs. DOS has an API of its own, as do Windows 3.1 and Windows 9*x*, so today's layered operating systems often support multiple APIs to allow backward compatibility.

An API is the published set of legal tasks that an operating system can do for an application—examples include opening a file, reading a keystroke, or ending a program. Of course, since we are dealing with computers, there are *i*'s to be dotted and *t*'s to be crossed. For example, one operating system might open a file with the command `DOSOPENFILE`, and another might open a file with the `makefile` command. Those two commands do the same thing, but they do it in different operating systems in much the same way that you express the idea *hello* differently in different languages.

Windows NT in its various forms, OS/2, and Windows 3.*x* all used different APIs, and so developers have always had to decide which API to focus their efforts on. Because of the large size of the Windows market, most vendors work first in Windows and then port their applications from Windows to some other operating system. An application trying to access one of today's operating systems from anything other than the APIs will crash. (I say *today's* operating systems because it was possible under DOS to jump into the operating system at any old place, leading to a host of compatibility nightmares for people trying to build "compatible" PC computers.)

In between the APIs and the device drivers is the kernel, which manages the whole thing.

A Client-Server, Microkernel Operating System

The only thing wrong with the previous model is that virtually all the applications themselves must live in kernel mode. That *does* make securing the operating system a bit harder, at least when compared with a *client-server* or *micro*kernel architecture, which is depicted in Figure 21.2. (It's called client-server because parts of the operating system treat each other as clients or servers.)

Notice that Figure 21.2 distinguishes between kernel mode and user mode. The basic layered operating system presented in the preceding section puts everything but the applications in the kernel mode. The client-server or microkernel model puts only the bare minimum (hence the *micro* part of microkernel) in kernel mode. One reason that the client-server model seems worth the effort is that operating system designers want their systems to be robust and stable.

One way to accomplish those goals is to simply write operating systems without bugs in them. (Now that we've had a little laugh, let's look at another way.) Another way is to exploit the memory protection functions built right into today's processor chips. Kernel mode programs are scary in that they can scribble all over *any* part of the system's memory. Also, user mode programs can be imprisoned in memory areas, and if they try to escape by exceeding their bounds, the CPU hardware automatically sounds the alarm.

One of the major goals of the client-server model is, then, to minimize the number of parts that run in kernel mode. There is, of course, a downside to the client-server model, one that can significantly affect performance and that I'll consider in the next section.

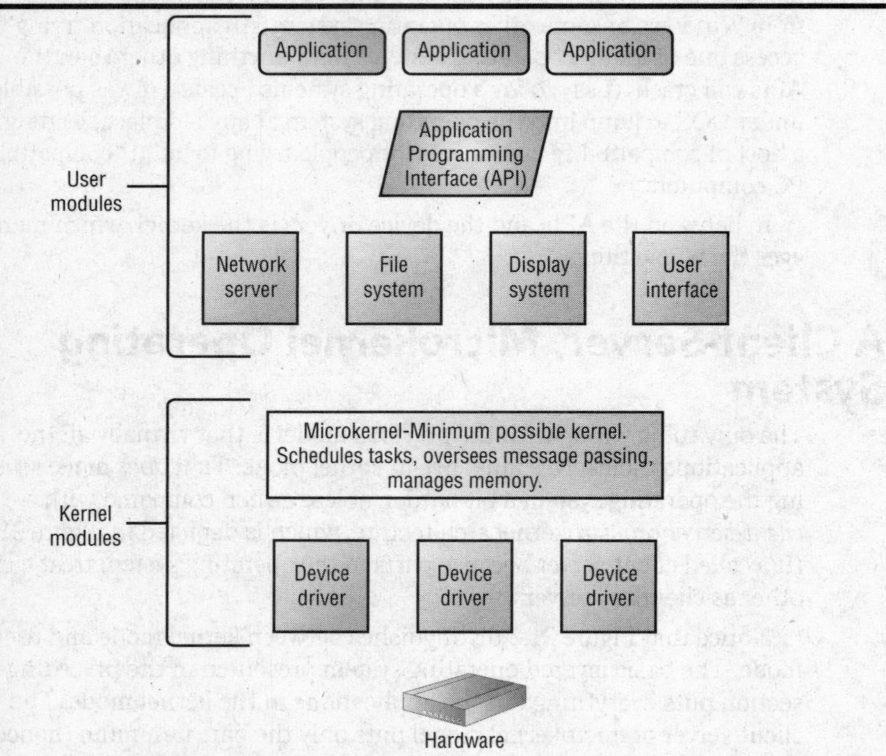

FIGURE 21.2: The microkernel or client-server operating system model moves more of the software into the user mode.

The Cost of Client-Server

The processor requires a bit of time—a few tens of microseconds—to shift between kernel mode and user mode. Although that may not sound like very much, consider that a 1000MHz microprocessor can sometimes get *10,000 instructions* to execute in 10 microseconds. Consequently, every user/kernel mode shift is expensive in terms of operating system performance.

Now consider that in a microkernel operating system, user modules cannot see other user modules (applications that don't run in kernel mode) and cannot directly communicate with them. This necessitates mode shifts. For example, imagine that an application wants to tell the operating system to read a keystroke. To do this, it needs to make an API function call, because the APIs are the authorized doorways into the operating system. In a simple layered model, the application simply calls the API, which takes care of communicating with the operating system. But the lines of communication aren't so straightforward in a microkernel model, where the communication flow looks more like Figure 21.3.

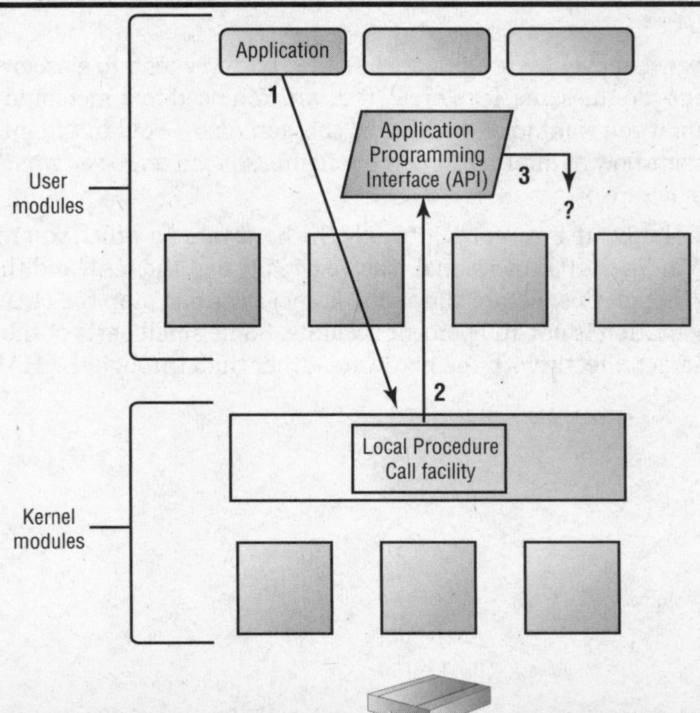

FIGURE 21.3: User module communication in a microkernel model

In the microkernel model, the application, instead of calling the API, calls a piece of the microkernel whose only job is to pass messages (in Windows XP Professional, it's called the *Local Procedure Call* facility or *LPC*). The LPC forwards the message to the API.

Here's the path of the message: The message goes from the application across the user/kernel boundary to the LPC, and from the LPC back to the API across the user/kernel boundary again. That's the point at which the API knows to ask the operating system to do something, and this of course generates another user/kernel mode shift. Further, accessing the network, the file system, the display, or the user interface involves piles of mode shifts. The latter are all user modules as well, so messages passed between them must go through the user/kernel boundary.

The NT Compromise

A pure microkernel model, then, would be tremendously inefficient because of the massive number of context shifts it requires. So NT has always used a kind of modified microkernel structure, as you see in Figure 21.4.

Now, whenever we see a figure like this, our eyes tend to glaze over; lest *yours* do the same, let's break it down. You need to understand this diagram if you want to stay with this chapter. Also, I couldn't fit an important flow of information on the figure, so read on to see what's *not* in this picture.

The Hardware box represents only the hardware on which you're running Windows XP Professional. You've already met the HAL and the kernel. Although this picture shows the kernel as sitting atop the HAL, that representation is not 100 percent accurate. Some small parts of the kernel interact directly with the hardware rather than through the HAL.

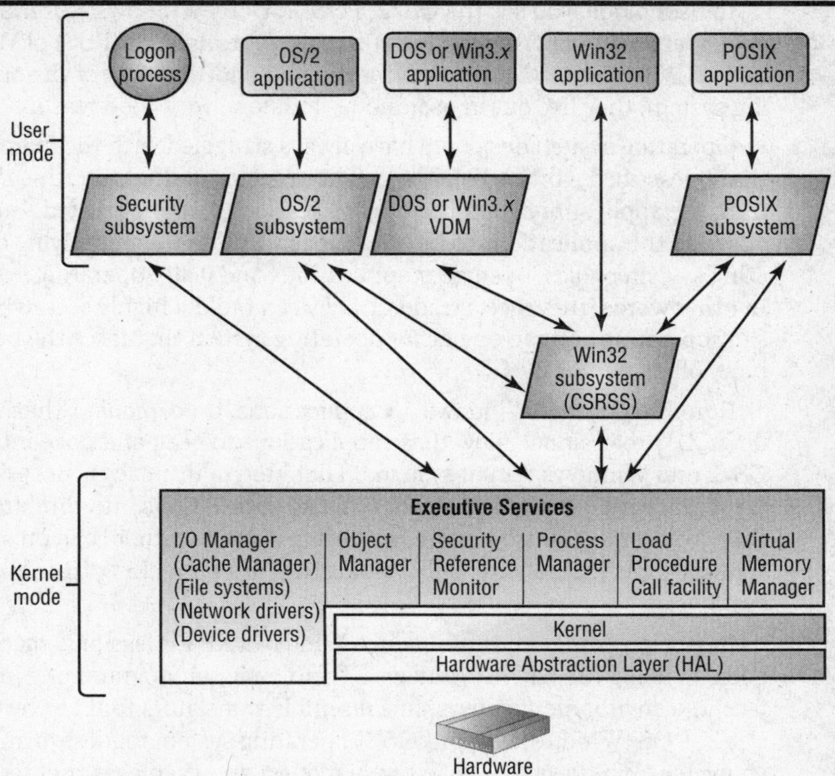

FIGURE 21.4: The Windows XP Professional modified client-server structure (simplified)

The I/O Manager is vitally important because:

- It contains all the device drivers that keep the hardware working.
- It contains most of the networking part of Windows XP Professional.
- It contains the file systems—FAT, FAT32, CDFS, UDFS, and NTFS.

Windows 2000 Executive Services is just a catch-all phrase for a few modules that are important to Windows XP Professional and that live in kernel mode. They are also called Windows 2000 Executive functions. I'll get to all of them a bit later.

In user mode, you see the OS/2, POSIX, DOS/Windows 3.*x*, and client-server (Win32) subsystems (usually abbreviated CSRSS) of Windows XP Professional. Although they're an important part of the operating system, they live out in user mode—and for a very good reason.

Operating system designers have always struggled with the dilemma that I described a bit earlier. They want to segregate the operating system from the applications, because the applications can't be trusted. But allowing the applications to be more closely knit to the underlying operating system makes for smaller applications and faster operating systems. In other words, they face a tradeoff: they can build a highly secure but slow operating system, or a faster operating system that faces the possibility of nastier crashes.

Running OS/2 or Windows 3.*x* applications, then, *requires* that Windows XP Professional allow these applications to peek and poke into the OS/2 and Windows 3.*x* subsystems. That kind of intimacy is necessary for Windows XP Professional to fool those applications into thinking that they are running on their native operating systems rather than on simple Windows XP Professional subsystems that are mimicking the native systems.

In fact, any program running on a Windows XP Professional machine ends up using the native Windows XP Professional programming interface; the environment subsystems resemble translators that convert an OS/2, DOS, Windows 3.*x*, or POSIX operating system request to an equivalent Windows XP Professional request and then pass that request to Windows XP Professional. The front end for requests to Windows XP Professional is the CSRSS. The word for the native Windows XP Professional programming interface, by the way, is *Win32*—something I'll have more to say about a bit later.

But first, let me clear up something *very important* that underscores yet again the cost of using even a hybrid client-server approach as Windows XP Professional does. Look at the lines running between the subsystems, the CSRSS, and the Windows XP Professional Executive. They're not actually correct because I've depicted each environment subsystem communicating directly with CSRSS—do you remember why? Take a look at Figure 21.5, and you'll see what I'm talking about.

Figure 21.5 illustrates how just one user mode subsystem, the DOS/Windows 3.*x* subsystem, communicates with another user mode subsystem, the CSRSS. Figure 21.4 shows a double-sided arrow between the DOS/Windows 3.*x* subsystem and the CSRSS. But two user modules can't directly communicate—*pass messages* is the more accepted Windows XP Professional term—under Windows XP Professional. Instead, the DOS/Windows 3.*x* subsystem must pass a message to the Windows XP Professional Executive, which lives in kernel mode, which then passes the message to CSRSS.

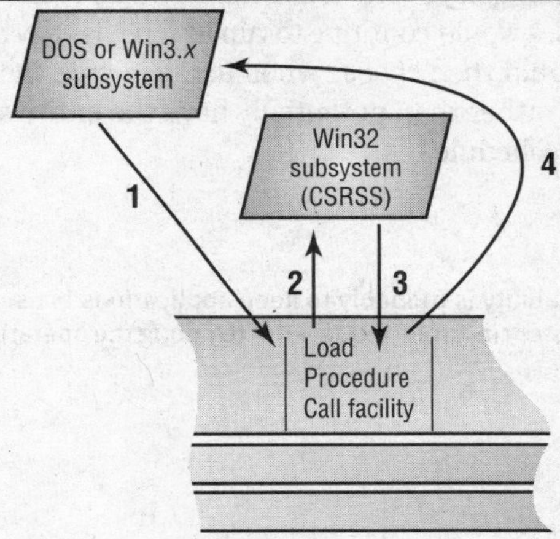

FIGURE 21.5: A more accurate view of subsystem communication in the Windows XP Professional modified client-server structure

Similarly, CSRSS can respond only to a request from the DOS/ Windows 3.*x* subsystem by first sending a message to the Windows XP Professional Executive, which then forwards the note to the DOS/Windows 3.*x* subsystem. Here you see that I'm 'fessing up for having oversimplified things a bit. Go back to Figure 21.4 and visualize all of the user mode communications that are represented as double-headed arrows as really being four single-headed arrows. I didn't want that oversimplification to cause you to miss exactly *how* expensive the client-server model is in terms of user/kernel shifts.

Is the Microkernel a Bad Compromise?

The whole idea of a microkernel or client-server operating system is that it is a stable approach, which puts drivers and subsystems all at arm's length, so to speak—out in user mode (ring 3 on Intel systems). And if they crash, they crash only themselves.

Well, yes, that of course sounds good, but to a certain extent, it's a moot point. If the keyboard driver is in user mode and it crashes, then certainly it has crashed only itself and the kernel continues to run. But what can you do with an operating system without a functioning keyboard?

On yet another hand, some of the things that you want to do might be possible even without a working keyboard. On a Windows 2000 Server machine, your server processes would continue to run as long as they didn't need keyboard input. You could then *choose* when to take down the server and bring it back up, rather than potentially have the entire system crash on the errant driver's schedule.

TIP

The best approach for stability is probably to keep applications in user mode and put the operating system in kernel mode—but to debug the operating system extremely well.

NOTE

You can tell whether an error occurred in user mode or kernel mode. Kernel mode errors lead to blue screens. User mode errors lead to Dr. Watson messages.

NT 4's Additional Architectural Change

All this discussion of where different operating system pieces should go is particularly relevant to NT from version 4 to the present. Prior to this release, Microsoft put the Windows NT native programming subsystem, the Win32 API, out in user mode–but with NT 4, Win32 moved to kernel mode.

Microsoft said that it made the change to improve NT's performance as a workstation operating system, and the switch did, indeed, improve NT's performance. Animation-based Windows 3.1 programs that ran painfully slow under Windows NT 3.51 and earlier versions ran at about the same speed under NT Workstation 4 as they do under Windows 95. XP's fairly fast at games as well.

Mainly, there were three pieces of NT that moved from user mode to kernel mode:

- USER, the user interface manager

- GDI, the graphics manager
- The video display drivers

USER is a set of routines that responds every time a user clicks or drags a user control. (*Control* is the generic phrase for a window, button, slider bar, radio button, check box, list box, combo box, or toolbar.) The GDI (Graphics Device Interface) is a set of routines that handles much of the low-level work required to keep a graphical user interface going. GDI routines manipulate bitmaps, colors, cursor shapes, icons, and fonts. Every time your word processor wants to show you a line of text in Times Roman, GDI puts those characters on the screen.

NOTE

Whenever you load a bitmap as wallpaper, you see another example of GDI at work.

Both GDI and USER are central, integral parts of Windows NT and they're pretty well debugged. Putting them into kernel mode, then, is probably a good idea. But the display drivers, well, that's another story.

I've already said that the only times I have ever seen Windows XP Professional crash were when I loaded a badly written SCSI or EIDE driver. Because those drivers are part of the I/O Manager, they live in kernel mode, which is why they can blue-screen the system when they fail.

Display drivers, in contrast, weren't able to kill a Windows NT machine in versions 3.51 and earlier. That changed in NT 4 (and continues in Windows XP Professional) because the display drivers now live in kernel mode. Again, a reasonable person could say, "Hey, wait a minute, *who cares*? After all, what can you get done on a computer that doesn't have a display driver?" And again, I answer that a server has very little use for a display driver. Windows 2000/NT Server works just fine no matter how strange the screen looks; after all, the file and application server part comes up automatically, and you needn't even log into an NT Server machine for it to act as a file server.

My worry is that display drivers are, like disk drivers, often not written by people inside Microsoft, and so they don't get tested as well. Not, mind you, that Microsoft is any paragon of virtue when it comes to bug-free code—although NT's pretty darn good that way—but because a Microsoft tester has access to thousands of different machines, a huge network, and the ear of people with intimate knowledge of the innards of

NT. A Microsoft tester is in a good position to beat the stuffing out of a display driver. In contrast, a display driver programmer at a video board company wouldn't have access to nearly that number of resources. When working at a company whose focus is hardware, testers often see software drivers as a kind of necessary evil—and the result is a display driver that hasn't been properly tested.

So, in the end analysis, what's the best course of action for *you*? Well, ultimately, Microsoft's decision to put the Win32 subsystem into kernel mode has meant that we get a snappier response out of our desktop applications on NT 4 and now Windows XP Professional. Yes, it probably means some small reduction in stability in NT/2000, but that problem probably comes from the drivers. I suggest, therefore, confining video board purchases to the boards on the Hardware Compatibility List (HCL)—they've been beaten around and are presumably fairly trustworthy.

In the end analysis, moving graphic and printing drivers into kernel mode was probably a bad idea. But Microsoft built some entirely new tools while creating Windows XP Professional that allowed them to really run drivers through the wringer. The result is that Windows XP Professional's kernel mode components are pretty reliable, and so you won't see too many blue screens under XP. The new *user* mode modules, however, may bedevil us, so I've found in general that Windows XP Professional means fewer blue screens but more frequent visits from the good Dr. Watson.

By the way, those driver-testing tools shipped *with* Windows XP Professional in the form of `verifier.exe`. It's a cool tool that lets you put a particular driver under intense scrutiny and prove pretty reliably whether it's buggy or not. Just choose Start ➢ Run, type **`verifier`** in the Open box, and press Enter. You'll see that it lets you put any kernel mode tool under the microscope.

Working with the Major Modules in Windows XP Professional

By now, you've met some of the major components in Windows XP Professional. But I haven't been able to work *all* of them into the discussion yet, so let me make amends for that now.

The HAL, Kernel, and I/O Manager

The HAL, kernel, and I/O Manager are some of the pieces of Windows XP Professional you've already met. The HAL enables many dissimilarly designed computers to look like Windows XP Professional. The HAL also smoothes out any differences created by running Windows XP Professional with a single processor on some machines and as many as 64 processors on other machines.

The kernel is the central manager, the part that knows at any moment which processes are running in the system, what memory they take up, what their priority is, and what (if anything) they're waiting for. Part of the system's memory management takes place in the kernel as well, and you'll read about how Windows XP Professional manages memory in a few pages.

The I/O Manager contains the network system, including the *redirector* (which makes it possible for a workstation to use resources on the network) and the server. The network board drivers are part of the I/O Manager as well, as are the file systems, the Cache Manager, disk interface drivers, and other device drivers.

The Windows XP Professional Executive

Remember back a few pages when I showed you an overview of the structure of Windows XP Professional? I included a piece of Windows XP Professional that is a kernel mode piece but didn't say much about it. That piece is called the Windows XP Professional Executive, and I'll describe it here.

The Executive consists of Windows XP Professional modules that were deemed important enough to live in kernel mode, ring 0 on an Intel processor. They are as follows:

- Local Procedure Call (LPC) facility
- Process Manager
- Object Manager
- Security Reference Monitor
- Virtual Memory Manager

The LPC facility is the part of the Windows XP Professional Executive that manages the messages passed between one user mode module and another—recall that two user mode modules can't communicate directly with each other.

The Process Manager has the job of handling the nitty-gritty detail of starting and shutting down processes (programs or parts of programs). Whenever you start a program, the Process Manager does much of the hard work. After the Process Manager starts a process, the process is usually handled by the kernel until the process terminates, at which time the process is, again, handled by the Process Manager—think of it as both obstetrician and undertaker for processes. The Process Manager oversees the creation and destruction of processes and a kind of subprocess called a *thread*.

The Object Manager, well, manages objects. Hmmm, let's try that another way. Windows XP Professional is built atop the whole notion of *objects*. Everything—and I mean *everything*—is implemented as an object. A file is viewed by Windows XP Professional as an object, as is a serial port, a process, and many of the programming constructs in Windows XP Professional.

Defining these elements as objects serves two purposes. First, making something into an object gives it properties in common with other objects, so Windows XP Professional offers a uniform way of accessing all of them. You see, in most operating systems, grabbing a serial port and communicating with it involves massively different code than grabbing a file and reading it. By putting an object interface on everything in Windows XP Professional, Microsoft made it a bit easier for programmers to use different parts of the operating system. So simplifying programmers' lives is the first benefit of an object-oriented operating system; the second is security.

By creating a single point of contact between an application program and a peripheral (another program, a file, an input/output device, and so on), Windows XP Professional makes the tasks of tracking which program uses which object and checking whether that program has the *right* to use that object much easier for itself. Keeping track of what objects are in the system and who's using them and deciding whether programs can access objects are the jobs of the Object Manager.

The Security Reference Monitor is the part of the Windows XP Professional Executive that oversees the security modules in Windows XP Professional.

The Virtual Memory Manager is the parking lot attendant for all the processes running in Windows XP Professional. It's the program that makes sure that every process has all the memory that it needs—even if the system doesn't *have* enough memory! You'll see how the Virtual Memory Manager accomplishes this feat a little later in this chapter.

Having exhausted all the modules in kernel mode under Windows XP Professional, we can now move on to the pieces that live in user mode. They're called the environment subsystems and the security subsystems.

Environment Subsystems

The pieces that enable you to run programs reside within user mode modules in Windows XP Professional; they are called *environment subsystems*. Here's a quick look at them.

Win32

Although Windows XP Professional is built to run programs from several other, competing, operating systems, it also has a programming interface of its own. Even before Windows XP Professional existed, Microsoft sought to get the programming industry as a whole to agree on which programming interface would serve the needs of programmers in building most programs.

The result was the Win32 API. First built for Windows for Workgroups 3.1 and Windows NT 3.1, Win32 is the closest thing that Windows XP Professional has to a native programming interface, but it's not totally owned by Windows XP Professional.

NOTE

Microsoft knew that Windows *9x* and Windows NT would have separate lives in the marketplace, but the company didn't want to have to write both NT and Windows *9x* versions of the applications. (Microsoft knew also that third-party programmers wouldn't want that either.) So it set out to create a programming interface that could sit atop either Windows *9x* or Windows NT/2000/XP. Win32 is the result.

The different structures of the two Windows—Windows 9*x* and Windows XP Professional—mean in practice that Windows XP Professional can do some things that 9*x* can't, and vice versa. As a result, writing a program that runs under Windows 9*x* but not under Windows XP Professional is possible—and those programs are out there; watch for them.

Another way in which the 9*x* and Windows XP Professional implementations of Win32 differ significantly is in how Windows 9*x* applications run on non-Intel platforms—they *don't*. What I mean is this: If you're running Windows XP Professional on an IA64 processor, you can also run DOS and Windows 3.1 programs, even though you don't have a Pentium or like processor. They work simply because Windows XP Professional on an IA64 system includes software to emulate the Intel processor command set on a RISC chip. When running a DOS program on an IA64, you'll see that it runs, but it runs very slowly.

NOTE

The *x*86 emulator runs the DOS or Windows 3.1 program by loading the first pieces of code and then examining the next few statements in the DOS or Windows 3.1 program. It then converts those statements to the native processor language of the RISC system and gives those statements to the RISC chip to execute. When the RISC chip is done, it goes back to the emulator program for more. This simultaneous translation of *x*86 opcodes (short for operation codes) to RISC opcodes is impressive, but slow.

If you want to run a Win32 program on your IA64, you've got to find out if the software vendor has written it for the IA64 in the first place. Although virtually every Win32 application has been built to run on the *x*86 line, most Windows XP Professional applications never get translated to IA64. Windows XP Professional's much-vaunted portability is of value only if software vendors take the short extra time needed to recompile their programs for both platforms—and, sadly, most have not.

As Windows 9*x* programs are usually also Windows XP Professional programs, RISC users are in the odd position of being pretty much guaranteed compatibility with Windows 3.1, but not with Windows 9*x*. Too bad we don't have an *x*86 emulator for Win32 code, isn't it?

NOTE

Buggy and *x*86-only programs aside, a number of types of programs will not run under both NT and 9*x*. But the Win32 API supports enough NT and 9*x* programs to be called a common programming interface.

The Win32 programming interface is a bit different in NT Workstation 4 and Windows XP Professional than it was in previous versions; as mentioned earlier, Microsoft moved the Win32 programming interface from user mode to kernel mode in version 4.

WOWEXEC

Windows XP Professional doesn't run Windows 3.1 programs natively; rather, it runs a large program that supports old Windows 3.1 programs called the "Win16 on Win32," or WOW. A program called WOWEXEC creates the WOW environment. You already know that Windows XP Professional can run Windows 3.1 programs, and I don't intend to belabor the point here. But there are some useful side effects caused by the way that Windows XP Professional runs Windows 3.1 programs that make XP *superior* to 3.1 for running its 3.1 programs. Specifically:

- Windows XP Professional optionally provides separate memory spaces for each Windows program.
- Windows XP Professional separates the Windows modules far enough from the system that a Windows 3.1 application basically *cannot* crash the system.
- Windows XP Professional multitasks Windows 3.1 applications far better than does Windows 3.1 or Windows 9*x*.

Separate WOWEXECs By default, all Windows 3.1 programs run in the same WOWEXEC module. To make WOWEXEC as backward-compatible as possible, Windows XP Professional enables Windows 3.1 applications to do a certain amount of fiddling around in their "operating system"—that is, in WOWEXEC, not in Windows XP Professional. As a result, a Windows 3.1 application *could* trash WOWEXEC. For example, you might find that a Windows 3.1 application just stops responding. It doesn't change the screen, you can't choose menu items, and you can't close it down. You *can*, of course, always press Ctrl+Alt+Del and tell the Task Manager to shut down any application, whether it's a Windows XP Professional or a Windows 3.1 application.

When you tell Windows XP Professional to shut down an application, it often returns a dialog box that says "This application is not responding" and advises you to either wait a bit and try again (a fruitless endeavor in my experience) or tell it to force the application to shut down. The second choice often does the trick.

Sometimes, however, it doesn't, and Windows XP Professional offers to go a step further, shutting down the whole of WOWEXEC. Be aware that this step shuts down not only the errant Windows 3.1 application, but also any other Windows 3.1 applications.

You have an option when running a Windows 3.1 application under Windows XP Professional to run the application in a separate memory space. *Separate memory space* means that Windows XP Professional creates a completely separate WOWEXEC for that one application. That's potentially good because no matter how crazy that application gets, it cannot damage anything except itself. That extra protection isn't without a cost, however. Each WOWEXEC takes up some memory, so running many Windows 3.1 applications, each in its own memory space, places a greater strain on your system's available RAM than if you run all of them in a single WOWEXEC.

Sturdier Multitasking Those separate WOWEXECs obviously improve the crash-proof nature of Windows XP Professional. But they offer something else as well: better multitasking.

Under Windows 3.1, all applications multitask using a method called *cooperative multitasking*. Explaining cooperative multitasking works best when using an unlikely analogy—a vaudeville show.

Windows 3.1 applications multitask in much the same way as vaudeville performers. The kernel—the stage manager in Windows 3.1—shoves an application out onto the Desktop, hoping that it won't stay there for long. A cooperative application runs only for a few tenths of a second at most, yielding to the kernel. The kernel can then select the next application to get some CPU time, and so on. Some Windows 3.1 applications, however, aren't very cooperative. They just slap the hourglass up on the screen and continue to work away, oblivious to the other applications that are waiting to run.

In vaudeville, the stage manager had a course of action: *the hook*. With the hook, a stage manager could yank a performer off stage. Sadly, Windows 3.1 lacks a hook.

A SHORT DETOUR INTO VAUDEVILLE

Back before TV and movies were popular, but after Americans started getting more leisure time and more income, more and more road shows started popping up around the country. Around the turn of the century, the most common format for these road shows was the variety show, with a dozen or so acts, each running for three to six minutes. These became known as vaudeville shows.

CONTINUED ➞

Now, the trick to managing a variety show is to understand that while *some* people will be spellbound by the guy who's balancing plates on poles, *others* came to see the woman whose dog can do square roots. As a result, each act can't go on for very long, or there won't be enough time for the other acts. The job of making sure that the schedule is rigidly adhered to falls to the stage manager. Standing just in the wings, he directs each act out onto the stage and, when time is up, he signals the performer to exit.

Now, here's where the cooperative part comes in.

The performer really *shouldn't* have to be reminded that his time is up, but sometimes it happens. Some performers feel that they're making the crowd happy and should be allowed to overstay their time on stage. A cooperative performer puts those thoughts aside for the good of the show, however, and takes her bows. Less cooperative performers don't.

To maintain compatibility with Windows 3.1, Windows XP Professional also lacks a hook in WOWEXEC. Consequently, a Windows 3.1 application can monopolize all the CPU power allocated to WOWEXEC. However, a Windows 3.1 application cannot take all the CPU time under Windows XP Professional because Windows XP Professional gives only a percentage of its CPU power to WOWEXEC–and that restriction is very important.

For one thing, no matter how poorly behaved your Windows 3.1 application is, no matter how much of a CPU thief it is, it still can't affect your 32-bit applications. A rude application *can* keep your other Windows 3.1 applications from getting CPU time–but there's even a way to work around that. Think about it for a minute, and you'll see what it is: running separate WOWEXECs.

Separate WOWEXECs cost you in memory, yes, but they also get separate CPU time allocations from Windows XP Professional, which means that you can use Windows XP Professional to get around Windows 3.1's uncooperative multitasking nature. Put each one of your Windows 3.1 applications in its own separate memory space, and they'll multitask like a charm. Oh, by the way, that cooperative multitasking problem doesn't pop up with Win32 applications; you might say that they're all built with a preinstalled hook.

OS/2 and POSIX

Windows XP Professional is a platform for client-server applications, and many client-server applications were built to run atop LAN Manager or Unix. LAN Manager ran on OS/2 version 1.3, so backward compatibility with Microsoft's previous network product required that Windows XP Professional be able to run LAN Manager applications. The OS/2 subsystem makes sure that happens.

Similarly, Unix is a platform for many client-server applications. Windows XP Professional would like to be able to support those applications, but, sadly, Unix isn't one operating system; it's an umbrella name for many different companies' implementations of the whole idea of Unix. The closest we come to a "standard" Unix is a government implementation called POSIX, and so Windows XP Professional supports POSIX applications.

Virtual DOS Machines (VDMs)

No operating system could call itself Windows compatible if it didn't support DOS programs; Windows XP Professional does that through a system called Virtual DOS Machine, or VDM. *How* Windows XP Professional achieves compatibility is an interesting story.

DOS programs have two basic needs: unrestricted access to 1MB of memory and unrestricted access to 64K of I/O addresses.

I'm sure you know what a memory address is, so I'll lay aside for the moment discussion of how Windows XP Professional solves that problem for DOS. But many people don't understand I/O addresses, so let me take a minute to explain them. All hardware devices, both chips on the motherboard and add-in cards, have hardware or I/O addresses. It's not unusual for us to say something like, "The communications program uses COM1," when we mean that the communications program sometimes needs to send data out of a serial port. It finds that serial port somewhere. From the CPU's point of view, nothing is actually called COM1. Instead, the CPU recognizes a piece of hardware at a particular address—hexadecimal address 3F8, in the case of COM1.

Windows XP Professional programs don't control a communications port by directly sending data to I/O address 3F8. Instead, they let the operating system do the controlling. Rather than sending the commands to COM1 to tell the modem to dial, for example, Windows XP Professional programs instruct the operating system to tell the modem to dial a particular number. Windows XP Professional applications, therefore, don't have to control hardware directly. DOS programs see the matter differently.

Virtually all DOS programs choose not to leave hardware control to the operating system and instead twiddle the hardware directly via that hardware's I/O addresses. Now, that could be a problem for Windows XP Professional because Windows XP Professional doesn't want any software addressing hardware directly except for the operating system itself. Disallowing DOS programs from communicating directly with I/O addresses, however, would make about 99 percent of the DOS programs crash, which would damage somewhat Windows XP Professional's claim to be DOS compatible. What, then, to do? The answer: Make use of *virtual device drivers*, or VxDs.

A VxD is a piece of operating system software that essentially shields the hardware from the program. When an application program, such as a DOS program, tries to access I/O address 3F8 directly, the action triggers a VxD for that address. As the VxD was attached by Windows XP Professional's designers to I/O address 3F8, that particular VxD is designed to handle serial port I/O. VxDs exist for the keyboard, the display screen, the hardware timer circuitry, the parallel port, you name it—just about all the standard PC hardware.

But what about the *not*-so-standard hardware? What kind of VxD support does Windows XP Professional have for it? Well, that's sort of a problem. Keyboards, mice, parallel ports, and the like are all pretty standard, so writing VxDs for them was possible. But no real market leader or standard in fax boards exists, so Windows XP Professional can't include a VxD for fax boards. Result: a number of DOS-based or Windows 3.1–based fax programs don't run under Windows XP Professional. (Actually, Windows XP Professional has a VxD that handles many fax boards, but not all of them.) Other examples of devices that lack VxD support: factory automation interfaces and proprietary boards. If Windows XP Professional runs across a DOS program that tries to access an address that Windows XP Professional doesn't have a VxD for, Windows XP Professional terminates the DOS program. This inability to run some DOS apps costs Windows XP Professional in terms of compatibility, but it's the price to pay for stability.

Managing Memory in Windows XP Professional

Let's wrap up this chapter with a quick look at how Windows XP Professional allocates memory to applications in its quest to be the most stable operating system around.

All Windows XP Professional applications start life being told that they have access to 2GB of RAM. Not only is that not true (I've seen Windows XP Professional machines with more than 2GB of RAM, but not many), but NT keeps on telling this little lie to *all* the applications running under NT!

NOTE

To be precise, Windows XP Professional applications (or, rather, Win32 applications, as there's really no such thing as a Windows XP Professional application) can work within a memory space equal to 2048MB, *minus* 128K. You'll see in a moment why that 128K is reserved.

The Numbers behind Windows XP Professional's Memory Requirements

Windows XP Professional requires that any machine it uses support a 32-bit memory structure, and 232 bits is 4096MB, or 4GB. The first chip on which Microsoft implemented NT, however, was the MIPS chip, which supports 4GB but with a requirement—applications can't have more than 2GB of that 4GB total, and the operating system must get the other 2GB. It's dumb, but it's not the dumbest thing I've ever seen built into an operating system. Microsoft decided to follow suit and designed Windows XP Professional to require the same thing.

NOTE

Just as an aside here, in my opinion the decision to restrict apps to 2GB max was a severely dumb move. No other 32-bit CPU that I know of imposes this limitation, and there's no a priori good reason to impose the limitation. Incorporating it into the architecture of Windows XP Professional makes about as much sense as saying that my Honda Civic is a hatchback and gets good mileage, so you should buy only hatchback cars for good mileage.

Remember how I mentioned in a previous note that, to be precise, 128K of that 2GB is not available? That's because Microsoft defines the memory space of each Win32 program as 2GB but restricts the bottom 64KB and top 64KB of that memory; no program can address it. *Why* Microsoft restricts that space reflects a small stroke of genius, and the story is told in the following section.

THE VIRTUAL MEMORY MANAGER AS PRODUCER

Have you ever seen Mel Brooks's movie or play *The Producers*? It's a farce about a crooked producer who comes up with a surefire way to make a pile of money. He finds a number of rich people who'd like to back a Broadway play and, talking to each person privately, sells 90 percent of the interest in the play over and over again. By the time he's done, he's probably sold 1,000 percent of the play to unsuspecting investors. Then he sets off to create a play that will definitely flop, allowing him to tell the unwitting investors that oh, well, that's how it goes, as the play closes on its first night—and the crooked producer walks away with all the investment money. Of course, the plan backfires; the play is a big hit, and the producer encounters an endless string of problems.

Windows XP Professional's Virtual Memory Manager is kind of like that producer.

Memory Mistakes That Programmers Make

Every programmer makes mistakes. Some mistakes are, however, more likely and more prevalent than others. Here are two of them: accidentally filling a memory address pointer to all zeros and then trying to write data, and accidentally filling a memory address pointer to all ones and then trying to write data.

The first error would lead a program to damage data in the bottom 64KB of its memory space. The second error would lead a program to damage data in the top 64KB of its memory space. By including those two memory address areas but marking them off-limits to a program, Microsoft guarantees that any accidental attempts at writing in the bottom or top 64KB—a symptom of a common programming error—*must* trigger an error message. A very clever feature.

Virtual Memory

And what if a Windows XP Professional application tries to *use* all 2GB of its memory space? Well, obviously most of us don't have computers with that much RAM. So, Windows XP Professional relies on an old dodge that operating systems have been using for years—*virtual memory*. All processors that run Windows XP Professional support virtual memory via *paging*. Here's how the dodge works.

First, CPUs divide their memory spaces into areas called *pages*. The 386, 486, Pentium, and Pentium Pro use 4KB pages, as do the MIPS and PowerPC chips. The Alpha uses 8KB pages. The Pentium and Pentium Pro have an option that enables them to use 4096KB pages, but probably no one uses that feature.

Second, CPUs enable their operating systems to re-address any given page. If a page is physically addressed as (for example) address 2000KB–2004KB, there's nothing saying that a program *using* that page must think that its address is 2000KB–2004KB. The CPU can just say to the program, "Oh, you needed address 124KB through 128KB? Well, here it is," and hand it that memory that is actually addressed from 2000KB–2004KB. In that case, we'd say that the *physical address* of the block is from 2000KB–2004KB but the *logical address* is 124KB–128KB. *Physical* and *logical* are the common words, but if they're not too clear, just substitute *actually* and *appears,* as I do: The memory that is actually at address range 2000KB–2004KB appears to be in the range 124KB–128KB.

TIP

The value of virtual memory can't be overstated.

Suppose you have a computer that's running 15 programs of various sizes and you exit from a random 7 of those programs. Unless all the programs were sitting right next to one another, your computer's RAM is probably *fragmented*—you have a block of used space, then a block of unused space, a block of used space, a block of unused space, and so on. So you load another program, and it wants *all* that space. Your operating system wants to give that RAM to the application all in one piece, so what does it do?

Well, on earlier operating systems, your system would defragment its memory, in a process somewhat like the DEFRAG command in MS-DOS 6.*x* or the SpeedDisk application in Norton Utilities. That's a tricky operation, because it means that you have to move an application *while* the application is working; it's like tuning a car while it's running down the road at 65 mph. The ability to just re-address a block of memory with some bogus address and then tie that bogus address to a piece of software (and, best of all, to have that piece of software *believe* you) enables you to avoid defragging in the Norton Utilities way. Instead, all an operating system has to do is to grab all the free RAM, assign it contiguous memory addresses, and voila! Instant block of contiguous memory.

Now let's put those two facts together and see how CPUs help with virtual memory. First, I kind of indicated that the CPU lies about a memory block's address only when necessary; not so. An inveterate liar from way back, the CPU insists on *always* supplying logical, not physical addresses to Win32 programs. Ignoring Mark Twain's advice that if you always tell the truth, you never have to remember anything, the CPU maintains *page tables,* which remember the physical and logical addresses of all the system's memory. In the page table is a bit that says whether a page is located in memory.

In effect, the CPU can hand out a bogus 2GB to each and every application regardless of how much or how little RAM exists on the system. Also, at any given moment, a lot more pages than the computer could *ever* supply have been handed out to applications. And if an application tries to access a page that's not in RAM at the moment, the Virtual Memory Manager swings into action. It has a large file called the *paging file* (stored on the hard disk as `pagefile.sys`), which acts as a holding tank for RAM pages. You see, if you're loading a 10MB application and you already have a 15MB application loaded but only 15MB of RAM available, the Virtual Memory Manager takes the pages for the now-dormant 10MB application and writes them to the paging file. That leaves space to put the entire 15MB application into RAM, at least for a moment or two. And if only some of the pages in both applications are being used or if the sum of the used pages for both applications is less than 15MB, you can load 25MB of applications into 15MB of RAM!

What's Next?

One important reason for using Windows XP Professional is its networking capabilities. In the next chapter, I'll provide more specifics about network architecture, including details on topologies and protocols, and discuss how to choose between a client-server and a peer-to-peer network.

Chapter 22

Network Architectures

By now, you're fully aware that the operating system on your computer is Windows XP Professional and that it was designed as a *network* operating system. Before you set up a network, though, you need to do some planning and some thinking about how it will be set up. The best way to approach this task is to delve into topologies. A *topology* is the layout of a network, and there are two types:

Physical topology Describes how the computers connect to each other. You can think of a physical topology as an actual map of how your computers and cables might look in an aerial photograph. The physical topology includes the cables, connectors, NICs (Network Interface Cards), and hubs. If it is a part of the network and you can tangibly touch it, it is part of the physical topology of your network.

Adapted from *Mastering Windows XP Professional* by Mark Minasi

ISBN 0-7821-2981-1 1056 pages $39.99

Logical topology Describes how signals pass between networked computers or how information passes from node A to node B. The same words (bus, ring) are used to describe specific physical and logical topologies, so be sure you understand the distinction.

After you've mastered the various specific topologies available in each of these two categories, we'll move bravely to the *protocols* that can be used for networking your computers. I make no bones about it: protocols for sending information across your network are easily the most technically intensive part of this chapter. So make sure you block out an hour of your time to get through it, and have a strong cup of coffee on hand. But I promise you, if you make it through this section of the chapter, the ride is all downhill from there.

Physical Topologies

If you wanted to, you could conceivably run cables from each network node to all other network nodes. Technically, assuming that you had enough places to plug in all those cables, this configuration could work fine. The only real problem is the amount of cable you would use.

If you draw a diagram for yourself, you can easily see how connecting all the computers in a network directly to one another could quickly get very complicated. For example, take a look at Figure 22.1. With 5 computers, you would need 10 cables, which doesn't seem too bad, really; but if you added just 3 more computers, you would have to connect 18 more cables! It gets worse: 10 computers require 45 cables; 25 computers require 300 cables.

To figure out how many cables your organization would need to interconnect all your computers this way, take the number of computers (n), multiply it by ($n-1$), and then divide the result by 2. Hence:

Number of cables = $n\ (n-1)\ /\ 2$

As you can see, the number of cables adds up quickly. If you don't want to spend your entire budget on cable, therefore, you need to devise a more efficient way of linking your network nodes. Most networks use a star topology or a bus topology.

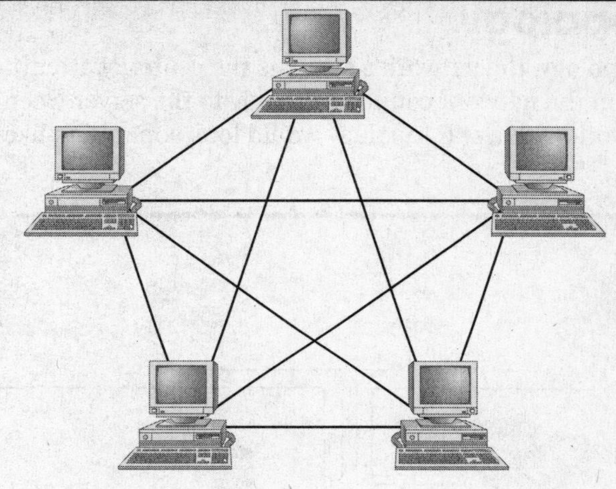

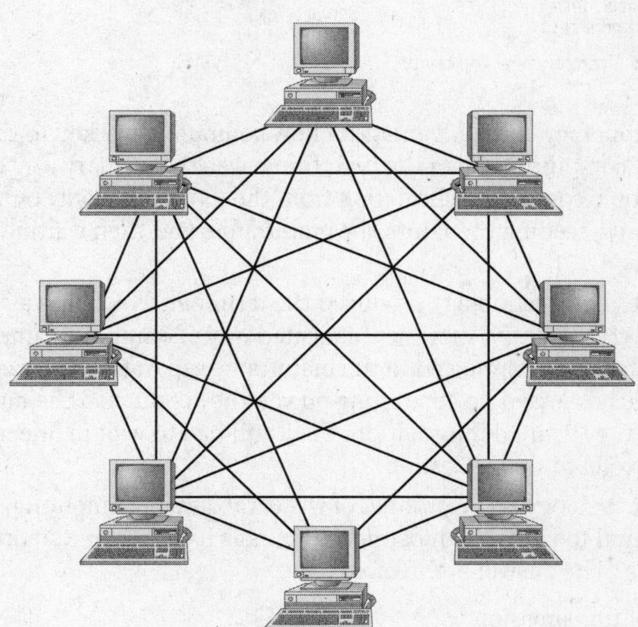

FIGURE 22.1: Direct-cabling requirements for a five-node network and an eight-node network

The Star Topology

In the star topology, the network's server is the center of attention. Each workstation on the network connects directly to the server. Seen from above, a network with a star topology would look something like Figure 22.2.

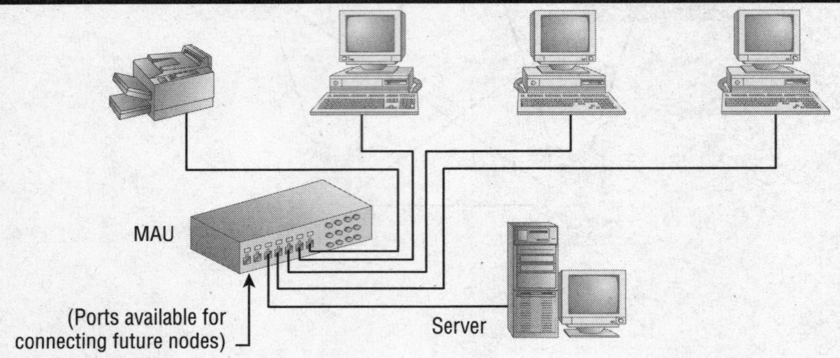

FIGURE 22.2: Star physical topology

The star topology takes advantage of how computers worked in the early days of computing, when the mainframe was the primary way to network. People could get information from the mainframe only by punching cards, feeding them into the mainframe, and then waiting for their answer.

Eventually, new technology produced the terminal, which was a slightly (but only slightly) more sophisticated way of doing the same thing. Each terminal connected to the mainframe separately, and because the terminals possessed no computing power, they contacted the mainframe when they wanted information. They still had to wait in line for the mainframe to get to their question.

If the star topology is the product of the early days of computing, why is it still around today, when most new terminals have become smart workstations? The answer is threefold:

- Ease of transmission
- Ease of troubleshooting
- Ease of cabling

Getting to the Hub of the Problem

The centerpiece of the star topology is a hub, a multistation access unit (MAU), or a concentrator. All three of these devices provide a centralized location where all the cables in your physical star meet. Any node that is connected to these devices can talk to any other node that is connected. Thus, the similarity of these three devices, but how are they different?

Hub A *hub* is a device that provides a meeting location for all your cables. Any device attached to the hub has physical access to any other device that is connected to the hub. Hubs generally fall into one of two categories: passive or active.

> **Passive hub** Provides a central location where all your cables meet; it provides no additional functions.
>
> **Active hub** Provides a central location where all your cables meet as well as at least one other function. The other function can be acting as a repeater (which is the most common) or acting as a bridge or router.

Multistation Access Units (MAUs) IBM generally refers to its hubs as multistation access units (MAUs). MAUs serve the same functions as hubs and are used to accommodate the IBM connector. Most MAUs are active by design.

Concentrators *Concentrators* are like build-it-yourself active hubs. A concentrator is a big box with expansion slots in it. An average concentrator could have up to 16 expansion slots. If you want the concentrator to be a straightforward hub, you can purchase a port card with 4, 8, or 16 ports to which you can attach computers. You can put your first port card in slot 0. Assuming that your port card had 8 ports on it, you would then be able to attach as many as 8 devices to the concentrator. This would be a good setup for a small network. The advantage of a concentrator is the capability to add more port cards as your network grows. If you want to add another small department of six people, add another 8-port card in slot 1.

And the fun is just beginning. As your network grows, you may have to provide a gateway service to your mainframe system in your office. No problem—just purchase a gateway card and put it into slot 2. Now all 16 of your current users (8 attached to slot 0 and 8 attached to slot 1) can go through the gateway card to get to the mainframe system. If distance between nodes is becoming a problem, add a repeater card so that all network packets are repeated as they flow through the hub. You can keep adding cards to the concentrator as your needs grow. If you are concerned that you might run out of slots, fear not. There is a slot specifically reserved for a backbone card that enables you to connect one concentrator to another so that they act as one large concentrator.

Of hub, MAU, and concentrator, the concentrator is the most expensive, but it does provide the greatest flexibility in terms of growth for your network.

NOTE

In practice, the preceding terms are often used interchangeably. For instance, many folks use the term *hub* when they are referring to a concentrator. In the previous paragraphs, I've given the true definitions of each term, but some of you may think those definitions are wrong because you've been hearing the industry use the terms loosely and often incorrectly. So don't be thrown when you are looking through articles or catalogs and you see mention of an 8-port stand-alone concentrator with no space to add additional cards. It is just the industry's way of keeping us on our toes. For the rest of this book, I bow to common usage and use the term *hub* to refer to all three options.

Star Topology Continued

On a network with a star topology, the server never has to wonder how to get information back to the terminal that asked the question. The server just finds the port to which the node in question connects and relays the information.

The star topology is nice for awkwardly arranged networks. As a simple example, imagine a network with four computers: three workstations and one server. If one workstation is upstairs and two are downstairs but in separate rooms, cabling the network is relatively easy if you don't have to worry about connecting all the nodes to each other and can concentrate on connecting the individual workstations to the hub.

Of course, the star topology has one major drawback—the large amount of cable it uses. Having a centralized hub isn't the most cable-efficient arrangement, so if you're concerned about cable costs and your nodes are close together, you might want to consider the bus topology.

TROUBLESHOOTING A STAR TOPOLOGY

Another big advantage to the star topology is that it's easy to troubleshoot. As you'll see in the discussion of the bus topology, if your bus network fails, you will have difficulty pinpointing exactly where the problem lies without a node-to-node search. On a star network, in contrast, finding the source of a problem is easy. If one node doesn't work, the problem probably lies somewhere between the port of the hub and the node. You should check to see if the problem lies with:

- The terminal itself
- The cable between the hub and the terminal
- The port on the hub that services the troubled terminal

First, check whether the NIC is configured correctly. Ensure that no hardware conflicts exist in terms of I/O addresses, IRQs (interrupt requests), or DMA (direct memory access) channels. You may also want to run a memory test on the workstation and run a hard drive testing utility.

If none of the network nodes work, the problem probably lies with the server, and it's time to hope that you planned for fault tolerance and that you did your backups.

The Bus Topology

The bus topology, known in the Mac world by the more descriptive term *daisy chaining*, is much more cable efficient than the star topology. In the bus topology, the cable runs from computer to computer, making each computer a link of a chain. You can run a bus topology in three ways. Ethernet is the best-known example of a logical bus topology; the others are called thicknet (10Base-5) and thinnet (10Base-2), based on the type of cable that you use to connect the network.

Thicknet, sometimes referred to as *frozen yellow garden hose* because of its stiffness and color, uses a thick, central cable as a sort of backbone for the network; then from the backbone it runs thinner cables known as *taps* or *drops* to the network's nodes, as depicted in Figure 22.3. What connects the thinner cable to the thicknet cable is a transceiver. In generic terms, a *transceiver* is a device that connects one cable type to a dissimilar cable type.

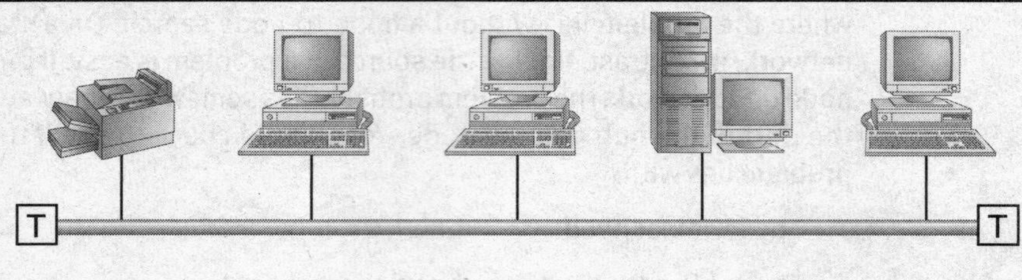

FIGURE 22.3: A thicknet configuration

The *T*'s at either end of the network in Figure 22.3 indicate the terminators.

The thicknet configuration is typically used in mainframe and minicomputer networks, but its popularity is diminishing as PCs get smarter and mainframe-based networks less common.

Thinnet, on the other hand, eschews the backbone idea and connects all network devices directly. Rather than using thick cable, thinnet uses the more flexible coaxial cable, as depicted in Figure 22.4. Thinnet is becoming a more popular networking topology than its thick counterpart, if for no other reason than that the thick cable in thicknet is a pain to work with—it's very stiff and clumsy.

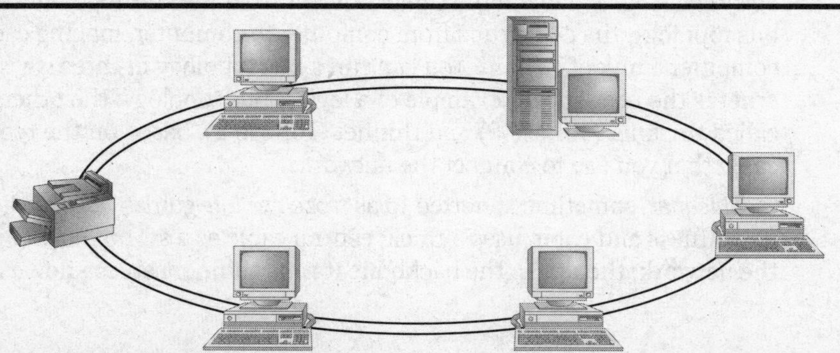

FIGURE 22.4: A thinnet configuration

The biggest potential problem with a bus network is that you have to tell it when to quit. If you haven't terminated your network, your network can't transmit. Nor can it transmit if even one node on the network is malfunctioning, because the system depends on every node being in proper working order so that it can pass the data along.

There is an important distinction between a node malfunctioning and a node being off. If the node is off, data will pass through the T-connector to the next active node. In this case, the network is unaware that an inactive node is present. However, if the node is on, or active but malfunctioning, problems will occur. The active node will still attempt to process a packet but will do it inaccurately, thus slowing down the whole network or bringing it to a screeching halt.

The bus topology does have one great advantage over the star topology: it's cable efficient and therefore can save you money on the most expensive part of your network. On the other hand, it can be difficult to implement if your network is not neatly lined up in a row. As I discussed in the section on the star topology, if the network is spread haphazardly over a building, running individual cables from each node to a hub could be a lot easier than trying to connect all the nodes to one another.

Another big minus to the bus topology is troubleshooting. If *one node* is down, the network can't relay messages, and the network stops dead. This factor not only makes your network vulnerable to failures (remember, the only way an entire star network dies is if the server or hub dies), but also makes it difficult to troubleshoot. To find a problem on a bus network, you might need to inspect every node on the segment to make sure that the cables are securely fastened, that no one tried to reboot or log off when a signal was being passed, or that any number of other things are in order.

Logical Topologies

Logical topologies (occasionally referred to as *electrical topologies*) describe the way in which a network transmits information from one node to the next node—as opposed to physical topologies, which merely represent what your network looks like. This topic is not all theory, however; the way you want your network to transmit information can directly affect your options when it comes to purchasing NICs and cabling.

As we head into logical topology, remember that the physical topology does not have a direct bearing on the logical topology. You can have a physical bus and a logical ring, a physical star and a logical bus, and so on.

The best way to visualize a logical topology is by way of an analogy. If you had a 400-page document that absolutely, positively had to be sent across the country overnight, you would probably send it via Federal Express. In the process of sending this document, you would have to use a FedEx envelope and addressing slip. When addressing the FedEx package, you would have to provide a source address, a destination address, and the document.

Your network needs the same pieces of information: source address, destination address, and data. All this information taken together constitutes the *packet*. The logical topology has to handle how this packet is going to be sent across the network. It's a three-step process:

1. The logical topology determines the format of the packet, just as FedEx has predetermined the format of its address slip. You must have the addresses in a certain format.
2. The logical topology determines how much information the packet will carry, just as FedEx says that only 30 pages can be sent in its letter envelope.
3. The logical topology determines the method of tracking the packet across the network, just as FedEx has its own tracking system.

Actually, in regard to step 3 of the process, some logical topologies do not track the packet at all; they just hope for the best. Other topologies track the packet along each step of its path.

Bus Topology

As mentioned earlier, Ethernet is probably the best-known example of a logical bus network; it certainly is the most popular LAN type. Ethernet is an example of a *logical* bus topology, but—as you'll see in a minute—it is not always a *physical* bus topology. (Yes, I keep hammering that home, but the concept isn't easy to grasp.)

How does the bus topology work? Simply put, each time a node on the network has data for another node, it broadcasts the data to the entire network. The various nodes hear the broadcast and look to see if the data is for them. If it is, they keep it. If it's not, they pass it down again until it reaches the correct destination.

Whatever anyone on the bus says, everyone hears. It's something like the old telephone party lines, in which several neighbors shared a telephone number. A distinctive ring was assigned to each person on the line so that everyone could answer their own calls. If your code was, say, three quick rings, and you heard the telephone ring three quick rings, you could pick it up and know it was for you. On the other hand, if you heard two long rings and one short ring, you'd know that the call was for your neighbor Burt and ignore it. In all cases, everyone heard the rings but only one person responded—the person whom the call was for.

The bus topology works in a similar fashion. Every Ethernet card has a 48-bit address peculiar to itself, and each piece of data that travels the network is directed to the address of the card in the node that should receive the data. All nodes on the network can see the data, but if it's not addressed to them, they ignore it and pass it down until it reaches the correct destination. (Bus networks work better than the old party lines that way—your neighbor's machine can't eavesdrop on data not sent to it.)

So now you know how data finds its destination on the network, but how do networked computers send the data in the first place? On a bus network, every workstation can send out information in a package called a *packet*. Data transmitted on a network of *any* type must conform to a strict format called the *Data Link Layer Frame format,* which that network type uses for arranging data. Ethernet's format looks like Figure 22.5.

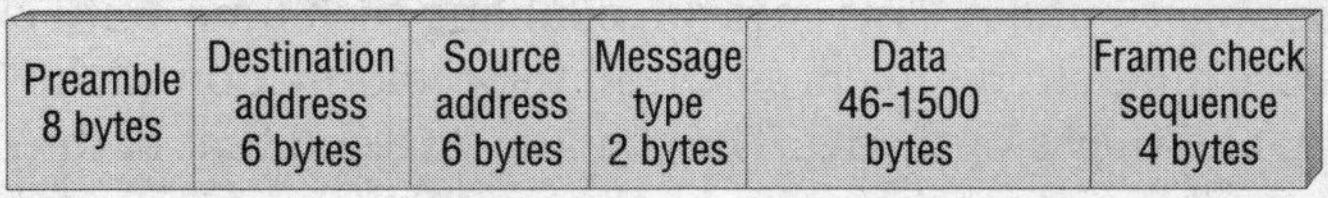

Preamble 8 bytes	Destination address 6 bytes	Source address 6 bytes	Message type 2 bytes	Data 46-1500 bytes	Frame check sequence 4 bytes

FIGURE 22.5: The composition of a Data Link Layer Ethernet frame

Each packet can be no more than 1,518 bytes, just to make sure that one workstation doesn't hog the network for too long. Before a workstation broadcasts to the network, it listens to see if anyone else is using the network. If the coast is clear, the workstation broadcasts.

What if the coast isn't clear? Ethernet is the topology that has to worry about that situation. When a node has a packet to send across the network, it "listens" to the cable to hear if any frequencies are going across the cable. If the sending node, I'll call it node A, detects a frequency on the cable, it will wait for the current packet to go by and then send its packet. If node A detects that the line is free, it will go ahead and send its packet.

The biggest problem with this broadcast method is distance. If the distance between node A and node B is too great, the nodes might not "hear" each other on the line and might both send packets at the same time. What follows is known as a *packet collision*. If a collision occurs, it will cause a frequency "ripple" on the cable. The first node to detect this increased frequency ripple sends out a high-frequency signal, which cancels out all other signals. This signal tells all nodes that a collision has occurred and that all nodes on the network should stop sending packets. At this point each node waits a random amount of time and then tries broadcasting again. Nodes can repeat this wait-and-listen routine as many as 16 times before giving up.

The way that nodes decide when to resend their data is actually pretty neat. The system is known by the unfortunate name of *truncated binary exponential backoff*. (No, unlike almost everything else in the LAN world, it doesn't have a convenient and commonly used abbreviation.) In English, this name means that after two nodes collide, each node on the network randomly generates a whole number between 1 and 2, multiplies that number by 0.5, and then waits that number of milliseconds before retransmitting. Of course, the first time out the chances are 50-50 that nodes A and B will pick the same number, so they might have to retry again. The next time, A and B randomly pick a number between 1 and 4 and do the same thing. If they pick the same number again, they'll pick a number between 1 and 8. This goes on, doubling each time, until either A and B choose different numbers and send their information or the 16 tries are up and they stop trying. The chances are good that both A and B will get to send their data, however, by the time they get to the 16th try. The delay could be up to half a second, which for a network that transmits data at 10 million bits per second is an eternity. A bus network rarely needs that many retries.

How likely are collisions? Having cable no longer than it's supposed to be decreases your chance of a collision because the nodes can "hear" other nodes broadcasting more easily; but the way the bus logical topology works *increases* the likelihood of packet collisions. Consider: if a node can't broadcast until the network is clear and more than one node has information to send, what's going to happen as soon as the line is free? Both nodes will leap to get their information out first, and the result is a collision.

Keep in mind that all this processing takes place at the Ethernet NIC. Therefore, if you are going to use the Ethernet topology, all your nodes must have Ethernet cards. Ethernet can run on top of a physical bus, physical star, or physical ring.

Ethernet isn't the only example of a bus topology, but it is the most used. For a while, AT&T marketed a one-megabit-per-second (Mbps) version of Ethernet called StarLAN. StarLAN is now a 10Mbps network, but now and then you'll see installations using the old StarLAN. Another, perhaps better known example is the LocalTalk/AppleTalk network built into Macintosh computers. LocalTalk transmits at only 250,000bps but employs many of the basic design principles found in Ethernet.

Token Ring Topology

IBM originally bought the design for the Token Ring logical topology from Olaf Soderblom, a Dutch scientist. The original Token Ring used a 4Mbps signaling speed, but in 1989 IBM released a 16Mbps version. Other Token Ring networks are available but they are not as well known as IBM's, partially because they were late getting on the market. In addition, other companies developing their own Token Ring systems have to decide whether to fight or accommodate Soderblom's claim of proprietary rights. At this point, the battle is still in progress.

Although the Token Ring network has a ring logical topology, it uses a connected star system like that of 10Base-T Ethernet for its physical topology. Instead of hubs, Token Ring uses devices called either concentrators or, more commonly, multistation access units (MAUs), as discussed previously.

NOTE

Don't confuse these MAUs with an Ethernet adapter's *media attachment unit*—a transceiver connecting to the Attachment Unit Interface (AUI) port.

A Token Ring board attaches to the MAU with a D-shell type connector on one side and an odd-looking IBM connector on the other. The Token Ring connector plugs into the MAU. Eight PCs can attach to a MAU, and then those MAUs attach to *other* MAUs. Token Ring networks do not have terminators; instead, one end of the cable plugs into the board, and the other end plugs into the MAU.

As with the hubs for 10Base-T, you can most easily arrange your Token Ring network so that cables extend from a central wiring closet (a place where all the cables can be gathered together) on each floor to workstations on that floor, and the MAUs go into the wiring closet. The cables between the MAU and the network device can be as long as 45 meters, providing enough space for most floor plans to be cabled with a wiring closet.

Remember that Ethernet is a broadcast system; that is, what one station says, all stations hear. But Token Ring doesn't work that way. In Token Ring, every station must repeat what it hears from the previous station, making a kind of "bucket brigade" of data.

The heart of the Token Ring topology is the token packet. To avoid packet collisions, the token topologies ensure that only one workstation can send information across the network at any given time. The method used to ensure that only a single transmission occurs is the token packet, or "talking stick." Only the node that has control of the token packet can send information across the network.

How does the token move around the network? When a workstation is done with the token, it releases it to whatever station is next in line. If nobody grabs the token, the workstation releases it a second time. If nobody responds to the token for a second time, the workstation sends out a general query, known as a *solicit successor frame*, over the network, asking, "Who's supposed to get the token next?" If a workstation responds, the sending workstation addresses the token to that workstation and passes the token. Because no single node can transmit for longer than it takes for a piece of data to make a complete circuit of the network, no one ever waits more than one circuit's worth of information before getting a chance to transmit. Unlike Ethernet, where collisions could conceivably keep other nodes from transmitting by tying up the network, Token Ring ensures that everyone gets a turn.

The fact that Ethernet *broadcasts* and that Token Ring *repeats* affects the kinds of cable that each network topology uses. Fiber-optic lines are not well suited to broadcasting but work well for point-to-point communications. Consequently, Token Ring is better suited to fiber usage than Ethernet is unless you use some kind of star configuration such as 10Base-T Ethernet. Token Ring is designed to support a variety of cable types, but most commonly uses IBM Type 1, IBM Type 2, and IBM Type 3 cables.

When a Bus Is Not a Bus: 10Base-T

To really understand how a network can use one physical topology and another logical topology, let's take a look at 10Base-T, a kind of Ethernet network that has a bus logical topology and a star physical topology. Figure 22.6 shows how a 10Base-T network is cabled.

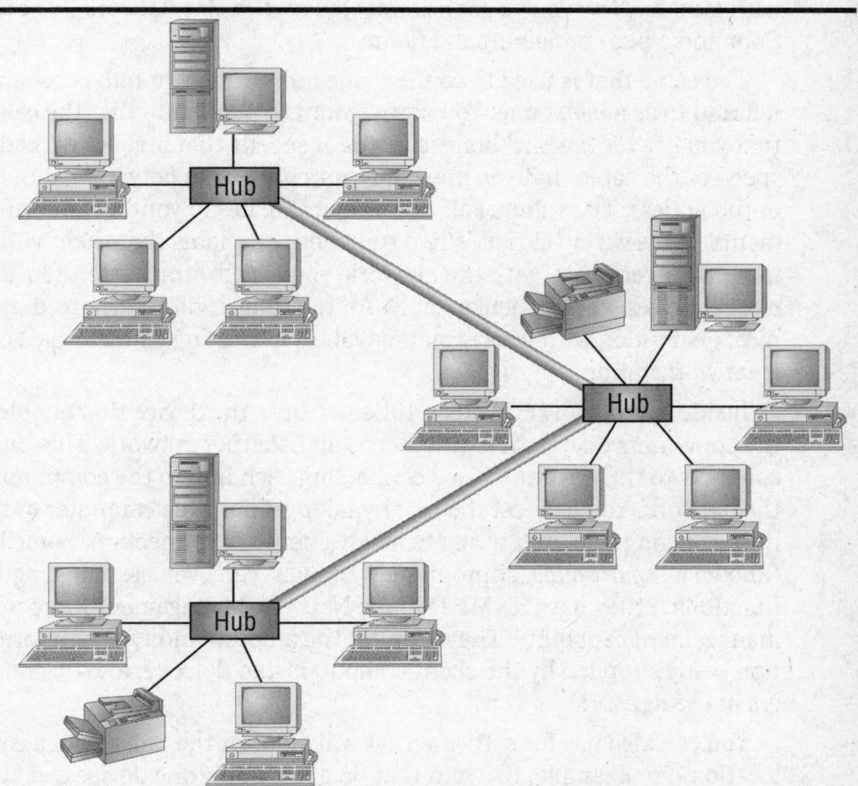

FIGURE 22.6: A 10Base-T distributed star configuration

10Base-T looks like a set of stars connected by a bus. It still behaves as if it were a bus—it broadcasts to the network—but it's cabled like a star, using unshielded twisted-pair (UTP). Therefore, this network is a *logical* bus but a *physical* star. Why does 10Base-T use this connected-star approach? It might seem contrary to logic, because a star network involves more cable than a bus and so should not be a preferred cabling scheme from a cost-of-wiring point of view.

But this connected-star approach has a major benefit: it is easy to troubleshoot. Suppose you're setting up a network in a building with multiple floors. On each floor, you create a wiring closet. You then run cables (the 10Base-T specifications limit each cable's length to no more than 100 meters) from the wiring closet to each workstation on that floor. Next, you connect each floor's wiring closet to the next floor's wiring closet with a cable. Now you've got a connected star—a star network on each floor and a bus connecting the floors.

The cable that is used to connect one hub to another hub is generally referred to as a backbone. You always want to make sure that the cable that you use for the backbone is rated for speeds that meet or exceed the speed of the cable that you are using throughout the network (from hub to the nodes). The value of all this extra cable lies in your test instruments in the wiring closet. When someone complains that their workstation no longer works with the network, you can go straight to the wiring closet and test the particular cable. All the cables will be arranged in a nice, neat order, with clearly marked labels indicating which cable goes to what workstation.

Inside each wiring closet is a 10Base-T hub, the device that enables all the computers on a floor to interact as an Ethernet network. This hub connects to the next hub, thus connecting each hub to the computers on the network. You can test the hub by taking a portable computer to the hub, plugging it in, and trying to make a network connection. Some hubs (known as *smart hubs*, appropriately enough) can even assume diagnostic functions if they have SNMP (Simple Network Management Protocol) management capability. They monitor the amount and type of information being supplied by the client computers and detect errors on computers in the network.

You can also pay for software that will monitor the hubs from a central location. For example, I've said that on a LAN only one device can "talk" at a time. One particular type of hardware failure makes a computer chatter away endlessly, locking up the network, but a smart hub detects this failure and disconnects that malfunctioning computer from the network.

Of course, the connected star approach of 10Base-T would simplify this debugging step even if you didn't have a smart hub; you could simply connect a portable computer to the hub—and then try to use the network. If the network is busy because of a chattering computer, disconnect one of the computers at the hub and try the portable again. Because all the connections are right at your fingertips, you need only a minute or two to test all the connections to find the chatterer.

IEEE's Topological Protocols

In 1980, the Institute of Electrical and Electronics Engineers (IEEE) attempted to make some sense out of all the conflicting standards, protocols, and manufacturing methods of cabling and logical topologies. The following sections, though not exhaustive, should give you a feel for some of the characteristics of these standards and how the IEEE committees work. Some of this information also appears elsewhere in the book, so don't worry if something looks familiar.

The 802.3 Standard

When the IEEE 802.3 committee met, Ethernet standards were already a powerhouse in the cabling configuration field, thanks to industry acceptance. However, the 802.3 committee was reluctant to force all new networks' topologies to follow the strict Ethernet standard as set out by Xerox and DEC, so it said, "Let's try to come up with an Ethernet-*like* standard," and the 802.3 standard was born. The 802.3 standard includes the older Ethernet protocol specifications in addition to changes in the basic structure of the data packets.

Although all Ethernet-type networks use the 802.3 standard, 10Base-2, which uses both a physical and a logical bus topology, is the most common. It uses 50-ohm coaxial baseband cable and can send data at

10Mbps. Information travels the network in packets consisting of the following parts (see Figure 22.7):

Preamble Eight bytes of information used to coordinate the rest of the information in the packet.

Start delimiter Indicates that the frame is about to begin.

Destination address The network address of the workstation or workstations that are to receive this information.

Source address The address that enables the receiving workstation or workstations to recognize the workstation that sent the information.

Type or length The type of information that is held within the data part of this packet, whether it is graphics information, ASCII text information, or any other type of data. If the type is not listed, this field will contain the length of the packet.

This information is crucial to the sending process because the receiving station can't understand bitmaps if it's expecting text (or vice versa). Think of what happens when you drink orange juice when you're expecting milk. It doesn't taste like either one, and you probably can't identify it, at least not right away.

Actual data The data can be anywhere from 46 to 1,500 bytes long.

Frame-check sequence A "packing slip" to verify that the rest of the packet reached its destination intact.

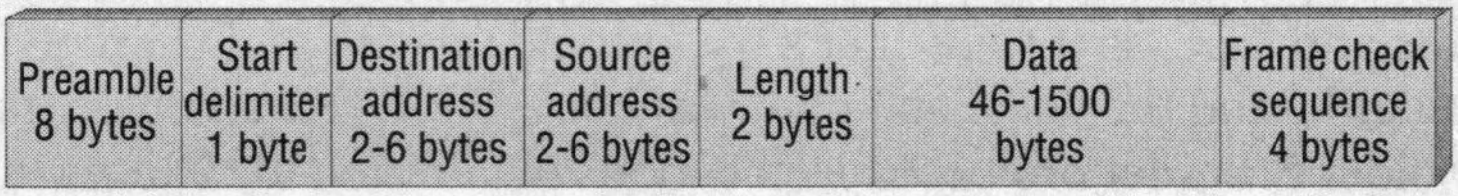

Preamble 8 bytes	Start delimiter 1 byte	Destination address 2-6 bytes	Source address 2-6 bytes	Length 2 bytes	Data 46-1500 bytes	Frame check sequence 4 bytes

FIGURE 22.7: The composition of an 802.3 frame

Not only did the IEEE 802.3 committee have to determine how information would travel through the network and the kind of cable and topology that would best suit the method of data travel, it had to determine how far the cables could stretch before the data faded or corrupted. The committee found that length to be 185 meters (607 feet) per cable segment. This length clearly limits the distance between workstations and may affect the choice of network type in some situations.

TIP

Remember, the length issue is important because it determines how far one workstation can be from another workstation or how closely the workstations have to be grouped together. If the workstations are too far apart, the information will fade away or become corrupted in transit. To avoid this problem, welcome to the wonderful world of repeaters. Recall that a repeater is simply a device that is placed periodically throughout the network to enhance or to strengthen the signal. As the signal reaches its length threshold, a repeater gives the signal a boost so that it can be sent another set distance before it hits the workstation that is to receive the information or before another repeater needs to enhance the signal again.

Carrier Sense Multiple Access/Collision Detection (CSMA/CD)

The 802.3 standard's most salient feature is the Carrier Sense Multiple Access/Collision Detection (CSMA/CD) designation. CSMA/CD gets to the heart of a basic Ethernet problem: how can you send vast amounts of information simultaneously across the network without causing collisions? After all, the network can handle only one packet at a time.

The best way to understand why Ethernet needs CSMA/CD is to visualize a warehouse that stocks large boulders. Each clerk sits alone in a room with a boulder the size of the one in *Raiders of the Lost Ark*. The halls of this warehouse are pretty narrow, so the boulders only just fit—there's certainly no room for two to pass each other. Before the clerks can move the boulders, they have to listen outside their doors to make sure that no one else is moving a boulder in the corridor. Because the clerks have to move the boulders around fairly often, they spend a lot of time listening and then leaping out the door as soon as it's quiet—which, of course, leads to collisions because all the other clerks are doing the same thing. When the boulders collide, each clerk has to go back to their storeroom and wait for quiet before trying again.

Your Ethernet LAN works in much the same way. If you send one packet of information from one workstation to another workstation, the network has no trouble controlling the flow of this packet. If more than one workstation tries to broadcast at the same time, however, the packets will collide, the transmission will abort, and the workstations will have to try transmitting again.

CSMA/CD provides a means for reducing packet collision. Before transmitting, CSMA/CD broadcasts a signal known as the *carrier-sensing signal* to see if any other workstations are broadcasting. If not, it gives the workstation the "all clear," and the workstation transmits its packet. If, however, the carrier-sensing signal (as shown in Figure 22.8) detects another workstation's transmittal, CSMA/CD tells the workstation to wait before broadcasting.

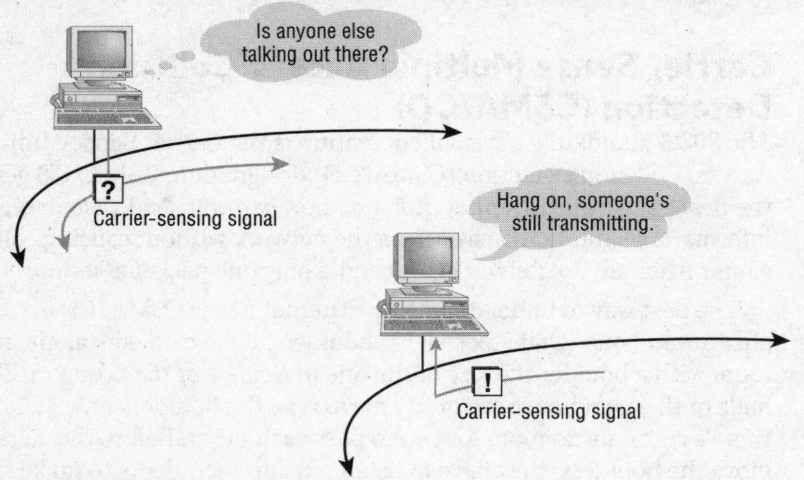

FIGURE 22.8: The carrier-sensing signal at work

This process works fine as long as network traffic isn't heavy and the LAN's cables aren't any longer than they're rated for. If either of those conditions exist, collisions are likely to happen regardless of CSMA/CD. CSMA/CD isn't in charge of making sure that only one workstation transmits at a time; it's in charge of making sure that all workstations are quiet before one transmits. If two workstations happen to *begin* transmitting at the same time, there's nothing that CSMA/CD can do to prevent the collision.

If two packets collide, CSMA/CD tries to avoid a repeat collision, as shown in Figure 22.9. As I discussed earlier, each workstation chooses a random number between 1 and 2 before transmitting again. If the workstations choose the same number, they each choose a number between 1 and 4 and try again. This process goes on until either the workstations have both successfully completed their transmissions or they've tried 16 times without success. If they flunk out by the sixteenth try, both workstations have to pause and give the other workstations a chance to transmit.

In short, CSMA/CD can't prevent every collision, but it tries to minimize the time that collisions tie up the network.

Another Ethernet protocol called 802.2 is a variation on this theme. People use 802.3 primarily in a Novell environment because it is faster than 802.2. However, 802.3 is proprietary to the IPX (Internetwork Packet eXchange) protocol from Novell. In a heterogeneous environment with different types of servers and network operating systems, 802.2 is preferred because it is more universal in nature.

How CSMA/CD Prevents Repeat Collisions

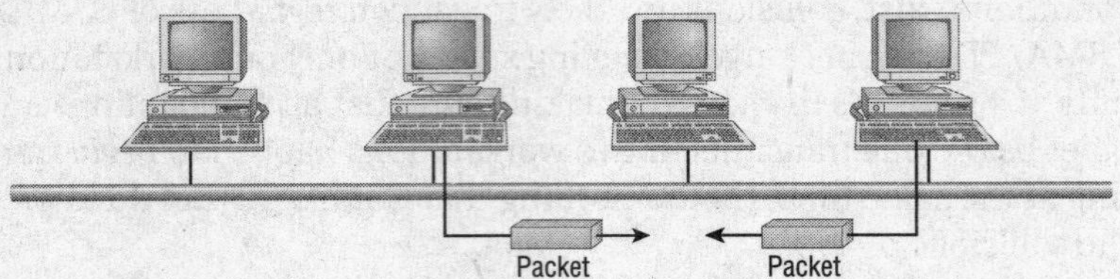

Two packets, not having heard each other, both start down the network.

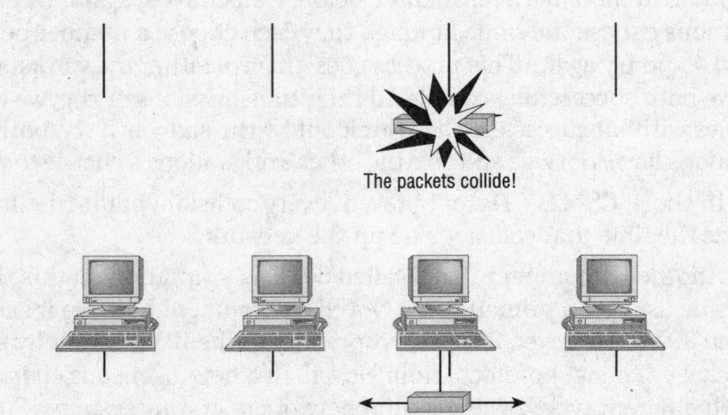

The node closest to the collision detects it and sends out a jamming signal, notifying all nodes that a collision has taken place.

Each node on the network waits a random number of milliseconds before transmitting, in hopes that they won't coincidentally wait the same amount of time and send packets at the same time again.

FIGURE 22.9: How CSMA/CD prevents repeat collisions

The 802.4 Standard

In an effort to design a standard that was less prone to collisions than the 802.3, the IEEE 802.4 subcommittee designed a combination bus/ring topology that transmitted information via a token. Using the bus physical topology and the ring logical topology, the 802.4 standard is designed on the principle that computers are prone to the same fallibility as humans: Give 'em half a chance, and they'll talk right on top of each other. To get around this problem, the 802.4 committee designed a token that the network could use in much the same way that discussion groups use "talking sticks"—whoever's got the stick has the floor (usually for a preset period of time) and no one else can talk until they've got the stick. So it is with the 802.4 standard.

Only the workstation that has the token can send information, and after that workstation has received acknowledgment of the receipt of that information, it must then pass the token to the next workstation in line. How does the network determine who's next in line? In the 802.4 standard, the network keeps track of who gets the token next. Just as the business manager could get the talking stick more often than the person in charge of office decorations, it's possible for some workstations to have priority over others to get the token.

The method of controlling collisions isn't the only way in which the 802.4 standard differs from the 802.3 standard. An 802.4 packet, also called a token bus, looks different from an 802.3 packet. The 802.4 contains a preamble, a start frame delimiter, frame control, destination address, source address, information, frame check sequence, and frame delimiter, as shown in Figure 22.10.

Preamble	Start Frame Delimiter	Frame Control	Destination Address	Source Address	Information	Frame Check Sequence	Frame Delimiter

FIGURE 22.10: The composition of an 802.4 frame

Although the token bus combination avoids collisions, the 802.4 standard still has some disadvantages that have kept it from common usage. Most shortfalls of the token bus format come from malfunctioning hardware, which can result in the token being lost, or from shadowed tokens that make it look as though the network has multiple tokens. Imagine a board meeting with more than one talking stick!

The 802.5 Standard

The IEEE 802.5 committee developed the 802.5 standard in conjunction with IBM. This standard is specifically designed for Token Ring networks that use the token specification to pass information from one workstation to another. As you'll remember from the earlier discussion of the Token Ring LAN, the 802.5 standard uses a star physical topology and a ring logical topology.

As in the 802.4 standard, the workstations on a Token Ring network use a token to determine which workstation gets to transmit. If a workstation doesn't need to transmit anything, it passes the free token to the next workstation, and so on until a workstation needs to transmit something.

Data travels from the originating workstation to every node on the network in succession. Each workstation examines the address on the data packet. If the data is for that station, the workstation keeps a copy of the data and sends the original on. If the data isn't for that station, it merely sends it to the next workstation on the network. When the sending workstation gets back the copy of its first data packet, it knows that it's time to stop transmitting and passes the free token to the next workstation.

The 802.5 standard has some qualities to recommend it. With a smart hub, the Token Ring protocol also allows for malfunctioning hardware—a nice feature that the token bus standard doesn't have. If a workstation malfunctions, either not releasing the token when its turn is up or jabbering over the network, the smart hub can recognize trouble and cut that workstation from the LAN, enabling the rest of the network to function normally. An 802.5 network can also extend for longer distances than either the 802.3 or the 802.4 because the packet travels from one workstation to another and is retransmitted at every step; therefore, it never has very far to go before being retransmitted.

The 802.11b Standard

In recent years, several hardware companies have developed technology that enables computers to plug into a network without cables or connectors.

And, indeed, in some circles 2001 is being called the year of the wireless LAN. This is primarily the result of the acceptance of the IEEE 802.11b standard, which specifies a carrier sense media access control and physical specifications for 5.5 and 1Mbps wireless LANs. A number of products are on the market, and you'll find a review of several of the most popular at `www.nwfusion.com/reviews/2001/0205rev.html`.

Peer-to-Peer versus Client-Server

In the computing world, some issues are so divisive that debates about them have something of the quality of religious argument. If you don't believe me, have you ever eavesdropped on an argument between a diehard Mac user and a PC aficionado?

To date, the peer-to-peer versus client-server debate hasn't reached this point of passion, but some people *really* believe in one or the other, sometimes for no other reason than one technology is the first that they ever encountered. If you'd like to take a slightly more intellectual look at the debate, read on.

Neither type of network is perfect for all situations. Client-server networks have better security whereas peer-to-peer networks are more flexible and are often cheaper. Windows XP supports both platforms.

Client-Server Networks

Client-server networks are similar in some ways to the old mainframe/terminal networks. In each, a central computer is in charge of the network and handles all requests. The main difference is that the client computers are able to compute on their own (assuming that they're PCs), unlike the dumb terminals. Figure 22.11 shows a client-server network configuration.

FIGURE 22.11: An example of a client-server network

For large organizations, client-server networks have several advantages:

They are often more upgradeable than peer-to-peer networks. Client-server networks are often more flexible than peer-to-peer networks. They have more options available to them and more software is written for client-server networks than for peer-to-peer. In addition, more industry information is available, which is helpful when you're trying to figure out a problem.

They give their administrators better control of the network. In peer-to-peer networks, each user is, to an extent, their own administrator. Client-server networks are controlled by an administrator who decides which peripherals and files each user may attach to.

They are infinitely expandable. Peer-to-peer networks can expand easily but don't work well with more than about 15 nodes. Client-server networks, on the other hand, can expand to hundreds of machines, even tens or hundreds of thousands in a wide area network (WAN).

They are more secure from unauthorized access. Client-server networks use much tighter and more efficient security than peer-to-peer networks use. Most client-server networks require a user to provide a password and a logon ID before accessing the network from a client computer. That password and ID give that user access only to the files and devices that the user is authorized to access. In addition, the password and ID tell the file server exactly what kind of file access that user has (read-only or full) and how they can manipulate files, by moving them or marking them for other users to share.

Client-server networks have their liabilities, of course. They're generally much more expensive per node than peer-to-peer networks, and they are harder to set up. Even for an experienced administrator, setting up the server could entail hours of work. And adding new clients to the network can be time consuming.

Expense and administration aside, however, client-server networks are best suited for large companies. Let's take a look at some of the kinds of servers you might see on a client-server network.

Disk Servers

A *disk server* is a central repository for files and data, attached to the network like any other node and appearing to each workstation as another local hard disk.

Saving information to a disk server is just like saving information to a local hard disk, but retrieving information from the disk server is a bit more complex. On a stand-alone workstation, in order to retrieve information from the hard disk, the computer must look up the file's location in the File Allocation Table (FAT) or the Master File Table (MFT), depending on whether you are using the FAT file system or the NTFS (New Technology File System) file system. After the computer finds the file's location, it moves the read/write heads to that location on the hard disk and copies the file into memory.

NOTE

As you will recall from either Chapter 2 of this book or from your own experience installing Windows XP Professional, you must decide which file system you want to use—NTFS, FAT, or FAT32. MFT is the NTFS version of the FAT.

It's not quite as easy to retrieve information from a disk server. You see, the disk server keeps its *own* FAT or MFT, and any time a workstation wants to retrieve information from the disk server, the disk server must send a copy of its FAT or MFT to the workstation. The workstation then stores a copy of the FAT or MFT in memory. To access information on the disk server, the workstation will first get a copy (to keep) of the disk server's FAT or MFT and then use that copy to see where the file is on the disk server's hard disk. Thus, when a workstation accesses a disk server, the following drama occurs.

The disk server can probably see the potential hazard. The whole point of a network is to give a number of people access to the network's capabilities, right? However, the first time someone accesses the disk server, the user will get a copy of the FAT or MFT as it looked *at that time*. Every time anyone adds or deletes a file from the server's hard disk, the FAT or the MFT changes. Therefore, if you get a copy of the disk server's FAT or MFT at 8:00 in the morning, by 2:30 that afternoon it's likely that your copy no longer matches the original. Because the disk server's CPU uses its outdated map to search for the data on the hard disk, your data retrieval could slow down or grind to a halt.

To get around this potential hazard, disk servers are usually divided or partitioned into several volumes, each volume reserved for a different workstation. In order to share information, it's saved on the "read-only" public volume, protecting the FAT's or the MFT's integrity on the disk server.

File Servers

Disk servers, as you can see, can be complicated and are potentially dangerous to work with. These days, *file* servers are much more common. File servers are a more complex animal than their predecessor. A file server usually has its own operating system, forming a shell around the disk operating system environment. This operating system filters out network commands and DOS commands, translating DOS commands to network commands, and vice versa.

File servers and disk servers are similar in function; that is, they provide a central place for workstations to store data. The main difference between a file server and a disk server is that a file server maintains its own FAT or MFT and does its own searching for files on its hard disk. When a workstation requests a file, the file server checks its FAT or MFT to see where the file is located on the hard disk and then moves the hard drive's rewrite heads to that location. After copying the data from the hard disk, the file server sends the copy of the file to the workstation that made the request.

The difference between a disk server and a file server could perhaps be expressed like this: When a workstation asks a disk server for a file for the first time that day, the disk server rummages in its drawer and finds a map of the storeroom where it keeps the files, telling the workstation, "Go ahead and get the file, kid, but keep the map; I've got better things to do than keep you supplied with maps." Every time a workstation gets something from the storeroom or returns something, the storeroom gets a little reorganized, but because it has an automatic update, the disk server always hands out accurate maps. When workstations come back to look for files using their old maps, however, it's quite possible that the storeroom will be rearranged and that they won't be able to find anything.

The file server, on the other hand, would rather find things itself than have a bunch of workstations rummaging through its hard disk. When a workstation asks for a file, the file server says, "I'll send it right out—no, really, I'd rather do it." It then finds the file, makes a copy of it for the workstation, and sends it through the network to the workstation that requested it.

File servers have a number of advantages over disk servers. First, because file servers don't need to copy the FAT or the MFT to the workstation, only one record of file locations exists, and the file server maintains it. Second, the server no longer has to divide its hard disk into volumes, so the server's entire disk can be shared with all workstations. This arrangement, as you recall, was *not* the case with the disk server.

NOTE

The server's entire disk *can* be shared with all workstations but isn't necessarily. File servers generally have stringent security measures that restrict file access to users with the proper access rights. The files a user can access depend on his or her access rights.

Dedicated and Nondedicated File Servers When you hear discussions of file servers, you'll sometimes hear people talking about dedicated file servers and nondedicated file servers. A *dedicated file server* has its own hard disk drive, and its only goal in life is to be a file server. By dedicating a computer as a file server, you restrict its memory to file server functions. A *nondedicated file server,* on the other hand, is a workstation that moonlights as a file server—its memory is divided between workstation functions and file server functions.

Why would you want a dedicated file server? A dedicated file server is faster, safer, and more efficient than one also being used as a workstation.

- It's faster because all the memory and all the processes that this computer does are file-server related.
- It's safer because no one's using the machine as a workstation and possibly crashing it (everyone crashes *sometimes*).
- It's more efficient because it does not have to divide its time between being a file server and being a workstation.

In short, dedicating your file server greatly improves your network's performance. Of course, the downside of a dedicated file server is that it can be expensive, because you must buy a computer just to hold and maintain the integrity and security of your information. Because your file server will have a lot of demands on it, you're going to want something fast with a big hard disk, and that type of machine isn't cheap.

The expense of a dedicated file server gives nondedicated file servers their place in life. A lower price tag is just about the only advantage you get from using your file server as a workstation. Nondedicated file servers tend to be slower than dedicated ones because any time the server needs CPU time to perform workstation tasks, the other workstations have to wait to access the server. This wait time can slow down your entire network.

Also, if your file server crashes—something far more likely to happen on a server that someone's using for a workstation than one used only for administration purposes—you can lose data all over your network. Having worked on networks with both dedicated and nondedicated file servers, I can honestly say that dedicated is a better bet if you can afford the extra machine. Nondedicated file servers may be a viable option for very small networks, but if you have 50 or 100 nodes on your network, the risk of data loss is more expensive than the extra machine. In the long run, the cost of buying an extra computer to be a dedicated file server will turn out to be less than that of losing your network's data.

If you *must* use a server as a workstation, it's best to make it a server that won't cause disaster if it crashes. Many nondedicated servers today are printer servers, fax servers, or e-mail servers. If one of those crashes, it's a pain in the neck but probably won't cause the annual report to go down in flames.

Peer-to-Peer Networks

Peer-to-peer networks represent an entirely different concept in networking. Rather than giving every computer on the network a central storage ground, peer-to-peer networking connects a group of totally independent computers, as depicted in Figure 22.12. Each computer generally keeps its applications on its own hard disk so that if something happens to the network, it simply breaks down into a group of individual yet functional computers. If one workstation goes down, life can go on for the rest of the network if all users keep their needed files at their own workstation. In other words, a peer-to-peer network enables every workstation to lead a double life: to be a workstation *and* a file server.

FIGURE 22.12: An example of a peer-to-peer network

NOTE

In the next chapter, I'll get into the details of using Windows XP Professional to connect a peer-to-peer network.

Peer-to-peer networks give their users many of the same capabilities that client-server networks do. Each user decides what capabilities and peripheral devices they will share with the rest of the network and then shares them. You can share things selectively, saying, perhaps, "Accounting gets to use the C drive, and Personnel gets to use the printer," and you can attach passwords to your resources so that unauthorized people can't access them. On the subject of sharing resources, remember that because important information on a peer-to-peer LAN is distributed throughout the network, you'll have to leave networked machines on and logged on to the network as long as anyone is working who needs the information on those machines.

Judging Peer-to-Peer Packages

When shopping for a peer-to-peer network operating system, you should keep three things in mind:

How good are its communications abilities? Most peer-to-peer packages include their own e-mail and chat capabilities, allowing both e-mail and real-time communications. A good package provides users with a list of other users available for chats and has both single-mode and multimode chat utilities.

How capable is its resource sharing? Although peer-to-peer networks often expect each workstation to keep its own applications on file, you may prefer to locate some applications centrally and let people pick them up from another machine. You'll also be sharing devices such as drives, CD-ROMs, and printers. The best packages notify users when a workstation with shared resources leaves the network.

How suitable is it for small-office use (since that's likely what you'll be using it for)? Because peer-to-peer networks rarely have network managers, you'll want a network that is as easy to control as possible. A good peer-to-peer should be easy to install and set up and have good print and file management tools to control shared resources. Although peer-to-peer networks are not famous for their security, you'll also want some way of controlling access to shared resources.

Understanding Peer-to-Peer Operations

We have explored how a client-server network operates, but how does a peer-to-peer network work? On a stand-alone machine, when you ask your operating system to access the drive, it can do it directly. The application talks directly to the operating system, which sends the information to the BIOS, which sends the information to the computer's disk.

The operating system needs no go-between to help it access information and peripherals on its own computer.

If you're working on a network, however, the situation is a little different. The operating system needs help accessing information on other computers on the network. Its helper is called the *redirector* (or the *shell,* if you're a Novell user).

Weighing the Advantages of Using a Peer-to-Peer Network

At first glance, client-server networks seem to have all the advantages. When you look again, however, you discover that isn't necessarily the case. For small networks, peer-to-peer has a number of advantages:

- It doesn't require a dedicated workstation (although using one is still a good idea for the reasons I discussed earlier).
- It's an easy way to connect and share information on the workstations that you already have in your office.
- It's cheaper than duplicating your purchases of printers, CD-ROMs, and so on, for every person in the office, and probably more efficient for printer sharing than products such as print buffers and physical print spoolers.
- It costs less than a client-server LAN and doesn't require a degree in engineering to set up and administer.

In short, peer-to-peer networking does not offer the flexibility or the complete security of a file server workstation relationship, but for a small installation, it will probably more than fit the bill.

WHAT'S NEXT?

You should now have enough information under your belt to describe your needs to any network cabler you might run into. What more is there to know? Well, for starters, in the next chapter I'll discuss how to set up a Windows XP Professional peer-to-peer network and how to connect to a domain.

Chapter 23

Setting Up and Configuring a Peer-to-Peer Network and Working with Domains

One of the most powerful features of Windows XP Professional is its capability to attach to and become part of a networking environment. In this chapter, we'll look at many of the decisions you will need to make in order to get the networking features to run reliably in that environment. You'll learn how to set up a simple peer-to-peer Ethernet network (including what to do if Windows XP doesn't detect your network interface card); how to configure your Windows 98/Me, Windows XP Professional, and Windows XP Home Edition machines using the Network Setup Wizard; and how to manually configure your Windows 95 and NT Workstation machines. You'll also learn

Adapted from *Mastering Windows XP Professional* by Mark Minasi.
Note: This chapter, originally titled *Connecting to Windows XP Peer-to-Peer Networks and Domains*, has been retitled to better represent its coverage.
ISBN 0-7821-2981-1 1056 pages $39.99

how to allow users to share documents and printers and how to create profiles for users and hardware. For those of you working with more complex networking environments, this chapter covers how to connect to a domain, as well as how to connect to Unix and Macintosh networks. Finally, the chapter wraps up with a section on troubleshooting your network.

SETTING UP A NETWORK

The whole idea of a network is to share things: space on a large disk drive, a particular file on that disk drive, a printer, and so on. Networks provide two major benefits. One, they can increase user productivity and collaboration. Two, they can save companies money on hardware and software. Imagine the cost difference of buying one color laser printer for the marketing department as opposed to buying one for each associate! As an example, let's consider a small office that needs to do some sharing.

In our office, Jennifer has more storage capacity on her machine than Joe does on his, but the office laser printer is attached to Joe's PC. Jennifer and Joe work on the office accounting system, so they need to share the accounting files—or they'll have to pass floppies back and forth via sneakernet. Because Jennifer has more disk space, they put the accounting files on her machine. So, the network problems that we need to solve are as follows:

- Sharing Joe's printer with Jennifer
- Sharing Jennifer's disk with Joe

Let's solve their problem with a basic peer-to-peer network. Microsoft generally refers to peer-to-peer configurations as *workgroups* (as opposed to *domains*). With this type of network, Jennifer makes her hard disk available on the network, and Joe makes his printer available on the network. Assuming that both computers are running Windows XP Professional, here's how to get Joe onto Jennifer's disk and Jennifer onto Joe's printer:

1. Jennifer tells the Windows XP Professional networking software, "Offer the Acctng subfolder on my C drive to anyone who wants it. Call it Acctng." In Microsoft enterprise networking terminology, Acctng becomes the *share name* of that folder on Jennifer's machine (GTW09), and it's the name that others will use to access the resource over the network.

In a few pages, I'll show you exactly how to share such a resource on the network so others can access it, but for now, remember this: a machine (named GTW09) is sharing a resource called Acctng with anyone on that network who's able to use it.

NOTE

Here's an important concept in Microsoft networking: You must name each machine in the network, whether it is a server or a workstation. Often you will hear this name referred to as a NetBIOS name. You also must name each user (in our example, Joe and Jennifer). Because the PCs need names, we may as well name the PCs with their inventory numbers, which in this example are DELL05 and GTW09. Another common naming scheme is to name the computer based on the physical location within the company. A computer in the east wing, row L station 6 could be called EL06.

TIP

Naming machines after their users is a bad idea, because PCs may be reassigned to other users.

2. Joe then tells the networking software on his PC, "Attach me to the Acctng resource on Jennifer's machine."
3. Joe, meanwhile, tells his computer to share the printer on his LPT1 port, giving it a name—again, a share name—of JOLASER. Joe's machine is called DELL05, so the UNC name of that printer will be `\\DELL05\JOLASER`.

NOTE

UNC stands for Universal Naming Convention. In the printer's UNC name, `\\DELL05` is the *machine* name, and `\JOLASER` is the *share* name. UNCs are used all the time in networking and always follow a `\\computername\sharename` format.

4. Jennifer then tells her networking software to make a network connection to JOLASER on Joe's machine, and to create it on her LPT1 port.

From now on, whenever Jennifer tells an application program to print to a laser printer on LPT1, the network software will intercept the printed output and will direct it over the network to Joe's machine. The networking software on Joe's machine will then print the information on Joe's printer.

I've left out some of the "how do we do this?" information; it's coming right up.

WAYS TO CONNECT A PEER-TO-PEER NETWORK

In the next section of this chapter, I'll show you how to connect a network that uses an Ethernet hub, which I discussed in the previous chapter. You can, however, connect a peer-to-peer network in a couple of other ways:

- By using an internal modem, a DSL modem, or a cable modem to configure a home phone line network. A network adapter with a converter is installed in each computer, and each computer is plugged in to a phone jack using a telephone cable.
- By using a wireless connection, which I described in Chapter 22.

For some detailed information about these types of connections, open Help and Support Center, click the Home and Small Office Networking link, and then click the Hardware Requirements for Home and Small Office Networking link. You'll also find some excellent information on this topic at www.homepna.com.

Windows XP Professional is designed to work in a variety of networking situations. XP makes the perfect network client for both home and office users. It doesn't matter if your network servers are running NetWare, Unix, or some other platform; Windows XP Professional will play nice with a variety of network operating systems. Windows XP Professional can also act as a server in a pinch—although you're better off going with a true server product for a long-term solution.

Connecting Your Ethernet Network

In the first part of this chapter, I'm going to show you how to set up a simple peer-to-peer Ethernet network that solves the problems of Joe and Jennifer that I just described. Using the information in the previous chapter, you first need to design your network, and then you probably need to go shopping—either on the Internet or at one of many computer centers that are springing up all over the place.

You need a Network Interface Card (NIC) for each computer on the network, a hub, and some cables. Many computers that you buy these days come with NICs already installed. If you have an older computer, though, you'll probably need to purchase a NIC. You can even buy a starter kit that contains everything you need—probably for less than $50. With that and a couple of screwdrivers, you're ready to get started. Follow these steps:

1. Turn off and unplug each computer that will be part of your network.
2. At each computer, open the case, and insert a NIC in an empty slot, screwing the card in securely so it won't come loose.
3. Replace the case.
4. Insert one end of the cable into the RJ-45 socket on the card and insert the other end of the cable into the hub. The hub number is not important as long as you don't plug it into a port labeled "Uplink" or "Crossover"—avoid those.

NOTE

One way to avoid using a hub altogether is to buy a *crossover* cable. Plug one end of the crossover into one machine, and plug the other end into your second machine. The major drawback with this is that you can only have two computers on your network. Although hubs are rather inexpensive, this is an alternative if money is really an issue.

5. Plug the hub into the power supply.

6. Turn on the hub and all connected computers. You'll see some lights start blinking on the hub. Most hubs will have a light for each port indicating whether it detects a connection, along with a power light and traffic indicators.

Because Windows XP Professional is Plug and Play, when you restart your computer after inserting the NICs, the system automatically loads the device drivers you need for the NICs. For the most part, Windows XP is very good about automatically detecting network cards after installing them and rebooting. In this respect, Windows XP is very user friendly. However, Windows XP is still a fairly new product. Not all network adapters have XP drivers available, and the NIC may not be detected. What do you do?

First of all, don't panic. Windows XP can sometimes use Windows 98 or Windows 2000 drivers. If your NIC came with a diskette or a CD with drivers on it (it should have), try the 98 or 2000 drivers by using the Add Hardware Wizard. In Control Panel, click Add Hardware, and follow the on-screen prompts. If those drivers don't work, look on the manufacturer's Web site to see if they have anything, be it advice or drivers, available for people in your situation. The absolute worst-case scenario is that you'll have to take the NIC back and get a different brand, but this is unlikely. Stick with name-brand parts, and you should never run into a problem that serious. Now you're ready to configure your network.

TIP

Always check to make sure that the hardware you're purchasing is on the hardware compatibility list (HCL).

Configuring Your Network

After successfully installing your network adapters, you need to take some common steps to get the network running properly. Among those steps are to name your computer and workgroup, add protocols necessary for communication (TCP/IP is installed by default, so you may not need to add more), and configure protocol parameters, such as IP addresses. Using the Network Setup Wizard simplifies these configuration processes.

Using the Network Setup Wizard

Setting up a peer-to-peer network has never been easier than it is with Windows XP Professional. You simply follow the steps in the Network Setup Wizard, and in a very few minutes you're done. The only catch is that the other computers on your network must be running one of the following operating systems:

- Windows 98
- Windows Millennium Edition
- Windows XP Professional
- Windows XP Home

If the other computers on your network are running some other operating system, you'll need to manually configure the network because the Network Setup Wizard is provided on the four operating systems listed earlier. Running the Network Setup Wizard not only will connect your computers to each other, but will also configure all computers to access the Internet through one host computer.

I'll show you how to manually configure the network in the next section.

If your network hardware is installed and working properly, you're ready to begin. Log on as a Computer Administrator user on the host machine (the one that will share its Internet connection). (If you're not sure how to log on as a Computer Administrator user, find out how in the beginning of Chapter 3.) Once you're logged in, connect to the Internet, and then follow these steps:

1. Click Start ➢ All Programs ➢ Accessories ➢ Communications ➢ Network Setup Wizard to start the Wizard.

2. At the Welcome screen, click Next.
3. At the Before You Continue screen, look at the checklist, make sure you have completed your preparations, and then click Next to open the Select a Connection Method screen.

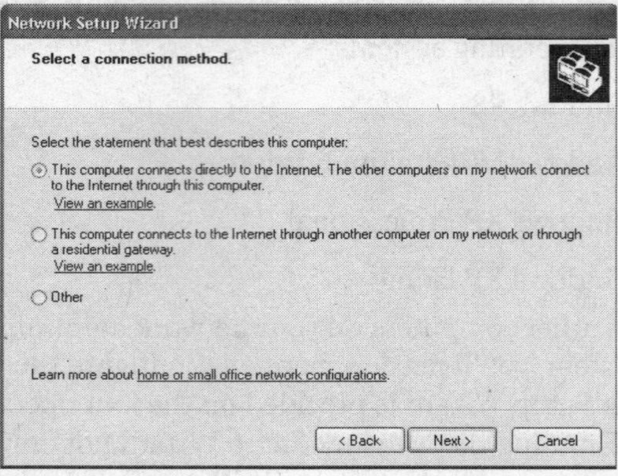

NOTE

If you do not have two connections (one for the Internet and one for your local network), you will not be able to make this computer a gateway.

4. Select the statement that best describes the setup of your system, and then click Next. What you do next depends on the configuration of your network. In this example, we've specified that this computer will connect directly to the Internet. For most small or home offices, where computers are connecting through a modem, DSL line, or cable modem, this is the appropriate choice. If you are participating on a large corporate network or otherwise have a proxy server or a firewall for Internet access, you will need to choose the second option listed. If you're still not sure which option is right for you, Windows XP will provide you with examples to help you decide.

Now you need to configure the other computers on your network. Running the Network Setup Wizard on the other computers will make them look for a host computer with a shared Internet connection. Therefore, your host computer will need to be up and running and connected to the Internet. Follow these steps at each computer:

1. Insert the Windows XP Professional CD in the CD-ROM drive.
2. At the opening screen, click Perform Additional Tasks.
3. At the next screen, click Set Up a Home or Small Office Network, and click Yes to continue.
4. The Wizard will give you some information on what it can do. Click Next on the next two screens to continue.
5. Select the network connection you wish to use. If your NIC is installed properly, it should be listed in the Connections box. Click Next to continue.
6. Since you have already set up your host computer, choose the option This Computer Connects to the Internet through Another Computer on My Network or through a Residential Gateway, and click Next.
7. Provide a description and name for this computer, and click Next.
8. Enter your workgroup name. Make sure that all computers on your network have the same workgroup name. Click Next to continue.
9. Click Next a few more times, and finally Finish. The Wizard will end and offer to reboot your machine for you.

NOTE

To run the Network Setup Wizard on a Windows 98 or Windows Me computer, you will need a Windows XP CD-ROM.

Configuring Windows 95/NT Workstation Machines

If you're using Windows 95 or Windows NT Workstation on your other network computers, you'll need to configure those computers manually. Follow these steps:

1. Right-click Network Neighborhood, and choose Properties from the shortcut menu to open the Network dialog box.

2. In The Following Network Components Are Installed list in the Configuration tab, you need to see at least the following (you may see more, and that's OK):
   - TCP/IP
   - Identification
   - File and Printer Sharing for Microsoft Networks

NOTE

For the remainder of this discussion, we are going to assume that this is a new installation and none of the required protocols are installed. We will begin by adding TCP/IP.

3. Click Add to open the Select Network Component Type dialog box. Select Protocol and click Add again. Under Manufacturers, select Microsoft. In the right pane, scroll down and click TCP/IP. Click OK twice.
4. Insert the CD-ROM disk for your appropriate operating system. Click OK. At this point, you may have to provide the path to the operating system files. For Windows 95 it should be x:\Win95; for Windows 98, x:\Win98; for Windows 98 Second Edition, x:\Win98_SE; and for Windows NT, x:\i386. Replace x: with your CD-ROM drive letter; for example, if your CD-ROM drive is D, replace x: with **d:**.
5. Right-click Network Neighborhood and choose Properties from the shortcut menu to open the Network dialog box.
6. In The Following Network Components Are Installed list in the Configuration tab, select TCP/IP Your network adapter. Click Properties.
7. You will see two choices: Obtain an IP Address Automatically or Specify an IP Address. Select one, depending on the following criteria:

   Obtain an IP Address Automatically Use this setting if you have a Dynamic Host Configuration Protocol (DHCP) server (a server that automatically assigns IP addresses to client machines) or if this machine is connected to an

Internet Connection Sharing host (Windows 9*x*, Windows 2000, or Windows XP).

Specify an IP Address Enter your IP address and subnet mask. If you are designing a network that is not connected to the Internet, you can choose any address you want. For example,

```
IP address:        131.107.2.102
Subnet Mask:       255.255.255.0
```

The numbers above the 255s in the subnet mask determine the network number. In this example, 131.107.2 is the network number. The network number *must* be the same for all the computers in the network. The number above the zero in the subnet mask is the host number. This number must be *different* on each computer in the network. If you're not sure which network numbers to use, here are a couple of examples you can use:

```
IP address:    10.  0.  0.  X
Subnet Mask: 255.255.255.  0
```

or

```
IP address:   172. 16.  1.  X
Subnet Mask: 255.255.255.  0
```

Of course, X is not a number. You can use any number between 1 and 254 to replace the X, but just make sure that each computer gets a unique number. Duplicate addresses on a network can cause a variety of communication problems. After you have made your selection and specified an IP address and subnet mask, click OK.

Identification

If you are going to connect your computers to share information, you must configure the Identification tab. This tab sets the computer name for the computer and configures your computer in a workgroup (a group of computers that can share information). Follow these steps:

1. Select the Identification tab.

2. In the Computer Name text box, enter a name. This name can be a maximum of 15 characters and must be unique within your network.
3. In the Workgroup text box, enter a workgroup name. This name *must be the same* for each computer in the network. If you're at a loss for a name, use WORKGROUP or SYSTEM.

NOTE

Capitalization of the workgroup name does not matter; *instructors* is identical to *Instructors*, which is identical to *INSTRUCTORS*. Also, do not give a machine the same name as any other machine in your environment.

4. Click OK.

File and Printer Sharing for Microsoft Networks

File and Printer Sharing for Microsoft Networks needs to be installed on Windows 98 machines for them to share resources on a network. Without it, Windows 98 machines can still be clients on a network; that is, retrieve files from and use printers on remote machines. However, they will not be able to host their own resources.

Windows NT machines also have the ability to share resources. However, Windows NT calls its server service "Server" and its client service "Workstation." These services are installed and configured by default on Windows NT machines.

Windows XP machines can share resources by default and do not require additional configuration of File and Printer Sharing for Microsoft Networks.

Configuring Windows XP Manually

The previous section dealt with how to configure Windows 98 and NT machines to participate on your Windows XP network. If your network contains just Windows XP machines, you don't need to configure the networking parameters yourself. Simply use the Network Setup Wizard and have it take care of everything for you.

However, some people don't trust all the automated features of computer and network setups. Although this may be obsessive, there's really nothing wrong with it. If you're one of those people who like to know everything that's going on in their machine, and therefore want to configure things manually in XP, here is some advice.

TIP

Double-checking your IP parameters and manually setting up your networking options are useful troubleshooting techniques if you are having communication problems on your network.

IP Configuration

Windows XP also has two options for configuring IP addresses, much like previous versions of Windows operating systems. The first option is to obtain an IP address automatically (through a DHCP server), and the second option is to configure addresses manually. If you want to configure addresses manually, the information on IP addressing in the "Configuring Windows 95/NT Workstation Machines" section in this chapter will help you in XP.

Automatically obtaining an IP address can happen in one of two ways. First, if your network has a DHCP server, you will obtain an address from it. I'm guessing that if you have just a small office in your home, you don't have a DHCP server. That's okay. Let's say that you set your Windows XP machine to obtain an IP address automatically, but Windows XP cannot locate a DHCP server (which makes sense, because you don't have one). Windows XP will automatically assign an IP address and subnet mask to your machine. The address will be in the 169.254.X.X range, with a subnet mask of 255.255.0.0. This feature is called Automatic Private IP Addressing (APIPA).

NOTE

Windows 98, 2000, Me, and XP support APIPA.

You should be careful of one thing when using APIPA, though. Let's say that you have manually configured one computer with an address of 131.107.2.102 and a mask of 255.255.255.0. Another computer on the same network gets an APIPA-assigned address of 169.254.225.128, along with a mask of 255.255.0.0. Those two computers will not be able to talk to each other using TCP/IP. The reason for this is they have different network addresses, so they each think the other is physically somewhere else, when they're really on the same physical network. The computers will be confused and won't talk.

To manually configure IP addresses on your Windows XP Professional computer, right-click My Network Places, and choose Properties from the shortcut menu. In the new window that opens, right-click Local Area Connection, and click Properties again. Highlight TCP/IP, and choose Properties. Select the Use the Following IP Address radio button, and enter your IP address, subnet mask, and default gateway (if necessary). You can specify an address for a DNS server as well, or you can obtain that server's address automatically.

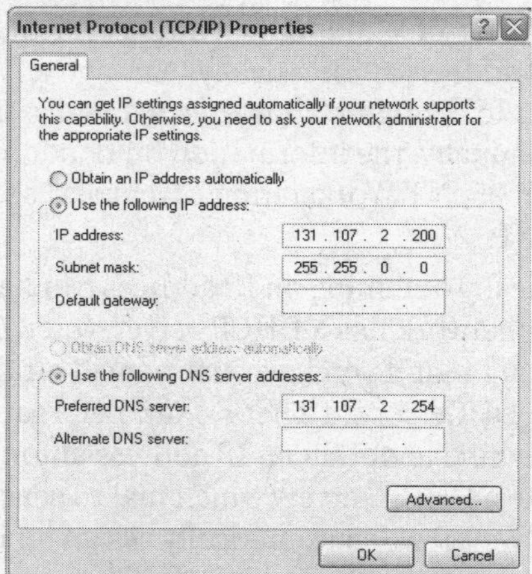

Identification

Windows XP Professional does not have an Identification tab like Windows 98 and NT did. Instead, right-click My Computer, choose Properties, and then choose Computer Name. Here you will see your computer name, as well as the workgroup or domain name. You can also change that information here.

System Restore | Automatic Updates | Remote
General | Computer Name | Hardware | Advanced

Windows uses the following information to identify your computer on the network.

Computer description: Test

For example: "Kitchen Computer" or "Mary's Computer".

Full computer name: TEST.

Workgroup: MSHOME

To use the Network Identification Wizard to join a domain and create a local user account, click Network ID. [Network ID]

To rename this computer or join a domain, click Change. [Change...]

Changes will take effect after you restart this computer.

[OK] [Cancel] [Apply]

CREATING SHARES

When you configure your network using the Network Setup Wizard, the Shared Documents folder and any printer directly connected to your computer are shared automatically. Before users on your network can get to other resources on your computer, you must share those resources. To do this, you must be logged on as an administrator or have a user account with local administrator privileges. You can create shares using Explorer or Computer Management. Using Explorer is simple and direct, so in this section that's what I'll use.

NOTE

To open Computer Management, in Control Panel click Performance and Maintenance, click Administrative Tools, and then click Computer Management.

A share can be a folder, a drive, a program, a file—any resource on your computer that you want other people to be able to use over the network. For this example, I'm going to share a folder. Here are the steps:

1. In Explorer, right-click the folder, and choose Sharing and Security from the shortcut menu to open the Properties dialog box for that folder at the Sharing tab:

NOTE

The file system that the shared resource is on is irrelevant in terms of operating system access, even though it may impact security. For example, Windows 98 does not have the ability to read NTFS volumes locally. However, a Windows 98 machine can access a shared folder located on an NTFS partition elsewhere on the network.

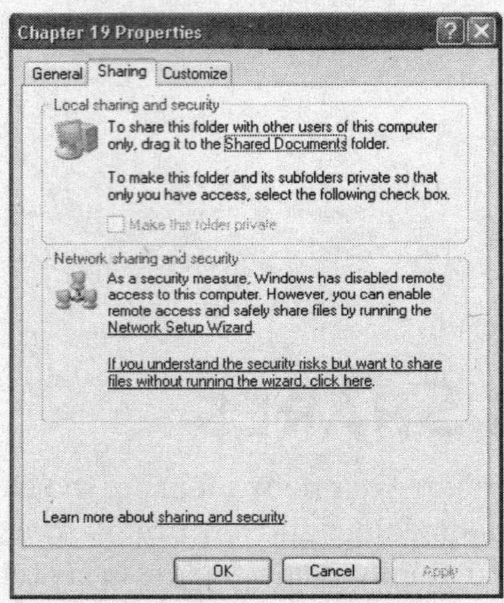

2. Before you can share the folder, you have to enable sharing. To do so, you can run the Network Setup Wizard by clicking that link in the Network Sharing and Security section, or you can click the If You Understand the Security Risks but Want to Share Files without Running the Wizard, Click Here link. Clicking this second link opens the Enable File Sharing dialog box:

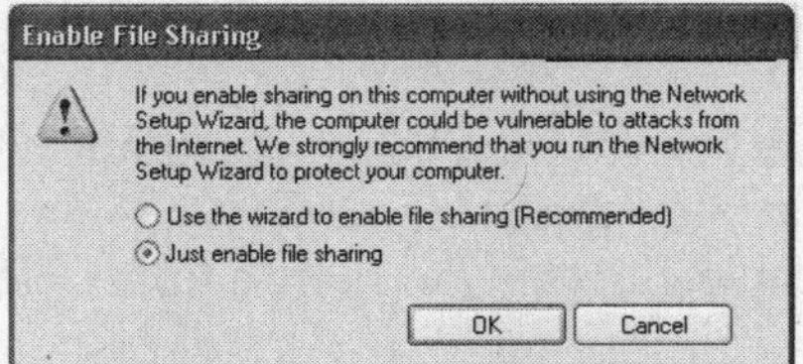

Click the Just Enable File Sharing option, and then click OK.

3. Back in the Sharing tab, you'll see the following after you click the Share This Folder on the Network check box:

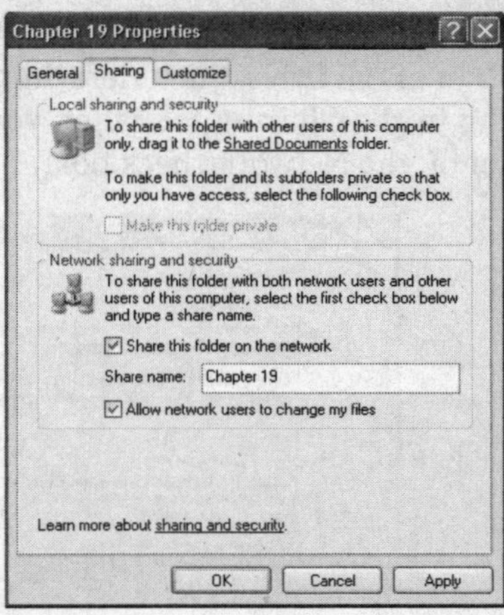

4. In the Share Name box, you can accept the name that Windows XP Professional suggests or enter another name.

5. If you want others on your network to be able to read the contents of the folder but not change them, clear the Allow Network Users to Change My Files check box.

6. Click OK.

7. Back in Explorer you'll see that the folder now has a hand under it to indicate that it is a shared folder.

Although Microsoft does not recommend sharing a drive, you can still do so. Follow these steps:

1. Choose Start ➢ My Computer to open the My Computer window.

2. Right-click the drive you want to share, and then select Sharing and Security from the shortcut menu to open the Properties dialog box for that drive at the Sharing tab:

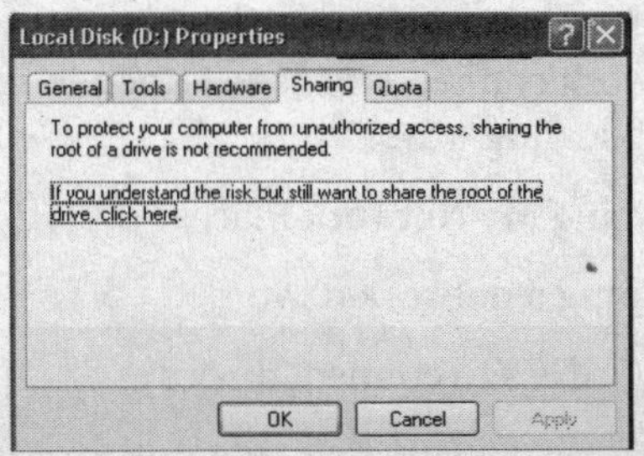

3. Click the If You Understand the Risk but Still Want to Share the Root of the Drive, Click Here link. You'll then see the following in the Sharing tab when you click the Share This Folder on the Network check box:

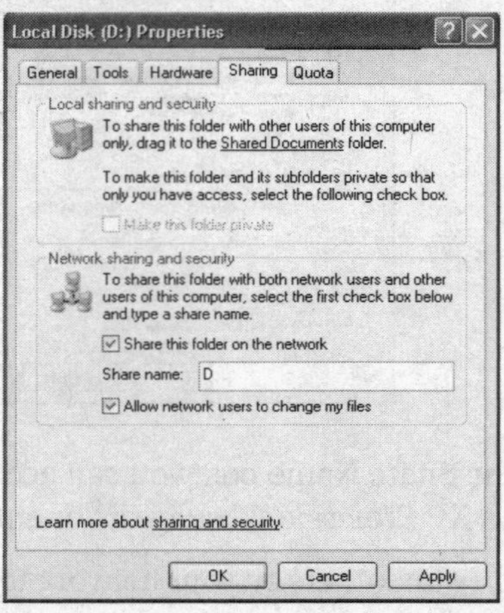

4. If you want others on your network to be able to read the contents of the drive but not change them, clear the Allow Network Users to Change My Files check box.
5. Click OK. The Setting Folder Permission dialog box will show the progress of sharing the drive.
6. Back in the My Computer window, you'll see that the drive now has a hand under it to indicate that it is shared.

ATTACHING TO NETWORK RESOURCES

After your network is configured for sharing, one of the easiest ways to test your network connections is to attach to network resources. You can do so in the following ways:

- By browsing My Network Places
- By mapping a network drive
- By using UNCs to connect directly

Browsing My Network Places

Click My Network Places on the Start menu to open a window that displays the options on your network. Click View Workgroup Computers under Network Tasks to display other computers on your network. Then, double-click a computer to view and connect to its shared resources.

Mapping a Network Drive

Mapping a network drive involves assigning a drive letter to a network location. For example, if you frequently connect to another user's shared folder, you might assign it an unused drive letter on your computer.

When you frequently access particular network resources, mapping a drive to the network share is a great way to ensure that they're easily available. When you map a drive, you're telling your computer, "make the `docs` shared folder on `server1` my drive letter L." Drive L then appears in My Computer under Network Drives, and all you need to do to access it is to double-click it. Remember that the information is still physically stored on the other machine. All you've done is make a logical pointer on your machine pointing to the physical resource. It's purely for the sake of convenience. One of the benefits to networking is being able to back up your files and folders on another computer. You'll find that some applications won't recognize other network drives unless they are mapped—so that's another reason you need to know how to map network drives.

To map a drive, follow these steps:

1. On the Start menu, right-click My Network Places, and choose Map Network Drive to open the Map Network Drive dialog box:

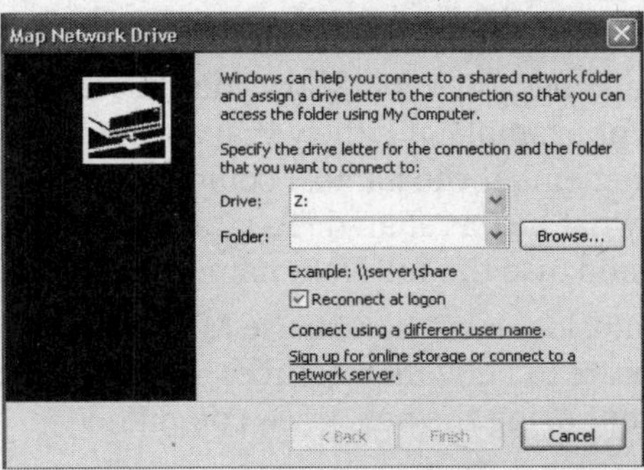

Part iv

2. From the Drive drop-down list, select an unused drive letter.
3. From the Folder drop-down list, select the folder you want to map to, or click Browse to find the folder on your network.
4. If you want to use this mapping every time you log on, leave the Reconnect at Logon check box selected.

NOTE

Clicking the Connect Using a Different User Name link opens the Connect As dialog box. I'll discuss that option later in this chapter.

5. Click Finish. The drive now appears in My Computer under Network Drives along with your local drives.

To disconnect a mapped drive, follow these steps:

1. In My Computer, choose Tools ➢ Disconnect Network Drive to open the Disconnect Network Drive dialog box.
2. Select the network drive you want to disconnect, and click OK.

Making a Direct Connection via a UNC

At the beginning of this chapter, I mentioned UNC names. Using UNC names is yet another way to attach to network resources. You do this in one of two ways. One way is to click the Start menu and choose Run. The other way is by executing `net use` statements at the command prompt. But before you can attach to resources on the network, you need to know which resources are available.

If you are using the `Run` command from the Start menu, type **`\\`*`computername`*** and it will show you the resources available on that machine. For example, if I knew that Joe had shared his printer but I could not remember the name, I could type in **`\\DELL05`**, hit Enter, and I would see what he has shared. To attach to a network resource using the `Run` command, use the full UNC name, like **`\\GTW09\acctng`**.

We already looked at how to use My Network Places and the `Run` command to locate to network resources, but you can also do so at the command prompt using the `net view` command.

NOTE

So far in this chapter, I've been talking primarily about how to set up and configure a Windows XP Professional peer-to-peer network, although some of the information, such as mapping network drives, applies equally to a client-server network and domains, which I'll discuss in the last part of this chapter. This section, however, contains information that sometimes applies to workgroups and sometimes applies to domains. You know which kind of network you have, so you'll know which instructions apply to your situation.

NOTE

In environments with lots of shared resources, complex group and permission issues can arise. For information on groups and permissions, see Chapter 24, "Living with Windows XP Professional Strict Security."

Here's how to use the `net view` command:

1. To display a list of the machines on your network, type **`net view`** at the command prompt.
2. To display a list of the resources on a particular machine, append the name of the machine. For example, if the machine name was spiritwolf, you'd enter **`net view \\spiritwolf`**.
3. To view the resources of a machine in another domain, for example, the server spiritwolf in the domain hq, you'd enter the following:
   `net view \\spiritwolf /domain:hq`
4. To display a list of all the domains on the network, simply enter **`net view /domain`**.

Using Net Use: Connecting to Other Drives and Printers

After you've browsed the network with the `net view` command, you can connect to all the available goodies (or disconnect from those you don't want) with the `net use` command. Use this command to connect to network resources as drives D through Z and printer ports LPT1 through LPT9.

WARNING

Drive letters can only be used once. So if your CD-ROM is drive D, you will only have drive letters E through Z available.

To display information about the workstation's current connections, type **`net use`** without options, and you'll see something like this:

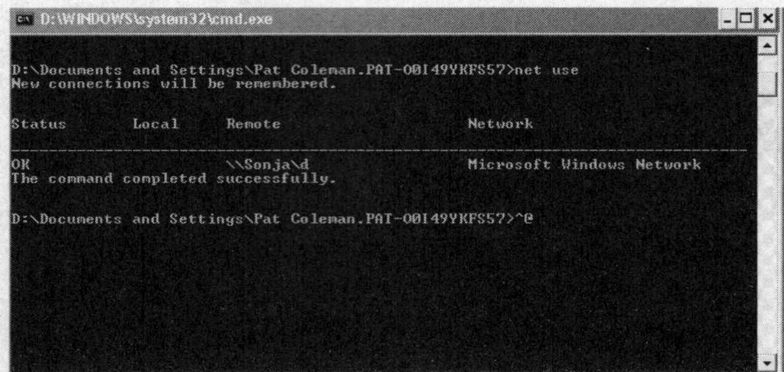

Connecting to a Resource in the Local Domain

To connect to a shared resource, such as a printer shared as lexmarko on server spiritwolf, type **`net use lpt1: \\spiritwolf\lexmarko`**.

Using Long Filenames in UNCs

If you wanted to connect to a folder called Wpfiles on the spiritwolf server and make that your E drive, you'd substitute **`E:`** for **`lpt1:`** and **`Wpfiles`** for **`lexmarko`** in the preceding example. Your command would be **`net use E: \\spiritwolf\wpfiles`**. You get to specify the port name or drive letter that you want to connect a resource to, but again, you're restricted to drive letters D through Z and ports LPT1 through LPT9.

If the computer you're getting the resource from has a blank character in its name (that is, the computer name has two words in it), you must put the name in quotation marks, like this:

```
"\\eisa server"
```

If a password (let's say it's "artuser") is attached to the resource that you're trying to connect to, you need to include that in your connection command, like this:

```
net use lpt1: \\ted\hp4m artuser
```

Or, if you want the computer to prompt you for the password so that it isn't displayed on the screen, append an asterisk:

```
net use lpt1: \\ted\hp4m *
```

Creating a Drive Mapping for Your Home Folder

To connect to your home folder (the folder on the server that has been assigned to you, assuming there is one), type the following:

```
net use /home
```

with the (optional) password on the end as just explained.

If you want to make the connection for another user, rather than for yourself, add the user's name (Frank) to the end of the line, like this:

```
net use lpt1: \\ted\hp4m user:frank
```

Passwords go before the user's name in the statement. If the user for whom you are making the connection is in another domain, the user part of the statement looks like this:

```
user:domainname/frank
```

where `domainname` is the name of that user's home domain.

Connecting to a Resource in Another Domain

If you want to connect to a resource in a domain that is not your usual one, you must first log on to that domain. One way to do this is to have a user account for yourself in the second domain. Managing multiple accounts for one person can get extremely cumbersome, so it's not the best setup. Another way is to have a trust relationship between your domains. Trust relationships allow users in one domain the potential to access resources in the other domain. I say potential because we still have to deal with permissions.

Think of trust relationships in human terms. If I trust you, I may let you drive my car (my resource). However, you still can't drive my car until I give you the keys (permissions). But if I don't trust you, there's no way I am handing you my keys! After you've logged on to the proper domain, the process of connecting to resources is the same as described above.

Using Other Switches

No matter what kind of connection you make, you can make it persistent (that is, have it reconnect automatically every time you reboot your machine) by adding the switch `/persistent:yes` to the end of the command. If you don't want it to be persistent, use `/persistent:no` instead.

If you don't specify one or the other, the default is whatever you chose last. If you want to make all future connections persistent, type the following:

```
net use /persistent:yes
```

(Or type **`:no`** if you want all future connections to be temporary.) Typing `/persistent` by itself at the end of the line won't do anything.

To disconnect from a resource, type the following:

```
net use devicename /delete
```

where *`devicename`* is the connection (such as D or LPT1). You don't have to provide a password or say anything about persistency to disconnect from a resource.

Using Profiles

Windows XP Professional uses two types of profiles: user and hardware. Although each serves a specific purpose, both types of profiles are used to customize the computing environment. In this section, we'll look at how to create and manage them.

Creating Hardware Profiles

If you use a laptop for business, you likely have encountered the following problem. When you bring your laptop into the office, you would like your computer to recognize the NIC and maybe an external monitor and keyboard. But when you take your laptop on the road, you want it to know that you do not currently have any of the "office" devices attached. Most laptops get their information by timing out on each device, which adds five minutes to the boot process and wastes time, not to mention wasting valuable battery life.

A feature of Windows XP Professional that is designed to alleviate this problem is a hardware profile. You can create a profile of the hardware that is attached to your machine when you are in the office and specify a different hardware profile for when you are on the road. And the fun doesn't stop there. You can create profiles for all the places in which you use your computer.

To create a hardware profile, follow these steps:

1. On the Start menu, right-click My Computer, and choose Properties from the shortcut menu to open the System Properties dialog box.
2. Select the Hardware tab, and click Hardware Profiles to open the Hardware Profiles dialog box:

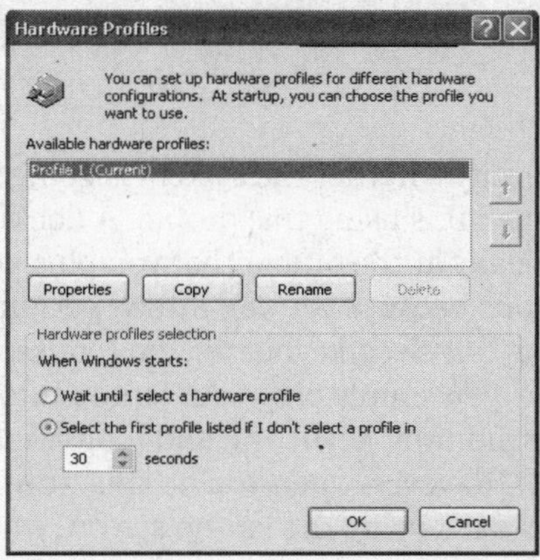

3. To create a new hardware profile, choose a configuration from the Available Hardware Profiles list, and then click Copy to open the Copy Profile dialog box.
4. Give the hardware profile a new name, and click OK. (I'll show you how to configure a profile a bit later in this section.)

TIP

When naming hardware profiles, use an intuitive naming pattern. As an example, "Office" and "On the road" are certainly better alternatives than "Profile 1" and "Profile 2."

5. To play with the docking properties of this profile, click Properties to open the Properties dialog box for the profile you are creating.

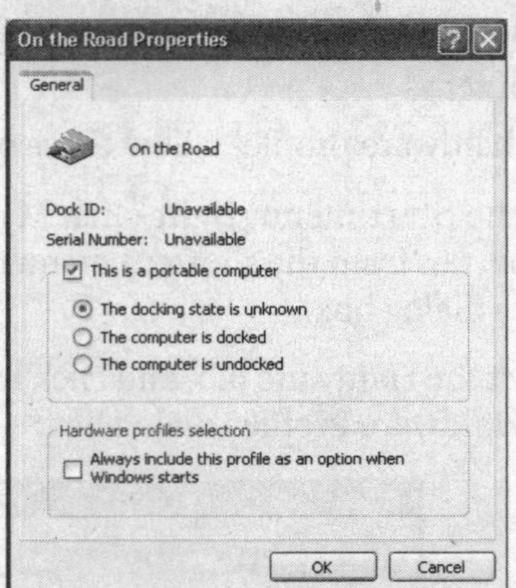

You can specify whether the system is going to be attached to a docking station when it is using this profile. A docking station is a box on your desk (usually at the office) that you plug your laptop into. You use docking stations because you can attach peripherals to them, such as a larger monitor, full-sized keyboard, and mouse. Then, when you come into the office, you simply plug your laptop into the dock, and you can use the larger monitor, keyboard, and mouse instead of the smaller ones on the laptop. However, when you do this, your laptop needs to know that sometimes it's using the laptop screen, whereas other times it's using the larger monitor. You tell the laptop this by configuring the docking properties.

If Windows XP Professional is not able to automatically detect the docking status of your laptop when in this profile, The Docking State Is Unknown option is selected. You can also strictly specify the state if it is always docked when using this profile or if it is *not* always docked when using this profile.

If this computer is a desktop, uncheck This Is a Portable Computer. When you've set your options, click OK to close the Properties dialog box, and then click OK twice more.

Managing Hardware Profiles

Now that you have created your hardware profile, you can begin to enable the services and devices that will be available through it. When you reboot your computer, choose a hardware profile. To enable or disable devices or services in this profile, follow these steps:

1. In Control Panel, click Performance and Maintenance, click Administrative Tools, and then double-click Computer Management to open the Computer Management window.

2. Expand System Tools, and then select Device Manager to display the list of devices in the pane on the right.

3. Expand the device you're interested in. Double-click the device that you want to enable or disable to open its Properties dialog box.

4. In the General tab, use the Device Usage drop-down list to enable or disable a device in the current hardware profile or in any (or all) hardware profiles, and then click OK.

5. To enable or disable services, expand Services and Applications, and then select Services to display the list of the services in the pane on the right:

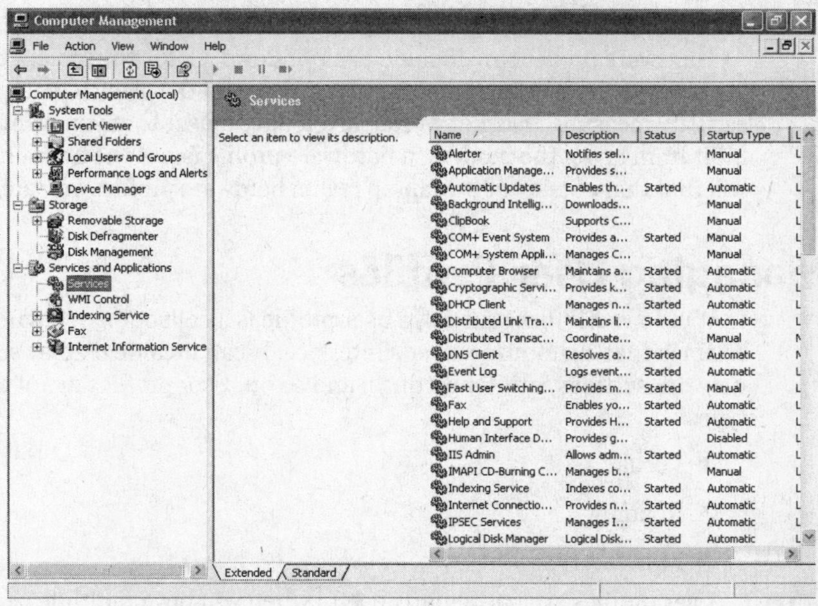

6. Double-click the service that you want to manage to open its Properties dialog box, and then click the Log On tab:

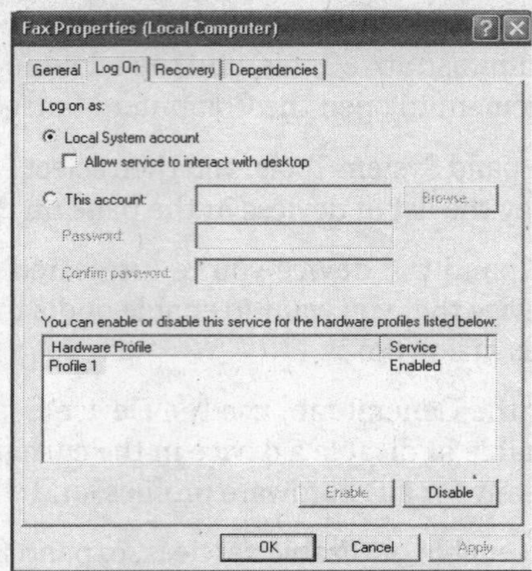

7. Select the specific hardware profile, click Enable or Disable, and then click OK.

Hardware profiles are included in Windows XP for convenience. They are intended to be a useful option for those who travel with laptops, not a security measure. In other words, if you have a user that you want to prohibit from using the modem, a hardware profile is not the answer. You will find that outside of the laptop realm, hardware profiles are rarely used.

Managing User Profiles

In Windows XP Professional, a user profile is a collection of environment settings that customize a user's interface. It can include display settings, network settings, printer settings, and so on. User profiles are of three types:

- Local
- Roaming
- Mandatory

User profiles are particularly useful when you have multiple users using the same workstation, or users that don't have an assigned desk location. If you and I use the same machine (you work days and I work the swing shift), you want to be able to have your settings (wallpaper, icons, printer and network connections) every time you log in. So do I. User profiles is the answer.

The first time you log on to a computer, whether it's yours or that of someone else on your network, Windows XP Professional creates a *local user profile* for you that is specific to that machine. Since this is the first time you are logging on to this machine, Windows XP gives you what is called the *default user profile*. When you log off, any changes you've made to the environment during the sessions are saved in your local user profile. Local user profiles only apply to a local machine, hence their name.

A *roaming user profile* can only be created by your system administrator and is stored on the server. A roaming user profile contains settings that are specific to you and is loaded whenever you log on to any computer on the network. Local user profiles and roaming user profiles contain the same types of information. The only differences are that a roaming profile is stored on a server (as opposed to the local machine), and roaming profiles follow you no matter where you log in. You must have a domain to use roaming user profiles.

TIP

If your network uses roaming user profiles, educate users to *not* store large files on their desktop, which is part of their profile. Every time they log on, the profile needs to be copied from the server it's stored on to the local machine. If there are large files as part of that profile, logging on to the network could take an excruciatingly long time.

A *mandatory user profile* specifies settings for an individual or a group of users and can only be created or modified by your system administrator. There is a major philosophical difference between mandatory user profiles and the other two we have discussed. With local and roaming profiles, users are allowed to customize their settings any way they choose. While this allows for freedom and personalization, people are known to abuse these types of privileges. With a mandatory user profile, the user gets a specified environment every time they log on. They are allowed to make changes, but every time they log off and back on, their settings are back to defaults. Most of the time, when users realize that their changes are not being kept, they will simply stop making changes at all.

NOTE

Mandatory user profiles will only work if you are implementing them across a network. They will not work locally.

Please note that mandatory profiles do *not* keep users from making changes to their desktop settings. Mandatory profiles just don't save those changes that the user does make. If you want to keep people from changing desktop settings at all, you need to use either Local Security Policy or Group Policies (which can affect an entire network).

To customize the default user profile so that each new user of the machine gets the same settings, follow these steps:

1. Log on to the computer as a new user.
2. Establish the desired settings, such as Start menu options, network connections, and so on, and then log off the computer.
3. Log back on to the computer as Administrator.
4. Right-click My Computer, and choose Properties from the shortcut menu to open the System Properties dialog box.
5. Click the Advanced tab, and then click Settings in the User Profiles section to open the User Profiles dialog box:

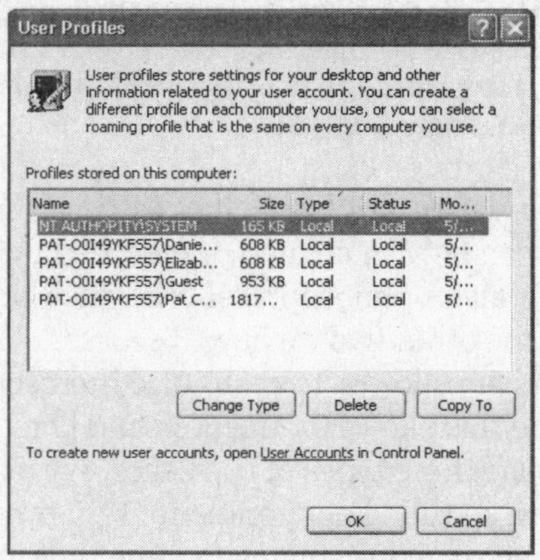

6. Highlight the profile that you want each new user to use, and then click Copy To to open the Copy To dialog box:

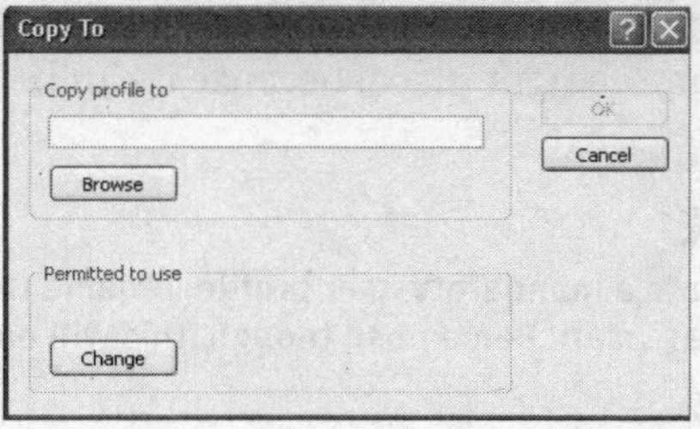

7. In the Copy Profile To box, enter the following path:
   `%SYSTEMROOT%\Documents and Settings\Default User`

8. Click OK, and then click OK again.

If you should happen to delete a profile folder in the Documents and Settings folder, Windows XP Professional will react as if the user has never logged on to the system before. When the user logs on again, Windows will create a new profile folder for the user. This feature can be useful if the user has placed icons and information all over the Desktop and is now complaining that it keeps coming up as a mess. You can simply delete the profile folder, and a new one will be created the next time that user logs on. It will be the default environment as created in the Default User folder.

Understanding Windows XP Professional Profiles versus 9x Profiles

If you've used Windows 9*x*, you know that it also has user profiles. Windows 9*x* stores a lot of its user environment information in a file called `user.dat` that is in the Windows folder. If you are in an NT Server or NetWare environment, you can easily network your user profiles so that your wallpaper, icons, Start menu, and so on can follow you around the network, regardless of which Windows 9*x* machine you sit at.

Windows XP Professional profiles are controlled by a file called `ntuser.dat`. Profiles are really a collection of folders and files stored on the computer, but if the `ntuser.dat` file is deleted or corrupted, the profile will not work properly. Also, each user that uses the computer gets their own profile folder, located in `C:\`*`%systemroot%`*`\Documents and Settings`. If Joe and Jenny have both logged on to this machine, it will have a `\Joe` folder and a `\Jenny` folder in Documents and Settings. The Joe and Jenny folders will each contain an `ntuser.dat` file, which controls their individual profiles. If you're going to delete someone's profile, make sure you're in the right place, because it can be confusing!

NOTE

To create a mandatory user profile, rename the user's `ntuser.dat` file to `ntuser.man`. Remember, though, this will only work across a network, not locally.

Profiles are specific to an operating system, so Windows XP profiles will work only if you are sitting at a Windows XP Professional machine, and Windows 9*x* profiles work only if you are sitting at a Windows 9*x* machine.

Connecting to a Domain

Although peer-to-peer workgroups have beauty in their simplicity, there are some limitations. As an example, did you know that with Windows XP, Microsoft has limited workgroups to 10 computers? For larger networks, you will need to create a domain.

Before you can connect to a domain, you will need to get the following information from your system administrator:

- Your domain username
- Your domain password
- The name of the domain that you will join
- Your computer name (you may have to provide the computer name to the administrator, especially if you configured it in a workgroup)

Once you are armed with this information, you can join a domain using the Computer Name Changes dialog box in System Properties or the Network Identification Wizard. Since using the Wizard is more descriptive, I'll walk through the process using it next. If you want to use the Computer Name Changes dialog box, follow these steps to open it:

1. Click Start, right-click My Computer, and choose Properties from the shortcut menu to open the System Properties dialog box.

2. Click the Computer Name tab, and then click Change to open the Computer Name Changes dialog box.

3. In the Member Of section, click the Domain option, and then enter the name of the domain. Click OK to close the Computer Name Changes dialog box, and then click OK again to close the System Properties dialog box.

Now, let's step briskly through the Wizard:

1. In the System Properties dialog box, click the Computer Name tab, and then click Network ID to start the Network Identification Wizard.

2. At the Welcome screen, click Next to open the Connecting to the Network screen.

3. Click the option that tells Windows XP Professional this computer is part of a business network, and then click Next to open the next Connecting to the Network screen.

4. Click the My Company Uses a Network with a Domain option, and then click Next.

5. Be sure that you have all the information listed on the Network Information screen, and then click Next.

6. On the User Account and Domain Information screen, enter your domain username, your domain password, and your domain name. Click Next.

7. On the Computer Domain screen, enter the name of your computer and your new domain, and click Next.

8. You'll see the Domain User Name and Password dialog box. Enter a username, password, and domain that has sufficient permissions to add this Windows XP Professional machine to the domain (the account must have Administrator rights in the domain), and then click OK. At this point, Windows XP Professional creates a machine name within the domain. Depending on your network, this could take a few minutes. When Windows XP Professional has created the machine name, it will return you to the User Account dialog box. Click Next.

9. On the Access Level Wizard, select the type of access that you want for the local computer. You can choose from three radio buttons: Standard User, Restricted User, and Other. Standard users can modify the computer and install applications but have no rights to read files that do not belong to them. Restricted users can save documents but have no rights to modify the computer or add applications. The Other option allows you to insert the user into a different group, such as Administrators, which would grant complete rights to the entire Windows XP Professional computer. Select a radio button, and then click Next.

10. The final dialog box, Completing the Network Identification Wizard, will appear. Click Finish and then click OK to reboot.

After the computer reboots, follow these steps to log on to the domain:

1. At the Windows logon prompt, press Ctrl+Alt+Del as you normally would to log on to Windows XP Professional.

2. Enter a username to log on to the domain (this is not always the same name as the local username), enter a password, and select the appropriate domain. You can either type in the domain name or select it from the drop-down list that Windows XP Professional automatically builds for you. If your domain name does not appear, click the Options button.

3. Click the OK button to complete the domain authentication process.

One thing to keep in mind is that you need sufficient permissions within the domain to add your computer to the domain. Normally, only domain administrator types have this ability, and it's not as though they want to give out the domain administrator password to everyone. If your user account does not have the necessary rights to join your computer to the domain, you may need some assistance from your network administrator.

Attaching to Network Resources Using Login Scripts

A very common way in which you will attach to network resources is through network drive mappings that the network administrator created in a login script. Often drive letters such as H and M are pointing to files on a file server on the network. The good news is, login scripts run automatically every time you log in (hence their name); therefore, they require no thinking on the part of the user.

You will be able to distinguish between network drives and local hard drives by the icon associated with the drive. Network drives have the little T-connector and cable beneath the icon. From time to time, you may see a drive with a red *X* across it. This symbol indicates that you formerly had a drive mapped to this drive letter, but the system cannot find the network location at this time. This situation happens most frequently if you are accessing the network remotely via a modem, but could also be a sign of connectivity problems.

Using the Connect As Option

You can use the Connect As dialog box to attach to a resource with another user account. (Click Start, right-click My Network Places, choose Map Network Drive from the shortcut menu to open the My Network Drive dialog box, and then click the link Connect Using a Different User Name.) By default, when you map a network drive, you are attached to the resource using the same user account that you originally use to log on to the workstation. But what if you are attaching to another server and you do not have an account on that server? This happens a lot to administrators.

If you have an administrator called Sheila Sanders, Sheila will have an account on her primary server that she logs on to. In addition, Sheila may need to attach to other servers that have resources she wants to use, even though she doesn't have an account on those servers. Another classic example would be that Sheila logs on to a Windows XP server as Sheila but has an account named SSanders on a NetWare server.

To resolve this issue, Sheila could log on to the Windows XP server as Sheila, but when she maps a drive to a Novell server, she could use the Connect As dialog box to connect to the NetWare server as SSanders. If the Sheila password on the Windows XP server and the SSanders account on NetWare are the same, Sheila gets direct access to the NetWare directory. If the passwords are different, Sheila will be prompted to enter a password for the NetWare server when she clicks OK to map the network drive.

Connecting to Non-Microsoft Networks

Thinking that Microsoft-based operating systems are the only ones in existence on networks is shortsighted. Although it's an oversight that Microsoft would surely allow you to maintain, now is a good time to discuss connecting to non-Microsoft operating systems and networks. This section specifically looks at connecting to Unix and Macintosh networks.

TIP

When working with multiple platforms, try to keep uniform usernames for all of your users. In other words, Sheila Sanders may have an easier time accessing resources if her account name is SSanders on all platforms, instead of Sheila on one and SSanders on another.

Entering the Dark Place That Is Unix

Right now, you may be thinking, "But I don't know much about Unix, much less how it networks!" That's okay. By now, you have some knowledge of general networking principles, and the principles do not change from platform to platform. You still need to find a way to make the machines talk, and you still need to make resources available across the network.

Probably the biggest difference if you're using a Unix-based machine is the interface. Although there are some graphical interfaces for Unix (such as X-Windows and Gnome), most of the time Unix is run from a command prompt. Don't be scared of the dark place, just be able to type some and you'll make it through. The good news is, accessing Unix-based resources from a Microsoft Windows XP Professional machine is incredibly similar to accessing Windows-based resources.

Microsoft offers two Unix interoperability products: Services for Unix 2.0 and Interix 2.2. The one you will be dealing with most is Services for Unix, which allows you to integrate your Windows XP Professional machine into a Unix environment. If you want to run Unix-based applications or logon scripts on your Windows XP Professional machine, you will need Interix.

NOTE

For purposes of this discussion, Unix and Linux support require the same configurations.

The first thing you need to look at when trying to connect to a Unix-based machine is the network protocol. Unix uses TCP/IP by default, and so does Windows XP Professional. First problem solved. Just make sure the machines are configured properly.

NOTE

One of the great things about the TCP/IP protocol is that it's universal. Whether you're using Windows, Unix, or any other operating system, the rules for configuring addresses don't change. Therefore, if you're trying to communicate with a Unix machine, just make sure that all computers have the same network address, but a unique host address. If you've forgotten how this works, take a look at the "Configuring Windows 95/NT Workstation Machines" section earlier in this chapter.

The next thing to look at is how the computers make requests. Windows XP Professional uses a protocol called Common Internet File System (CIFS) to make requests of the server. Unix uses the Network File System (NFS) protocol. Since the two are incompatible, we need to figure out a way to make the two platforms talk. Enter Services for Unix.

NOTE

Services for Unix is an umbrella term for two separate products: File Services for Unix and Print Services for Unix.

Services for Unix contains many components—more than is necessary to cover here. Probably the most important ones are Client for NFS and Server for NFS. When you install Services for Unix on your Windows XP machine, these services allow you to not only request stuff from an NFS server but to host resources for NFS clients as well. Specifically, Services for Unix allows you to access files and printers on a Unix server, as well as have Unix machines access your files and printers. Every Windows XP Professional machine that needs to access Unix resources will need to have Services for Unix installed.

NOTE

Services for Unix is an optional add-on product that must be purchased from Microsoft.

Here's one way to install Services for Unix (if it's been purchased):

1. Right-click My Network Places.
2. Select the Advanced menu, then choose Optional Networking Components.
3. Place a check next to Other Network File and Print Services, and click Next.
4. Windows XP will copy necessary files to your hard drive, and close the dialog box.

Printing in Unix is also slightly different from Microsoft printing. Installing Services for Unix installs two critical printing components: Line Printer (LPR) and Line Printer Daemon (LPD).

The LPR service is what is used to send print jobs to the print server, which is LPD. Daemon, in Unix terms, simply refers to a server service. If you wanted to, you could use LPR from a command prompt to send print jobs to an LPD server. It's easier to map to the printer, though. Here's how to add an LPT port:

1. Click Start, and choose Printers and Faxes.
2. Under Printer Tasks, select Add a Printer, which opens the Add Printer Wizard. Click Next.
3. Choose Local Printer Attached to This Computer, and clear the Automatically Detect check box.
4. Click Create a New Port, and for the port type, choose LPR Port. Click Next.

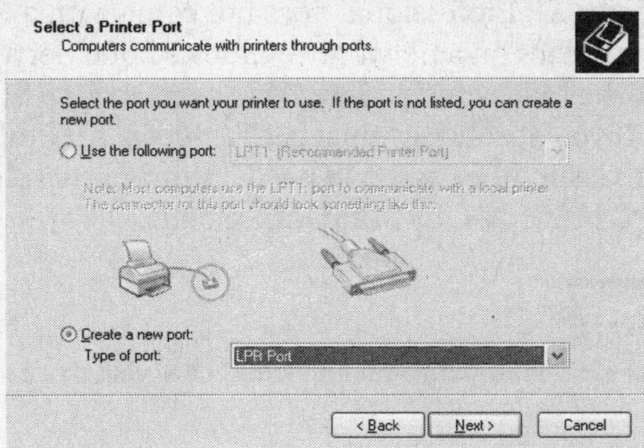

5. In the Name or Address of Server Providing LPD box, enter the DNS name or IP address of the host providing the LPD service (the Unix printer). You will also need to provide the name of the printer or print queue. Click OK.

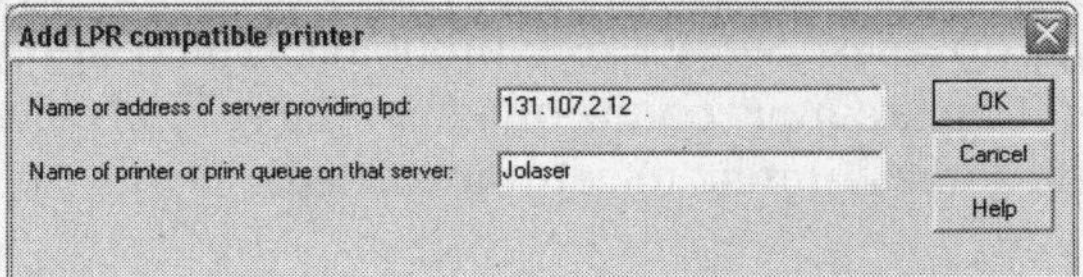

6. The Wizard will finish the installation for you.

Macintosh Networks

Networking professionals will tell you that the words "Macintosh" and "network" should never be used in the same sentence. Native Macintosh networking is horribly slow by today's standards, and creating Macintosh-accessible volumes on NT servers could cause crashes and headaches. Because of these issues, Macs don't have a good name in the PC-networking arena.

But for all the flak Macs get regarding networking, they make excellent graphics and design machines. Besides, most of the Macintosh networking components, including the NIC, are built-in.

Macintosh computers use the AppleTalk networking protocol by default. Fortunately, however, Macs also support TCP/IP. It's recommended that if you want to network with Macs, you should use the TCP/IP protocol. Windows XP Professional does not support the AppleTalk protocol.

Windows XP Professional does not come with any products or services to support Macs on a network. Windows 2000 Server comes with Services for the Mac, which allows Mac users to save files on Windows 2000 servers. If you absolutely must get Windows XP Professional and Macs talking to each other, you will need a third-party solution. One such solution is PC MACLAN, by Miramar Systems.

NOTE

For more information about PC MACLAN, visit `http://www.miramar.com`.

TROUBLESHOOTING NETWORKS

Entire books have been written on the topic of troubleshooting networks. It's such a voluminous topic that it requires a lot of attention. To that end, there is no way this chapter can teach you everything you need to know to troubleshoot network problems. The best training for troubleshooting is simply hands-on experience. That said, this section will give you some pointers to get you started.

Receiving the Error Message "No Domain Server Was Available"

When logging on to the server, you may get an error message stating that no domain server is available to authorize you to log on to a domain. Often this error message will prevent you from seeing some resources in My Network Places and prevent you from accessing the network entirely.

NOTE

The title of this section is a good example of a specific error message. Whenever you receive specific error messages, write them down. They are invaluable to have when searching your resources for a solution. You're never going to know how to fix everything right away, but if you know where to look for help, you'll be a lot further ahead in the game.

TIP

A good place to get started is Microsoft's Knowledge Base. It has a lot of articles about known error messages and may be able to help you. Go either to Microsoft's Web page (`www.microsoft.com`) and click the Support link, or to `support.Microsoft.com`. You will be able to type in your error message and search through all of Microsoft's products, or choose the specific product you are interested in. The support page also provides a download area for patches, and newsgroups for you to post questions.

This message appears when the system is unable to contact a domain controller for the domain that you are logging on to. The obvious problem could be that the server is down. Another common cause of this error is that a bridge, router, or gateway is malfunctioning in your environment; so check the hub and the bridges to make sure they are operating normally.

Easily the most common occurrence of this problem is when TCP/IP is the primary transport protocol in your environment. If the workstation is on one physical segment of the network and the domain controller is on another segment of the network, often the client machine is unable to see the server via NetBIOS. To test this situation, see if you can ping the server's address. If you can ping the server by using its IP address but are unable to contact the server for domain logon authentication, you have determined the cause of your dilemma.

One common solution is to install a Windows Internet Naming System Server (WINS Server) in your environment. It will handle the NetBIOS computer name to IP address name resolution (in much the same way that a DNS server handles IP host name to IP address conversions). Once the Windows Internet Naming Service is installed on a server, the Windows XP Professional computer must point to the WINS Server. To point the client to the WINS Server, follow these steps:

1. Right-click My Network Places and select Properties to open the Network Connections folder.
2. Right-click Local Area Connection and select Properties to open the Properties dialog box for your connection.
3. Double-click Internet Protocol (TCP/IP) to open the Internet Protocol (TCP/IP) dialog box.
4. On the General tab, click the Advanced button to open the Advanced TCP/IP Settings dialog box. Select the WINS tab.
5. Click Add to open the TCP/IP WINS Server dialog box.

6. In the WINS Server box, enter the IP address of the WINS server, and click Add.
7. Click OK and then click OK twice more. Close Network Connections.

While installing WINS is a common solution to this problem, it has a few drawbacks. One, it means you must have an additional server available to run this service. Yes, WINS can be installed on a server that's already doing something else, like a file or print server, but why pile more work on that machine? Two, Microsoft is moving away from using WINS, and moving toward DNS for all name resolution situations.

That said, if your network has a DNS server (which it must if you are running a Windows 2000 or XP domain), configure your clients to use the DNS server. This should already be the case, and if the clients can find the DNS server, and the DNS server has the records it's supposed to have, you won't encounter this error message.

TIP

If your client computers are getting their IP configuration information from a DHCP server, the addresses of WINS and DNS servers can be supplied along with the IP address, subnet mask, and other parameters.

Configuration Testing

You will want to test your configuration if you can't connect to machines you think you should be able to. The last section dealt with a specific problem, whereas in this section, the issue is a bit more ambiguous. Keep the following principles in mind when troubleshooting networks:

- Isolate the problem before fixing it.
- Be familiar with the tools you have available.
- Always check the obvious things (i.e., connections) that could be wrong, no matter how silly it may seem.

All the changes you have made in the network configuration will require you to reboot your system. When the system restarts, you will know if Windows XP Professional can see the network during the logon procedure. You may see error messages, for example, if your TCP/IP address went awry or if the domain controller refuses to validate you into the domain. Even if no errors are immediately apparent, take a look in Event Viewer for potential conflicts. Event Viewer is a great tool for helping track down problems. To open Event Viewer, follow these steps:

1. In Control Panel, click the Performance and Maintenance category, click Administrative Tools, and then double-click Computer Management to open the Computer Management window.
2. In the Computer Management pane, expand System Tools, and then expand Event Viewer.
3. Click System to display events in the pane on the right.
4. Look for red stop signs or yellow exclamation points. If you see one of these symbols, double-click it to open the Event Properties dialog box for that event, which will look similar to the following:

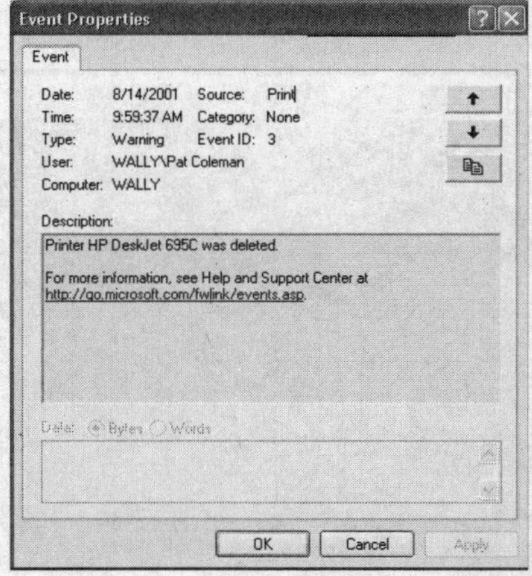

5. If the information in the Event Properties dialog box isn't sufficient to solve the problem, check the configuration of the component. In some cases, you may need to remove and reinstall it.
6. Click the Close button to close the Computer Management window.

TIP

When using Event Viewer to troubleshoot network problems, start at the top of the list and work down until you find event ID number 6005 with a source of eventlog. This represents the last time you booted the computer. The most likely source of your problems will be the event immediately above or immediately below the 6005 event. You should focus most of your efforts resolving these before moving on to the others.

The ultimate test of your configuration is being able to attach to all the resources you need. Looking in My Network Places, clicking Entire Network, and then double-clicking Microsoft Windows Network can give you insight into which parts of the networks you can and cannot communicate with.

If you believe you need to troubleshoot your TCP/IP configuration, you will want to use the IPCONFIG utility. Type **`ipconfig /all`** at the command prompt, and you will get a report that looks similar to the one in Figure 23.1.

```
Command Prompt
Microsoft Windows XP [Version 5.1.2505]
(C) Copyright 1985-2001 Microsoft Corp.

D:\Documents and Settings\Pat Coleman>ipconfig /all

Windows IP Configuration

        Host Name . . . . . . . . . . . . : wally
        Primary Dns Suffix  . . . . . . . :
        Node Type . . . . . . . . . . . . : Unknown
        IP Routing Enabled. . . . . . . . : No
        WINS Proxy Enabled. . . . . . . . : No

Ethernet adapter Local Area Connection:

        Connection-specific DNS Suffix  . :
        Description . . . . . . . . . . . : 3Com EtherLink XL 10/100 PCI TX NIC
(3C905B-TX)
        Physical Address. . . . . . . . . : 00-50-04-98-B6-29
        Dhcp Enabled. . . . . . . . . . . : No
        IP Address. . . . . . . . . . . . : 192.168.20.2
        Subnet Mask . . . . . . . . . . . : 255.255.255.0
        Default Gateway . . . . . . . . . : 192.168.20.80
        DNS Servers . . . . . . . . . . . : 192.168.20.80

D:\Documents and Settings\Pat Coleman>
```

FIGURE 23.1: An `ipconfig /all` report

`Ipconfig /all` reports all the vital information regarding your TCP/IP connection, even down to lease duration of your IP address if you are using DHCP on your network. If `ipconfig` reports an address that is unfamiliar to you, or reports no information at all, then you may have found your problem.

For testing TCP/IP configurations, the `ping` utility is commonly used. Follow this procedure to test your IP configuration and network connection:

NOTE

Some of these tests assume that your LAN is connected to the Internet.

1. Test that you've installed the IP software by pinging the built-in IP loopback address. Type **`ping 127.0.0.1`**. If that fails, you know that you've done something wrong in the initial installation, so check that the software is installed on your system. This test does not put any messages out on the network; it just checks that the software is installed. By the way, the same thing happens if you ping your IP address, except that pinging your address also tests the network card.

   If that fails, your TCP/IP stack probably isn't installed correctly, or perhaps you mistyped the IP number (if it failed on your specific IP address but not on the loopback), or perhaps you gave the *same* IP number to another workstation.

2. Ping your default gateway to see that you can get to it, because it should be on your local subnet. For example, if your gateway were at 199.34.57.2, you would type **`ping 199.34.57.2`**, and you should get a response.

3. If you can't get to the gateway, check that the gateway is up and that your network connection is all right. Nothing is more embarrassing than calling in outside network support, only to find that your LAN cable fell out of the back of your computer.

4. Ping something on the other side of your gateway, such as an external DNS server. (Ping me, Mark Minasi, if you like: 199.34.57.1. I ought to be up just about all the time.) If you can't get there, it's likely that your gateway isn't working properly.

5. Next, test the name resolution on your system. Ping yourself *by name*. Instead of typing something such as **`ping 199.34.57.35`**, you'd type **`ping nec.Mmco.Com`** (the machine you're on at the moment). That tests HOSTS and/or DNS.

6. Then, ping someone else on your subnet. Again, try using a DNS name, such as `mizar.Ursamajor.Edu`, rather than an IP address. If that doesn't work, use the IP address. If the IP address works, but the host name doesn't, you've got a problem with the HOSTS file or DNS.

7. Finally, ping someone outside your domain, such as `house.gov` (the U.S. House of Representatives), `www.yahoo.com`, or `orion01.Mmco.Com`. If that doesn't work but all the pings inside your network work, you've probably got a problem with your Internet provider.

WARNING

While pinging Web sites can help test connectivity, some Web sites do not allow pings in to their network. They block pings off as a security measure. So, the site may be up, but you won't get a response from a ping. `Microsoft.com` is a good example of this.

If you're successful on all these tests, your TCP/IP connection should be set up properly.

Quick Advice

As mentioned previously, troubleshooting is best learned by doing. There really is no good substitute for experience. To make things easier, though, there are some quick tips you can always keep in mind when troubleshooting a network:

- Always check your connections. Try another network cable if possible.
- Check and double-check your IP configuration, including IP address, subnet mask, default gateway, and DNS server addresses.
- Run `ipconfig` and `ping`. Make sure you're set up properly, and see what, if anything, you *can* connect to.

- Look in Event Viewer for any errors.
- Use your help and online resources.
- Delete and reinstall the network adapter if necessary.

Also, the Windows Help and Support center has a lot of good information, including Wizards, to assist in your troubleshooting. Take one step at a time, and if you make configuration changes, change one thing, test, and then change another if necessary. Don't change a bunch of stuff all at once, because you'll never know which change was the right one. One last thing–if you see someone troubleshooting a problem, and they say something like, "Huh, that's not supposed to happen," or "That's weird...," think about how silly a statement that *really* is. If everything was working as advertised, then why are they troubleshooting in the first place?

WHAT'S NEXT?

In this chapter, we've looked at how to set up and configure a network, create shares, attach to network resources, use user profiles and hardware profiles, connect to a domain, and troubleshoot your network when things go awry. But an important aspect of networking is still missing: how to set up rights and permissions for shares and for files and folders. I'll discuss this in detail in the next chapter, because, as you well know by now, security is the main reason people migrate to Windows XP Professional in the first place.

Chapter 24

Living with Windows XP Professional Strict Security

In the previous chapter, I walked you through the steps for creating and configuring a network, but one big piece of the networking pie is still missing: securing the resources on your network. From its inception, the NT family of operating systems was designed with security as a primary feature, and, of course, this architectural element is omnipresent in the Windows XP Professional.

Adapted from *Mastering Windows XP Professional*
by Mark Minasi
ISBN 0-7821-2981-1 1056 pages $39.99

Unlike some other operating systems, Windows XP Professional requires you to create a user account for yourself right on your PC before you can do anything on that PC. Yes, the idea that you must create your own user account on your personal PC before you can do anything with the PC is unusual—after all, most of us are accustomed to requiring network accounts, but not particular accounts on a workstation. But—as your father might say when you complain that something you don't like isn't fair—get used to it!

The user account is an integral part of Windows XP Professional and has some great benefits. For example, suppose you and Sue share a computer. You can set up the computer so that you own a folder on the hard disk and Sue owns another folder on the hard disk, and *it is completely impossible for Sue to access your data* (and vice versa) unless you give her permission.

In addition, you can restrict access to files and folders by setting permissions. As you may recall, in Windows XP Professional you can use the FAT, FAT32, or NTFS file system. If you use either FAT system, you can exercise only a limited amount of control over file and folder access, but if you use the NTFS system, you can exercise a great deal of control—whether the files are on your local computer or on your network.

In this chapter, we'll first look at how to set up user accounts, and then we'll look in detail at establishing permissions for shares, files, and folders.

Understanding User Accounts in Windows XP Professional

As you have just read, you must create separate user accounts on a Windows XP Professional machine before any user can log on to the workstation—and, unlike Windows 9*x*, Windows XP Professional won't let you get anywhere until you log on.

If your computer is part of a Windows XP Professional client-server network, two types of user accounts are available: domain accounts and local accounts. A domain account gives you access to the network and to the network resources for which you have permission. The manager of the server normally sets up domain accounts, which are stored in a directory on the server. The directory can either be Active Directory or a Windows NT domain directory.

A local user account is valid only on your local computer; local user accounts sit in a database called the *Security Accounts Manager*, or SAM. You create user accounts with the Users and Passwords applet, which you'll meet later in this chapter.

In this chapter, I'm going to talk about local user accounts only. If you happen to be the administrator of a domain on a network and you need help creating domain user accounts, take a look at *Mastering Windows 2000 Server,* Third Edition (Sybex, 2001).

Before I get into how you change or create an account, we need to look at the types of accounts in Windows XP Professional. The two broad categories are users and groups. A user account identifies a user on the basis of their user name and password. A group account contains other accounts, and these accounts share common privileges.

User accounts are of three types:

Computer Administrator This account has full and complete rights to the computer and can do just about anything to the computer. The Computer Administrator account was created during installation and setup of Windows XP Professional. The Computer Administrator account cannot be deleted. You'll need to log on as Computer Administrator when you want to create new accounts, take ownership of files or other objects, install software that will be available to all users, and so on.

Limited This account is intended for use by regular old users, those who should not be allowed to install software or hardware or change their user name. Someone with a limited account can change their password and logon picture.

Guest This built-in account allows a user to log on to the computer even though the user does not have an account. No password is associated with the Guest account. It is disabled by default, and you should leave it that way. If you want to give a visitor or an occasional user access to the system, create an account for that person, and then delete the account when it is no longer needed.

As I said earlier, a group is an account that contains other accounts, and a group is defined by function. Using groups, an administrator can easily create collections of users who all have identical privileges. By default, every Windows XP Professional system contains the following built-in groups:

Administrators Can do just about anything to the computer. The things that they can do that no other type of user can do include loading and unloading device drivers, managing security audit functions, and taking ownership of files and other objects.

Backup Operators Can log on to the computer and run backups or perform restores. You might put someone in this group if you wanted them to be able to get on your system and run backups but not to have complete administrative control. Backup operators can also shut down the system but cannot change security settings.

Guests Have minimal access to network resources. As I mentioned earlier, creating user accounts for occasional users is a much safer bet than using Guest accounts.

Network Configuration Operators Can manage network configuration with administrative-type access. Although they do not have administrative access to your system, these users can modify network and dial-up connections.

Power Users Can create new printer and file shares, change the system time, force the system to shut down from another system, and change priorities of processes in the system. They can't run backups, load or unload device drivers, or take ownership.

Remote Desktop Users Have the right to log on remotely.

Replicator Enables your computer to receive replicated files from a server machine.

Users Can run programs and access data on a computer, shut it down, and access data on the computer from over the network. Users cannot share folders or create local printers.

HelpServicesGroup A group of users for the Help and Support Center.

IIS_WPG The Internet Information Services Worker Process Group; this group is available only if you have installed IIS. A member of this group can manage the IIS Web server (not content, just service).

Understanding User Rights

But what's this about shutting down the machine or loading and unloading drivers? Well, actually, the notion of a *user right* is an integral part of how Windows XP Professional security works. Basically, the difference between regular old users and administrators lies in the kinds of actions that they can perform; for example, administrators can create new user accounts but regular old users cannot. In Windows XP Professional terminology, the ability to perform a particular function is a user right. To take a look at the user rights in Windows XP Professional and the types of users to whom they are assigned, follow these steps:

1. In Control Panel, click Performance and Maintenance, click Administrative Tools, and then click Local Security Policy to open the Local Security Settings window.

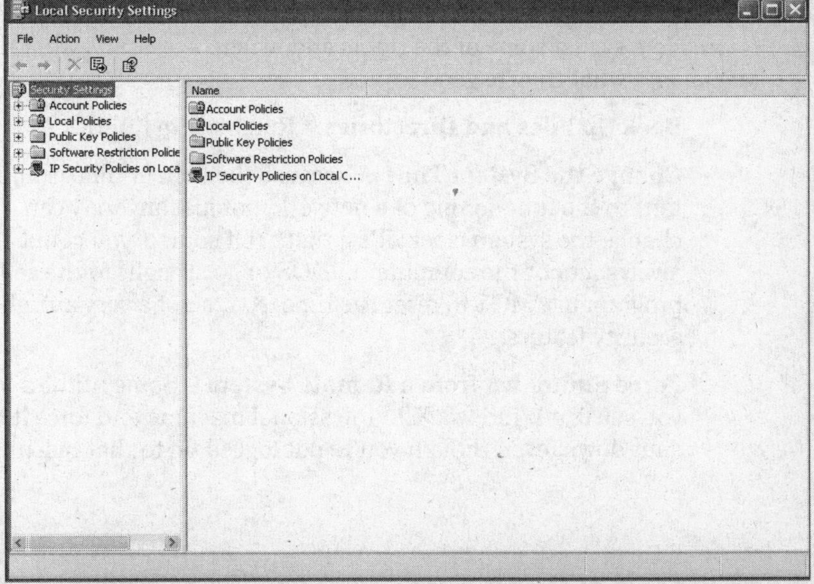

2. In the Security Settings pane, expand Local Policies, and then click User Rights Assignment to display a list of user rights in the pane on the right:

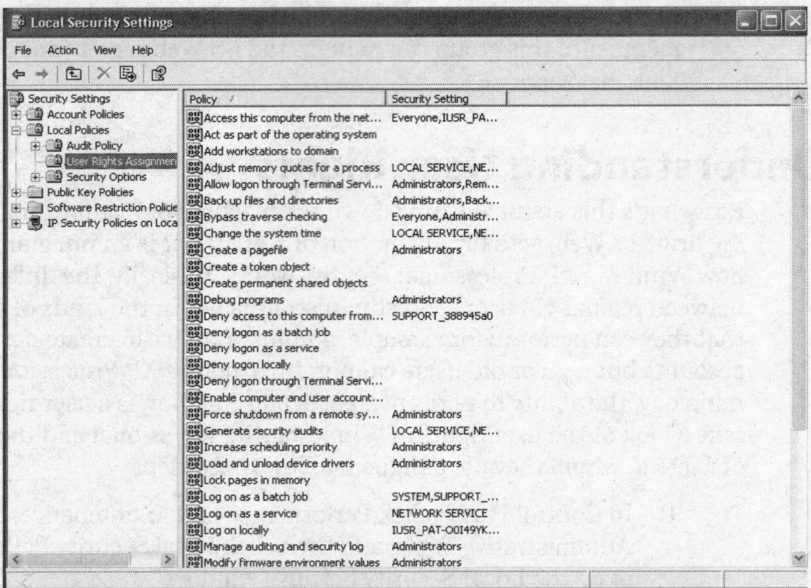

Most user rights are self-explanatory, but a few can use some clarification. Here's a list some of the rights and, where necessary, what they mean and what they're good for:

Back Up Files and Directories Run backup utilities.

Change the System Time Because the system time is important to the functioning of a network, not just anybody can change the system clock; it's a right. (Of course, you could always reboot the computer in DOS or go straight to the setup program in CMOS to reset the time, so it's not a very airtight security feature.)

Force Shutdown from a Remote System Some utilities let you select a Windows XP Professional machine and force it to shut down, even though you're not logged on to that machine.

(One such utility comes with the Resource Kit.) Because you wouldn't want just anybody doing a forced shutdown, Microsoft made this a right.

Load and Unload Device Drivers A device driver is not only a video driver or SCSI driver; a device driver may be part of a software application or operating system subsystem. Without this right, you'll often be unable to install new software, and you'll usually be unable to change drivers or add and remove parts of the operating system.

Log on Locally Sit down at the computer and log on.

Manage Auditing and Security Log You can optionally turn on a Windows XP Security Log, which will report every single action that woke up any part of the security subsystems in Windows XP Professional. In general, I don't recommend using the Security Log because the output is quite cryptic and can be *huge*; logging all security events can fill up your hard disk quickly, and the CPU overhead of keeping track of the log will slow down your computer. You can't enable any security logging unless you have this right.

Restore Files and Directories As the name states.

Take Ownership of Files or Other Objects If you have this right, you can seize control of any file, folder, or other object even if you're not *supposed* to have access to it. This right is obviously quite powerful, which is why only administrators have it.

NOTE

The user right to Take Ownership of Files or Other Objects is the secret to the administrator's power. You can do whatever you like to keep an administrator out of your data, but remember that the Computer Administrator can always take ownership of the file, and as owner, do whatever they want to the file including changing permissions. You cannot keep an administrator out; you can only make it difficult to get in.

Creating a User Account

Okay, now that you understand about the types of accounts and the concept of rights, let's create a new user account. You can do so in a couple of ways: using the Users and Passwords applet and using Computer Management. I'll start with the steps for creating a new user account with the Users Accounts applet:

1. Log on as Computer Administrator.
2. Choose Start ➢ Control Panel to open Control Panel, and then click User Accounts to open User Accounts.
3. Click the Create a New Account link to open the Name the New Account screen:

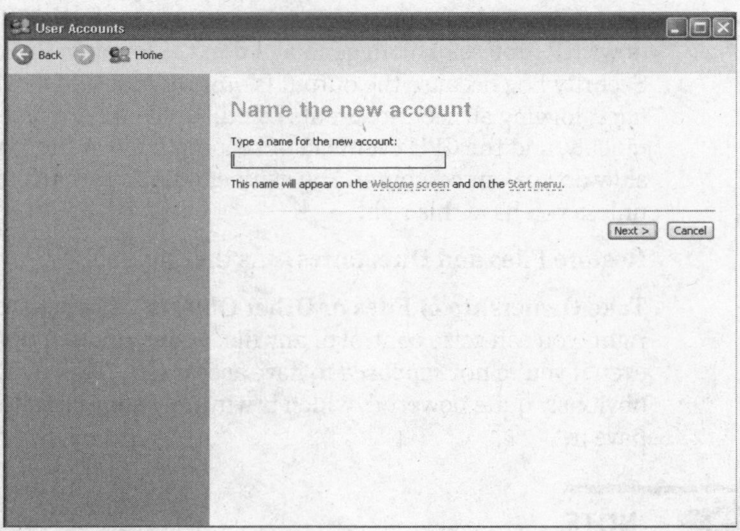

4. Enter a user name for the person, and then click Next.

NOTE

In Windows XP Professional, a user name can be a maximum of 20 characters and is not case sensitive.

5. Specify the type of account you want this user to have, and then click Create Account.

6. Back in User Accounts, click Change an Account, click the account you just created, and then click Create Password to open the screen on which you can create a password for the account.

NOTE

In Windows XP Professional, a password can be a maximum of 127 characters if you are in a pure Windows XP Professional environment. If you have Windows *9x* machines on your network, keep the password to a maximum of 14 characters. Passwords are case sensitive.

7. In the Type a New Password box, enter a password, and then enter it again in the Type the New Password Again to Confirm box. If you want, you can then type a hint (which can be seen by anyone using this computer) to trigger your remembrance of the password if you forget it.

8. Click Create Password to establish the password for the new user account.

To gain more control over the process of managing user accounts on Windows XP Professional, you will need to use the Local User Manager. In Control Panel, click Performance and Maintenance, click Administrative Tools, and then click Computer Management to open the Computer Management window. In the Computer Management (Local) pane, expand System Tools, expand Local Users and Groups, and then select Users to display a list of users in the right pane. Choose Action ➢ New User to open the New User dialog box, as shown in Figure 24.1.

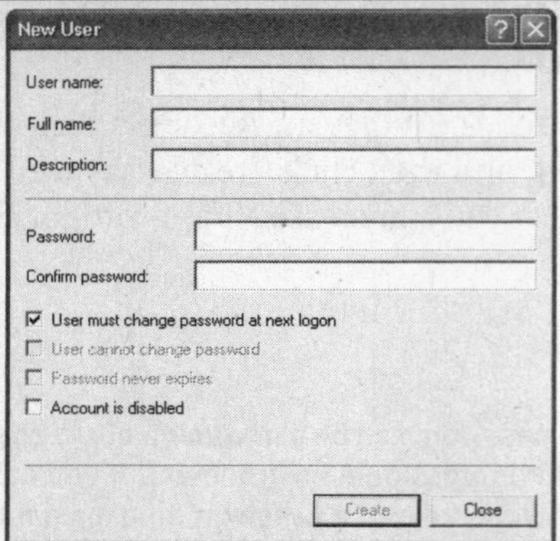

FIGURE 24.1: Use the New User dialog box to add a new user to your system.

Now follow these steps:

1. Enter a user name for this new account.
2. Enter the person's full name.
3. Enter a description.
4. Enter and confirm a password.
5. Set the password options. The default option is User Must Change Password at Next Logon. This option means that only that user will know the password, which means better security. If you uncheck this option, the other two options become available. Select User Cannot Change Password if this account will be used for a service or for someone that you do not want to give the ability to change their own password. Select Password Never Expires if this password should be considered "permanent" and not have an automatic expiration.
6. The final option is to specify whether the account should be disabled. This is often a good idea if you want to change other properties of the account before it can be used, such as setting permissions on files and folders that this user will use. If this is the case, check the Account Is Disabled box.
7. When all options are selected, click Create to complete the process of making the new user account.

NOTE

To enable a disabled account, in the Local Users and Groups window, right-click the account, and choose Properties from the shortcut menu to open the Properties dialog box for that account. Clear the Account Is Disabled check box.

Creating a Group Account

The process of creating a new group account is similar to creating a new user account. Local groups are useful for assigning permissions to resources. To create a new group account, follow these steps:

1. In Control Panel, click Performance and Maintenance, click Administrative Tools, and then click Computer Management to open the Computer Management window.
2. Expand System Tools, expand Local User and Groups, right-click Groups, and choose New Group from the shortcut menu to open the New Group dialog box:

3. Type a name for the group in the space provided. The name can contain any numbers or letters and can be a maximum of 256 characters. The name must be unique in the local database.
4. Enter some text in the Description field that will describe the membership and purpose of this group.

5. Click the Add button to open the Select Users dialog box:

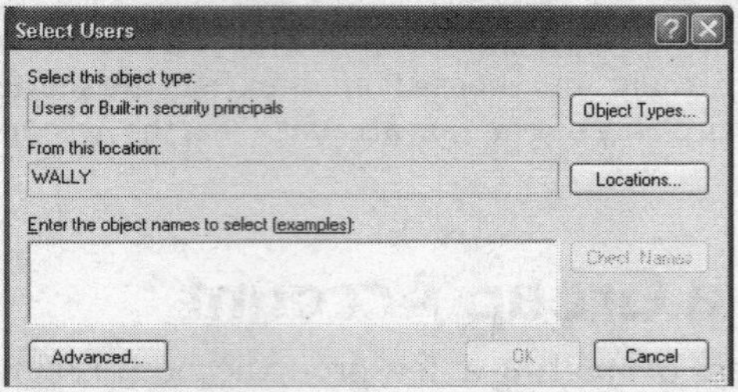

6. In the Enter the Object Name to Select box, enter the name of the user you want to add to the group, and then click OK. Repeat step 5 and this step to add more users to the group.

7. Back in the New Group dialog box, click Close, and then close Computer Management.

SETTING PERMISSIONS

The capability to restrict access to data is a really great feature of NT and Windows XP Professional. Prior to NT, my experience with operating systems of all kinds was that if you could gain physical access to a computer, you could get to its data; before NT, the only way to secure data with any confidence was to put the data on a server and put the server behind a locked door.

But network security is only as good as you make it. If a person can gain physical access to your machine, they can remove your hard disk and have all your data. Data security includes educating users to protect passwords and to apply permissions responsibly.

In this section, I'm going to show you how to set permissions at the share level and at the file and folder level. Remember, however, that you can establish file and folder security only if you are using the NTFS file system.

NOTE

To set permissions on a shared resource, you need to disable simple file sharing, which is enabled by default. In an Explorer window, choose Tools ➢ Folder Options to open the Folder Options dialog box. Click the View tab, and then in the Advanced Settings list, clear the Use Simple File Sharing (Recommended) check box.

Setting Share-Level Permissions

In the previous chapter, I showed you how to share resources on your computer with others on your network. Now we need to look at what kind of access you want to give those who use your shared resources. To do this, you set the permissions.

To set share permissions, follow these steps:

1. In Explorer, right-click the shared resource, and choose Sharing and Security from the shortcut menu to open the Properties dialog box for the share at the Sharing tab.
2. Click the Permissions button to open the Permissions dialog box:

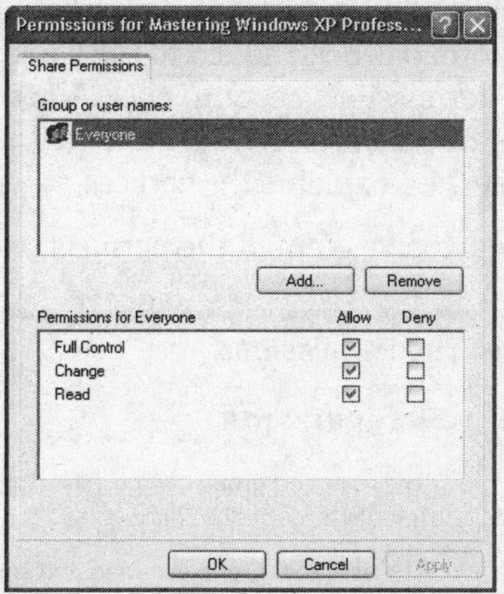

NOTE

The default shared permission in Windows XP Professional is for the Everyone group to have Full Control. In a secure environment, be sure to remove this permission before assigning specific permissions to users and groups.

3. Click Add to open the Select Users or Groups dialog box, in which you can select which groups have access to a shared file or folder:

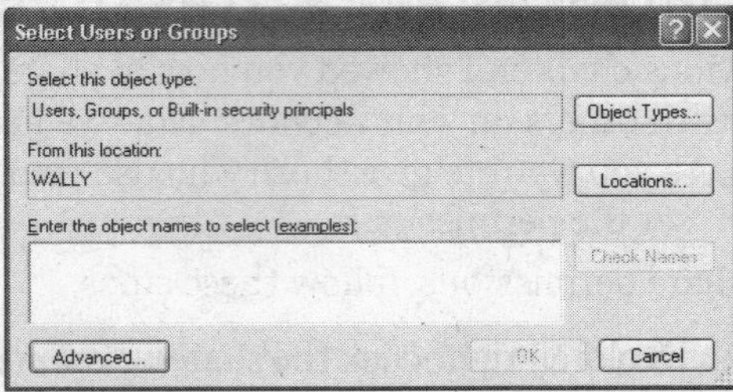

4. In the Enter the Object Name to Select box, enter the name of the user or group to whom you are granting permission, and click OK.

5. Back in the Permissions dialog box, you'll see that the user or group has been added to the Group or User Names list. In the Permissions section, click Allow or Deny to specify the type of permission you want to grant this user or group. Table 24.1 explains the choices.

6. When you've granted the permissions, click OK.

TABLE 24.1: File Permissions

PERMISSION	DESCRIPTION
Full Control	The assigned group can perform any and all functions on all files and folders through the share.
Change	The assigned group can read and execute, as well as change and delete, files and folders through the share.
Read	The assigned group can read and execute files and folders but cannot modify or delete anything through the share.

Types of File and Folder Permissions

Share-level permissions determine who can access resources across the network and the type of access they will have. However, you can still assign more detailed permissions to the folders and files that can be accessed through the share. In addition, by using file- and folder-level permissions, you can restrict access to resources even if someone logs on to the system.

MULTIPLE GROUPS ACCUMULATE PERMISSIONS

You might have one group in your network called Accountants and another called Managers, and they might have different permission levels—for example, the Accountants might be able to only read the files, and the Managers might have Change access, which in NT was called Read and Write access. What about the manager of the Accounting department, who belongs to both the Managers and the Accountants groups—does he have Read access or does he have Change access?

In general, your permissions to a network resource *add up*—so if you have Read access from one group and Change from another group, you end up with Read *and* Change access. However, because Change access *includes* all the things that you can do with Read access, there's no practical difference between having Read and Change and having only Change access.

You've already seen that network shares have three types of permission levels: Read, Change, and Full Control. The permission types for files and folders are much more extensive, and each primary type includes still other types. Here are the primary types:

Read Allows you to view the contents, permissions, and attributes associated with a resource. If the resource is a file, you can view the file. If the resource is an executable file, you can run it. If the resource is a folder, you can view the contents of the folder.

Write Allows you to create a new file or subfolder within a folder if the resource is a folder. To change a file, you must also have Read permission, although you can append data to a file without opening the file if you have only Write permission.

Read & Execute Allows you the permissions associated with Read and with Write and also allows you to traverse a folder, which means you can pass through a folder for which you have no access to get to a file or folder for which you do have access.

Modify Allows you the permissions associated with Read & Execute and with Write, but also gives you Delete permission.

Full Control Allows you the permissions associated with all the other permissions I've listed so far and lets you change permissions and take ownership of resources. In addition, you can delete subfolders and files even if you don't specifically have permission to do so.

List Folder Contents Allows you to view the contents of folders.

If these levels of access are a bit coarse for your needs, you can fine-tune someone's access with what Microsoft calls *Special Access*. To modify the special access permissions for a file or folder, follow these steps:

1. In Explorer, right-click the resource whose permissions you want to modify, and choose Properties from the shortcut menu to open the Properties dialog box for that resource.
2. Click the Security tab, and then click Advanced to open the Advanced Security Settings dialog box:

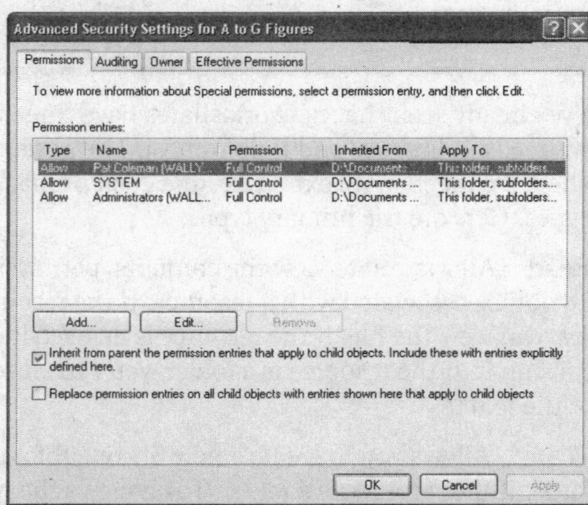

NOTE

If you don't see the Security tab in the Advanced Security Settings dialog box, in the Explorer view of My Computer choose Tools ➢ Folder Options to open the Folder Options dialog box. Click the View tab, and in the Advanced Settings list, clear the Use Simple File Sharing (Recommended) check box, and click OK.

3. Click Edit to open the Permission Entry dialog box:

Here's a description of each of these permissions:

Full Control As its name indicates and as discussed earlier in this chapter.

Traverse Folder/Execute File You can change folders through this folder, and you can run this file.

List Folder/Read Data You can read the contents of a file and display the contents of a folder.

Read Attributes You can display the current attributes of a file or folder.

Read Extended Attributes You can display the extended attributes of a file or folder, if there are any.

Create Files/Write Data You can write data to a new file. When applied to a folder, this permission means you can write files into the folder, but you can't view what's already in the folder.

Create Folders/Append Data You can create new folders in this location, and you can append data to existing files.

Write Attributes You can modify the attributes of a file or folder.

Write Extended Attributes You can create extended attributes for a file or folder.

Delete Subfolders and Files You can remove folders contained within the folder you're working in, and you can remove the files contained in them.

Delete You can delete files.

Read Permissions You can display the current permissions list for the file or folder.

Change Permissions You can modify the permissions for the file or folder. This permission is normally only included in Full Control.

Take Ownership You can claim ownership of a file or folder.

These levels of granularity make security considerations more difficult to grasp initially, but they give a skilled administrator much finer control over how files and folders will be accessed.

To prevent someone from accessing a file or folder, you have two choices. The first, and usually the best, is to simply not grant the person access to the file or folder. That means, don't add their account to the list of permissions. The second method is to add the person's account to the permissions list, but check Deny for each permission. This creates an explicit No Access–type permission.

NOTE

The special access items are all check boxes, not radio boxes, so you can mix and match as you like.

Assigning File and Folder Permissions

Now that you know something about the types of permissions you can place on files and folders, let's walk though the steps to assign them:

1. In Explorer, right-click the file or folder for which you want to establish permissions, and choose Properties from the shortcut menu to open the Properties dialog box for that file or folder.
2. Click the Security tab:

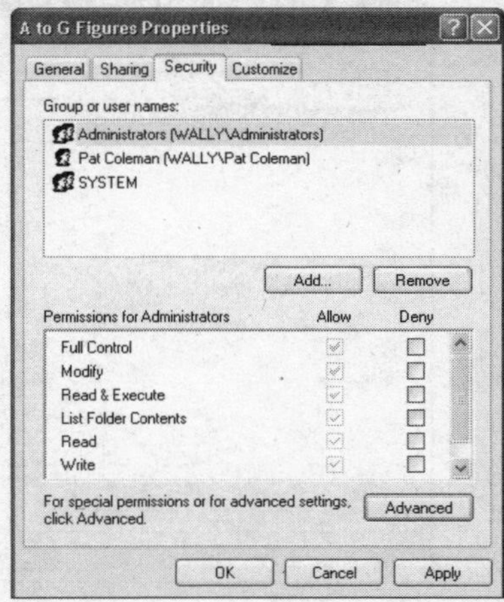

3. Click Add to open the Select Users or Groups dialog box.
4. In the Enter the Object Name to Select box, enter the name of the user or group to whom you are granting permission, and click OK.
5. Back in the Properties dialog box, you'll see that those groups or users have been added to the Group or User Names list. Click OK.

Auditing Files and Folders

In addition to assigning file and folder permissions, Windows XP Professional lets you keep track of who accessed a file and when. You can audit everyone or only specific users or groups. To enable, set up, and view auditing, you need to be logged on as an administrator. Enabling auditing is a bit of a pain, but you have to do it before you can set up auditing. Bear with me, and follow these steps:

1. At a command prompt, type **`mmc /a`** and press Enter to open the Microsoft Management Console.
2. Choose File ➢ Add/Remove Snap-in to open the Add/Remove Snap-in dialog box:

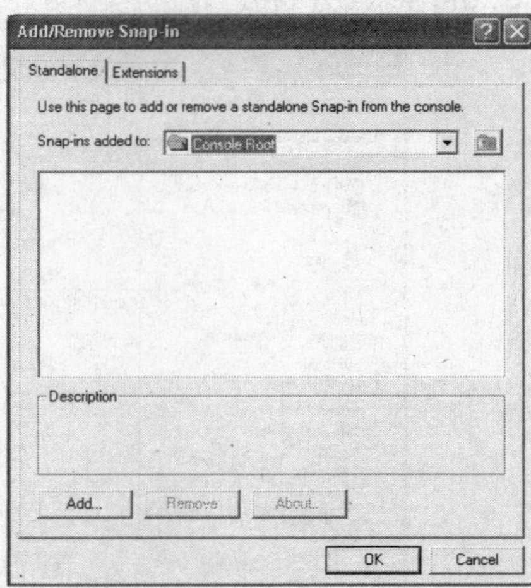

3. Click Add to open the Add Standalone Snap-in dialog box:

4. In the Snap-in list, select Group Policy, and then click Add to start the Group Policy Wizard:

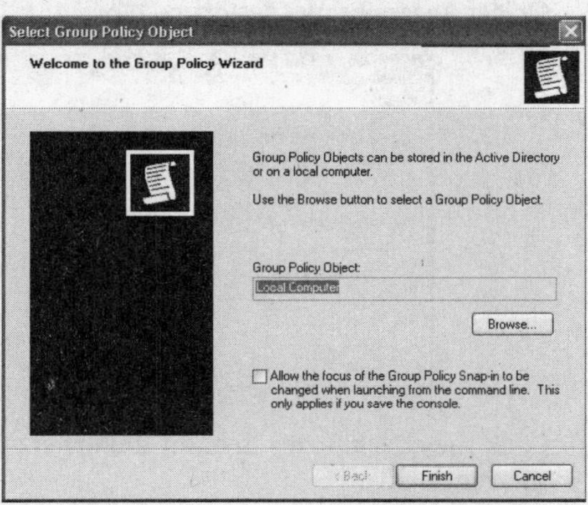

5. If Local Computer is not selected in the Group Policy Object box, browse for it, and then click Finish.
6. Back in the Add Standalone Snap-in dialog box, click Close.
7. Back in the Add/Remove Snap-in dialog box, click OK.
8. Now back in the MMC, expand Local Computer Policy, expand Computer Configuration, expand Windows Settings, expand Security Settings, expand Local Policies, and then click Audit Policy. You'll see the following:

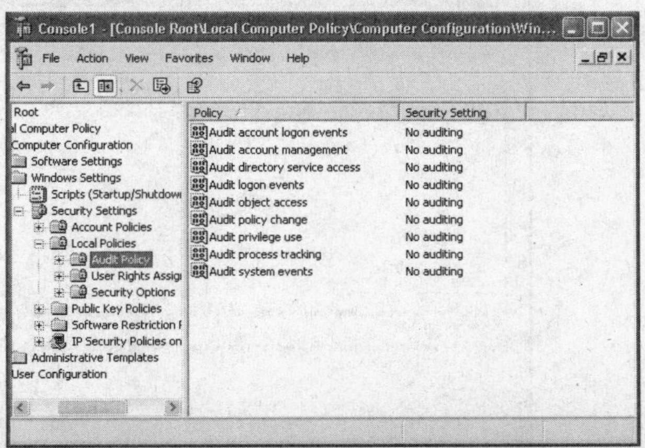

9. In the pane on the right, right-click Audit Object Access, and choose Properties from the shortcut menu to open the Audit Object Access Properties dialog box:

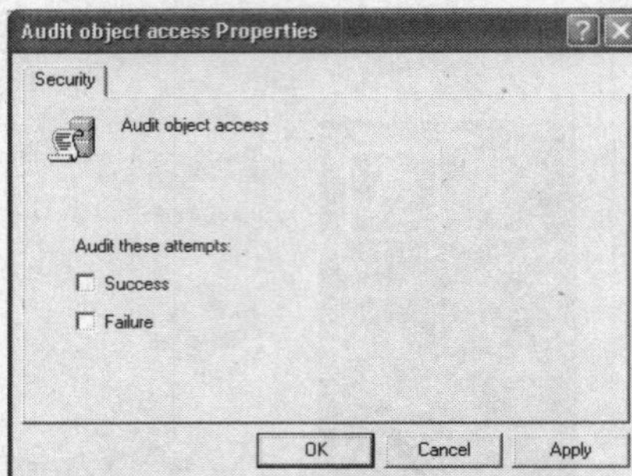

10. Click the check boxes to audit for success and failure, and then click OK.

11. Close the MMC.

Whew! Now you're ready to set up auditing. Follow these steps:

1. In Explorer, right-click the share you want to audit, and choose Properties from the shortcut menu to open the Properties dialog box for that share.

2. Click the Security tab, click the Advanced button to open the Advanced Security Settings dialog box, and then click the Auditing tab:

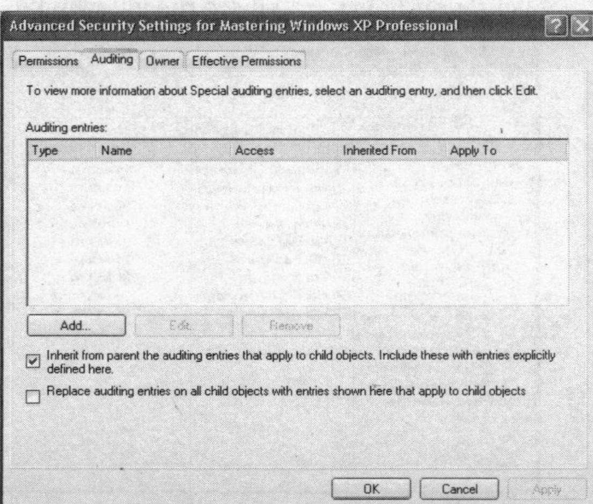

3. Click Add to open the Select User or Group dialog box.
4. In the Enter the Object Name to Select box, enter the name of a user or a group to audit, and then click OK to open the Auditing Entry dialog box:

5. Select the entries that you want to audit, and then click OK three times.

To take a look at the events you've selected to audit, follow these steps:

1. In Control Panel, click Performance and Maintenance, click Administrative Tools, and then click Event Viewer to open the Event Viewer window.
2. In the pane on the left, select Security Log to display a list of audited events in the right pane.

UNDERSTANDING OWNERSHIP

Ownership—what a confusing concept. *Ownership* is a process by which you can take exclusive control over a file or a folder; and you can do all of this with a click of a button. But before you get power drunk with the possibilities, let's take a closer look at what being the owner of a file really means.

Defining Ownership

Now, having worked with NT since its inception, I don't mind telling you that the whole idea of a folder or file's "owner" seemed a bit confusing until I finally figured out the definition. Here's a definition—and from this point on, let me shorten the term *file* or *folder* to *object*:

> **Minasi's Definition of an Owner** An object's owner is a user who can *always* modify that object's permissions.

Ordinarily, only an administrator can control settings such as an object's permissions. But you want your users to be able to control objects in their own area, their own home folder, without having to involve you at every turn. For example, suppose you want to give another user access to a folder in your home folder. Rather than having to seek out an administrator and ask the administrator to extend access permissions to another user, you as the owner can change the permissions directly. Ownership lets users become mini-administrators, rulers of their small fiefdoms.

To find out who owns an object, follow these steps:

1. In Explorer, right-click an object, and choose Properties from the shortcut menu to open the Properties dialog box for that object.
2. Select the Security tab, and then click Advanced to open the Advanced Security Settings dialog box.
3. Select the Owner tab.

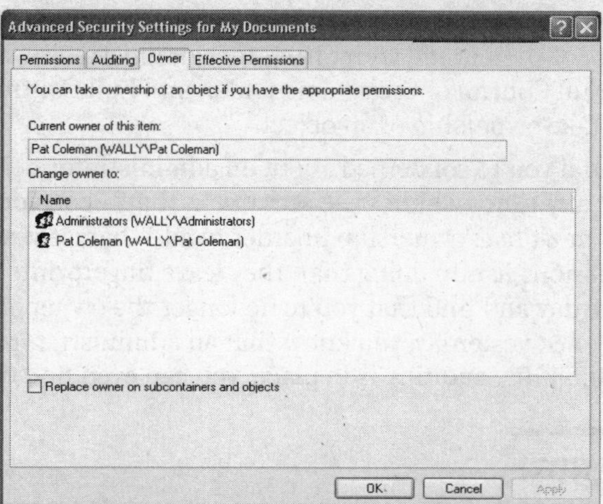

Taking Ownership

Users can't force themselves onto the permissions list for an object, but if they have the Take Ownership permission they *can* become the owner, and once they are the owner, *then* they can add themselves to the permissions list.

If you highlight your name in the Change Owner To list and click OK, you can become the owner of the object, but you can't see what's in the object because you are still not on the permissions list.

NOTE

Owners of files can't necessarily access those files. All that the owners of files can do is change the permissions on those files.

Okay, then, how do you get to the object? Well, since you are an owner, you can change permissions. So you will add yourself to the permissions list and *then* gain access to the object.

Now, why were you able to do that? Because of a user right that all administrators have by default: Take Ownership. Perhaps if you were a more user-oriented than administrator-oriented company, you could remove the Administrators group from that right. By doing so, however, an administrator would be unable to poke around a user's area.

Further, users can always shore up their security just a bit by taking control of their home folder from the administrators. Recall that users have Full Control of their home folder, and Full Control includes the ability to take ownership of an object.

And if you're concerned about an administrator being able to take control at any time—where's the security in that?—consider that an administrator must *take* ownership in order to add themselves to the object's permissions list. In doing that, they leave fingerprints behind; if you log on one day and find that you're no longer the owner of something that you owned yesterday, you know that an administrator has been snooping—and if file auditing is in place, you can even find out who snooped.

NOTE

You can't *give* ownership; you can only exercise the permission to take ownership. If an administrator were to take ownership of a file, they could not edit the file and then give ownership back to the original owner.

To summarize permissions and ownership:

- By default, new files and new subfolders inherit permissions from the folder in which they are created.
- A user who creates a file or a folder is the owner of that file or folder, and the owner can always control access to the file or folder by changing the permissions on it.
- When you change the permissions on an existing folder, you can choose whether those changes will apply to all files and subfolders within the folder.
- Users and groups can be denied access to a file or a folder simply by not granting the user or group any permissions for it.

WARNING

It is possible to lock out everyone including the operating system itself if you do not apply permissions correctly.

WHAT'S NEXT?

Before we leave this part of the book, we need to take a look at one more important networking component–telecommuting. As more and more of us connect to our main office from home or on the road, the security of the data we transmit and receive becomes an issue. In the next chapter, I'll discuss how to use the features of Windows XP Professional to set up and ensure the safety of telecommuting transactions.

Chapter 25

Secure Telecommuting

In this chapter, we'll take a look at a common scenario—a corporate user who wants (or needs) to telecommute a portion of the time and needs to do so as securely as possible. We'll look at some of the common threats that a telecommuting user must face, along with what Windows XP Professional can do to protect against those threats.

Adapted from *Mastering Windows XP Professional*
by Mark Minasi

ISBN 0-7821-2981-1 1056 pages $39.99

Telecommuting Overview: Risks and Rewards

As telecommuting becomes more commonplace, the risks and rewards associated with it are becoming more apparent. The rewards are obvious: no dealing with traffic jams, being able to work in your bathrobe (if you want to), no office distractions, and so on. The risks, however, are a little less obvious. One of the biggest problems is the risk involved when corporate data is moved outside the corporation's walls.

The risks of telecommuting fall into three distinct areas:

- The interception of corporate data
- The impersonation of an authorized user
- The potential abduction of confidential data

It's interesting to look at the irony of the situation. Corporations are increasing their efforts to secure their data within their walls, but at the same time they are allowing more and more employees to telecommute. I can imagine that people who want to steal corporate data will eventually start to focus their efforts on telecommuting workers instead of the corporation's main systems, because most telecommuters make much easier targets.

The interception of data is an obvious threat: as data passes from your Windows XP Professional computer into your corporation's main systems, someone eavesdrops on the data transmission and reads the data. If your transmission is crossing the Internet, it will travel through many systems outside your company's control before it reaches its final destination. The same is true with dial-up modems, although the risks are slightly less as your traffic is being carried over the telephone network (a bit more secure). Still, risks do exist, and the main way to deal with the risk of data interception is through data encryption between the source and destination computers. I'll talk about some of the ways you can protect against data interception by encrypting transmissions leaving your Windows XP Professional computer.

The impersonation of a user is also a threat. If someone obtains your username and password, and if your account has dial-in access, that person can log in to your company's systems under your account, effectively impersonating you. Although the problem of account/password discovery happens within the corporation's walls as well (for example, users writing passwords on yellow sticky notes and attaching them to their monitors), it becomes more of a problem when a user's account is granted dial-in access. The pitfalls of this type of security breach are many–corruption of data, deletion of data, abduction of data, and the introduction of malicious viruses, just to name a few. You can take steps to prevent user impersonation. Some of them are built into Windows XP Professional, and others are security measures that your corporation must implement, and we'll take a look at a number of possible solutions later in this chapter.

Finally, the risk of having data abducted is also a threat. Corporate espionage is a significant problem in many large organizations (although corporations usually keep silent about it since reporting it would have a negative impact on the company's stock price). Again, although corporations are taking significant steps to increase the security of their data within the company's walls, they are allowing users to keep copies of some data on their own home computers or laptops. Instead of targeting a corporate network, it will eventually be easier for someone to target a telecommuting user if they want to obtain a copy of sensitive corporate data. After all, which would be more difficult–breaking into a company and trying to steal a computer, or breaking into someone's home and stealing their computer or laptop? We'll take a look at some of the utilities provided in Windows XP Professional that will allow you to secure data on your system so that even in the worst-case scenario–your computer is completely stolen–your company's sensitive data won't fall into the wrong hands.

Protecting against the Interception of Data

If you are telecommuting, odds are you are connected to your corporation's network in one of three ways: directly–through some sort of wide-area network connection, indirectly–through an analog dial-up networking connection, or through a high-speed digital connection or possibly a virtual private network (VPN). No matter how you are connected, you can take steps to secure your communications.

Securing RAS Dial-In Sessions

The dial-in scenario is probably familiar if you've been using computers for any length of time. You install a modem, you define a dial-up networking entry to call into a remote network, and then your computer initiates a connection over your phone line. This is a relatively secure means of communicating with a remote network, but it still could be compromised: someone could tap into your phone line and record the data conversations traveling back and forth between your computer and the remote computer. Therefore, the primary means to protect RAS (remote access server) dial-in sessions is via encryption. Windows XP Professional makes it easy to implement (and require) encryption on any dial-up networking connection.

NOTE

Encryption is the process of encoding information so that it is secure from unauthorized access. Decryption is the reverse of this process.

Assuming you have a working dial-up networking connection, setting up encryption is relatively easy. Follow these steps:

1. Choose Start ➢ Connect To ➢ Show All Connections to open the Network Connections folder.
2. Right-click the icon for your dial-up connection, and choose Properties from the shortcut menu to open the Properties dialog box for that connection.
3. Click the Security tab, click the Advanced (Custom Settings) option button, and then click the Settings button to open the Advanced Security Settings dialog box:

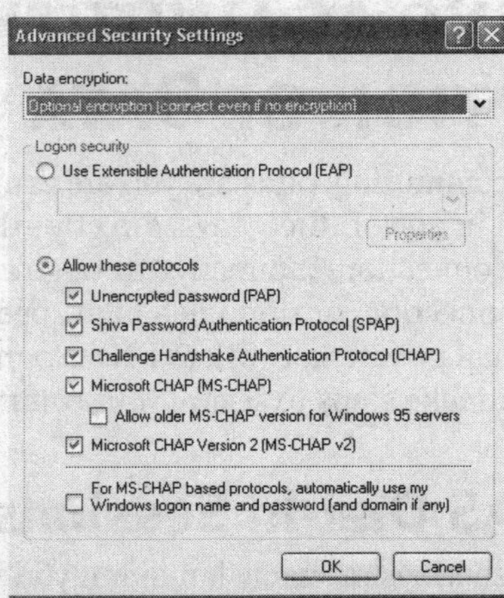

You'll notice that the very first item in the Advanced Security Settings dialog box is the Data Encryption drop-down list box. This option has four possible settings:

No Encryption Allowed This setting will attempt to force your computer into a nonencrypted communication session. If the remote system that you are dialing into will allow any type of connection (encrypted or not), you will be able to connect. However, if the remote system will accept only encrypted connections, you will not be able to connect.

Optional Encryption This setting will defer to whatever is required by the remote system you are calling into. If the remote system does not require encryption, this setting will let you connect. If the remote system does require encryption, this setting will also let you connect.

Require Encryption Enabling this setting will implement a 40-bit encryption channel between your Windows XP Professional computer and the remote system. If the remote system cannot support encryption, your session will immediately disconnect, and you'll see a disconnection error message.

Maximum Strength Encryption Enabling this setting will require a strong (128-bit) encryption channel between your Windows XP Professional computer and the remote system. You will see this option only if you purchased Windows XP Professional in the United States. If the remote system cannot support strong encryption, your session will immediately disconnect with an error message.

Enabling a data encryption option ensures that all your communications are kept private, even if someone is able to intercept them.

To enable encryption on your dial-up connection, select one of the protocols in the Logon Security section of the Advanced Security Settings dialog box.

Virtual Private Networking Connections

Virtual private networking (VPN) connections are—by definition—meant to be private. VPNs were originally developed as a means to route confidential, private data across untrusted networks. As a result of the reach and popularity of the Internet, VPNs have enjoyed a considerable amount of success in the current market.

One of the better analogies I've found for explaining the concepts of a virtual private network is to refer to them as "pipes." To conceptualize VPNs, think of two pipes, one large and one small. Now, imagine that the small pipe actually runs *inside* the large one. It starts and ends at the same places the large pipe does, and it can carry materials on its own completely independently of whatever is happening in the large pipe. As a matter of fact, the only thing the small pipe is dependent on the large pipe for is the determination of the start and end points. Beyond that, the small pipe can operate independently of the large pipe in terms of direction of travel, materials it carries, and so on.

To add another layer to this analogy, let's assume that the large pipe is made of a transparent material and that the small pipe is made of metal. Anyone taking a look at the pipe-within-a-pipe would easily be able to see whatever is moving through the outside (large) pipe. However, whatever is traveling through the inside pipe would remain a mystery.

If this is starting to make sense, you should be thinking to yourself that the large pipe represents the unsecured network (that is, the Internet) and that the small pipe represents the virtual private network. VPN is a way of tunneling data packets through a connection that already exists but that can't be used on its own for privacy reasons. Obviously, the Internet is a perfect example of a network that often can't be used on its own for privacy reasons.

To establish a VPN connection to your corporate network, your company must have set up a VPN server capable of receiving those connections. (More information on setting up a virtual private networking server is available in *Mastering Windows 2000 Server*, Sybex, 2001.) If your company has set up a VPN server for you to dial in to, you will need to know the answers to the following questions:

- Which authentication type does it require?
- Which encryption strength does it require?
- What is the IP address or DNS (domain name service) name to connect to?

Once you know the answer to these questions, you can set up a VPN connection on your Windows XP Professional computer.

Since a VPN (typically) runs over the Internet, the first thing you must have on your system is a functional Internet connection. Whether your connection is a dial-up modem or a dedicated cable/xDSL connection is mostly irrelevant. Assuming you have an Internet connection in place, you can easily create a VPN connection. Follow these steps:

1. Choose Start ➢ Connect To ➢ Show All Connections to open the Network Connections folder.
2. In the Network Tasks bar, click the Create a New Connection link to start the New Connection Wizard.
3. Click Next to open the Network Connection Type screen:

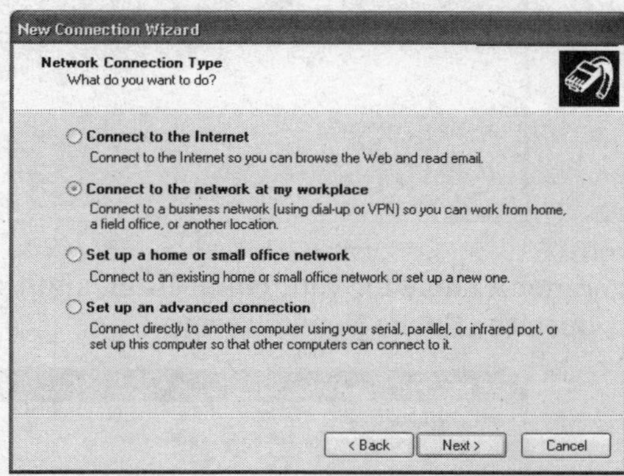

4. Select the Connect to the Network at My Workplace option, and then click Next to open the Network Connection screen:

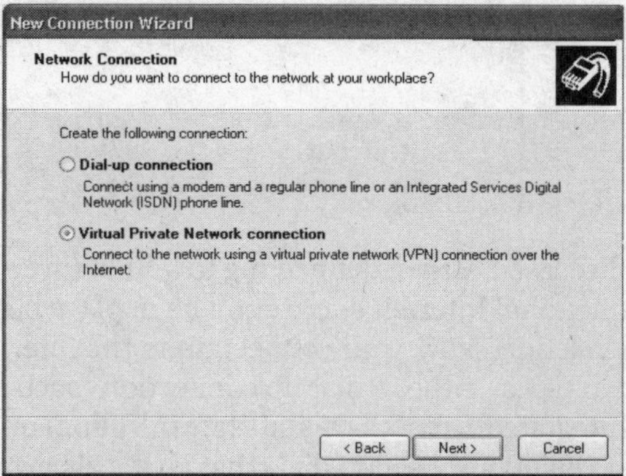

5. Click the Virtual Private Network Connection option, and then click Next to open the Connection Name screen:

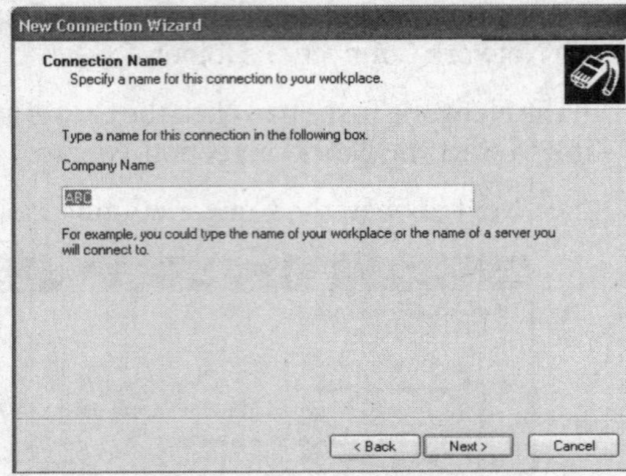

6. Enter a name for your connection, and then click Next to open the Public Network screen:

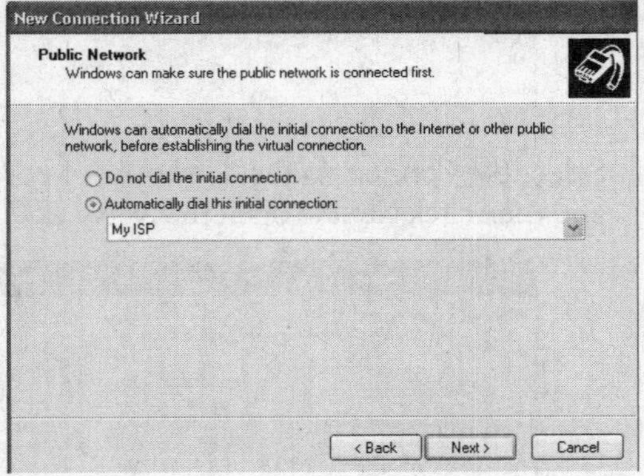

As I discussed earlier, connecting to a VPN (over the Internet) requires that a functional Internet connection be in place before establishing the VPN connection. Now, your connection to the Internet will most likely be one of two types—either a dial-up connection (such as a modem or an ISDN [Integrated Services Digital Network] line) or a dedicated connection that you do not need to dial (that is, it's always there, always on). If you are using a dial-up connection to connect to the Internet, you can instruct Windows XP Professional to automatically establish that connection first before initiating your VPN connection by selecting the Automatically Dial This Initial Connection option. Select your Internet dial-up connection from the drop-down list, and then any time you launch your VPN connection, Windows XP Professional will automatically log you in to the Internet. If you have a direct connection to the Internet (cable, xDSL, other), simply skip this step by selecting the Do Not Dial the Initial Connection option. When you are finished with this step, click Next to open the VPN Server Selection screen:

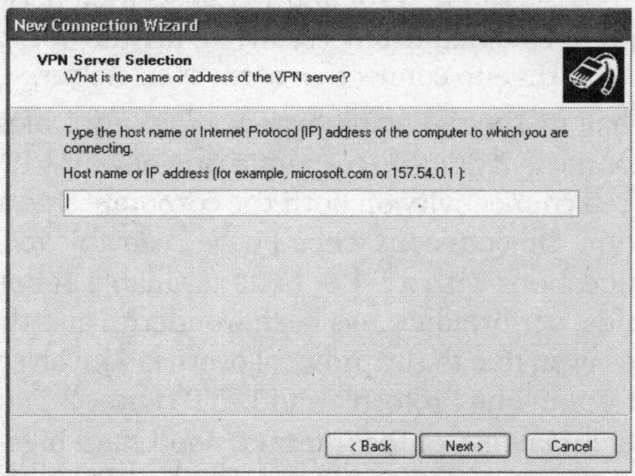

Since virtual private networks function over the Internet, you will connect to a VPN either via an IP address or a DNS name (which resolves into an IP address). Enter the name of your target VPN server, or enter the IP address of the destination system, and then click Next to finish your VPN connection.

In the final screen of the Wizard, specify whether you want a shortcut to this connection on your Desktop, and click Finish. You have now successfully created a VPN connection.

Now, if your corporation has implemented their VPN server correctly, it should be set up so that you can't connect unless your connection is encrypted. Assuming that is the case, you may need to set the appropriate encryption level for your VPN connection the same way you would set one for a RAS connection (as discussed earlier in the chapter).

Once you've got everything correctly defined on your system, you should be able to double-click your VPN icon on your Windows XP Professional system and get connected—securely—to your corporate network. Once you're connected, you should be able to navigate throughout your company's corporate network just as if you were sitting in the office.

VPN Performance Considerations

Our look at virtual private networking wouldn't be complete without taking a bit of time to discuss performance issues. Although virtual private networking is a neat technology, some performance drawbacks are associated with it.

In the right set of circumstances, virtual private networking can provide fast, reliable, and secure connections to your company's network from across the Internet (or another unsecured network). However, in the wrong set of circumstances, virtual private networking can make an already slow dial-up connection seem even slower.

So what are the right circumstances? In my professional opinion, high-speed connectivity on the corporate side of your VPN, and preferably high-speed connectivity on both the corporate side and your personal connection. On occasions when I have been able to implement VPN circuits at locations with a T-1 or better available at both the company and client ends, performance has been wonderful and the connections reliable. However, due to the protocol overhead involved with PPTP (Point-to-Point Tunneling Protocol) and L2TP (Layer 2 Tunneling Protocol) and the inherent latency of the Internet, don't have high-performance expectations if you are planning to implement a VPN with a dial-up modem.

If you are using a dial-up modem, nothing will ever be faster than a direct dial-in connection. Period. Dial-in connections are simple. There's no encryption, and there's no VPN protocol overhead involved. Plus, your traffic does not have to cross through a countless number of routers before reaching its destination. Simply put, with a direct dial-in connection your packets go out of your computer, across the phone line, and directly into the corporate network.

If you are implementing a VPN connection over a dial-up modem, your packets must first be encrypted. They must then be bundled into a VPN protocol and then bundled again into another TCP/IP packet. After that, they are transmitted across the Internet, where they will probably pass through anywhere from 4 to 12 routers before reaching the VPN server at your corporation. Once the VPN server receives the packet, it must unpackage all the payload and then decrypt it. Although computers can do this quickly, it does add overhead to the process.

How much overhead? Well, there are no official numbers to go by, but I'd say you can expect a decrease in your performance ranging anywhere from 10 to 50 percent. Now, without getting into all the technical details, it is worthwhile to note that this isn't entirely Microsoft's fault; after all, they can't be blamed for the fact that the Internet can be inherently slow at times (or can they?). However, even with the worst-case scenario of a 50 percent reduction in performance, if there is 1Mb worth of bandwidth available on each side of the VPN, the effective speeds of the network are still roughly in the 500Kbps range—a very respectable amount. However, if you're using a 56K modem on your Windows XP Professional workstation (which probably won't connect much faster than 48Kbps), you can easily see how a 50 percent performance penalty can make a connection go from "slow" to "unusable."

Everything in life is a trade-off, and it will be up to you to decide if this will work adequately enough for your needs. After all, what is adequate to one person might be great to another and unacceptable to yet another. In either case, expect a performance penalty when implementing virtual private networking and plan accordingly.

Protecting against the Impersonation of a User

Compromising a valid user's account name and password is a network administrator's worst nightmare. An unauthorized user—posing as a valid one—can steal, compromise, or sabotage data from the company's network. If that user has remote dial-in access capabilities as well, the problem is even worse as someone can dial in from anywhere in the world and make trouble for the network. Therefore, it is important to prevent your user ID and password from falling into the wrong hands.

Common Sense Guidelines

It still amazes me how many times I run into users who have written their usernames and passwords on a yellow sticky note and then stuck the note to their monitor. Talk about a security nightmare! Even if people don't stick their passwords on their monitors, users have a tendency to write them down on cards in their wallets or put them into an organizer such as a Palm. The first measure of good security is to never write your username and password down. If, for some reason, you must do so, at least write them on separate sheets of paper and store them in different places. Don't store them with each other.

Another common security problem is users who choose passwords that are easily guessed. For example, it's common for many people to use simple things for passwords, such as the type of car they drive, their favorite sport or a favorite athlete, their mother's maiden name, their middle name, and so on. All those types of passwords can be easily guessed if someone is determined enough.

The best types of passwords are complex combinations that have nothing whatsoever to do with you. You can make your passwords a bit more complex—but still easily remembered—by substituting letters, numbers, or symbols in place of actual words. This is the same type of logic that people use to spell out phrases on custom license plates. For example, you could use the phrase "No soup for you today!" as a password (with all due respects to the *Seinfeld* "Soup Nazi" episode) by using "nosoup4u2day". Such a password is still easily remembered, but is much harder to guess. Other suggestions for substitutions are:

- Instead of the word "to" or "too," use the number 2.
- Instead of the word "for," use the number 4.
- Instead of the word "at," use the @ symbol.
- Instead of the word "and," use the & symbol.
- Instead of the word "you," use the letter U.
- Instead of the word "are," use the letter R.

I'm sure you get the point. The object is to keep the password something that you can remember while making it difficult to compromise. I've had good success using this formula.

Encrypted Authentication

If you are dialing into a remote network—either via a direct dial-in line or a VPN connection—Windows XP Professional must pass your user credentials (your username and password) to the remote system for authentication. The remote system will then check those credentials to determine if your account has been granted dial-in access. But how does Windows XP Professional send your credentials to the remote computer?

The answer can be found in the Advanced Security Settings dialog box. As you can see in that dialog box, Windows XP Professional can send your user credentials to the remote system in a number of ways, as long as the remote system is able to understand. Some of these authentication methods are encrypted, and some are not.

Extensible Authentication Protocol (EAP) Since security and authentication is a constantly changing field, embedding authentication schemes into an operating system is impractical at times. To solve this problem, Microsoft has included support for Extensible Authentication Protocol, which is simply a means of "plugging in" new authentication schemes as needed. Presumably, any type of extensible authentication would be encrypted, but that could vary from one case to the next.

Unencrypted Password (PAP) Password Authentication Protocol (PAP) is one of the first options and is also one of the least secure. It is no more secure than a simple conversation from your server saying "What is your name and password?" to the client, the client responding with "My name is Mark and my password is 'let-me-in.'" There is no encryption of authentication credentials whatsoever.

Shiva Password Authentication Protocol (SPAP) SPAP is an encrypted password authentication method used by Shiva LAN Rover clients and servers. Windows XP Professional can provide SPAP authentication if needed.

Challenge Handshake Authentication Protocol (CHAP) Defined in RFC (Request for Comments) 1334, and later revised in RFC 1994, CHAP is a means of encrypting authentication sessions between a client and server. Since this protocol is defined by an RFC, it enjoys a broad base of support among many operating systems and other devices.

Microsoft CHAP (v1 and v2) (MS-CHAP) Microsoft's derivative of CHAP, or Challenge Handshake Authentication Protocol. An encrypted authentication method that also allows you to encrypt an entire dial-up session, not just the original authentication, which is important when it comes to setting up virtual private networking sessions.

Caller-ID/Callback Security

Although Caller-ID/callback security isn't an option for Windows XP Professional, it is worth discussing in terms of security. Simply put, let's assume that you have dial-in access to your corporate network, and the worst-case scenario comes true—someone obtains your user ID and password. Caller-ID and callback security can still provide your corporation with some level of protection. Both features work by verifying that you are actually calling from an authorized phone number—a phone number that has been predefined by the administrators of your corporate network.

Caller-ID Security If the dial-in systems on your corporate network can support it, your account can be set up with a Caller-ID–based security option. In this scenario, when the computers on your corporate network receive your incoming call, they take note of the phone number. Once you provide a username and password authentication, your username is checked for an associated Caller-ID number. If the two numbers match, your call is granted. If the two numbers don't match, your call is denied. Therefore, even if someone has your username and password, this type of security can protect your corporation's computers. The drawback is that whenever you want to connect to your company's network, you must be calling in from the approved number.

Callback Security This functions in a similar manner to Caller-ID security, but is a bit more secure (I've read that Caller-ID information can be spoofed with the correct equipment). With callback security enabled, your user account is associated with a call-back number. When you initiate a dial-in session to your company's network, you will provide your username and password. The system that verifies your dial-in credentials will see that you have a call-back number associated with your account and immediately disconnect you. After it disconnects you, it will then initiate a call to your system and establish the connection. This is a very secure method of verifying a dial-in user; however, it comes at the price of having to always log in from the same phone number.

If you are concerned that your account credentials might fall into the wrong hands, talk to your network administrators to see if either of these options are available for your dial-in system. Windows 2000 Server supports both of them.

Third-Party Products: SecurID, SafeWord

Although this is a book about Windows XP Professional, I want to mention two products that fall into the "extremely cool" category of security products: SecurID from RSA Security and SafeWord from Secure Computing.

The nature of these two products is similar—they are what's known as a "second factor" authentication method. What that means is that your "first factor" of authentication—your username and password—is not good enough to obtain access to a resource; you must authenticate yourself in another (second) manner before access is granted. You can think of a second factor authentication as being similar to having two different locks on a door—a regular one and a deadbolt. You won't be granted access until you can provide the correct authentication (a key) for both.

How they work—from a user perspective—is quite simple. When you start a dial-up networking session, you are prompted for your username and password. That is your first authentication. After successfully negotiating a dial-in connection to your corporation's network, you are then prompted for a second authentication—a second "password," if you will. What's unique about this second password is that it's a different password every time.

SecurID works through a small key fob that has a digital readout on it. Every 60 seconds, a new number appears on the readout. The key fob is given to a user and must be used to gain access to the company's network. Let's take a look at a typical example.

Let's assume that a user named Wendy is trying to dial in to her company's network. Now, Wendy has a password for her account—let's assume that it's "arlington". Wendy also has a SecurID key fob that has been assigned to her. At the moment she is trying to sign in, her key fob is displaying the six-digit number 378265. As an added measure, Wendy also has a four-digit "pin" number assigned to her. Let's assume that she used 1234 for her pin number.

When Wendy dials in, she'll type in her username and password (wendy/arlington) just as in a normal dial-up connection. Her Windows XP Professional system will dial in to the company's network and negotiate a connection. Once the connection is negotiated, Wendy will be prompted for her SecurID passcode. At the moment she is logging in, the correct passcode for her will be "1234378265". Her passcode is validated by a SecurID server within the company's network, and if the passcode is correct, she is granted access to the network. The SafeWord system also functions on a similar, one-time password concept.

As you can see, this is an *extremely* secure means of authenticating a user. If someone manages to obtain Wendy's username and password, they are useless without her SecurID key fob. And even if someone were to obtain the key fob itself, it would still be useless without knowing Wendy's individual pin number.

Protecting against the Abduction of Data

Okay, I'll admit it, the word "abduction" sounds a bit too much like an *X-Files* episode, but the word just fits so well with the concept I am trying to get across. In any case, the abduction of data is simply someone without authorization copying corporate data off your system. You know, your typical corporate espionage stuff.

As I stated earlier in the chapter, I can imagine that this will become more and more of a problem as companies allow increasing amounts of data outside their corporate walls. After all, who is it more difficult to steal data from—the well-guarded and physically secured corporate network, or Joe the account executive walking out of the building late at night with his laptop? A quick bop on Joe's head and a grab of the laptop would compromise all the data stored on the laptop.

Or would it? Windows XP Professional contains encryption technologies that specifically address this type of situation. The encrypting file system (EFS) can ensure that no one other than you will be able to read your encrypted files if your computer is ever stolen.

The encryption capabilities available in Windows XP Professional (right out of the box) are very good. And with a few additional precautions, you can make sure that they are absolutely secure—that no one will be able to ever read your encrypted files.

NOTE

It goes without saying that if someone gets hold of your username and password, all bets are off. As far as Windows XP Professional is concerned, if someone logs in with your username and password, it must be you! Windows XP Professional will gladly decrypt all your files in that scenario. So, it's critical to make sure that your password is not discovered.

Encrypting Files with EFS

Encrypting data is merely a matter of a few clicks of the mouse, and an entire folder or folder structure can be protected from prying eyes. Having said that, you should try to follow a few "best practices" principles when working with EFS:

Don't encrypt the Windows XP Professional folders. This would have a significant impact on your system—most likely it wouldn't boot. Fortunately, EFS will always try to prevent you from encrypting system files, but you probably shouldn't even try to in the first place.

Don't encrypt your My Documents folder. This runs 100 percent contrary to Microsoft's suggested practices. The reason I recommend that you *don't* encrypt your My Documents folder is because there are almost no visual clues in the Windows interface that a file or folder has been encrypted. I've already read a few accounts of users who were "playing around" with EFS and followed Microsoft's suggestions to encrypt the My Documents folder, but months later they forgot that they had done it. Because of some sort of failure (in one instance, a simple HAL [hardware abstraction layer] upgrade), the users reloaded Windows XP Professional. Guess what? Since they hadn't taken the additional step to back up their recovery keys, all their documents were irrecoverable. Gone. Personally, I like to make a folder called Encrypted Stuff, which gives me an obvious visual reminder that anything within that folder will be encrypted.

Encrypt your Temp folder. Your temporary folder (which can usually be found by typing `SET` at a command prompt and looking for the TEMP= and TMP= folders) is often a repository for fragments of your data, documents, and so on. Sometimes programs don't properly clean up after themselves, and they leave fragments of your files in this folder. If this folder is encrypted, no leftover fragments can be used by anyone else.

Encrypt entire folders, not just files. As I mentioned earlier, I like to make a special folder on my machine and call it Encrypted Stuff—then I just copy everything into it that I want protected.

Encrypting files and folders is really quite simple. Follow these steps:

1. Click Start, right-click My Computer, and choose Explore from the shortcut menu to open an Explorer-type window.
2. Right-click the file or folder, and choose Properties from the shortcut menu to open the Properties dialog box for that item.
3. Click the Advanced button to open the Advanced Attributes dialog box:

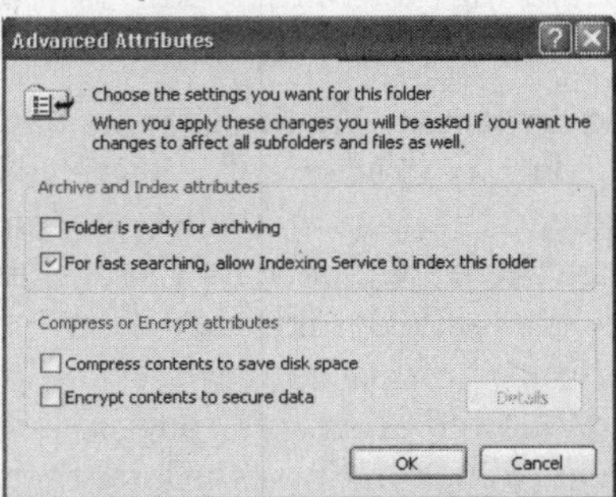

   Notice the two check boxes at the bottom of this dialog box: Compress Contents to Save Disk Space and Encrypt Contents to Secure Data. These two items are mutually exclusive, meaning that if you compress a file you can't encrypt it, and if you encrypt a file, you can't compress it.

4. If necessary, uncompress the file, and check the Encrypt Contents to Secure Data check box.
5. Click OK, and then click OK again to encrypt the file.

It almost seems too easy, doesn't it? Well, don't take my word for it—try logging in as someone else and see if you can read the file. You can't. Even if you have full access to the file under another user account, you won't be able to open the file, copy it, or do anything else with it. Only the user account that encrypted the file can decrypt it.

WHAT'S NEXT?

This chapter completes our look at the networking world according to Windows XP Professional. The next part of this book concerns an even more advanced topic—the Windows XP Professional Registry. If you are an occasional or novice Windows user, you will seldom have any reason to deal with the Registry. But if you are a power user or a system administrator of even a small network, you need to know what the Registry is and how and when to use it. In the next chapter, Peter Hipson starts by explaining what the Registry is and why it even exists.

PART V
Working with the Registry

Chapter 26

What Is a Registry and Why?

Some Windows users know exactly what the Registry is: a system designed to cause users and administrators to lose their hair. I know this is true because I can no longer feel the wind ruffling through my hair. Oh, I feel the wind; I just don't feel the hair.

Revised and adapted from *Mastering Windows 2000 Registry* by Peter D. Hipson

ISBN 0-7821-2615-4 752 pages $39.99

The Registry, like Windows, was evolutionary. The Registry was preceded by a pair of flat-text files, called `Win.ini` and `System.ini`. These two files live on even today in Windows XP, though they are virtually unchanged from Windows NT version 4. The first Registry to appear in Windows was created to solve a number of problems: poor performance (retrieving information from the original flat-text `.ini` files was cumbersome), size limitations (the `.ini` files could be only so large), and maintenance problems (the `.ini` files were organizationally impaired!).

Today, the Windows XP `.ini` files contain only a few entries used by legacy 16-bit applications. They are of no importance to us, and we ignore them. It's the Registry that is the most important system, because it contains the heart and soul of Windows XP. Without the Registry, Windows XP would be nothing more than a collection of programs, unable to perform even the basic tasks that we expect from an operating system. Every bit of configuration information that Windows XP has is crammed into the Registry. Information about the system's hardware, preferences, security, and users—everything that can be set is set in there.

Windows 2000 placed a limit on the Registry, so it couldn't grow to an infinite size (that's *infinite* in a loose manner of speaking, given that—sadly—disk size looks likely always to be finite). If the Registry grew too big for its current size allocation, Windows 2000 displayed a message telling you that you were low on Registry quota. By default, Windows 2000 set the Registry size to 25 percent of the paged pool size; for most computers, the paged pool size is approximately equal to the amount of installed RAM, up to a maximum of 192MB. Windows 2000 would then adjust this size based on the currently installed RAM. You could also change the Registry size manually via the Virtual Memory dialog box (which you'd reach from the Performance Options dialog box, which in turn you'd reach from the System Properties dialog box) or by setting the `RegistrySizeLimit` and `PagedPoolSize` entries in the Registry.

Windows XP does away with the Registry size limit and lets the Registry data consume any available amount of paged pool memory space and disk space. So if necessary you can store huge amounts of data in your Registry. But you probably have better uses for your disk space.

NOTE

Microsoft limits the size of any object that is stored in a Registry data key to 1MB. This limit is basically only meaningful for REG_BINARY objects, because strings and such are unlikely to become this large. If you find that you must store more than 1MB in a Registry object, you will need to store the information in a file and store a pointer to the file in the Registry. Without this limitation, the Registry could easily grow to be the largest file on your system.

ORGANIZATION

The Registry is organized into five major sections. These sections are called *hives*, which are analogous to root directories on your hard drive. Each hive, by definition, has its own storage location (a file) and log file. If necessary, a given hive can be restored without affecting the other hives in the Registry.

Inside a hive you find both keys and subkeys (which are analogous to directories and subdirectories on your hard disk). A key may have information, or data, assigned to it (referred to as a *value entry*), making the key analogous to a file on your hard drive as well.

A key or subkey may have zero, one, or more value entries, a default value, and from zero to many subkeys. Each value entry has a name, data type, and a value:

- The entry's name is stored as a Unicode character string.
- The entry's type is stored as an integer index. The type is returned to the querying application, which must then map this type to the type that the application knows.
- The entry's value is stored as necessary to allow efficient retrieval of the data when needed.

Both the Windows operating system and applications store data in the Windows Registry. This practice is both good and bad. It is good because the Registry makes an efficient, common storage location. Here's the bad part: as more and more applications and systems store information in the Registry, it grows larger, and larger, and larger.

It is most unusual for the Registry to get smaller—I'm unaware of any application that does a really complete job of cleaning up all of its own

Registry entries when the application is uninstalled. Many applications leave tons of stuff in the Registry when they are uninstalled, and not many applications clean up unused entries as a routine process. The end result is that the Registry will grow, like Jack's magic beanstalk, as time goes on.

NOTE

From time to time in these chapters, I'll refer to hives, keys, subkeys, and values using the generic term *object*. When you see *object*, assume that the item could be any valid item in the Registry!

Hives and Their Aliases

There are a number of hives in the Windows XP Registry and accepted abbreviations for each:

- HKEY_CLASSES_ROOT, a.k.a. HKCR
- HKEY_CURRENT_USER, a.k.a. HKCU
- HKEY_LOCAL_MACHINE, a.k.a. HKLM
- HKEY_USERS, a.k.a. HKU
- HKEY_CURRENT_CONFIG, a.k.a. HKCC

NOTE

If you've used the Registry in a version of 32-bit Windows earlier than Windows 2000, you may remember there was a hive called HKEY_DYN_DATA. This hive, which had no abbreviation, disappeared in Windows 2000, though Microsoft had originally intended to include information about Plug and Play in this hive. So where is PnP data saved if the HKEY_DYN_DATA hive is gone? Windows 2000 supports PnP, as does Windows XP—but in these operating systems Microsoft has integrated PnP data with the main Registry rather than have a separate hive.

Each hive begins with HKEY_. HKEY is an abbreviation of "hive key," though the significance of this is not terribly important in understanding the Registry. The H also signifies that the name is a "handle" for a program to interface with the Registry. These handles are defined in the file `winreg.h`, included with the Windows SDK (Software Development Kit).

The Registry contains duplication—sort of. For example, you'll notice that everything in HKEY_CURRENT_USER is also contained in the hive HKEY_USERS. But these aren't two different sets of the same information; rather, they're two names for the same set of information. Microsoft needed to make some parts of the Registry appear to be in two places at one time. But they didn't want to copy these sections, because that could have created problems with keeping each section current. Instead, they created an alias, or another name, for some Registry components. The alias points to the original component and is updated whenever the original is. These aliases are created solely by Windows. You, as a user, can't create an alias in the Registry no matter how hard you try!

The most common alias is the Registry hive HKEY_CURRENT_USER. It is an alias either to the .DEFAULT user in HKEY_USERS or to the current user in HKEY_USERS. If you take a quick peek at HKEY_USERS, you will see several keys there: one is .DEFAULT and the others are named with long strings of characters. These are SIDs (security identifiers), which Windows uses to identify users. One of these subkeys for the currently logged-on user consists of just the SID, while the other consists of the SID suffixed with _Classes. For example, on one of my XP Professional computers, my account has the two subkeys HKEY_USERS\S-1-5-21-13967357-152049171-1708537768-1004 and HKEY_USERS\S-1-5-21-13967357-152049171-1708537768-1004_Classes.

NOTE

The default user, used when no user is logged on, has only one subkey, named .DEFAULT.

There are also other aliases in the Registry. For example, the Registry key HKEY_ LOCAL_MACHINE\System\CurrentControlSet is an alias to one of the other control sets—ControlSet001, ControlSet002, or sometimes ControlSet003. Again, this is that same magic; only one Registry object is there, it just has two names. So remember that when you modify a specific Registry key or subkey, another Registry key or subkey may magically change also!

Data Values

A value may contain one or, in some instances, more than one data item. The only type of multiple-item value entry that the Registry editor can handle is REG_MULTI_SZ, which may contain zero, one, or more strings.

Data is stored in a number of different formats. Generally the system uses only a few simple formats, while applications, drivers, and so forth may use more complex types defined for a specific purpose. For example, REG_RESOURCE_LIST is a complex Registry type used primarily by drivers. Though it would be inefficient, all Registry data could be considered to be REG_BINARY data.

Data types for value entries include the following:

- REG_BINARY
- REG_COLOR_RGB
- REG_DWORD
- REG_DWORD_BIG_ENDIAN
- REG_DWORD_LITTLE_ENDIAN
- REG_EXPAND_SZ
- REG_FILE_NAME
- REG_FILE_TIME
- REG_FULL_RESOURCE_DESCRIPTOR
- REG_LINK
- REG_MULTI_SZ
- REG_NONE
- REG_QWORD
- REG_QWORD_LITTLE_ENDIAN
- REG_RESOURCE_LIST
- REG_RESOURCE_REQUIREMENTS_LIST
- REG_SZ
- REG_UNKNOWN

Applications may access each of these data types. Additionally, some applications store data in formats that only they understand. Actually, there is a provision in the Registry that allows the storing application to assign a specific type to the Registry data. Any application or component that doesn't understand the format would simply treat the data as a REG_UNKNOWN type and read the data as binary.

NOTE

Oops, did I say something special? Yes! Don't forget that applications can and do store data in the Registry.

How the Registry Is Used

How does Windows use the Registry? When is the Registry first opened and used?

The Registry is a tree-based hierarchical system that offers quick access to data stored in almost any format. Actually, the Registry is a rather flexible database. Registry information comes from a number of sources:

- From installing Windows
- From booting Windows
- From applications, systems, and user interaction

Every component of Windows uses the Registry, without exception. There is a set of APIs that are used to allow both Windows and other applications to access Registry information easily and quickly.

Windows starts to use the Registry at the very beginning stages of system boot-up. The Windows boot process is based on which file format is installed, though the important parts are identical in either case. The unimportant parts are the loading of the specific drivers to read the NTFS file system.

The Windows boot process consists of the following steps:

1. The system is powered up, the video is initialized, and the hardware self-tests are performed. The BIOS performs these tests, which are called POSTs (power-on self-tests). Usually, the memory test is the most visible one; its progress is shown on most computer screens.

2. After running POST, the system will initialize each adapter. If the adapter has its own built-in BIOS, the adapter's BIOS will be called to perform its own initialization. Some adapters, such as Adaptec's SCSI adapters and network adapters from manufacturers such as 3Com and Intel, will both display messages and allow the user to interact. Some adapters that don't have a BIOS won't be initialized until Windows loads their drivers much later in the boot-up process.

3. After all the adapters that have a BIOS have been initialized, the system boot loader reads in the sector located at the very beginning of the first bootable disk drive and passes commands to this code. This sector is called the *boot sector*, or the MBR (Master Boot Record), and it is written by the operating system when the operating system is installed.

4. The code in the MBR then loads the NTLDR file—the NT boot loader. (This file has no extension, though it is an executable file.) Once NTLDR is loaded, the MBR passes control to the code in NTLDR.

5. NTLDR then switches into 32-bit mode (remember an Intel *x*86 processor always boots into 16-bit real mode). It then loads a special copy of the necessary file system I/O files and reads in the file `boot.ini`.

6. The file boot.ini has information about each operating system that can be loaded. Remember, Windows XP supports multiboot configurations. It is trivial to create a Windows XP installation that can boot Windows XP, Windows 2000, Windows NT, and Windows Me, Windows 98, or Windows 95. The boot loader can even boot two or more different copies of Windows XP with either the same or different version numbers. NTLDR then processes the boot.ini file. If the computer has a multiboot configuration, the boot loader displays the list of operating systems available so that the user can select which of them to load. If the computer has only Windows XP installed (and only one copy of it), the boot loader goes ahead and loads Windows XP. Either way, let's assume that Windows XP will be loaded.

7. When you select Windows XP to be loaded, NTLDR loads the file NTDETECT.COM. This program then collects information about the currently installed hardware and saves this information for the Registry. Most of this information is stored in the HKEY_LOCAL_MACHINE hive.

8. Once NTDETECT has detected the hardware, control is passed back to NTLDR, and the boot process continues. At this point, the Registry has been substantially updated with the current hardware configuration and stored in HKEY_LOCAL_ MACHINE\Hardware.

9. If there has been a boot problem that Windows is aware of, or if you press the F8 key from the boot menu, Windows displays the Windows Advanced Options Menu, from which you can choose the Last Known Good Configuration item to force Windows to use the last configuration with which the computer booted successfully. This configuration is stored in the Registry hive HKEY_LOCAL_MACHINE.

10. Following the detection of NTDETECT, NTLDR will load and initialize the Windows NT kernel, load the services, and then start Windows.

11. When the kernel is loaded, the HAL is also loaded. (The HAL–Hardware Abstraction Layer–is used to manage hardware services.) Next, the Registry system subkey HKEY_LOCAL_MACHINE\System is loaded into memory. Windows scans the Registry for all drivers with a start value of zero. This includes those drivers that should be loaded and initialized at boot time.

12. At the next stage, kernel initialization, you see a screen identifying the version of Windows XP that's booting, followed by a screen with the message *Windows is starting up*. Again, the system scans the Registry and finds all drivers that must be started at the kernel initialization stage.

13. From this point, Windows starts various components and systems. Each component and system reads the Registry and performs various tasks and functions. The final stage is to start the program that manages the user logon, WinLogon. WinLogon allows the user to log on and use Windows XP.

Once Windows XP is booted, both the operating system and applications use the Registry. The Registry is dynamic, but usage of the Registry may be dynamic or static. That is, some Registry items are read one time and never reread until the system is restarted. Other items are read every time they are referenced. There is no fixed rule as to what is read each time it is needed and what is not, but to be on the safe side, follow these guidelines:

- Application-related data is probably read when the application starts. If you change application-based data, restart the application. In fact, the best path to follow is this: Do not change application-based data while the application is running.
- User-interface data is sometimes dynamic, sometimes static. With user-interface data, the way to go is to change the data and wait to see the results of the change. If the change doesn't appear, try logging on again.
- System data is usually either static or otherwise buffered. Many system-related Registry changes won't become effective until the system is restarted. Some system data is rewritten, or created, at start-up time, precluding changes by users. Many of the items in `HKEY_LOCAL_MACHINE` may be reset at system boot time, especially those items that are hardware related.

A Note on Terminology

The Registry is made up of hives, keys, subkeys, and value entries. Well, actually, depending on the source, you may be faced with hives and data keys; or keys and items; or just data keys; or who knows what else.

There is some indication that Microsoft wants to drop the original term for a Registry section—the *hive*—and replace this term with the word *key*. In the Windows NT Resource Kit, Microsoft makes the following definition:

> The registry is divided into parts called *hives*. A hive is a discrete body of keys, subkeys, and values rooted at the top of the registry hierarchy. Hives are distinguished from other groups of keys in that they are permanent components of the registry; they are not created dynamically when the system starts and

> deleted when it stops. Thus, HKEY_LOCAL_MACHINE\Hardware, which is built dynamically by the Hardware Recognizer when Windows NT starts, is not a hive.

In the Windows XP documentation, Microsoft says a hive is:

> A section of the registry that appears as a file on your hard disk.

These definitions are absolute and state exactly what is a hive and what is not. However, in the real world, no one follows this exact definition. Many authors call all holders of information *hives* (or *sub-hives*) and call data objects *keys*. Others never refer to hives at all and instead call all holders *keys*, or *subkeys,* and refer to data objects as *values*.

Virtually every definition leaves something to be desired. To call the thing that holds data a "value entry" sometimes makes it awkward to refer to the contents. Consider these examples:

> The value entry named `asdf` contains the value `1234`.

> The value called `asdf` contains the value `1234`.

The following example is much more readable:

> The value entry `asdf` is a REG_DWORD with a value of `1234`.

Is there a need to distinguish between what Microsoft calls a "hive" (a top-level, permanent, Registry component) and what Microsoft calls a "key"? When does a hive become a key, and is this important? I can't think of any context in which anything is gained by making this distinction. Referring to the top-level objects as *hives* certainly frees up the term *key* to be used elsewhere, but why not stick to one term?

Table 26.1 compares Registry terminology against the terminology used for the Windows file system—and gives the terminology I'll be using in the chapters in this part of the book.

TABLE 26.1: Registry Terminology Explained

Context	Root Collections	Subcollections	Objects	Data
Disks	Root directories		Files	Data
Older Registry terminology	Hives	Sub-hives	Data keys	Data
Newer Registry terminology	Hives	Keys/subkeys	Value entry	Data
Registry terminology in this book	Hives	Keys/subkeys*	Value entry	Data

***Just to keep things easy to read, I'll use the term *key* to refer to both keys and subkeys.**

Hints and Kinks from the Experts

In each of these chapters, I'll present a few hints and kinks from the experts. These experts are a number of people who have a lot of experience working with the Windows Registry. They have learned from their experiences and the experiences of others.

For example, every expert will tell you the same thing: The minute you start tinkering with the Registry, you will create a mess that is so bad that only a clean reinstall (or restoration from a backup) will fix it. To restore the backup, you would boot from your Windows XP CD, choose the Repair option, and restore the Registry–not a full backup. (If you did want to restore a full backup, it would only work if you'd selected to back up System State data.)

The first time I had a serious Registry problem, I'd change something, and things would just get worse. Some Registry problems cannot be "hacked," or fixed manually. The only fix for these problems is to either reinstall or restore the system. However, this type of situation is unusual. My experience has been that these problems happen only when hardware (like the Registry's drive) fails or an incredibly errant program totally trashes the Registry. Neither of these happens very often at all.

Most users make minor tweaks or fixes in the Registry. Most of the time, things go okay. Sometimes things go awry. Through it all, we toast the Registry, and then it's back to the proverbial drawing board. Such is life...but it's as well to be prepared. In the next chapter, I'll show you how to back up your Registry so that you can recover from toasting episodes.

WHAT'S NEXT?

Now that you know what the Registry is and why it's important, you need to know how to use it, how to back it up, and how to restore it—all topics that I'll deal with in the next chapter.

Chapter 27

README.1ST: PREVENTING DISASTER!

Preventing disaster is an important thing to do. No one wants a system failure or to have to reinstall Windows.

You are reading this chapter for your own particular reason. Perhaps, as I am recommending, you are here because you want to do everything possible to prevent a disaster with your Windows installation. Or maybe you really, really want to recover from an existing disaster. If you are recovering from a problem, you may want to skip to the section later in this chapter titled "Restoring the Registry." For those of you who never do anything wrong, read on.

The Registry has always been the one part of Windows that virtually every user has neither understood nor trusted. Just when things go well, the Registry gets corrupted, and it is time to reinstall everything.

Revised and adapted from *Mastering Windows 2000 Registry* by Peter D. Hipson

ISBN 0-7821-2615-4 752 pages $39.99

The Windows XP operating system is quite robust. However, many things can cause problems. For example, a hard drive failure (even a small soft error on the system drive in the Registry files), a controller failure, or a more complex memory bit that sometimes doesn't set correctly all can cause many problems with Windows and the Registry.

WARNING

Windows XP is robust, but our hardware is not. Most Pentium systems do not have memory parity. Though earlier PC systems used memory parity, this feature disappeared quietly a few years back when memory prices were painfully high and there was a serious effort to keep computer prices to a minimum. Most of the newest computers now do support parity for their memory; many of the systems still in use do not, and as a result, routine memory errors won't be detected until it is much too late.

In this chapter, we'll cover a number of potential problem areas:

Backup: You'll learn a number of ways to back up that pesky Registry.

Restoration: What's difficult even under the best of conditions will be made simpler after you've perused these pages.

Recovery techniques: You'll discover ways to recover from a Registry failure and retain as much of the existing installation of Windows XP as possible.

Hints and kinks from the experts: This is stuff from the Resource Kit and a few ideas from some experts on how to keep things going well.

What's the Deal with the Registry, Anyway?

One of the biggest problems with the Registry is that Windows uses it constantly. The entire process of backing up and restoring the operating system is much more difficult because Windows must have the Registry files open as a restore is being done.

There are several ways to solve this problem: One solution is to use the backup program supplied with Windows XP. Another is to use an after-market backup program. Such a backup program has to contain the code necessary to do Registry backups and restores.

TIP

Oh, joy! The backup program included with Windows XP allows backing up to media other than tape drives. Now you can back up to other hard drives (a technique that I use), Zip drives, and other storage media.

However, these techniques may not work well under your circumstances. You may already have had a Registry failure, and there may be no Registry backup to rely on for recovery. Backing up and recovering the Registry without a tape backup is excruciatingly difficult using previous versions of the backup program.

The backup program included with Windows XP Professional lets you create an Automated System Recovery (ASR) disk that you can use to restore your Windows installation—including the Registry—as a last resort. But you can also use the files that the ASR disk uses for recovery in other recovery techniques. That's because Windows XP does not store any Registry information on the ASR (Microsoft recognized that the Registry was becoming too large to store on a typical diskette). The directory `%systemroot%\repair` (the same location in which they are stored in Windows NT 4 and Windows 2000) holds all the Registry files that are backed up.

Restoring the Registry from the `%systemroot%\repair` directory requires the Windows XP installation program. It's not that bad; you don't have to reinstall Windows, but the installation program will restore the Registry from the backup, if necessary.

The menu that you can access when you boot up Windows XP also allows a user to restore parts of the Registry based on copies of the Registry saved from previous sessions.

TIP

Always, always make sure that you back up the Registry whenever you install new software or hardware or remove anything from your computer. If you do not back up the Registry, and you restore a previous copy from an old backup, the system will not work as expected! See "Backing Up the Registry" later in this chapter for instructions on backing up the Registry.

Where Exactly *Is* the Registry?

In order to back it up, you need to know where the Registry is located. Sometimes you get to the Registry as if by magic—the standard Registry editors don't tell you where the Registry is; they simply load it automatically. However, many times you need to know where to find the Registry files. They're not too difficult to find; the Registry's files are in the `%systemroot%\system32` directory and the `%systemroot%\system32\config` directory.

ENVIRONMENT VARIABLES

Every Windows XP installation automatically has some shortcut variables installed that are accessible to the user and the system. These variables are called *environment variables*. One environment variable, `%systemroot%`, contains the drive, path, and directory name for the directory that Windows XP was installed in. Another environment variable, `%systemdrive%`, contains the drive on which Windows XP is installed.

Using these environment variables makes it easy to write batch files and to otherwise locate components of your current Windows XP installation. For example, you might type at a command prompt:

```
CD %systemroot%
```

This command would then change to the directory that Windows XP was installed in.

Using the environment variables also can be very useful when writing software that must be run on a number of different Windows XP installations, especially when these installations are made to different drives or directories.

The following files are critical components of the Registry. These files are backed up to the `repair` directory, so that they may be restored as necessary in the event of a Registry failure.

These two files are stored in the `%systemroot%\system32` folder:

`Autoexec.nt`: Used to initialize the MS-DOS environment unless a different startup file is specified in an application's PIF.

`Config.nt`: Used to initialize the MS-DOS environment unless a different startup file is specified in an application's PIF.

The following files are stored in the `%systemroot%\system32\config` directory:

`Default`: The default Registry file.

`SAM`: The SAM (Security Accounts Manager) Registry file.

`Security`: The security Registry file.

`Setup.log`: The file that contains a record of all files that were installed with Windows XP. Certain components of Windows XP use the information in this file to update the operating system.

`Software`: The application software Registry file.

`System`: The system Registry file.

An additional file is used to reconfigure security when the Registry must be repaired. This is contained only in the `repair` directory, and not in the `%systemroot%\system32\config` directory:

`SecSetup.inf`: The out-of-the-box default security settings.

In a typical Windows XP installation, the `%systemroot%\system32\config` directory contains these files:

`AppEvent.Evt`: The application(s) event log file.

`Default`: The default Registry file.

`Default.sav`: A backup copy of the information contained in the default Registry file.

`netlogon.ftl`: A file containing network logon information.

`SAM`: The Security Accounts Manager Registry file.

`SecEvent.evt`: The security event log.

`Security`: The security Registry file.

`Software`: The application software Registry file.

`Software.sav`: A backup copy of the information contained in the software Registry file.

`SysEvent.evt`: The system events log.

`System`: The system Registry file.

`System.sav`: A backup copy of the information contained in the system Registry file.

`Userdiff`: Migrates preexisting user profiles from previous versions of Windows to Windows XP.

In the Registry, the most important files are those with no extensions—these are the current Registry files.

The files in the `%systemroot%\system32\config` directory that have the extensions `.log` or `.sav` contain a history that may be viewed with the Event Viewer program. For example, files with the extension `.sav` were saved using the Last Known Good booting process. Files with the `.log` extension are records of changes made to the Registry when Registry auditing is turned on. Though the `.log` and `.sav` files are not strictly necessary to have a working Windows XP installation, it is best to consider each of these files a member of a complete set.

WARNING

Be careful not to replace one file in the Registry without replacing all the others. It is simply too easy to get one file out of sync with the remaining Registry files, and this would spell disaster.

SIDE TRIP: RESTORING WINDOWS XP OR 2000

Restoring a copy of Windows XP or 2000 from a backup can be a difficult process. First, without a working copy of Windows XP or 2000, you can't run the backup and restore programs. This means you have to install a new copy of the OS to be able to run the restore program. You'd then use this copy of Windows XP or 2000 to restore the original system from the backup. Some users will reformat the drive, reinstall Windows XP or 2000 into the same directory that the original installation was made to, and restore on top of this new installation. There's nothing wrong with doing this, as long as you remember one critical point: If you installed any Windows XP updates or Windows 2000 service packs on your original installation, these updates or service packs must also be installed on the new installation being used to run the restoration program. If you don't install the updates or service packs, Windows XP or 2000

CONTINUED ⟶

restores system files from the original installation (with the updates or service packs) on top of the new files (without the updates or service packs); the files will be out of version sync with the existing operating system files and the Registry. This will usually cause the restore to crash without much of a warning as to what happened.

To perform a full restore of Windows XP or 2000 (and everything else on the drive) do the following:

1. Reformat the drive. Remember that you're doing a full restore here, and nothing that was on the drive is considered valuable at this point.
2. Install Windows XP or 2000, using your original distribution CD-ROM.
3. Install the updates or service packs that were installed with the version of Windows that is being restored. Remember that if the service packs are cumulative, you need only reinstall the last service pack. For example, if Service Pack 3 was installed on Windows 2000, it will not be necessary to install Service Packs 1 and 2. You only need to reinstall Service Pack 3.
4. Reinstall your backup/restore program, if necessary, and begin your restoration process.

Backing Up the Registry

Generally, two of anything is better than one. It's easier to ride a bicycle than a unicycle. However, it is even easier to drive a car—you don't even have to keep your balance. Where the Registry is concerned, keeping *at least* two copies of it is a good idea. I'd recommend that you keep at least four:

- The copy created by the Windows XP Professional backup program, stored in `%systemroot%\repair`. The Windows Setup program is able to use this copy to restore the Registry.
- A backup copy of the Registry files found in `%systemroot%\repair`, saved in a safe and convenient location. Consider a Zip disk or some other type of removable storage media for this copy.

- One (or more) backup copies, created using a backup technique on a type of media that is compatible with the backup and restore program of choice. (I'll discuss backup methods to use in the next section.)
- A copy of the Registry files contained in `%systemroot%\system32\config` stored on separate media, such as a different drive, diskettes, a Zip drive, CD-RW, or some other easily accessible, writable media. Try to avoid media requiring special drivers and such, because these drivers may not work when you need to restore that pesky Registry. This copy may only be made by dual-booting into another copy of Windows XP or Windows 2000 (or into Windows 9*x*–Windows 95, Windows 98, or Windows Me–if the drive is FAT formatted).

NOTE

In Windows NT 4, keep the special copy created by the RDisk utility that is stored in the Windows NT directory `%systemroot%\repair`. This copy of the Registry can only be used by the Windows NT Setup program to repair an existing copy of Windows NT. Also keep the copy created by the RDisk utility that is stored on the Windows NT ERD. Again, this copy of the Registry can only be used by the Windows NT Setup program to repair an existing copy of Windows NT. Windows 2000 and Windows XP don't support RDisk. Instead, the Registry backup, ASR-creation functionality (for Windows XP), and ERD-creation functionality (for Windows 2000) are incorporated into the finally-useful-for-everyone Backup program.

Be absolutely sure you keep these copies secure. Lock 'em up, stash 'em away. Oh, and by the way, that lock on your desk drawer is not good enough; use a good fireproof safe or strong box.

DANGER, WILL ROBINSON, DANGER!

Throughout this chapter we talk about backing up the Registry, saving the Registry to diskettes, other drives, and tapes. That's all well and good. However, you must remember that the Registry contains sensitive information.

CONTINUED →

The Registry is the heart and soul of the Windows operating system. It contains information critical to both the operation and security of Windows. There are many ways that someone could use your backup Registry files to breach your system's security, perhaps costing you money or (gasp!) your job.

Be absolutely sure you maintain the highest levels of security for any copies of the Registry that you make. If saved to external media (diskettes, tapes, or Zip drives, for example), make sure these copies are securely locked up. Why? Someone could, with little effort, completely subvert system security and then use the backup copies of the Registry to hide their actions.

I recommend you use a quality fireproof safe or a strong box for storing your Registry backup copies. Me, I use a fireproof, locked strong box inside a federal government–rated Mosler safe—and I don't think I'm being overly protective, either.

Backup Techniques

Windows XP and Windows 2000 support two different file systems. The first file system, called FAT (File Allocation Table), is identical to the file system used with DOS and Windows 9*x*. The FAT file system is not secure and offers no resistance to hackers and others who want to access files improperly. There are several flavors of the FAT file system: FAT12, FAT16, and FAT32. Windows XP and Windows XP fully support FAT32 and FAT16. This support allows compatibility with the large-disk support in Windows 98 and Windows Me.

The second file system, NTFS (NT File System), is unique to Windows 2000 and Windows XP. Though it is possible to read an NTFS drive from DOS or Windows 9*x* using shareware utilities, it is generally not possible to write to an NTFS drive unless you are using Windows 2000 or Windows XP. However, System Internals (see their Web site at `http://www.sysinternals.com`) has two utilities that allow you to write to an NTFS volume from DOS or Windows 9*x*.

Back Up to Tape or Other Media

The Windows XP backup program, Backup (`NTBackup.exe`), is one of a whole slew of compatible backup programs that allow backing up the system Registry to tape, diskettes, other hard drives, or for that matter, any Windows XP–supported writable media. The process is straightforward and can be done as part of a regular backup cycle, or whenever desired. Just select the System State check box in the backup tree to back up the Registry using Backup. When it stores the System State, Backup saves the following items:

- Boot files—the files used to boot the system
- COM+ Class Registration database—the COM+ classes' registration
- Registry—the set of files that comprise the configuration of Windows XP

For a Windows 2000 Server system, Backup saves the following items as well.

- Active Directory—the database of information about objects on the network
- SysVol—a shared directory that contains the server's public files that will be replicated on all other domain servers on the network

Using Backup is simple if you are familiar with creating and restoring tape backups. However, there are a few difficulties in using backups of the Registry. First, to keep the Registry backup easily accessible, it would be wise to place the Registry backup on its own media. If the media is inexpensive, this is a viable practice, but if you are paying an arm and a leg for media, this can be costly, because each Registry backup is relatively small as far as backups go.

Second, the Registry backups must be kept secure; perhaps more secure than standard backups. Everyone's situation is different; just realize that unrestricted access to the Registry would allow someone to have unrestricted, unaudited access to everything else as well.

Finally, tape backups are sometimes slow. Stick the tape in the drive and the first thing that happens is that the tape gets rewound (to re-tension it). This process alone can take some time—time that is not available when you are working on getting a server up and running. Consider instead backing up the Registry to a local hard drive other than the system drive.

Backing Up Using *copy* or *xcopy*

You can't copy back the current Registry while Windows is using the Registry. Period. Therefore, to restore the Registry using either `copy` or `xcopy`, you have to shut down Windows and start another operating system, such as DOS, Windows 9*x*, Windows 2000, or a second copy of Windows XP. Which operating system you use depends on which file system is being used on the computer. If the file system is FAT, you should start DOS or Windows 9*x*. If the file system is NTFS, you should start Windows 2000 or a second copy of Windows XP.

Backing up the Registry with `copy` or `xcopy` is easier than using Backup. Run the Backup program and create an ASR disk. Then simply copy the backup of the Registry found in the `%systemroot%\repair` directory to another location. Then (this is optional, but can't hurt), `xcopy` the current Registry files in the `%systemroot%\system32\config` directory using the `/c` option, which tells `xcopy` to ignore errors. (Since the currently opened Registry cannot be copied, these files will generate an error.)

Backing Up If You're Using FAT

If you're using the FAT file system, you can simply boot a DOS, or Windows 9*x* (if you're using FAT32), diskette that was formatted with the `/s` option. This will give you a DOS command prompt that allows you to read from and write to the hard drive quite easily.

To create a bootable disk, simply use the Windows 9*x* or DOS `FORMAT` command with the `/s` system option. Then copy the `xcopy` command's files (`xcopy*.*`) to the diskette, too. You can then boot this disk in the Windows XP computer, allowing unrestricted accesses to all FAT drives that are installed on that computer. When using Zip drives, it may be necessary to add DOS drivers for these drives to your boot diskette.

NOTE

If the system is already configured for dual-booting, you probably can use the second operating system instead of using a boot diskette. It probably won't matter which alternate operating system is installed (DOS, Windows 9*x*, or even Windows NT); all will work fine for the purpose of backing up the Registry. There is no need for boot diskettes in this situation.

After booting into a command prompt, it is a simple task to copy the Registry files to a safe location, such as another hard drive, a set of diskettes (the Registry won't fit on a single diskette), a Zip drive, a CD-RW drive, or other supported media.

NOTE

If your computer will boot from its CD-ROM drive, and you have a CD-RW drive, consider creating a bootable CD instead.

Backing Up If You're Using NTFS

If you're using the NTFS file system, you face a much more difficult problem. NTFS is a secure file system that cannot be easily accessed using other operating systems such as DOS or Windows 9*x*. Files on an NTFS drive may only be written by Windows 2000 and Windows XP and not by other operating systems. Sure, there are utilities that allow NTFS to be accessed from Windows 9*x*. However, the mode of access is read-only; there is no chance of a restore that way.

To be able to access the Registry files on an NTFS drive, it is necessary to install a second copy of Windows XP or a copy of Windows 2000. Actually, this is not a major problem because everyone should have at least two installations of Windows XP. Windows XP supports multiple boot configurations quite effectively. To create a multiple boot installation of Windows XP, simply follow these steps:

1. Ensure that you have sufficient space on your hard drive for a second copy of Windows XP. Your second copy of Windows XP will need only to be the basic operating system—so the amount of disk space will be relatively modest compared to a full installation. ("Relatively modest" means that you should get change from a gigabyte, depending on how much additional software and features you install.)

2. Begin your installation from the Windows XP CD or from a local or network source of files. When prompted for a destination, simply specify a new directory.

WARNING

Don't install to the same directory that your current working installation of Windows XP is installed into. That won't create a second copy of Windows XP—it'll just overwrite your working installation.

3. The Windows Setup program will configure the Boot Manager (creating new entries in the boot menu) so that you are able to choose which copy of Windows XP you want to boot.

CUSTOMIZING THE BOOT MENU

Once you install a second copy of Windows XP, your boot menu will list both copies of Windows XP. This can be confusing since the descriptions will be almost identical.

The solution is to customize the boot menu. The boot drive's root directory contains a file called `boot.ini`. This file includes the boot options for each copy of Windows that is installed. Before you can edit `boot.ini` directly, you need to clear the Hide Protected Operating System Files check box and select the Show Hidden Files and Folders option button on the View tab of the Folder Options dialog box (choose Tools ➢ Folder Options from an Explorer window). But you can also open `boot.ini` for editing more easily as follows: Press Winkey+R to display the System Properties dialog box. Click the Advanced tab. Click the Settings button in the Startup and Recovery group box to display the Startup and Recovery dialog box. Then click the Edit button in the System Startup group box. Windows opens `boot.ini` for editing in your default text editor (for example, Notepad).

CONTINUED ➞

The `boot.ini` file includes a text string that describes the installation:

```
[boot loader]
timeout=30
default=multi(0)disk(0)rdisk(0)partition(3)\WINDOWS
[operating systems]
multi(0)disk(0)rdisk(0)partition(3)\WINDOWS="Microso
ft Windows XP Professional" /fastdetect
multi(0)disk(0)rdisk(0)partition(4)\WINDOWS="Microso
ft Windows XP Professional backup" /fastdetect
multi(0)disk(0)rdisk(0)partition(2)\WINDOWS="Microso
ft Windows XP Home Edition" /fastdetect
multi(0)disk(0)rdisk(0)partition(1)\WINDOWS="Microso
ft Windows XP Home Edition backup" /fastdetect
```

You can modify anything in the quoted strings. A suggestion is to call your backup installation of Windows XP Professional just that—"Windows XP Professional backup," as in the example above.

The `default=` line toward the beginning of `boot.ini` specifies the version of Windows that will be booted by default. You can change this manually if you like doing things the hard way, but it's much easier to change the selection in the Default Operating System drop-down list in the Startup and Recovery dialog box. Windows XP changes `boot.ini` automatically when you close the Startup and Recovery dialog box.

When you reinstall Windows, the Windows Setup program automatically makes the latest installation the default operating system. Use the Startup and Recovery dialog box to change this if necessary.

To *copy* or to *xcopy*, That Is the Question

Users of FAT file systems can access the Registry with a DOS boot disk, and users of either FAT or NTFS can gain access with a second copy of Windows XP or a copy of Windows 2000 as described above. Once a method to access the Registry has been established, it is a simple task to completely back up the Registry.

Typically, I'll use a command window (a "DOS box," or command prompt), because I use NTFS and have a second copy of Windows XP installed. Here's how I back up the Registry on my main Windows XP Professional box.

Using the `md` (make directory) or `mkdir` command, I create a new directory called `\RegBU` on another drive (my system has five hard drives):

```
md d:\RegBu
```

I then use the `copy` command (or `xcopy`) to copy the Registry files in the `\system32` directory and the `\system32\config` directory to the `RegBU` directory.

This example would save a backup to a subdirectory on the D: drive. This is a good solution if the system (G:) drive becomes unreadable, because the backup copy will still be accessible. Other alternatives include backing up to a removable (Zip) drive or a network drive on a different computer.

If things are going well, I also use PKZIP to back up the Registry files to a set of diskettes. In my system, the files in my `config` directory are just over 16MB in size. Am I typical? No. I only have a few users in my user database, so my Registry is smaller than most. PKZIP is able to compress the files down to only two diskettes, which is a reasonable number. Of course, if I used a Zip drive, I could put these files on a single cartridge, but in my case that would be a waste of space.

Once you've copied your Registry files to a safe location, simply remove the boot diskette (if you used one) and reboot the computer. This will give you a copy of the Registry that is restorable later using an almost identical technique: boot to DOS and restore the files.

TIP

What is a safe location? A safe location typically would be to another drive, a Zip drive, or perhaps even diskettes. Diskettes present a small problem in that the Registry files are typically going to be a total of 10 to 20MB in size. Using a utility such as PKZIP allows you to write these large files to a number of diskettes while at the same time compressing them, reducing the number of diskettes required to a minimum.

Using the Registry Editor to Back Up the Registry

Using the Registry Editor, you can make an additional copy of the Registry and restore it by double-clicking a single icon.

NOTE

If you are a system administrator and you have Windows *9x* systems, the technique described below will work for these computers as well.

WHEN ONE IS BETTER THAN TWO: WINDOWS XP HAS ONE REGISTRY EDITOR TO WINDOWS 2000'S TWO

Remember how I was saying that two of anything is usually better than one? Well, here's a case of the opposite. Windows 2000 had *two* programs for editing the Registry, RegEdit and RegEdt32. Both identified themselves as "Registry Editor," but RegEdt32 offered various capabilities that RegEdit didn't, including a separate window for each hive open and the ability to set security on hives. In turn, RegEdit had a single killer feature—a status-bar readout of the full path to the current key—that was great when you were spelunking deep in the Registry and needed a quick check on where you'd gotten to.

So when you were planning to work with the Registry in Windows 2000, you needed not only to know which key you'd be working with but which of the two Registry Editors would serve you best. Windows XP makes things a bit simpler by providing a single Registry Editor, RegEdit, that integrates the best of the features from both the older versions of RegEdit and from RegEdt32. In case you're used to using RegEdt32 in Windows 2000, Windows XP provides a stub for RegEdt32, so that if you open the Run dialog box, enter **regedt32**, and click the OK button, XP runs RegEdit for you instead.

If you follow the steps outlined shortly, you can create a copy of the system Registry that includes everything except the `Security` and `SAM` Registry keys. When backing up a Windows XP workstation on a network, Registry Editor will usually use this technique to save everything needed. There are other methods to back up the security database, though those methods are awkward and somewhat difficult to manage: it is easier to use the techniques described earlier in the chapter to do a complete Registry backup. Because the `Security` and `SAM` keys are not backed up, this is not a complete backup technique. Rather, this is an interesting technique for backing up the other major parts of the Registry—one that is very easy and quick to do.

To use Registry Editor to back up the Registry, follow these steps:

1. Run Registry Editor. Either go to a command window and type the command **`regedit`**, or choose Start ➢ Run to open the Run dialog box, type **`regedit`** in the Open input area, and click the OK button.
2. After Registry Editor starts, note that My Computer is highlighted. If My Computer is not highlighted, click it to highlight it. This ensures that the entire Registry, not just part of it, is backed up.
3. Choose File ➢ Export.
4. Registry Editor will display the Export Registry File dialog box. Using the dialog box's toolbar, navigate to the Desktop, type a name or the file (for example, **`Registry`**) and click Save.
5. Exit Registry Editor.

Notice that unlike earlier versions of Registry Editor, the version that is supplied with Windows 2000 and Windows XP will write the Registry file out in Unicode format (each character is two-bytes long). Editors and utilities that do not understand Unicode character sets will have difficulty working with this file. To convert a Unicode text file to one-byte text format, use the `type` command, with the output redirected to a new file. For example:

```
type "file in unicode.reg" >"file in text.txt"
```

This is easy and almost painless. Using this technique to back up the Registry immediately after installation allows you to restore the system to a known state very easily and quickly. Simply double-click the file you created in step 4, above, and this file will be reloaded as the current Registry.

NOTE

The saved Registry file may be placed anywhere you desire. In some cases, placing a Registry restore capability on the user's Desktop is tantamount to courting disaster. Some users will click it just to see what will happen. One solution is to hide the file or save it to an offline storage location.

RESTORING THE REGISTRY

To restore the Registry, you must consider how the Registry was saved. There are four ways to save a Registry, each of which differs in just how much of the Registry was saved and where the Registry was saved:

- You can use a backup program to copy the Registry to a tape or other offline location. The backup program will then restore the Registry backup to its original location.
- You can copy the Registry (as described above), creating identical copies of the Registry that can then be recopied back to the original Registry locations. This requires that you use a second operating system (or a second copy of Windows XP) to copy the files back.
- The Backup program saves the Registry to the `%systemroot%\repair` directory. You can then use the Windows Setup program to restore these files.
- You can use Registry Editor to save the Registry in a text file with an extension of `.reg`. Windows knows that this is a Registry file (because the `.reg` file type is a registered extension) and will reload the file automatically into the Registry if the file is double-clicked in Explorer or from the Desktop. From a command prompt, enter the command **`start filename.reg`**, where *filename* is the name of the Registry backup file.

Restoring from Tape

Restoring a tape backup is a simple though time-consuming process. When you use a backup and restore program compatible with Windows XP, make sure that you select the option to restore the local Registry. You will have to make the decision about restoring other files at this time based upon your circumstances. If you suspect that other system files may be corrupted, or if you are simply not sure of the state of the system, I would recommend repairing Windows XP or restoring the entire operating system and the Registry at the same time. If you know that the Registry is the only damaged component, simply restoring the Registry and not other system files may save some time.

Restoring from Other Media Supported by Backup

Restoring backups saved on other media (such as disks, diskettes, Zip drives, etc.) is a simple and often fast process. Use the Windows XP Backup program, and select System State from the list of backed up items to restore.

NOTE

It is not possible to restore only part of the System State data; you must restore it all.

If your backup includes files in addition to the System State, you can restore those files at the same time. You will have to make the decision about restoring these other files based on your circumstances. If you suspect that other system files may be corrupted, or if you are simply not sure of the state of the system, I would recommend repairing Windows XP or restoring the entire operating system and the Registry at the same time. If you know that the Registry is the only damaged component, simply restoring the System State and not other system files may save a certain amount of time.

If you're using another backup program, simply follow the instructions provided with the program. The same general cautions about which files to restore (only the System State or the entire operating system) still apply. The main difference between most backup programs is the user interface.

NOTE

When restoring, be especially cautious that you do not restore the wrong version of the System State. Generally, you would want to make sure that you restore the most current working version of the Registry.

Recovering a Copied Registry

A Registry that has been backed up using `copy` or `xcopy` is restored in the opposite manner from which it was backed up. For example, if you have the NTFS file system, you would have to restart the system using your backup copy of Windows XP.

FAT and NTFS

When restoring a Registry on a FAT-based file system running Windows XP, it's necessary to boot DOS, Windows 9*x*, Windows 2000, or a second copy of Windows XP. If you have a dual-boot installed (either DOS or Windows 9*x*), it will be OK if you use the dual-boot to get to the other operating system.

If you are restoring the Registry on an NTFS system, dual-boot into the backup copy of Windows XP that you installed to back up the Registry.

WARNING

Once running the alternate operating system, find your latest working copy of the Registry *before* you copy it over the Registry that you think is corrupted, and back up the current Registry to another location. Take this precaution just in case the current Registry is not the problem (it happens) and the backup copy is not as good as you think it is.

You can follow these steps to restore your Registry from a backup you have created:

1. Boot to another operating system: Windows XP, Windows 2000, DOS, or Windows 9*x* for FAT; Windows XP or Windows 2000 for NTFS.
2. Save the current Registry to a safe location just in case it is not the problem.
3. Copy your saved Registry (from wherever it was stored) to the Registry location.
4. Boot the original version of Windows XP and test to see if the restoration worked. If it didn't, keep reading, more golden tips are coming up soon.

Using Automated System Recovery (ASR)

If you can't use the Recovery Console (discussed toward the end of this chapter) to restore a damaged part of your Registry, you may have to fall back on the ASR diskette and your backup of your system files. Automated System Recovery is new in Windows XP, but it seems to work well—providing, of course, that your backup is up to date.

To restore the system Registry from your backup and the ASR diskette requires running the Windows Setup program. Take the following steps:

1. Insert your Windows XP installation CD in your CD drive.
   - If necessary, configure your computer's BIOS to boot from the CD drive before the floppy drive or hard drive.
2. Insert your ASR diskette in your floppy drive.
3. Reboot your computer.
4. When your computer prompts you to boot from the CD, choose that option. Windows Setup launches.
5. When Windows Setup prompts you to press the F2 key to launch Automated System Recovery (ASR), press the F2 key. Windows Setup reads the files from the floppy disk and uses them to rerun the installation using the saved settings.

Using Setup and the Repair Command to Recover

When it first starts, Setup examines the hard drive and looks for already-installed copies of Windows XP and their `repair` directories. Once the examination is complete, Setup will give you three choices:

- Set up Windows XP, invoked by pressing Enter.
- Repair a damaged Windows XP installation using Recovery Console, by pressing R.
- Quit, because this was all just a big mistake, by pressing F3.

Now, we know that we are in trouble at this point—the only choice is whether it might be possible to recover from the problems without doing a complete reinstallation of Windows XP.

The Repair option looks tempting—but that's repairing Windows manually using the Recovery Console, which I'll discuss later in the chapter. In this section, we're looking at the automated repair section that Windows XP offers.

Press Enter. Windows Setup then displays the license agreement. Press the F8 key when you're comfortable with its contents. Windows Setup then scans the computer's hard disks. If it finds an installation of Windows XP that it thinks you might want to repair, it displays a screen such as that shown in Figure 27.1.

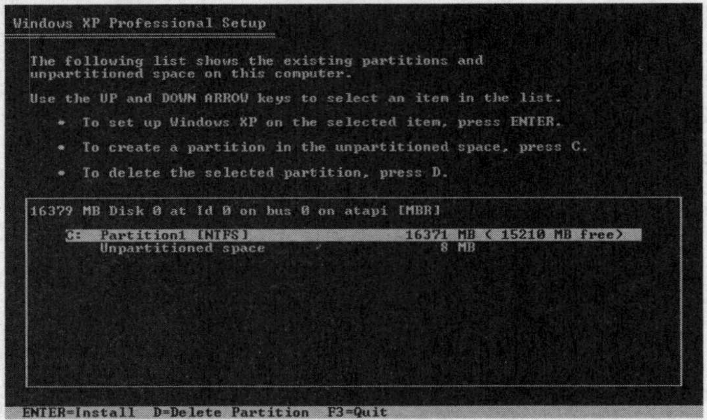

FIGURE 27.1: If Windows Setup finds an installation of Windows XP on the computer's hard disks, it offers you the option of repairing it.

Let's say that we are going to try to repair. First, we select the repair option, by pressing R. At this stage, the Setup program switches to repair mode and continues. Windows Setup examines your disks, deletes the files that it will replace, and copies replacement files from the CD.

Setup then reboots and continues the installation process as for a regular installation using an answer file, except that the answers are coming from the installation of Windows that's being repaired rather than from the answer file.

Loading a *.reg* File

Any `.reg` file created by Registry Editor (discussed earlier) is usually loaded by simply double-clicking the `.reg` file in the Explorer program or on the Desktop.

You can also go into Registry Editor to load the `.reg` file. From the Registry Editor main menu, select File ➢ Import, use the resulting Import Registry File to select the file, and then click the Open button. Actually, when you double-click a `.reg` file, Windows XP starts Registry Editor to do the Registry file load. The main advantage of loading a Registry file from the Registry Editor menu is that you're able to see the effect of the Registry load in Registry Editor.

A `.reg` file, being a text file, may be *carefully* edited. Did I emphasize *carefully* enough? Realize you are making a Registry change if you modify the `.reg` file and then reload it. And make certain that the editor you use understands Unicode. Notepad will work fine, just remember not to use the default `.txt` file extension that Notepad uses when saving the file.

Realize that you will not be able to use this technique if you are unable to boot or run Windows. This is another good reason to have multiple backups of the Registry in different formats.

NOTE

When restoring the Registry, several errors are displayed. Some errors will state "System Process - Licensing Violation" and advise the user that the system has detected tampering with the product registration component of the Registry. Click OK when these messages appear and also when another error stating that it was not possible to write to the Registry shows up. This final error is actually an artifact of the licensing violation errors and does not indicate a failure of the entire process.

To make the restored Registry active, it is necessary to restart Windows. (Windows caches most of the Registry while it is running.) There is no prompt to restart. However, some changes to the Registry will not be reloaded until the system is restarted. Select Start ➢ Turn Off Computer and then click the Restart button in the Turn Off Computer dialog box.

NOTE

It is not uncommon for applications to update the Registry using a `.reg` file during program installation time. This is one method used by software developers. Why? Simple: this allows the Registry to be repaired, restoring the application's default values without having to reinstall the entire program.

The Recovery Console

New in Windows 2000 and appearing again in Windows XP, the Recovery Console is a tool that allows recovery from a number of failures. In versions of Windows that didn't have the Recovery Console, all we could do was to boot another copy of Windows and hack our way around, replacing files, even Registry components, in the blind hope that we would somehow fix the problem.

The Recovery Console is a powerful, simple (no, that's not an oxymoron!) feature that is supplied with Windows 2000 and Windows XP. Now, realize that the Recovery Console is not installed by default. You can either run the Recovery Console from your Windows XP CD by booting your computer from the CD after disaster has struck or install the Recovery Console on your computer before disaster strikes so that you can use the Recovery Console without your Windows XP CD. Before you ask—you can't install the Recovery Console from the Recovery Console itself.

Installing the Recovery Console

If you want the Recovery Console available when your Windows XP CD isn't, you need to install the Recovery Console. So, let's install the Recovery Console right now.

NOTE

It is not possible to install the Recovery Console at the same time as Windows XP. You must first install Windows XP and then install the Recovery Console. If you have multiple copies of Windows XP installed on your computer, it is only necessary to install the Recovery Console one time—the Recovery Console will work with as many copies of Windows XP as are installed.

Follow these steps to install the Recovery Console:

1. Insert the Windows XP distribution CD, and change into the `i386` directory.
2. Run `winnt32.exe`, using the `/cmdcons` option. Typically, no other options are needed, though some users may want to specify source options, especially if installing from a network share rather than a hard drive.

3. The `winnt32.exe` program will present the Windows Setup dialog box shown in Figure 27.2. This dialog box allows you to cancel the installation if you need to. Note that multiple installations of the Recovery Console will simply overwrite previous installations; in such cases, no error is generated.

   - If the computer has an Internet connection available, Windows Setup connects to Windows Update and retrieves any relevant updated files.

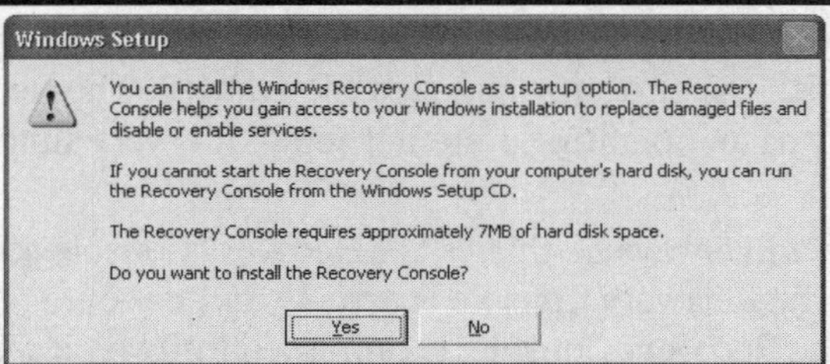

FIGURE 27.2: Setting up the Recovery Console using `winnt32 /cmdcons` bypasses all other setup options.

4. If there are no errors, the dialog box shown in Figure 27.3 is displayed. The Recovery Console is ready for use at this point.

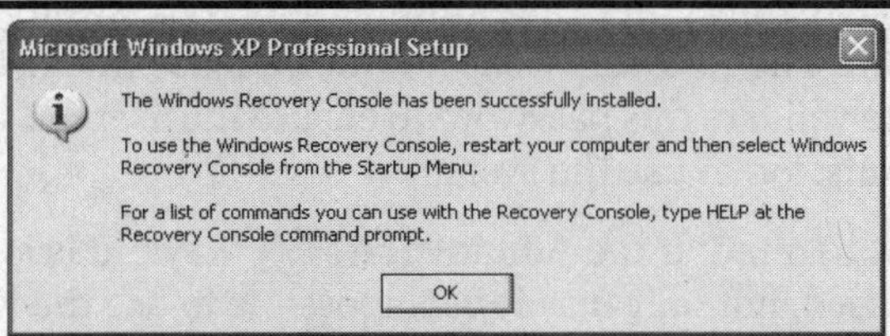

FIGURE 27.3: The Recovery Console has been successfully installed.

What's in the Recovery Console?

The Recovery Console consists of a minor modification to the `boot.ini` file, and the addition of a *hidden* directory on the boot drive. The added directory's name is `cmdcons`. The change to the `boot.ini` file is simply the addition of an additional line providing for a new boot option:

```
C:\CMDCONS\BOOTSECT.DAT="Microsoft Windows Recovery Console"
/cmdcons
```

This option consists of a fully qualified file name (`c:\cmdcons\boot-sect.dat`), a text description (`Microsoft Windows Recovery Console`), and a boot option (`/cmdcons`).

NOTE

The `cmdcons` directory is always located on the boot drive, not on the system drive, unless the boot drive is also the system drive.

As everyone should be well aware, the Windows Boot Manager is able to boot virtually any operating system (assuming that the operating system is compatible with the currently installed file system). The Recovery Console does qualify as an operating system, though it is very simple—and limited.

A major question will always be this: is the Recovery Console secure? In most situations, the Recovery Console is actually quite secure. The user, at startup of the Recovery Console, is prompted for two pieces of information:

- They must specify which Windows XP installation or Windows 2000 installation is to be repaired (assuming that there is more than one Windows XP installation or Windows 2000 installation!)
- They must successfully enter the Administrator's password for that installation. The Recovery Console will then use the installation's SAM to validate this password to ensure the user has the necessary permission to use the system.

A question comes to mind: If the Administrator's password is lost or otherwise compromised, not only may it be impossible to use the Recovery Console, but anyone with access to the compromised password would be able to modify the system with the Recovery Console. This is not really an issue, though. If the Administrator's password is lost, that's life. It will be difficult, if not impossible, to recover the password. If the security of the Administrator's password is compromised, it will be necessary to repair the damage—changing the password is mandatory in this case. In either case, the Recovery Console is no less secure than Windows XP is.

In the `cmdcons` directory, there are more than one hundred files. Most of these files are compressed and will be uncompressed by the Recovery

Console when needed. Here's a list of the most important of the uncompressed files found in this directory:

```
C:\cmdcons\autochk.exe
C:\cmdcons\autofmt.exe
C:\cmdcons\biosinfo.inf
C:\cmdcons\BOOTSECT.DAT
C:\cmdcons\disk101
C:\cmdcons\disk102
C:\cmdcons\disk103
C:\cmdcons\disk104
C:\cmdcons\kbdus.dll
C:\cmdcons\ksecdd.sys
C:\cmdcons\migrate.inf
C:\cmdcons\ntdetect.com
C:\cmdcons\NTFS.sys
C:\cmdcons\setupldr.bin
C:\cmdcons\setupreg.hiv
C:\cmdcons\spcmdcon.sys
C:\cmdcons\system32
C:\cmdcons\txtsetup.sif
C:\cmdcons\winnt.sif
C:\cmdcons\system32\ntdll.dll
C:\cmdcons\system32\smss.exe
```

The files `disk101`, `disk102`, `disk103`, and `disk104` are disk image identifier files, and they contain nothing but a single space and a carriage return/line feed. The `BOOTSECT.DAT` file is the bootable boot sector image file. The `migrate.inf` file contains information used to update the Registry if needed. The `setupreg.hiv` file is used to update the Registry; however, this file is in a special format usable only with certain applications. The `cmdcons` directory also contains the subdirectory `system32`. This subdirectory contains two files, `ntdll.dll` and `smss.exe`.

You probably noticed that I described the files listed above as the "most important" of the uncompressed files. That's because the `cmdcons` directory contains a host of uncompressed keyboard-mapping files. Apart from `kbdus.dll`, which appears in the above list and contains the U.S.

keyboard layout, you'll find a wide range of keyboard mappings for different languages and layouts. For example, `kbduk.dll` contains the U.K. keyboard layout, and `kdbdv.dll` contains the assorted Dvorak keyboard layouts.

Using the Recovery Console

Once the Recovery Console is installed, it will appear in the startup menu as the last item in the list, named "Microsoft Windows Recovery Console."

WARNING

It is strongly recommend that the Recovery Console not be invoked unless absolutely necessary! The commands available in the Recovery Console are powerful, and if used improperly, they can destroy a Windows installation.

To use the Recovery Console, follow these steps:

1. Boot the system.
2. When the startup menu is displayed, select "Microsoft Windows Recovery Console."
3. Select the installation to be repaired if there are multiple Windows XP or Windows 2000 installations.
4. Enter the correct administrator password for the installation to be repaired.
5. Use any Recovery Console commands (see the section after next) needed to do the repair.

When you're done repairing the installation, simply enter the **`exit`** command to exit the Recovery Console and restart the computer.

Starting the Recovery Console from the Installation CD-ROM

The steps to start the Recovery Console for computers that either do not have the Recovery Console installed or cannot be booted (perhaps due to errors in the partition table, or MBR) are:

1. Boot the system, using the CD-ROM disk or diskettes as appropriate.

2. When the Welcome to Setup text screen is displayed, select Repair by pressing the R key.
3. Select the installation to be repaired if there are multiple Windows XP or Windows 2000 installations.
4. Enter the password for one of the Computer Administrator accounts on the Windows XP installation or the Administrator account on the Windows 2000 installation to be repaired.
5. Use any Recovery Console commands (see the next section) needed to do the repair.

When you're done repairing the installation, enter the **`exit`** command to exit the Recovery Console and restart the computer.

Recovery Console Commands and Options

When the computer is started in the Recovery Console mode, a prompt similar to a command prompt is the only interface available to the user. The Recovery Console's functionality is limited, and it supports only the following commands:

`attrib` Changes file attributes. The read, hidden, and system attributes may be either set or cleared as desired.

`batch` Allows execution of a set of Recovery Console commands that have been saved in a text file. The filename and extension both must be specified for the `batch` command to work. This command allows specifying an output file as well.

`bootcfg` Lets you work with the boot configuration and recovery. You can scan for Windows installations, add a Windows installation to the boot list, set a default boot entry, or enable redirection in the boot loader.

`chdir (cd)` Works identically to the command session's `cd` command, changing the current working directory to the directory specified or, if no directory is specified, displaying the current working directory.

`chkdsk`	Works similarly to a command session's `chkdsk` command. Two options are available: `/p` specifies that the drive is to be checked regardless of whether the dirty flag is set; `/r` specifies that `chkdsk` should repair any bad sectors found.
`cls`	Works identically to the command session's `cls` command—clears the screen.
`copy`	Copies a file from a source location to a destination location. The file, if compressed, is uncompressed when copied. No wildcards are permitted with the `copy` command. There are no options to this command.
`delete (del)`	Works much like a command session's `delete` command. This command deletes the specified file or files. It will only work in the system directories of the installation being repaired, in hard drive root directories, and with local installation source files.
`dir`	Works similarly to a command session's `dir` command. This command will display the names of files and subdirectories in the location specified. The `dir` command has no options, listing file sizes, modification dates, and attributes.
`disable`	Used to disable a service or device driver. The service or device driver to be disabled is marked as `SERVICE_DISABLED` to prevent it from being started when the system is subsequently restarted.
`diskpart`	Manages partitions on disk devices. This command is able to add or delete partitions as desired. When adding a partition, a command parameter specifies the size of the partition in megabytes.
`enable`	Used to enable a service or device driver. The service or device driver to be enabled is marked with the user specified service type: `SERVICE_AUTO_START`, `SERVICE_DISABLED`, `SERVICE_DEMAND_START`, `SERVICE_BOOT-START`, or `SERVICE_SYSTEM_START`.
`exit`	Ends the Recovery Console session and reboots the computer.

`expand`	Works similarly to a command session's `expand` command. This command allows expanding files from a source CAB file. Three options are available: `/d` displays the contents of the CAB file; `/f` lets you identify the files to expand from the source (using wildcards if necessary); and `/y` suppresses any overwrite warnings that may be given.
`fixboot`	Repairs or replaces the (optional) specified drive's boot sector.
`fixmbr`	Repairs or replaces the (optional) specified drive's master boot record.
`format`	Works similarly to a command session's `format` command. This command allows formatting disks using FAT, FAT32, and NTFS. One option, `/q`, allows quick formatting without a scan when the drive is known to be good.
`help`	Lists the available Recovery Console commands.
`listsvc`	Displays a list of services and drivers that are currently available on the computer.
`logon`	Run automatically when the Recovery Console is first started, this command is used to log on to an installation of Windows XP.
`map`	Used to display a list of all drive mappings. This command's output is very useful for the `fixboot`, `fixmbr`, and `fdisk` commands.
`mkdir (md)`	Works similarly to the command session's `md` (`mkdir`) command. This command allows creating directories within the system directories of the currently logged-on installation, removable disks, root directories of hard disk partitions, and local installation sources.
`more`	Works like the command session's `type` command. Displays the file's contents on the screen. There are no parameters for the `more` command.
`net use`	Allows you to map a network share to a drive letter.

`rename (ren)`	Allows the user to rename a file. This command does not support wildcard specifications.
`rmdir (rd)`	Works similarly to the command session's `rd` (`rmdir`) command. This command allows deleting directories within the system directories of the currently logged-on installation, removable disks, root directories of hard disk partitions, and local installation sources.
`set`	The Recovery Console supports a limited set of environment variables. These variables affect Recovery Console commands only.
`systemroot`	Changes to the current installation's `%systemroot%` directory. Functionally equivalent to `cd %systemroot%` in a normal command session.
`type`	Works like the command session's `type` command. This command displays the file's contents on the screen. There are no parameters for the `type` command.

Hints and Kinks from the Experts

Here's another installment of good stuff from the Windows gurus.

Why Don't My Changes to the Registry Take Effect?

Always reboot. Reboot after restoring any Registry values. Windows does not reload many values except at boot time. There's nothing worse than wondering why your "fix" didn't work when Windows was simply not loading it. (In case you're wondering, this is why the installation routines for many programs require a reboot to take effect.)

Users Never Have a Current System State Backup!

In most sites, users rarely have a current System State backup when they need one. Give them one with this procedure. Use the scheduler (the AT command or a good one like OpalisRobot) on each workstation to schedule a save of the System State. The batch file to schedule is:

```
net use x: /delete
net use x: \\YourServer\RepairShare$ /persistent:no
if not exist x:\%computername% md x:\%computername%
REM - Use NTBackup to save the system state!
REM - '/l: f' used to create a full backup log.
ntbackup backup systemstate /f "x:\%computername%\System
State" /l:f

net use x: /delete
exit
```

where `%computername%` is a subdirectory of the hidden share on the server (one for each workstation). When you need the System State for that workstation, just reattach the share to the target system.

The scheduler must be run under the system context and allowed to interact with the desktop or under the context of an administrative user. If you use the system account, you can't schedule the copy because the system account has no network access. Use a ROBOT account that is a member of the Administrator group with a non-blank, non-expiring password. Use full path names for all files.

Here is a sample schedule for workstation wsA:

```
AT \\wsA 01:00 /interactive every:M,T,W,Th,F,S,Su
\\YourServer\RepairShare$\Repair.bat
```

You can dress up the `Repair.bat` with logging, messaging, and so on.

WHAT'S NEXT?

In Chapter 26, I talked a bit about Registry terminology—hives, keys, subkeys, and value entries. In the next chapter, I'll provide an overview of the Registry and then look in detail at some important keys.

Chapter 28

Anatomy of the Registry: The Blood, Gore, and Guts

In Chapter 26, I talked a little about what the Registry is and the terminology used for its various components. In this chapter, I'll get into more of the details of what actually is in the Registry. If you're only interested in how to use (or recover) the Registry, but not *what* the Registry is, you could skip this chapter. However, if you're unsure about this, I'd recommend reading it anyway.

Revised and adapted from *Mastering Windows 2000 Registry* by Peter D. Hipson

ISBN 0-7821-2615-4 752 pages $39.99

Now humor me for just a moment; I think I'm going to back up my Registry. In fact, it is a good time for *you* to do a backup as well, since it is entirely possible that at any time you might have some kind of problem (or disaster) with the Registry and really need that backup copy to restore it. Choose Start ➢ All Programs ➢ Accessories ➢ System Tools ➢ Backup to start the Backup or Restore Wizard, select the Let Me Choose What to Back Up option button on the What to Back Up page, select the System State check box under the My Computer object on the Items to Back Up tab, and then create an Automated System Recovery disk.

Next, let some time pass by...

Ah, that feels better. I've got a fresh backup copy of my Registry just in case I do something stupid, and so do you—not that we ever do anything stupid, right?

The Registry is subdivided into a number of clearly defined sections, called *hives*:

- HKEY_CLASSES_ROOT
- HKEY_CURRENT_USER
- HKEY_LOCAL_MACHINE
- HKEY_USERS
- HKEY_CURRENT_CONFIG

Some hives are less important than others. For example, on a Windows 2000 Server machine, a damaged Security Accounts Manager key (SAM) could probably be recovered easily without serious, permanent problems. You might lose the entire user database, so no users would be able to log onto the server. However, as long as you can log on as Administrator, the worst case is that you would have to enter the other user information again. The default SAM Registry will contain at least the initial Administrator user ID and password, which you would have to know.

However, say you lose the system component of the Registry without adequate backup. In that case, it is unlikely that you'll be able to recover without reinstalling Windows, and that would be a painful experience at best.

OF HIVES AND BEES—A REGISTRY OVERVIEW

As I discussed in Chapter 26, the Windows XP/2000/NT Registry (and the Registry for Windows 9*x*) is arranged into logical units called *hives*. Though I can't vouch for its truth, legend has it that some unnamed programmer at Microsoft seemed to see a logical relationship between the various keys in the Registry and the structure of a beehive. Now me, I just don't see this, so let's consider the two following alternative analogies:

- The Registry is arranged just like the folders and files contained on your hard drive. Hives are analogous to root directories, and keys are like subdirectories and files. In fact, this relationship is almost 100 percent parallel: Hives are usually shown separated by backslashes (just like directories on the drive) from keys, and keys typically (but not always) have values. Remember, a file may also be empty.
- The Registry is arranged as a hierarchical database, nothing more, and nothing less. If you are a database person, this view of the Registry might make more sense to you. In truth, the database arrangement is more like the Registry's actual construction.

Specific data is assigned to a key. As I've mentioned, some Registry keys don't have a value set; this is also acceptable.

WARNING

Be careful not to delete empty keys just because they are empty. Even though they don't have a value, their presence in the Registry may be necessary for the health and well being of Windows XP. Never, ever, delete a key unless you know that there will be no adverse side effects.

The Registry Hives

The Registry is divided into five hives, and every one is named with the prefix `HKEY_`. Each hive embodies a major section of the Registry that has a specific functionality. Each hive is separate from the other hives and is typically stored as a file in the directory `%systemroot%\system32\config`. Hive storage files have no extension or file type, making them easier to find. These hives are discussed next.

Hives, Keys, and Values

In these chapters, I use a terminology similar to that used when referring to disk drives, directories, subdirectories, files, and the contents of files. Often Microsoft confuses the issue somewhat. I try to keep it clear:

Hive: A hive is similar to a root directory on a drive. Inside a hive there are keys (like files and subdirectories). A hive is the highest level; a hive cannot be a sub-hive inside another hive. An example of a hive in the Registry is HKEY_LOCAL_MACHINE.

Key: A key is similar to a subdirectory or a file and is found inside a hive. Inside a key there can be other keys (like files) that contain values or other keys (like subdirectories) that contain both values and keys. A key will have either a hive or key as a parent above it, and zero or more keys contained within it. Sometimes Microsoft refers to a key as a *sub-hive*. An example of a key in the Registry is HKEY_LOCAL_MACHINE\SAM.

Value: A value is similar to a file's data. Each key will have one value (though the value may consist of many parts) or no value set at all. There is also something called the *default value* (sometimes called the *unnamed value*), an object that may or may not be assigned a value.

HKEY_CLASSES_ROOT

The HKEY_CLASSES_ROOT hive contains information about both OLE and various file associations. The purpose of HKEY_CLASSES_ROOT is to provide for compatibility with the existing Windows 3.*x* Registry.

The information contained in HKEY_CLASSES_ROOT is identical to information found in HKEY_LOCAL_MACHINE\Software.

HKEY_CURRENT_USER

The HKEY_CURRENT_USER hive is used to manage specific information about the user who is currently logged on. This information includes:

- The user's Desktop and the appearance and behavior of Windows to the user.
- All connections to network devices, such as printers and shared disk resources.

- Desktop program items, application preferences, screen colors, and other personal preferences and security rights. They are stored for later retrieval by the system when the user logs on.

All other environment settings are retained for future use.

By accessing the roaming user profile, Windows is able to make any workstation that the user logs onto appear the same to the user. Domain users need not worry about having to set up or customize each workstation that they will be using.

The information contained in HKEY_CURRENT_USER is updated as users make changes to their environments.

HKEY_LOCAL_MACHINE

The HKEY_LOCAL_MACHINE hive contains information about the computer that is running Windows XP. This information includes applications, drivers, and hardware. There are five separate keys contained within HKEY_LOCAL_MACHINE:

Hardware: The key used to save information about the computer's hardware. To allow new hardware to be added easily, the Hardware key is always re-created when the system is booted. Changes to this key are not meaningful. Contained within the Hardware key are the following three subkeys:

Description: Contains information about the system, including the CPU, FPU, and the system bus. Under the system bus is information about I/O, storage, and other devices.

DeviceMap: Contains information about devices (keyboards, printer ports, pointers, and so on).

ResourceMap: Contains information about the HAL (Hardware Abstraction Layer). Remember, HAL is not a talking computer on a spaceship, HAL is the hardware. Also contained are I/O devices, drivers, SCSI adapters, system resources, and video resources.

SAM: The Security Accounts Manager (SAM) stores information about users and domains in the SAM key. This information is not accessible using any of the resource editors. Rather, this information is better managed using the administrator's User Manager program.

Security: Contains information about local security and user rights. A copy of the SAM key is found in the Security key. As with SAM, the Security key is not accessible using the resource editors, and the information is best modified using the administrator's tools.

Software: Contains information about installed system and user software, including descriptions. There are generally subkeys for each installed product in which the products store information—including preferences, configurations, MRU (most recently used files) lists, and other application-modifiable items.

System: Contains information about the system startup, device drivers, services, and the Windows XP configuration.

HKEY_USERS

The HKEY_USERS hive contains information about each active user who has a user profile. A minimum of two subkeys are in the HKEY_USERS key: .DEFAULT and information for the currently logged-on user. The purpose of the .DEFAULT key is to provide information for users who log on without a profile. Information for the current user is stored under the user's SID (security identifier).

Personal profiles are contained in the %sysdrive%\Documents and Settings\Default User folder, unless roaming profiles are used, in which case a copy will be stored there, but the original will reside on a server.

HKEY_CURRENT_CONFIG

The HKEY_CURRENT_CONFIG hive contains information about the system's current configuration. This information is typically derived from HKEY_LOCAL_MACHINE\System and HKEY_LOCAL_MACHINE\Software, though HKEY_CURRENT_CONFIG does not contain all the information that is contained in the source keys.

NOTE

As I noted in Chapter 26, the HKEY_DYN_DATA hive no longer exists in Windows 2000 and Windows XP. In Windows NT 4, this hive was intended to contain information about the system's PnP (Plug and Play) status. However, since Windows NT 4 does not support PnP, this key is empty.

Registry Key Data Types

Values have different data types:

REG_BINARY: Represents binary values. They may be edited or entered as hexadecimal or binary numbers. Figure 28.1 shows the Registry Editor's Edit Binary Value dialog box.

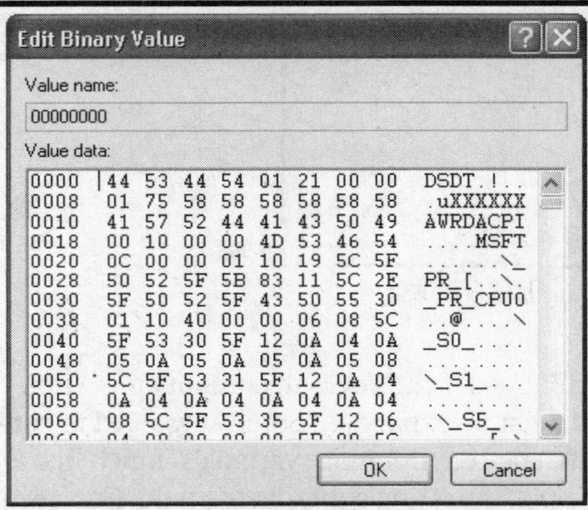

FIGURE 28.1: The Edit Binary Value dialog box

You can also use the Binary Data dialog box (see Figure 28.2) to get a better view of binary data but not to edit it.

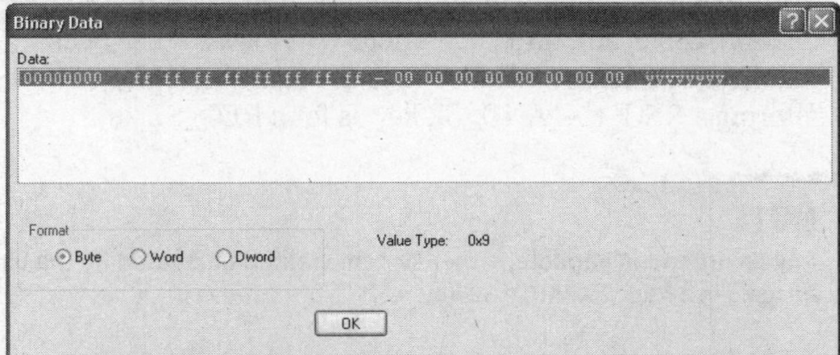

FIGURE 28.2: The Binary Data dialog box

REG_SZ: Used for Registry keys that contain strings. Editing is easy; just type in the new string. Case is preserved, but realize that the string is initially selected, so be careful not to inadvertently delete it. Strings are of fixed length and are defined when the key is created. Figure 28.3 shows a string being edited in the Edit String dialog box. A string key may be made longer by adding more characters to the string; it will be reallocated if this happens.

FIGURE 28.3: The Edit String dialog box

REG_EXPAND_SZ: Used if the key is to contain an environment variable that must be expanded. Some keys need to contain values that reference environment variables, much like a batch file—for example, if a string contains the field `%systemroot%\system32`, and it is necessary for the `%systemroot%` part of the string to be replaced with the value that is assigned to it in the environment. To do this substitution, this string must be defined as a REG_EXPAND_SZ type string. The result of the expansion would then be passed to the requestor. `%systemroot%` is a standard environment variable containing the location, drive, and directory where Windows XP has been installed. The Registry Editor uses the same dialog box for entering a REG_EXPAND_SZ key as for a REG_SZ key.

NOTE

Any environment variable, either system created or created by the user, may be used in a REG_EXPAND_SZ key.

REG_DWORD: A 32-bit value. The value is entered as decimal or hexadecimal. The Edit DWORD Value dialog box (shown in Figure 28.4) allows us to enter only valid numeric data to help save us from sloppy typing.

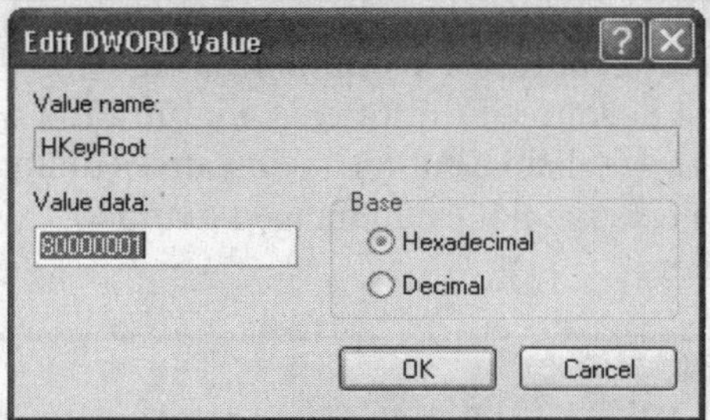

FIGURE 28.4: The Edit DWORD Value dialog box

REG_MULTI_SZ: Used to store multiple strings in a single Registry key. Normally, a string resource in the Registry can contain only one line. However, the multi-string type allows a string resource in the Registry to hold multiple strings as needed. Figure 28.5 shows multiple strings being edited, with two lines present in this example.

NOTE

The Windows *9x* Registry editor does not support the REG_MULTI_SZ type. Editing a REG_MULTI_SZ item with the Windows *9x* Registry editor can corrupt the data the item contains.

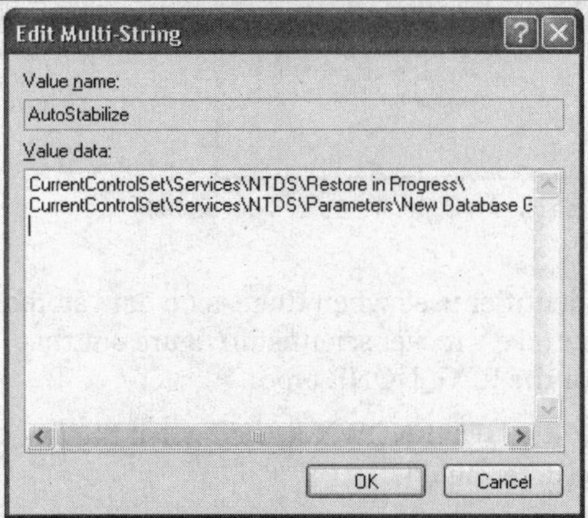

FIGURE 28.5: The Edit Multi-String dialog box

REG_FULL_RESOURCE_DESCRIPTOR: Used to manage information for hardware resources. No one should edit the items that appear in the Resource Editor fields. Figure 28.6 shows a disk resource object displayed in the Resources dialog box. However, these objects are not ever changed manually with the resource editors.

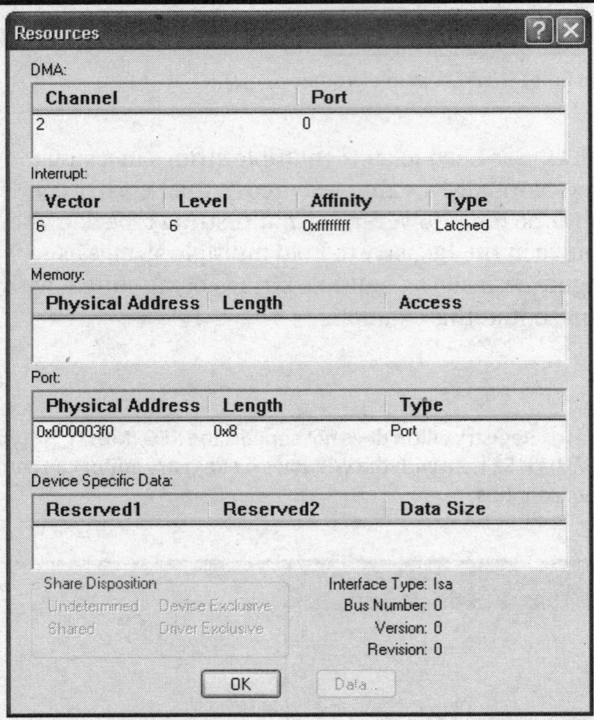

FIGURE 28.6: A disk resource shown in the Resources dialog box

REG_NONE: An identifier used when there is no data stored in the key. It doesn't take a rocket scientist to figure out that there is no editor for the REG_NONE type.

REG_UNKNOWN: REG_UNKNOWN is used when the key's data type cannot be determined.

HKEY_LOCAL_MACHINE: The Machine's Configuration

The HKEY_LOCAL_MACHINE hive contains information about the current hardware configuration of the local computer. The information stored in this hive is updated using a variety of processes, including the Control Panel, hardware and software installation programs, and administrative tools, and is sometimes automatically updated by Windows XP.

It is important not to make unintended changes to the HKEY_LOCAL_MACHINE hive. A change here could quite possibly render the entire system unstable.

NOTE

All the settings in the HKEY_LOCAL_MACHINE hive are recomputed at boot time. If a change has been made, and the change is causing problems, first try rebooting the system. The Windows Boot Manager should rebuild the HKEY_LOCAL_MACHINE hive at reboot time, discarding any changes made.

HKEY_LOCAL_MACHINE\Hardware: The Installed Hardware Key

HKEY_LOCAL_MACHINE\Hardware contains information about the hardware configuration of the local machine. Everything hardware related (and I do mean everything) will be found in this hive.

In Windows XP, the HKEY_LOCAL_MACHINE\Hardware key is subdivided into several keys:

Description: Contains descriptive information about each device, including both a general description and information about basic configurations and so on.

DeviceMap: Contains information about devices, including the location in the Registry where a device's full configuration is saved.

ResourceMap: Contains translation information about each major component that is installed in the system. Most keys contain a set value entries named .Raw and .Translated.

NOTE

If your computer supports ACPI (Advanced Configuration and Power Interface), you'll also see an ACPI key under \Hardware. This key includes keys for the Differentiated System Description Table (DSDT), Firmware ACPI Control Structure (FACS), Fixed API Description Table (FADT), and Root System Definition Table (RSDT).

DESCRIPTION

Within HKEY_LOCAL_MACHINE\HARDWARE\Description is a wealth of information about the installed hardware. The only subkey, System, describes the CPU and I/O fully. Items in the Description key are always redetected at boot time. The following subkeys are contained in the System subkey:

> **CentralProcessor**: The CentralProcessor subkey contains information about the CPU. This includes speed, which is an identifier that contains the CPU's model, family, and Stepping. Also included in this subkey is vendor information; for example, a "real" Intel CPU has the VendorIdentifier string GenuineIntel.
>
> **FloatingPointProcessor**: The FloatingPointProcessor subkey describes the system's FPU (floating point unit) in a set of entries similar to that of the CPU. The fact that the typical CPU has an integral FPU is not considered here; the FPU will be listed separately, regardless.
>
> **MultiFunctionAdapter**: The MultiFunctionAdapter subkey describes the system's bus (PCI), any PnP BIOS installed, and other devices, including the controllers for disk drives, keyboards, parallel and serial ports, and the mouse. For a mouse that is connected to a serial port, the mouse will be found under the serial port, while a mouse that is connected to a PS/2 mouse port will be shown connected to a pointer controller as a separate device.

Typically, the Description key can be used to determine what hardware is installed (and being used) and how the installed hardware is connected. However, some devices, such as storage devices (non-IDE hard drives, SCSI devices, non-IDE CD-ROM drives, video, and network interface cards), are not listed in HKEY_LOCAL_MACHINE\Hardware\Description. Instead, they are listed in HKEY_LOCAL_MACHINE\Hardware\DeviceMap. Why? Because these devices are not detected at boot-up stage; instead, they are detected when they are installed.

DeviceMap

The HKEY_LOCAL_MACHINE\Hardware\DeviceMap subkey contains information about devices, arranged in a similar fashion to the HKEY_LOCAL_MACHINE\HARDWARE\Description subkey discussed earlier. In the Devicemap subkey, the following subkeys are found:

KeyboardClass: Contains the address of the subkey that manages information about the keyboard itself.

PARALLEL PORTS: Contains the address of the subkey that manages information about the parallel ports.

PointerClass: Contains the address of the subkey that manages information about the system mouse.

Scsi: A complex subkey with information about each SCSI interface found on the computer. A note about what is considered a SCSI port is in order. Actually, Windows XP pretends that IDE devices, as well as many CD-ROM devices that are connected to special interface cards, are SCSI devices. This is a management issue. Windows is not converting these devices to SCSI, nor is it using SCSI drivers; rather, Windows is simply classing all these devices under a common heading of SCSI.

SERIALCOMM: Contains the address of the subkeys that manage information about the available serial ports.

VIDEO: Contains the address of the subkey that manages the video devices. There are typically two devices defined in VIDEO: one is the currently used adapter, and the second is a backup consisting of the previously installed (usually the generic VGA) adapter's settings to use as a backup in the event of a problem with the video system.

ResourceMap

The ResourceMap subkey is used by all the various hardware device drivers to map resources that they will use. Each ResourceMap entry will contain information about the usage of:

- I/O ports
- I/O memory addresses
- Interrupts
- Direct memory access (DMA) channels
- Physical memory installed
- Reserved memory

The ResourceMap subkey is divided into subkeys for each class of device (such as Hardware Abstraction Layer), and under these subkeys lie subkeys for different devices.

The key in ResourceMap called PnPManager contains Plug-and-Play information.

The System Resources key contains information on the computer's physical memory and reserved memory.

HKEY_LOCAL_MACHINE\SAM: The Security Access Manager

HKEY_LOCAL_MACHINE\SAM contains information used by the Windows XP security system. It also contains user information (permissions, passwords, and the like). The SAM key is mirrored in HKEY_LOCAL_MACHINE\Security\SAM; making changes to one changes the other.

NOTE

Can't see the SAM key or the Security key? In Registry Editor, select the subkey you cannot see and then select Edit ➢ Permissions. Next, change the Permissions list from Special Permissions to Full Control. Close the Permissions dialog box and choose View ➢ Refresh to refresh the display in Registry Editor.

In Windows XP, this information is set using the Microsoft Management Console (MMC), Local Users and Groups branch. In a Windows 2000 system that's a domain controller; the SAM is not used (we have the Active Directory services now). The SAM subkeys (both in HKEY_LOCAL_MACHINE\SAM\SAM and HKEY_LOCAL_MACHINE\Security\SAM) should only be modified using the MMC in Windows XP or Windows 2000. However, attempts to modify information that is in the SAM subkeys typically result in problems. For example, users will be unable to log on, wrong permissions will be assigned, and so on.

WARNING

Don't attempt to modify the SAM or Security key unless you have made a full backup of your Registry, including the SAM and Security keys, as described in Chapter 27.

HKEY_LOCAL_MACHINE\Security: The Windows 2000 Security Manager

The key HKEY_LOCAL_MACHINE\Security contains information relevant to the security of the local machine. This information includes:

- User rights
- Password policy
- Membership of local groups

This information is typically set using Local Users and Groups in Computer Management.

NOTE

Under Windows NT 4, the Security subkeys should only be modified using the User Manager or the User Manager for Domains. With Windows 2000 Active Directory, only the Active Directory administrative programs (Active Directory Users and Computers) should be used. Attempts to modify information in the Security key typically result in problems. For example, users are unable to log on, wrong permissions are assigned, and so on.

HKEY_LOCAL_MACHINE\Software: The Installed Software Information Manager

The HKEY_LOCAL_MACHINE\Software Registry key is the storage location for all software installed on the computer. The information contained in

HKEY_LOCAL_MACHINE\Software is available to all users and consists of a number of standard subkeys as well as a few subkeys that may be unique to each computer.

One computer on my network, a Windows XP Professional machine, has the following subkeys in HKEY_LOCAL_MACHINE\Software. These subkeys correspond to items that I have installed on my computer:

Adobe: Contains information about the copy of Adobe's Acrobat program that I recently installed.

Creative Tech: Contains information about the Sound Blaster Live card installed in the computer.

Federal Express: Contains information about the FedEx online access and support I have on my computer. All of my FedEx airbills are produced by computer, making shipments much easier.

Intuit: Contains information specific to the financial software that is Intuit's specialty.

Qualcomm: Contains information specific to the Eudora e-mail program. The nice thing about Eudora is that there is a free version for private use.

The following are system subkeys probably installed on your computer; however, some of these subkeys, such as ODBC and Clients, may not be present on some minimal installations:

Classes: Contains two types of items. First are file-type association items. For example, a typical association entry might have the name DIB, with a string that associates this name with the application Paint Shop Pro. Second are COM (Common Object Model) associations. For example, the extension .doc is associated with Microsoft Word or with WordPad, the default viewer for .doc files. Both WordPad and Word may be embedded in other applications. For instance, Outlook, Microsoft's upscale e-mail system, can use Word-formatted documents and embed either Word or WordPad to display and edit these documents.

Clients: Contains client-server relationships. For example, Microsoft Outlook is a multipurpose program with e-mail, a calendar, contact lists, news, and other features. Each of these parts of Outlook has a complex series of calling protocols that are defined in the Clients subkey.

`Microsoft`: Stores a number of items that pertain to Microsoft products or parts of Windows. There can be as few as 20 or as many as 100 entries in the `Microsoft` subkey.

ODBC: Stores items that pertain to Open Database Connectivity, which allows applications to retrieve data from a number of different data sources. Many users install ODBC, either realizing that they are installing it or as a side effect of installing another product.

`Program Groups`: This subkey contains one value entry, `ConvertedToLinks`, which is used to indicate whether the program groups were converted. A value of one (`0x00000001`) shows that the conversion is complete. Even a system installed on a new computer that didn't require conversion will have this value.

`Secure`: If you say so. The `Secure` subkey is the location in which any application may store "secure" configuration information. Only an Administrator can modify this subkey, so mere mortal users can't change secure configuration information. Not many, if any, applications use the `Secure` subkey.

`Windows 3.1 Migration Status`: Used to indicate if the computer was upgraded from Windows 3.*x* to Windows NT 4, 2000, or XP. Though at one time there were many upgrades, more users today are likely to be doing clean installations— virtually all existing Windows 3.*x* systems have already been upgraded. This key contains two subkeys: `IniFiles` and `REG.DAT`. These values show whether the `.ini` and `Reg.dat` files have been migrated successfully to later formats.

HKEY_LOCAL_MACHINE\System: The System Information Manager

The `HKEY_LOCAL_MACHINE\System` subkey is used to hold startup information used by Windows when booting. This subkey contains all the data that is stored and not recomputed at boot time.

The `HKEY_LOCAL_MACHINE\System` key (a.k.a. the `System` key) is organized into control sets (such as `ControlSet001`, `ControlSet002`, and `CurrentControlSet`) containing parameters for devices and services.

(The key Clone, present in prior versions of Windows NT, is not found in Windows 2000 and Windows XP.)

The main control sets are:

ControlSet001: The current and the default control set used to boot Windows normally. Mapped to CurrentControlSet at boot time, ControlSet001 is the most critical component in the Registry in the normal boot-up process.

ControlSet002: A backup control set from the Last Known Good boot that is used to boot from when the default control set (ControlSet001) fails or is unusable for some reason.

ControlSet003: ControlSet003 (and ControlSet00*n*, where *n* is greater than 3) is a backup control set from the Last Known Good boot that may be used to boot from when the default control set (ControlSet001) fails or is unusable for some reason.

CurrentControlSet: The CurrentControlSet is the control set Windows 2000 has booted from. It is usually mapped to ControlSet001.

NOTE

The Clone control set found in NT 4 is the volatile copy of the control set (usually ControlSet001) that was used to boot the system. Created by the system kernel during initialization, this key is not accessible from the Registry editor.

There are several other items in the HKEY_LOCAL_MACHINE\System key:

MountedDevices: Contains items for each locally attached storage device that is available to the system.

Select: Contains four subkeys. It also has information on which control set was booted and which subkey is the Last Known Good set. Also, if there is a "failed" control set, the failed control set's identity will be found in the Select subkey.

Setup: Contains information used by Setup to configure Windows. This information includes locations of drives and directories, the setup command line, and a flag telling if setup is currently in progress.

The HKEY_LOCAL_MACHINE\System key is critical to both the boot process and to the operation of the system. Microsoft has created a number of tools and processes that help protect the HKEY_LOCAL_MACHINE\System key information. These include the Last Known Good boot process, which allows mapping in a known (or so we hope) copy of the control set, which in turn allows the system to boot if the original control set is too damaged to be booted.

WARNING

Do not, I repeat, *do not*, boot using the Last Known Good control set unless it is necessary! Any changes made to the system during the previous session will be lost, gone, forever and ever!

When modifying the control sets, be aware of the process of booting and creating the control sets. Generally, modifying a backup control set won't affect the system.

WHEN IS THE CURRENT CONTROL SET THE LAST KNOWN GOOD CONTROL SET?

At some point in the boot process, the current control set will be copied into the Last Known Good control set. In Windows XP, the process of replacing the Last Known Good control set is done after the initial logon is performed. This allows the system to catch any problems related to the logon process.

HKEY_USERS: Settings for Users

Current user configurations are saved in HKEY_USERS. In HKEY_USERS there are three keys. The first key, .DEFAULT, is the default user profile. This profile is used when no user is currently logged on. Once a user logs on, their profile is loaded and stored as the second and third keys found in HKEY_USERS.

The second key, the user profile for the user who is currently logged on, appears as something like this:

```
S-1-5-21-682003330-764733703-1708537768-1003
```

The second key is the key for a specific user's profile. The profile is the user's own profile and is created the first time the user logs onto Windows XP.

The third key looks something like:

```
S-1-5-21-682003330-764733703-1708537768-1003_Classes
```

This key contains information about the various classes registered for the current user.

These last two long, magical Registry keys need some explanation. The number, as a whole, is called a SID (security identifier). There is a lot of information in a SID. For example, the ending one-, two-, three-, or four-digit number is used to identify both the user, and for some users, the type of user.

But it's not just users that Windows tags with SIDs. If you look at the Registry for a fresh installation of Windows XP Professional, you'll see one of these long SIDs—the SID for the identity under which you logged on. But you'll also see a number of shorter SIDs, including `S-1-5-18`, `S-1-5-19`, and `S-1-5-20`—plus `CLASSES` entries as appropriate (for example, `S-1-5-19_CLASSES`). These SIDs are for system services. For example, the SID `S-1-5-18` is used by the Local System service.

So far, so good. But because SIDs are used not only in all versions of Windows XP (Home and Professional, at this writing) but in all versions of Windows 2000 (Professional, Server, Advanced Server, and Datacenter Server), and because they're used for different categories of groups, users, and services, there are a lot of different ones. The following tables detail those you're likely to run into if you're using a Windows XP Professional system connected to a Windows 2000 Server system.

Table 28.1 lists a number of general user types that might be assigned. In these chapters, the most commonly seen value is 500, which is assigned to me, the system administrator account.

TABLE 28.1: Common SID Values

User Group	SID
DOMAINNAME\ADMINISTRATOR	S-1-5-21-*xxxxxxxxx-xxxxxxxxxx-xxxxxxxxxx*-500
DOMAINNAME\GUEST	S-1-5-21-*xxxxxxxxx-xxxxxxxxxx-xxxxxxxxxx*-501
DOMAINNAME\DOMAIN ADMINS	S-1-5-21-*xxxxxxxxx-xxxxxxxxxx-xxxxxxxxxx*-512
DOMAINNAME\DOMAIN USERS	S-1-5-21-*xxxxxxxxx-xxxxxxxxxx-xxxxxxxxxx*-513
DOMAINNAME\DOMAIN GUESTS	S-1-5-21-*xxxxxxxxx-xxxxxxxxxx-xxxxxxxxxx*-514

General users might be assigned SIDs ending in four-digit numbers starting at 1000. My domain has a user called Pixel, whose SID ends in 1003, and another user, Long, whose SID ends in 1006. Get the picture?

There are also a number of built-in and special groups of SIDs, as shown in Tables 28.2 and 28.3.

TABLE 28.2: The Built-in Local Groups

Built-in Local Groups	SID
BUILTIN\ADMINISTRATORS	S-1-2-32-*xxxxxxxxx-xxxxxxxxxx-xxxxxxxxxx*-544
BUILTIN\USERS	S-1-2-32-*xxxxxxxxx-xxxxxxxxxx-xxxxxxxxxx*-545
BUILTIN\GUESTS	S-1-2-32-*xxxxxxxxx-xxxxxxxxxx-xxxxxxxxxx*-546
BUILTIN\POWER USERS	S-1-2-32-*xxxxxxxxx-xxxxxxxxxx-xxxxxxxxxx*-547
BUILTIN\ACCOUNT OPERATORS	S-1-2-32-*xxxxxxxxx-xxxxxxxxxx-xxxxxxxxxx*-548
BUILTIN\SERVER OPERATORS	S-1-2-32-*xxxxxxxxx-xxxxxxxxxx-xxxxxxxxxx*-549
BUILTIN\PRINT OPERATORS	S-1-2-32-*xxxxxxxxx-xxxxxxxxxx-xxxxxxxxxx*-550
BUILTIN\BACKUP OPERATORS	S-1-2-32-*xxxxxxxxx-xxxxxxxxxx-xxxxxxxxxx*-551
BUILTIN\REPLICATOR	S-1-2-32-*xxxxxxxxx-xxxxxxxxxx-xxxxxxxxxx*-552

TABLE 28.3: The Special Groups

SPECIAL GROUPS	SID
\CREATOR OWNER	S-1-1-0*x-xxxxxxxx-xxxxxxxxx-xxxxxxxxx-xxx*
\EVERYONE	S-1-1-0*x-xxxxxxxx-xxxxxxxxx-xxxxxxxxx-xxx*
NT AUTHORITY\NETWORK	S-1-1-2*x-xxxxxxxx-xxxxxxxxx-xxxxxxxxx-xxx*
NT AUTHORITY\INTERACTIVE	S-1-1-4*x-xxxxxxxx-xxxxxxxxx-xxxxxxxxx-xxx*
NT AUTHORITY\SYSTEM	S-1-1-18-*xxxxxxxx-xxxxxxxxx-xxxxxxxxx-xxx*

Naturally, there are many more SID codes and definitions. Tables 28.1–28.3 simply show a few of the more commonly used SIDs.

NOTE

Remember to differentiate between the HKEY_USERS hive and the HKEY_CURRENT_USER hive. HKEY_CURRENT_USER contains a pointer that references the current user in HKEY_USERS.

The content of a user's profile, as it is found in the HKEY_USERS hive, is interesting. For example, the following keys are present in a typical user's profile (usually, there is nothing to guarantee that they will all be present, or that others might not be added):

`AppEvents`: Contains information about events (an event is an action like closing, minimizing, restoring, or maximizing) in a key called `EventLabels`. This information includes a text label for the event, such as the label "Close program" for the event close. These labels are used for a number of purposes, but one that most of us see is in the Control Panel's Sounds and Audio Devices applet. A second section in `AppEvents` is `Schemes`, which lists labels for each application that uses specific sounds for its own events.

`Console`: Contains the default command-prompt configuration. You can customize this configuration for each command prompt individually; you can also change the global default, which is then used for all new command prompts. For an example of command-prompt customization, open a command window and select Properties from the System menu. The Registry offers more configuration settings than the Properties dialog box.

`Control Panel`: Contains information saved by many of the Control Panel's applets. Typically, these are default, or standard, values that are saved here, not user settings, which are stored elsewhere.

`Environment`: Contains the user environment variables for a user. Generally, you set user and system environment values in the Environment Variables dialog box (choose Start, right-click My Computer to open the System Properties dialog box, click the Advanced tab, and then click the Environment Variables button).

`EUDC`: Contains the definitions and other information about end user defined characters (EUDC). The program `eudcedit.exe` lets users edit/design characters that are specific to their needs. If you haven't used end user–defined characters, you won't see this key.

`Identities`: Contains the information to link users and software configurations. Most configurations are Microsoft based, such as Outlook Express.

`Keyboard Layout`: Contains the keyboard configuration. Most users, at least those in the United States., will have few or no substitutions. However, users who are using special keyboards or non–U.S. English keyboards will have some substitutions for special characters found in their languages.

`Network`: Contains mappings for each network drive connected to the computer. Information about the connections includes the host (server), remote path, and username used for the connection. The `Network` key is not typically found in the `.DEFAULT` key because users with no user profile are not automatically connected to a remote drive.

`Printers`: Contains mappings for each remote (network) printer connected to the computer. Information about the printer connection includes the host (server) and the DLL file used to manage the connection. The `Printers` key is typically not found in the `.DEFAULT` key because users with no user profile are not automatically connected to a remote printer.

RemoteAccess: Contains the various remote access configurations. The connections are managed using the Control Panel's Network Connections applet.

SessionInformation: Contains information about the current user session, including the number of programs the user is running. The SessionInformation key is found only for "live" users; it is not found in the .DEFAULT key or for system services.

Software: Contains information about software installed, including components such as Schedule, Notepad, and so on. Also included in Software is Windows itself, with configuration information specific to the currently logged-on user.

SYSTEM: Contains information about items such as backup configurations and files that are not to be backed up.

UNICODE Program Groups: Contains information about program groups that use Unicode. More commonly found on computers configured for languages other than English, Unicode is the scheme for displaying characters from both English and non-English alphabets on computers.

Volatile Environment: Contains information about the logon server that will be placed in the environment. One typical item is the LOGONSERVER environment variable. All items in Volatile Environment are dynamic; that is, they are created each time a user logs on. Other dynamic environment information might be contained in this key as well.

HKEY_CURRENT_CONFIG: The Current Configuration Settings

The Registry hive HKEY_CURRENT_CONFIG is created from two Registry keys, HKEY_LOCAL_MACHINE\System and HKEY_LOCAL_MACHINE\Software. As it is created dynamically, there is little value in modifying any of the objects found in the HKEY_CURRENT_CONFIG hive.

The HKEY_CURRENT_CONFIG hive is composed of two major subkeys:

Software: Contains current configurations for some software components. A typical configuration might have keys under Software for the current version of Windows, for example.

System: Contains information about hardware. The most common device found in this key is the video display adapter (found in virtually all configurations) and sometimes information about the default video modes as well. The video mode settings contained here are typical for any video system: resolution, panning, refresh rates (didn't you wonder where refresh rates were saved?), and BitsPerPel (color depth).

Generally, you would modify the source settings for a hardware device in HKEY_LOCAL_MACHINE\System\ControlSet001\Hardware Profiles\Current\System\CurrentControlSet\Services\<device>\Device0, where <device> is the device being modified. For example, my Matrox Millennium is listed under the device name MGA64.

TIP

For more information about the source for HKEY_CURRENT_CONFIG, take a look at HKEY_LOCAL_MACHINE, described earlier in this chapter.

HKEY_PERFORMANCE_DATA: The Performance Monitor Settings

Ever wonder where the Windows 2000 and Windows XP Performance Monitor information is contained? Since Windows 9*x* uses HKEY_DYN_DATA to store performance data, and Windows 2000 and Windows XP do not, the performance data must be somewhere. There is a final "hidden" Registry hive, named HKEY_PERFORMANCE_DATA. This hive, which is simply not accessible except to applications written specifically to access performance data, is primarily dynamic in nature. To find the answer to this question, check out Chapter 11 of *Mastering Windows 2000 Registry*, "The Performance Monitor Meets the Registry."

NTUSER: The New User Profile

Windows XP's installation process will create a default user profile and configuration. This information is located in `%systemdrive%\Documents and Settings\Default User`. Whenever a new user logs onto a workstation or domain, this default user profile is copied to the user's profile. After that, the user modifies their profile to their own requirements and needs.

As an example, Windows XP's default language is typically U.S. English. (There are other language editions of Windows XP; for this example, I'm assuming the U.S. English version.) Whenever a new user logs on, the user will have U.S. English as his or her language, even if the system administrator has selected a different, non-English locale.

The default user profile is saved in the disk directory at `\Documents and Settings\Default User`. In Windows NT 4, the default user information was stored in `%systemroot%\Profiles\Default User`. User information is always saved in a file named `NTUSER.DAT`. There is an entire configuration for new users in this directory—check out the Start menu, Desktop, and other directories, too. You will find that interesting modifications can be made that enable new users to become proficient quickly without spending too much time customizing their computers.

WARNING

This technique is an advanced use of the Registry editor and you must exercise care not to inadvertently modify the wrong Registry or the wrong keys. Back up the Registry *before* doing the following.

This technique works on Windows XP Professional for local accounts. If you have a Windows 2000 Server or Windows NT 4 Server, you can use a similar technique with a couple of twists:

- First, to make this new user profile accessible to remote users, (that is, all users other than those who log on locally) you must copy the `Default User` directory to the share named Netlogon. This share is typically located in the directory at `%systemroot%\sysvol\sysvol\`, in a directory that is named for the server. (For Windows NT 4 users, look in `%systemroot%\system32\Repl\Import`.) One way to copy these files is to create a new custom profile and copy the new custom profile using the User Profiles tab in the Control Panel's System applet.

- Second, if there are BDCs (Backup Domain Controllers), you would actually edit the file in the `Export` directory (same initial path) because this directory is locally replicated to the Import directory and to the other BDC `Import` directories, although it might be located elsewhere. The NetLogon share can be located quickly by typing

  `net share`

  at a command prompt. The computer's shares will be displayed.

Follow these steps to modify the default new user profile in your new `Default User` directory (remember to create a new `Default User` directory, saving the current `Default User` directory as a backup):

1. Start Registry Editor as usual.
   - In Windows 2000 Server or Windows NT Server, you need to use RegEdt32 rather than RegEdit for this process, as RegEdit is unable to load the `NTUSER.DAT` file.
2. Select the HKEY_USERS hive by clicking it in the left pane of Registry Editor.
   - In Windows 2000 Server or Windows NT Server, click the title bar of the HKEY_USERS on Local Machine window to make the window active.
3. Choose File ➢ Load Hive. Windows displays the Load Hive dialog box, which is a common Open dialog box by another name.
   - In Windows 2000 Server or Windows NT Server, choose Registry ➢ Load Hive from the RegEdt32 menu.
4. Open the hive named `NTUSER.DAT` found in `%systemdrive%\Documents and Settings\Default User` (on Windows XP Professional) or `%systemroot%\Profiles\Default User` (on Windows 2000 Server or Windows NT Server).
5. Registry Editor or RegEdt32 will prompt for a new key name. Use the name **NTUSER**.

6. Change whatever keys in NTUSER need to be modified. There will be a slew of changeable items in the new profile, including AppEvents, Console, Control Panel, Environment, Keyboard Layout, Software, and Unicode Program Groups. When adding new keys, do be careful to ensure that all users have at least read access to the new keys. No read access means that the key won't be accessible to the user.

TIP

To set the permissions for a key, select the key, and then select Edit ➢ Permissions in Registry Editor or Security ➢ Permissions in RegEdt32. Ensure that the group Everyone has at least read access. Resist the urge to give everyone more than read access to this key, too. Too much power can be a dangerous thing!

7. After making all modifications to NTUSER, choose File ➢ Unload Hive (in Registry Editor) or Registry ➢ Unload Hive (in RegEdt32).
8. Exit Registry Editor or RegEdt32.
9. In Windows 2000 Server or Windows NT Server, save this profile in the NetLogon share location.

New users will then get this new profile each time they log on.

Hints and Kinks from the Experts

Another installment of good stuff from the Windows gurus. In your search for more information, frequent their sites on the Internet (see Appendix C, "Where Can I Get More Help?" of *Mastering Windows 2000 Registry*).

How Can I Tell What Changes Are Made to the Registry?

Using Registry Editor, you can export portions of the Registry. This feature can be used as follows:

1. Start Registry Editor.

2. Select the key you want to monitor.
3. Select File ➢ Export. Registry Editor displays the Export Registry File dialog box.
4. In the Export Range section, select whether you want to export the whole of the Registry (the All option button) or the selected hive (the Selected Branch option button).
5. Enter a filename and click the OK button.
6. Perform the change (install some software or change a system parameter).
7. Perform steps 1 through 4 again using a different filename.
8. Run the two files through a comparison utility such as `windiff.exe`.
9. If you are using WinDiff, select File ➢ Compare Files, and you will be prompted to select the two files to compare.
10. Once the files are compared, a summary will be displayed stating whether there are any differences. To view the changes, double-click the message.
11. Press F8, or select View ➢ Next Change, to view the next change.

You have now found what changed.

(Courtesy of John Savill.)

WHAT'S NEXT?

Although you've already used Registry Editor in this chapter, the next chapter will take a more detailed look at this powerful tool and show you how to use it efficiently when you are working with the Registry. The next chapter will also give you some special tips for working with the Registry.

Chapter 29

Registry Tools and Tips: Getting the Work Done

There are a number of excellent Registry tools for users of Windows XP. First, Windows XP provides a serviceable Registry editor. This Registry editor calls itself Registry Editor, lives in an executable file named `regedit.exe`, and combines most of the best features of the two Registry editors included with Windows 2000. (Why did we need two Registry editors for Windows 2000? Well, each had its advantages and disadvantages. RegEdit was the Registry editor created for Windows 95, and RegEdt32 was the "native" Windows 2000 Registry editor. RegEdit offered a few functions that RegEdt32 didn't, such as importing and exporting Registry files and pretty good search capabilities; similarly, RegEdt32 offered features that RegEdit didn't, such as a multiple-document interface that displayed each of the main hives in the Registry in its own window, read-only mode, and security-configuration options.)

Revised and adapted from *Mastering Windows 2000 Registry* by Peter D. Hipson

ISBN 0-7821-2615-4 752 pages $39.99

If you're working with Windows 2000, both of these Registry editors are valuable. I use either one depending on what I am doing, and my mood. I find RegEdit easier to use, while RegEdt32's got much more power. Not included with Windows 2000, the Windows 2000 Resource Kit offers a number of excellent tools, too. The Registry tool, REG, is run at the command prompt. REG allows flexible manipulation of the Registry, replacing earlier versions of a number of the other Resource Kit components.

If you are still using older Resource Kit components in legacy support systems, there is no urgent need to change or migrate to the newer tools that are contained in the Windows 2000 Resource Kit. However, it is not recommended that the older utilities be used when updating support facilities, but that the new tools be integrated wherever possible.

Many of the Resource Kit utilities are command-prompt driven. However, being experienced users, we are not afraid of a command prompt, are we?

TIP

Found a program you don't know about? When in doubt, enter a command with either no options or a /? option, and the command should display some form of help. Not all commands display significant help, and some do not provide any help at all. However, the Resource Kit utilities won't cause damage if this help convention is used.

REGISTRY CHANGES ARE PERMANENT!

Before we get started, here's a quick warning: All changes made with the Registry Editor are immediate and, for all intents, permanent! Though you can go back and manually undo a change made with the Registry Editor, everything that you change with the Registry Editor affects the current Registry. Unlike RegEdt32 in Windows 2000, the Registry Editor in Windows XP does not have a read-only mode. There is no safety net, nothing to catch your bloopers, and generally you'll have to clean up your own mess.

In other words, you are editing the real, working, live, honest-to-goodness Registry—not a copy. There is no Save command in the Registry Editor; you type in a change, and it is saved right then and there.

So, make sure you have a backup of the Registry files before diddling with the Registry.

USING THE REGISTRY EDITOR

Using the Registry Editor is as simple as starting it. From a command prompt, typing **`regedit`** and pressing Enter will start the program. You can also select Start ➢ Run, type in **`regedit`**, and click the OK button to start the Registry Editor. If you plan to run the Registry Editor frequently, consider creating a shortcut to it on the Start menu or on your Desktop.

Once started, the Registry Editor will display the current Registry (see Figure 29.1). By default, the Registry Editor opens the local Registry. However, it is possible to open a Registry on a remote computer by selecting File ➢ Connect Network Registry and entering the name of the computer whose Registry is to be opened.

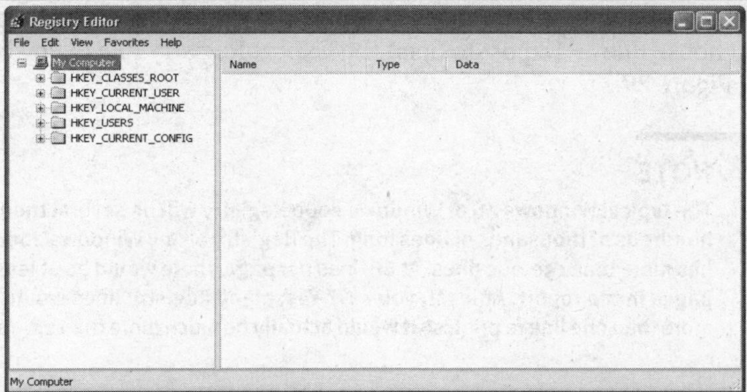

FIGURE 29.1: The Registry Editor opens the current, local Registry automatically.

The Registry Editor has a straightforward set of menus. The File menu allows you to import and export Registry files, save and load text-based `.reg` (Registry) files, connect to and disconnect from a network Registry, and print the current branch or the entire Registry.

RegEdit in Windows 2000 included two improvements that Microsoft has carried through to the Registry Editor in Windows XP. First, there's a new column in the right-hand display of values and data that lists each value's type. Although the Registry Editor will display the names of all the data types available to Windows XP, you are still restricted to editing string, binary, and DWORD data types. Second, the Favorites menu lets you place subkeys into a list of favorites. This gives you the ability to navigate quickly to a subkey.

The Edit menu allows you to create a new key or value entry in the string, binary, DWORD, multi-string, and expandable string data types. If you need to create any other Registry data type, you'll have to use a different program. The Edit menu also allows you to delete an object, change permissions on an object, rename a key or subkey, or copy the name of the currently selected key. At the bottom of the Edit menu are Find and Find Next options.

Importing and Exporting Registry Hives and Keys

The ability to export a Registry hive or key (or the entire Registry, if necessary) is a powerful feature of the Registry Editor. Once a Registry is open, select a hive or key (or My Computer to export the entire Registry) and choose File ➢ Export to open the Export Registry File dialog box (see Figure 29.2).

NOTE

The typical Windows XP or Windows 2000 Registry will be several thousand to hundreds of thousands of lines long. The Registry on my Windows 2000 server has more than 130,000 lines. At 66 lines per page, there would be at least 2,000 pages in the report. At least, you say? Yes, many Registry lines would require more than one line to print, so it would actually be much more than 2,000 pages.

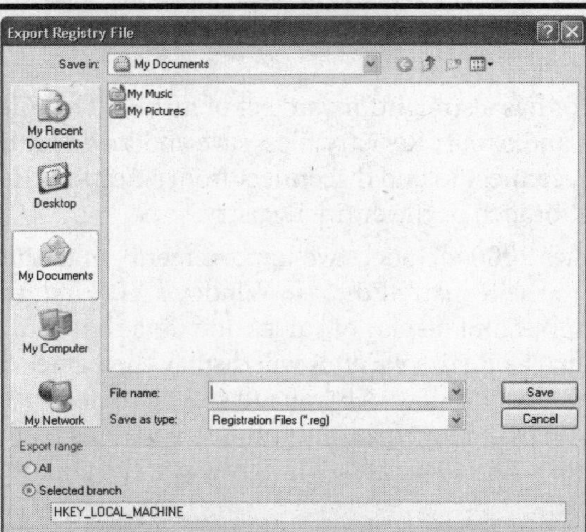

FIGURE 29.2: Exporting the currently selected hive or key is easy!

A hive is exported into a Unicode text-based file. This file has no comments; some of the Resource Kit Registry tools do comment exported sections of the Registry. However, the file may be opened with most any text editor (such as Notepad), searched, and even (carefully) modified. Any changes made to the exported text file may be incorporated into the Registry by simply importing the modified file.

Importing a file that the Registry Editor had previously exported is as simple as selecting File ➢ Import and specifying the name of the Registry file to import.

WHAT IS AN EXPORTED REGISTRY FILE?

A Registry file exported by the Registry Editor will start with a line that reads "Windows Registry Editor Version 5.00." The line following will be the first hive exported in a hierarchical format:

```
Windows Registry Editor Version 5.00
[HKEY_LOCAL_MACHINE]
[HKEY_LOCAL_MACHINE\HARDWARE]
[HKEY_LOCAL_MACHINE\HARDWARE\ACPI]
```

Generally, a full export of a Registry will start with an export of the HKEY_LOCAL_MACHINE hive, as the above example shows.

The contents of an exported Registry are arranged in the file as a hive and key combination (fully qualified, enclosed in brackets), with the data value name in quotes and the value following the equal sign:

```
[HKEY_LOCAL_MACHINE\HARDWARE\DESCRIPTION\System\Floa
tingPointProcessor\0]
"Component
Information"=hex:00,00,00,00,00,00,00,00,00,00,00,00
,01,00,00,00
"Identifier"="x86 Family 6 Model 8 Stepping 3"
"Configuration
Data"=hex(9):ff,ff,ff,ff,ff,ff,ff,ff,00,00,00,00,00,
00,00,00
```

This example shows the three value entries that FloatingPoint-Processor contains.

Why export the Registry? First, while the search capability in the Registry Editor is reasonably powerful, it's far from optimal. (Well, that's my opinion!) Loading an exported Registry file into an editor allows you to quickly search for strings using the editor's search capability.

Another benefit is that it is easy to export the Registry before installing an application or system extension. After an installation, it is also a good idea to export the Registry. Then, using one of the system comparison tools (such as FC or WinDiff), you can compare the two versions of the Registry and see what the installation has changed. Bingo—a quick way to see what's happening to the Registry on installations.

Loading and Unloading

The Registry Editor lets you load a subkey into the current Registry. You can modify this subkey and then unload it. But why would you want to do this?

There are several reasons for loading and unloading keys into the Registry Editor. A classic example is given in Chapter 28. This example, configuring a modified new user profile, concerns the file `NTUSER.DAT`. In `NTUSER.DAT` is the `HKEY_CURRENT_USER` hive. Within this hive are settings, such as internationalization, colors, schemes, and other items. Windows 2000's or Windows XP's installation process will create a default user profile—nothing spectacular, a very plain configuration. Whenever a new user logs on to a workstation (or domain), this default user profile will be copied to the user's profile. After that, the user may modify this default profile to his or her requirements and needs. Of course, you might want to establish some organizational defaults, such as a company scheme.

WARNING

The techniques shown next are an advanced use of the Registry Editor. Back up the Registry *before* doing the following.

The default user profile is saved in the following disk directory:

- For new Windows 2000 and Windows XP installations: *`%systemdrive%`*`\Documents and Settings\Default User` (this directory may have the hidden attribute set, so that it is not displayed when using either Explorer or a command session)
- For Windows NT 4, and for Windows 2000 and Windows XP installations that are upgraded from Windows NT 4: *`%systemroot%`*`\Profiles\Default User\`

The name of the user profile is NTUSER.DAT. There is an entire configuration for new users in the directory *%systemdrive%*\Documents and Settings\Default User; check out the Start Menu, Desktop, and other directories, too. You will find that interesting modifications can be made that enable new users to become proficient quickly without spending too much time customizing their computers.

First, if you're working on a server, to make this new user profile accessible to remote users (users other than those who log on locally), you must copy the Default User directory to the share named NetLogon. This share is typically located in the directory at *%systemroot%*\sysvol\sysvol.

Placing files in Export will cause replication to copy them locally to Import, along with any BDCs (Backup Domain Controllers). Note that the share might be located elsewhere. The NetLogon share can be located quickly by typing the following command at a command prompt:

```
net share
```

The computer's shares will be displayed.

One process to copy these files is to create a new custom profile, and then copy the new custom profile using the System applet's User Profiles tab.

WARNING

If you are even slightly smart, you'll make a backup copy of the NTUSER.DAT file *before* you make any changes in it!

As I mentioned in the previous chapter, do the following to modify the default new user profile. (Remember to create a new Default User directory, saving the current Default User directory as a backup.)

1. Start the Registry Editor using either a command prompt or by selecting Start ➢ Run.
2. Click the HKEY_USERS key to make it active.
3. Choose File ➢ Load Hive.
4. Open the hive file in *%systemdrive%*\Documents and Settings\Default User. (If your system is configured, or installed, with different directory names, choose the correct name.) This hive has a filename of NTUSER.DAT.

5. The Registry Editor will display the Load Hive dialog box to prompt for a new Key Name. Use the name NTUSER.

6. Change whatever keys in NTUSER need to be modified. There will be a slew of changeable items in the new profile, including `AppEvents`, `Console`, `Control Panel`, `Environment`, `Keyboard Layout`, `Software`, and `Unicode Program Groups`. When adding new keys, do be careful to ensure that all users have at least read access to the new keys. No read access means that the key won't be accessible to the person named "user."

TIP

To set the permissions for a key, select the key, and then choose Edit ➢ Permissions. Ensure that the Everyone group has at least read access. Resist the urge to give everyone more than read access to this key. Too much power can be a dangerous thing!

7. After making all modifications to NTUSER, select the NTUSER key and choose File ➢ Unload Hive. Unloading the hive overwrites the existing file `NTUSER.DAT`. (You did back up the original file, right?)

8. Exit the Registry Editor.

Now each time a new user logs on to this computer, the user will get this new profile. If you're working on a server, save the profile to the Netlogon share location. Thereafter, each time a new user logs on to the network, the user will get this new profile.

CAN'T FIND THE LOCATION FOR THE NTUSER.DAT FILE?

Remember that the `NTUSER.DAT` file will have the hidden attribute, so it will not normally be displayed in either a command window or in Explorer. Either tell Explorer to display hidden files or, at a command prompt, use the `dir` command with the /ah option to display hidden files and directories.

Worse comes to worst, open a command window (tough to do this in Explorer) and, in the root of the system drive, use the command:

```
DIR /ah /s ntuser.dat
```

CONTINUED ⟶

This command will list all copies of the NTUSER.DAT file, allowing you to change the appropriate one. One thought, though: don't change the "current user" NTUSER.DAT file—it won't work! Windows will rewrite the file when the user next logs off, causing any changes you made to disappear!

Connecting to and Disconnecting from Remote Registries

When the Registry Editor starts, it opens the local Registry automatically. But once you've started the Registry Editor, you can open the Registry on a remote computer (see Figure 29.3). Actually, you can connect to many remote registries at one time. With a remote Registry connected, you may not close, or disconnect, the local Registry. This leaves it up to the user to make sure that if changes are made, they are made in the correct Registry.

NOTE

The computer with the remote Registry must be on the network, and both computers must be running the Remote Registry service. (This service is started by default in Windows XP Professional.)

Hopefully, this will make remote Registry maintenance somewhat easier. Some functionality doesn't span multiple registries (such as searching), but generally everything that may be performed on a local Registry may be also performed on a remote Registry.

TIP

Once finished with a remote Registry, it is a very good idea to disconnect from it. This may help prevent unexpected modifications to the wrong Registry.

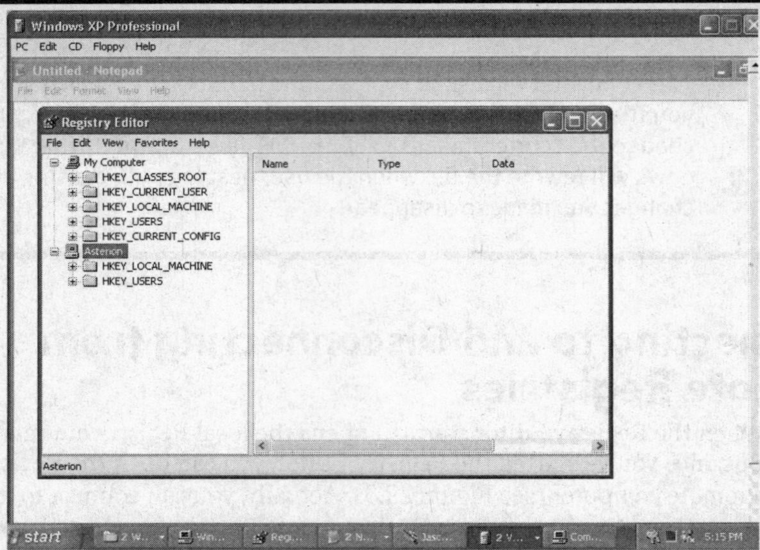

FIGURE 29.3: A remote Registry and the local one open at the same time in the Registry Editor

Printing the Registry

The Registry Editor lets you print a Registry hive or key. As mentioned previously, printing an entire Registry is not a swell idea—you'd have to make a major investment in paper and printer supplies. Typically, a Registry would require thousands of pages to print.

Printing sections of a Registry hive can be very useful if a paper record is needed or if you need something to take to a meeting. The limit of a printed Registry hive or key is that searching it might be difficult.

Printing is easy: select the hive or subkey you want to print, and then select File ➢ Print from the Registry Editor's main menu. The Print dialog box, shown in Figure 29.4, allows you to edit the branch to be printed (with the currently selected object as the default). The results of printing a Registry report are almost identical to exporting, with the exception that a printed report lacks the initial header line that's found in an exported Registry file.

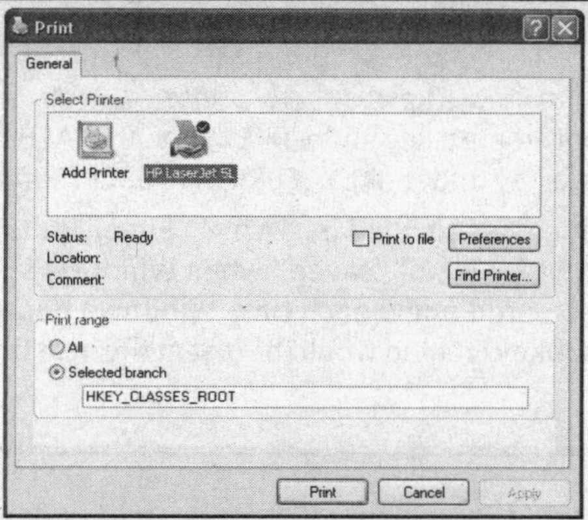

FIGURE 29.4: The Registry Editor's Print dialog box ready to print the hive HKEY_CLASSES_ROOT

TIP

Is it very readable? Generally not. The Registry Editor's print facility is basic and simply wraps lines at 80 characters. Any line more than 80 characters long will wrap and be difficult to read. A better solution is to export the Registry to a file, load the file into a word processor, format it so that it is readable, and print it from the word processor.

Creating, Deleting, and Renaming Entries

The Registry Editor allows you to quickly create, delete, or rename an entry. Entries may consist of keys, subkeys, or value entries.

Creating a New Key

You can quickly create a new key by following these steps:

1. Select the hive or key in which the new key is to be created.

WHY CAN'T I CREATE A KEY HERE?

Not all hives allow you to create keys directly under the hive itself. For example, you cannot create a key under HKEY_LOCAL_MACHINE, though you can create a key under HKEY_CURRENT_USER.

The first question that comes to mind is, "Why?" Simply put, the HKEY_LOCAL_MACHINE hive is not "saved" when Windows shuts down. Rather it is re-created anew each time Windows boots—therefore, any key or subkey created would be lost at the next boot-up time.

2. Select Edit ➢ New ➢ Key or right-click in the right pane and choose New ➢ Key from the shortcut menu.
3. The Registry Editor will create the new subkey, giving it a default name of New Key #*n* where *n* is a number beginning with 1. You will have the opportunity to edit the new subkey's name, which you should do at this time. Give the subkey a meaningful name or the name that is expected for this subkey.

Once the new subkey has been created, it may then be populated with additional subkeys and value entries.

NOTE

A hive, key, or subkey may contain both value entries and other subkeys at the same time.

Creating a Value Entry

You can quickly create a new value entry by following these steps:

1. Select the hive or key in which the new value entry is to be created.
2. Select Edit ➢ New and then choose String Value, Binary Value, DWORD Value, Multi-String Value, or Expandable String Value, depending on the type of data that this value entry will have. You should select the data type for your key.

3. The Registry Editor will create the new value entry, giving it a default name of `New Value #n` where *n* is a number beginning with 1. You will have the opportunity to edit the new value entry's name, which you should do at this time. Give it a meaningful name or the name that is expected for it. Press the Enter key to save the new name.

TIP

At any point, you may rename a key or value entry by right-clicking the item to be renamed and selecting Rename from the shortcut menu.

4. To enter data into the new entry, double-click the entry. The correct edit box will be displayed, allowing you to edit the data.

Once the new value entry has been created, its data may be entered as necessary.

NOTE

A key need not have a data value entered. A key is valid without any data, though no-data defaults vary depending on the type of data the key contains: String values (including multi-string values and expandable string values) have a zero-length string as their default. Binary values have a zero-length binary value (which is different from having a value of zero). DWORD values have a value of zero.

Figure 29.5 shows the Registry Editor with a new subkey containing another subkey, a string value, a binary value, a DWORD value, a multi-string value, and an expandable string value. Note that I've named the initial subkey `Test Key`.

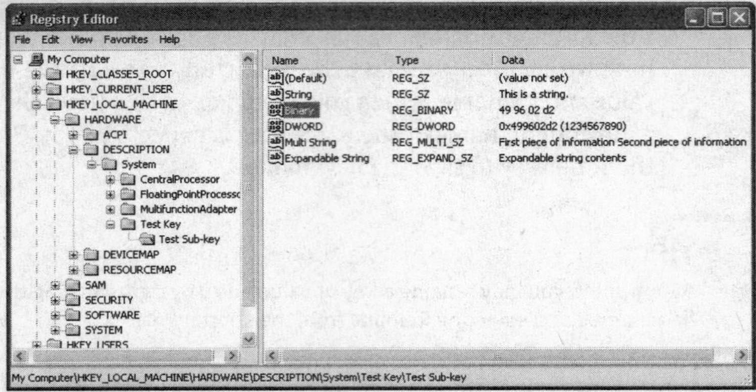

FIGURE 29.5: The Registry Editor after creating the subkey called `Test Key` and a further subkey called `Test Sub-key`

In the example, each of the new value entries were given names to match the type of data stored in them. Each one can be edited at any time. Selecting the key or value entry and choosing Edit ➢ Rename allows you to change the name; selecting the value entry and choosing Edit ➢ Modify allows you to change the value entry's contents. You may also double-click the value entry or right-click (also known as a *context-click*) on the item and choose Modify to change the value.

NOTE

Around this point, you may be wondering how you can create a data value with a data type not supported by the Registry Editor. Here's how: Create a `.reg` file (export the subject key) and edit the `.reg` file with any compatible text editor. Entries may be created in the format: `"entry name"=hex(n):hh hh ...`, where *`entry name`* is the name for the data value, *n* is a number corresponding to the type desired, and *hh* is one or more pairs of hex data. Data types are described in Appendix B of *Mastering Windows 2000 Registry*.

Copying Key Names

Is this as simple as it seems? A long, convoluted name without having to type it? Yes, it is!

Copy Key Names, found in the Registry Editor's Edit menu (and from the key's shortcut menu if you right-click the key and select Copy Key Name), will copy the key's name to the Clipboard. The information is copied in text format and may then be pasted into other applications or word processors as needed. For example, when the new subkey created for Figure 29.5 is copied, the following text will be placed into the Clipboard:

```
HKEY_LOCAL_MACHINE\Hardware\Description\System\Test Key\Test
Sub-key
```

This means it is not necessary to manually type in long Registry keys into other applications and documents. This feature, for example, was a great help when writing these chapters.

Searching: Find and Find Next

Searching a Registry is one of the most important tasks you'll have to undertake. Before you make a modification, do debugging, or start browsing, it is usually necessary to search for something.

Now, as I've mentioned previously, the Registry Editor's search capabilities are a bit limited. (If it's any consolation, RegEdt32 in Windows 2000 is even more limited in its searching capabilities.)

TIP

The Registry Editor searches downward only. If what you are searching for is located above the current selection, you'll never find it. When in doubt, start at My Computer, and you can be assured that the search will include the entire Registry.

Searching allows you to look at keys, data value names, and data value contents. You may choose to search any or all of these (see Figure 29.6), and the search may also be limited to whole strings only, which applies to searching text strings exclusively.

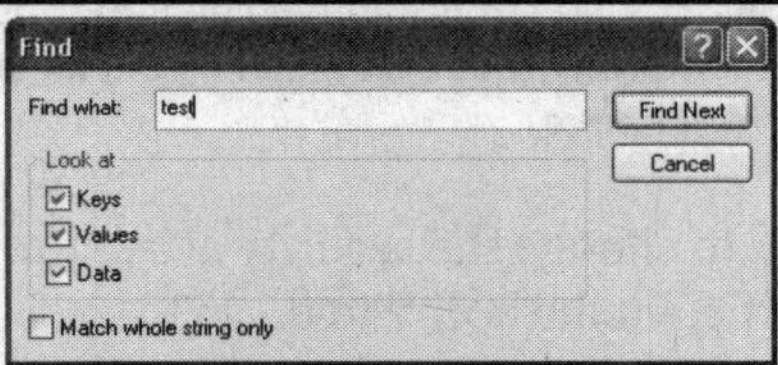

FIGURE 29.6: The Registry Editor searches downward only.

TIP

The Registry Editor's search is not case specific, so strings to be searched for may be entered in lowercase if desired. This is nice, since the case of many Registry entries is rather mixed.

Once the search finds the item searched for, it will stop on the word(s) found and close the Find dialog box. You can search for the next instance of the search item by pressing the F3 key or by choosing Edit ➢ Find Next.

If the search is unable to find the string entered, the Registry Editor will display a message box telling you that it has finished searching through the Registry (see Figure 29.7). Click the OK button to dismiss this message box.

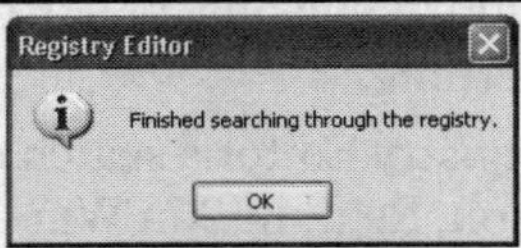

FIGURE 29.7: If the search is unsuccessful, the Registry Editor displays this dialog box.

Security

Security is paramount in a Windows 2000 or Windows XP installation. The Registry, just like the NTFS file system, can be protected from unauthorized access. This can be a critical issue, because Windows 2000 and Windows XP support remote Registry editing.

NOTE

It is possible to make changes in a Registry from another computer without the recipient of these changes even knowing that a change has been made (that is, until they see the results of the change).

The Registry Editor allows you to change the security attributes for a hive and any keys, if you have sufficient authority to do so.

Initially, when you select Edit ➢ Permissions, the Permissions For dialog box is displayed (see Figure 29.8). Basic security is set in this dialog box, while advanced functionality (permissions, auditing, and owner) is set in the Advanced Security Settings dialog box.

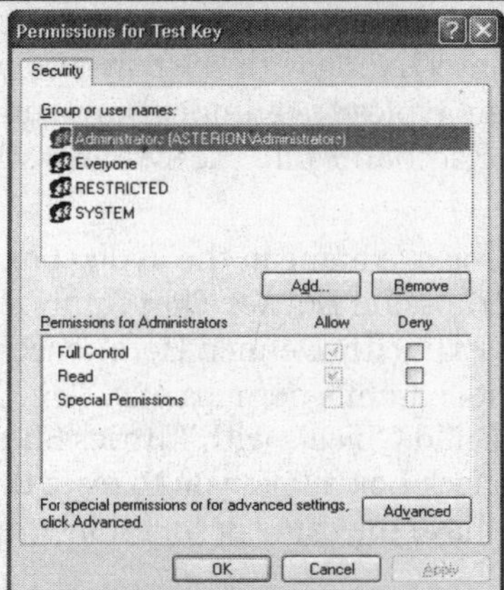

FIGURE 29.8: Setting the permissions for `Test Key` in the Registry Editor

Clicking the Advanced button of the Permissions For dialog box displays the Advanced Security Settings dialog box, shown in Figure 29.9. The Advanced Security Settings dialog box has four tabs: Permissions, Auditing, Owner, and Effective Permissions.

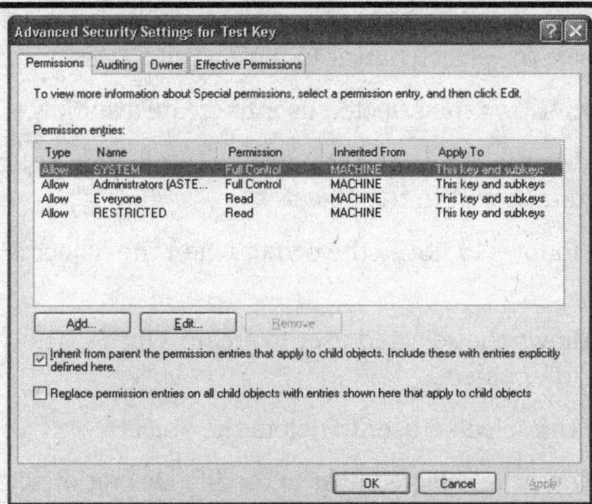

FIGURE 29.9: Specific users and administrative units can have their own permissions.

The Permissions Tab

The currently selected object is displayed along with the current permissions granted. Default permissions are typically, but not always, ones that everyone can read; the Administrator accounts and the system both have full control.

The Permissions tab will list the object's name in the dialog box's title bar. The "Inherit from Parent the Permission Entries That Apply to Child Objects. Include These with Entries Explicitly Defined Here" check box allows the current object to include its parent's permissions. The "Replace Permission Entries on All Child Objects with Entries Shown Here That Apply to Child Objects" check box allows you to reset the permission entries so that child objects have the same permission entries as the current parent object.

You set detailed permissions by clicking the Edit button on the Permissions tab of the Advanced Security Settings dialog box and working in the resulting Permission Entry dialog box (see Figure 29.10). In the list box are the current permissions, organized by name. Select one name (each must be modified separately) and set the type of access. The selections include the following:

Query Value: Allows the selected user to have read access.

Set Value: Allows the selected user to have write access.

Create Subkey: Allows the selected user to create a subkey.

Enumerate Subkeys: Allows the selected user to obtain a list of subkeys contained within the object.

Notify: Tells Windows to notify the owner when the object is modified.

Create Link: Allows the selected user to create a link to the object from another object.

Delete: Allows the selected user to delete the object.

Write DAC: Allows the selected user to modify Discretionary Access Control information.

Write Owner: Allows the selected user to modify the owner record information.

Read Control: Combines the Standard Read, Query Value, Enumerate Subkeys, and Notify Permissions.

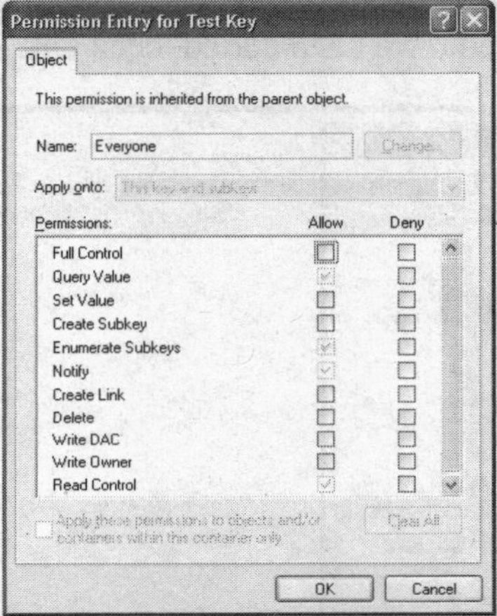

FIGURE 29.10: Permissions are customized on a user-by-user basis in the Permission Entry dialog box.

WARNING

Of course, the standard warnings apply: *Do not grant more permission than is necessary to do the job.* Understand which permissions are being granted (see the above list) and consider granting permissions temporarily, removing anything granted as soon as it is not necessary.

The Auditing Tab

The word *auditing*, when mentioned with the word *government*, generally gets us weak in the knees and starts us sweating profusely. However, auditing Registry interaction can be somewhat less troublesome and very beneficial to the user.

Auditing, like permissions, is based on users. You set up auditing on the Auditing tab of the Advanced Security Settings dialog box (see Figure 29.11). For an object that has not had any auditing set, the list will be blank. The first thing to do is to select the "Inherit from Parent the Permission Entries That Apply to Child Objects. Include These with Entries Explicitly Defined Here" check box. Next, click the Add button and use the Select User or Group dialog box (see Figure 29.12) to add new users to the list. In the Select User or Group dialog box, both groups and individual users can be selected. Select one name in the Name list and click the Add button to add that name to the list of names to be audited. Once all names to be audited have been added, click OK.

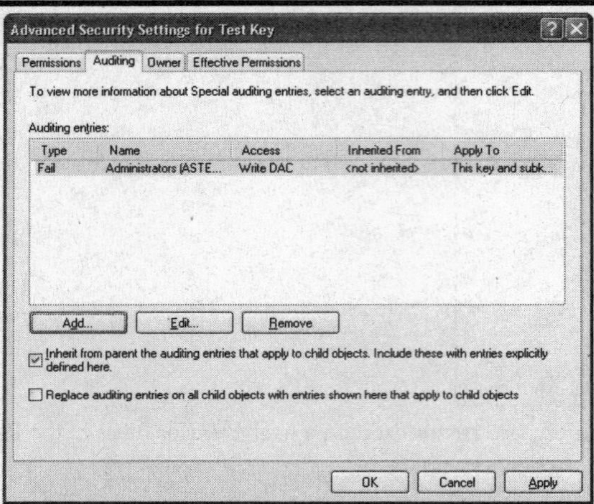

FIGURE 29.11: The Auditing tab of the Advanced Security Settings dialog box, on which you set auditing permissions

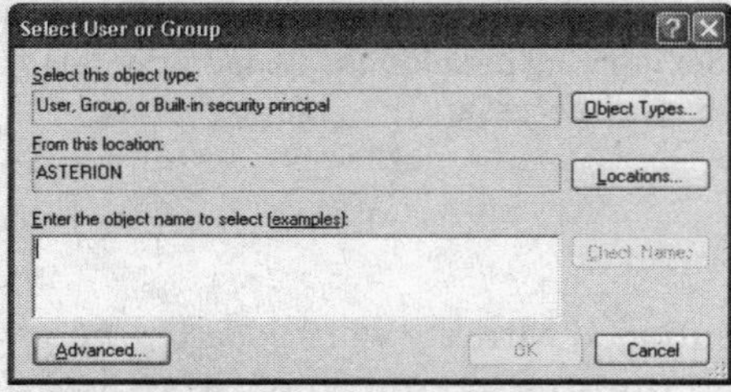

FIGURE 29.12: Add users or administrative units to be audited in the Select User or Group dialog box.

Next, on the Auditing tab, select one of the names in the Auditing Entries list, and click the Edit button. Then set specific permissions in the Auditing Entry dialog box. Events that may be audited include:

Query Value: Audited whenever the user or group in the Name list reads the object.

Set Value: Audited whenever the user or group in the Name list writes to the object.

Create Subkey: Audited whenever the user or group in the Name list creates a key.

Enumerate Subkeys: Audited whenever the user or group in the Name list enumerates a list of keys contained within the object.

Notify: Audited whenever the user or group in the Name list does anything that generates a notification to the owner.

Create Link: Audited whenever the user or group in the Name list creates a link to the object from another object.

Delete: Audited whenever the user or group in the Name list deletes the object.

Write DAC: Audited whenever the user or group in the Name list modifies the Discretionary Access Control information.

Write Owner: Audited whenever the user or group in the Name list modifies the owner record information.

Read Control: Audited whenever the user or group in the Name list does anything that includes the standard Read, Query Value, Enumerate Subkeys, or Notify Permissions.

You can audit successful actions, failed actions, or both by selecting the appropriate check boxes in the Successful column and the Failed column in the Auditing Entry dialog box:

Successful: Whenever an operation succeeds, auditing information is saved. This mode is useful when creating a log of information about changes to the Registry. Auditing successful operations can help you go back and determine which changes were made to the Registry to try to fix the problem.

Failed: Whenever an operation fails, auditing information is saved. Whenever security is an issue (any time there is more than one user), auditing failed operations can help point to attempts to compromise system security.

TIP

Select successful auditing for critical objects that shouldn't be changed often. Select failed auditing for any object that is security related.

The Owner Tab

I own things, you own things. To keep the records straight, there are things like titles for cars, deeds for property, and other documents that trace ownership of anything that is non-trivial. With computers, especially Windows 2000 and Windows XP, ownership is an important thing. I "own" my computer, and I probably don't want you messing with it.

When you're using NTFS on a drive, you can set ownership for files. In addition, objects in the Registry may have ownership. Ownership implies ultimate control: the owner can restrict access, audit, do whatever he or she wants.

The Owner tab of the Access Control Settings dialog box (see Figure 29.13) allows you to take "ownership" of a Registry object.

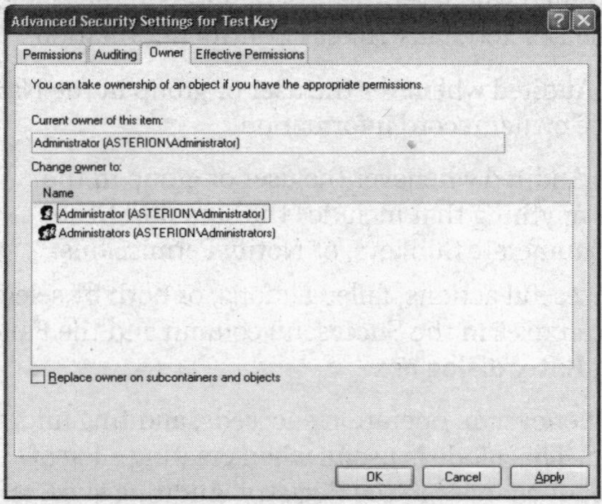

FIGURE 29.13: The Owner tab of the Advanced Security Settings dialog box lists the current owner and allows ownership to be set to the current user.

The owner of any object may allow or disallow another user from taking ownership; however, once another user has ownership, the original owner's rights are terminated.

NOTE

Both the current owner and the system administrator may assign ownership of the object to a user or to the system administrator.

The Effective Permissions Tab

With all the different permissions that you can set (as described in the previous sections), it can be hard to see exactly which permissions any given group or user has. To help you keep permissions straight, the Effective Permissions tab of the Advanced Security Settings dialog box (see Figure 29.14) lets you view the permissions currently in effect for the selected user or group.

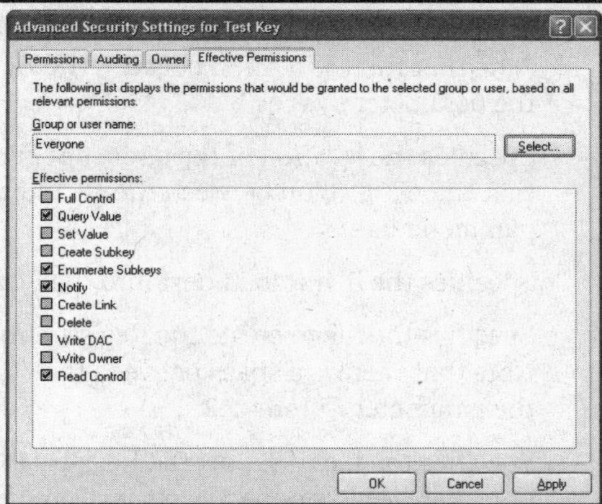

FIGURE 29.14: The Effective Permissions tab of the Advanced Security Settings dialog box gives you a quick way to see which permissions a user or group currently has.

Using the Registry Editor from the Command Line

The Registry Editor may be used from the command line, without user interaction. The commands that the Registry Editor uses include those described below. (Note that not all commands may be available under all operating systems.)

To import a Registry file into the Registry Editor, use the command:

```
REGEDIT [/L:system] [/R:user] filename1
```

To create a Registry object from a file, use the command:

```
REGEDIT [/L:system] [/R:user] /C filename2
```

To export a Registry (or part of the Registry), use the command:

```
REGEDIT [/L:system] [/R:user] /E filename3 [regpath1]
```

To delete part of a Registry, use the command:

```
REGEDIT [/L:system] [/R:user] /D regpath2
```

In all the above commands, the parameters are:

`/L:system`	Specifies the location of the `system.dat` file. Note that there is a colon between the `/L` and the parameter `system`.
`/R:user`	Specifies the location of the `user.dat` file. Note that there is a colon between the `/R` and the parameter `user`.
`filename1`	Specifies the file(s) to import into the Registry.
`/C filename2`	Specifies the file to create the Registry from. Note that there is a space between the `/C` and the parameter `filename2`.
`/E filename3`	Specifies the file to export the Registry to. Note that there is a space between the `/E` and the parameter `filename3`.
`regpath1`	Specifies the starting Registry key to export from (defaults to exporting the entire Registry).
`/D regpath2`	Specifies the Registry key to delete. Note that there is a space between the `/D` and the parameter `regpath2`.

WARNING

Be careful; be very careful. Running the Registry Editor in the command-line mode can be damaging to the Registry—it is possible to utterly destroy the Registry with a single command.

Tips for Using the Registry Editor

The Registry Editor offers the ability to export the Registry, or parts of the Registry, to a text file. This file may be used for any of the following:

- A snapshot of the condition of the Registry at the time the export was made.
- A limited backup of the Registry that might have value in restoring the Registry in the event there is a failure.
- A file that when compared with another export file, using FC or WinDiff, can quickly show differences between the two versions of the Registry.
- A file that can be edited using any text editor (Notepad, for example); the results of the editing could then be incorporated into a Registry using the Registry Editor's import facilities.

The Registry Editor allows adding simple keys, subkeys, and values (with limited data types) to any Registry. Though the Registry Editor won't add, edit, or create the more complex data types that Windows XP supports (such as the data type REG_FULL_RESOURCE_DESCRIPTOR, and so on), much work with the Registry is done using the simple character and numeric data types.

Installing Remote Registry Editing on Windows 95, Windows 98, and Windows Me

Though Windows NT Workstation and Windows 2000 Professional have remote Registry editing installed already, Windows 95, Windows 98, and Windows Me do not. The installation process is similar on all three operating systems, though the source of the necessary drivers differs on Windows 95 and Windows 98—and Windows Me doesn't include them. (You'll recall that Windows Me was positioned firmly as a consumer operating system, with Windows 2000 Professional as its corporate counterpart—so presumably Microsoft deemed Windows Me not to need remote

Registry editing. But you can install it using the files from the Windows 95 or Windows 98 CD.)

You have to install a network service to enable remote Registry editing. This service, REGSERV, is found in the following location:

- Windows 95: Look on the Windows 95 distribution CD, in the directory `\admin\nettools\remotreg`, for the `regserv` program files.
- Windows 98: Look on the Windows 98 distribution CD, in the directory `\tools\reskit\netadmin\remotreg`, for the `regserv` program files.

In each operating system, the installation is identical:

1. Open Control Panel.
2. Start the Network applet.
3. Click the Add button on the Configuration tab.
4. Select Service from the list, and click the Add button.
5. Click the Have Disk button, and provide the directory information as given above.
6. Select Microsoft Remote Registry.
7. Install the Remote Registry service, and reboot the computer when prompted.

TIP

The Remote Registry service files are identical in Windows 95 and Windows 98. Either will work with either version of the operating system.

Hints and Kinks from the Experts

Here's a key hint: restricting access to a remote Registry.

How Do You Restrict Access to a Remote Registry?

Access to a remote Registry is controlled by the ACL on the key `winreg`. To set access, follow these steps:

1. Start the Registry Editor.
2. Move to `HKEY_LOCAL_MACHINE\System\CurrentControlSet\Control\ SecurePipeServers`.
3. Check for a key called `winreg`. If it does not exist, create it (select Edit ➢ Add Key).
4. Select the `winreg` key by clicking it.
5. Select Edit ➢ Permissions. Windows displays the Permissions for `winreg` dialog box.
6. If the user is listed in the Group or User Names list box, select their entry. Otherwise, click the Add button and use the Select Users, Computers, or Groups dialog box to add the user to the Group or User Names list box. Then select their entry.
7. Select the Read check box in the Allow column in the Permissions For list box to give the user read access.
8. With the user's entry still selected, click the Advanced button. Windows displays the Advanced Security Settings for `winreg` dialog box.
9. Double-click the user's entry on the Permissions tab to display the Permission Entry for `winreg` dialog box, in which you can select which actions the user can perform.
10. When you've finished specifying permissions, click the OK button to close the Permission Entry for `winreg` dialog box. Then click the OK button to close the Advanced Security Settings for `winreg`, and click the OK button to close the Permissions for `winreg` dialog box.

You can set up certain keys to be accessible even if the user does not have access by editing the value `HKEY_LOCAL_MACHINE\System\CurrentControlSet\Control\ SecurePipeServers\winreg\Allowed Paths`. You can add paths to this list.

(Courtesy of John Savill.)

NOTE

For more information, see article Q153183 in the Microsoft Knowledge Base.

WHAT'S NEXT?

This chapter completes our look at the Registry. The next part of the book focuses on how to maintain and troubleshoot Windows XP Professional. The first chapter in that part begins by discussing how to manage the disks and the drives on your computer system.

Maintaining and Troubleshooting Your Disks and Drives

Chapter 30
Managing Your Disks and Drives

This chapter discusses how to manage your disks and drives, showing you how to understand and undertake the key actions you'll need to perform with them. These actions range from formatting a disk to converting a disk's file system to NTFS; from using compression to free up disk space on an NTFS disk to using quotas to prevent users from grabbing more than their fair share; and from defragmenting your disks to creating and deleting partitions.

Revised and adapted from *Mastering Windows XP Home Edition* by Guy Hart-Davis

ISBN 0-7821-2980-3 1024 pages $39.99

FORMATTING A DISK

Be it hard, removable, or floppy, a disk needs to be formatted before it's usable. *Formatting* imposes a file system on the disk's physical sectors, arranging them into logical clusters that Windows can access and manipulate.

You use the same procedure for formatting hard, removable, and floppy disks. By contrast, recordable (CD-R) and rewritable (CD-RW) discs and writable DVDs need a different kind of formatting because they use different file systems.

To format a disk, follow these steps:

1. Open an Explorer window. (Usually, choosing Start ➢ My Computer gives you the best view for formatting disks.)
2. Right-click the disk and choose Format from the shortcut menu. Windows displays the appropriate Format dialog box for the disk:
   - For a local hard disk, Windows displays the Format Local Disk dialog box (shown in Figure 30.1).

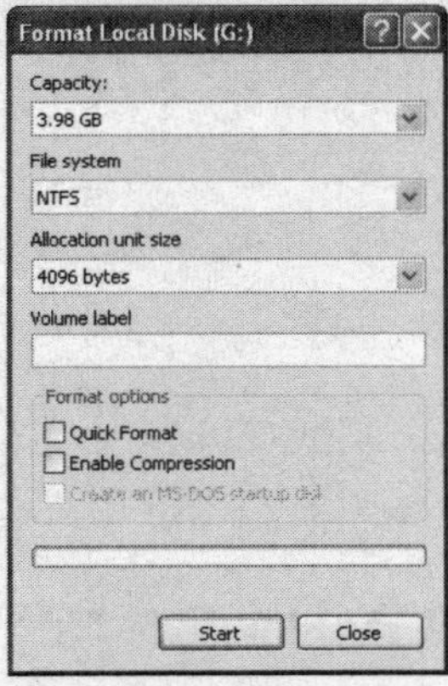

FIGURE 30.1: In the Format Local Disk dialog box, specify the file system to use for the disk.

   - For a floppy disk, Windows displays the Format 3 1/2 Floppy dialog box.

- For a removable disk, Windows displays a dialog box named after the drive's name. For example, for a Zip 100 drive, Windows displays a Format ZIP-100 dialog box.

3. If you're formatting a floppy disk, make sure that the Capacity drop-down list is showing approximately the right size for the disk. You shouldn't be able to change this setting for a hard disk, but you should check it in case Windows XP is having trouble reading the disk, which could indicate a physical problem with the disk.

NOTE

Good news: Windows XP fixes a problem with previous versions of Windows, in which a format operation would grind to a halt if an Explorer window was showing the contents of the disk you tried to format. This problem was especially annoying when you displayed the disk in Explore mode to check that it didn't contain anything worth keeping, and then issued a command from the Folders Explorer bar while the contents were still displayed in the right pane.

4. In the File System drop-down list, choose the file system with which to format the disk: NTFS or FAT32 for a hard disk. You'll recall from Chapter 2 that NTFS offers advantages of security and stability over FAT32 and that the main reason for using FAT32 is if you need an operating system not based on NT—for example, Windows 9*x*—to be able to read the disk.

5. In the Allocation Unit Size drop-down list, you can specify the cluster size for the disk. By default, Windows selects the Default Allocation Size item. Typically the options for NTFS are 512 bytes, 1024 bytes, 2048 bytes, and 4096 bytes. You shouldn't need to specify the cluster size, but see the next sidebar if you're curious as to why not.

6. In the Volume Label text box, you can enter a name for the volume. FAT32 volume names can be a maximum of 11 characters, and NTFS volume names can be a maximum of 32 characters. There's no obligation to enter a volume label, but doing so makes the volume easier to identify. (This tends to be less important for a floppy disk than for a hard disk volume, especially if you label the outside of the floppy.)

7. In the Format Options section, select the Quick Format check box if you want to skip scanning the disk for bad sectors. Skipping the scan speeds up the format significantly, because it means that all Windows has to do is remove the files from the disk. But it's almost always a good idea to perform the scan by running a standard format. The only exception is if you've very recently scanned the disk for bad sectors and it's come up clean.
8. If the Enable Compression check box is available, you can select it to enable compression on the drive. Compression is available only on NTFS drives. The section "Using Compression to Free Up Space," later in this chapter, discusses the pros and cons of compression.
9. Click the Start button. Windows displays a warning dialog box (shown in Figure 30.2) checking that you're sure you want to format the disk.

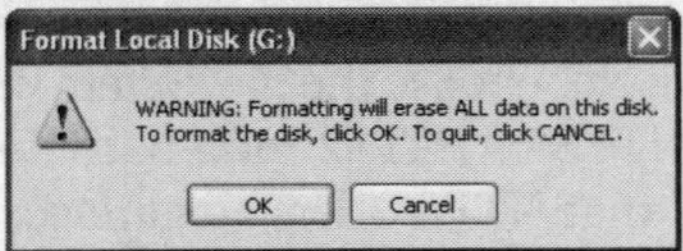

FIGURE 30.2: Because you're about to wipe the contents of the disk, Windows double-checks with this warning dialog box to make sure you know what you're doing.

10. If you *are* sure, click the OK button. Windows starts the formatting operation.
11. When Windows has finished formatting the disk, it displays a Formatting Local Disk dialog box (or a Formatting 3 1/2 Floppy dialog box, or a Formatting ZIP-100 dialog box, or whatever), such as that shown in Figure 30.3, to tell you that the format is complete.

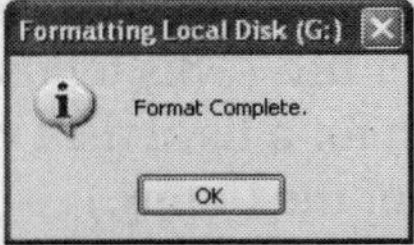

FIGURE 30.3: Windows displays a dialog box such as this when it has finished formatting the disk.

12. Click the OK button. Windows closes the Formatting Local Disk dialog box and returns you to the Format Local Disk dialog box (or whichever variant of the Format dialog box was previously displayed).

13. Click the Close button. Windows closes the Format Local Disk dialog box.

You can now use the formatted disk to store files.

NOTE

The Create an MS-DOS Startup Disk check box lets you create a floppy disk that boots DOS. You can't do much from DOS to an XP computer, so you probably won't need to use this capability.

EXPERT KNOWLEDGE: WHAT IS THE CLUSTER SIZE, AND SHOULD YOU SPECIFY IT?

The *cluster size* is the smallest amount of disk space that you can allocate for storing a file. Windows uses clusters as a logical overlay to let it get at the physical sectors on the disk in which the information is actually stored. Most files take up multiple clusters; the smaller the cluster size, obviously enough, the more clusters a file of any given size takes up.

In the days when both disks and files were smaller than they are today, cluster size used to be more of an issue than it is now. Operating systems that used the FAT16, such as DOS and Windows 95, essentially weren't able to create enough clusters to handle large disks efficiently: For a drive of 120MB, FAT16 uses a 2KB cluster size, which is fine; for a 512MB drive, 16KB, which is—let's say—lavish; and for a 3GB drive, 64KB, which is prodigal. Any space not used in the cluster is wasted, so if you stored a 1KB file on that 3GB drive under FAT16, you were wasting 63KB—far worse overheads, so to speak, than in the Mall of America.

CONTINUED →

Unlike FAT16, FAT32 and NTFS *can* create enough clusters to handle even large disks, so cluster size shouldn't be an issue with Windows XP. As mentioned a moment ago, you can specify cluster sizes of 512 bytes (0.5KB), 1KB, 2KB, and 4KB: all good, small sizes. If you're creating files smaller than 4KB these days, you're doing well—and in any case, hard disks have grown so much that occasionally wasting a few KB seldom causes much pain anymore.

The best cluster size depends on the size of the disk in question. If you're familiar with the cluster size recommended for the size of disk you have, you *can* specify the cluster size you want to use. But because Windows is preloaded with information about cluster sizes, it's usually best to let Windows allocate the cluster size automatically. To do so, leave the Default Allocation Size entry (the default) selected in the Allocation Unit Size drop-down list.

Changing the Computer's Name, Description, and Workgroup

Each computer has a name and a description and belongs to a workgroup (unless your computer is part of a domain):

- The name isn't the name for My Computer (which you can rename to anything you want without affecting anything more than the user interface): It's the name by which the computer appears on the network (if any) to which it's attached. The name is partly for your benefit, partly for the benefit of other users, partly for that of Windows, and partly for that of other computers on the network: It enables you, other users, Windows, and the other computers to identify your computer.
- The *description* is entirely for your and other users' benefit: It's a text field that lets you describe the computer identified by the name. Windows doesn't assign a description by default, so the computer doesn't have a description until you enter one.

- The *workgroup* is a logical collection of computers intended to work together. By default, the Windows XP Professional setup routine adds your computer to a workgroup named MSHOME.

You can change the computer's name, description, and workgroup easily enough. To do so, follow these steps:

1. Press Winkey+Break. (Alternatively, display the Start menu, right-click the My Computer item, and choose Properties from the shortcut menu.) Windows displays the System Properties dialog box.
2. Click the Computer Name tab (shown in Figure 30.4), which shows the description, computer name, and workgroup name.

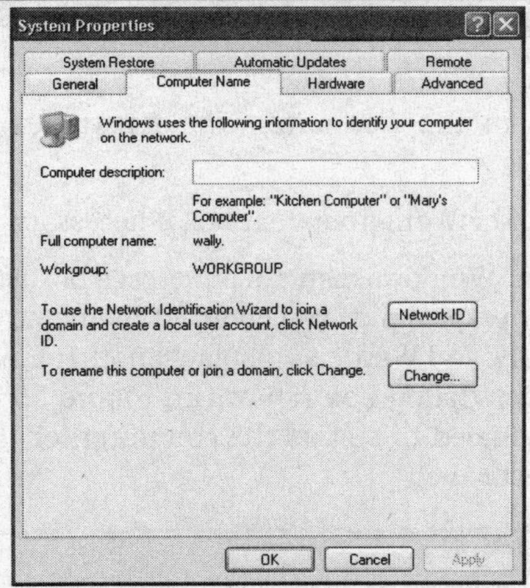

FIGURE 30.4: You can change the computer's name on the Computer Name tab of the System Properties dialog box.

3. In the Computer Description text box, enter the description for the computer.
4. To change the computer name or workgroup, click the Change button. Windows displays the Computer Name Changes dialog box (shown in Figure 30.5).

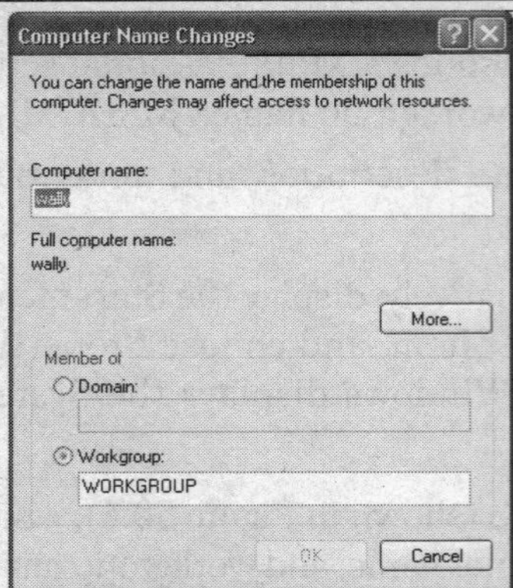

FIGURE 30.5: Use this Computer Name Changes dialog box to change the computer's name or workgroup.

5. Change the name in the Computer Name text box if necessary.
6. Change the name in the Workgroup text box if necessary.
7. Click the OK button. Windows displays a message box welcoming you to the workgroup (if you changed the name or workgroup). Click OK, and Windows displays another Computer Name Changes dialog box (shown in Figure 30.6) telling you that you need to restart the computer for the changes to take effect.

FIGURE 30.6: When you change the computer's name or workgroup, Windows displays this Computer Name Changes dialog box telling you that you'll need to restart the computer.

8. Click the OK button. Windows closes the second Computer Name Changes dialog box, returning you to the System Properties dialog box. The Computer Name tab now displays a warning telling you that changes will take effect after you restart the computer.

9. Click the OK button. Windows closes the System Properties dialog box. If you need to restart your computer, Windows displays the System Settings Change dialog box (shown in Figure 30.7).

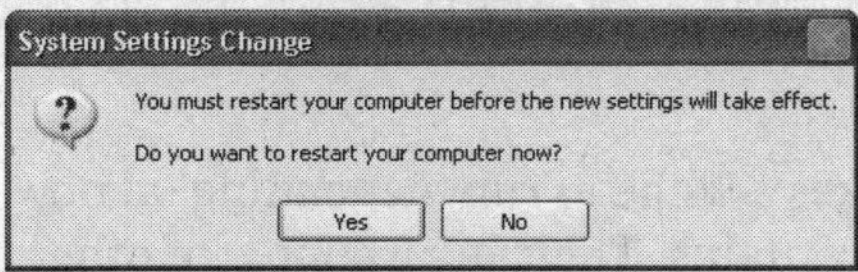

FIGURE 30.7: If you need to restart the computer to make the changes stick, Windows displays the System Settings Change dialog box to remind you.

10. Choose the Yes button if you want Windows to restart your computer straight away. Choose the No button if you want to take any other actions and then restart the computer yourself.

Converting a Disk to NTFS

If you need to use Windows' security features, compression (discussed next), or quota management (discussed later in this chapter), your volumes need to be NTFS rather than FAT. Windows provides a tool for converting a disk from FAT or FAT32 to NTFS, so you can convert your volumes at any time. This is a one-way process, in that you can't convert the disk back to FAT unless you reformat it (which involves removing all the data from the disk), so it's not something to try idly or on a whim.

The best time to convert a disk from FAT to NTFS is when you install Windows XP. The second-best time is when you need to format the disk, because formatting overwrites all the contents of the drive anyway. But if you want to maintain a dual-boot system with Windows 9*x* until you're sure that Windows XP suits you, you'll need to keep one or more drives formatted with FAT, which means that neither of these options is viable—unless you're prepared to blow away the contents of the FAT disk when you decide to commit to NTFS.

To convert a FAT disk to NTFS without affecting the data on it (other than the file system on which the data is stored), open a command prompt window (choose Start ➢ All Programs ➢ Accessories ➢ Command

Prompt) and issue a `convert` command. The syntax for the `convert` command is as follows:

```
convert drive: /FS:NTFS
```

As you'd guess, *`drive:`* here is the letter of the drive to convert. For example, the following command converts the D drive:

```
convert d: /FS:NTFS
```

The `convert` command takes a while to run, depending on how big the drive is and how much it contains. There are a couple of other things that you should know about it:

- `convert` needs a modest amount of space for the conversion, so the disk can't be stuffed to the gills with files when you convert it. (If the disk *is* stuffed—which isn't a great idea anyway—you just need to move some of the files off the drive temporarily while you perform the conversion. You can then move the files back onto the drive.)
- If you don't want to specify permissions for the files and folders on the converted drive, add the `/NoSecurity` flag to the command. You won't usually want to do this.
- Converting the system volume to NTFS requires two reboots. The conversion happens after the reboot, and Windows then reboots itself again.

Using Compression to Free Up Space

To save disk space, you can *compress* files, folders, or even an entire drive that uses NTFS. (You can't compress a FAT32 drive.) How much disk space you save depends on the types of file you're compressing. Anything that's already compressed—for example, a Zip file or a compressed multimedia file such as an MP3 music file or an MPEG movie—won't compress much, if at all. Files such as Word documents or Excel spreadsheets compress nicely, as do uncompressed graphics (for example, TIFF files).

The advantage of compression is, obviously enough, that it saves space so that you can pack more information on your drives. To counterbalance this advantage, compression has two main disadvantages: First, your computer will take longer to access a compressed file, folder, or drive; and second, you cannot encrypt a compressed file or folder.

Unless your computer is state-of-the-art fast, it's probably not wise to compress files that you need to play at full speed. For example, multimedia files may not play back without hiccups if you compress them.

Compressing a File or Folder

To compress a file or a folder, follow these steps:

1. Right-click the file or folder and choose Properties from the shortcut menu. Windows display the Properties dialog box for the file or folder.
2. On the General tab, click the Advanced button. Windows displays the Advanced Attributes dialog box (shown in Figure 30.8).

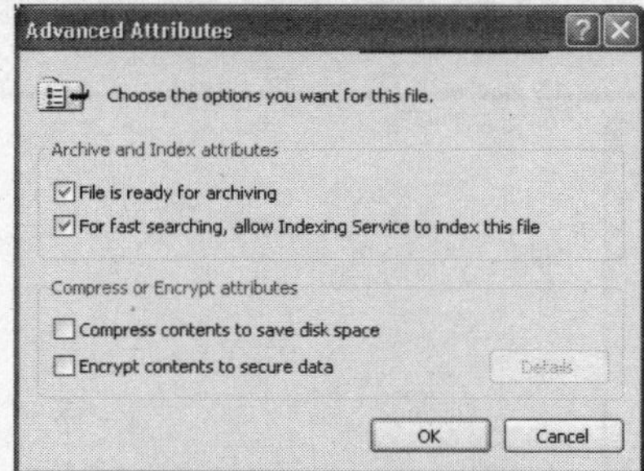

FIGURE 30.8: To save space, you can compress a file or folder by selecting the Compress Contents to Save Disk Space check box in the Advanced Attributes dialog box.

3. Select the Compress Contents to Save Disk Space check box.
4. Click the OK button. Windows closes the Advanced Attributes dialog box.
5. Click the OK button. Windows closes the Properties dialog box.

You can work with compressed files or folders without uncompressing them.

Compressing a Drive

Compressing individual folders (let alone individual files) is a slow business and may not save you a large amount of space. You'll usually get better results from compressing a whole drive.

To compress an NTFS drive, be sure you are logged on as an administrator or as a member of the Administrators group, and then follow these steps:

1. Right-click the drive and choose Properties from the shortcut menu. Windows displays the Properties dialog box for the drive.
2. On the General tab, select the Compress Drive to Save Disk Space check box.
3. Click the Apply button. Windows displays the Confirm Attribute Changes dialog box (shown in Figure 30.9), asking if you want to apply this change only to the root of the drive or to its subfolders and files as well.

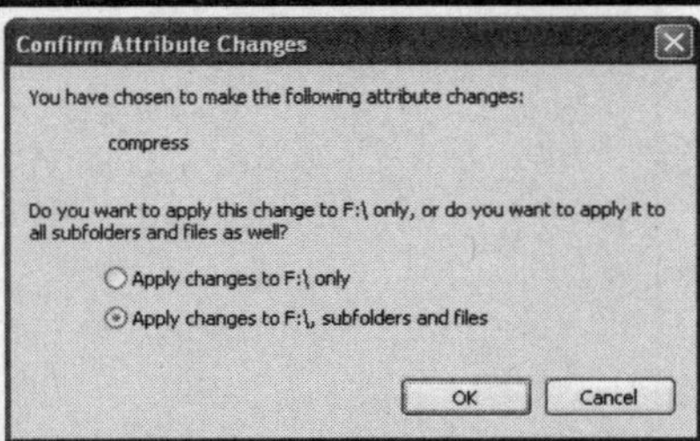

FIGURE 30.9: To compress a drive and its contents, select the Apply Changes to *N*:\, Subfolders and Files option button in the Confirm Attribute Changes dialog box.

4. Select the Apply Changes to *N*:\, Subfolders and Files option button.
5. Click the OK button. Windows closes the Confirm Attribute Changes dialog box, displays the Applying Attributes dialog box, and starts compressing the drive.
   - If Windows displays the Error Applying Attributes dialog box telling you that an error occurred applying the attribute to (in other words, compressing) a file because

the file is being used by another process, choose the Ignore button, the Ignore All button, the Retry button, or the Cancel button as appropriate.

6. When compression is complete, click the OK button in the Properties dialog box for the drive. Windows closes the dialog box.

You can work with a compressed drive without uncompressing it.

SETTING ARCHIVING AND INDEXING FOR A FILE OR FOLDER

Apart from compression, the Advanced Attributes dialog box (shown in Figure 30.10) for a file or folder offers two other options:

File/Folder Is Ready for Archiving check box Select this check box (or leave it selected) to specify that the file or folder can be archived. Nothing will happen to the folder until you use a program (such as Backup) that checks the archiving status of files.

For Fast Searching, Allow Indexing Service to Index This File/Folder check box Select this check box (or, again, leave it selected, as the case may be) to include this file or folder in any indexing operations you tell Windows to perform. By indexing your files, you can create a database that lets you search more quickly for files matching specified criteria.

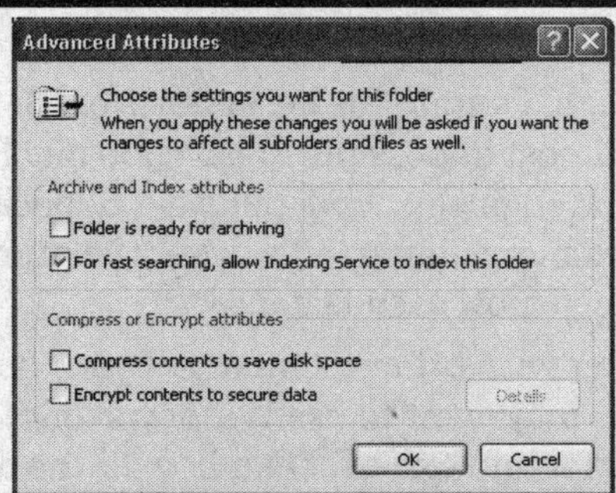

FIGURE 30.10: You can set further attributes, including archiving and indexing options, in the Advanced Attributes dialog box.

When you've finished choosing settings in the Advanced Attributes dialog box, click the OK button. Windows closes the Advanced Attributes dialog box. Then click the OK button. Windows closes the Properties dialog box for the file or folder.

Encryption

When you encrypt a file or a folder, you jumble its contents so that it cannot be read until it is decrypted. In Windows XP Professional, only the user that encrypts a file or folder can decrypt it. You encrypt a file or folder using the Encrypt Contents to Secure Data check box in the Advanced Attributes dialog box, which we looked at in the previous section.

TIP

A quick and easy way to encrypt files is to move them to an encrypted folder. For example, you might create a folder and name it Encrypted Stuff. When you then want to encrypt a file, simply move the file to that folder.

Using Quotas to Apportion Disk Space

As you know, it's not possible to get too thin, to be too rich, or to have too much disk space. Actually, the first two parts of this aren't really true anymore: Most people reckon Cameron Diaz is too thin and Bill Gates is too rich. (But that's their business and is protected by freedom of expression.)

The third part still holds, though: Despite the best efforts of IBM, Seagate, and their competitors, it's almost impossible to have too much disk space these days. However fast the engineers work out ways to pack more information on a platter and stack more platters in a drive, the number and size of files people want to keep grow even faster.

If you're sharing your computer with other members of your family, or with people in your office, you may want to use Windows' quota-management tools to make sure that no one user can hog all the disk space. Quota management may seem a formal and officious thing to implement, but it's easy to do; it can have a salutary effect on users' behavior; and it can help keep your computer running smoothly by preventing it from running out of disk space. Best of all, when you've set quotas on a disk, it appears to the user as if the section of the disk available to them is all the disk space there is. For example, if you have an 80GB drive and set a quota of 20GB per user, each user gets the impression of having a 20GB drive. If you want, you can keep them in ignorance about the rest of the drive.

Quota management is easy—but you need to know three important things in order to get it right:

- You can use quotas only on NTFS volumes.
- Quotas work on whole volumes, not on individual folders.
- If you implement quotas on your system volume, don't prevent users from using more than their allotted quota of disk space. Windows writes information to disk on the system partition when booting. Implementing capped quotas can prevent Windows from booting. You'll get entertaining errors as the Network Service and System try desperately to exceed their quotas to do your bidding.

To set quotas, take the following steps:

1. Right-click the volume for which you want to set quotas and choose Properties from the shortcut menu. Windows displays the Properties dialog box.
2. Click the Quota tab (shown in Figure 30.11 with several choices made).

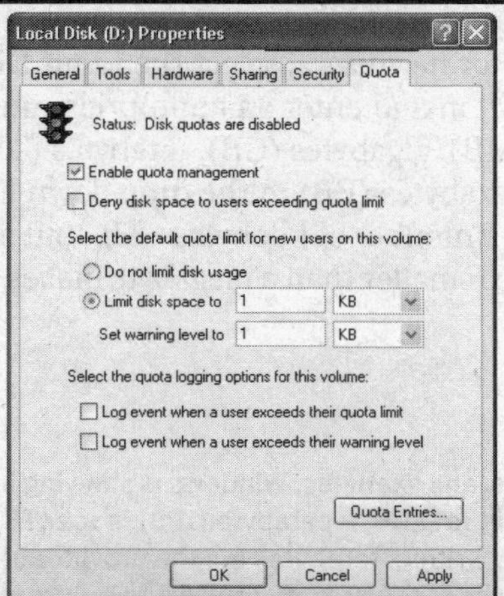

FIGURE 30.11: Use quotas to prevent any user from using up more than their fair share of drive space.

NOTE

If your system is not part of a domain, the Security tab may not be displayed in the Properties dialog box for a drive. To display this tab, in an Explorer window, choose Tools ➢ Folder Options to open the Folder Options dialog box. Click the View tab, and in the Advanced Settings list, clear the Use Simple File Sharing (Recommended) check box and then click OK.

3. Select the Enable Quota Management check box. Windows enables the other controls on the Quota tab.
4. If you want to prevent a user from using more than their allotted amount of disk space, select the Deny Disk Space to Users Exceeding Quota Limit check box.

WARNING

Be aware that denying disk space to a user could cause them to lose work or be forced to delete an existing file in order to save a new file. Think carefully before you use this option; and if you use it, make sure that users understand quotas and their implications before they discover the limitations the hard way.

5. In the Select the Default Quota Limit for New Users on This Volume area, specify whether to limit disk space for new users:
    - If you don't want to limit disk space, select the Do Not Limit Disk Usage option button.
    - To limit disk space for new users, select the Limit Disk Space To option button and enter an appropriate number of megabytes (MB), gigabytes (GB), terabytes (TB), petabytes (PB), or exabytes (EB) in the drop-down list. (You can also enter a number of kilobytes—KB—but any amount of disk space smaller than a megabyte makes no sense.)

NOTE

By offering terabytes, petabytes, and exabytes, Windows is showing it's ready for the future. A terabyte (1TB) is 1024GB, a petabyte (1PB) is 1024TB, and an exabyte (1EB) is 1024PB. At this writing, terabytes are the province of serious servers, petabytes are the province of server farms, and exabytes are provinces *of server farms.*

- If you limit disk space, use the Set Warning Level To text box and drop-down list to specify the limit at which Windows warns the user that they're about to run out of disk space. This limit should be a little less than the amount of disk space they're limited to—enough less that the user will need to create several files of the size they usually work with between triggering the warning and reaching the limit. For this setting, you may want to accept the default that Windows offers or manually set a bigger cushion of your own. You can use decimal places with the same unit in the Set Warning Level To text box or select the next smaller item in the drop-down list so that you can work with whole numbers.

6. In the Select the Quota Logging Options for This Volume area, select the Log Event When a User Exceeds Their Quota Limit check box or the Log Event When a User Exceeds Their Warning Level check box if you want Windows to log these events.
7. Click the Quota Entries button. Windows displays the Quota Entries window (shown in Figure 30.12). The first time you display this window, the only quota it lists is the one for your user identity or the Administrators group.

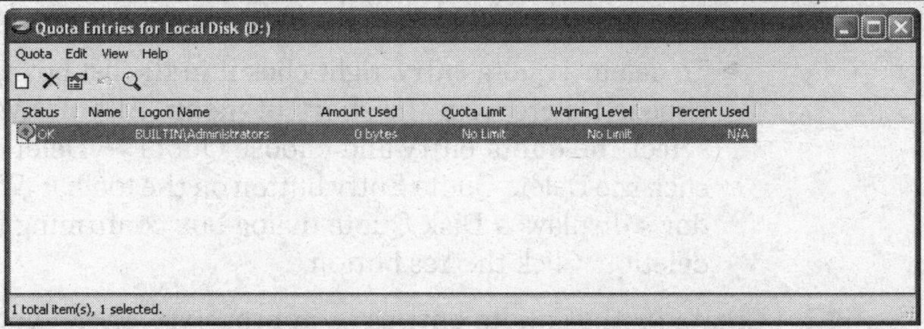

FIGURE 30.12: Once you've enabled quotas, use the Quota Entries window to set quotas for each user.

8. Choose Quota ➢ New Quota Entry or click the New Quota Entry button. Windows displays the Select Users dialog box.

9. Enter the username in the Enter the Object Names to Select list box and click the OK button. Windows displays the Add New Quota Entry dialog box (shown in Figure 30.13).

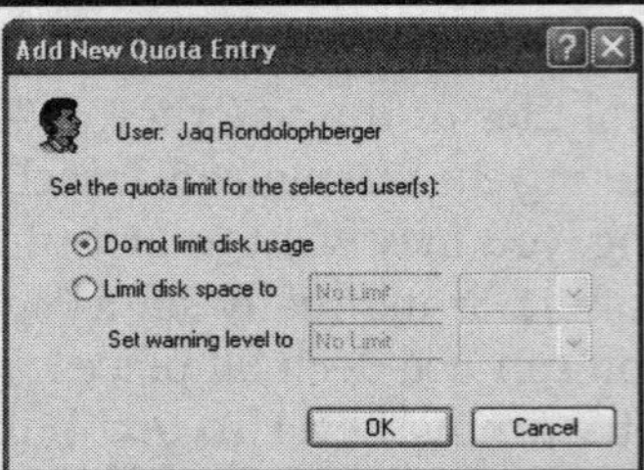

FIGURE 30.13: Use the Add New Quota Entry dialog box to specify the quota limits for the user.

10. Set a disk space quota and warning level as described in step 5.
11. Click the OK button. Windows closes the Add New Quota Entry dialog box and adds the quota entry to the Quota Entries window.
    - To change an existing quota entry, double-click it in the Quota Entries window. Windows displays the Quota Settings dialog box for the user. Change the quota settings or warning level and click the OK button.
    - To delete a quota entry, right-click it in the list box and choose Delete from the shortcut menu. Alternatively, select the quota entry and choose Quota ➢ Delete or click the Delete Quota Entry button on the toolbar. Windows displays a Disk Quota dialog box confirming the deletion. Click the Yes button.
12. Create further quota entries as appropriate, then choose Quota ➢ Close. Windows closes the Quota Entries window and displays the Properties dialog box.
13. Click the Apply button to make Windows apply the quotas, or click the OK button to make Windows apply the quotas and close the Properties dialog box.

If disk quotas are not currently enabled, when you click the Apply button or the OK button to apply the quotas, Windows displays the Disk

Quota dialog box (shown in Figure 30.14). This dialog box warns you that when you enable quotas, Windows needs to rescan the volume to update disk usage statistics, and that this process can take several minutes. Click the OK button to enable quotas.

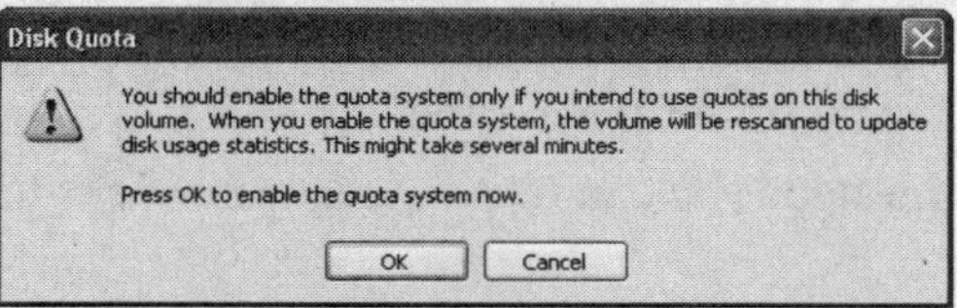

FIGURE 30.14: If the quota system isn't enabled for the volume, Windows displays the Disk Quota dialog box warning you that it will need to rescan the volume.

When you've set a quota on a volume, Explorer shows the user the amount of space that remains to them on the volume, not the actual amount of space available on the volume. When a user reaches their warning level, they see a message telling them that they're running out of space.

If you chose to deny disk space to users exceeding their quota limit, they'll see a message such as that shown in Figure 30.15 when they take an action that will exceed their quota limit. Notice that the message isn't that the user is over quota—it's simply that there isn't enough space on disk.

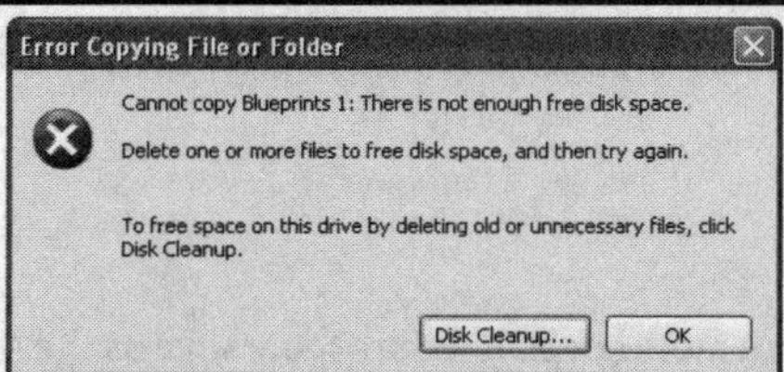

FIGURE 30.15: When a user takes an action that will exceed their quota limit, Windows tells them there's not enough space on the disk.

TIP

If you need to apply the same quotas to several volumes, choose Quota ➢ Export to export quotas from one volume to a file. From another volume, choose Quota ➢ Import to import the quota settings file.

Disk Maintenance

Like cars, hard disks can take a fair amount of abuse these days, but the better you treat them, the better performance they give you and the longer they last. Unlike cars, hard disks thrive on running all the time; but like cars, they don't appreciate fragmentation or crashes—and they appreciate a little cleaning-up from time to time.

This section details the steps you can take to keep your disks in good order.

Defragmenting Your Disks

As you know, data is stored on your hard disk in physical areas called sectors that are mapped into logical areas called clusters. Each cluster contains a relatively small amount of information so that Windows can use the clusters efficiently. As a result, most files occupy more than one cluster. These clusters can be located just about anywhere on the partition of the drive that contains the volume. Ideally, all the data in a file is stored in contiguous clusters, so that the hard disk's heads can read the data without having to move too far. The farther the hard disk's actuator arm has to move to allow the heads to read the clusters that make up the file, the slower the file is to load.

When files are stored in widely spread-out clusters, the volume is said to be *fragmented*. To improve disk performance, you *defragment* (or *defrag*) it using a disk *defragmenter* (or *defragger*). A defragmenter rearranges the data on the disk so that each file occupies contiguous clusters wherever possible.

NOTE

Related to defragmenters but more specialized are tools such as the Microsoft Office optimizer, which defragments a specific set of files and arranges them in a location on the hard drive that the disk heads can quickly access.

Depending on how fragmented a volume is, and how big it is, defragmentation can take anything from a few minutes to a few hours. You *can* work on your computer while defragmentation is going on, but you'll find the computer responding more slowly than usual, and any files that you create, move, or copy may slow down the defragmentation process. Because of this, the best time to defragment a volume is when you're going to leave your computer for a few hours—for example, when you hear the siren song of the mall, an extended lunch hour, or an endless meeting.

To start Disk Defragmenter, choose Start ➢ All Programs ➢ Accessories ➢ System Tools ➢ Disk Defragmenter. Alternatively, right-click the drive icon in an Explorer window, choose Properties from the shortcut menu, display the Tools tab in the Properties dialog box, and click the Defragment Now button. Figure 30.16 shows Disk Defragmenter. The list box shows the volumes on your computer, their session status (whether they're being analyzed or defragmented), file system, capacity, amount of free space, and percentage of free space.

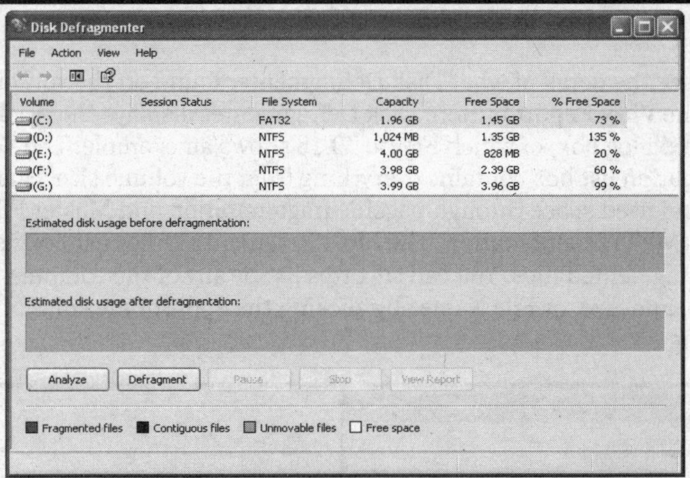

FIGURE 30.16: Use Disk Defragmenter to defragment your drives.

NOTE

You can also run Disk Defragmenter from a Computer Management window. Doing so can be handy if you're working with Computer Management already, but otherwise it conveys no particular benefits. But you need to know about this because, once you access Disk Defragmenter in a Computer Management session, Disk Defragmenter stays active. Now, you can run only one instance of Disk Defragmenter at a time, so if you start Disk Defragmenter while Computer Management is running, Windows displays a Disk Defragmenter message box telling you that "This version of Disk Defragmenter does not support running more than one instance." If you've forgotten about the Computer Management session, this message box seems to come out of the blue. (If you're not running Computer Management, this message box may mean that another Computer Administrator user is running Disk Defragmenter.)

Typically, you'll want to start by analyzing a volume. Select it in the list box and click the Analyze button. Disk Defragmenter examines the volume and displays the Disk Defragmenter dialog box (shown in Figure 30.17) with its recommendations.

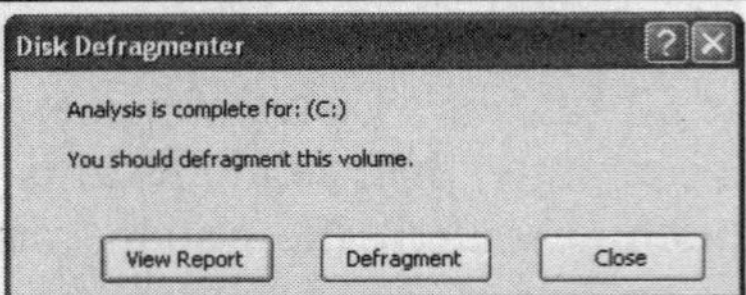

FIGURE 30.17: The Disk Defragmenter dialog box tells you the result of the analysis and makes a recommendation.

To see the detail of what Disk Defragmenter found on the volume, click the View Report button. Disk Defragmenter displays the Analysis Report dialog box, of which Figure 30.18 shows an example. The Volume Information list box contains everything from the volume size, cluster size, and used space through pagefile fragmentation and Master File Table (MFT) fragmentation. The Most Fragmented Files list box lists the most fragmented files. You can sort this list by any of the columns—Fragments, File Size, or File Name—by clicking the appropriate column heading.

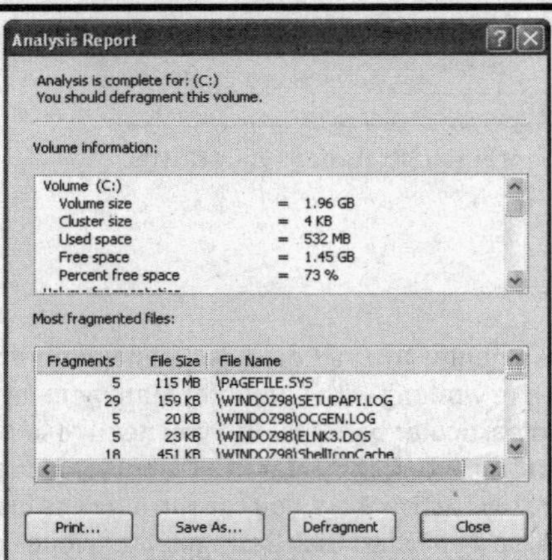

FIGURE 30.18: The Analysis Report dialog box provides a large amount of information about the volume and the most fragmented files it contains.

From the Analysis Report dialog box, you can use the Print button to print a copy of the analysis report or the Save As button to save it to a file. More likely, though, you'll want to click the Defragment button to defragment the drive (if Disk Defragmenter recommends doing so) or the Close button to close the dialog box.

If you click the Defragment button in the Analysis Report dialog box or the Disk Defragmenter dialog box, Windows closes the dialog box and starts defragmentation. While defragmentation is running, the status bar provides information on the percentage completed and the file currently being moved. (Unfortunately, Disk Defragmenter doesn't offer a full-screen graphical view of the process like Windows 9*x* defragmenters did.) You can use the Pause button and Stop button to pause or stop defragmentation.

When defragmentation is complete, Disk Defragmenter displays another Disk Defragmenter dialog box telling you so. Click the View Report button to display the Defragmentation Report dialog box containing a report (similar to the Analysis Report dialog box's report) on the volume's status, or click the Close button to close the dialog box.

How often you need to run Disk Defragmenter depends on how actively you use your computer and how often you create, modify, or delete files. Under normal usage, running Disk Defragmenter anything from once a week to once every couple of months will keep your files adequately defragmented. Experiment with Disk Defragmenter to establish a schedule that works for you. If Disk Defragmenter says that a volume doesn't need defragmenting, decrease the frequency with which you run Disk Defragmenter.

Cleaning Up Your Disks with Disk Cleanup

Most Windows programs create temporary files that they use to store information temporarily when you're running them. Some programs remember to get rid of these files when you exit them. Others forget. And if your computer loses power or crashes, even the well-behaved programs don't have a chance to get rid of temporary files.

Windows' Disk Cleanup feature provides an effective way to remove from local drives not only these temporary files but also temporary Internet files, downloaded program files, offline Web pages, and the contents of the Recycle Bin. (Disk Cleanup does not work on network drives.)

Close all programs you're running, and then start Disk Cleanup by choosing Start ➢ All Programs ➢ Accessories ➢ System Tools ➢ Disk Cleanup. (Alternatively, right-click a drive and choose Properties so that Windows displays the Properties dialog box. Then click the Disk Cleanup button on the General tab.) If your computer has multiple hard drive volumes, Disk Cleanup displays the Select Drive dialog box. (If your computer has a single hard drive volume, Disk Cleanup goes ahead and calculates how much space you will be able to free up on the drive.) In the Drives drop-down list, select the drive you want to clean up, and then click the OK button. Disk Cleanup examines the disk (which may take a few minutes) and then displays the Disk Cleanup dialog box (shown in Figure 30.19).

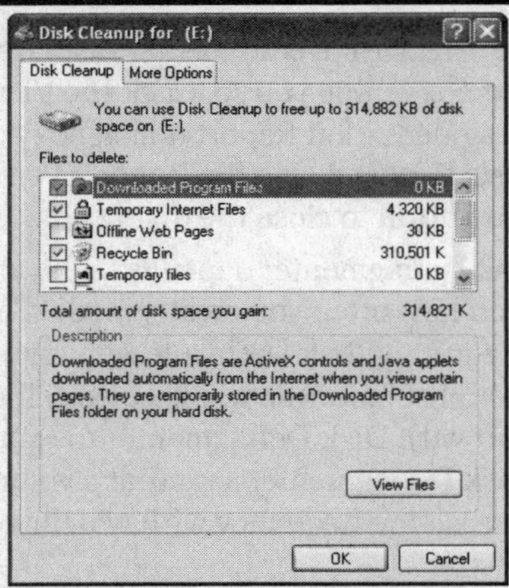

FIGURE 30.19: Disk Cleanup presents a list of the items you can remove to clean up your disk.

As you can see in the figure, the Disk Cleanup page of the Disk Cleanup dialog box lists the items you can remove and how much space you can recover by doing so. Which of the following items appear in the list depends on the drive's contents:

Downloaded Program Files ActiveX controls and Java applets downloaded by Internet Explorer so that it could display pages that needed them. If you delete these files, Internet Explorer may need to download the controls and applets again when you next access pages that need them, which may slow down your browsing a bit. You can click the View Files button to have Windows display an Explorer window containing the files.

Temporary Internet Files These files are the components of Web pages that Internet Explorer has downloaded and has stored on your hard drive so that it can retrieve them quickly when you access the same sites again. Deleting these files means that Internet Explorer will need to download them again the next time you access one of the sites, which will slow down your browsing. Again, you can click the View Files button to have Windows display an Explorer window containing these files–but be warned that there are usually thousands of them, and that the format in which they appear is less than informative.

Offline Web Pages This item appears only if you use offline favorites in Internet Explorer. These files hold the information for the cached copies of your offline favorites. If you use offline favorites extensively, these files may take up a lot of space. If you delete these files, you won't be able to view your offline favorites until you synchronize them again–and synchronizing them will probably reclaim most of the disk space that deleting these files freed up.

Recycle Bin These files are the contents of the Recycle Bin. As usual, make sure that you want to get rid of these files before you tell Disk Cleanup to delete them. You can click the View Files button to have Windows display an Explorer window showing the contents of the Recycle Bin.

Temporary Files These files are temporary storage files that should have been deleted by the program that created them. You can delete with impunity any temporary files that aren't currently being used. (Disk Cleanup leaves alone any temporary files still in use.)

WebClient/Publisher Temporary Files These files are temporary storage files kept by the WebClient/Publisher service. Deleting these files may affect WebClient/Publisher performance, but you won't lose any information by doing so.

Compress Old Files To free up some space, you can tell Windows to compress files that you haven't used for a while. If you select this check box, select the Compress Old Files item, then click the Options button that appears in the Disk Cleanup dialog box and use the Compress Old Files dialog box (shown in Figure 30.20) that Windows displays to specify when to compress files. (The default setting is 50 days.)

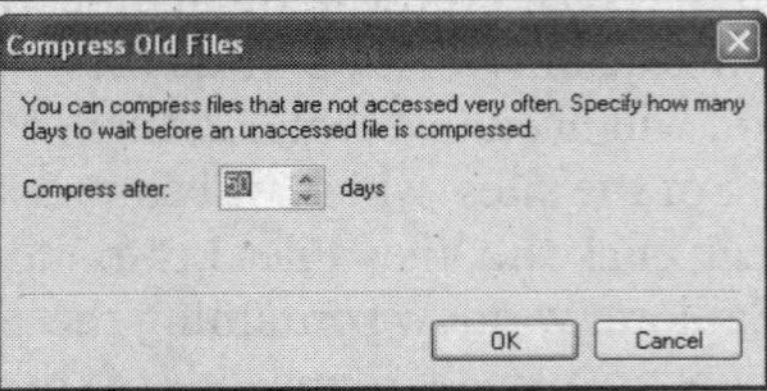

FIGURE 30.20: If you choose to have Windows compress old files to free up space on your hard drive, specify in the Compress Old Files dialog box how long the files should remain unaccessed before Windows compresses them.

Catalog Files for the Content Indexer These files are leftover catalog files from indexing. There's no downside to deleting them—they don't contain the current index.

Select the check boxes for those items you want to delete and click the OK button. Disk Cleanup displays a Disk Cleanup for *N*: dialog box to confirm that you want to perform the actions (for example, deleting the files). Click the Yes button. Disk Cleanup performs the cleanup.

Checking a Disk for Errors

Once you've cleaned unnecessary files off your hard disk, it's a good idea to check it for errors. Errors typically occur when sectors go bad, which can happen through natural selection (some disks age more quickly in parts) or unnatural intervention (such as physical damage resulting from the disk being bumped or receiving an electrical spike).

To check a disk for errors, follow these steps:

1. Close all programs that are on the disk or that might be accessing the disk. (In practice, it's best to close all programs for the time being.) Close any files open from the disk.
2. In an Explorer window, right-click the drive and choose Properties from the shortcut menu. Windows displays the Properties dialog box for the drive.

3. Click the Tools tab.
4. Click the Check Now button. Windows displays the Check Disk dialog box (shown in Figure 30.21).

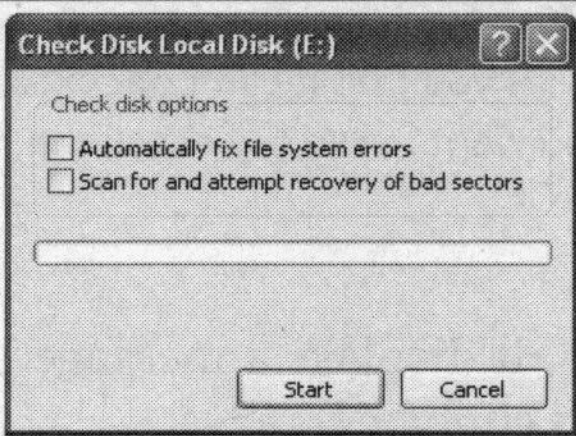

FIGURE 30.21: In the Check Disk dialog box, specify whether to automatically fix errors in the file system and whether to detect bad sectors and attempt to recover their contents.

5. If you want Windows to repair file-system errors, select the Automatically Fix File System Errors check box.
6. If you want Windows to scan for bad sectors and attempt to recover information from them, *and* repair file-system errors, select the Scan for and Attempt Recovery of Bad Sectors check box.
7. Click the Start button to run Check Disk. Windows displays the Checking Disk dialog box while it performs the checks.
   - If you see a Checking Disk dialog box such as that shown in Figure 30.22 telling you that "the disk check could not be performed because the disk check utility needs exclusive access to some Windows files on the disk" and asking whether you want to schedule the disk check to take place the next time you restart the computer, select the Yes button. This dialog box typically appears when you're checking a system volume: Because Windows is constantly using the volume, Check Disk can't get exclusive access to it.

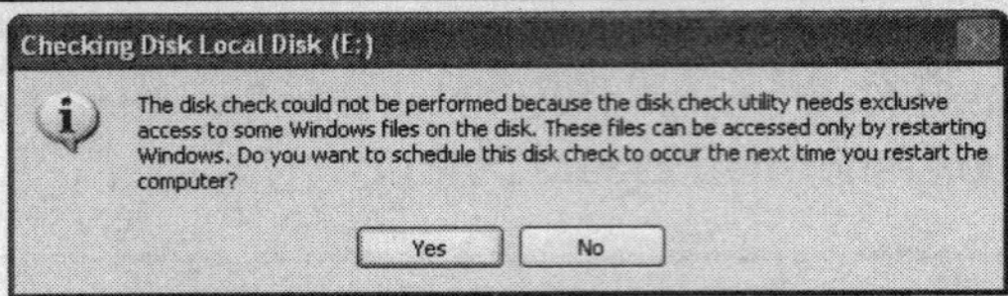
Checking Disk Local Disk (E:)

The disk check could not be performed because the disk check utility needs exclusive access to some Windows files on the disk. These files can be accessed only by restarting Windows. Do you want to schedule this disk check to occur the next time you restart the computer?

Yes No

FIGURE 30.22: The Checking Disk dialog box tells you that it can't get exclusive access to the disk and asks if you want to run the check the next time you restart the computer.

8. When Check Disk has finished, it displays a message box telling you that the disk check is complete.
9. Click the OK button. Check Disk closes and returns you to the Properties dialog box.
10. Click the OK button. Windows closes the Properties dialog box.

Scheduling Your Maintenance Tasks with the Scheduled Task Wizard

Windows includes a Scheduled Task Wizard that runs you through the process of scheduling the running of just about any program that you want to run at a particular time. This is particularly useful for tedious maintenance tasks–though of course you can also use the Scheduled Task Wizard to schedule regular games of FreeCell or DOOM should you feel the need.

Creating a Scheduled Task

To create a scheduled task, open the Scheduled Tasks folder by choosing Start ➢ All Programs ➢ Accessories ➢ System Tools ➢ Scheduled Tasks. (Alternatively, choose Start ➢ Control Panel, click the Performance and Maintenance link, and click the Scheduled Tasks link.) Start the Scheduled Task Wizard by double-clicking the Add Scheduled Task item. Then follow the screens that the Wizard presents through these steps:

- Choose the program to run.

- Enter a name for the task. If you want, this can be the name of the program, or you can enter a descriptive name—whatever works for you.
- Specify the frequency with which to perform the task: Daily, Weekly, Monthly, One Time Only, When My Computer Starts, or When I Log On.
- Specify the time of day, the frequency, and the days of the week for the task. For example, you might choose to run Disk Defragmenter at 2:00 AM every Friday.
- Specify the user under whose name to run the task and the password (if applicable) for that user. Usually, you'll want the task to be run under your own name. But you might want to use another username only for maintenance tasks. That way, you could let other users know they shouldn't use the computer when that user was logged on, so that the maintenance tasks wouldn't slow down their use of the computer (and vice versa).

Setting Advanced Properties for a Scheduled Task

The Scheduled Task Wizard gives you access to most of a task's properties, but not to all of them. To set further properties than the Wizard offers—for example, to set multiple schedules for the same task—use the task's Properties dialog box.

On the last page of the Scheduled Task Wizard, you can select the Open Advanced Properties for This Task when I Click Finish check box if you want to have the Wizard open the task's Properties dialog box automatically. Alternatively, double-click the task in the Scheduled Tasks folder (which resides under Control Panel). Windows displays the task's Properties dialog box.

The Properties dialog box for the task has three pages: Task, Schedule, and Settings:

- The Task page shows the program assigned to the task, the folder in which the task starts, and the username under which the task runs. There's also a Comments text box in which you can add comments to the task. For example, you might note any changes to the task and why you've made them. Clear the Enabled (Scheduled Task Runs at Specified Time) check box to prevent a task from running.

- The Schedule page shows the current schedule or schedules for the task. Select the Show Multiple Schedules check box if you need to set up more than one schedule for a task. (Alternatively, you can set up multiple separate tasks doing the same thing at different times. But using multiple schedules for the same task is neater and usually more efficient.) To specify an end date or a duration for the task, click the Advanced button and work in the Advanced Schedule Options dialog box.
- The Settings page contains three sections of advanced settings not offered by the Scheduled Task Wizard:

  Scheduled Task Completed section For a one-time task, select the Delete the Task If It Is Not Scheduled to Run Again check box if you want Windows to delete the task automatically once it has run successfully. To prevent a task from running for an inordinately long time, select the Stop the Task if It Runs for *NN* Hours *NN* Minutes check box and specify appropriate values in the two text boxes.

  Idle Time section This section contains three self-explanatory options for making sure the task runs when the computer is idle rather than when it is in use: the Only Start the Task if the Computer Has Been Idle for At Least *NN* Minutes check box and text box; the If the Computer Has Not Been Idle That Long, Retry for Up to *NN* Minutes check box and text box; and the Stop the Task if the Computer Ceases to Be Idle check box.

  Power Management section If you don't want to drain your portable's battery by running the task on battery power, select the Don't Start the Task if the Computer Is Running on Batteries check box and the Stop the Task if Battery Mode Begins check box. If you want Windows to wake your computer from its questionably deserved slumber in order to perform the task, select the Wake the Computer to Run This Task check box.

Changing a Scheduled Task

To change the details of a scheduled task, double-click the task in the Scheduled Tasks folder and work in the task's Properties dialog box. (See the previous section for details of the settings you can change.)

Preventing a Scheduled Task from Running

To prevent a scheduled task from running, clear the Enabled (Scheduled Task Runs at Specified Time) check box on the Task tab of the Properties dialog box for the task.

To delete a scheduled task, right-click it in the Scheduled Tasks folder and choose Delete from the shortcut menu. (Alternatively, select the task and click the Delete This Item link in the Folder Tasks list.) Select the Yes button in the confirmation message box.

Managing Disks with Disk Management

Formatting disks and converting their file system is all very well—but what if you need to create or delete a partition? For these tasks, Windows provides a Computer Management snap-in called Disk Management.

Starting Disk Management

Take the following steps to start Disk Management:

1. Choose Start ➢ Control Panel.
    - Alternatively, click the Start button to display the Start menu, right-click the My Computer item, and choose Manage from the shortcut menu. Windows opens the Computer Management window. Go to step 5.
2. Click the Performance and Maintenance link. Windows displays the Performance and Maintenance screen.
3. Click the Administrative Tools link. Windows displays the Administrative Tools screen.
4. Double-click the Computer Management shortcut. Windows opens a Computer Management window.
5. Expand the Storage item in the console tree if it's not already expanded.
6. Click the Disk Management item. Computer Management starts the Disk Management snap-in, which displays information about your disks. Figure 30.23 shows an example.

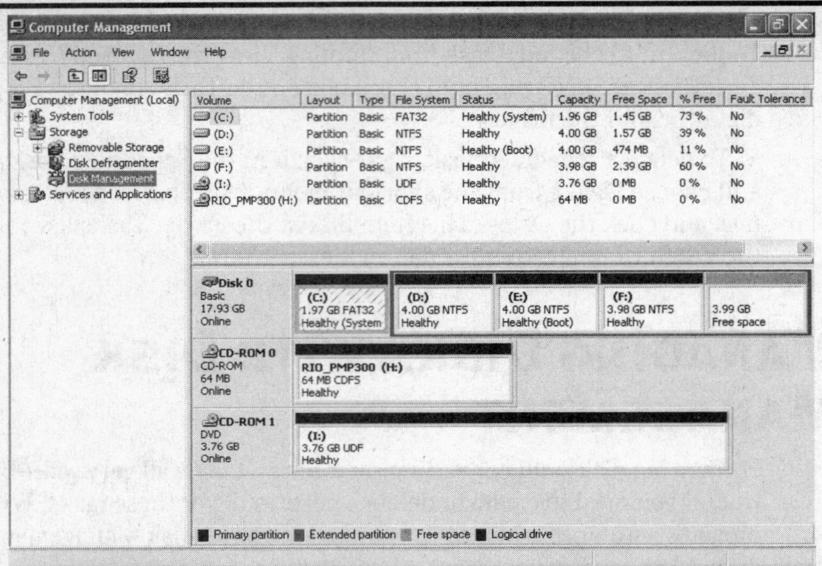

FIGURE 30.23: Use Disk Management to manage your disks.

As you can see in the figure, the top section of the right-hand pane lists the volumes currently defined on the system, giving the following information about each volume:

- The letter for the volume (for example, C:)
- The volume's layout—whether it's a full disk or a partition
- The type (basic or dynamic)
- The file system (FAT32, NTFS, CDFS, UDF, and so on)
- The status—for example, Healthy (Boot) for a boot volume in good condition
- The capacity in megabytes, gigabytes, or larger units
- The amount of free space
- The percentage of the volume free
- Whether fault tolerance is used on the volume
- The overhead consumed by fault tolerance (if it's used). You can't see this column in the figure, because it's off the right side of the screen.

Below this list, Disk Management shows a graphical representation of each physical disk attached to the computer and how it's broken down. For example, in the figure, Disk 0 (the first hard disk—computer counting begins at 0) has a FAT32 C: drive, three NTFS drives, and a chunk of free space. Then there's a CD-ROM drive that shows up as CD-ROM 0 and a DVD drive that shows up as CD-ROM 1.

EXPERT KNOWLEDGE: DYNAMIC DISKS AND FAULT TOLERANCE

That bit about basic disks and dynamic disks may have raised your eyebrows a bit—especially since Disk Management shows that your computer has basic disks. But don't worry—the term refers to the disk's configuration rather than to its capabilities. If you bought the largest and fastest hard drive on the block, it'll still be the largest and fastest until the engineers release something better, no matter that it uses the basic disk configuration.

A *basic disk* is one configured to support primary partitions, extended partitions, and logical drives (within extended partitions). A *dynamic disk* is one configured so that you can use fault tolerance or create multidisk volumes on the fly.

Fault tolerance is a feature typically implemented only in servers or high-end workstations. It uses multiple disks to avoid the possible loss of information when disk problems occur. Windows 2000 Server and Windows XP Professional implement software fault tolerance through Redundant Array of Inexpensive Disks (RAID). Fault tolerance involves *overhead*—extra space used to keep extra copies of information so that it isn't lost if hardware fails.

Creating a Partition

If you have free space available, you can create a partition in it. Below is an example of creating a new logical drive using that free space shown back in Figure 30.23. The options available to you will depend on your disk configuration.

1. Right-click the free space and choose New Logical Drive from the shortcut menu. Computer Management starts the New Partition Wizard, which displays an introductory page.

2. Click the Next button. The Wizard displays the Select Partition Type page (shown in Figure 30.24).

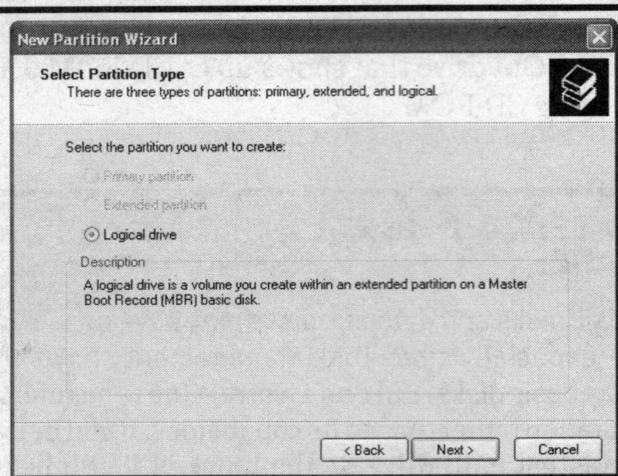

FIGURE 30.24: On the Select Partition Type page of the New Partition Wizard, specify which type of partition to create (if there's a choice).

Select the partition type (you may not have a choice, as in the figure) and click the Next button. The Wizard displays the Specify Partition Size page (shown in Figure 30.25).

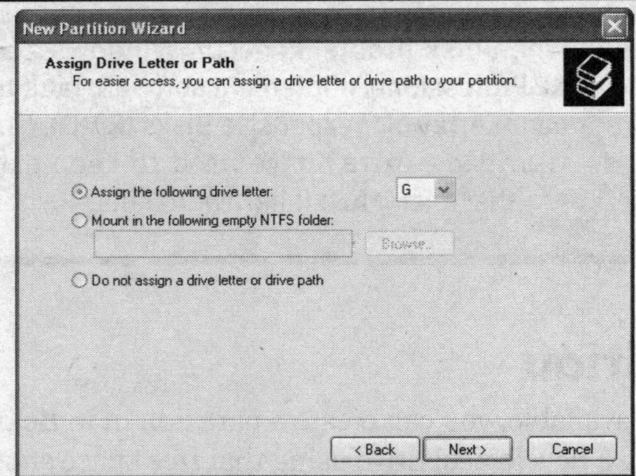

FIGURE 30.25: On the Specify Partition Size page of the New Partition Wizard, specify the size of the partition.

4. In the Partition Size in MB text box, enter the size of partition you want to create. The Wizard suggests using all the

space available, which you may well not want to do. The read-out above the text box shows the minimum and maximum sizes possible.

5. Click the Next button. The Wizard displays the Assign Drive Letter or Path page (shown in Figure 30.26).

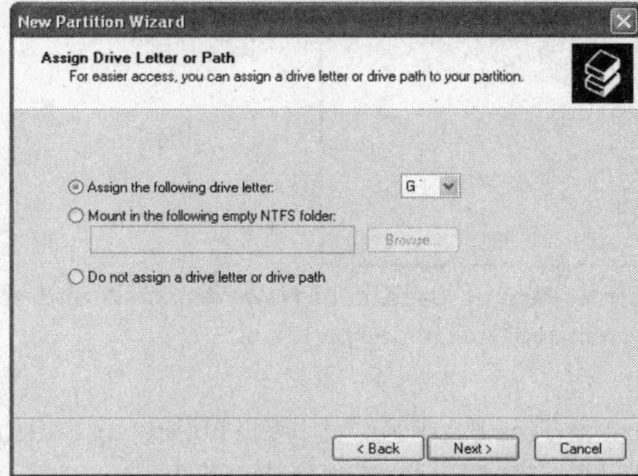

FIGURE 30.26: On the Assign Drive Letter or Path page of the New Partition Wizard, specify the drive letter to use for the partition.

6. Leave the Assign the Following Drive Letter option button selected and specify the letter in the drop-down list.

   - Instead of assigning a drive letter, you can select the Mount in the Following Empty NTFS Folder option button and specify the folder in the text box. This option tends to be of more use for servers than for home or home-office computers.

   - Instead of doing either of the above, you *can* avoid assigning a drive letter or path by selecting the Do Not Assign a Drive Letter or Drive Path option button. The only reason to do this is if you're planning to assign letters (or paths) later after creating other partitions. In order to access the partition through the Windows interface (for example, from Explorer or from an application), you'll need to assign a drive letter or path to it sooner or later—and it may as well be sooner.

7. Click the Next button. The Wizard displays the Format Partition page (shown in Figure 30.27).

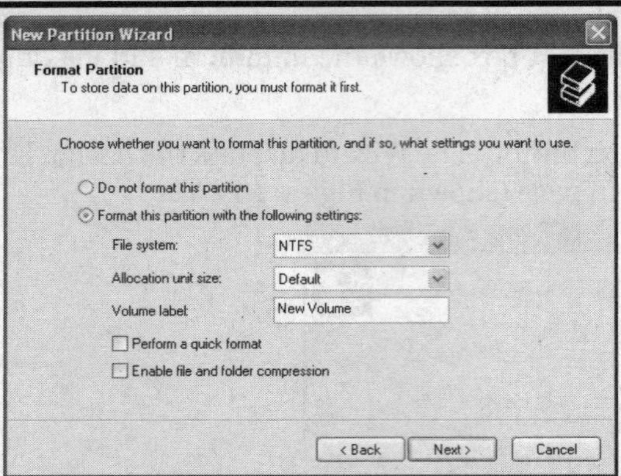

FIGURE 30.27: On the Format Partition page of the New Partition Wizard, specify the file system and label for the partition.

8. Leave the Format This Partition with the Following Settings option button selected and choose settings:
   - Choose the file system (preferably NTFS, but FAT32 or FAT if necessary) in the File System drop-down list.
   - Leave the Allocation Unit Size drop-down list set to Default unless you've got a very good reason to change it.
   - Enter the label for the volume in the Volume Label text box. (The Wizard suggests `New Volume`, but you should be able to come up with something more descriptive. Again, you have 20 characters for the label on an NTFS volume and 11 characters for that on a FAT or FAT32 volume.)
   - Select the Perform a Quick Format check box if you've checked the disk for errors recently and found none. If not, it's better to perform a full format, including the check for errors.
   - Select the Enable File and Folder Compression check box if you want to use compression on the volume.
9. Click the Next button. The Wizard displays the Completing the New Partition Wizard page (shown in Figure 30.28).

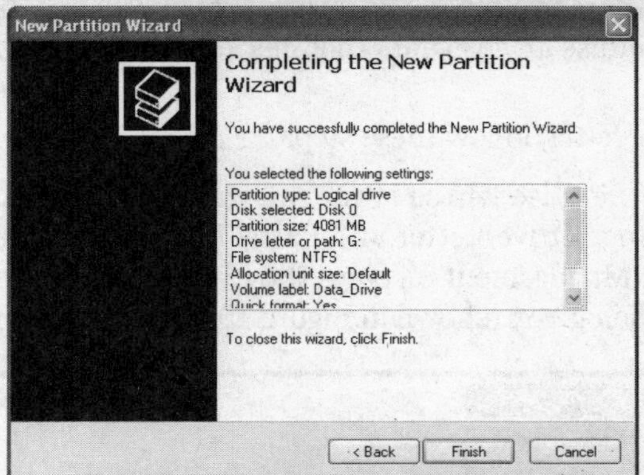

FIGURE 30.28: On the Completing the New Partition Wizard page of the New Partition Wizard, double-check the choices you made.

10. Click the Finish button. The Wizard closes, creates the partition, and formats it. You'll need to wait for the formatting to finish before you can use the volume.

Deleting a Partition

To delete a partition and dispose of all its data, right-click the partition and issue the Delete command from the shortcut menu. For example, if it's a logical drive, choose the Delete Logical Drive item on the shortcut menu. Disk Management displays a Delete Logical Drive dialog box such as that shown in Figure 30.29. Click the Yes button to proceed.

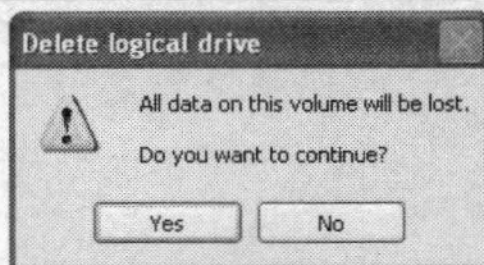

FIGURE 30.29: Disk Management double-checks that you're sure you want to delete a drive.

Changing the Drive Letter

Disk Management also lets you change the drive letter for a volume other than your system volume or boot volume. This capability comes in handy if you get your drive letters in a tangle. Be aware, though, that changing the drive letter will confuse any program that has learned the path to files on this drive.

To change the drive letter, follow these steps:

1. Right-click the drive whose letter you want to change and choose Change Drive Letter and Paths from the shortcut menu. Disk Management displays the Change Drive Letter and Paths dialog box (shown in Figure 30.30).

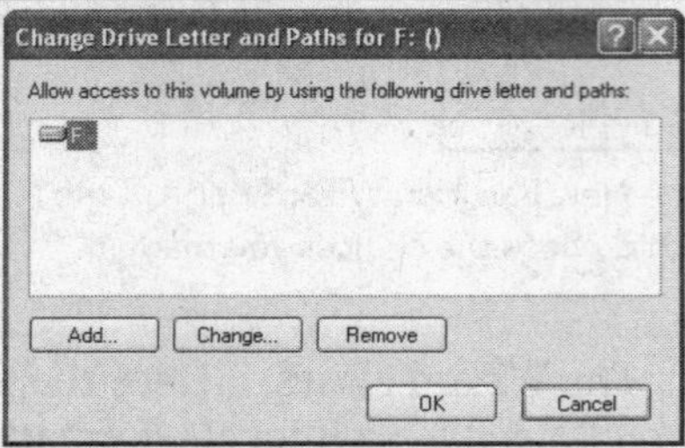

FIGURE 30.30: Use the Change Drive Letter and Paths dialog box to change the drive letter for a drive.

2. To change the drive letter, select it (if it's not already selected) and click the Change button. Disk Management displays the Change Drive Letter or Path dialog box (shown in Figure 30.31).

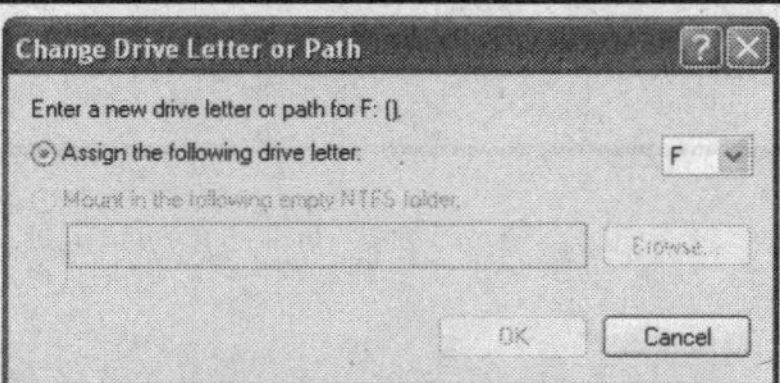

FIGURE 30.31: Specify the drive letter or path in the Change Drive Letter or Path dialog box.

3. Make sure the Assign the Following Drive Letter option button is selected, then select the letter in the drop-down list.

   Click the OK button. Disk Management displays the Confirm dialog box (shown in Figure 30.32), warning you that changing the drive letter might prevent programs from running.

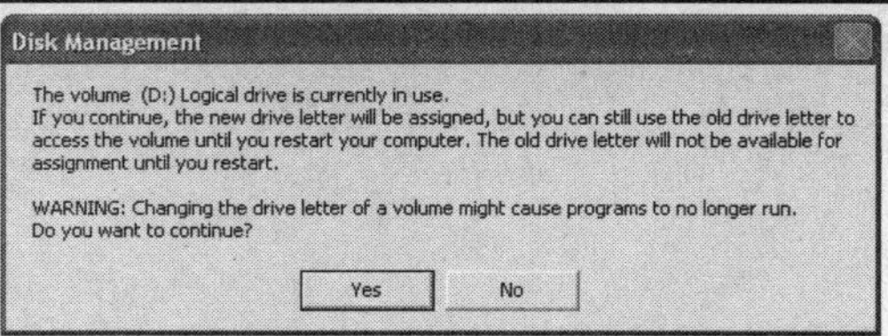

FIGURE 30.32: Confirm the change in the Confirm dialog box.

5. Click the Yes button. If files on the drive are open, Disk Management displays the Disk Management dialog box shown in Figure 30.33 telling you that you can continue to use the old drive letter until you reboot and asking if you want to continue.

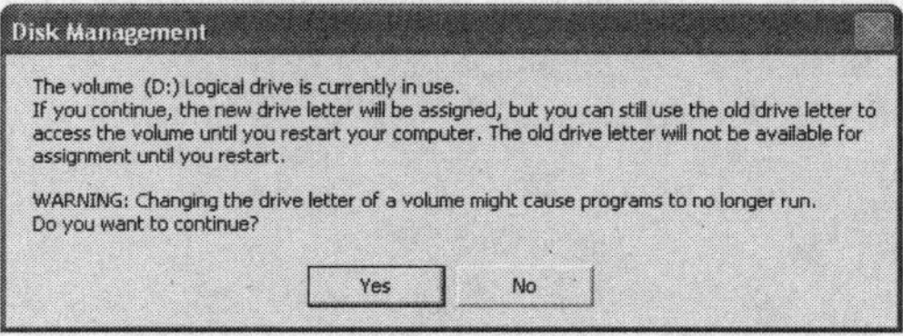

FIGURE 30.33: Read the small print in the Disk Management dialog box and signal your willingness to proceed.

6. Click the Yes button. Disk Management makes the change.
7. Change other drive letters if necessary, then restart your computer so that you can start using the new drive letter assignments.

Exiting Disk Management

When you've finished working in Disk Management, choose File ➢ Exit to close the Computer Management window.

What's Next?

This chapter has discussed how to manage your disks and drives. The next chapter continues the topic of how to manage your computer and focuses on how to manage hardware, drivers, and power.

Chapter 31

Managing Hardware, Drivers, and Power

This chapter discusses how to install hardware on your computer and how to install, update, and roll back device drivers, the software that makes hardware function. It also covers how to configure power management on your computer and how to install an uninterruptible power supply.

Windows XP greatly simplifies the software end of the process of adding hardware. If the hardware is hot pluggable, Windows locates and loads the correct driver automatically. If the hardware is conventional, you use the Found New Hardware Wizard (if Windows finds the hardware) or the Add Hardware Wizard (if you have to tell Windows that the hardware is there) to install the software for the device. This chapter shows you how to use these Wizards and notes special considerations for installing common types of hardware.

Revised and adapted from *Mastering Windows XP Home Edition* by Guy Hart-Davis

ISBN 0-7821-2980-3 1024 pages $39.99

What Hardware Can You Use with Windows XP?

One of Microsoft's goals in designing Windows XP was to make it capable of picking up the hardware compatibility mantle of Windows 98 and Windows Me, each of which supported an impressive range of hardware both (relatively) ancient and modern. As a result, Windows XP supports a very full range of hardware right out of the box, and it includes compatibility-tested drivers for many products. A *driver* is a piece of software that enables it and Windows to communicate with each other.

By using the Windows Update feature to keep your copy of Windows up to date, and by downloading new drivers from hardware manufacturers' websites as necessary, you can also add the latest hardware to Windows XP. The devices you're more likely to have problems with are legacy devices more than a few years old, particularly those from smaller companies or from companies that have gone out of business.

To check whether a hardware item is compatible with Windows XP, open Help and Support Center (choose Start ➢ Help and Support), click the Compatible Hardware and Software link on the Home page, and use the search options on the Compatible Hardware and Software page.

Using Hot-Pluggable Devices

Hardware devices that use USB, FireWire, and PC Card connections are *hot pluggable*—you can plug in and unplug the device while Windows is running without any adverse effects. Windows automatically loads and unloads drivers for hot-pluggable devices as needed.

NOTE

Limited users and Guest users can install hot-pluggable devices. In most cases, only Computer Administrator users can install devices that are not hot pluggable.

Installing a Hot-Pluggable Device

When you plug in a hot-pluggable device for the first time, Windows displays a pop-up from the notification area to let you know that it has noticed the device. Figure 31.1 shows an example.

FIGURE 31.1: Windows displays a notification area pop-up message when it notices you've plugged in a hot-pluggable device.

Windows then automatically looks for a driver to let Windows and the device communicate with each other. It first checks in its capacious driver cache, which contains a wide variety of preinstalled drivers. If it draws a blank there, and if your computer is connected to the Internet, it checks the Windows Update site for a driver for the device; if it finds a driver, it downloads it and installs it. If Windows is able to find a suitable driver in either the driver cache or Windows Update, it unpacks and installs the driver, displaying a pop-up identifying the device as it does so. Figure 31.2 shows an example of such a pop-up.

FIGURE 31.2: If Windows can find a driver for the hot-pluggable device, it loads it.

When the driver is installed and working, Windows displays a pop-up telling you that the hardware is ready to use. Figure 31.3 shows an example of such a pop-up.

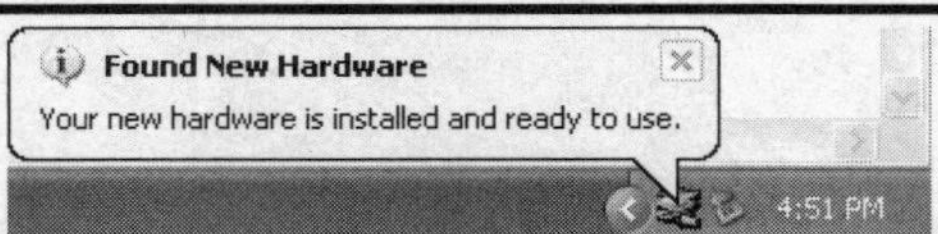

FIGURE 31.3: Windows lets you know when the device is ready to use.

If Windows can't find a driver for the device, it starts the Found New Hardware Wizard, so that you can supply the driver for the device manually. See "Using the Found New Hardware Wizard" later in this chapter for a walkthrough of using the Found New Hardware Wizard.

Removing a Hot-Pluggable Device

Removing a USB device or FireWire device is as simple as unplugging it. Windows notices that you've removed the device and unloads its driver.

To remove a PC Card device, you're supposed to use the Safely Remove Hardware feature. But often you can simply unplug the PC Card without causing any problems.

Plugging a Hot-Pluggable Device in Again

When you plug a hot-pluggable device in again, Windows notices it and loads the driver without displaying any pop-up.

Using the Found New Hardware Wizard

For devices that aren't hot pluggable, or for hot-pluggable devices for which Windows can't find a suitable driver, you use Windows' two hardware Wizards, the Found New Hardware Wizard and the Add Hardware Wizard.

When Windows discovers some hardware new to it (or that Windows thinks it doesn't know about), it starts the Found New Hardware Wizard. Figure 31.4 shows the first page of the Found New Hardware Wizard.

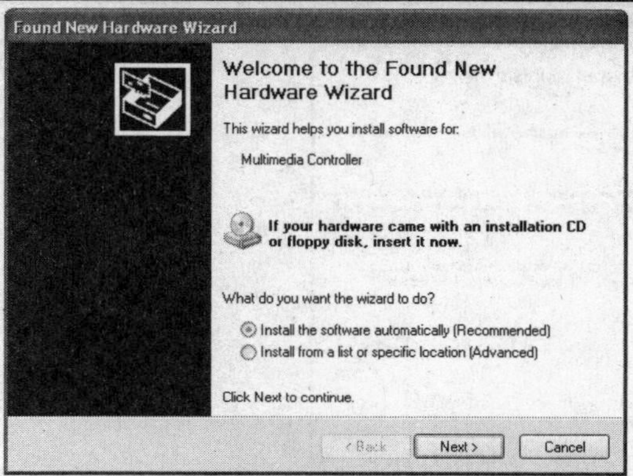

FIGURE 31.4: Windows displays the first page of the Found New Hardware Wizard when it discovers new hardware. Choose whether to install the software for the hardware automatically or specify the details of the software you want to install.

As you can see in the figure, the Wizard lists the type of hardware it has found—in this case, Multimedia Controller. If the Wizard can't identify the type of hardware, it displays *Unknown device*.

The What Do You Want the Wizard to Do? list gives you two options:

Install the Software Automatically Select this option button (which is usually selected by default) if you want the Wizard to try to install the software needed for the hardware. This is usually a good option: The Wizard often manages to set up the hardware, and if it doesn't, you can easily return to this stage and try the second option. Click the Next button. The Wizard searches for the software and installs it automatically.

Install from a List or Specific Location Select this option button if you want to specify a particular driver for the hardware. Then follow the procedure described in the next section.

If the Found New Hardware Wizard *doesn't* find the software it needs, it displays the Cannot Install This Hardware page (shown in Figure 31.5).

FIGURE 31.5: The Found New Hardware Wizard displays the Cannot Install This Hardware page if it can't find the software needed for the device. Click the Back button if you want to return to the start of the Wizard so that you can try the procedure manually.

At this point, you have three choices:

- If you want to give up on installing the software for this hardware completely (or at least for the foreseeable future), make sure the Don't Prompt Me Again to Install This Software check box is selected. Then click the Finish button. The Wizard closes itself and makes a note not to find this piece of hardware again.
- If you want to give up on installing the software for the time being, clear the Don't Prompt Me Again to Install This Software check box. Then click the Finish button. Each time you restart Windows (or run the Add Hardware Wizard), the Found New Hardware Wizard will offer to install the hardware. These offers get old fast, but you may sometimes want to leave the installation of hardware for a day or two while you dig out the driver disk, download a new driver manually, or run Windows Update to see if it can find a driver.
- To try to identify the necessary software yourself, click the Back button to return to the start of the Wizard. Then follow the steps below.

Installing a Driver from a Specific Location

To install a driver from a specific location, take the following steps:

1. On the first page of the Found New Hardware Wizard, select the Install from a List or Specific Location option button.
2. Click the Next button. The Found New Hardware Wizard displays the Please Choose Your Search and Installation Options page (shown in Figure 31.6).

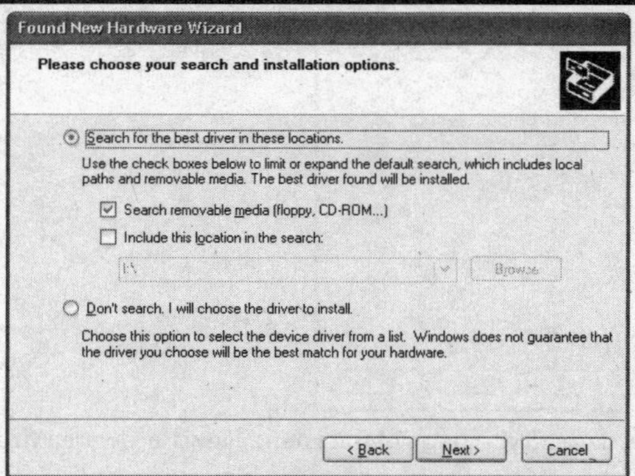

FIGURE 31.6: On the Please Choose Your Search and Installation Options page of the Found New Hardware Wizard, choose whether to search for a driver or specify a particular one.

3. Choose whether to let the Wizard search for a driver or to specify a specific driver:
   - To let the Wizard search, leave the Search for the Best Driver in These Locations option button selected. Then select the Search Removable Media (Floppy, CD-ROM) check box if you want the Wizard to search your floppy and CD-ROM drives. (Insert a floppy or CD at this point if appropriate.) Alternatively, or additionally, select the Include This Location in the Search check box and use the text box, drop-down list, or Browse button to specify the location to search.
   - To specify a driver yourself, select the Don't Search. I Will Choose the Driver to Install option button.

4. Click the Next button.
   - If you chose to search for a driver, the Wizard searches for one, installs it (if it finds one), and displays the Completing the Found New Hardware Wizard page.
   - If you chose to specify a driver, the Wizard displays the Hardware Type page (shown in Figure 31.7).

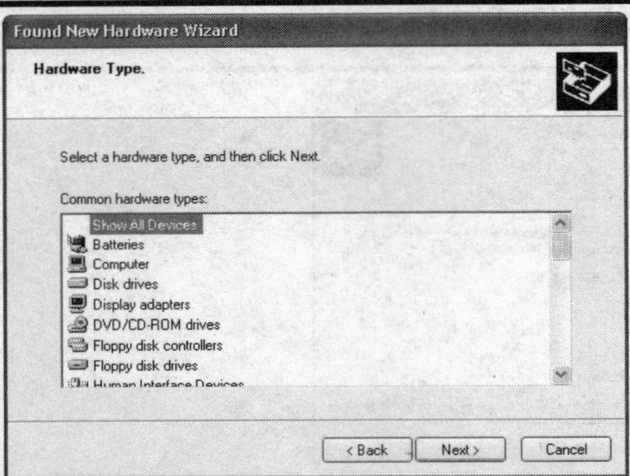

FIGURE 31.7: On the Hardware Type page of the Found New Hardware Wizard, choose the type of hardware you're installing.

5. In the Common Hardware Types list box, select the type of hardware you're installing. The list is extensive, but if the device doesn't fit any of the descriptions, select the Show All Devices item.

TIP

If you're installing a driver from a floppy or a CD, it's not crucial that you get the hardware type right. The function of this page is to display the appropriate list of manufacturers and devices on the Select the Device Driver You Want to Install for This Hardware page of the Wizard.

6. Click the Next button. The Found New Hardware Wizard displays the Select the Device Driver You Want to Install for This Hardware page. Figure 31.8 shows this page with all devices shown.

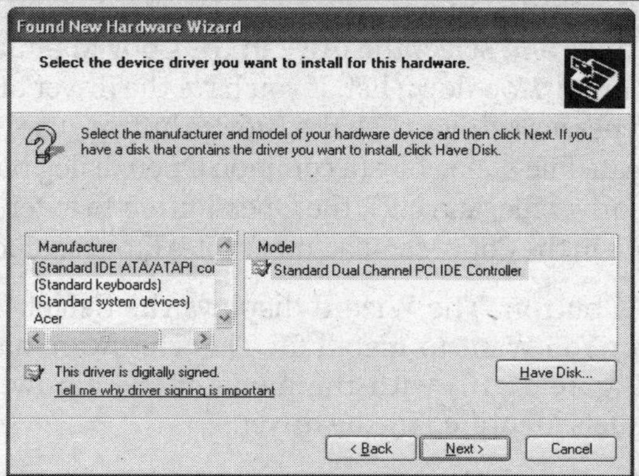

FIGURE 31.8: On the Select the Device Driver You Want to Install for This Hardware page, select the manufacturer and device, or use the Have Disk button to identify the driver by its file.

7. If Windows has a driver for the device, you can select it by selecting the manufacturer in the Manufacturer list box and the device in the Model list box. But usually the Found New Hardware Wizard will have identified the driver if Windows has it already, so you'll be visiting this page of the Wizard only if you need to install a driver that Windows *doesn't* have. Click the Have Disk button. Windows displays the Install From Disk dialog box (shown in Figure 31.9).

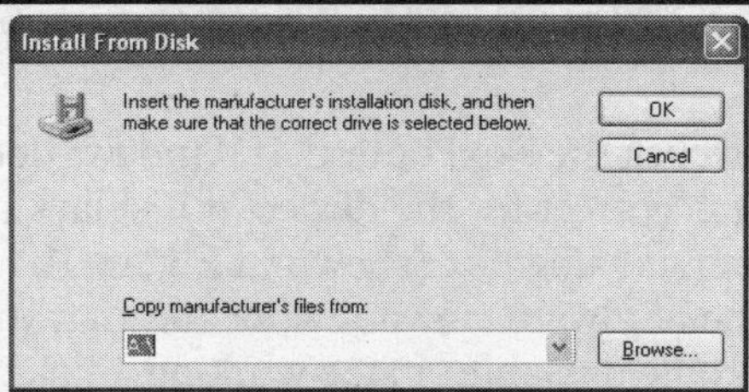

FIGURE 31.9: Use the Install From Disk dialog box to provide a driver of your own.

8. If you have the driver on a floppy or a CD, insert it in the appropriate drive and select the drive in the Copy Manufacturer's Files From drop-down list. If you have the driver on a local drive or network drive, click the Browse button, use the resulting Locate File dialog box (a common Open dialog box) to locate the driver file, and click the Open button to enter its name and path in the Copy Manufacturer's Files From text box.

9. Click the OK button. The Wizard displays the Select the Device Driver You Want to Install for This Hardware page (shown in Figure 31.10) with the name of the hardware model or models identified by the driver.

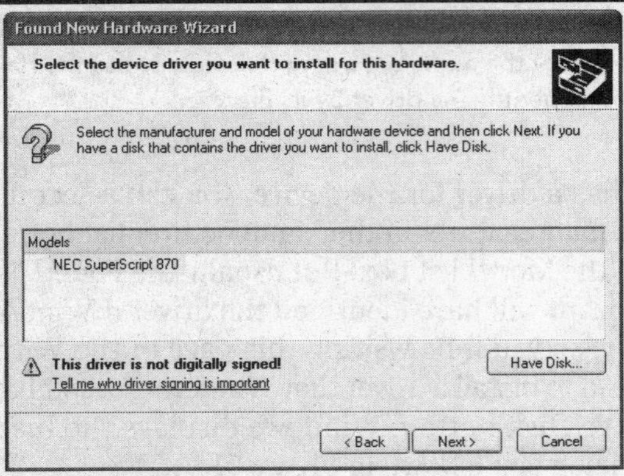

FIGURE 31.10: When you specify the driver to use, the Wizard displays the Select the Device Driver You Want to Install for This Hardware page.

10. Select the driver and click the Next button. If Windows doesn't think the driver is correct for the device, it displays the Update Driver Warning dialog box (shown in Figure 31.11), warning you that the hardware may not work and that your computer might become unstable or stop working. Click the Yes button if you're sure you want to install this driver. Otherwise, click the No button and select another driver.

NOTE

If the Wizard can't find hardware information in the location you specified, it displays the Select Device message box telling you that the location you specified doesn't contain information about your hardware. The Wizard then displays the Install from Disk dialog box again so that you can specify a different location for the file. If you get to this stage, you're probably stuck. You can click the Cancel button to close the Install from Disk dialog box and return to the Select the Device Driver You Want to Install for This Hardware page so that you can select a built-in driver, but that's about it. Click the Cancel button to cancel the Wizard.

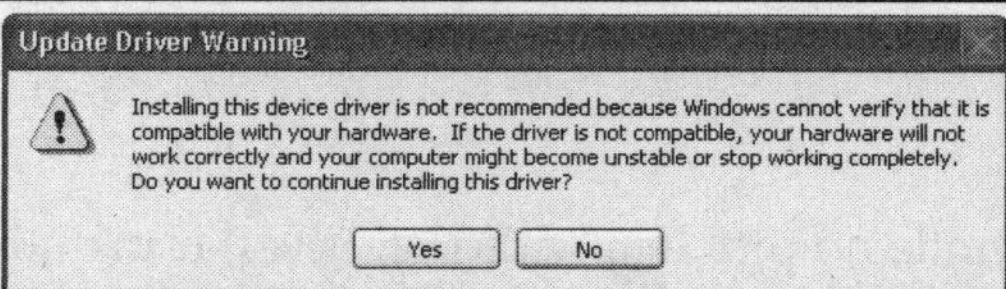

FIGURE 31.11: The Update Driver Warning dialog box warns you if you've chosen a driver that appears not to match your device.

11. The Wizard checks to make sure that the driver you're installing has passed the Windows Logo testing to verify its compatibility with Windows XP. (See the next Note for an explanation of Windows Logo testing.) If the driver has passed Windows Logo testing, all is well; if it hasn't passed, the Wizard displays the Hardware Installation dialog box (shown in Figure 31.12), warning you of the problem and strongly discouraging you from installing the driver. If you're sure the driver is okay, click the Continue Anyway button. If you have any doubts about the driver, click the STOP Installation button.

NOTE

Windows Logo testing isn't testing a logo, as its name implies, but rather a Windows compatibility test. When a product passes the test, the manufacturer is allowed to display the Designed for Microsoft Windows logos on the product. Drivers that pass Windows Logo testing are digitally signed by Microsoft to verify their compatibility. The Wizard checks for the digital signature and raises Cain if it's not there.

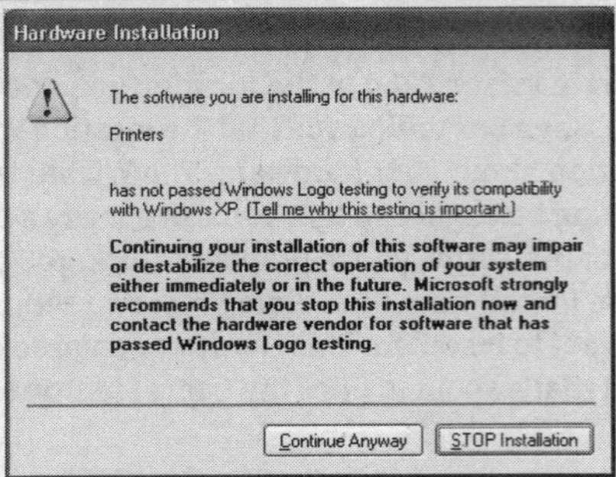

FIGURE 31.12: If the driver you're installing hasn't passed Windows Logo testing, the Wizard displays the Hardware Installation dialog box to warn you.

12. If Windows finds no problem with the driver, it installs it and displays the Completing the Found New Hardware Wizard page.
13. Click the Finish button. The Wizard closes itself, and the hardware is ready for use.

If the Found New Hardware Wizard is unable to install the device, it displays the Cannot Install This Hardware page, telling you what the problem was. Figure 31.13 shows an example in which the driver file ("the third-party INF"—*inf* is short for *initialization file*) didn't contain digital signature information.

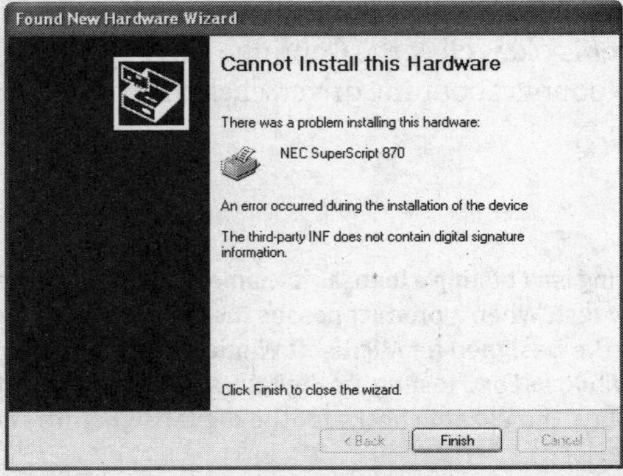

FIGURE 31.13: The Found New Hardware Wizard displays the Cannot Install This Hardware page if it runs into a problem installing the device.

NOTE

Help and Support Center contains a system for referring searches for drivers that don't come with Windows or with the hardware device. When you plug in a new hardware device, and Windows finds that it doesn't have a driver for it and you can't supply a driver, Windows invites you to send information about the hardware to Microsoft. Once you've sent the information, you can take a variety of actions depending on what information is available. For example, you might be able to view a list of compatible devices (if any), search for information on compatible devices or Knowledge Base articles about the hardware, or find a link to the vendor's website.

Running the Add Hardware Wizard

If Windows doesn't find the new hardware you install, run the Add Hardware Wizard so that you can add the hardware manually. As you'll see, there's considerable overlap between the Add Hardware Wizard and the Found New Hardware Wizard, so don't be surprised if some of the steps in this list duplicate those in the previous section.

To run the Add Hardware Wizard, take the following steps:

1. Choose Start ➢ Control Panel. Windows displays Control Panel.
2. Click the Printers and Other Hardware link. Windows displays the Printers and Other Hardware screen.
3. Click the Add Hardware link in the See Also pane. Windows starts the Add Hardware Wizard, which displays the Welcome to the Add Hardware Wizard page.
4. Click the Next button. The Wizard searches for new hardware and displays the The Following Hardware Is Already Installed on Your Computer page (shown in Figure 31.14).

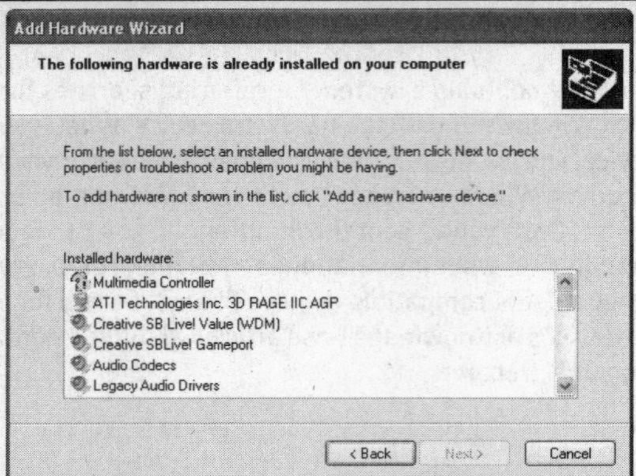

FIGURE 31.14: On the The Following Hardware Is Already Installed on Your Computer page of the Add Hardware Wizard, select the Add a New Hardware Device item.

NOTE

If the Add Hardware Wizard doesn't find any hardware it didn't already know about, it displays the Is the Hardware Connected? page, which asks whether you've already connected the hardware to the computer. Select the Yes, I Have Already Connected the Hardware option button or the No, I Have Not Added the Hardware Yet option button as appropriate. If you select the Yes, I Have Already Connected the Hardware option button, the Wizard displays the The Following Hardware Is Already Installed on Your Computer screen. If you select the No, I Have Not Added the Hardware Yet option button, the Wizard displays the Cannot Continue the Add Hardware Wizard screen, which offers to turn off the computer for you so that you can connect the hardware and try the Add Hardware Wizard again.

5. If the device you want to install is listed in the Installed Hardware list box, select it. If it's not, select the Add a New Hardware Device item in the list box—the last item in the list.
6. Click the Next button. The Wizard displays the The Wizard Can Help You Install Other Hardware page (shown in Figure 31.15), offering to search for the hardware.

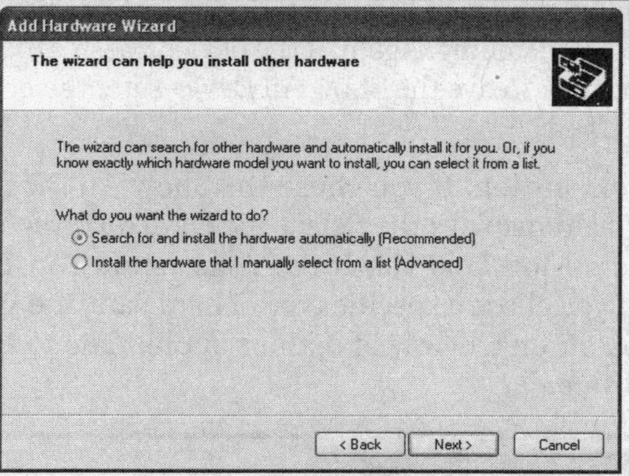

FIGURE 31.15: The Add Hardware Wizard offers to search for the hardware, but usually you'll do better to select it manually.

7. Select the Install the Hardware That I Manually Select from a List option button.
8. Click the Next button. The Wizard displays the From the List Below, Select the Type of Hardware You Are Installing page (shown in Figure 31.16).

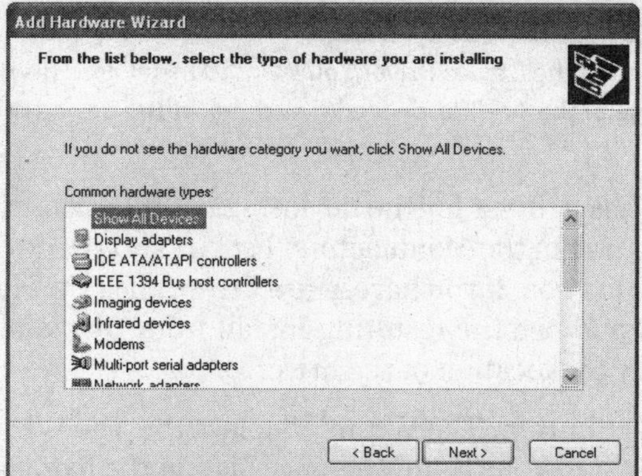

FIGURE 31.16: On the From the List Below, Select the Type of Hardware You Are Installing page, select the category of hardware that you're installing.

9. In the Common Hardware Types list box, select the type of hardware you're installing. Again, if the device doesn't fit any of the descriptions, leave the Show All Devices item selected (as it is by default).

10. Click the Next button. If you chose the Show All Devices item, the Wizard displays the Select the Device Driver You Want to Install for This Hardware page (shown in Figure 31.17). If you chose a specific type of hardware, the Wizard leads you off on a byway of options appropriate to that type of hardware.

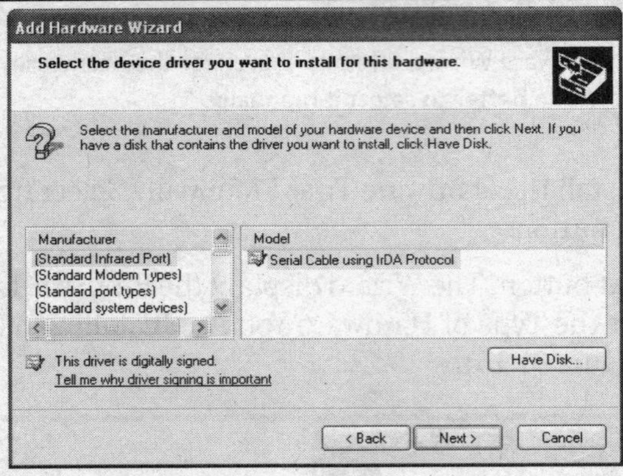

FIGURE 31.17: On the Select the Device Driver You Want to Install for This Hardware page of the Add Hardware Wizard, select the device driver.

11. If Windows has a driver for the device, select it by selecting the manufacturer in the Manufacturer list box and the device in the Model list box. If you have a new driver, click the Have Disk button and use the resulting Install from Disk dialog box to specify the location of the driver.

12. Click the Next button. The Wizard displays the The Wizard Is Ready to Install Your Hardware page, listing the hardware that's lined up for installation.

13. Click the Next button. The Wizard installs the hardware and displays the Completing the Add Hardware Wizard page (shown in Figure 31.18).

FIGURE 31.18: The Completing the Add Hardware Wizard page of the Add Hardware Wizard lists the hardware that the Wizard has successfully installed.

14. Click the Finish button. The Add Hardware Wizard closes itself. The hardware should be ready for use.

Working with Hardware Drivers

Without a functional driver, Windows can't use any piece of hardware. And using the wrong driver or a badly written driver can make Windows unstable or even make it crash.

Hardware manufacturers frequently release new versions of drivers for their hardware to improve performance, to banish bugs, or both. If you want to keep your hardware running to the best of its capacity, check the manufacturers' sites and the Windows Update site for updated drivers. In theory, Windows Update should be able to supply you with the latest drivers for most of your hardware. In practice, you can probably get the latest drivers more quickly by haunting the hardware manufacturers' websites and newsgroups.

To view, change, or uninstall the driver for a device, display the Driver tab of the Properties dialog box for the device. The easiest way to display the Properties dialog box for the device is to go through Device Manager.

Opening Device Manager

To display the Device Manager window, take the following steps:

1. Press Winkey+Break or click the Start button, right-click the My Computer item, and choose Properties from the shortcut menu. Windows displays the System Properties dialog box.
2. Click the Hardware tab.
3. Click the Device Manager button. Windows displays the Device Manager window (shown in Figure 31.19).

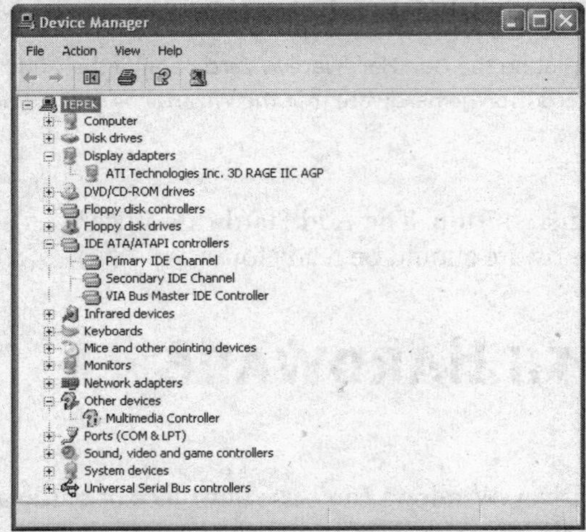

FIGURE 31.19: Use Device Manager to access hardware devices you want to configure.

As you can see in the figure, Device Manager presents a categorized tree of the devices on the computer in its default view. Any device that isn't working or has a problem is marked with a question-mark icon, like the Multimedia Controller that appears in the figure. When all is well with a category of device, Device Manager presents the category collapsed. In the figure, the Display Adapters category and the IDE ATA/ATAPI Controllers category are expanded to show their entries.

You can change the view by displaying the View menu and choosing Devices by Type (the default view), Devices by Connection, Resources by Type, or Resources by Connection from the menu. You can display hidden devices by choosing View ➢ Show Hidden Devices.

If you leave Device Manager open while you plug in a hot-pluggable device, you may need to refresh the listing in Device Manager to make it list the device. To do so, choose Action ➢ Scan for Hardware Changes.

To check or set properties for a device, double-click its entry in Device Manager (or right-click the entry and choose Properties from the shortcut menu). Windows displays the Properties dialog box for the device.

Checking the Details of a Driver

The Driver tab of the Properties dialog box for a device shows some details of the driver: the provider of the driver (the company that supplied the driver to your computer), the date, the version, and the *digital signer*—the owner of the digital certificate applied to the driver. Figure 31.20 shows an example of the Driver tab of the Properties dialog box for a graphics card driver.

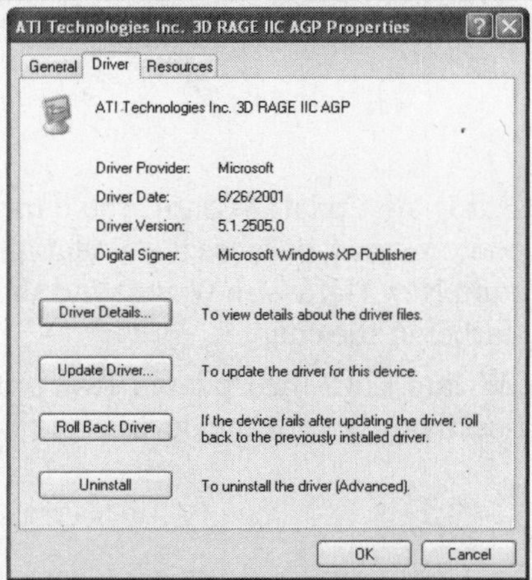

FIGURE 31.20: The Driver tab of the Properties dialog box shows some information about the driver.

To display further information, click the Driver Details button. Windows displays the Driver File Details dialog box, which displays further information: the filenames and paths of the driver files, the provider (the company that originally provided the driver), the file version, the copyright information, and the digital signer (again). Figure 31.21 shows an example of the Driver File Details dialog box.

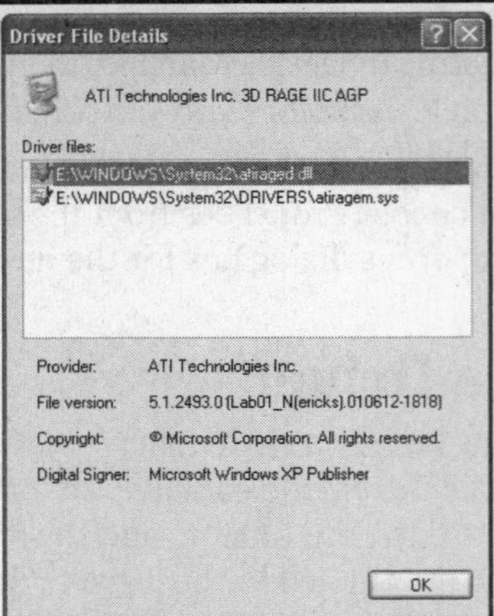

FIGURE 31.21: The Driver File Details dialog box contains further information about the driver, including the filenames and paths of the driver files.

Updating a Driver

To update a driver, you use the Hardware Update Wizard. You'll have no problems with the Hardware Update Wizard, because it's essentially another manifestation of the Found New Hardware Wizard and the Add Hardware Wizard that you met earlier in the chapter.

To run the Hardware Update Wizard, click the Update Driver button on the Driver tab of the Properties dialog box for the device.

Rolling Back a Driver

If a new driver you've installed doesn't work, or doesn't improve things, revert to the previous driver by using the driver rollback feature. To use the rollback feature, click the Roll Back Driver button on the Driver tab of the Properties dialog box for the device.

DISABLING A DEVICE

If you want to stop using a device temporarily, you can disable it. For example, you might want to disable a device that you think is making Windows unstable.

To disable a device, right-click it in Device Manager and choose Disable from the shortcut menu. Windows displays a confirmation message box such as that shown in Figure 31.22. Click the Yes button. Windows closes the message box and disables the device.

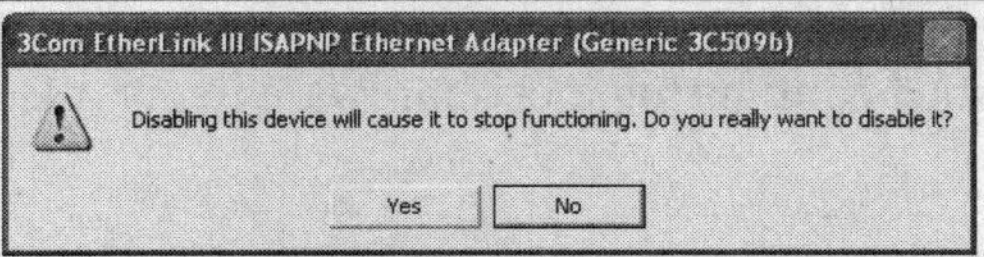

FIGURE 31.22: Windows displays a confirmation message box when you instruct it to disable a device.

UNINSTALLING A DEVICE

If you want to stop using a device permanently and remove it from your computer, uninstall it first. To do so, right-click the device in Device Manager and choose Uninstall from the shortcut menu. Windows displays the Confirm Device Removal dialog box, of which Figure 31.23 shows an example. Click the OK button. Windows closes the dialog box and uninstalls the device.

FIGURE 31.23: Windows displays the Confirm Device Removal dialog box for confirmation when you uninstall a device.

NOTE

You can also uninstall a device by clicking the Uninstall button on the Driver tab of the Properties dialog box for the device.

Adding Specific Hardware Items

The following sections discuss considerations for adding particular hardware items that need configuration beyond the driver. Many hardware items do not.

The easiest place to start configuring most hardware items is Device Manager.

Adding a CD Drive

The Properties dialog box for a CD-ROM has two settings on its Properties tab (shown in Figure 31.24):

CD Player Volume slider Drag the slider to set the volume you want the CD player to deliver when playing audio CDs. This setting controls the output of the CD drive. You can control the output volume from your sound card by using Volume Control

Enable Digital CD Audio for This CD-ROM Device check box Select this check box if you want to use digital output rather than analog output from the CD drive for audio CDs. Digital output typically gives you higher audio quality, especially when you're copying audio CDs to your hard drive. Most newer CD-ROM drives and just about all DVD drives support digital output, but some older CD-ROM drives don't. If digital output doesn't work for you, clear this check box to return to analog output.

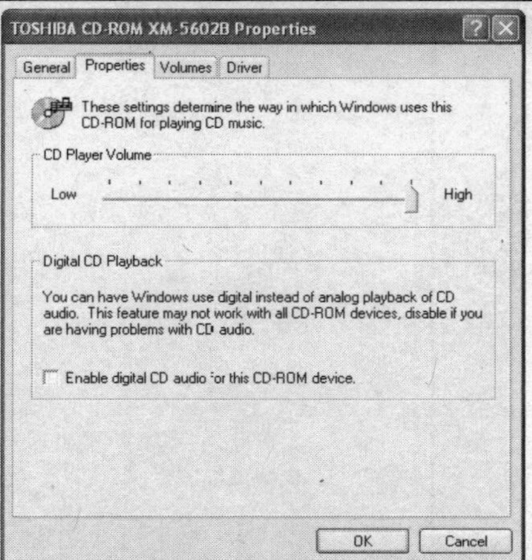

FIGURE 31.24: On the Properties tab of the Properties dialog box for a CD-ROM drive, you can set the CD's volume and specify whether to use digital CD audio.

Adding a DVD Drive

Because DVD drives can play CDs, it should come as no surprise that the Properties dialog box for a DVD drive contains the same Properties tab as the Properties dialog box for a CD drive. (See the previous section for a discussion of the two controls this Properties tab contains.)

The Properties dialog box for a DVD drive also contains a DVD Region tab (shown in Figure 31.25), which displays the DVD encoding region currently set for the DVD player. To change the region, select the country you want in the list box and click the OK button.

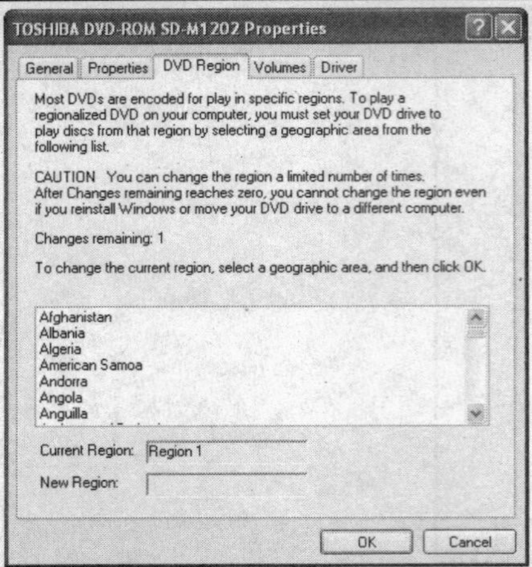

FIGURE 31.25: The DVD Region page of the Properties dialog box for a DVD drive displays the current encoding region.

Adding a Removable Drive

The first time you plug in a removable drive or local drive and Windows finds pictures or audio files on it, Windows displays the Removable Disk dialog box or Local Disk dialog box to let you specify whether you want to set a default action to take with files of this type. Figure 31.26 shows an example of the Removable Disk dialog box for a CompactFlash card in a PC Card adapter. The CompactFlash card contains picture files, so the Removable Disk dialog box contains actions that Windows can take with picture files: Print the Pictures, View a Slideshow of the Images, Copy Pictures to a Folder on My Computer, Open Folder to View Files, or Take No Action.

Select the action you want to take. If you want Windows to take this action for every disk you add that contains this type of file, select the Always Do the Selected Action check box. Then click the OK button. Windows closes the Local Disk dialog box or Removable Disk dialog box and takes the action you specified.

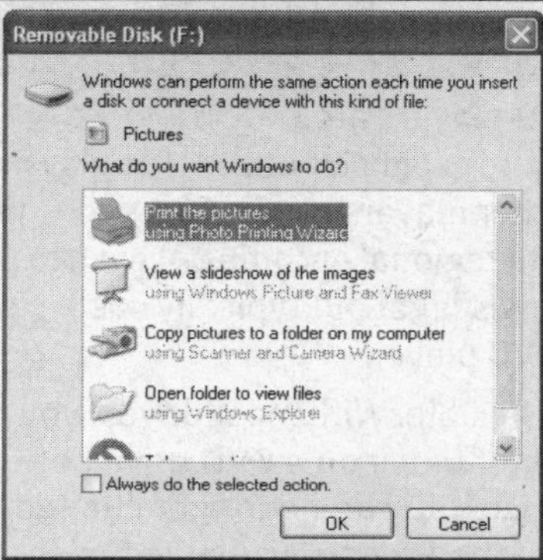

FIGURE 31.26: In the Local Disk dialog box or Removable Disk dialog box (shown here), you can specify which action you want Windows to take for a particular content type when you add a local disk or removable disk.

EXPERT KNOWLEDGE: DVD ENCODING REGIONS

In case you've managed to avoid the question of DVD encoding regions: As far as DVDs are concerned, the world is divided into eight regions or *locales*. Region 1 is the U.S., Canada, and U.S. Territories. Region 2 is Europe, Japan, South Africa, and the Middle East. Region 3 is Southeast Asia, East Asia, and Hong Kong. Region 4 is Australia, New Zealand, the Pacific Islands, South America, Central America, Mexico, and the Caribbean. Region 5 is Eastern Europe, Mongolia, North Korea, the Indian subcontinent, and Africa. Region 6 is China. Region 7 is "reserved" (for off-world use, perhaps). And Region 8 is for international vessels such as airplanes and cruise ships.

DVD players are encoded to play only DVDs for their region. Almost all DVDs are encoded for the region in which they're intended to be sold. (There are also *all-region DVDs* that'll play in any region.) So to play a DVD, you need a player with a matching region code.

CONTINUED →

Most consumer-electronics DVD players are coded for one region only. Some players—typically more expensive ones—can play discs for two, more, or all regions. Other players can be *chipped*—modified—to play DVDs with different regional encoding or even to play any regional encoding. Chipping is legal but typically costs a proportion of the cost of a cheap DVD player.

PC DVD drives are a little more flexible. With most drives, you can switch region a certain number of times on a DVD drive before it goes into a locked state in which you can no longer change the region. The DVD Region page of the Properties dialog box for the DVD drive displays the number of times you can change the region again. Use them sparingly.

Why do DVDs have regional encoding anyway? In theory, it's to let the movie studios control the release of the movie in different countries. For example, U.S.–made movies are usually released in the U.S. several months before they're released in Europe, and DVDs and videos of the movie are often released in the U.S. while the movie is still running in Europe. Regional encoding prevents most of the Europeans from viewing the movie on DVD until it's released with Region 2 encoding.

In practice, regional encoding also enables the distributors to charge different prices for DVDs in different countries without being undercut by imported DVDs from the least expensive regions. For example, at this writing, DVDs in Region 2 are substantially more expensive than those in Region 1, and the European Union is investigating whether this constitutes price-fixing.

Adding a Modem

Windows automatically loads the driver for a USB modem, a PCI modem, or a PC Card modem if it can find the driver. It sometimes loads the driver for a serial modem too, but other times, it fails to notice that you've added it. If this happens, run the Add Hardware Wizard manually and specify the details of the modem.

Specifying Your Location

The first time you go to use a modem, Windows displays the Location Information dialog box (shown in Figure 31.27) demanding your location information unless you've given it already.

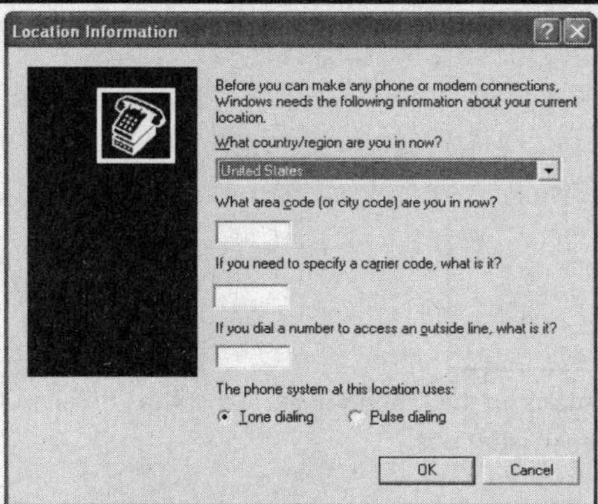

FIGURE 31.27: Sooner or later, Windows prompts you for information about your location. Supply it once, and you should be free from all future demands.

Specify the details: your country and region; your area code or city code; any carrier code you need to enter; any number you dial to access an outside line; and whether the phone system uses tone dialing (the norm for most modern exchanges) or pulse dialing. Then click the OK button. Windows closes the Location Information dialog box.

Specifying Phone and Modem Options

After you close the Location Information dialog box, Windows displays the Phone and Modem Options dialog box with the Dialing Rules tab foremost. Figure 31.28 shows this tab of the dialog box.

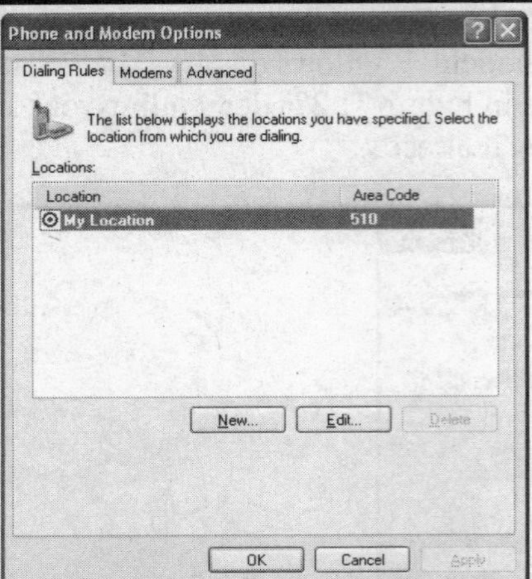

FIGURE 31.28: Edit your locations on the Dialing Rules tab of the Phone and Modem Options dialog box.

Windows provides you with a default location named My Location with the area code you specified in the Location Information dialog box. Rename this location to something descriptive (for example, *Home* or the name of the city or town): Click the Edit button and enter the new name in the Location Name text box on the General tab of the Edit Location dialog box that Windows displays. Click the OK button. Windows closes the Edit Location dialog box. Click the OK button. Windows closes the Phone and Modem Options dialog box.

NOTE

For a laptop or other computer you take traveling, you'll probably want to create other locations as well.

Adding a Video Card

When you install a new video card, Windows may detect it on boot-up and display the Found New Hardware Wizard so that you can install the correct driver for it. Other times, you may have to change the video driver manually by using the Hardware Update Wizard.

After installing the driver for the new video card, you usually need to restart Windows. When you log back in, Windows displays the Display Properties dialog box so that you can test and apply the screen resolution and color quality you want.

Adding a Monitor

Adding a monitor tends to be simplicity itself, involving only a couple of cables. But Windows identifies many monitors simply as Plug and Play Monitor, assigning them a generic driver. This driver works well enough for undemanding programs, but to get the best performance, use the Hardware Update Wizard to install the latest driver for your specific type of monitor.

If you're seeing corrupt images on your monitor, or if the mouse pointer doesn't respond properly to conventional stimuli, or if DirectX isn't working, you may need to change the graphics hardware acceleration on your computer or disable write combining. (*Write combining* is a method of shunting more information from the video card to the monitor at once. It can cause screen corruption by providing the monitor with more information than it can handle.) To do so, take the following steps:

1. Right-click open space on the Desktop and choose Properties from the shortcut menu. Windows displays the Display Properties dialog box.
2. Click the Settings tab.
3. Click the Advanced button. Windows displays the Monitor and Graphics Card Properties dialog box.
4. Click the Troubleshoot tab (shown in Figure 31.29).

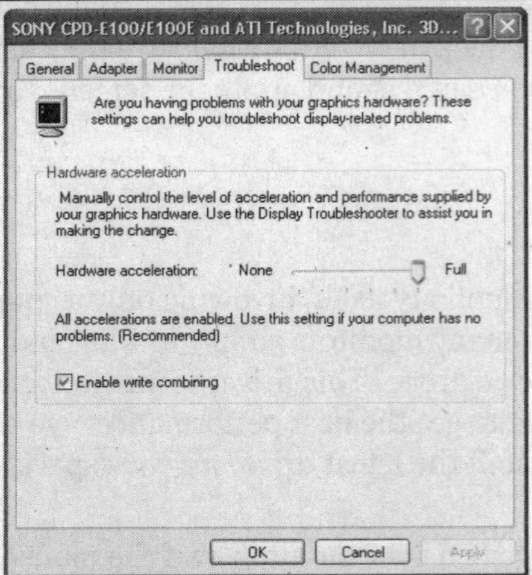

FIGURE 31.29: If you see corrupt images on the screen, try reducing hardware acceleration or disabling write combining on the Troubleshoot tab of the Monitor and Graphics Card Properties dialog box.

5. Move the Hardware Acceleration slider one notch at a time from Full (or wherever you find it) toward None until the problems disappear. At each setting, click the Apply button, and check your computer to see what effect the change has had.
6. Alternatively, or additionally, try clearing the Enable Write Combining check box to prevent screen corruption. Click the Apply button and see what effect the change has had.
7. When the screen seems to be behaving as it should, click the OK button. Windows closes the Monitor and Graphics Card Properties dialog box, returning you to the Display Properties dialog box.
8. Click the OK button. Windows closes the Display Properties dialog box.

Setting Up and Using Multiple Monitors

Like Windows 98 Second Edition, Windows Me, and Windows 2000 Professional, Windows XP lets you attach multiple monitors to your computer to increase the amount of Desktop space available to you. This feature can make both work and play much easier—but it can also lead you to loading your desk with more monitors than it can comfortably provide a footing for.

This discussion of using multiple monitors concerns only desktop computers to which you can add one or more extra graphics cards. But Windows XP includes a feature called DualView that lets you use multiple monitors with portable computers and graphics cards with multiple outputs.

WARNING

Setting up multiple monitors can be a tricky and frustrating business. With some combinations of motherboards and graphics cards, you need to install the graphics cards in the right sequence in order to get them to work. Others work fine immediately. Others never work. Before you try to implement multiple monitors, check the hardware compatibility list (HCL) at the Microsoft website, `www.microsoft.com`, for details of the graphics cards that are known to work in multiple-monitor configurations with Windows XP.

To use multiple monitors, you need to make sure that your graphics cards work together (some graphics cards don't) and that your computer's motherboard supports multiple monitors (some motherboards don't). In most cases, you'll want to use an AGP graphics card and one or more PCI graphics cards, but two or more PCI graphics cards without an AGP card can provide a satisfactory solution as well. The monitors, by contrast, don't need to know about each other—each gets its own input, so each can believe it's the only monitor in town if it wants to. So any monitors should do. You can mix CRTs and LCDs provided that the graphics cards in question can handle the monitor to which they're connected.

NOTE

In the 1990s, large monitors were so expensive that it was much cheaper to buy two, three, or even four small monitors than one large one. That's now changed, at least with cathode-ray tube monitors (LCD monitors are still prohibitively expensive). 19-inch monitors are reasonably affordable, and even 21-inch and 22-inch monitors are worth thinking about if you need a serious amount of Desktop space. But there's no reason you shouldn't have a monster monitor and a couple of satellite monitors if you want—or even two or more monsters....

To set up multiple monitors, power down your computer and insert the new graphics card. (You *can* install multiple graphics cards and monitors at a time, but unless you're very lucky and everything works, you'll be looking at some doubly confusing troubleshooting.) Connect the second monitor, then power everything on. Don't be surprised if the bootup display appears on the second monitor rather than your primary one. After you log in to Windows, it should discover the new hardware, which will trigger a Found New Hardware notification area pop-up followed by the Found New Hardware Wizard. If Windows affects not to have noticed the new hardware, run the Add Hardware Wizard manually to add the graphics card and monitor.

Next, display the Settings tab of the Display Properties dialog box. For each monitor you want to use (hint: all of them), select the monitor and then select Extend My Windows Desktop onto This Monitor. Once you've done that, let Windows know where the monitors are positioned in relation to each other by dragging the monitor icons into their relative positions. If you get confused as to which monitor is which, click the Identify button to have Windows flash up the number of each monitor on the monitor. Then set the screen resolution, color depth, and refresh rate for each monitor as usual.

Once you close the Display Properties dialog box, you should have a substantially enlarged Desktop. By default, the Taskbar appears on your primary monitor (the one that shows the boot sequence), but you can drag it to any of the other monitors as you see fit.

Maximizing a window maximizes it for the monitor it's currently (or mostly) on. You can extend a "normal" window across two or more monitors by dragging its window border to the appropriate size.

Configuring Power Management

If you have a laptop computer and use it on the road, power management tends to be an exciting part of your computing life. You've probably developed strategies to maximize your battery life while traveling, such as dimming the screen or slowing down the processor when you can accept poorer performance in the interests of longevity.

If you have a desktop computer, power management tends to be a much less stimulating topic, because leaving your computer running usually isn't a problem. But to keep your computer healthy, to keep your (or your employer's) electrical bill to a minimum, and perhaps to contribute to keeping the polar icecaps in place, it's a good idea to configure power management on your computer.

Windows XP offers a variety of power-management settings, from power schemes and hibernation to attaching an uninterruptible power supply (UPS) to your computer. The following sections discuss these options.

To configure power management, open the Power Options Properties dialog box as follows:

1. Right-click the Desktop and choose Properties from the shortcut menu. Windows displays the Display Properties dialog box.
2. Click the Screen Saver tab.
3. Click the Power button. Windows displays the Power Options Properties dialog box.

NOTE

Because the Power Options Properties dialog box displays different tabs depending on how your computer is configured, the following sections show the Power Options Properties dialog box from different computers.

Choosing a Power Scheme

First, choose a power scheme and adjust it as necessary:

1. Display the Power Options Properties dialog box as discussed in the previous section. By default, the Power Schemes tab (shown in Figure 31.30) is displayed.

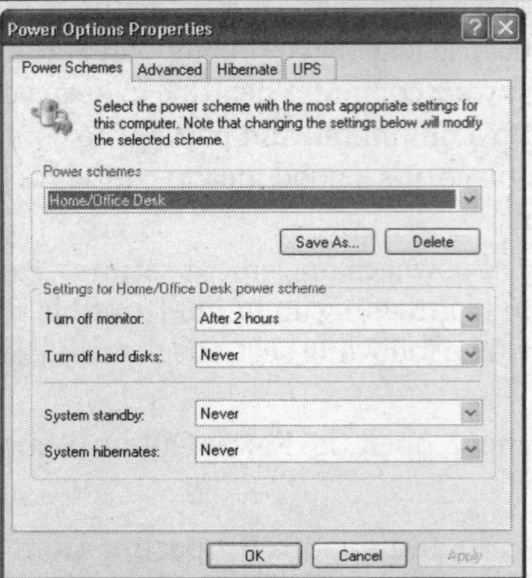

FIGURE 31.30: Choose basic power-management options on the Power Schemes tab of the Power Options Properties dialog box.

2. In the Power Schemes drop-down list, select the power scheme that seems best to describe your computer's role: Home/Office Desk, Portable/Laptop, Presentation, Always On, Minimal Power Management, or Max Battery. The Presentation scheme never turns off the monitor and is intended for computers left to run kiosk-style presentations (for example, at a trade show). The Always On scheme is useful for a computer that's acting as a server. The Minimal Power Management scheme aims to get the maximum performance out of a computer without worrying about conserving power.

3. The Settings for Power Scheme section contains adjustable settings for the power scheme. Which settings there are depends on which of your computer's components are designed for power management. For most computers, Windows offers the Turn Off Monitor drop-down list and the Turn Off Hard Disks drop-down list. If your computer offers power features for standby and hibernation, the Settings for Power Scheme section displays a System Standby drop-down list and a System Hibernates drop-down list as well.

NOTE

If you adjust the settings for a power scheme, you can save your custom power scheme by clicking the Save As button and specifying the name for the scheme in the Save Scheme dialog box that Windows displays.

4. Click the Apply button to apply the power scheme to your computer.

Choosing Advanced Power Options

The Advanced tab of the Power Options Properties dialog box (shown in Figure 31.31) offers various advanced power-management options. Which of these options you see depends on the hardware configuration of your computer.

Always Show Icon on the Taskbar check box Select this check box to make Windows display a power icon in the System Tray. This option is most useful for laptop computers, as you can see at a glance whether the computer is plugged in (Windows displays a plug icon) or running on battery power (a battery icon).

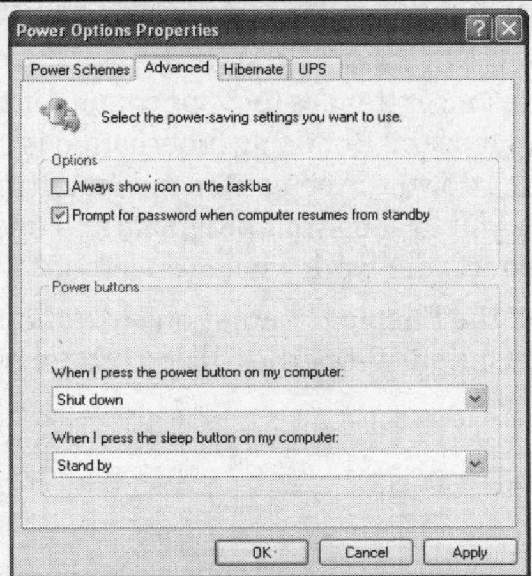

FIGURE 31.31: If necessary, choose further power-management options on the Advanced tab of the Power Options Properties dialog box.

Prompt for Password when Computer Resumes from Standby check box Select this check box if you want Windows to make you enter your password when you wake the computer from a standby state.

When I Press the Power Button on My Computer drop-down list In this drop-down list, select the action you want Windows to take when you press the Power button on your computer when Windows is running. The options are Do Nothing, Ask Me What to Do, Sleep, Hibernate, and Shut Down.

When I Press the Sleep Button on My Computer drop-down list In this drop-down list, select the action you want Windows to take when you press the Sleep button on your computer. As for the Power button, the options are Do Nothing, Ask Me What to Do, Sleep, Hibernate, and Shut Down.

Enabling and Disabling Hibernation

Hibernation suspends your computer in its current state with programs and documents open. When you tell your computer to hibernate, it writes all the data held in RAM to a hibernation file on the hard disk. This way, even if the computer's battery runs out, all your information is safe. (If the battery *does* run out, hibernation saves you no time over shutting the computer down.)

The more RAM you have, the longer it takes for your computer to enter hibernation and to emerge from it again. But using hibernation is usually substantially faster than shutting down the computer and restarting it, especially as hibernation allows you to keep your programs and documents open, so that you can restart your work where you left off.

To enable hibernation, select the Enable Hibernation check box on the Hibernate tab of the Power Options Properties dialog box (shown in Figure 31.32).

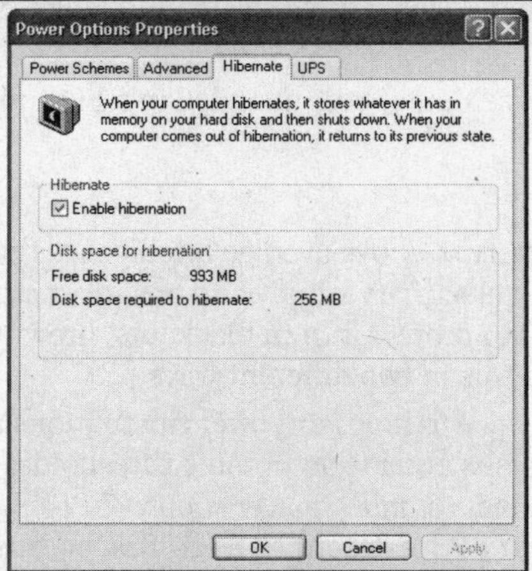

FIGURE 31.32: Use the Hibernate tab to enable and disable hibernation.

Enabling and Disabling Advanced Power Management

If your computer supports Advanced Power Management (APM), Windows displays an APM tab in the Power Options Properties dialog box. On this tab, you can toggle APM on and off by selecting and clearing the Enable Advanced Power Management Support check box.

NOTE

For portable computers, Windows includes an Alarms tab in the Power Options Properties dialog box.

Configuring Windows to Use an Uninterruptible Power Supply

One of the great benefits of a laptop computer is that its battery protects it from data loss when a power outage occurs. To get similar protection in a desktop computer, you need to attach a separate device—an uninterruptible power supply (UPS). A UPS is about the most important hardware add-on purchase you're likely to make for your computer, so this section discusses in some depth which features you should look for in a UPS.

Like backup media, a UPS is seldom if ever included in a PC bundle.

What Is a UPS?

A *UPS* is essentially a large battery of above-average intelligence that sits between your computer and the electricity supply and ensures a steady power stream to your computer to protect it from blackouts, brownouts, and surges. Different UPSes do this in two different ways.

The simpler way is for the device to monitor power fluctuations and kick in when the power supply falls outside acceptable thresholds. Technically, this type of device is called a *standby power supply (SPS)* rather than a UPS, but you'll often hear SPSes described as UPSes, because consumers will pay more money for them that way.

The more complicated—and better—way is for the device to feed power to the computer continuously, charging itself when the power supply is running within acceptable parameters. This device is technically a UPS. This way of supplying power is better because the UPS delivers conditioned power to the computer all the time, protecting it better from fluctuations and avoiding the critical moment of changeover from main power to battery power that can be a drawback with an SPS.

Choosing a UPS

If you're looking for a UPS, keep these features in mind:

Operating system support Make sure the UPS is designed for use with Windows XP. With operating system support and an appropriate system management port (discussed next), the UPS can warn Windows XP when the electricity supply has failed. Windows can then shut itself down automatically if the computer is unattended. (More on this in a moment.)

System management port Make sure the UPS has an appropriate system management port for your computer. Many UPSes use a serial port connection. Others use a USB connection.

Indicators for line voltage and battery power The UPS should have an indicator to indicate when the incoming power to the UPS is okay, and another indicator to indicate when the devices attached to the UPS are running on battery power.

(Many UPSes also sound an alarm when battery power is being used.)

Multiple power outlets Make sure the UPS has enough outlets for all the devices you want to plug into it directly.

Enough power and battery life Before buying the UPS, work out how much power and battery life you need it to have. Make a list of the computers and devices you'll need to have plugged into the UPS, then use a power-supply template such as that on the American Power Conversion Corporation Website (`www.apc.com`) to calculate the number of volt-amps (VA) you'll need to keep the equipment running. (You can simply add up the voltages listed on the equipment, but be aware that the power-supply rating on your computer equipment shows the maximum power rather than typical power usage.) Then decide the amount of time you'll need to shut down the computers once the power alarm goes off. Generally speaking, the more power and battery life you need, the more the UPS will cost. If you just want a few minutes to allow you to shut down Windows under control (or to have Windows shut itself down), a modest and inexpensive UPS may fit the bill.

TIP

Unless you're convinced that you'll need to print during a power outage, don't plan to plug your printer into your UPS. Printers are power hogs. Laser printers are such power hogs that they can kill a UPS.

Installing a UPS

Once you've bought a UPS and lugged it home, power down your computer and install the UPS. Bring up the computer again, log on to Windows, and display the UPS tab of the Power Options Properties dialog box (shown in Figure 31.33).

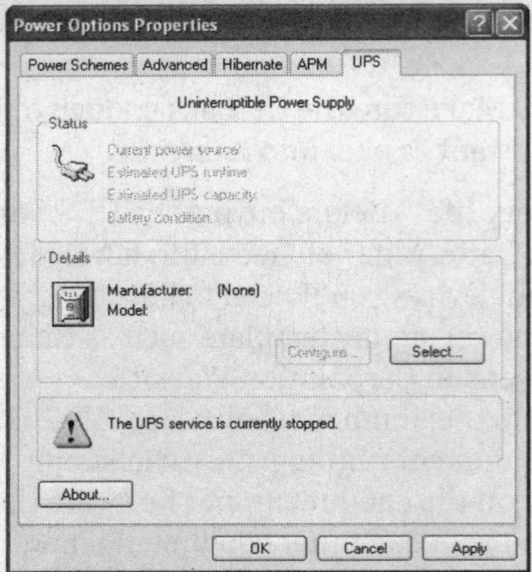

FIGURE 31.33: The UPS page of the Power Options Properties dialog box

To let Windows know about your UPS, take these steps:

1. Click the Select button. Windows displays the UPS Selection dialog box (shown in Figure 31.34 with American Power Conversion chosen in the Select Manufacturer drop-down list).

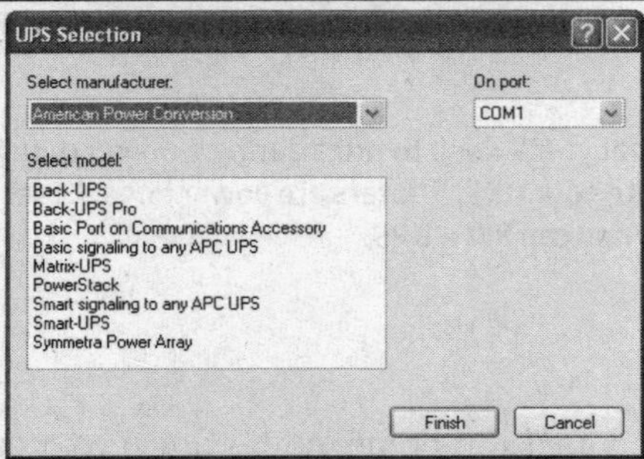

FIGURE 31.34: Use the UPS Selection dialog box to specify which UPS you're using and the port it's connected to.

2. In the Select Manufacturer drop-down list, choose the manufacturer of your UPS. If the manufacturer isn't listed, choose the Generic item.
3. If the manufacturer was listed, specify the model of UPS in the Select Model list box, and select the port in the On Port drop-down list. Click the Finish button. Windows closes the UPS Selection dialog box, returning you to the Power Options Properties dialog box.

4. If the manufacturer wasn't listed, select the Custom item in the Select Model list box. Then click the Next button. Windows displays the UPS Interface Configuration dialog box (shown in Figure 31.35). Consult your documentation, then choose settings for Power Fail/On Battery, Low Battery, and UPS Shutdown as appropriate. Then click the Finish button. Windows closes the UPS Interface Configuration dialog box, returning you to the Power Options Properties dialog box.

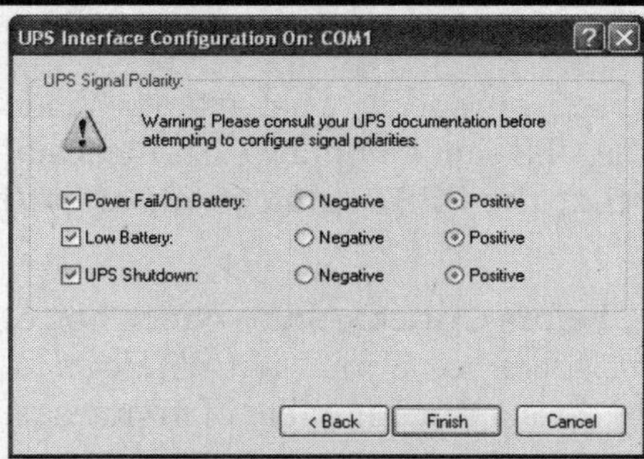

FIGURE 31.35: If Windows doesn't list the manufacturer of your UPS, use the UPS Interface Configuration dialog box to configure signal polarities for the UPS.

5. In the Power Options Properties dialog box, click the Configure button. Windows displays the UPS Configuration dialog box (shown in Figure 31.36).

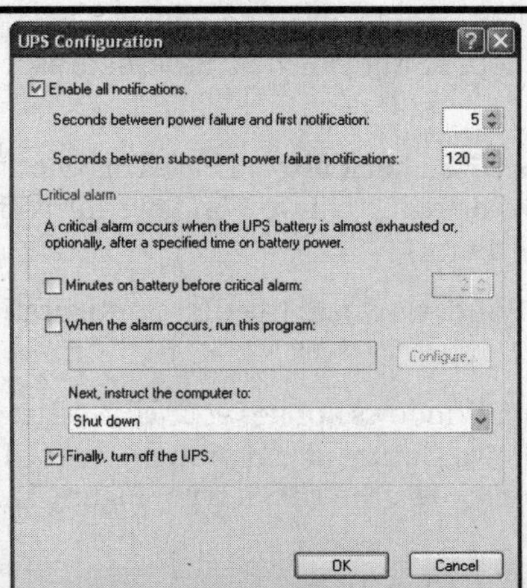

FIGURE 31.36: Use the UPS Configuration dialog box to choose settings for the UPS.

6. Select or clear the Enable All Notifications check box as appropriate. Adjust the value in the Seconds between Power Failure and First Notification text box and the Seconds between Subsequent Power Failure Notifications text box to suit your needs. For example, if your electricity supply suffers from mini-outages of a few seconds each, you might choose to increase the Seconds between Power Failure and First Notification setting to a value such as 20 or 30 seconds so that the UPS raises the alarm only for a more serious outage than usual.

7. In the Critical Alarm section, specify what actions Windows should take when the UPS sends Windows a critical alarm, warning Windows that the UPS is almost out of battery power.

   Minutes on Battery before Critical Alarm check box and text box Select this check box if you want Windows to sound an alarm after the specified number of minutes running on battery power.

   When the Alarm Occurs, Run This Program check box and text box If you want Windows to run a program when an alarm occurs, select this check box and specify the program in the text box. For example, you might want to run a custom shutdown utility or use a program to send a warning to users of connected computers.

   Next, Instruct the Computer To drop-down list In this drop-down list, choose Shut Down or Hibernate as appropriate.

   Finally, Turn Off the UPS check box Leave this check box selected (as it is by default) to have Windows turn off the UPS (and stop the alarm).

8. Click the OK button. Windows closes the UPS Configuration dialog box.

9. Click the Apply button. Windows applies your UPS settings. The Status section shows status information on your UPS, and the Details section shows the UPS's type. Figure 31.37 shows an example.

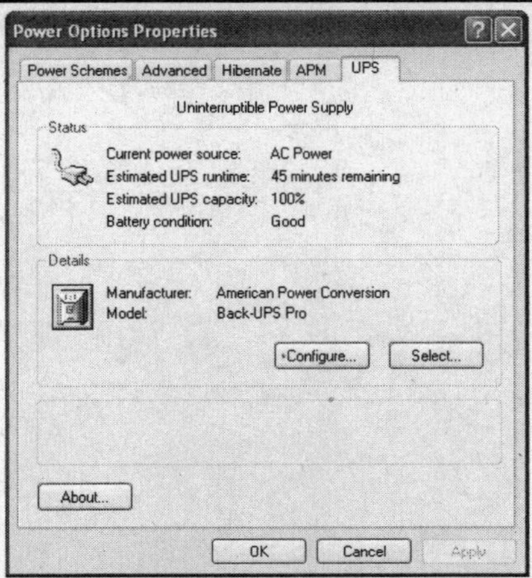

FIGURE 31.37: When you've configured the UPS, the Status section on the UPS tab of the Power Options Properties dialog box shows you the UPS's estimated runtime and capacity.

10. Click the OK button. Windows closes the Power Options Properties dialog box.

What's Next?

Although Windows XP Professional is arguably the most stable Windows implementation to date, things sometimes do go wrong. The next chapter starts by giving you some troubleshooting guidelines and then goes on to discuss how to optimize Window and how to dual-boot Windows XP Professional with another operating system.

Chapter 32

Troubleshooting, Optimizing, and Dual-Booting Windows

You've read a number of times already in this book that Windows XP is much more reliable than Windows 9*x*—and it's quite true. But things still sometimes go wrong with Windows XP: a program hangs; you start getting bizarre error messages about some strangely named component not having done something it should; or Windows starts to slow down, behave oddly, or become unstable.

Revised and adapted from *Mastering Windows XP Home Edition* by Guy Hart-Davis

ISBN 0-7821-2980-3 1024 pages $39.99

This chapter discusses how to use the tools that Windows provides for dealing with untoward occurrences such as these. It also discusses some steps you may want to take to optimize Windows in the hope of keeping it running smoothly and as swiftly as your hardware permits. And it shows you how to set up a dual-boot arrangement so that you can use both Windows XP and another operating system on your computer.

Dealing with Program Hangs

When a program hangs, it'll usually be very obvious. The program stops responding to direct stimuli (keystrokes and mouse commands issued in its window) and indirect stimuli (for example, commands issued via the Taskbar or via another program). If you move another program window in front of the hung program's window and then move it away, the hung program's window fails to redraw correctly, leaving either parts of the window that you've moved or a blank, undrawn area on the screen.

Ending a Program

Sometimes Windows notices when a program has hung and displays the End Program dialog box automatically so that you can choose whether to end the program. Other times, you'll need to use Task Manager to tell Windows to end the program. To do so, take the following steps:

1. If you have Task Manager running already, switch to it. If not, press Ctrl+Alt+Delete. Windows displays Task Manager with the Applications tab foremost.
2. Select the task you want to end.
3. Click the End Task button. If Windows can end the task easily, it does so. Otherwise, Windows displays the End Program dialog box, of which Figure 32.1 shows an example.

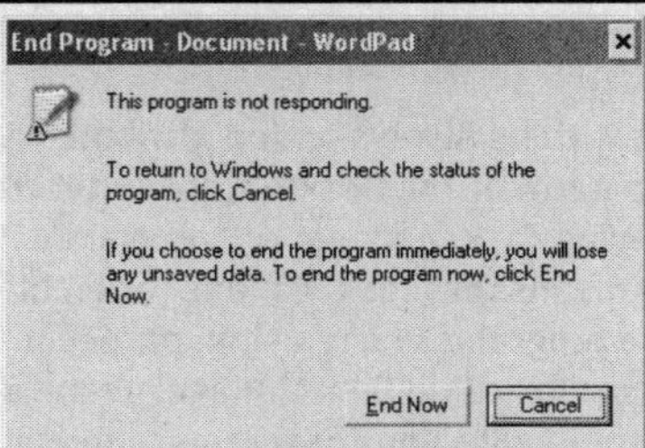

FIGURE 32.1: If Windows can't close the program easily, it displays the End Program dialog box to let you end it forcibly.

4. Click the End Now button. Windows ends the program. You lose any unsaved data in the program.
5. After clearing up the debris and virtual shrapnel left by the program, Windows displays a message box such as that shown in Figure 32.2, inviting you to tell Microsoft about the problem, with the implication that doing so will help them prevent such problems from recurring in the future.

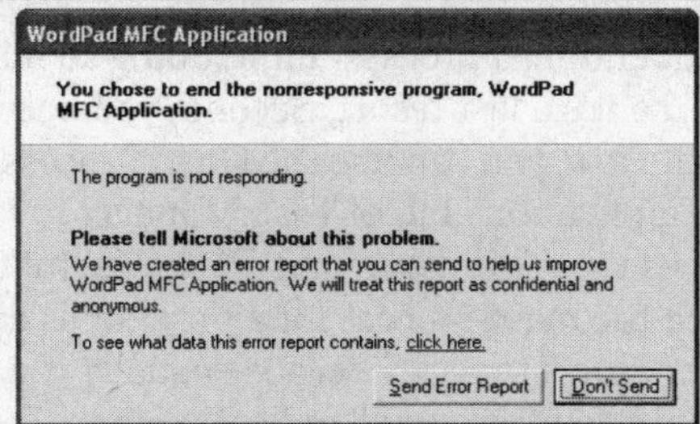

FIGURE 32.2: Windows displays a dialog box such as this one when you've used the End Program dialog box to end a program. Choose whether to send Microsoft information on the problem.

6. Click the Send Error Report button or the Don't Send button as appropriate. (To see details on what information you'll be sending to Microsoft, click the Click Here link before dismissing the dialog box.)

You can turn off or tweak this error reporting if you want. See "Enabling and Disabling Error Reporting" later in this chapter.

NOTE

By default, Task Manager appears with its Always on Top attribute on, so that it always appears as the topmost window on the Desktop, no matter which program window is active. Always having Task Manager on top makes it easy to keep track of Task Manager, but it means that Task Manager often blocks dialog boxes or error messages in the programs you're using, particularly at low screen resolutions such as 800×600. If you find Task Manager useful and often keep it open to see what's happening with your programs, choose Options ➢ Always on Top to remove the check mark from the Always on Top menu item and make the Task Manager window behave like a normal program window. (To turn Always on Top back on, repeat the command.) Also on the Options menu are two other items that are both on by default: Minimize on Use, and Hide when Minimized.

Ending a Process or a Process Tree

Instead of ending a program, you can end a process. A *process* is the executing environment in which program components called *threads* operate. Many programs run as a single process much of the time, but others involve multiple processes.

There are two problems with ending a process. First, doing so may make your computer unstable, so it's a last resort. Second, you need to know which process does what. Now, you can use the Go to Process command from a program on the Applications tab of Task Manager to identify the process on the Processes tab. This command can be useful for learning the name under which the main process for a program is executing, but it's not much use for ending a process, because usually you'll do much better to end the program itself from the Applications tab. Ending the program takes out all the processes associated with the program. So the only reason to end a process directly is if it doesn't have its associated program listed on the Applications tab. This is the case for a system process, but it's not a good idea to end a system process unless you're certain what it's doing. But if you overload Windows, it can sometimes get confused about which programs are running and lose a program's listing from the Applications tab while keeping its process or processes going.

If this happens, you can end a process by selecting it on the Processes tab and clicking the End Process button. Windows displays the Task Manager Warning dialog box shown in Figure 32.3 warning you that ending the process may make your system unstable or lose your data. If you're prepared to risk such consequences, click the Yes button. Windows terminates the process.

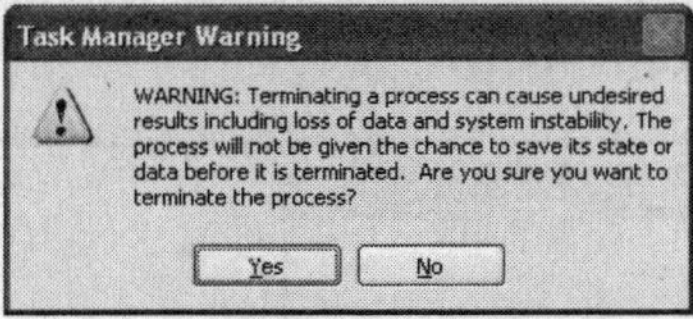

FIGURE 32.3: Windows displays this Task Manager Warning dialog box when you tell it to end a process.

To end all the processes associated with a process, right-click the process and choose End Process Tree from the shortcut menu. Windows displays the Task Manager Warning dialog box shown in Figure 32.4 with a variation of its message about the possible undesirable results of stopping processes. Click the Yes button if you want to continue. Windows stops the processes.

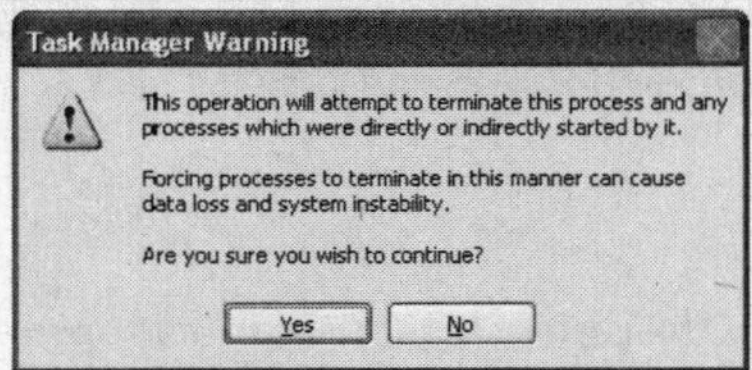

FIGURE 32.4: Windows displays this Task Manager Warning dialog box when you tell it to end a process tree.

Using Event Viewer to Identify Problems

If your computer seems to be behaving strangely, you can use Event Viewer to try to pinpoint the source of the problem.

Take the following steps to open Event Viewer:

1. Choose Start ➢ Control Panel. Windows displays Control Panel.
2. Click the Performance and Maintenance link. Windows displays the Performance and Maintenance screen.

3. Click the Administrative Tools link. Windows displays the Administrative Tools screen.
4. Double-click the Event Viewer shortcut. Windows starts Event Viewer (shown in Figure 32.5).

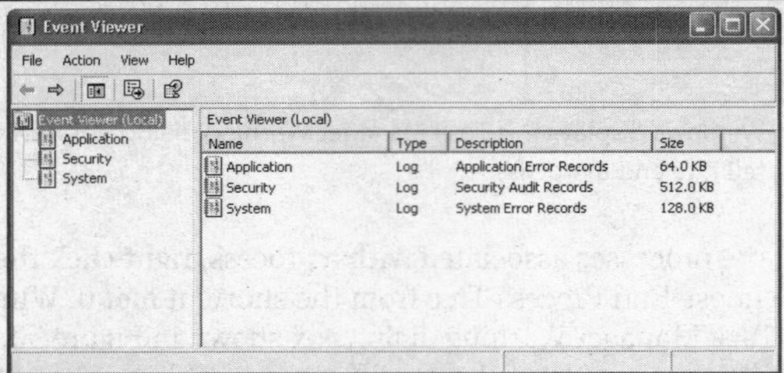

FIGURE 32.5: Use Event Viewer to identify problems and to learn what's happening behind the scenes in your computer.

As you can see in the figure, Event Viewer contains three logs: the Application Log, the Security Log, and the System Log.

NOTE

Event Viewer automatically opens the current logs. You can also open old logs by choosing Action ➢ Open Log File. Event Viewer displays a common Open dialog box with two peculiarities: a Log Type drop-down list and a Display Name text box. Navigate to the log and select it. Then select the appropriate type of log—Application, Security, or System—in the Log Type drop-down list. The Display Name text box automatically displays *Saved* Type *Log*, where *Type* is the log type selected (for example, *Saved Application Log* for an Application Log). You can change this description as necessary. Click the Open button. Event Viewer opens the log file and adds it to the left pane. (You can also rename it here by using standard Windows editing techniques, such as selecting the name and pressing the F2 key.)

The System Log

The System Log contains information about Windows processes. The System Log uses the following three types of events:

Error events A notification that an error has occurred. Errors can be anything from mildly serious (for example, "The device

U.S. Robotics 56K FAX EXT disappeared from the system without first being prepared for removal") to seriously serious (for example, a system error described only by forbidding error codes).

Warning events A notification that something has gone wrong, but not disastrously so. For example, you might see a warning that "The browser was unable to retrieve a list of servers from the browser master on the network." This isn't bad—it just means that the browser (a service that finds out which resources are available on the network) has to find another browser master (a computer that's coordinating information on available resources).

Information events Events worth noting in the System Log but that are not considered errors and do not merit warnings. For example, when you start Windows, it starts the event log service, and logs this as an Information event. Other examples include Windows' starting to use a network adapter that it has detected is connected to the network, or that the browser has forced an election on the network because a master browser was stopped.

The System Log is stored in the `SYSEVENT.EVT` file in the `\Windows\system32\config\` folder.

The Application Log

The Application Log contains information about programs running on the computer. Like the System Log, the Application Log supports three types of events: Error events, Warning events, and Information events. Program developers specify the events that their programs raise and which event type each event has.

The Application Log is stored in the `APPEVENT.EVT` file in the `\Windows\system32\config\` folder.

The Security Log

The Security Log contains information on security-related events such as Account Logon actions, Logon/Logoff actions, Policy Change actions (initiated by the System object), and System Events (such as the loading of authentication packages). You can also enable auditing on files and folders, which lets you track which users take which actions on those files and in those folders.

The Security Log is stored in the (you've guessed it) SECEVENT.EVT file in the \Windows\system32\config\ folder.

Viewing an Event Log

To view one of the three event logs, select it in the left pane of the Event Viewer window. Event Viewer displays the events in the log in the right pane. Figure 32.6 shows an example of viewing the System Log.

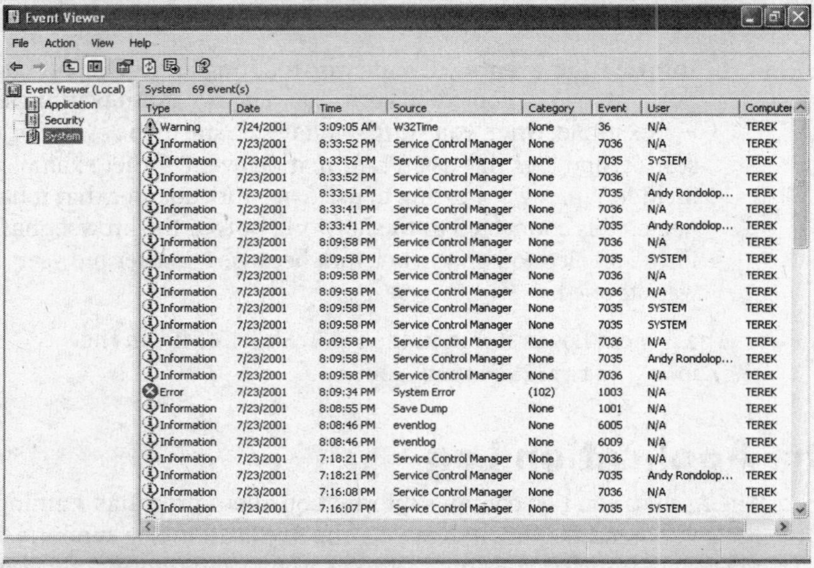

Event Viewer

File Action View Help

Event Viewer (Local)
Application
Security
System

System 69 event(s)

Type	Date	Time	Source	Category	Event	User	Computer
Warning	7/24/2001	3:09:05 AM	W32Time	None	36	N/A	TEREK
Information	7/23/2001	8:33:52 PM	Service Control Manager	None	7036	N/A	TEREK
Information	7/23/2001	8:33:52 PM	Service Control Manager	None	7035	SYSTEM	TEREK
Information	7/23/2001	8:33:52 PM	Service Control Manager	None	7036	N/A	TEREK
Information	7/23/2001	8:33:51 PM	Service Control Manager	None	7035	Andy Rondolop...	TEREK
Information	7/23/2001	8:33:41 PM	Service Control Manager	None	7036	N/A	TEREK
Information	7/23/2001	8:33:41 PM	Service Control Manager	None	7035	Andy Rondolop...	TEREK
Information	7/23/2001	8:09:58 PM	Service Control Manager	None	7036	N/A	TEREK
Information	7/23/2001	8:09:58 PM	Service Control Manager	None	7035	SYSTEM	TEREK
Information	7/23/2001	8:09:58 PM	Service Control Manager	None	7036	N/A	TEREK
Information	7/23/2001	8:09:58 PM	Service Control Manager	None	7036	N/A	TEREK
Information	7/23/2001	8:09:58 PM	Service Control Manager	None	7035	SYSTEM	TEREK
Information	7/23/2001	8:09:58 PM	Service Control Manager	None	7035	SYSTEM	TEREK
Information	7/23/2001	8:09:58 PM	Service Control Manager	None	7036	N/A	TEREK
Information	7/23/2001	8:09:58 PM	Service Control Manager	None	7035	Andy Rondolop...	TEREK
Information	7/23/2001	8:09:58 PM	Service Control Manager	None	7036	N/A	TEREK
Error	7/23/2001	8:09:34 PM	System Error	(102)	1003	N/A	TEREK
Information	7/23/2001	8:08:55 PM	Save Dump	None	1001	N/A	TEREK
Information	7/23/2001	8:08:46 PM	eventlog	None	6005	N/A	TEREK
Information	7/23/2001	8:08:46 PM	eventlog	None	6009	N/A	TEREK
Information	7/23/2001	7:18:21 PM	Service Control Manager	None	7036	N/A	TEREK
Information	7/23/2001	7:18:21 PM	Service Control Manager	None	7035	Andy Rondolop...	TEREK
Information	7/23/2001	7:16:08 PM	Service Control Manager	None	7036	N/A	TEREK
Information	7/23/2001	7:16:07 PM	Service Control Manager	None	7035	SYSTEM	TEREK

FIGURE 32.6: Use Event Viewer to find out which events have occurred on your system.

To view the details of an event, double-click it (or right-click it and choose Properties from the shortcut menu). Windows displays the Event Properties dialog box (shown in Figure 32.7). The dialog box shows the date, time, type, user (if appropriate), computer, source, category, and ID number of the event. The Description text box displays the description of the event, and the Data text box displays any data for it. You can toggle the display of the data between bytes and words by clicking the Bytes option button or the Words option button. With the dialog box open, you can use the Previous Event button (the up-arrow button) and the Next Event button (the down-arrow button) to display the details for the previous event or next event, or the Copy Event Details to Clipboard button (the button below the Next Event button) to copy the details of the event to the Clipboard.

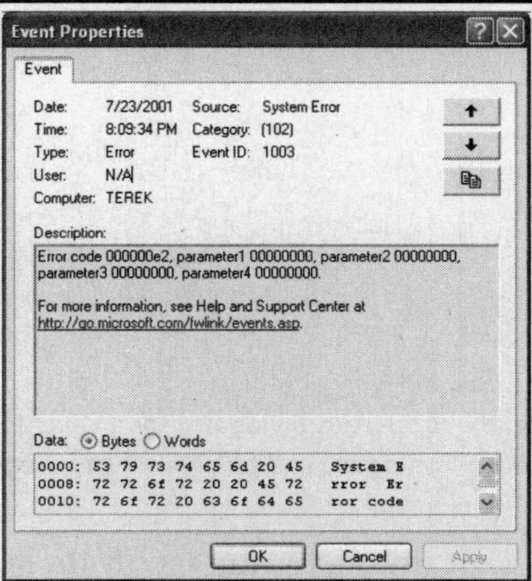

FIGURE 32.7: Use the Event Properties dialog box to view the properties for an event.

Managing the Event Logs

As you can imagine, event logs grow in size, particularly when many events occur that need logging. Windows offers features to keep the size of your event logs under control.

To manage the event logs, follow these steps:

1. Right-click the event log in question and choose Properties from the shortcut menu. Windows displays the Properties dialog box for the log. Figure 32.8 shows the General tab of the Properties dialog box for the Application Log.

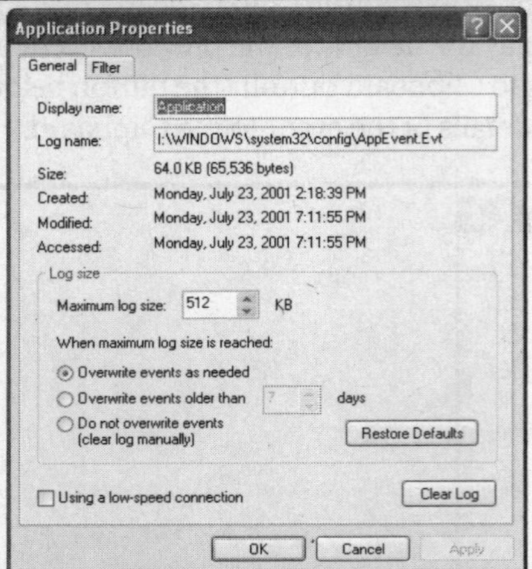

FIGURE 32.8: Use the General tab of the Properties dialog box for an event log to specify a maximum size for the log file and which events to overwrite.

2. In the Maximum Log Size text box, you can specify the maximum size to which the file can grow. The default size is 512KB, but you can set any size from 64KB upward. Having the log file grow to a couple of megabytes shouldn't be a problem unless you're backing it up from another machine, but there's no particular reason to keep a large amount of log-file data.

3. In the When Maximum Log Size Is Reached area, select one of the option buttons to specify what Windows should do when the log file reaches its maximum size:

   Overwrite Events As Needed Select this option button to have Windows delete the oldest event to make room for the newest event, thus keeping the log file around its maximum size.

   Overwrite Events Older than *NN* Days Select this option button (the default setting) to make Windows overwrite events older than a particular number of days in order to make room for new events. If you archive your log files, set the number of days in the text box to match your frequency of archiving. The default setting is 7 days. Be aware that if the log file reaches its maximum size within the allotted number of days and contains no events older than that number of days, Windows stops writing events to the log file. (This isn't usually a good idea.)

Do Not Overwrite Events Select this option button if you want to prevent Windows from overwriting any events. This means that you'll need to clear the event log manually. Until you clear the log, Windows writes no more events to the log once it has reached its maximum size.

4. If your computer is connected to the network via a modem and is receiving event information from other computers (or is transmitting event information to other computers), select the Using a Low-Speed Connection check box. This option reduces the amount of information transmitted.
5. Click the OK button. Windows applies your changes and closes the Properties dialog box for the event log.

Filtering the Event Log

Your event logs can fill up quickly, especially when there's something wrong with your system or with a program. To find particular events, you can use the Filter tab of the Properties dialog box to apply filters. Follow these steps:

1. Right-click the event log in question and choose Properties from the shortcut menu. Windows displays the Properties dialog box for the log.
2. Click the Filter tab (shown in Figure 32.9).

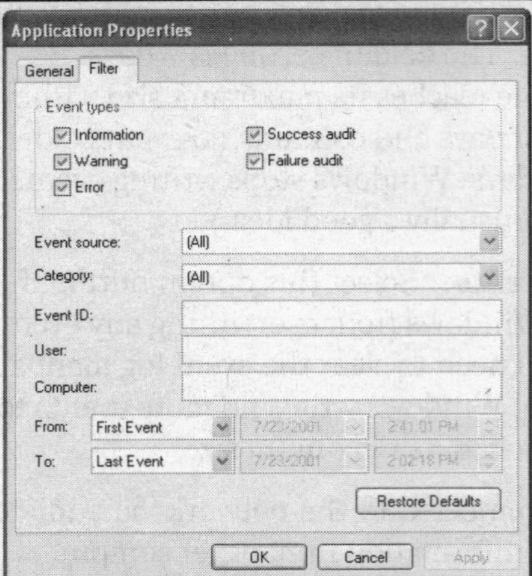

FIGURE 32.9: Use the Filter tab of the Properties dialog box for a log to filter the types of events displayed.

3. In the Event Types group box, select the check boxes for the types of events you want to see. Clear the other check boxes.
4. Use the controls on the lower two-thirds of the tab to specify the details of the events you want to see.
5. Click the OK button. Windows applies your choices and closes the Properties dialog box.

Clearing the Event Log

To clear a log, right-click it in Event Viewer and choose Clear Log from the shortcut menu. Alternatively, display its Properties dialog box and click the Clear Log button on the General tab.

Event Viewer displays an Event Viewer dialog box asking if you want to save the log before clearing it. Click the Yes button or the No button as appropriate.

Optimizing Performance

This section discusses steps you can take to optimize the performance of your computer and of Windows. These steps range from getting more RAM (if you need it), through setting suitable performance options for your computer, to specifying the size and location of the paging file. You should also defragment your disk or disks as discussed in Chapter 30.

RAM: Do You Have Enough?

If your computer's performance seems disappointing, make sure that your computer has plenty of RAM to run Windows itself plus all the programs that may be running in the background. As mentioned earlier in the book, 128MB is usually enough for running a single-user session at reasonable speed, and 256MB is usually enough for several user sessions running conventional programs. If you want multiple users to be able to open large programs or large files at the same time, you might need 384MB or 512MB.

If your computer is light on RAM, consider adding more. At this writing, RAM prices have reached an all-time low, and you can get 256MB of SDRAM for less than $100.

There are various ways of finding out how much RAM you have on your computer. Normally, when the computer starts, you'll see the boot routine take a quick count of the RAM. (Some computers hide this part of the boot process behind a custom splash screen.)

Once Windows is running, the easiest way to find out the amount of RAM is to display the System Properties dialog box (press Winkey+Break, or right-click the My Computer item on the Start menu and choose the Properties item from the shortcut menu) and look at the Computer section of the General tab.

Choosing Performance Options

Next, make sure that Windows is configured to give the best performance possible for your needs.

As mentioned in Chapter 1, getting the best performance out of Windows XP on a computer that isn't screamingly fast is partly a question of choosing the right balance between visual delight and speed: the more graphics and visual effects that Windows XP is using, the slower their display will be, and the heavier the demands placed on the processor as well as the graphics subsystem.

You also need to give the foreground program as much of a boost as possible, make sure that memory usage is optimized for programs rather than system cache, and set an appropriate size for your paging file.

To set performance options, follow these steps:

1. Press Winkey+Break. Alternatively, choose Start ➢ Control Panel, click the Performance and Maintenance link, and then click the System link. Windows displays the System Properties dialog box.
2. Click the Advanced tab (shown in Figure 32.10).

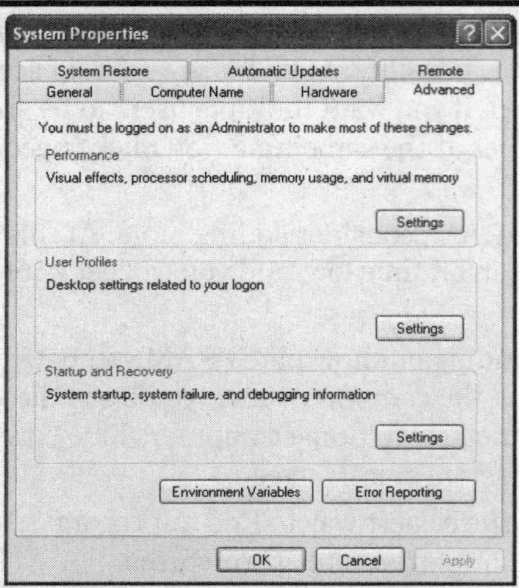

FIGURE 32.10: The Advanced tab of the System Properties dialog box is the starting place for setting performance options.

3. Click the Settings button in the Performance section. Windows displays the Performance Options dialog box.
4. On the Visual Effects tab of the Performance Options dialog box (shown in Figure 32.11), select one of the option buttons:
   - Select the Let Windows Choose What's Best for My Computer option button to have Windows apply the mixture of settings it deems most appropriate to your computer's speed and your graphics card's capabilities.
   - Select the Adjust for Best Appearance option button to turn on all the effects.

- Select the Adjust for Best Performance option button to turn off all the effects.
- Select the Custom option button if you want to apply a custom set of effects. Then select the check boxes for the effects you want to use. Most of the effects are self-explanatory—for example, the Animate Windows when Minimizing and Maximizing check box controls whether Windows animates windows when minimizing and maximizing them. (In fact, this item isn't precisely named, as the effect is applied to windows that are being restored as well as minimized or maximized—but no matter.) The fewer visual effects you use, the better the performance you'll enjoy, but the plainer and less subtle the Windows interface will seem.

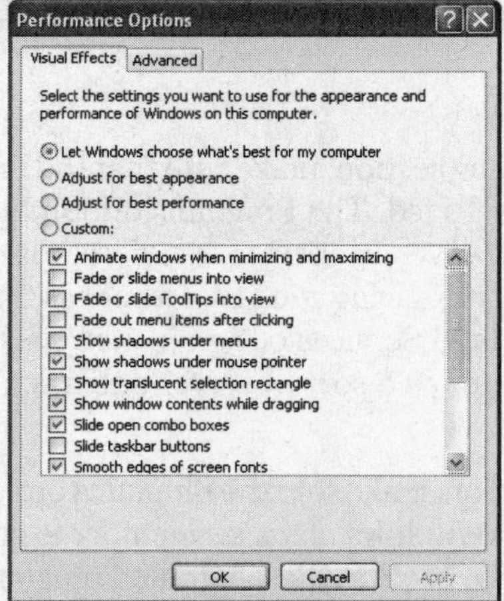

FIGURE 32.11: You can improve performance by turning off unnecessary visual effects on the Visual Effects tab of the Performance Options dialog box.

5. Click the Advanced tab (shown in Figure 32.12).

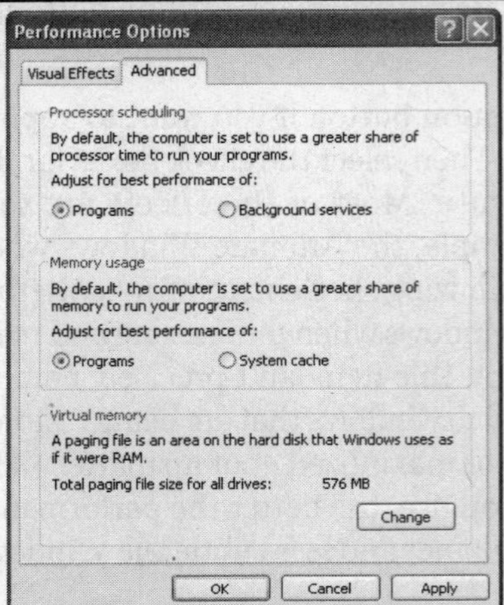

FIGURE 32.12: On the Advanced tab of the Performance Options dialog box, make sure that processor scheduling and memory usage are optimized for applications.

6. In the Processor Scheduling section, make sure that the Programs option button is selected. The Programs option button causes Windows to give priority to the foreground program—the active program—giving you faster response time in it. (Select the Background Services option button only if you're using this computer as a sort of server and are not running programs on it.)
7. In the Memory Usage section, make sure the Programs option button is selected so that Windows manages memory to give the maximum performance boost to the foreground program. Select the System Cache option button only if you want to optimize the system cache performance at the expense of program performance.
8. If necessary, change the size of the paging file by following the instructions in the next section.
9. Click the OK button. Windows applies your changes and closes the Performance Options dialog box.
10. Click the OK button. Windows closes the System Properties dialog box.

Specifying the Size and Location of the Paging File

The *paging file* is space reserved on the hard disk for Windows to use as virtual memory. *Virtual memory* involves storing memory information on the hard disk so that more information can be loaded into memory (both real and virtual) at the same time. Windows juggles virtual memory automatically, swapping information between the RAM and the paging file, so its use should be imperceptible to you. (You'll hear the hard drive working, of course; but then the hard drive works so much when Windows is running that you'll hear it even when no virtual memory swapping is taking place.)

Being able to load more information into memory at a time is good, but because the hard drive is much slower to access than RAM, storing memory information in virtual memory makes your computer run more slowly than it would if it were to store all memory information in RAM. Even if you have a huge amount of memory, Windows XP still requires you to use virtual memory. Given that RAM is at a new historic low price at this writing, making 512MB or 768MB of memory borderline affordable, this is a bit disappointing—but that's the way it is.

Windows automatically creates the paging file on the drive that Windows itself is installed on, going on the general assumption that this is a convenient place to have it. It may not be, and you may want to move the paging file.

The paging file takes up anything from about 100MB to a gigabyte or more. By default, the paging file is initially set to 1.5 times the amount of RAM in the computer: a 96MB paging file for a computer with 64MB RAM; 192MB for 128MB RAM; 384MB for 256MB RAM; and so on. So if you have a small drive or partition, you may want to move the paging file off it when you start running low on disk space. You can also split the paging file between different partitions if you're running low on space on all the partitions.

You might also want to move your paging file to a faster drive than the drive it's currently on. For example, if you had a small but screamingly fast SCSI drive in your computer as well as a slower but much larger EIDE drive, you might want to move the paging file to the SCSI drive to improve performance. (This would work for a large and fast SCSI drive as well—but you'd probably have installed Windows on that drive in the first place, so the paging file would already be there.) Similarly, you may be able to improve performance by moving the paging file to an otherwise unused EIDE drive, should you have one hanging around.

The paging file is called PAGEFILE.SYS. It's a hidden and protected operating system file, so if you feel the urge to look at it, you'll need to select the Show Hidden Files and Folders option button and clear the Hide Protected Operating System Files check box on the View tab of the Folder Options dialog box in order to see it. (To display the Folder Options dialog box, choose Tools ➢ Folder Options in an Explorer window.)

NOTE

If you look for the paging file, you may also see the hibernation file, HIBERFIL.SYS. (Your computer will have a hibernation file only if your computer supports hibernation.) By default, the hibernation file is stored on the same drive as the paging file, and is approximately the same size as the amount of RAM your computer contains. For example, if the computer has 256MB RAM, the hibernation file will be about 256MB as well. That's because Windows writes the contents of RAM to the hibernation file before entering hibernation—RAM doesn't store information when it's powered down.

As you've undoubtedly guessed, you shouldn't delete the paging file (even if you can see it). In fact, Windows XP won't let you delete it—if you try to do so, it prevents you with an Error Deleting File or Folder message box telling you that the file "is being used by another person or program" and suggesting that you close any programs that might be using the file (but not any people!) and try again. You *can* delete the paging file by booting another operating system and attacking it from there, but there's little point in doing so—you can manage the paging file easily enough by following the procedure described next.

To specify the size and location of the paging file, follow these steps:

1. Click the Change button in the Virtual Memory section on the Advanced tab of the Performance Options dialog box. Windows displays the Virtual Memory dialog box (shown in Figure 32.13).

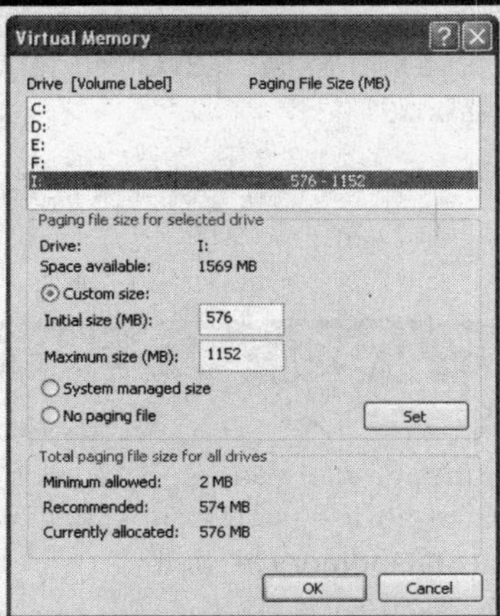

FIGURE 32.13: In the Virtual Memory dialog box, you can specify the size of the paging file and the drive on which to locate it.

2. In the Drive list box, select the drive (or one of the drives) that contains the paging file.
3. In the Paging File Size for Selected Drive list box, specify the size of the file:
   - If you want Windows to manage the paging file's size, select the System Managed Size option button.
   - If you want to manage the paging file's size yourself, select the Custom Size option button. Enter appropriate values in the Initial Size text box and the Maximum Size text box, based on the Recommended readout and the Currently Allocated readout in the Total Paging File Size for All Drives group box. Click the Set button.
   - To remove the paging file from this drive, select the No Paging File option button. Click the Set button.
4. Specify paging file sizes for the other drives as appropriate by repeating steps 2 and 3.
5. Click the OK button. Windows closes the Virtual Memory dialog box and returns you to the Advanced tab of the Performance Options dialog box.

6. Click the OK button. Windows closes the Performance Options dialog box and returns you to the Advanced tab of the System Properties dialog box.

You'll need to restart Windows before your changes to the paging file take effect.

EXPERT KNOWLEDGE: WHAT HAPPENS WHEN YOU RUN OUT OF VIRTUAL MEMORY?

The main point of having virtual memory, of course, is to prevent you from running out of physical memory—as far as possible. But what happens if you run out of virtual memory as well?

Between the memory used by Windows itself, the memory any running program occupies, and the memory taken up by whatever data files you've got open, RAM itself goes quickly enough. It's easy to chew up 128MB of RAM on a single-user session. And if a couple of other users have sessions running in the background, perhaps with a few large graphics files open for editing between them, 256MB can disappear faster than a sixteen-inch pepperoni pizza waylaid by teenagers.

Of course, Windows doesn't allocate the RAM just like that to itself, the programs, and the files. Instead, it monitors your memory usage the whole time, doling out RAM and virtual memory as it judges best to keep itself running (the first priority) and the programs you're using in the foreground responding smoothly. As you work, Windows is constantly shunting pages of memory from RAM to the paging file on the hard disk and vice versa, trying to keep ahead of the game.

If you want to get a rough picture of what's happening in memory and the page file, open Task Manager (right-click the Taskbar and choose Task Manager from the shortcut menu). Look at the PF Usage readout and the Page File Usage History graph on the Performance tab to see how much memory is being used. That reading is in megabytes or gigabytes. Then look at the Physical Memory (K) section, which lists the total memory, available memory, and system cache. These figures are in kilobytes, so you'll need to divide by 1024 to get exact megabytes, but dividing by 1000 will give you figures close enough for government work.

CONTINUED →

The illustration below shows the computer struggling. You can see that the CPU usage has been high but has dropped a bit. Memory usage is massive and has been steadily increasing. And there's only a pathetic amount of physical memory unused and available: less than 1 percent of the total.

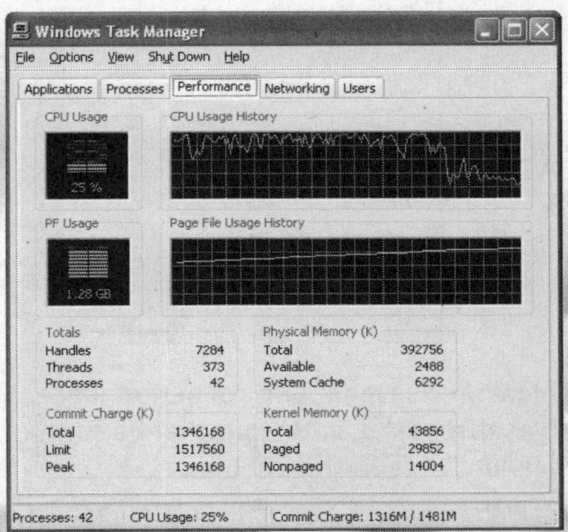

Then display the Processes tab and look at what's going on there. Select the Show Processes from All Users check box so that you see all the processes that are going on. Then choose View ➢ Select Columns to display the Select Columns dialog box. Select the Virtual Memory Size check box and click the OK button. Task Manager adds the VM Size column to the columns displayed. You can then sort the running processes by the Mem Usage column or by the VM Size column to see how much memory and virtual memory each is taking up. The illustration below (which doesn't show processes from all users) explains why the computer in the above illustration was struggling: Two processes have absurdly large virtual machines. Also, check out the Commit Charge readout at the bottom of the Taskbar window. There's a runt's helping of memory left, and that's all.

CONTINUED ⟶

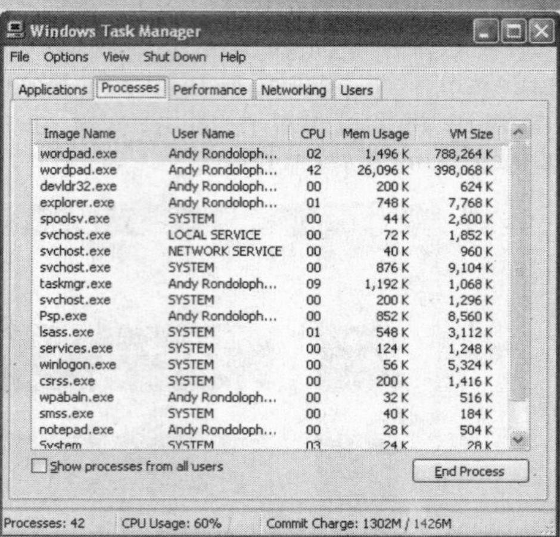

For more precise monitoring of performance, use the Performance tool, as discussed in "Monitoring Performance with the Performance Tool" later in this chapter.

If you watch the readouts in Task Manager, you'll see that Windows tries to keep some RAM available for as long as possible. When most of the RAM is gone, the amount of virtual memory consumed grows faster to accommodate your memory demands. But if you keep using up more memory (for example, by opening large files), and you've set a maximum size for your paging file, you'll eventually run out of virtual memory as well as RAM.

When you run out of virtual memory, Windows XP displays the Windows Virtual Memory Minimum Too Low pop-up in the notification area (shown on the next page), telling you that it is increasing the size of your virtual memory paging file and that, while this is happening, requests for memory may be denied. Windows is serious about denying requests for memory—it starts responding glacially slowly, and you'll probably be less frustrated if you leave it alone until it has finished increasing the size of the paging file. Click the pop-up to dismiss it, and then sit back for a minute or two. Again, if you have Task Manager open, you can see Windows increasing the size of the paging file—the size of the second Commit Charge figure on the Processes tab will increase to show the new amount of memory available.

CONTINUED ➡

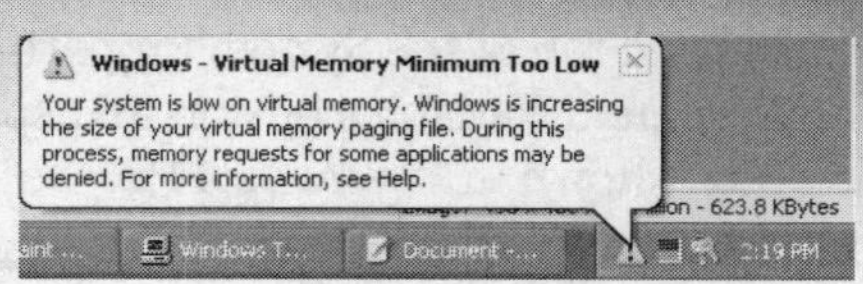

Once Windows has grabbed more memory for the paging file, and has written as much data to disk as it must in order to get things moving again, it'll become more responsive—but probably only a *bit* more responsive. You can try to start using Windows normally again at this point, but in most cases you'll be better off reducing the amount of memory you're using. This could mean closing some programs; closing some big files; using the Users tab of Task Manager to log someone off and close their programs (losing any unsaved data if necessary); or shutting down Windows and restarting it. (Restarting Windows will also terminate any other user sessions and lose any unsaved data they contain.)

When Windows is struggling for memory, you'll see the Applications tab of Task Manager list programs as *Not Responding* when in fact they *are* responding but are doing so very slowly. You can use the End Task button to kill any program that really isn't responding, but it's usually better to wait a few seconds (or a few minutes) to see if the program comes back to life when Windows is able to feed it more memory.

If you start any memory-hungry program when Windows is struggling for memory, Windows may clobber the program without notifying you. Again, it's better to wait until Windows has stabilized itself and the programs that are currently running before you try to run any more programs.

TIP

You can set a different printer as the default printer at any time by right-clicking its icon in the Printers and Faxes folder and choosing Set As Default Printer.

Setting Environment Variables

From the Advanced tab of the System Properties dialog box, you can click the Environment Variables button to display the Environment Variables dialog box (shown in Figure 32.14).

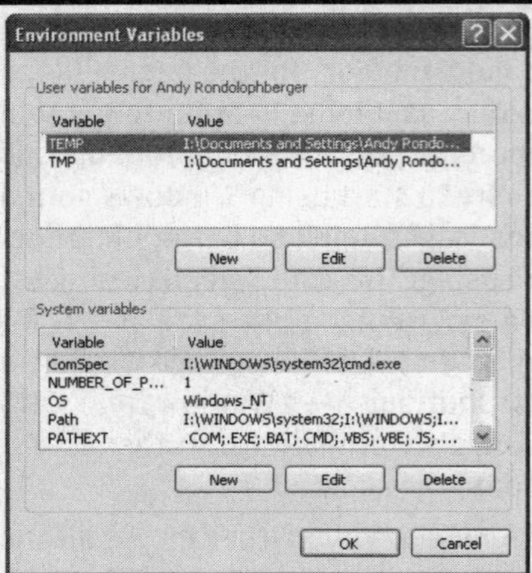

FIGURE 32.14: You can examine user variables and system variables in the Environment Variables dialog box.

Environment variables have largely been superseded by Registry values, so you probably won't need to do much in this dialog box. You *can* use the New buttons, the Edit buttons, and the Delete buttons to create, edit, and delete user variables and system variables, but you shouldn't need to do so. And you *can* find out some information about Windows and your system from the System Variables list box—but most of this information is more easily found elsewhere. For example, you'll find processor information in the System Info applet, which you can access from the Help and Support Center window.

Click the OK button or the Cancel button to close the Environment Variables dialog box when you've finished gazing at the wonders it offers.

Enabling and Disabling Error Reporting

If you've ever complained about software crashing on Windows, or about Windows itself crashing, you should like Windows XP's error-reporting features, which by default are set up to enable error reporting on Windows itself and programs running on it. You can turn off error reporting if it doesn't suit you, or you can choose to include or exclude specific programs from error reporting. For example, if you're developing a program, and it keeps crashing because you haven't programmed it right, you'd probably want to exclude it from error reporting on the grounds that Microsoft hadn't even heard of it yet (and they might not want to hear of it until you improve it).

To configure error reporting, follow these steps:

1. Click the Error Reporting button on the Advanced tab of the System Properties dialog box. Windows displays the Error Reporting dialog box (shown in Figure 32.15).

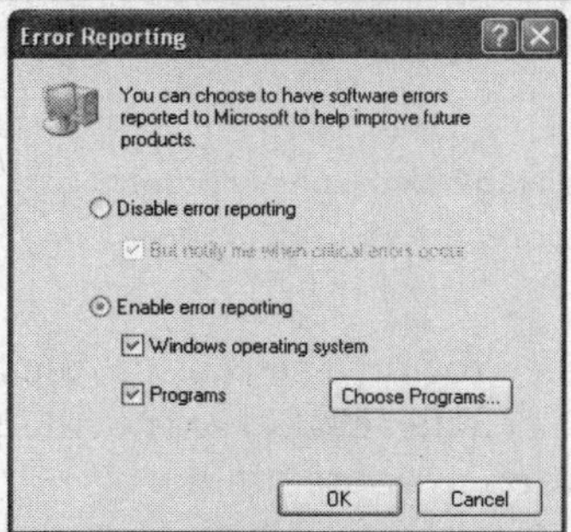

FIGURE 32.15: Use the Error Reporting dialog box and the linked dialog boxes to configure error reporting to your taste.

2. Select the Disable Error Reporting option button to turn off error reporting entirely. Otherwise, leave the Enable Error Reporting option button selected (as it is by default).
   - If you turn off error reporting, it's best to leave the But Notify Me when Critical Errors Occur check box selected so that Windows lets you know when something goes badly wrong.

3. In the Enable Error Reporting list, select or clear the Windows Operating System check box and the Programs check box as appropriate.

4. To specify which programs to include or exclude, select the Programs check box. Then click the Choose Programs button. Windows displays the Choose Programs dialog box (shown in Figure 32.16).

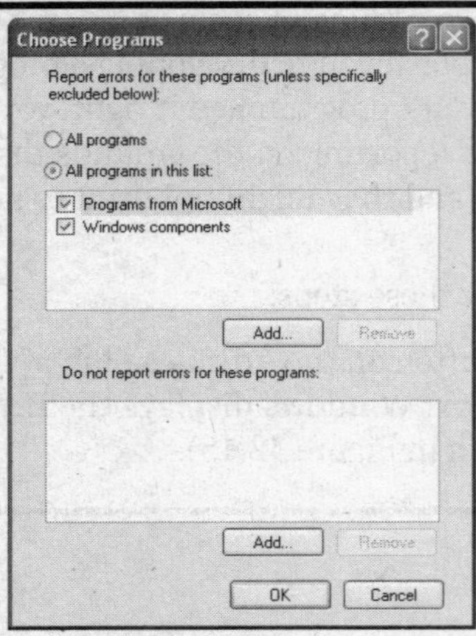

FIGURE 32.16: Use the Choose Programs dialog box to specify programs to include or exclude from error reporting.

5. In the Report Errors for These Programs area, select the All Programs option button (the default setting) or the All Programs in This List option button as appropriate.

6. If you selected the All Programs in This List option button, select or clear the check boxes in the list box to indicate the programs you're interested in. Use the upper Add button and the resulting Add Program dialog box to add programs to this list.

7. To exclude specific programs from error reporting, use the lower Add button and its Add Program dialog box to build a list of programs for exclusion in the Do Not Report Errors for These Programs list box. Select and clear the check boxes for the programs you add to the list as appropriate.

8. Click the OK button. Windows closes the Choose Programs dialog box.
9. Click the OK button. Windows closes the Error Reporting dialog box.

SETTING STARTUP AND RECOVERY OPTIONS

Windows XP includes several startup options that you should know about if you're running a dual-boot setup. (If you're not, just ignore these options: They don't apply to you at the moment.) And it lets you specify what it should do when it encounters a system failure—an error bad enough to crash the system.

To set startup and recovery options, follow these steps:

1. Click the Settings button in the Startup and Recovery section on the Advanced tab of the System Properties dialog box. Windows displays the Startup and Recovery dialog box (shown in Figure 32.17).

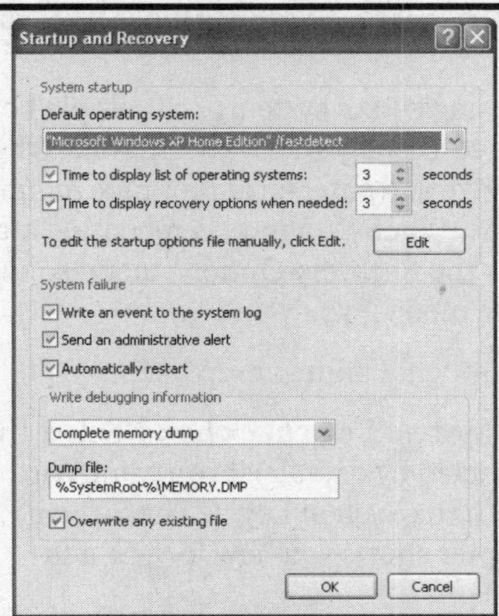

FIGURE 32.17: Use the System Startup options in the Startup and Recovery dialog box to specify the default operating system to boot and for how long Windows should display the boot list of operating systems. Use the System Failure options to specify what Windows should do if it suffers a system failure.

2. If you have a dual- or multiple-boot system, choose options in the System Startup section:

   - In the Default Operating System drop-down list, select the operating system that you want to boot by default.
   - If you want Windows to display the boot list of operating systems for a number of seconds before booting one, so that you can boot an operating system other than the default one, select the Time to Display List of Operating Systems check box and enter a suitable value in the text box. You can enter any value from 0 seconds to 999 seconds. The default value is 30 seconds, but most people find a shorter value more useful—long enough to give you time to select the operating system (or just tap a key) without needing pro-sports reflexes, but short enough to pass quickly if you just want to boot the default operating system.

TIP

You can edit the boot options file, `BOOT.INI`, manually by clicking the Edit button in the System Startup sections. The section "Creating a Dual-Boot Setup" at the end of this chapter discusses how to edit the boot options file.

3. Whether you're using a single-boot system or a multiple-boot system, leave the Time to Display Recovery Options When Needed check box selected, and enter an appropriate number of seconds in its text box. When Windows is rebooting after a failed boot, it displays the Recovery Options menu so that you can restart it in Safe mode if you want.

4. Choose options in the System Failure group box:

   Write an Event to the System Log check box Select this check box (which is selected by default) if you want Windows to write an event to the System Log. ("The System Log" earlier in this chapter shows you how to view and interpret the System Log.)

   Send an Administrative Alert check box Select this check box (which is selected by default) if you want Windows to display an Alert dialog box when a system failure occurs. Having a visual indication of narrowly averted or impending disaster can concentrate the mind wonderfully.

Automatically Restart check box Select this check box (which is selected by default) if you want Windows XP to automatically reboot if there's a system failure. (Windows reboots after writing that event to the System Log and sending an administrative alert, of course–if you left those check boxes selected.)

TIP

It should go without saying that these recovery options aren't a panacea. Any crash serious enough to be called a system failure will almost invariably result in the loss of any unsaved data sitting around in the programs affected. Besides, despite sitting stably on the New Technology bedrock of Windows NT and 2000, Windows XP still suffers occasional lockups, particularly with misbehaved hardware drivers. If your system hangs (freezes), you'll probably need to reboot it manually, because the auto-reboot functionality will be frozen as well. After rebooting, you'll find that no event was written to the System Log and no administrative alert was sent, because Windows was just as blindsided by the hang as you were.

Write Debugging Information section In the drop-down list, select the type of debugging information that you want Windows to write in the event of a crash. Your choices are None, Small Memory Dump, Kernel Memory Dump, and Complete Memory Dump. The None choice turns off the writing of debugging information. A Small Memory Dump creates a file with a name built of the prefix `MINI`, the date in MMDDYY format, a hyphen, the number of the dump, and the DMP extension. For example, the first dump on Christmas Day 2001 is named `MINI122501-01.DMP`. The dump file is stored in the directory specified in the Small Dump Directory text box and contains the smallest possible amount of memory information to be useful for debugging. With each crash, Windows creates a new file. A Kernel Memory Dump dumps only the kernel memory into a file called `MEMORY.DMP` by default and needs between 50 and 800MB of space for the paging file on the boot volume (not on another volume). A Complete Memory Dump, as its name suggests, dumps all the information contained in system memory when the crash occurred. Again, this goes into a file named MEMORY.DMP by default. To create a complete memory dump, you need to have a paging file on the boot volume (again, not on another volume) of at least the size of your computer's RAM plus 1MB (for example, a paging file of at least 97MB if your computer has 96MB RAM). Choose the location and name for the dump file in the text box in the Write Debugging Information group box, and select the Overwrite Any Existing File check box if appropriate. (This check box isn't available for Small Memory Dump, because this option creates a sequence of files automatically.)

NOTE

A small memory dump happens instantaneously. A kernel dump takes a bit longer. A complete memory dump takes anything from a few seconds to a minute or two. For a kernel dump or a complete dump, Windows displays a Blue Screen of Death with a percentage counter as it writes the contents of memory to disk. When this is done, the computer reboots (if you've left the Automatically Restart check box selected).

5. Click the OK button. Windows closes the Startup and Recovery dialog box.

Monitoring Performance with the Performance Tool

As you saw earlier in the chapter, you can monitor performance to some extent by using Task Manager—and if any program gets out of hand, you can shut it down without much difficulty from there. But if you want to see more precisely what's happening on your computer, use the Performance tool instead.

To run Performance, take the following steps:

1. Choose Start ➢ Control Panel. Windows displays Control Panel.
2. Click the Performance and Maintenance link. Windows displays the Performance and Maintenance screen.

3. Click the Administrative Tools link. Windows displays the Administrative Tools screen.
4. Double-click the Performance shortcut. Windows starts Performance (shown in Figure 32.18).

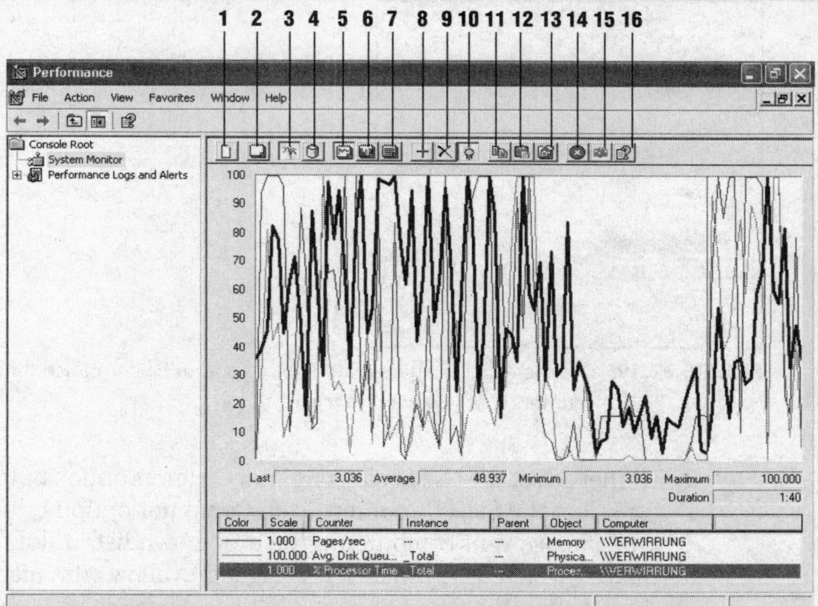

1. New Counter Set Button
2. Clear Display Button
3. View Current Activity Button
4. View Log Data Button
5. View Graph Button
6. View Histogram Button
7. View Report Button
8. Add Button
9. Delete Button
10. Highlight Button
11. Copy Properties Button
12. Paste Counter List Button
13. Properties Button
14. Freeze Display Button
15. Update Data Button
16. Help Button

FIGURE 32.18: If Task Manager doesn't give you the detail you need on your computer's performance, use the Performance tool to monitor performance.

In grayscale (as printed here), this looks like a spider taking a polygraph test, but in color (on a monitor), it's easy enough to read. As you can more or less see in the figure, Performance starts you off in Graph view tracking three counters: Pages/Sec, Avg. Disk Queue Length, and % Processor Time (listed in the list box at the bottom of the window).

You can add further counters by taking the following steps:

1. Click the Add button. Windows displays the Add Counters dialog box (shown in Figure 32.19).

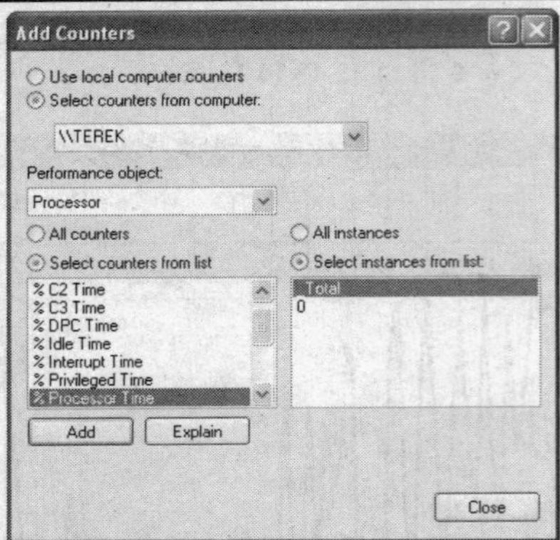

FIGURE 32.19: Use the Add Counters dialog box to add to Performance the counters that you want to track.

2. Either select the Use Local Computer Counters option button or select the Select Counters from Computer option button and choose your computer in the drop-down list. It doesn't matter which. Performance is designed to allow administrators to monitor computers remotely.
3. In the Performance Object drop-down list, select the category of item you want to monitor. For example, you might select Memory. Windows displays a list of the counters available for that performance object in the left list box.
4. With the Select Counters from List option button selected (as it is by default), select the first counter in the left list box and click the Add button to add it to the Performance window.
   - Click the Explain button to display a window explaining the meaning of the current counter.
5. Add further counters by repeating steps 3 and 4.
6. Click the Close button. Windows closes the Add Counters dialog box.

To remove a counter from Performance, select it in the list box at the bottom of the Performance window and press the Delete key or click the Delete button.

To highlight a counter with a thick black line, select the counter in the list box and click the Highlight button.

TIP

Once you've set up a view in Performance that shows the items you want to track, you can add it to your favorites by choosing Favorites ➢ Add to Favorites, specifying the name for the favorite in the resulting Add to Favorites dialog box, and clicking the OK button.

When you've finished using Performance, choose File ➢ Exit. Windows closes Performance.

Using the System Restore Feature

Windows' System Restore feature provides a way of recovering from the consequences of installing the wrong hardware driver (or a buggy driver) or a dysfunctional piece of software.

How System Restore Works

System Restore uses a system of *restore points* that include information about the state of the computer's software configuration when the restore point was created. Windows creates some restore points automatically at quasi-regular intervals and before you install some drivers and programs, and you can create restore points manually whenever you want to. For example, you might choose to create a restore point manually before you install a new driver or program, just in case Windows doesn't create a restore point and things turn out for the worse.

If your computer starts misbehaving, you can return your computer to one of the restore points before whatever change precipitated the trouble. You run System Restore and specify the restore point. Windows then restores the computer's software configuration using the information stored in the restore point.

System Restore is very impressive technology, but it can't fix every problem. It affects only your system files (as opposed to your data files), so rolling back the computer to an earlier state doesn't delete any data files that you've created or downloaded in the meantime. Likewise, returning to a restore point doesn't reinstate any data files that you've deleted since that point in time.

Adjusting the Amount of Space System Restore Takes Up

As you'd guess, System Restore stores the restore-point information in files on your hard disk. The more restore points Windows creates automatically and you create manually, the more space they take up. Windows automatically reserves space on each hard drive volume for System Restore files. System Restore needs at least 200MB in order to do any good. By default, it claims anywhere between 12 percent and 20 percent of each drive.

That's a serious investment of space, and you don't really need to use System Restore on any drive but the one that contains your Windows files and program files. Once you've gotten your computer fixed up with the hardware and software you need, and everything seems to be working to your satisfaction, you may want to reduce the amount of space devoted to System Restore. To do so, take the following steps:

1. Press Winkey+Break; or click the Start button, right-click the My Computer item on the Start menu, and choose Properties from the shortcut menu. Windows displays the System Properties dialog box.
2. Click the System Restore tab. Figure 32.20 shows two examples of the System Restore tab, because the tab shows different controls depending on whether your computer has one hard drive (as in the left example) or multiple hard drives (as in the right example). Windows displays *Monitoring* for a drive you're monitoring and *Turned Off* for a drive on which you've turned off System Restore.
3. If you have only one hard drive, drag the Disk Space to Use slider to specify the amount of space to use for System Restore.

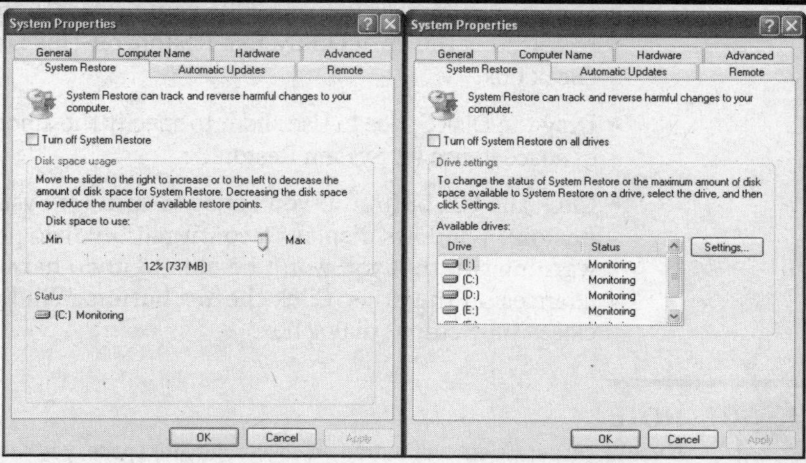

FIGURE 32.20: On the System Restore tab of the System Properties dialog box, you can turn off System Restore or adjust the amount of space it takes up.

4. If you have multiple hard drives, follow these steps for each drive:

    - Select the drive in the Available Drives list box and click the Settings button. Windows displays the Settings dialog box for the drive. Figure 32.21 shows an example of the Settings dialog box for a system drive (on the left) and an example for a nonsystem drive (on the right).

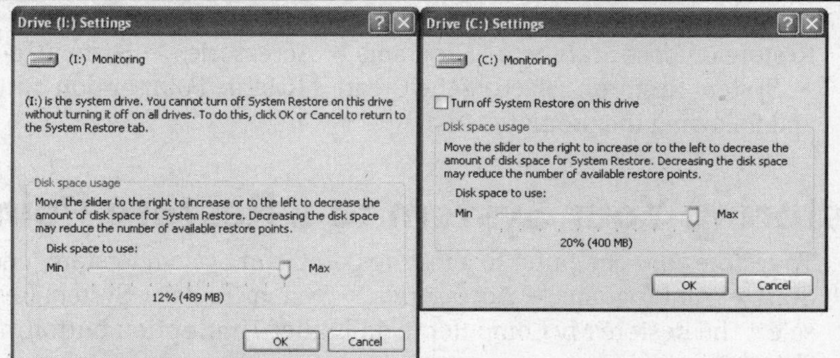

FIGURE 32.21: If you have multiple drives, use the Settings dialog box to choose settings for each drive. The Settings dialog box on the left is for a system drive. The Settings dialog box on the right is for a nonsystem drive.

- For a nonsystem drive, you can turn off System Restore by selecting the Turn Off System Restore on This Drive check box.
- Drag the Disk Space to Use slider to specify the amount of space to use for System Restore.
- Click the OK button. If you chose to turn off System Restore, Windows displays a confirmation dialog box warning you that you won't be able to undo harmful changes on the drive. Click the Yes button. Windows closes the Settings dialog box.

NOTE

If you're desperate enough to trade recoverability for space, you can turn off System Restore by selecting the Turn Off System Restore check box or the Turn Off System Restore on All Drives check box. But usually it's a much better idea to keep using System Restore but devote less space to it.

5. Click the OK button. Windows closes the System Properties dialog box.

Setting System Restore Points

Windows automatically creates restore points called *system checkpoints* periodically—usually one or two a day. It also creates restore points automatically when you install certain types of software.

You can create system checkpoints manually by running System Restore (choose Start ➢ All Programs ➢ Accessories ➢ System Tools ➢ System Restore), selecting the Create a Restore Point option button, and following the prompts.

Restoring Your System to a Restore Point

To restore your computer to a restore point, run System Restore (choose Start ➢ All Programs ➢ Accessories ➢ System Tools ➢ System Restore), select the Restore My Computer to an Earlier Time option button, and follow the prompts.

After restoring your system to the restore point, check your system to make sure that it's running properly. If the restoration didn't produce the effect you wanted, run System Restore again. You can either choose a restore point further in the past or undo your last restoration.

Restoring the Last Known Good Configuration

System Restore can work wonders—provided that your system can boot Windows. But if your system can't boot Windows, you need to take other measures. Your first step should be to try restoring the Last Known Good Configuration. When you reboot, you'll see a message that says, "For troubleshooting and advanced startup options for Windows XP Professional, press F8." If you press F8, you'll see a menu on which Last Known Good Configuration is one of the choices. Use the arrow key to scroll down to this item, and then press Enter. This should make your machine bootable, but if it doesn't, try using Recovery Console as described in the next section.

Repairing a Windows Installation Using Recovery Console

If using the Last Known Good Configuration does you no good, or if you want to go nuclear without taking conventional recovery steps, try Recovery Console. Recovery Console gives you a command prompt skeleton of Windows XP that you can use to perform basic file maintenance (for example, replacing a corrupted system file) or to issue repair commands for getting Windows running again.

To start Recovery Console, take the following steps:

1. Boot from your Windows XP CD as if you were installing Windows XP from scratch. Wait while Setup loads all the files required for setup.
2. On the Welcome to Setup screen, press **R**. Setup displays the Recovery Console, which presents you with a numbered list of the operating systems that it has identified on the computer. The operating systems are identified by the drive and

folder that contains them rather than by type, so make sure you select the right one if the computer has multiple operating systems installed.

3. Type the number of the operating system you want to recover and press the Enter key. (To cancel out of Recovery Console, press the Enter key without typing a number.) Setup prompts you for the Administrator password for the account.

4. Type the password for a Computer Administrator account and press the Enter key. (If your account doesn't use a password, just press the Enter key.) Setup displays a command prompt to the system root folder for the operating system.

The command prompt doesn't look very exciting, but it gives you the entrée to the operating system that you need to fix Windows XP. Recovery Console supports regular DOS commands. For example, you can use the COPY command to copy files from a floppy or from a CD (for example, the Windows XP CD) to replace files.

Recovery Console also supports commands for taking the following actions:

Partitioning the disk Invoke the DISKPART command to display a partitioning screen that you can use to create and delete partitions.

Creating a new boot sector Use the FIXBOOT command to create a new boot sector on a partition you specify and make that partition active.

Repairing the master boot record Use the FIXMBR command to repair the master boot record on the drive. (If you don't know what the master boot record is, you probably shouldn't be using this command.)

Listing the devices and services on your computer Use the LISTSVC command to list the devices and services on your computer.

Enabling and disabling devices Use the ENABLE command and the DISABLE command to enable or disable a specific device or service. (Use the LISTSVC command to list the devices or commands that you can enable or disable.)

Logging on to a different operating system Use the LOGON command to log on to another operating system so that you can repair it.

Returning to the system root folder Use the SYSTEMROOT command to return to the system root folder.

To exit Recovery Console and restart your computer, issue the EXIT command and press the Enter key.

Creating a Dual-Boot Setup

If you want to run not only Windows XP but also another operating system on your computer, you'll probably want to create a dual-boot setup or multiboot setup. Windows XP includes a boot loader that makes dual-booting relatively simple—provided that either the other operating system cooperates or you install Windows XP after the other operating system.

EXPERT KNOWLEDGE: EXTRACTING A COMPRESSED FILE FROM A CABINET FILE

If Windows won't boot because it has corrupted a vital system file (or you've somehow managed to delete a vital system file), you'll need to replace the system file in order to get Windows working again.

The best place to get a replacement system file is your Windows CD. If you don't have a second PC handy on which to extract the file from the compressed cabinet file that contains it, you can use the DOS-based EXTRACT command from Windows *9x* to extract the file.

The basic syntax for the EXTRACT command is as follows, where *cabinet* is the name of the cabinet file and *filename* is the name of the file to extract:

```
EXTRACT cabinet filename
```

To display a directory listing of the contents of the CAB file, use the following syntax, where *cabinet* is the name of the cabinet file:

```
EXTRACT /D cabinet
```

Creating a Dual-Boot Setup with Another Version of Windows

To create a dual-boot setup with another version of Windows, follow the procedure described in "Performing a New Installation of Windows XP" in Chapter 2. Setup automatically creates a dual-boot setup with the previous version of Windows. When you boot your computer, Windows displays the Please Select the Operating System to Start screen, from which you specify which of the operating systems should boot.

Choosing System Startup Options for Booting Windows

When you've created a dual-boot setup as described in the previous section, you can specify which of the operating systems the boot loader boots by default. You can also edit the boot menu (which is stored in the `BOOT.INI` file) to change the order in which the operating systems are listed and the way in which they are listed. You may also need to remove boot menu items that have become superfluous or confusing.

To choose system startup options, take the following steps:

1. Press Winkey+Break. Alternatively, choose Start ➢ Control Panel, click the Performance and Maintenance link, click the Other Control Panel Options link, and click the System link. Windows displays the System Properties dialog box.
2. Click the Advanced tab.
3. Click the Settings button in the Startup and Recovery section. Windows displays the Startup and Recovery dialog box (shown in Figure 32.17, earlier in the chapter).
4. In the Default Operating System drop-down list, select the operating system that you want to boot by default.
5. If you want Windows to display the boot list of operating systems for a number of seconds before booting one, so that you can boot an operating system other than the default one, select the Time to Display List of Operating Systems check box and enter a suitable value in the text box. You can enter any value from 0 seconds to 999 seconds. The default value is 30 seconds.

6. If you want to change the names and descriptions of the items on the boot menu, click the Edit button. Windows opens the `BOOT.INI` file in a Notepad window. Figure 32.22 shows an example of a `BOOT.INI` file open in Notepad.

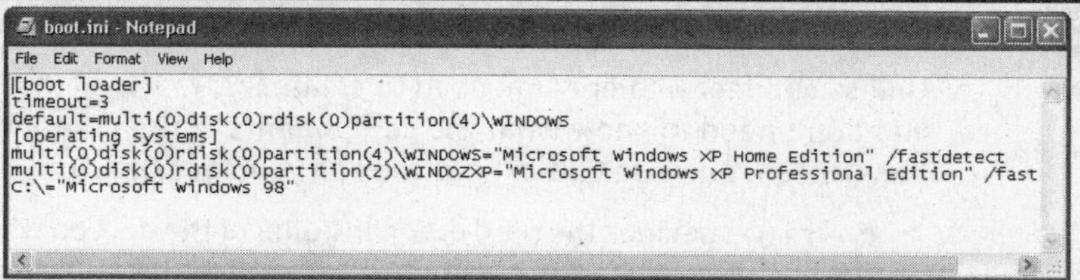

boot.ini - Notepad
File Edit Format View Help
[boot loader]
timeout=3
default=multi(0)disk(0)rdisk(0)partition(4)\WINDOWS
[operating systems]
multi(0)disk(0)rdisk(0)partition(4)\WINDOWS="Microsoft Windows XP Home Edition" /fastdetect
multi(0)disk(0)rdisk(0)partition(2)\WINDOZXP="Microsoft Windows XP Professional Edition" /fast
C:\="Microsoft Windows 98"

FIGURE 32.22: You can edit the `BOOT.INI` file to change the list of entries displayed and the order in which they're listed.

- Edit the descriptions of the operating systems as necessary within the double quotation marks. For example, you might add to the name of an operating system a note about when it should be used:

```
multi(0)disk(0)rdisk(0)partition(1)\WINDOWS="Windows XP
Professional - test configuration" /fastdetect
```

WARNING

Don't change any of the disk, volume, or partition information. Doing so may prevent Windows from booting.

- To change the number of seconds the boot menu is displayed, change the `timeout=` value. (It's usually easier to do this in the Startup and Recovery dialog box.)
- Similarly, you *can* change the `default=` line to change the default operating system, but it's usually much easier to use the Default Operating System drop-down list in the Startup and Recovery dialog box.
- Press Ctrl+S or choose File ➢ Save to save the `BOOT.INI` file, and then press Alt+F4 or choose File ➢ Exit to close it.

7. Click the OK button. Windows closes the Startup and Recovery dialog box.

8. Click the OK button. Windows closes the System Properties dialog box.

EXPERT KNOWLEDGE: *MULTI(), RDISK()*, AND */FASTDETECT*

Unless you feel a compelling need to create `BOOT.INI` manually, you don't need to know what the components of the boot menu items mean. But if that's a curious look on your face, read on.

- `multi()` specifies the hard disk controller of the disk on which the operating system in question is installed. Numbering starts at zero (because it's computer-counting).
- `disk()` specifies the hard disk on which the operating system is installed. `disk()` is used only when `scsi()` is used; otherwise, it's included in the boot menu item but has no function. Again, numbering begins at zero.
- `rdisk()` specifies the hard disk on which the operating system is installed. Once again, numbering begins at zero.
- `partition()` specifies the partition on which the operating system is installed. Just to be confusing, numbering starts at 1.

If Windows XP or Windows 2000 is installed on a FAT32 partition, there's also a `signature()` component to the boot menu item. This specifies the disk controller.

If the operating system is installed on a SCSI disk without an active BIOS, the boot menu item has a `scsi()` component that specifies the hard disk controller.

The `/fastdetect` switch turns off the detection of serial mice. You can also use this switch with a specific COM port to turn off detection on that port—for example, `/fastdetect=COM1`.

Setting Up a Dual-Boot with Linux

The Windows XP boot loader handles previous installations of Windows deftly, but it's not designed to work with Linux (or indeed OS/2, Solaris, BeOS, or other non-Microsoft operating systems). If you want to dual-boot Windows XP and Linux, you need to take a different approach.

You can install Linux either before installing Windows XP or after installing Windows XP. In either case, you'll need to keep your partitions straight so that the later installation doesn't overwrite the earlier installation. When installing Linux after Windows XP, make sure that you don't install Lilo (the *Li*nux *Lo*ader) on the master boot record (MBR). Doing so overwrites the Windows XP boot loader, which prevents Windows XP from starting at all.

This means that (obviously enough) you shouldn't use an automated installation routine that's designed to take over the whole disk for Linux. For most installations of Linux, you'll need to choose a custom installation. For example, for Red Hat, specify a Custom System on the Install Type screen, and partition the drive manually with Disk Druid (or fdisk if you're feeling bold). On the Lilo Configuration screen, select the First Sector of Boot Partition option button instead of the Master Boot Record option button in the Install Lilo Boot Record On list. Also, make sure the Create Boot Disk check box is selected.

If you don't mind leaving a floppy disk dangling around your floppy drive, you can also boot Lilo off a floppy. Windows XP boots regularly when the floppy drive is empty.

EXPERT KNOWLEDGE: SERIOUS MULTIBOOTING

The methods discussed in this section work well enough for setting up a dual-boot arrangement or a multiboot arrangement with a modest number of operating systems. But if you need to install serious numbers of operating systems on the same computer, it's worth investing in a heavy-duty boot manager such as System Commander from V Communications (`www.v-com.com`). System Commander lets you install more than 100 operating systems on the same computer. (You'll have a hard time finding that many different operating systems, but you can also install multiple copies of the same operating systems to get the numbers up.)

INDEX

Note to the Reader: Throughout this index **boldfaced** page numbers indicate primary discussions of a topic. *Italicized* page numbers indicate illustrations.

Symbols & Numbers

A

B

C

D

F

G

I

J

K

L

N

P

S

U

V

W

X

Y

Z

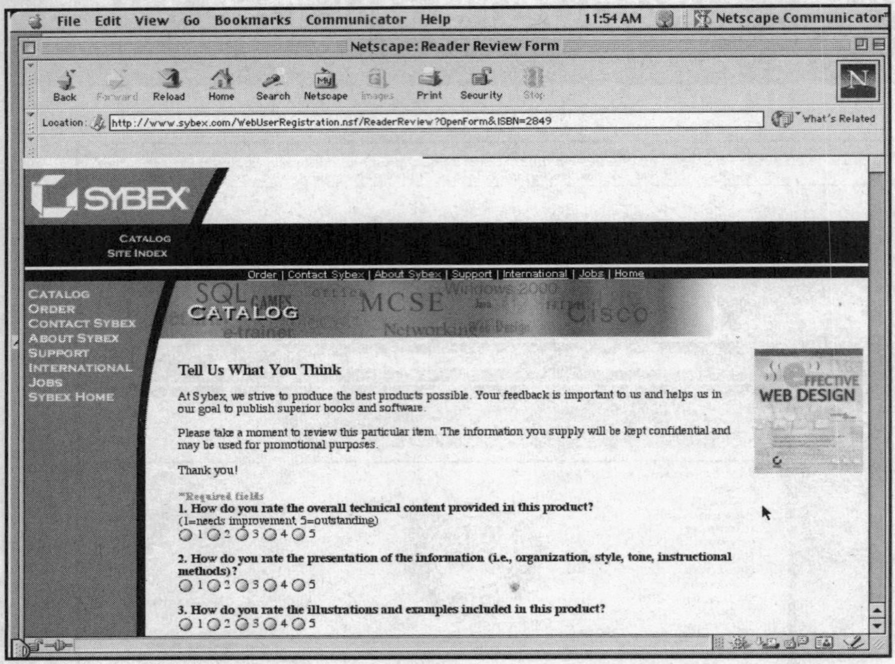

About the Contributors

Some of the best–and best-selling–Sybex authors have contributed chapters from their books to *Windows XP Professional Complete.*

Pat Coleman is a Technical Editor and author who writes about the Internet, Windows and Windows applications.

Peter Dyson is a writer and software engineer with more than 20 years of experience in software development and technical support. His more than two dozen books include *Windows 98 Instant Reference, The Dictionary of Networking* and *Unix Complete*, all from Sybex.

Guy Hart-Davis has written dozens of computer books, including *Word 2000 Developer's Handbook, Mastering VBA 6, Word 97 Macro & VBA Handbook* and two editions of the best-selling *MP3—I Didn't Know You Could Do That* and *MP3 Complete*. He is well into his second decade of rebooting Windows PCs.

Peter Hipson is an author, consultant, and teacher. When not writing computer books, he can often be found teaching computer science at the local college, where he says he "ruins the lives of hundreds of unsuspecting college students every year." An avid Microsoft beta tester, he finds time to test and use virtually every product Microsoft produces.

Mark Minasi, MCSE, is recognized as one of the world's best teachers of NT/2000. He teaches NT/2000 classes in 15 countries and is a much sought-after speaker at conferences. His firm, MR&D, has taught tens of thousands of people to design and run NT networks. Among his eight other Sybex books are *Mastering Windows* 2000 *Server 3rd Ed., Mastering Windows NT 4 7th Ed.*, and *The Complete PC Upgrade and Maintenance Guide*, which has sold a million copies and been translated into 12 languages.

Faithe Wempen has authored over 20 computer books on topics including Microsoft's Windows Me, Windows 98, Office, Access, and PowerPoint. Skilled at instructing newbies, Wempen's Indianapolis-based training operation teaches beginners how to use PCs. Wempen is A+ certified, earned her master's degree in English from Purdue University, and has taught writing and composition.